DATE DUE

THE INDIAN SLAVE TRADE

THE RISE OF
THE ENGLISH EMPIRE
IN THE AMERICAN SOUTH, 1670–1717

ALAN GALLAY

YALE UNIVERSITY PRESS/NEW HAVEN & LONDON

Designed by Mary Valencia.
Set in Garamond and Trajan types by Integrated Publishing Solutions, Grand Rapids, Michigan.
Printed in the United States of America by Vail-Ballou Press, Binghamton, New York.

Library of Congress Cataloging-in-Publication Data
Gallay, Alan.
The Indian slave trade : the rise of the English empire in the American south, 1670–1717 / Alan Gallay.
p.   cm.
Includes bibliographical references and index.
ISBN 0-300-08754-3 (cloth : alk. paper)
ISBN 0-300-10193-7 (pbk. : alk. paper)
1. Slave trade—Great Britain—History—17th century. 2. Slave trade—Southern States—
History—17th century. 3. Indian slaves—Southern States—History—17th century. 4. Indians,
Treatment of—Southern States—History—17th century. 5. Indians of North America—Southern
States—Social conditions. I. Title.
HT1162.G35 2002
381′.44′0975—dc21
2001005270

A catalogue record for this book is available from the British Library.

The paper in this book meets the guidelines for permanence and durability of the Committee
on Production Guidelines for Book Longevity of the Council on Library Resources.

10 9 8 7 6

FOR
CYRANA

The savage who told me all of this is a man of the Maugoulacho nation who is living with the Mauvilla nation. He had assured me that the English were in those nations every day, and that they take pack horses burdened with clothing, guns, gunpowder, shot, and a quantity of other goods which are sold or traded to the savages for cured deer hides, for fresh deer hides with hair, and for the buffalo that are covered in a fine wool being gray in color like a mouse. But the greatest traffic between the English and the savages is the trade of slaves which the nations take from their neighbors whom they war with continuously, such that the men take the women and children away and sell them to the English, each person being traded for a gun. This greatly destroys the nations which are our neighbors.

—Charles Levasser, 1700

CONTENTS

PREFACE

The French cartographer Guillaume Delisle never visited the New World. Delisle's father was the king's official cartographer and, as such, could give his son access not only to the documents that colonial officials sent to imperial administrators in France but also to returning officials, soldiers, and priests. At Versailles and in Paris, Delisle interviewed those who had visited New France, obtaining information on the location of waterways and Indian peoples and compiling demographic and geographic profiles of the North American continent. From these data he produced in 1703 a remarkably accurate depiction of the area that is now the United States.[1]

We can identify with his task as we reconstruct a distant world that we cannot visit, and attempt to make a representation that is coherent and valuable. Our map by its very nature must be selective, for everything cannot be represented—even if this were physically possible, the detail would overwhelm us. There must be outline, clarity, and substance; the entire picture, as well as individual sections, should provide guidance to those who will use the map in their work. Unlike the earliest mapmakers of the New World, who invented what they did not know, we are bound not to invent, although we can suggest what might have been, based on our interpretation of the evidence. The mapmakers of the early eighteenth century often provided detailed notations—editorial comments—to bring out the significance of their drawings. In a sense, that is what I do in this book. My task is to draw a picture of the South that captures a period of time: roughly 1670 to 1717. To give the depiction richness and depth, the book may occasionally read like political history or diplomatic history, but often it will read like cultural, intellectual, economic, demographic, or social history.

The colonial South is a distant world. As a place, the South still exists, much changed by roads and plows, buildings and people. But one can still have a sense of the earlier environment in places that have not undergone great alteration. Many salt marshes, bayous, and swamps maintain their essential character, even as forests and pine barrens disappear.

The many peoples of the colonial South are more foreign to us today than the environment they inhabited, although, as with the surviving remnants of landscape, aspects persist in their descendants. Unlike Delisle, we do not have living witnesses to interrogate, but we do have hindsight in our favor. Just as Delisle was able to reconstruct a cartographic representation of the New World that the people who lived there could not create—because they lacked the skills, resources, and perspective—so, too, do we have numerous advantages over those who experienced the colonial South firsthand. They could provide reams of information that are now lost, vantage points for understanding events, people, and ideas: but we have information that they did not possess; new methods for understanding societies, people, and systems of economy, diplomacy, and thought. We have the advantage of being able to step back and view the large picture, fitting remnants of the past into it, altering its outline and composition as it becomes clearer to us.

Historians must be detectives, social scientists, and philosophers. As detectives, we seek out information, decode fragments, and interrogate witnesses: the documents. We measure words against actions to reconstruct the patterns of thought by which past peoples construed reality. As social scientists, we fit individual behavior into group dynamics to delineate what is singular and what is indicative of the larger historical forces at work. As philosophers, we meditate on the meaning of that singular moment created by many forces converging and merging into something unique—yet linked to other singular moments by the common humanity of the participants.

My data come largely from the paper trail left by the English, French, and Spanish colonial empires. The bureaucracies of each received reports, letters, and statistics from colonial officials, private citizens, soldiers, and men of the cloth (whom I do not include with private citizens because they often functioned in a semiofficial capacity). Connected to these documents were those generated within the European colonies, sometimes for transmission to Europe and sometimes not, such as court proceedings, assembly minutes, commission records, economic transactions (deeds, conveyances, bills of sale), personal correspondence, diaries, books, pamphlets, and newspapers. To these we may add the archaeological record, paintings, maps, buildings, and oral histories, as well as the scholarly works in which these materials are collected and analyzed.

I have employed no single methodology for disclosing the patterns that exist in the evidence. My judgments on colonialism, colonists, and native peoples are drawn not only from an analysis of the evidence but also from observations made from reading about colonialism in different places in a variety of eras. I have also turned to ethnohistory, anthropology, and archaeology for an understanding of the native peoples who did not leave written materials about their lives before and just after contact with Europeans.

My method is contextual: to assess evidence within new contexts and from different perspectives. In my study of the South, I reconstruct contexts by repeatedly enlarging the geographic and human scope in which events occurred. For instance, when I examine the relationship between the Creek and the Apalachee, I broaden the geographic range in which the interaction took place, as involving not just the north Florida–Alabama–Georgia area in which these peoples connected but the entire South, and I move through each area slowly to see how their relationship might have been affected by or had impact upon the peoples there. Then I extend this analysis to other regions; a foray into the English imperial system might lead to Barbados or Massachusetts, or I might follow the trail through the Spanish empire to Cuba. This book, then, is largely about relationships between groups of people and how those relationships connect to larger historical forces and to other peoples and areas.

I occasionally meditate upon these group relationships, giving weight to location, as well as to the history, culture, and demography of each group. Trying to explain peoples' behavior is necessary for suggesting the map's contours. Some may think, by contrast, that I do not philosophize enough, that I have the responsibility of always separating good from evil, of creating a parable from which the moral of the story may easily be drawn. I wish that it were so simple. I have taken my cue from the French novelist Georges Simenon, whose prolific and dark work has as its central theme the ability of anyone to commit a hideous act if placed in circumstances in which they believe there is no other choice. It is often easy to identify those whose capacity to inflict pain on others comes so readily; history is full of these characters, as is this book—individuals concerned only with self-aggrandizement, willing for others to suffer that they may benefit. I do not wish, however, to place these characters into the same category as those whose behavior might also bear condemnation but whose options were few and for whom the consequences were not so clear. Instead, I believe that my task is to show the options and the circumstances and let readers judge for themselves.

Although this book is arranged somewhat topically, the story is told chronologically. Chronology helps keep grounded the wide-ranging story, which covers so many peoples, but it also arises from my conviction that the collapse of time damages the reconstruction of the past. This has been especially true in scholarly and public reconstructions of Native American history, where it is assumed that Indian societies were incapable of change and "doomed" to fall before the inexorable march of Western society. It is important to this study to show how quickly Native Americans adapted to the vast changes of the late seventeenth century and how many again adapted in the coming years. Because Native American life is dynamic, I have not included material from the 1740s, for instance, to discuss the 1710s, except in a few places, where culture and circumstances had not altered dramatically.

I am concerned with the longer processes of historical change and with placing this story into these larger contexts, but not at the risk of obscuring the focus on the lives of those recalled here. I feel an obligation to those I write about—an obligation to uncover and relate their lives as best I can. I have a special obligation in this case because so many of the peoples discussed here are so rarely heard about, and their stories are largely unknown. I feel no obligation to provide a brief, an argument to be used for or against them in historical debate. Rather, I hope to disclose the circumstances of their lives when their world underwent catastrophic or near-catastrophic change around the beginning of the eighteenth century. This obligation weighs heavily on me, and I admit it not for sympathy but as explanation. It recently has become de rigueur in the new narrative history for authors to plant themselves alongside those they write about. For some scholars, especially those who work in literary criticism, it is a way to bring honesty to their work. They are constantly analyzing themselves to better understand how they analyze others. At the root of this approach is an appreciation of the subjective nature of inquiry—that the perceiver can never be removed from the perceived.

I eschew this approach largely because of my obligation to those I write about. This book is not about me. It is true that as author, I cannot be separated from my subject matter. My authorial voice permeates every page. I bring subjectivity to the work—none of us can leave it out. Instead, we try to understand who we are and where we are coming from in our engagement with those we study.

I am neither Indian nor African nor Christian European, so I admit to bearing no especial affinity with the peoples of this book. I am male, however, and have been raised in the Western tradition, so I bring this baggage wherever I go. My removal from the time and cultures of the period may not make me any more objective, but it does allow me to be differently subjective from the people who experienced these events firsthand.

ACKNOWLEDGMENTS

This book would not have been possible without generous institutional support. Over the past ten years I have been favored with three grants that allowed me the opportunity to complete this manuscript and two edited books. The Andrew P. Mellon Foundation provided a year-long fellowship at Harvard University, during which time I began research for this book. Western Washington University granted a sabbatical during which I wrote the first half of the book, which was finished with the assistance of a fellowship from the National Endowment for the Humanities. Without the sustained period of research and writing allowed by these institutions, I am sure that this book would never have reached final form.

At Western Washington University, George Mariz, chair of the Department of History, assisted me with red tape, answered questions about English history and bibliography, and supported my efforts in numerous other ways. Bob Ballas of the Department of Foreign Languages kindly checked several of my translations of abstruse French documents. Eugene Hoerauf carefully turned my maps into finished products. Charles Grench, formerly of Yale University Press, gave assistance and encouragement at several important points in the review process. Connie and Carl Schulz graciously provided their hospitality while I conducted research in Columbia, South Carolina, as did my dear friend David Teasley in Washington, D.C. The members of the Northwest Early Americanists Workshop kindly provided valuable comments on Chapter 4.

Two colleagues' expertise improved the manuscript immeasurably. Chris Friday helped me think through many issues in Native American history, read and commented on the manuscript, and offered many invaluable suggestions. Leonard Helfgott meticulously examined two drafts, consistently prompted me to keep an eye on the large picture, and offered a plethora of ideas on how to best present the story. Although I am grateful for their contributions, it is their friendship that I value most.

Doug Egerton of Le Moyne University also read the entire manuscript, calling me to account for awkward prose and shoddy reasoning. For the past twenty years Doug and I have traversed southern history and enjoyed each other's company on research and other professional trips through the South. The journey is certainly a great part of the reward.

Peter H. Wood of Duke University gave his expert opinion and advice on two drafts of the manuscript. In particular, I appreciate his suggestions concerning tone, organization, and the elimination of text and footnotes that would allow the most important elements of the story to stand out. Anyone who works in the field of the colonial South owes a debt to Peter's work.

My wife, Carolina, created a perfect environment for me to study and write. In addition, she allowed me to inflict upon her the entire manuscript, which benefited immensely from her careful critique—no one is more offended by a poor sentence than she. She understands how much this book has meant to me, and I always will cherish her love and support.

A week after my daughter, Cyrana, was born, she moved cross-country to begin life in new surroundings. She has been a great traveler ever since, cheerfully tolerating being uprooted every two to three years as her father undertook teaching and research opportunities abroad and in other parts of America. I dedicate this book to her and to the soaring spirit within that loves life and learning.

NOTE ON THE TEXT
AND TERMINOLOGY

I have taken the liberty of correcting spellings in primary sources, except of proper names, and inserting commas and periods, all to make reading easier. I have not, however, Americanized the English spelling of words, nor have I corrected capitalization, wishing to retain some of the flavor of the original. Nor have I altered the text by adding words to quotations except when denoted by brackets. If I am unsure about the meaning of a word, I have inserted a question mark in brackets. If a word is no longer used or if the writer invented the word, but if the reader can probably gauge the meaning, I have usually left it as the writer wrote it or altered the spelling slightly.

Titles of pamphlets, maps, books, and laws are not altered; quotations from maps are also unaltered.

In 1670 the word *Carolina* officially referred to the area of both North and South Carolina but usually designated South Carolina, where most of the English colonists settled. The names North and South Carolina entered the English language before the official separation of the two territories because their settlements were markedly different. In this book, I use Carolina and South Carolina interchangeably to refer to South Carolina.

Generally I use the term *African* to describe slaves in South Carolina who came from Africa or the West Indies, reserving until the end of the book the use of *African American,* employed as a referent for slaves and free people of African descent living in the United States. Likewise, I refer to the early Carolinians from Europe as Europeans; at the end of the book they become Euramericans. I generally use the designations *white* and *black* to distinguish people of European and African descent.

Indian, Amerindian, and Native American are employed interchangeably. I have not used a final *-s* to pluralize the names of southern native groups, except for the Piedmont Indians of North and South Carolina. This is keeping with the linguistic style of many of these groups.

INTRODUCTION

Studies of the colonial South have made huge strides from the narrow histories of ruling elites that characterized the field before the mid-1970s. Peter H. Wood's landmark work, *Black Majority: Negroes in South Carolina from 1670 Through the Stono Rebellion* (1974), among its many accomplishments, moved African-American life to center stage.[1] With great skill, Wood uncovered a wealth of information about the slaves' significant contributions to early southern history, deftly displaying how Africans shaped not only their own lives but their masters', too. Never again could the South's history be written as a mere extension of elite whites' vision and behavior.

Wood employed an interdisciplinary methodology to tell the stories of those whose voices were often unrecorded in written records. This methodology has likewise been used to create ethnohistories of several southern native peoples whose lives were previously known and understood only dimly.[2] Aiding these works was a renaissance in archaeological studies that has shed light on life before European contact.[3] Native American histories can no longer be categorized by "before and after" pictures, in which Indians were depicted as monolithic cultures: unchanging and unchangeable. Instead, aboriginal peoples are now analyzed in the context of a long history that preceded engagement with Europe, a substantial proto-European contact era, and a post-

1

contact period; within each era, native peoples lived in dynamic societies as politics, economy, and social relations altered to meet new circumstances. Contrary to the myths of America's history that portray Indian peoples as incapable of adaptation, Native Americans readily met the challenges offered by the introduction of new technologies, peoples, and ideas. Their responses varied from one group to the next as geopolitical circumstances, local histories, and regional cultural traits combined to create a rich variety of peoples.

This reconstruction of Indian histories required an emphasis on internal dynamics rather than on a peoples' relationship with external forces. When historians did consider external forces, the people remained at the center, shading the portrayal. In the 1980s and 1990s, many scholars became so concerned with recapturing a native past that developed according to the Indians' rhythms and culture that the histories they produced remain largely divorced from those of Europeans and Africans in the region. Historians of the European colonies followed a similar pattern. Thus we have histories of Spanish Florida, French Louisiana, and English Carolina and "tribal" histories of Apalachee, Timucua, Choctaw, and Catawba; but no one has recently attempted to tie the entire South together.[4] Other historians have redefined the frontier interactions of the South to reveal a ubiquitous intermingling and a widespread exchange of goods and services among Europeans, Indians, and Africans.[5] Yet these studies have not addressed the larger geopolitical issues.[6] Rather than coming together in discrete encounters solely to trade goods, Native, European, and African life, I argue, became inextricably linked by a combination of forces that no one in the South could avoid. To understand these forces we must uncover the patterns and contexts of group and individual interactions. We must examine the subregions in which people lived and their connections to other subregions. We must look at a broader world, an Atlantic world, that impinged on the South. This larger picture illuminates the South's diverse peoples. From new vantage points, we can observe and assess the obstacles and opportunities created by local, regional, and international conditions. Southerners made many important choices: the range of their answers was molded by experience but also by new and complex historical currents, seen and unseen, that enveloped their lives.

For much of the colonial period, the European colonies of the South were fragile beachheads of powerful empires. Even after a century of settlement, Spain's mission system, stretching across the northern tier of Florida and along the Georgia coast, fell easily to English and Indian attacks. Likewise, through much of its history, French Louisiana tottered, undersupported and undercapitalized, on the brink of destruction. Its overextended mother country never sent enough free settlers to build a vibrant, secure, and self-sustaining society in the Mississippi Valley. South Carolina had much greater success: its plantation system ultimately prevailed in the region. But this was not inevitable. Between 1670 and 1730, the colony struggled to survive. Institutional weakness, political and economic uncertainty, and lawlessness characterized the colony, and many Carolina settlers shared no common purpose but to accumulate riches. Unlike Puritan New Englanders, they displayed little interest in building a community. Carolinians had neither patterned settlements nor a unifying religious vision. Whereas the Puritan elite created a highly repressive society to keep watch on personal behavior, Carolina's elite brooked no interference with individual activities in pursuit of wealth. No other mainland English colony endured such a long period dominated by an incorrigible and politically corrupt elite. For two generations, few men of wealth and power could be found who would obey laws, whether royal, proprietary, or local, that prohibited their moneymaking schemes. Thomas Jefferson once wrote that slavery turned the children of slaveholders into petty tyrants, but in South Carolina the culture of self-aggrandizement preceded and then was reinforced by slaveholding. From first settlement, South Carolina elites ruthlessly pursued the exploitation of fellow humans in ways that differed from other mainland colonies, and they created a narcissistic culture that reacted passionately and violently to attempts to limit their individual sovereignty over their perceived social inferiors. The radicalism of nineteenth-century South Carolina nullifiers, duelists, and fire-eaters was a product not just of slaveholding but of a singular history and political culture that evolved in the late seventeenth and early eighteenth centuries.

No one can deny that South Carolina's sister colony, Virginia, also had a distinctively brutal colonial history epitomized in its early years by a ruthless elite. Founded more than a half-century before Carolina, the Old Dominion (1607) also began as a privately owned colony, where local officials disregarded directives from England as they amassed and exploited human labor. Seventeen years after the settlement of Jamestown, the Virginia Company lost its colony to the Crown. A small ruling class maintained control over much of the labor and thus the economy and political system of this royal colony. With little interference from the mother country, the elite built a profitable, if harsh and unstable, plantation regime. Virginia went through massive social upheaval in Bacon's Rebellion (1676) but then moved toward stability in the eighteenth century. In contrast, South Carolina's Lords Proprietors retained ownership of their colony for a half-century: though local leaders displayed the same relentless pursuit of wealth (and labor) as in Virginia, they faced considerable hindrance from the colony's owners in England and an even greater challenge from powerful native peoples who inhabited the region. This marked one of the most important differences between Virginia and South Carolina: warfare, disease, and outmigration of native peoples allowed the plantation regimes of the Chesapeake colonies (Virginia and Maryland) to develop relatively free of outside interference. With local Indian groups too reduced to undermine the plantation system and European enemies too distant to attack, Virginia's domestic development proceeded unchecked by external physical threats. South Carolina, by contrast, became thoroughly enmeshed in imperial competition with Spanish Florida and French Louisiana, while its powerful Indian neighbors played an even larger role in influencing the colony's economic and political development.

At the time of South Carolina's colonization in 1670, the South's Native Americans were in the midst of vast political, social, and cultural changes that had begun in the fifteenth century with the collapse of many Mississippian chiefdoms. Smaller political units emerged amid vast intraregional migration. The entrance into the South of newcomers, both Indians and Europeans, led aboriginals to alter their polities and group strategies. The adaptive success of some, but not all, of the South's native peoples severely limited European power throughout the colonial era. In each colony, hundreds of colonials faced thousands of Indians—and the Native Americans usually had superior military power owing to their skills and knowledge of the terrain. The Europeans were forced into dependence on Indian allies to defend their colonies and to conduct military campaigns. The ability to create these alliances alleviated the Europeans' tenuous position but did not reduce their dependence. Indians secured the colonies against external and internal foes while providing the economic wherewithal for each colony's survival: Indians fed the colonists, worked for them, and exchanged valuable commodities that the Europeans sold to other parts of the world to gain the capital needed to construct plantations. At any time, native peoples could have destroyed the plantations and entire colonies. Neither Louisiana nor Florida nor Carolina could have resisted the powerful Indian confederacies. These confederacies, formed in the seventeenth century, grew and increased in power in the early eighteenth century. They chose not to conquer the Europeans because they perceived that they gained less by conquest than by trade or by raid. Southern Indians were not opposed to conquest in principle, for some did annihilate their enemies; but warfare was conducted for specific cultural and geopolitical purposes, and the removal of the European colonies did not meet those ends. In warfare, warriors hoped to prove their valor, obtain captives and booty, and achieve vengeance against enemies; the goals of each Indian group included all of these factors plus the need to maintain alliances and security. Warfare and diplomacy were pivotal in the welfare of native communities as in the European colonies.

Given the quickly changing geopolitical circumstances that arose from European colonialism, many native peoples reacted speedily and effectively to reach their goals. Thousands of others did not successfully adapt. Some refused, while others were killed or captured. Many tried to adapt in the face of difficult and dire circumstances, but events—and people—conspired against them. Europeans, too, could not always meet their goals. Spanish Florida never established a large plantation society; the colony barely survived through much of the first half of the eighteenth century. French Louisiana's plantation system also never met imperial expectations, and its development was much overshadowed by French success in Martinique, Saint Domingue, Guadaloupe, and Canada. But English South Carolina eventually prospered, though it took a long time for staple crop production to supersede the Indian trade (including the trade in Indian slaves) in economic importance.

The Europeans would not have survived, let alone thrived, had not Indian assistance reinforced the umbilical cord that connected each colony to its respective imperial systems. Without the constant influx of military assistance, supplies, and new colonists, the European beachheads would have withered. Spanish Florida relied on a combination of Indian labor and Crown grants. French Louisiana depended on periodic influxes of new soldiers to man its far-flung outposts and a large supply of trade goods to appease Indian peoples who otherwise would likely have destroyed the colony. South Carolina needed the English imperial system for markets to purchase its products and the items it obtained from the Indian trade. Without these markets, Carolina had no raison d'être. South Carolina colonists displayed little interest in pursuing a subsistence existence until the 1750s, when many Europeans of humble backgrounds emigrated to the colony's backcountry.[7] Before then, the colony mostly attracted people preoccupied by the search for exportable commodities that others, mainly Indians and Africans, produced.

The South's European colonies thus stood sustained by their imperial connections to their mother country and to other colonies, but also by the native peoples who not only outnumbered them but fed, protected, and traded with them. The colonies' futures were as uncertain as their present. Yet despite much inherent weakness, the English settlement at Carolina played an inordinately influential role in the region, an outgrowth of its colonists' skills in manipulating and negotiating with native peoples, but owing more to the strength of the English empire. The English enticed native peoples into alliance with their colonies by having trade goods of superior quality and quantity to those offered by France and Spain. The English empire was also able to consume as much of the natives' commodities as the natives could produce, including the trade in Indian slaves. This trade *infected* the South: it set in motion a gruesome series of wars that engulfed the region. For close to five decades, virtually *every* group of people in the South lay threatened by destruction in these wars. Huge areas became depopulated, thousands of Indians died, and thousands more were forcibly relocated to new areas in the South or exported from the region.

This book is about the creation of the Old South within a preexisting South, that is, the establishment of a British plantation system—a political, social, and economic way of life—that dominated the region in the nineteenth century but was born much earlier, in the colonial period. There were many plantation societies in the seventeenth- and eighteenth-century western hemisphere. From Jamaica to Brazil, the Chesapeake to Saint Domingue, Europeans responded to the international market economy by building slave-based plantations producing staple commodities. But the Old South can be personified only in part by its plantation economy; it must have had, or developed, other characteristics that made it an identifiable region. Several scholars have argued that the distinctions between North and South result from the ethnically different peoples who settled the two regions, but I believe that it is patently absurd to claim that the South was Celtic and the North was English. The cultural differences between the two could barely account for the differences between North and South. Culture undoubtedly plays a huge role in shaping society, but not apart from such other factors as geography, technology, and demographics. The English, Scots, Irish, Germans, French, and other Europeans who settled in South Carolina had more in common in regard to ideas of colonization, economy, slavery, and society than they had differences. And they shared this worldview with colonists in the mid-Atlantic and northern regions. Whether a colony was Spanish, English, French, or Dutch had greater impact than where in Europe the settlers came from, for each colonial system shaped its colonies in particular ways, but each was limited by the possibilities allotted by the locale. English Puritans, for instance, did not build plantations in New England because the environment did not support this economic system, but Puritans readily became planters in the South, the Chesapeake, and the West Indies. Anglicans and Puritans, Scots Highlanders and Lowlanders, Ulstermen and Scots-Irish all operated within the same basic cultural parameters in English colonies.

They adapted to their New World environments and built their lives based on how they were best able to fit their "European" desires to the resources available, which included capital, tillable land, labor, and access to markets. An environment cannot define a region apart from its human population, but it presents to its human inhabitants the realm of the possible.

This book is not an environmental history—but it is a geopolitical one. It examines the South as a region inhabited by a variety of peoples whose lives were unavoidably linked. In the South, events on one side of the region could and did have dramatic impact on events on the other side. At a minimum, there was a ripple effect that everyone felt. For example, Chickasaw relations with the Arkansas on the Mississippi River had an impact on Chickasaw relations with the Choctaw to the south, which in turn affected Choctaw interactions with the Creek to the east, which subsequently influenced Creek relations with the Apalachee and Spanish to the southeast, which shaped the Spaniards' relations with the Yamasee and Carolina to the north.

Geopolitical studies tend to emphasize the competition of states for control of natural resources and markets. In the late seventeenth-century South there was little competition on a regional scale for natural resources in the form of minerals and land, but there was rivalry for the control of another resource: human labor. The demands for labor that occurred in the South were only partly internal to the region—for the trade networks of the international market economy drew labor *out* of the South in the form of Native American slaves at the same time that it drew African laborers *to* the South's British plantations. Charles Town became a depot drawing Europeans, Africans, and European goods; animal pelts and Native Americans, wood and agricultural commodities flowed out. The linchpin that facilitated the inward and outward flow were captured Native Americans, a highly valuable commodity who could be sold to any European colony.

Native American societies are traditionally viewed as external to the plantation system. In this book I demonstrate that the drive to control Indian labor—which extended to every nook and cranny of the South—was inextricably connected to the growth of the plantations and that the trade in Indian slaves was at the center of the English empire's development in the American South. The trade in Indian slaves was the most important factor affecting the South in the period 1670 to 1715: its impact was felt from Arkansas to the Carolinas and south to the Florida Keys. It created a swirl of activity that involved almost all, if not all, of the South's many peoples. It forced migrations and realignments, bringing misery to thousands and wealth to others. It existed on such a vast scale that more Indians were exported through Charles Town than Africans were imported during this period. This fact alone forces us to reconsider the character and impact of English colonialism on the American South.[8]

The trade in Indian slaves creates a new context for understanding the institution of slavery. For the most part, slavery was not a moral issue to southern peoples of the late seventeenth century. Europeans, Africans, and Native Americans all understood enslavement as a legitimate fate for particular individuals or groups. All accepted that "others" could or should have that status, though what that status encompassed and how slaves were treated varied greatly from group to group. In the seventeenth century, slavery as an institution had minimal economic significance for American Indians and usually much less importance for Africans than for Europeans. In Native American societies, ownership of individuals was more a matter of status for the owner and a statement of debasement and "otherness" for the slave than it was a means to obtain economic rewards from unfree labor. For Europeans, issues of status and debasement were secondary to the desire to reap wealth, though later, status and debasement became mechanisms for perpetuating and extending slavery. The slave *trade*, however, was an entirely new enterprise for most people of all three culture groups. Much more than slavery in this era, the slave trade reveals the contours of ethical behavior as each group defined it. People had to decide whether they wished to hunt not just their enemies but people they had never met; some went further and captured their allies and friends.

Native Americans who participated in the slave trade as enslavers engaged in a far different enterprise than Native Americans who owned slaves. The Indian slave trade was a part of the English empire's colonial system, and it introduced Indians to the international market economy, though economic considerations were neither the sole, nor necessarily the primary, reason to become enslavers. Yet the profits to be made by enslaving one's neighbors were important. For southern Native Americans, capturing other Native Americans was a way to obtain European trade goods. The swift introduction of these commodities into the South did not drastically alter Indians' economy or way of life, at least initially. The trade goods largely filled existing functions more efficiently. European axes, pots and pans, guns, paint, and clothing made life easier but did not change its patterns.[9] Hunting and processing animal pelts and capturing human beings in raids were not new activities, but the scale increased dramatically. Indians spent more time hunting—animals and humans—than previously, but the European articles they received in return provided time-saving equivalents; for instance, building a canoe or piragua now took much less time than formerly. Indian dependency on European trade goods did occur, but the question is when and how fast. Indians became dependent on alcohol, which severely undermined the fabric of native communities,[10] and they employed European weaponry—when skills with the bow and arrow were lost, they could not be reclaimed. Overhunting and reliance on European textiles created a need for European cloth, scissors, thread, and buttons. Many southern Indians were dependent on European trade goods by the mid-eighteenth century, but that occurred after the period of concern here. Indians' involvement in the slave trade was therefore not a direct result of their dependence on trade goods; the issues are more complex and subtle.

The Indian slave trade provided the strongest link between the South's many peoples in the late seventeenth and early eighteenth centuries. It forced every group that lived in the South to make decisions about themselves and their relations with their neighbors. It led southern peoples to reassess their individual and group identities. The Indian slave trade also exposed southern peoples to a new ideology of group identity, race. Since the mid-eighteenth century, the shibboleth of "race," an artificial construct that has no biological meaning, has had great importance in southern, American, and world history. In the late seventeenth century, however, it was a term of little substance, a concept under formation. Indians, Africans, and Europeans had many identities, but membership in a "race" was not one of them. Ethnicity was itself a concept undergoing vast transformation, particularly in Europe, where a combination of forces (including religion) brought into question the nature of group identity.[11]

An important subtheme of this book is the examination of how some of these ethnic identities evolved. Similar to the artificial construction of race, ethnicity, too, is a social construct by which a group of people defines itself in opposition to others. Ethnic identity becomes apparent only when people are faced with an external threat that draws them together. An ethnic group can have many people or few and can contain one or more language groups. Ethnicity constantly evolves as its members redefine themselves; it is relational and situational, one of many identities simultaneously held by its members. Ethnicity has no inherent tie to land or religion—groups migrate and can alter their religion any number of times. There exists no "pure" ethnicity because of the redefinitions and changes that take place over time.

Culture, as opposed to ethnicity, describes the broad patterns of ideas, behavior, and thought processes that characterize people who have lived for centuries in a specific geographic area. Culture develops as a product of a region's environment and history. Within each region, culture varies from one area to the next, but neighbors develop similar characteristics from exchanging ideas and technology and from contending with similar environmental and geopolitical forces. Groups of people within a culture tend to emphasize the differences among themselves and their neighbors, whereas people from distant regions focus on those same groups' similarities. Scots Highlanders could speak at great length on the differences between themselves and Lowlanders or between one clan and another, but a Choctaw viewing both would think the distinctions trivial. In these pages I examine the interactions of cultures in the South, Native American, African, and European, and the evolution of several southern ethnicities, specifically among the region's aboriginal peoples and the British Carolinians. At the end of the seventeenth century, Carolinians were actively defining themselves. Every European empire faced this task as it contended with incorporating or excluding "alien" peoples in its colonies. Monarchy, colonial proprietors, the church, merchants, colonists, *and* indigenous peoples all contributed to the construction of ideologies of imperialism through their thoughts and actions. In South Carolina, the debate over the nature of empire and the definition of British, European, and non-European peoples reflected the basic divisions of Whig versus Tory in Great Britain; the Act of Union (1707) between England and Scotland invigorated a "reform" movement in the colony to incorporate indigenous peoples into the empire and alter the nature of relations between Europeans and Indians; the failures of reform in 1715 set the southern colonies to exclude the South's Amerindian peoples permanently from their society. In this way, the Yamasee War of 1715 becomes the watershed event of the South's "racial" history as it defines the place of racially cast peoples: Africans, Indians, and Europeans in that society.

THE GEOPOLITICS OF THE SOUTH: THE SUBREGIONS

The development of South Carolina, the institution of an Indian slave trade and the formation of Indian confederacies occurred within specific locales, the product of geopolitical forces that few understood. Culture, demography, economy and history indelibly shaped southern life within specific geographic subregions that were related to other subregions, which were all connected and influenced by external regions. For most southern peoples, their subregions defined the larger world in which they lived. Culture, trade, and various forms of knowledge filtered from one subregion to the next, but not until the arrival of the Europeans did events in distant subregions and areas external to the South have such an immediate and direct impact upon daily life.[12]

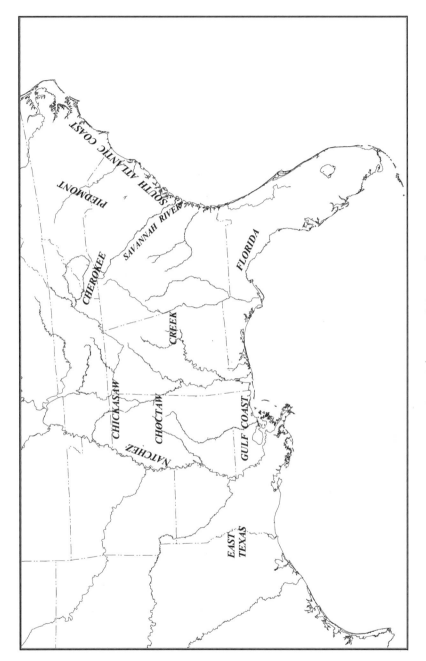

The subregions of the South

The *Florida* peninsula was the first subregion to have intensive and sustained contact with Europe. These contacts began in the early sixteenth century with the arrival of shipwrecked sailors and Spanish conquistadors. The planting of a permanent Spanish colony in 1565 at Saint Augustine led to the arrival of colonists, soldiers, and priests and to the extension of a mission system across northern Florida and the Georgia coast, creating a wall that protected the peninsula from land-based attacks. The powerful Indian peoples of north Florida who resided in the missions, were buttressed by the Spanish presence against enemies to the north and northwest, but they were also weakened by disease. Moreover, stormy relations with one another often undermined both the Indians' and Europeans' strength. A century later, repeated attacks from Europeans and by natives of neighboring subregions led to the collapse of the missions, opening a path for raiders from the north to infiltrate all the way to the Florida Keys. Both native and Spanish power on the peninsula declined significantly. Although Florida remained engaged in relations with other subregions of the South and became a long-standing thorn in the side to these areas, it remained, like most areas on the periphery, a secondary subregion in the regional geopolitics.

Immediately above Florida and to the west was the *Creek* subregion. In the area comprising modern-day southwest Georgia and central and northern Alabama, an array of native peoples converged to form the Creek Confederacy. Like most of the South's interior native peoples, these were agriculturists who spent considerable effort hunting to obtain meat and clothing. In the seventeenth century their main threats came from the Spanish-Indian alliance in north Florida, from the Westo Indians on the Savannah River, and probably from groups to their west that soon formed the Choctaw Confederacy. Because enemies surrounded them, the Creek might be assumed to have occupied a weak position, but they adapted well to the shifting geopolitical circumstances of the region and emerged as the premier locus of power in the mid-eighteenth-century South. This conglomeration of diverse peoples created a large and effective confederacy that well suited constituent interests for maintaining local autonomy within an alliance powerful enough to withstand external foes. The Creek are the best example of how the South's geopolitics shaped the political life of its people. The member groups had no reason to affiliate as a confederacy except to protect themselves from outsiders. Confederation met their needs, and it did so in a manner that neither eradicated nor significantly altered the individuals' and groups' traditional ways of life, social systems, and local polities.

To the west of the Creek, in modern-day central Mississippi, lived numerous groups that came together as the *Choctaw*. Similar to the Creek in culture, their situation differed in significant ways from their eastern neighbors. The Choctaw were more populous and less diverse than the Creek; they also appeared to the Europeans as much weaker militarily. Choctaw war parties tended neither to travel the great distances that the Creek ventured nor to be as offensively oriented. Hemmed in on the east by the Creek and on the west by the Mississippi River and the peoples who lived on its banks, the Choctaw had little compelling reason to undertake aggressive operations against their neighbors, save for the raids by which they obtained booty, fulfilled obligations, and kept enemies at bay. Unlike the Creek, they hardly pushed against neighboring subregions. As I explain in Chapter 6, the Choctaw used the terrain as their best defense against outsiders. Their greatest threat in the early colonial period arose from Chickasaw attacks from the north, which led the Choctaw into alliance with the French to the south. The Choctaw desired French goods and diplomatic assistance against the Chickasaw. Those goods were usually in short supply, and French mediation was of limited value. But Choctaw difficulties with the Chickasaw, the Creek, and the English forced them to accommodate to the French, whom they could easily have obliterated. In spite of their many enemies, their apparent offensive weakness, and the simmering internal problems that frequently threatened to explode, the Choctaw were the most powerful people west of the Creek, and their subregion was of major importance. All the subregions that surrounded them were weaker, except for the Creek, and all had to take into consideration Choctaw power. The Choctaw had the potential to destroy the peoples to the north, south, and west and to dominate the Mississippi River and the northern coast of the Gulf of Mexico. That they did not do those things made their inherent power no less formidable and their position no less important—all their neighbors recognized the potential. A Choctaw move in any direction had repercussions throughout the South.

Below the Choctaw and the Creek lived many Indian peoples along the northern coast of the Gulf of Mexico and near the mouth of the Mississippi River. In this *Gulf Coast* subregion lived the French and their allies, the *petite nations*. The latter comprised numerous small Indian groups with whom the French traded and provided mutual defense. Vulnerable to attacks from the north, and from Europeans by sea, neither Indians nor Europeans had the capacity to maintain this subregion against strong external threats; neither could they extend their power over neighboring subregions, for instance, by closing the Mississippi. The French, supported by their petite nation allies, generally fought a losing battle to spread their influence through the South.

Fortunately for the French, peoples in other subregions were desperate for help in the form of trade goods and alliance against the English, which the French supplied in varying degrees.

Up the Mississippi River, from roughly modern-day Natchez, Mississippi, to Memphis, Tennessee, was another subregion, which I label *Natchez,* after the people and place. In Natchez lived several groups that retained chiefdom characteristics long after they had disappeared elsewhere in the South. These peoples included the Natchez, Tunica, Taensa, and other smaller groups who lived among or near them. Also in this subregion, to the north, lived the Arkansas. All of these river peoples interacted with the French, who traveled the Mississippi between Canada and the Gulf of Mexico, and all were subject to slave raids inspired by English Carolina. These Mississippi River peoples had little direct contact with the Creek and other Indians east of the Choctaw and Chickasaw. As with Florida, this subregion was largely depopulated by the same factors that earlier struck the Florida peninsula: disease, slave raids, and warfare. Survivors migrated to the Gulf Coast, where they became petite nations, west into Louisiana, or east into the Creek Confederacy.

To the west of Natchez, in central Louisiana and *East Texas* lived many native peoples who developed important contacts with the French in Louisiana and the Spanish in New Mexico and Texas. This subregion had little impact on the rest of the South and was more a borderland between the South and New Mexico. Most of the inhabitants were culturally dissimilar to the Mississippian peoples, placing greater emphasis on hunting and gathering and less on settled agriculture. Arkansas, the area to the north of the Red River, was also a border area, but it was largely uninhabited at this time and mainly used as a hunting preserve by Indians living on all sides.

To the east of the Mississippi River and north of the Choctaw in northern Mississippi and southwest Tennessee was the *Chickasaw* subregion, inhabited by the Indians of that name. The Chickasaw bore much cultural and linguistic similarity to the Choctaw, with whom they often warred. The Chickasaw played a role in the South far above what their numbers would suggest. They became the chief slavers of Indians in the lower Mississippi Valley, selling their captives to the English traders from South Carolina. Chickasaw ties thus extended all the way to the Atlantic. But they also stretched both north and south. The ability of the Chickasaw to cut communication between Canada and Louisiana on the Mississippi River led to interaction with the French of Illinois and the Gulf Coast. Moreover, their endemic warfare with the Choctaw, and their periodic conflicts and accommodation with the Alabama and the Creek, ensured their great impact on the entire region. The

Chickasaw's location proved conducive to creating strong internal defensive works to protect against invasion. No major rivers ran through their subregion, making overland invasions by enemies difficult, slow, and detectable. By contrast, the Chickasaw found their location advantageous to penetrating Natchez and Choctaw subregions.

Far to the east of the Chickasaw were the *Cherokee*, who inhabited eastern Tennessee and western South Carolina. Their location in the Appalachian Mountains and its foothills isolated them somewhat from the rest of the South. The Cherokee made up one of the most populous of the southern confederacies, with three, and sometimes four, geographical divisions. In the late seventeenth century, they developed trade relations with Virginia, but entered the international market economy in a slower fashion than most of their neighbors. By the early eighteenth century, Cherokee attention had shifted to the east to Carolina and southward to the Creek, whereupon they played a significant but not a central role in the region. The Cherokee subregion remained on the periphery of the South's development, its main importance lying in its relationship to the subregions to the east, the Piedmont and the South Atlantic Coast.

Directly east of the Cherokee lay the *Piedmont* subregion, inhabited by the Piedmont Indians of North and South Carolina. These groups had little interaction with the Cherokee and with the groups that lived to the south of the Savannah River. Located on the northeastern periphery of the South, like the Indians of central Louisiana, they initially had little connection to the heartland, though this changed dramatically in the early eighteenth century with the growth of the English colonies and the outbreak of regional wars. The Piedmont Indians in the early colonial period lived somewhat isolated from the burgeoning English colonies, in spite of their proximity to them, and had intermittent contact with Iroquois from New York. The Iroquois traveled south along the east side of the Appalachians to trade, raid, and conduct diplomacy with Indian peoples throughout the South Atlantic. The Iroquois even interacted with the Creek and occasionally attacked the distant Chickasaw. In response to Iroquois raids, but even more to the growth of the English colonies, many of the Piedmont Indians joined together in the eighteenth century as the Catawba Confederacy. Throughout their history, even into the nineteenth and twentieth centuries, these groups maintained a low profile, usually but not always avoiding larger regional affairs.[13]

East of the Piedmont Indians, toward the coast of North Carolina lived the Tuscarora, a large Iroquoian people, and their numerous smaller neighbors. These Indians had little contact with natives below the Savannah River, having much more interaction with peoples to the north in Virginia. To the south of the Tuscarora lived the coastal Indians of South Carolina. These small groups came to be known as Settlement Indians to the South Carolina colonists, with whom they had much interaction. By the second quarter of the eighteenth century many were pushed out of the *South Atlantic Coast* subregion and either joined the Catawba or the Creek. The English colonies dominated the South Atlantic Coast subregion by 1717.

The last important subregion of the South lay along the *Savannah River* and extended into Georgia and the upper reaches of the Ocmulgee River. No other area of the South experienced as much population flux between 1670 and 1734. At times nearly deserted, at other times the area bustled with population and activity. On the Savannah at various and sometimes overlapping intervals could be found living Westo and Tuscarora from the north, Yamasee, Apalachicola, and Apalachee from the south, Chickasaw from the west, as well as Savannah (Shawnee), Yuchi, and Cherokee. The English established their most important trading posts along the river, which for them became a way station to the rest of the South, and which attracted Creek towns to migrate into northern Georgia in the early eighteenth century. The Savannah River subregion became a crossroads for trade and diplomacy; a launching ground and a target for major military engagements; and an area coveted for settlement by both Indians and Europeans. An extension of this subregion to the south, the modern-day state of Georgia, like Arkansas, was sparsely populated but used as hunting grounds through much of the colonial period, though the Creek had settlements in the southwest and central areas. Control of Georgia was disputed by the Creek, Spanish, English, and Savannah River Indians, and even the Cherokee made claim to the area as their hunting grounds.

From a geopolitical perspective, the Savannah River, Creek, and Choctaw subregions, which I label the *Central South*, were the critical areas of the region. Whoever controlled any of these three subregions had the potential to control the adjacent coastal subregions as well as the other inland subregions. Not until the invention of the steamboat did the coastal areas gain the technology for obtaining economic and military dominance over the Central South. The Mississippi River, for instance, was of secondary importance in the region because no group had the ability to use the river to extend its power in the region. The river was important to the French as a means for tying together their far-flung inland empire. But the difficulty of transporting goods upriver, and the ability of France to supply Louisiana via the Gulf of Mexico, did not make control of the river critical or essential, though the French sometimes viewed it in those terms.[14]

16

The South Atlantic Coast, the Florida peninsula, and the northern Gulf Coast subregions contained human populations (mostly Europeans and their Indian allies) who tried to exert their influence into the inland areas of the South, particularly into the Savannah River, Creek, Choctaw, Natchez, and Chickasaw subregions. European trade goods that were highly desired by the inland peoples entered through the coastal subregions. The inland groups in return exchanged items that the coastal groups desired, particularly for export: animal pelts and slaves. The groups who dominated coastal subregions competed with one another for access to and alliance with inland peoples; the inland peoples competed and fought one another for access and alliance with the dominant coastal groups. From a military standpoint, the coastal areas had the weakest position, for it was easier to attack and decimate the coastal groups than vice versa. In this regard, the Natchez resembled a coastal subregion, for the Mississippi gave enemies easy access to the Indian towns along the river.

The Creek area was probably the most important subregion of the entire South. The Creek developed enough power to influence the course of events in all directions. Neither the peoples to the west (the Chickasaw, Choctaw, and French) nor the peoples to the southeast (the Spanish and allied Indians) nor those to the northeast (English and allied Indians) could push effectively against the Creek, and most feared suffering at their hands. Other groups sought their alliance but usually settled for their neutrality. Creek towns along the Chattahoochee, Flint, Alabama, and other rivers had easy access to the Gulf of Mexico and thus the French and Spanish. The Creek also controlled the South's main east-west trade route and could cut relations between the Chickasaw and English. Eminently mobile, they could easily trade with or attack Charles Town, Saint Augustine, Mobile, Pensacola, or New Orleans. They could hem in the Cherokee to the north and control the Savannah River. The Creek had little influence on the far reaches of the South west of the Mississippi and in North Carolina, but indirectly their actions influenced these areas, too. The Creek had plenty of good land for hunting and farming and thus were not forced to expand their domain. All this good fortune is not to say that they were in any way all-powerful or always aware of their inherent strength. It took the Creek several decades to realize the extent of their power, and even then, Creek leaders found it hard to get all the constituent groups of the confederacy to act in concert. Moreover, their main enemy, the Choctaw, was something of an immovable force. The character of war between the two usually took the form of raid and counter-raid rather than any comprehensive assault that threatened the core of either group, but their mutual fear of widening hostilities kept each from overreaching in other directions.

The Europeans also recognized the key role played by the Creek and the importance of their subregion to the balance of power in the South. The Spanish, French, and English all hoped to expand inward. From Florida, the Spanish pushed against the Creek subregion in the seventeenth century but made little headway. Late in the century, the Spanish were put on the defensive, and once it became clear that they could not conquer the entire South, they sought to maintain Saint Augustine and Pensacola to anchor their colony while providing support for their Indian allies to resist the Creek, English, and Savannah River Indians. Toward that end they hoped to obtain Creek neutrality so that they could focus on the English and Savannah River Indians.

The French hoped to extend their influence over the Central South by controlling the Mississippi, which they expected would provide them the wherewithal for pushing the English out of the area. The French wished to make themselves the chief suppliers of goods to Indians. They dreamed of uniting Indians against the English and the Creek, if the latter resisted their leadership; but they never came close to brokering pan-Indian support.

The English had less clear goals in the Central South than the French and the Spanish. In South Carolina, private interests often set the agenda that guided colonial diplomacy. Whatever goals the English Crown and its agents possessed, the reality of English colonial life was that the pursuit of profits by English settlers was the force that most shaped colonial policies. Frenchmen and Spaniards both hoped to make profits in the South, and their officials were not above adapting imperial goals to their own personal interests. But in South Carolina, from first settlement, the quest for profits directed politics, diplomacy and warfare: the Crown's, proprietors', and colony's interests were barely considered. When local officials finally learned that allowing private interests to conduct diplomacy and Indian affairs was detrimental to the common good, they found these private interests too ensconced to overcome. The English colonials soon understood the weakness of their subregion and the power of the Indians, but it took a devastating pan-Indian war to expose their weakness and the importance of the Central South to their welfare.

The narrative that follows is divided into four parts. In the first part, I describe the South before the arrival of Europeans and the entry of the Spanish and French in the sixteenth century. This wave of "newcomers" was followed in the late seventeenth century by a second wave comprising the Westo and the English, who initiated the Indian slave trade, and the Yamasee and Scots, who played key roles in turning the Savannah River into a hive of activity and a focus for the British and Spanish imperial systems. Part 2 examines how southerners—Indians and Europeans—responded to the slave trade, adjusting to a rapidly changing world in which diplomacy and alliance were necessary for survival. This section investigates how Europeans and Indians communicated their interests and conducted relations. It probes the competition among English, French, and Spanish to control the South. It explores the evolution of British imperial ideology and how Native American peoples were drawn into European affairs, particularly by slaving. Part 3 then focuses on the evolution of South Carolina's Indian policies as the colony tried to rationalize Indian affairs to protect its burgeoning plantation economy. Part 4 explores the growth of English influence coupled with the ultimate failure of their Indian policies. It measures the impact of the Indian slave trade on its victims and the enslavers while tracing the rise of a pan-Indian movement against the British, pointing the way to the establishment of new relations among Europeans and Indians.

PART ONE

THE SOUTH TO 1701

1

THE MISSISSIPPIAN ERA

THE CHIEFDOMS

The South existed as a distinctive region from about the year A.D. 1000, when maize (*zea mays*) production increased substantially among the area's inhabitants. Easily storable and highly nutritional, maize bore little resemblance to today's corn, which has a much smaller percentage of the original caloric, mineral, and vitamin values.[1] Roasted, pounded into hominy, fried, boiled, and baked, corn was processed by southern Indians into dozens of dishes from which many people received more than half of their calories.[2] Archaeologists are unsure whether maturing political organization led to increased production or, more likely, increased production led to new and more sophisticated polities, but the results were the same: maize became the building block of the so-called Mississippian Cultures (1000–c. 1730),[3] the most complex societies north of Mexico.[4]

Maize allowed southern Indians to create permanent residences on stable farmsteads that were successively occupied for generations. Because of the rich soils and a favorable climate, southern farmers produced two crops of maize per year, a green corn harvested in summer and a second crop in autumn. Early in the Mississippian period, maize was stored in large belowground pits. The rise of chiefdom polities (c. 1000) led to the pooling and storage of the surplus in aboveground structures at local centers. Storage life was usually one to two years, perhaps longer. Chiefs redistributed maize to commoners during droughts and exchanged surplus maize for prestige items from neighboring peoples. Maize was also incorporated into religious ceremonies, some of which persisted into the historic period, notably the Green Corn ceremony celebrated by many southern peoples.[5]

Maize remained the South's preeminent food source even after European colonization. The Old South (early eighteenth century to mid-nineteenth century) built its wealth on cash crop staples: rice, cotton, tobacco, and sugar; but production of corn, rather than wheat, filled the basic dietary needs of humans and animals, shaping the region's culture, economy, and diet. Hominy, grits, and corn bread were more than just staples of southern cuisine. The ability to produce surplus corn was as important for Europeans as Indians— it meant that they could withstand the periodic ruin of their cash crops owing to bad weather and did not have to rely on food imports as did other plantation regions, notably the West Indies. The premier historian of southern agriculture, Lewis Cecil Gray, observed of the marriage between the South and maize: "Indian corn was universally grown from the earliest period of settlement. The taste acquired for it in the various forms in which it was prepared no less than its great economic advantages made it the staff of life for high and low."[6]

With the rise of maize, hunting and gathering did not end, but intensive agricultural production allowed the native peoples to spend less time attaining subsistence and more time in craft production, religious and leisure activities, and warfare. It also meant that some individuals did not have to engage in subsistence and could specialize as administrators, servants, artisans, and perhaps soldiers. Surplus and specialization led to multitiered societies of elites and commoners. Archaeologists agree that the chiefdom polities all shared this inegalitarian social structure, though class relations varied in each. The ethnohistorical record—the reports of the first Spanish explorers— describes chiefs of substantial kingdoms carried in litters. Chiefs had the power of life and death over their subjects, and they ritually sacrificed commoners in religious ceremonies and at the death of the highest-ranking elites.[7] Birth defined status, and at least some chiefs claimed descent from the sun, but personal skills, such as in warfare and hunting, could elevate an individual's rank within the hierarchy.

By comparing sites throughout the South and to other regions of the world, archaeologists can furnish much information on social and political organization. In general, they divide chiefdoms into two types: simple and complex. Simple chiefdoms were characterized by two-tiered organization, whereas the complex, or paramount chiefdoms, had three or more tiers. Paramount chiefdoms collected tribute from simple chiefdoms, thus the extra tier of organization. They generally had larger populations than simple chiefdoms, were highly organized, commanded huge amounts of labor, and conducted sophisticated military campaigns.[8] Although some survived into the historic period, the paramount chiefdoms, and the Mississippi culture in general, peaked in the South in the fourteenth century.

Chiefs established networks of power, marrying kin into nearby villages, from which they received tribute and labor. They also built and maintained power by monopolizing religious rituals—the group's ideology—which gave them and their birth lines the right to rule. Rituals and religious life centered on the thousands of mounds built by Mississippian peoples throughout the South—hence the name often ascribed to them: the Moundbuilders. The mounds served as burial grounds for individuals and as platforms on which to build temples and houses for chiefs. Many were multilevel and used for hundreds of years. Archaeological examination of the mounds and their contents provides much of what we know of precontact peoples, in addition to the records left by the early Spanish explorers. From the mounds and surrounding village sites, archaeologists can assess stages of occupation, hierarchy, political organization, subsistence, nutrition, and patterns of trade.

Examination of burials provides the most substantial record of hierarchical organization among the chiefdoms. From skeleton remains we have learned that elites often had a better and more balanced diet than commoners. Prestige goods—items produced outside the chiefdom, badges of office, and highly specialized craft items—signify elite burials. Among these prestige goods were columella pendants, sheet-copper hair ornaments and headdresses, robes, pearls, discoidals, and ear ornaments.[9] Fineware ceramics and marine-shell beads were others. John H. Blitz shows in his study of the Tombigbee River chiefdoms that the ability to produce and possess prestige goods was less distinct in the two-tiered simple chiefdoms than in the more stratified complex chiefdoms. In the simple chiefdoms, specialized craft production took place in small outlying villages, not just in local centers.[10] The complex chiefdoms, by contrast, had more specialization, and the chiefs had greater access to distant trade goods and raw materials because of their control over external relations.

Signs of warfare are evident from burial remains, the building of bastioned palisades, and the ethnohistorical evidence that records endemic warfare between neighboring peoples. The advent of the bow and arrow in the Late Woodlands era (A.D. 600–1000) led to improved fortifications. The

Mississippians constructed plastered palisades and wattle-and-daub houses to protect against fire arrows.[11] Extensive moats and bastions increased the strength of local centers. Some of the palisades were quite large and built to protect fields as well as housing and storehouses.[12] Cahokia, the largest known Mississippian center, used about twenty thousand logs in each of its four phases of palisades construction.[13] Blitz suggests that fortification construction drew labor from outlying villagers, who would have benefited from the protection of their surplus—thus illustrating the ability of certain chiefdoms to command and organize many laborers over a fairly large area.[14]

There is much disagreement about the causes of warfare.[15] It is unclear whether chiefdoms pursued warfare to control natural resources, obtain captives for labor, or for other reasons. Complex chiefdoms undoubtedly employed their military to undertake conquest and exact tribute. Raiding was more common than conquest, but the scale of warfare may have owed as much to geography and demography as to any other factors. For instance, in the South Appalachian area, where chiefdoms had both a great deal of land, and buffer zones between them, warfare was largely confined to raiding, and Indians had little knowledge of the core center of neighboring chiefdoms.[16] In contrast, in the central and lower Mississippi Valley, rival chiefdoms existed in close contact: warfare was extensive with conquest always a possibility.

Whether by raiding or conquest, if enemies reached one's mounds, then a disaster of the first magnitude occurred. Archaeologist David G. Anderson postulates that one reason why "major Mississippian centers, once abandoned, were not invariably occupied" was that desecration of mounds by invaders undermined elites' right to rule, for those rights were based on their genealogical-religious authority. Elites, Anderson argues, "were ideologically bound to remain about their place of origin."[17] This may explain how Spanish explorers hastened the decline of many chiefdoms in the sixteenth century. Spanish abuse of chiefs and disrespect for sacred sites undercut the sanctity of native leaders. Moreover, Hernando de Soto's *entrada* (royally sanctioned expedition), in particular, but others as well, brought into closer contact Indians from competing chiefdoms. These Indians traveled with the Spanish or went to meet them. They may have used their newly gained knowledge of their neighbors' core centers for attacking sacred places. It took just one successful attack on the mounds to wreak havoc and destruction on these politically unstable polities.

Mississippian chiefdoms varied in size and complexity, but they shared many characteristics. The riverine system of the southeast encouraged the movement of goods and ideas, particularly on the Mississippi, Tombigbee,

Coosa, and Savannah River watersheds, so even where extensive trade did not take place, there was enough exchange of goods and technology to create general cultural similarities. Religious iconography was similar throughout the region, particularly in the stylization of bird figures,[18] bilobed arrows, and square-cross gorgets, which leads scholars to perceive much affinity in belief systems, though the nature of those beliefs remains elusive.[19] A few scholars believe that resemblance between Aztecan and Mississippian symbols resulted from a network of direct exchange, but more believe that any shared morphology occurred discretely and not from direct contact.[20]

Cultural, political, and social development varied from place to place, in part, however, as a result of cycling. Anderson defines cycling as "the recurrent process of the emergence, expansion, and fragmentation of complex chiefdoms amid a regional backdrop of simple chiefdoms." He perceives constantly shifting centers of power in the southeast "as first one community and then another assumes prominence."[21] Cycling occurred for a variety of reasons. For one, the chiefdoms were politically unstable. Population growth, territorial expansion, and factional competition among elites all fed instability. A chief's death always presented the potential for internal problems.[22] The Spanish explorers recorded murders of claimants and their supporters; internal divisions also led to break-offs of villages and simple chiefdoms, usually to join other chiefdoms. Only with difficulty, and the threat of military reprisal, could paramount chiefs maintain influence and control over their more distant villages—which through new combinations could challenge a chiefdom's core. With this pattern of rise and fall there was no linear development to a more sophisticated political structure, and it is unclear what new factors would have been necessary for the southern chiefdoms to have evolved, if at all, into states,[23] without first having outside states organize chiefdoms into confederacies as a mode of control and taxation.

It also is unclear why so many of the major Mississippian centers disappeared by 1400. There is no archaeological evidence of severe climatic or environmental change or of epidemic disease or an increase in warfare. Likewise, the second wave of declension that occurred with the Spanish arrival in the sixteenth century is also difficult to document. Marvin T. Smith finds little archaeological evidence of pandemic disease in the early contact period in the South,[24] though he assumes that it must have taken place. Other archaeologists repeat Smith's speculations as authoritative proof that disease must have been widespread. There *is* much ethnohistorical evidence of disease in the seventeenth century—but we are nowhere close to making informed judgments on the impact of disease in the sixteenth century, when the Spanish first arrived. There may not be a link between disease and the collapse of the chiefdoms because (1) so many chiefdoms disappeared by 1400, not 1500, before Europeans brought new pathogens to the region, and (2) the large waves of pandemic disease of the seventeenth century occurred after the collapse of the chiefdoms encountered by the Spanish in the sixteenth century.[25] Moreover, the survival of the Natchez chiefdom into the early 1730s evinces that chiefdoms could and did exist side by side with European colonies. Chiefdoms also existed in similar form among some of the Natchez's neighbors, so it cannot be said that the European presence inherently caused the collapse of chiefdoms, either by disease or by the mere presence of a more sophisticated social and political system in the region. Disease and European expansion into the South might have contributed to some chiefdoms' disintegration, but there must have been other factors involved, because not all collapsed yet so many disappeared before European arrival.

Further disputes exist over the relationship of pre- and protocontact peoples to those of the historic period.[26] In many instances, postcontact peoples did not inhabit the same exact area as their ancestors. Migration, and the creation of new towns and political identities, was quite common throughout the precontact and colonial South. Towns and groups of towns broke from one chiefdom and joined another, and remnants converged into new towns. Sometimes entire areas became nearly depopulated as large-scale outmigration occurred. Anderson has analyzed this situation along the Savannah River, home to numerous Amerindians, "until a nearly valleywide organizational collapse occurred in the 15th century," except along the headwaters.[27] Likewise, the disappearance of the most significant and extensive chiefdom, Cahokia, near modern-day Saint Louis, is equally mysterious.[28] The disappearance of polities and the movement of peoples do not negate the ancestry of the historic-era southern Indians to the earlier chiefdoms. They were as much the same peoples as the English were born of Angles, Saxons, Normans, and others. Southern Indians of the historic period inherited their ancestors' Moundbuilder culture, technology, and religion. They continued to rely on the bow and arrow for hunting and fighting; they still lived in palisaded towns and built bastioned fortifications; maize was their dietary staple; kinship still defined a person's place in society, even as other identities altered; canoes and piraguas persisted as the main source of transportation for many; and the ancient game of chunky remained a favorite pastime. (Chunky was played with a stone and sticks set as goal posts on fields located at town centers.) Villages of small family homesteads characterized both precontact chiefdoms and postcontact bands. Warfare was endemic for both, with the capture of women an important goal of raiders. So what changed?

Although slaves were kept in both chiefdoms and bands, they were unimportant to the band economy, whereas there is evidence of chiefdoms employing unfree labor in the fields.[29] In bands (and probably in chiefdoms), the keeping of slaves was a mark of status as well "as a demonstration of the prowess of their captors."[30] Slaves had the further utility of demonstrating to free Indians an alternative, and undesirable, existence as an "other," an individual without substantive identity—and thus a reminder to all of the importance of kinship.[31] Europeans did not introduce slavery or the notion of slaves as laborers to the American South but instead were responsible for stimulating a vast trade in humans as commodities. Because of their previous history of raiding for captives, many southern Indians adapted to European slave trading practically overnight.

There were other important changes from the pre-European contact to post-European contact peoples: social stratification declined, tribute was no longer delivered to local centers, and towns entered into decentralized confederacies. Spiritual life undoubtedly also changed greatly. Except for the Mississippi River peoples who remained in chiefdoms and maintained temples, other southern Indians no longer built temples and retained a priesthood, whose work revolved in part around the temples. In spite of the loss of rituals, temples, and priestcraft, the spiritual substance largely survived. Southern native religion remained holistic: there was no separation between the sacred and the secular, as existed among Europeans. Respect for authority, the importance of kin identity, and the centrality of animals and the environment in the spiritual worldview all carried over from the Mississippian era. The Spanish encountered powerful chiefdoms, but the English arrived much later and except in Virginia did not interact with chiefdoms, and so they had much less of an idea of the historical development and basis of southern Indian cultures. Even if those Spanish who permanently settled Florida had little knowledge of the many chiefdoms encountered by the Spanish explorers of earlier decades, the later Spanish missionized the Apalachee, a powerful Florida chiefdom famed throughout the South. The Apalachee inflicted successive defeats on Spanish entradas, but they were in decline by the time of permanent colonization under Pedro de Menéndez de Avilés in 1565. As in other parts of their empire, the Spanish operated with an existing native polity to build their mission system and through that system quickly extended themselves across northern Florida.[32] In other words, they worked with, and gained knowledge of, chiefdom organization and culture. This contrasts with the English entry more than a century later into Carolina, where English settlers encountered relatively small bands, except for the powerful Westo, whose political culture was Iroquoian, not Mississippian. Thus, in the South, the Spanish interacted with large chiefdoms as well as small bands, whereas the English in the Carolinas had contact only with small bands, save for the large group of Iroquoian invaders from the north. This may have shaped English feelings of cultural superiority, for they saw in local Indian polities little that was recognizable in their own culture and thus deserving of respect. The Spanish, by contrast, appreciated the religious and political hierarchy of the chiefdoms they encountered, and though they condemned native religion and political structures, they saw in these recognizable institutions a building block for incorporating Indians into their own polities and church.

In sum, the outward forms more than the inner substance changed for southern Indians from the pre-European contact to postcontact eras. To the Europeans who engaged these peoples so different from themselves, the outward forms provided cultural clues on how contact and exchange could and should take place. The Spanish perceived, in some of the Florida Indians, structured societies in which priestcraft and politics were utterly entwined in a hierarchical structure akin to their own; the English could see nothing but anarchy in the Indians they met further north in Carolina; the French, arriving in the lower Mississippi Valley at the end of the seventeenth century, encountered both chiefdoms and bands, and they had the added advantage of sending many people who possessed long-term experience with a variety of native peoples in Canada, and even though that experience did not lead most French to accept indigenous cultures on their own terms, it allowed for some French to develop a keen understanding of native societies, at least keener than that generally held by the English and Spanish.

EARLY CONTACTS BETWEEN
NATIVE AMERICANS AND EUROPEANS

The Mississippian culture area largely corresponded with the South, extending from Oklahoma east into southern Illinois, south to the Gulf of Mexico, north to the Ohio River Valley, and east to the Atlantic Ocean. By the sixteenth century it had constricted from the west and north. Arkansas became a borderland between the West and the South as western hunters pushed Mississippians eastward, and the Ohio River country was no longer part of the region, although the Ohio fed into the Mississippi, as Algonquins and Iroquois took over the area. The South remained connected to the North and the lands of Algonquins and Iroquois through a corridor along the east side of the Appalachians, leading to trade, warfare, and migration, particularly of Tuscarora moving south into North Carolina and later by Westo settling on the Savannah River. Along this corridor lay Virginia, a border region outside the South but connected to it.[33] At the time of first contact with Europeans, Virginia's aborigines, mostly of the Powhatan chiefdom, were culturally halfway between the southern Indians and the northern Algonquins.[34] On the north-south corridor, Virginia received cultural transmissions from both directions, and unlike the Iroquois to the north, Powhatans rarely ventured southward or northward. Shut off by the Appalachians and unconnected to the South's river system, Virginia in the Mississippian and colonial eras had little impact on the region beyond the Jamestown colony's traders, who generally did not go farther than the Cherokee in the southern Appalachians. Not until the regionwide transformation brought about by the creation of the United States and later transportation developments was Virginia brought into the South.[35]

It is only by reading history backward, and faultily, that the Virginia area appears to be part of the South in the prehistoric and colonial periods. It is ordinarily assumed that Virginia had always been part of the South, and the most important part of that region, for it was the first English colony to develop a plantation society based on slave labor, and the colonies that formed south of it ostensibly imitated Virginia by doing the same. But slavery and plantations were ubiquitous in the European colonial world. Moreover, there was little migration by Virginians to the South, by which they could carry their ideas and institutions, until a much later period.[36] Certainly South Carolina had far more in common with Barbados than it did with Virginia: Carolina received European settlers, African slaves, trade goods, and its model for plantation agriculture from the West Indies.[37] Likewise, Saint Augustine's connections with Cuba and Louisiana's to the French sugar islands played influential roles in their development—both had little to no contact with Virginia, whose main axis of trade and cultural exchange was with Europe, not America. If the South is defined as an area of interrelationships, where affairs in any one corner of the region could dramatically affect the region, then Virginia clearly lay outside the colonial South. Virginia may be excluded from the pre-nineteenth-century South not just as a point of nomenclature but also to emphasize the lack of connectedness and influence of the Old Dominion on the region. As I show—Spanish Florida, French Louisiana, British Carolina, and the Indian peoples from the lower Mississippi Valley to the Atlantic and north to the southern Appalachians lived lives that were intimately connected: together they made up a specific region, their fate enmeshed by the area they inhabited. Interactions between Creek and Choctaw, for instance, had direct bearing on every other group of people, from the Cherokee in the southern Appalachians to the Apalachee in Florida and from the small Gulf Coast groups to the Chickasaw and peoples of the central Mississippi Valley. Virginia was almost unaffected by this relationship and also had minimal impact on any other peoples of the region, save for the Cherokee and some of the Piedmont Indians with whom they traded.

Spain had much greater impact on the South than Virginia through its explorers and the establishment of permanent settlements in Florida. Spanish exploration from the South Atlantic to the Mississippi Valley kindled European interest in the South while introducing Native Americans to European culture. The time lag between Spanish exploration of the region (mid-sixteenth century) and the steady influx of Europeans (late seventeenth century) might have had a long-term positive impact on southern Native Americans living distant from the Atlantic coast. The Mississippi Valley peoples had intensive contacts with Soto's entrada in the 1540s, and then more than a century elapsed before Europeans again entered the region. This allowed the Mississippi Valley peoples time to recover their numbers from any adverse reactions to newly introduced European microbes—and to develop resistance to those pathogens, so that when Europeans returned, the Indians were not decimated by Old World diseases.[38] This contrasted with the situation in Florida, where there was a persistent influx of Spanish explorers, shipwrecked sailors, and then colonists from the 1520s onward. Florida's indigenous population had little time to adapt to the pathogenic onslaught and suffered more dearly than did native people elsewhere in the South.

Archaeologists and historians tend to overemphasize the impact of the Spanish on the Native American peoples of the South outside of Florida and the South Atlantic coast. Whatever impact disease had—carried by Spaniards and their animals and trade goods—native populations away from Florida recovered quickly enough that the new political units could defend themselves ably against the Europeans. During the seventeenth century, the chiefdoms along the Atlantic seaboard and west to the Mississippi evolved into new political forms, mostly as confederacies—an alliance of towns whose connections were voluntary. These towns and confederacies were not as hierarchical or as organized as in the chiefdoms of the precontact period, but that made them no less effective for meeting the changing circumstances of southern life. If anything, these new decentralized confederacies of disparate towns and peoples were much superior to the rigid chiefdoms in their political flexibility. Southern Indians did not devolve into inferior polities, they evolved into societies that better suited their new world. The transformation from chiefdom to confederacy began with the splintering of the chiefdom into towns. These towns then affiliated to resist more powerful organized forces—both European and Indian—that entered the region. As they confederated, however, the towns did not create new centralized polities but retained their independence: their alliance was predicated on defense, though it could be employed for aggression against others. The egalitarian social structure and independence of towns gave individuals and groups more room for adjusting to the peoples, ideas, and goods that entered and transformed the region in the late seventeenth century and afterward. The challenges presented were enormous, and the less authoritarian societies of the postcontact period adapted quickly. Fluidity of opinion in egalitarian bands helped groups evade disasters that a stubborn elite, bound by ties to place, ideology, and political forms, might not have been able to avoid. Southern Indians did not consciously decide to form these new political units; the Choctaw, Cherokee, Creek, and Catawba confederacies were formed over time, as old traditions blended with new needs and circumstances.

Spain did play a role in the changes. Although Spanish settlement was confined largely to the Florida peninsula and along the Atlantic coast into Georgia, the raids of Spanish-allied Indians into Alabama helped unite in defense peoples who evolved into the Creek confederacy, though even there Spanish influence in sparking the creation of new political organizations might not have been paramount.[39] After the initial forays of Spanish explorers, Spain's influence did not reach much farther into the South than Florida, where it was of mammoth proportions.

The Spanish sought to repeat successes in Mexico and Peru in *La Florida*—to find precious metals and convert heathens. The search for exotic foods and pathways to the Orient also intrigued Spaniards.[40] Yet the first Spanish attempts were failures of great magnitude. Of the Pánfilo de Narváez expedition's six hundred men who landed at Tampa Bay in 1528—only a handful survived. One problem met by the explorers, and by subsequent Spanish forays, was the impressive military power of the Indians, whose bows and arrows were more than a match for the Europeans. Álvar Núñez Cabeza de Vaca, one of the few survivors of the Narváez fiasco, wrote of how "good armor" was of no "avail" against the Apalachee. This was owing to "the power and skill with which the Indians are able to project" arrows from bows "as thick as the arm, of eleven or twelve palms in length, which they will discharge at two hundred paces with so great precision that they will miss nothing." Cabeza de Vaca saw an "arrow that had entered the butt of an elm to the depth of a span," and other witnesses swore that they had seen red oaks, as thick as "the lower part of the leg, pierced through from side to side by arrows."[41] The Spanish also had difficulty adjusting to the Indians' style of warfare—they always had to be on guard for what the Europeans described as the Indians' reckless bravery. Rodrigo Ranjel, who served as private secretary to Hernando de Soto, recorded with amazement episodes of "great courage and boldness" on the part of the Apalachee. "For example," he recounted,

> two Indians once rushed out against eight men on horseback; twice they set the village on fire; and with ambuscades they repeatedly killed many Christians, and although the Spaniards pursued them and burned them they were never willing to make peace. If their hands and noses were cut off they made no account of it. . . . Not one of them, for fear of death, denied that he belonged to Apalachee; and when they were taken and were asked from whence they were they replied proudly: "From whence am I? I am an Indian of Apalache." And they gave one to understand that they would be insulted if they were thought to be of any other tribe than the Apalaches.[42]

Soto's destructive entrada (1539–1543) accomplished little but to alienate Indians. His force of more than six hundred traveled from Florida north to the Carolinas and west to the Mississippi, where Soto died of disease. Everywhere the Spanish went, Indians were introduced to the worst that Europe had to offer. Published reports by survivors detail the sadism, abuse, rapes, and murders committed by the conquistador and his men on their several-thousand-mile quest for precious metals and jewels.[43] Ranjel, one of those eyewitnesses, recalled that even where the invaders received a friendly reception, the Spanish found ways to spoil the situation. Welcomed by the female leader of Cofitachequi with numerous presents, Ranjel admitted that he and Soto sneaked into the Indians' temple and stole two hundred pounds of pearls.[44] They spent fifteen days with these Indians "in peace, and they played with them." The Indians "swam with the Christians and helped them very much in every way." But then the Indians fled because Soto "asked for women."[45] The Spanish and Indians reconciled their differences on this occasion, but many other encounters ended badly. As Ranjel summarized, somewhat rhetorically: "why," it must be asked, that "at every place they came to, this Governor [Soto] and his army asked for those tamemes or Indian carriers, and why they took so many women and these not old nor the most ugly . . . ravaging the land and depriving the natives of their liberty without converting or making a single Indian either a Christian or a friend." They had captured the women "for their foul use and lewdness," baptized them "more on account of carnal intercourse . . . than to teach them the faith." They held "chiefs and principal men captive," pillaged wherever they went, and enslaved Indians to carry what they stole. The reason Ranjel offered: none other than greed and lechery.[46]

These were not the only factors, however, for the Spanish explorers looked on the Indians as savage heathens who deserved brutal treatment. This perspective horrified many in Spain, and the Soto entrada in particular inspired a movement for reform spearheaded by Bartolmé de las Casas.[47] The Spanish crown responded favorably and ordered that on future expeditions the cross must accompany the sword, Amerindians could not be enslaved, and permanent settlements must be established. Success was not quickly forthcoming. In 1556, Juan Pardo landed north of the Savannah River on the Sea Islands of South Carolina in hopes of creating a base from which to search for mines and pathways to Mexico and to convert Indians. Pardo failed. Tristan de Luna Arellano then led a force of fifteen hundred colonists to Pensacola Bay in 1559, but a hurricane and other impediments led to another disaster.[48] By then, however, Spanish thinking shifted to building farms and homesteads and exploiting the land for its agricultural wealth. Additional impetus came from the need to control the Atlantic coast. Attacks from English, French, and Dutch corsairs in Atlantic and Caribbean waters forced the Spanish to reorganize their shipments of New World precious metals to Europe.[49] Spanish ships were notified of a predetermined date to meet in Havana, from which the royal navy would escort them home. The fleet then sailed up the Florida coast before heading across the Atlantic. Control of the Florida peninsula became crucial to the protection of Spain's American riches.

As the Spanish prepared to occupy Florida, they received word that the French planned to colonize the peninsula.[50] Admiral Gaspard de Coligny approved an expedition of mostly Huguenots led by Jean Ribaut, which landed in 1562. The French immediately set about searching for precious metals, but also established naval bases from which to prey on Spanish shipping. As French carpenter Nicolas Le Challeux reminisced of those who went: "They volunteered for a variety of reasons: some spurred by an honest desire to see Florida, hoping that the trip would enrich them; others were driven by the desire for adventure; some had nothing to lose; they preferred to tempt the raging seas than to remain in their current poor state and condition."[51]

The French built Fort Caroline near modern-day Saint Augustine and

Charlesfort near Port Royal, South Carolina.[52] Ribaut sailed to France for supplies and reinforcements but was captured and imprisoned in England in 1563.[53] (His visit to England played an important role in piquing the English's interest to establish a privateering base on the North American coast— which resulted in the settlement of the Roanoke colonies.) Released or escaped, Ribaut journeyed to France and then returned to Florida, where he learned that the Spanish were soon expected under the *Adelantado* (possessor of a contract from the monarch to wield civil and military authority over a territory) Pedro Menéndez de Avilés, charged to remove the French and erect a permanent military and civilian establishment. Ribaut decided that the French were better off meeting the Spanish at sea. His fleet unsuccessfully sought the enemy for five days, and on its return a storm dispersed the flotilla, shipwrecking many. When the Spanish arrived, they easily subdued the French fort and hanged its inhabitants. Though the French outnumbered Menéndez on the coast, he took full control. He accomplished this through trickery, with grievous results for the French. The widely scattered shipwrecked French parties all decided that they could not remain indefinitely on the beach and must surrender. Because the Spanish were so outnumbered, they insisted that the French submit in small parties. Promising no terms, the Spanish insinuated that the French would be treated as prisoners of war. Instead, after learning each man's occupation and religion, the Spanish treated the prisoners "like beasts being led to the slaughter."[54] With their hands tied behind them, hundreds of defenseless captives were stabbed to death.[55] Menéndez justified his actions to his king, claiming the French had been spreading "the odious Lutheran doctrine in these Provinces, and that I had [to make] war [with] fire and blood . . . against all those who came to sow this hateful doctrine." In spite of his professed religious motives, Menéndez spared sixteen men of the heretical faith whose special skills he required.[56]

The first meeting of Europeans in "La Florida" had concluded in an incredible display of violence. The competition for Florida and the South would hereafter be defined largely by warfare. Legal claims for territory had almost no meaning—brute force was to be the deciding factor. In this competition, Native Americans not only participated but often played the most significant role in determining the outcome. In Florida, French alienation of local Indians through perfidy had led the Indians to assist the Spanish against the French by showing the Spanish where the shipwrecked French parties lay. The alienation had occurred when the French changed sides in a local dispute between two groups of Indians, abandoning their erstwhile allies in the belief that the other group of Indians could lead them to hidden caches of riches. Europeans were slow to learn that the conquistador mentality would not work in the American South. There were no precious metals to obtain, and different circumstances from Mexico and Peru meant that Indians could not be dealt with so cavalierly. Natives had to be inveighed to ally through appeasement of their self-interests. The pursuit of material gain became a joint native-European enterprise. Though Europeans tried to dictate the terms of the partnership, many southern Indian peoples possessed enough power to ensure that their own interests were met.

INITIAL STEPS IN EUROPEAN COLONIZATION

After Menéndez's mass murder, the French abandoned colonization of the South and moved as far away as they could in their exploration and exploitation of North America—to Canada. Soon the English challenged the Spanish by planting colonies first at Roanoke Island in North Carolina and then on Chesapeake Bay in Virginia, locations close enough to provide succor to privateers plundering the Spanish Caribbean but far enough from Florida that the Spanish would have a hard time removing them.[57] In fact, however, English privateering had so declined by the time of the establishment of Jamestown that Spain had no imperative to destroy the Virginia colony, which soon grew beyond everyone's expectations.

Barring occasional attacks on Saint Augustine, which received unwelcome visits from Sir Francis Drake and from French corsairs who took revenge for the murder of their countrymen, the Spanish proceeded unimpeded from European interference and built a colony and mission system in Florida. Unlike the English to the north, the Spanish had great difficulty attracting settlers and never developed a local economy strong enough to support the military, religious, and civil establishments. For more than two centuries, the Spanish crown poured money into Florida to prevent other European powers from occupying the colony, and not just to protect the sealanes but also from fear that the peninsula could become a staging ground for assaults on Mexico. Thus, when the French reentered the South by descending the Mississippi at the end of the seventeenth century, Spain scoured the Gulf Coast in hopes of removing them and built Pensacola as a bastion, albeit a shaky one, of Spanish power.

By the mid-seventeenth century the Spanish perception of the South included only minimally the potentiality of the land to produce items needed elsewhere in the empire. Instead, Spain viewed Florida as a remote dominion of the empire, a drain on resources with little intrinsic value except to protect more valuable colonies. That goal was to be accomplished by moving to the missions and converting local Indians, which had the added advantage, the Spanish thought, of being good for the Spanish colonists' souls and the church they upheld. Unable to attract substantial numbers of settlers, the Florida establishment remained difficult to manage. Florida was placed under the administrative control of both Cuba and Mexico, funds and supplies were rarely forthcoming in a timely manner, and the colony suffered frequent hardships. Saint Augustine had little control over the peninsula apart from the Atlantic coast and north-central areas. Cuba usually had more contact with south Florida and the Tampa Bay area than did Saint Augustine. Pensacola was dependent on Mexico and sometimes had to rely on the French of Mobile, and later New Orleans, for assistance, after France and Spain became allies in the early eighteenth century.[58]

The Spanish, English, and French shared views of the South and its Indian peoples. They all sought alliances to enlist native help against enemy Indians and Europeans. All three empires wished to employ Indians for extracting riches from the region, whether through mining, hunting, or agriculture. They all saw Indians as peoples to be subdued, though not necessarily through military means. They perceived the South as a region that was part of a larger Atlantic world connected by ships and oceans to other colonies, to Europe, and to Africa.

The South's native peoples understood better than the Europeans the internal dynamics of group relationships in the region, but they did not have the same broad view of an Atlantic world that was largely unknown to them. Amerindians learned quickly of the competitive nature of the European powers and of the Europeans' love of precious metals, while developing their own desire for European alliances to obtain trade goods and assistance against their enemies.

The European presence powerfully affected the South's native peoples. Whatever effects disease had, the cosmology of native inhabitants had to contend with the sudden appearance of the strange, aggressive, and acquisitive newcomers. Just as Europeans, on encountering Native Americans, had to reconsider their world with such questions as, "Why did God hide the existence of these peoples from us?" so Native American worldviews were threatened by the Europeans. They had to contend with confident and arrogant newcomers arriving on huge ships, in possession of a wealth of iron goods, loud and powerful explosives, and strange clothing, and in the company of odd animals. These invaders entered their lands as if they owned everything and treated native peoples as inferior beings. The Europeans would have appeared as extraordinary people in possession of unfathomable stores of knowledge—yet equally mysterious would have been why, having such gifts, Europeans were so ignorant about other things, habitually short of supplies, and thoughtless, sadistic, violent, and untrustworthy. Indians would have had difficulty reconciling these factors and at the same time would have lost respect or confidence in their owns ways and leaders. For chiefs who claimed to descend from the sun and to wield great power over heaven and earth, the appearance of Europeans in possession of considerable power would have undermined their authority. Some chiefdoms survived the challenge, notably the Natchez, but the unstable nature of many chiefdoms made them unable to resist the influx of new ideas, peoples, and microbes—and not all of the new peoples and ideas were from Europe, for Indian groups from afar also migrated into the region.

2

CAROLINA, THE WESTO,
AND THE TRADE IN INDIAN SLAVES,
1670–1685

NEWCOMERS

When the English planted a settlement at Carolina in 1670, no one could envision the extent of its impact on the South.[1] Entering a region already in the throes of vast cultural, social, and political change, the English would provide the dominant societal framework that replaced the chiefdoms that had prevailed for so long. The changeover was not immediate, however. The Spanish mission system, the new Native American confederacies, and the surviving chiefdoms long operated in the region, but the English plantation model steadily expanded until it reigned over the South.

The process was neither fast nor inevitable, though the impact of English settlement was quickly felt. In 1670, Carolina's low country Amerindians could scarcely conceive of the potential impact of the English, although they had been exposed to the earlier French and Spanish colonies at Port Royal, giving them some familiarity with Europeans. Carolina's Amerindians might have thought that English settlement, if like Spanish settlement, would take up little land and would perhaps focus on trade and the search for precious metals. During the previous century, European visits to the area were transitory and their people peripatetic. Certainly Native Americans neither could predict nor understand the English plantation system soon to be established in Carolina, though rumors of English tobacco plantations probably filtered southward from Virginia. Whereas none of the previous European attempts at permanent colonization had succeeded, and even Spanish movement onto the Georgia coast would not have seemed all that threatening, Carolina natives would have perceived a greater threat arising from the peoples who migrated to the Savannah River from the north. These Indians, known as the Westo to the English and the Chichimeco to the Spanish, became the most powerful military force in the area to English, Spanish, and Amerindian alike.

The Westo had just migrated to the Savannah River from Virginia, where they were known as the Richahecrian. One anthropologist, Marvin T. Smith, believes them to have been displaced Erie (an Iroquoian group) from New York and Pennsylvania, who had been forced south by the Iroquois wars of 1654–1656.[2] The expansion of English Virginia westward pressured the Powhatans and other Virginia Amerindians, which forced the Westo to migrate again, but not before having established trade relations with English Virginians. From their new home along the Savannah, they aggressively attacked southern Indians to the east, southeast, and south. Smith claims that the Virginians' arming of the Westo gave them undue advantage, forcing the technologically inferior bands to the south to confederate as the Creek Indians. The new weaponry, however, could scarcely have provided the Westo with anything more than a psychological advantage, for the firepower of seventeenth-century guns paled in comparison to the bow and arrow, which could be shot more frequently and accurately.[3] The acquisition of guns alone is insufficient to explain why the Westo terrorized their neighbors. Instead, Westo aggression can be attributed to the two forced migrations in the fifteen years before they arrived on the Savannah and their desperate need to carve out living space. Just how many Westo migrated is unknown, though the Spanish reported that they had variously five hundred and two thousand gunmen, which implies a population of seventeen hundred to eight thousand. A group of Amerindians of that size required a large territory—hundreds of square miles, most of which was needed for hunting—to sustain itself.

The Westo relationship with Virginia traders also shaped the nature of their aggressiveness toward their neighbors. The Virginians offered trade goods to the Westo in exchange for captives.[4] It made more sense to the Westo to devote their energy to enslaving Amerindians than to hunting and processing pelts. Instead of killing their enemies or intimidating them to flee, the Westo sold them to the English, which not only removed their foes but gained them something in return. Their single-mindedness to gain land and their organizational skills, tactics, and trade connections gave them numerous

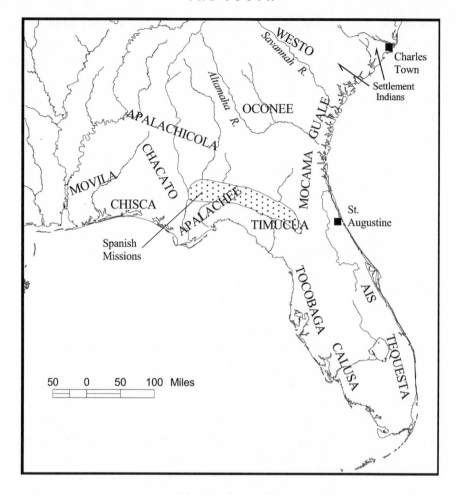

The South in 1670

advantages over the region's other Indians. They mortally wounded the Spanish mission system in Guale and Mocama (located on the Georgia and north Florida sea coast) while inducing some of Carolina's coastal Indians to welcome the English into the region as an ally.

Whatever expectations Indians had of the new English colony planted at Charles Town, its settlement was of a permanent nature, which quickly transformed the Carolina low country. Although the new European immigrants hunted and fished like the coastal Amerindians, they also introduced livestock, particularly cattle, which roamed freely before shipment to the West Indies. Both Amerindians and Europeans farmed, but the English cleared large areas of land for commercial agriculture, consciously aping other European colonies in their search for marketable agriculture commodities for sale abroad. English settlement also included African slave laborers transferred from West Indian plantations. Africans felled trees, erected buildings, and helped transform low country land to pasture and farm use. English settlement, although it provided coastal Indians with trade goods and a needed ally against the Westo, could not help but create resentment as it altered the landscape and drove away the nondomestic animals so necessary for Indian existence in the region. This forced low country indigenes to travel greater distances to hunt, while also leading many to work for the Europeans to obtain clothing, tools and other items that they formerly produced themselves.

The first English settlers largely hailed from other colonies, particularly Barbados. Although subsistence necessarily preoccupied their early efforts, they had not come to Carolina for that alone. With life in the West Indies as their model, and these same islands as their market, they moved to Carolina in search of rich land and commercial opportunities, using their slave labor to produce lumber, shingles, and staves, as well as beef and corn for export. In Peter H. Wood's words, Carolina became a "colony of a colony," providing sugar-rich Barbados with a nearby producer of food and other necessities.[5]

THE LORDS PROPRIETORS OF CAROLINA

The eight lords proprietors granted Carolina under patent from King Charles II in 1663 had complete control over the disposal of Carolina land and the structure and form of its government, as long as they approved no laws repugnant to the laws of England. The proprietors had the right to direct colonial relations with local Indians, which became a constant point of contention, not just between the proprietors and the colonists, but between the proprietors and their own appointed officials. During most of the proprietary period, the struggle for control over Indian affairs defined the colony's history and shaped the fortunes of all involved. The proprietors asserted their claims within the colony through the Fundamental Constitution, by which they established colonial government.[6] Largely the work of Proprietor Anthony Ashley Cooper, and his secretary, the philosopher John Locke, the constitution provided penalties of forfeiture of one's entire estate, moveable and unmovable property, as well as banishment, for anyone who claimed land by purchase or gift from any Indian or Indian nation.[7] The proprietors did not dismiss Indian ownership of land within their domain, but they believed that their patent gave them ownership of non-Indian land and the exclusive right to negotiate with Indians for land. This measure served as a statement of proprietary rights and precluded Indians from losing their land through settler trickery. Until they lost their patent, the proprietors clumsily but consistently tried to balance their interests with Indian rights.[8]

The proprietors explicitly ordered the local government not to disturb Indian lands. In 1669 they issued instructions that no one could take up land within two and a half miles of an Indian settlement on the same side of a river.[9] Division of the land into 12,000-square-acre parcels (baronies) reserved the village barony plus an adjacent barony for the Indians. In spite of the proprietors' expressed concerns, Indian land rights never assumed great importance in their plans. Ten years later, when the proprietors granted forty of these baronies (totaling 480,000 acres) to Sir John Cochrane and Sir George Campbell for the settlement of Scots Presbyterians in the Port Royal region, they instructed the Scots to reserve one or more squares for the Indians if they refused to leave, hardly adequate compensation for the many Indians in the area. The proprietors assured the Scots that they would "use their best endeavors to obtain the consent of the Indians concerned"[10] and to protect grantees from Indian claims. Indians possessed usufruct rights in English law over land cultivated and inhabited—the proprietors thus could not legally ride roughshod over Indian land—but these rights generally did not protect hunting land.[11]

The proprietors seem not to have realized or cared that leaving the Indians a 12,000-acre parcel in the midst of English settlement would not allow them to maintain their traditional way of life. Indians required large hunting preserves to obtain food and clothing. The proprietors were not unlike most other Englishmen in holding Indian hunting in contempt. In England hunting was a sport reserved for the elite; it rankled the English to see Indians partake in an activity reserved to the wellborn in their own society.[12] Most English colonists wanted Indian men to give up the bow and arrow for the plow and to alter the gender roles that had women working the fields and men hunting. Carolina, however, was different. The colony's economy for its first fifty years revolved around the Indian trade: colonists wanted Indians to hunt to bring in the animal skins and furs they could exchange for European goods. Indians were encouraged to hunt, not near the plantations, but to the west and south. This inconvenienced the "Settlement Indians," who received their name from living near and among the English colonists. The Europeans also preferred to have Indians move to the edges of European settlement because there they could provide a first line of defense against intruders.

Whereas the colonists envisioned local Indians as allies and trading partners who would remain external to Carolina, the proprietors wished to incorporate Indians who lived within their patent into their colony. "Hoping in time to draw the Indians into our government," the proprietors wanted to lure Indians through various enticements.[13] Inclusion would be on "enlightened" terms of religious tolerance. The Fundamental Constitution provided that although the "Natives . . . who will be concerned in our Plantation are utterly strangers to Christianity," their "Idolatry, Ignorance or Mistake gives us no right to expel or use them ill." The constitution tolerated all religions in part because the proprietors wanted to attract settlers. They foresaw that people arriving from other places "will undoubtedly be of different opinions concerning Matters of Religion." The Church of England would be the only church supported by government, and the constitution expressed the hope that all would convert, but this could only occur if non-Anglicans, "having an opportunity of acquainting themselves with the true and reasonableness of its Doctrines and the peaceableness and Inoffensiveness of its profession, may by good usage and persuasion . . . be won over to embrace and unfeignedly receive the truth."[14]

In this age of religious bigotry, wherein English high church Anglicans and Dissenters had spent the previous decades at one another's throats, trying to disenfranchise, disempower, penalize, and kill one another (as well as Catholics and the new sects that proliferated), this was a remarkable statement of tolerance, though not a unique one; Maryland and Rhode Island offered religious toleration, as did Pennsylvania, founded soon after Carolina. Still, Carolina's offer was far more liberal than that of most other colonies, and the colony's policies toward Indians were as liberal as Pennsylvania's and Rhode Island's. Under the Fundamental Constitution, native religion was treated no differently than any religion other than the Church of England, though, as we shall see, this "enlightened" approach toward Amerindians was shared less by Carolina colonists than by Pennsylvania Quakers. It was a view held by some Europeans but few American colonists, who tended toward religious bigotry where Indians were concerned.

THE RATIONALE FOR ENSLAVEMENT

Of much less concern to the proprietors was the African slaves whom the free colonists imported to the colony. The proprietors had no doubt that their colony would be built on enslaved African labor. They foresaw that some Africans would seek to convert to Christianity and that planters might prevent conversion out of fear that enslaving Christians would be illegal. The proprietors put slave owners at ease by stipulating in the Fundamental Constitution that conversion would not release slaves from their condition.[15]

Late seventeenth-century English considered African slavery a moral, legal, and socially acceptable institution. Copying the Spanish, Portuguese, and Dutch colonies, the English enslaved Africans on their plantations both in the West Indies and on the North American mainland. (Before establishing colonies, English had participated in the African slave trade, at least as early as the late sixteenth century, when John Hawkins provided Spanish colonies with slaves.)[16] Europeans were not alone in keeping slaves—many human societies of this era can be characterized by their exploitation of un-free labor—but the exploitation of non-European peoples by Europeans in the colonies was especially virulent and brutal. In England, the force of law and custom, together with the power of the state, allowed the ruling classes to rule with more ease: labor discipline was accomplished more easily at home than in foreign countries or new colonies, where the resentments of la-borers combined with a weaker government to lead those who controlled labor to employ force more often and heavily than they could have at home. Sixteenth- and seventeenth-century England employed brutal force in its Irish colony, under Oliver Cromwell especially, which provided a model for the treatment of non-English peoples in its American colonies. The English readily drew parallels between the Irish, whom they characterized as dark sav-ages beyond the pale of civilization, and Africans, whom they also considered savage and incapable of civilization.[17]

The English rationale for enslavement lay in the belief that captives taken in a "just war" could be offered enslavement as an alternative to death.[18] The narrowness of the options offered prisoners did not diminish the "voluntary" nature of the decision, for the captives had in effect forfeited their lives when they were captured. Captors considered themselves benevolent by giving cap-tives the choice of enslavement or death.[19] By the mid-seventeenth century, the English had added another rationale for enslavement by determining that the children of a slave mother inherited her condition so that slave status passed from one generation to the next. Two oddities characterized this ra-tionale. First, in law, children's status devolved from the father, not the mother. The change perpetuated enslavement by making status hereditary (a condi-tion contrary to most African slave traditions) and by not freeing the many mulattoes born from the union of free white males and slave females.[20] The second oddity lay in the original justification of enslavement as the product of capture in a just war. English planters had not captured their slaves in a just war or in any war: they had purchased them from slave traders. The Eng-lish thus extended the rationale for enslavement to the purchase of slaves cap-tured by other people in a just war. But had the Africans been captured in wars, just or otherwise? Some had, but many had not. Often African slaves were the victims of raiders whose sole intent was to capture free people to sell to slave traders.

In Europe, many viewed the enslavement of Native Americans somewhat differently from the enslavement of Africans, though both were subject to incipient racialization by Europeans who considered both as savages. Africans were deemed a "brutish people" whose inherent savagery and physical nature suited them to a life of labor.[21] Having Africans judged intellectually and spiritually inferior to all other humans, the slavers devoted little thought to elevating Africans' status or incorporating them fully within European or colonial societies. Indians, however, were romanticized as noble people who could be elevated to Christian civilization or perhaps could be left alone to live in their conceived state of purity. Many Europeans thought of Indians as their biological equals, positing that only circumstances of separation by the Atlantic had led to Indians' very different social and political development. Some Europeans opposed enslavement of the New World's indigenous peoples. Spain outlawed Native American enslavement in its empire in the sixteenth century, though local governments and Spanish colonists found ways to skirt the laws and keep Indians in various states of unfree labor.[22]

In England the sentimentality of the concept of the noble savage created opposition to enslavement but never involved the state or the established church as it did in Spain. In Spain, organized religion played an active role influencing, initiating, and administering government policy, and its empire's highly centralized system took a uniform approach to Indian slavery.[23] By contrast, in the English colonies jurisdiction over enslavement was a local consideration, not a matter of imperial policy. All English colonies with the notable exception of Georgia during its first twenty years permitted slavery.[24] Each colony created a body of laws to govern the institution, though slavery was practiced before laws defined its parameters.

In Carolina, the proprietors made distinctions between enslaving Africans and enslaving Indians. They distinguished between Africans and Amerindians because Africans would arrive in the colony as slaves for private use by free people, whereas Indians were indigenous, free, and in possession of existing rights to the land. But the proprietors' concerns were also practical: they worried that enslavement of Indians would initiate wars, which might not only prove expensive but bring unwanted attention from forces within England that might wish to take away their patent. The proprietors repeatedly urged their officials and colonists to treat Indians fairly, and they tried to create a society that would institutionalize and maintain justice for them.

As early as 1680 the proprietors ordered the Carolina government to ensure Indians equal justice with European settlers. They published regulations and distributed them widely so no one could claim ignorance. They suggested steep penalties for anyone interfering with Indian embassies and instructed the governor and council to establish a commission to meet at least every two months in Charles Town to hear all complaints.[25] Astute enough to recognize that presents would be necessary "to purchase their friendship and alliance,"[26] and that trade between settlers and natives would bind the two peoples, the proprietors also insisted that Amerindians receive retribution for offenses committed against them by the English, with perpetrators punished by the colony's government and forced to pay reparations. Establishing this system of justice proved nearly impossible given the views of colonists and local officials, who saw the exploitation of Indians as the easiest way to wealth. Nevertheless, the proprietors persisted, and officials made several attempts to protect Indians, though these usually arose out of expediency rather than any sense of justice. The ultimate failure of proprietary idealism arose from a combination of factors. Even when structures were in place to provide justice, the propensity to commit injustice, though sometimes punished, proved too overwhelming for proprietary and local governments to overcome. It was a question of will and resources. Government rarely possessed the will to devote the resources necessary to create a tolerant and equitable society. Could colonists who exploited Africans be expected to treat Indians any differently?

PROPRIETORS VERSUS COLONISTS: THE INDIAN TRADE

The proprietors had self-interested reasons to prevent abuses and keep colonists out of the Indian trade. They had reserved most of the Indian trade for themselves and did not want to share this moneymaking enterprise. They also thought that the trade would deter colonists from developing their landholdings. The proprietors believed their plan of colonization to be a reasonable arrangement: the colonists had the use of the land and its timber and in return were expected to pay a quitrent, a tax on their land.[27] The English settlers agreed with the scenario, but only to a point. Few could see any reason to pay the quitrent—a problem faced by proprietors and the royal government in other colonies. Moreover, establishing commercial agricultural enterprises took time; land had to be cleared, crops planted, crops and seed experimented with until colonists found what would thrive in the Carolina soil. Further, the cultivation of staples for export meant that labor had to be purchased, which in turn required capital. The more labor one commanded, the more quickly profits could be made. Some planters brought laborers, both slave and indentured servant, with them, but they always desired more and thus needed more capital. To obtain that capital, the planters looked to the Indian trade, where investment brought quicker returns. Animal pelts—hunted and processed by Indians—could be purchased by colonists with little effort of time and labor on their part. Indians who could be shipped easily to other colonies as slave laborers were even more valuable. The trade in Indians and pelts quickly tied Carolina into England's intercolonial network, for both commodities had value throughout the empire and thus could be exchanged for other commodities: tools, seed, manufactured goods, and African slave laborers.[28]

Two economies thus grew side by side in Carolina: a frontier exchange with Amerindians that brought in animal pelts and Indian slaves, which were then turned into needed capital and commodities to develop a plantation system, which produced food and wood products. At the heart of both economies lay slavery—slaves as laborers and slaves as saleable commodities. The proprietors made money from neither and perceived the transformation of Indians into commodities as the gravest threat facing the colony.

The English enslavement of Native Americans in Carolina occurred at first settlement, though colonial officials felt it necessary to justify themselves to the proprietors. To show compliance with custom, in December 1675, Carolina's Grand Council carefully explained to the proprietors why they had approved of the sale of Indians into slavery. The Sewee, they reported, "and other our Neighbouring Indians" had offered to sell their "Indian prisoners" to the colonists. These captives, "Lately taken, are Enemies to the said Indians who are in Amity with the English." It did not matter that the Indians were not at war with the English, only that they were taken in war and that their captors chose to sell them. Telling the proprietors that these Indians were enemies of friends demonstrated that they were not enslaving "innocent" Indians and that they were complying with their Indian allies' wishes. The council noted, undoubtedly for the proprietors' benefit, "that the said Indian prisoners are willing to work in this Country, or to be transported from hence,"[29] thus fulfilling both the custom of enslaving no one against their wishes and the proprietors' order that "no Indian upon any occasion or pretense whatsoever is to be made a Slave, or without his own consent be carried out of Carolina."[30]

Control over the Indian slave trade lay in the hands of the proprietors' appointed officials in Carolina. These appointees, who comprised the colony's elite, tried to keep the colonists out of the trade, but only so that they themselves could reap the profits. They heeded proprietary orders only when it coincided with their interests. They held no loyalty to the proprietors who had appointed them to office and granted them land. Instead, they chafed under proprietary prohibitions on the Indian trade, which aimed at keeping them from the area of opportunity that promised the quickest route to wealth.

Disregard of proprietary rules at the highest levels of colonial administration—the colony's governors and council members—had far-reaching effects on Carolina's development. With the governor and council typically placing their interests above those of the proprietors, there was little respect for the law. The colony's elite split into factions and jockeyed for power. Because there was so much conflict over the spoils of office, the elite could not maintain order among themselves. Local elites resorted to fighting, rioting, and illegal jailing to improve their position.[31] With almost total disdain for proprietary rules and imperial law, the colony became a haven for pirates who traded with elites,[32] probably for items they would have had little difficulty trading elsewhere—pelts and Indian slaves. Abuse of office led the proprietors frequently to remove governors, periodically heightening the intense competition for office and the inevitable vying for the ear of new governors. Neither Crown nor proprietors could force the Carolina elite to accept the rule of law, though English discontent over the colony's active participation in trade with pirates ultimately led to an imperial crackdown.

The contest for power among elites effected a struggle over who would control the Indian trade. Within the colony, colonists could trade with local Indians,[33] which they did for foodstuffs, pelts, and slaves. But the proprietors reserved for their agents the potentially profitable trade with the large tribes outside the colony, which local elites eyed greedily. The proprietors claimed a monopoly on this trade for several reasons: they believed that the Indians needed the trade and that the colonists seemed incapable of participating in it without taking advantage of the Indians; they fully expected trade abuses to lead to war or the desertion of their Indian neighbors to the Spanish; and they hoped, as noted, to see some return on their investment in the colony.[34] In April 1677 the proprietors forbade for seven years all trade with the Spanish and all Indians who lived beyond Port Royal, particularly the Westo and Cuseeta, "two warlike and fierce Nations . . . [with] who, if quarrels should arise," the colony would face grave danger.[35] Five proprietors signed an agreement to control the trade, each agreeing yearly to subscribe £100 for trade goods. Dr. Henry Woodward, who had initiated the trade and played a key role in Indian affairs in the colony's early years, agreed with the proprietors to conduct it for them in return for 20 percent of the profits. The Proprietors also licensed London merchants to trade with Spanish Saint Augustine and with Indians anywhere along the Carolina coast or Florida cape.[36]

COLONISTS VERSUS INDIANS:
CAROLINA WARS WITH THE KUSSOE

Carolina had more to worry about than trade and Indian slavery, for not all the local Indians welcomed the colonists. From first settlement of the colony, the Kussoe, for instance, had refused to ally with the English. The colony's Grand Council accused the "Kussoe and other Southerne Indians" of stealing "a great quantity of Corn." The council complained that the Kussoe refused to "comply with any fair entreaties to live peaceably and quietly." Among other things, the insolent Kussoe had threatened to join the Spanish "to cut off the English people in this place" and had intimidated "the more friendly sort of Indians" from "Amity or trading" with the colony. In October 1671 Carolina declared war on the Kussoe.[37]

The Grand Council never mentioned in its journals why the Kussoe were so unhappy with the English as to continually threaten them. They had frequent contacts with one another, enough that several colonists reported Kussoe murmurings and threats against them. The Kussoe lived about thirty miles upriver from Charles Town on the Ashley and Edisto Rivers.[38] From their perspective, the English, like the Westo, had settled the area unannounced, presumably with the approval of some low country Indians and with no attempt to negotiate a settlement with the others. The English had not yet recognized that their manner of claiming and settling land might antagonize the Kussoe and others. Because the English did not understand or refused to accept overlapping claims to land, they believed it adequate to obtain permission to settle from one group; they might not have seen fit to secure Kussoe permission.

Whether the English in fact knew the sources of discontent, they expected peace and amity with Amerindians on their own terms. The council offered peace to the Kussoe if they would agree to it and pay a ransom for two prisoners plus any others taken by Carolina troops.[39] The council made no attempt to negotiate differences, offering the Kussoe peace only if they would, in effect, pay reparations and accept English settlement and dominance. Instead, the Kussoe made themselves scarce. They appear infrequently in the historical record but often enough to allow us glimpses of the course they took during Carolina's early years. For three years they did not appear in the Grand Council's journal. One might assume that they had moved to the Piedmont or beyond or, like other small groups, had pushed southwest to join those who soon became known as the Lower Creek. Yet the Kussoe had not gone that far. They remained in the low country or the eastern Piedmont, out of the way of the English but not abandoning the region. As with many

Indian peoples in the history of European expansion, one response to foreign intrusion was simply "laying low." In 1671 this was not so hard to accomplish. Carolina was but a nascent colony, and the settlers' understanding of the topography was extremely limited. Offensive operations required knowing where to find the enemy or having Amerindian allies show the way and perhaps join the fight.

The Kussoe forced the Carolinians to seek them out—apparently. Three years after the declaration of war, the Grand Council alleged that the Kussoe "have secretly murdered three English men." Frustrated that "these Indians have no certain abode," they sent several "parties" to "use all means to come up with the said Indians." The council left it up to the soldiers whether to kill any or all of them.[40]

In the midst of the Kussoe war the colony had to contend with another group of low country Indians, the Stono. In the summer of 1674 the council had been "credibly informed" that the cacique (headman) of the Stono "hath endeavoured to confederate certain other Indians to murder some of the English Nation, and to rise in Rebellion against this settlement." The council sent a party to seize the cacique, but whether they succeeded is unknown.[41]

The record is equally unclear on how the Kussoe-Carolina war ended, but the two settled their differences in the colony's favor. The Kussoe were allowed to maintain a settlement in the Carolina low country. In return, Governor Joseph West (March 1671–April 1672, August 1674–September 1682, September 1684–Summer 1685) reported, the Kussoe had "to pay a deer skin monthly as an acknowledgment or else to lose our amity."[42] In other words, the Kussoe had to accept English dominance, represented symbolically each month by the payment of a skin. Their symbolic reduction was reflected in more material terms by the forced surrender of their most valuable lands: the rich soil along the Ashley and Edisto Rivers that would soon be the basis of the richest plantations on mainland North America. The Stono also made peace. They joined in a cession of land in 1682; by this time, the government had learned the expediency of getting more than one group of Indians to sign, and the signatories at this cession represented eight groups.[43] The Kussoe and the Stono, like other coastal Indians, remained in the low country but lost their best lands to the planters; most then lived in relative accord with the English by accepting their dominance until the Yamasee War of 1715, after which most joined the Creek to the south or the Catawba in the Piedmont. The Settlement Indians played an important role in the colony's history, but before we explore that role further it is essential to examine another group who did not entirely accept English settlement—the Westo.

THE WESTO

As already noted, the Westo arrived in Carolina shortly before the colony's founding and brought ties to the Virginians with them. These ties did not presume that the Westo would establish friendly relations with Carolina. English colonies often negotiated with Indian groups one by one, and Indians responded in kind. Virginia and Carolina traders operated independently of one another, answerable only to their respective governments. This independence of action did not mean that the Crown would approve of one colony's traders inciting Indians to war with another colony, but conflicts and conflict of interest did occur from the decentralization of English Indian policies. The Carolinians, to secure their financial and diplomatic interests, looked to replace the Virginians as trading partners with Indians from the Cherokee southward. For the remainder of the colonial period Carolina worked to exclude Virginia from the southern trade.[44] To a large extent the Carolinians succeeded, and needed to, for at stake were not only profits but the colony's well-being. For Virginia, by contrast, trade with southern Indians was mostly an economic concern, for those Indians were too distant to threaten the Old Dominion. In spite of Carolina's steadily growing preeminence in the trade, the Virginia traders retained a share, and during wars between Carolina and its neighbors, Virginians sometimes acted as a source of supplies for the colony's enemies.

Carolina needed to establish relations with the powerful Westo and replace the Virginians as trading partners. As anthropologist Marcel Mauss pointed out in *The Gift,* two neighboring peoples who do not engage in trade must necessarily exist in a warlike state.[45] Before trade ties could be established, however, warfare with the Westo had broken out in 1673. Westo attacks against Carolina coastal Indians extended to the English, and the fledgling colony was hard put to stop them. Carolina had to rely on neighboring Indians, not just for defense, but for offensive operations as well.

Carolina turned to the Esaw, a Piedmont people, who, according to Carolina's Grand Council, "are well acquainted with the Westo habitations, and have promised all the help they can afford." Whether the Esaw offered their assistance to gain the colony's goodwill or to enlist an ally against their own enemy is unknown, but it probably combined both motives. In desperate straits, the English laid aside their arrogance—they not only accepted Esaw assistance but let the Esaw determine the best way to subdue the Westo. Illustrating the serious nature of the task, the Grand Council instructed its four-man negotiating party to the Esaw, half of whom were council members, and thus among the most important personages in the colony, to go to the Esaw to "treat and agree with the said Indians as *they* shall find most convenient for the better carrying on of the said War, and for the discovery of those parts of this Country" where the Westo live.[46]

For reasons unknown the party did not leave for four months, but on their "safe" return, the council not only listened to their report but heard a "complaint . . . by neighbouring Indians" concerning the theft of goods by three white men, who were ordered to restore the goods and pay a fine of twenty shillings "to satisfy for their trespass." If they did not comply, a warrant of distress would be issued.[47] The need for an alliance with local Indians convinced the council to provide a modicum of justice for Settlement Indians. Carolina had to prove to local Indians that their property would be secured—and speedily. At the next meeting the council announced a system for settling property disputes that would avoid trials and allow Indians and English to settle their differences quickly. A complainant could "bring a Petition to the Secretaries Office," where a summons would be issued requiring both parties to "appear with their evidences before the Grand Councill." As long as both parties agreed to submit to the council's judgment, the parties could avoid a court case.[48] The system apparently did not work. Indians, suspicious of the process, did not flock to the council with cases. Even if they had, it is questionable whether European defendants would have agreed to submit to a council decision when they would have had a much better chance of winning a case in front of a jury of their peers. And it is questionable whether many Indians would have filed court cases in the unfamiliar English legal system. Still, the council's attempt signifies its recognition of the need to protect Settlement Indians' property.

The first war with the Westo ended in December 1674, when the Westo initiated an alliance by appearing at the plantation of Dr. Henry Woodward. Already known from Florida to Carolina as the most important Englishman in Carolina's diplomacy with Amerindians, Woodward had arrived in Carolina in 1666 under proprietor sponsorship to learn Indian languages and pave the way for English settlement. Two years later he was captured by the Spanish and imprisoned in Saint Augustine. He escaped, served as a surgeon on a privateer, and returned to Carolina in 1670. Woodward's linguistic and personal skills placed him in the key position as negotiator of trade and political relations with neighboring Indians.

Woodward's reputation had spread to the Westo, and they now made it clear to him that they desired both to end the hostilities and open trade. They escorted him to their towns on the west side of the Savannah River, above modern-day Augusta, where the Westo had arranged a reception. As Woodward entered the towns, the Westo saluted him with a volley of fifty to sixty small arms, thus displaying not only their firepower but their ability to obtain European arms. "The chief of the Indians made long speeches intimating their own strength (and as I judged their desire of friendship with us)." In a show of respect and hospitality, in the evening they "oiled my eyes and joints with bears oil," gave presents of deerskins, and feted Woodward with enough "food to satisfy at least half a dozen of their own appetites."[49] In this way the Westo showed Woodward that they wanted a new relationship with Carolina but that they made this offer from a position of strength, not weakness.

The host town featured double palisades on one side; only a single palisade defended the side that fronted the river. On the banks of the river "seldom lie less than one hundred fair canoes ready upon all occasions." Woodward was impressed to find the Westo well supplied with arms, ammunition, trading cloth, and other English goods they had obtained from the northward, for which they exchanged "dressed deerskins and young Indian slaves." The Westo hoped to establish a trade with Carolina, whose nearer location made the exchange of goods more convenient, hence more profitable. It also might have been much safer. Woodward learned that the Cherokee were the Westo's enemies, and if the Cherokee were obtaining goods from the Virginians, it would have been expedient for the Westo to procure goods from the Carolinians.[50]

The Westo could ill afford an alliance between the Cherokee and the Virginians. Cherokee numbers made them a grave threat. The Westo needed allies. Carolina was one possibility, but during Woodward's visit another arose. Two Savannah (Shawnee) Indians arrived from the vicinity of the Apalachicola River, near the Gulf of Mexico. The Savannah were a unique Indian group. Most inhabited a large number of towns in the Ohio River Valley. Probably as a result of the Iroquois Wars that began in the 1640s, many Savannah migrated to places as diverse as Florida, Georgia, Pennsylvania, and Maryland.[51] It was not unusual for Indian groups to splinter and move in myriad directions, but the Savannah found strength in diaspora and retained close ties among their towns, so that there was frequent reforming, moving, and splintering. Individuals unhappy with the living situation in one area could leave and move to another town or migrate with others and form new towns in other distant places—yet know that they could always return and join older Savannah establishments. Their diaspora and visiting from one town to another led to important ties with numerous peoples east of the Mississippi. Their language became a lingua franca, and their experiences made them particularly suited for initiating and leading the pan-Indian movement of the nineteenth century that extended from the Ohio Valley to the Gulf of Mexico.[52] Woodward thus witnessed a historic occasion: the Savannah establishing first contact with the powerful Westo and with Carolina.

The Savannah had remained outside the Spanish orbit in Florida and were seeking allies for themselves. Although the Savannah and the Westo could not understand each other's languages, they exchanged information by signs, and according to Woodward, the Savannah informed the Westo that the Cuseeta, Chickasaw, and Cherokee were going to attack them. It is questionable whether all three were preparing a concerted attack. In previous years the Westo had warred with the Cherokee and with Indians to the south like the Cuseeta, and they had probably sold captives from both groups to the Virginians. But this is the first evidence that the Westo had attacked the Chickasaw, which meant that they might have gone as far as the Mississippi in search of land and captives. The Westo did not take the warning lightly and prepared for the invasion.

The Savannah probably warned of the impending attack to earn Westo goodwill. They could not establish a relationship with Carolina without first opening one with the Westo, who ranged over the land between them and the English. The Savannah understood the value of European trade. Their towns in the Ohio Valley had had contacts with English traders by the 1670s, and the Spanish in Florida had provided them with trade goods, though in limited quantities. While the Westo were distracted by preparing for the invasion, the Savannah approached Woodward about striking up a trade, showing him beads they had obtained from the Spanish.

Woodward's visit to the Westo was a success, and it resulted in a profitable trade in Indian slaves that lasted from 1675 to 1680. The Westo preyed on Spanish-allied Indians in Guale and Mocama. They also continued to attack other groups, including the Settlement Indians. Carolina's need to retain an alliance with the coastal Indians precluded any permanent rapprochement with the Westo, who for unknown reasons would not or could not end their wars with the coastal Indians.[53] The Westo also continued their wars with the Cherokee, Chickasaw, Chisaca, Coweta, and Cuseeta.[54] The Carolinians thus learned that alliance with the Westo limited their options in opening positive relations with virtually any other southern Indians, for the Westo effectively blocked the pathways west and south and there was little chance that the Westo's enemies would trade with the Westo's English allies. The Savannah's meeting with Woodward was most unfortunate for the Westo. Once the English realized the desirability of trade with those Indians, the Westo became expendable, and the Savannah later would help destroy the Westo before replacing them on the Savannah River as allies of the English.[55]

THE PROPRIETARY PROGRAM OF REFORM

War with the Westo erupted again in the winter of 1679–1680. The proprietors learned of it in February from a ship's captain rather than from the Carolina government. They blamed the governor and council for not maintaining friendship with the Westo and for not protecting the Settlement Indians from them. Coupling amity with firmness, the proprietors averred, would have instilled in the Westo both love and fear of the colony. Carolina's failure to protect the coastal Indians had led to an escalation of violence that could not help but lead to war. The proprietors ordered their officials to make peace immediately with the Westo, though on safe and reasonable terms. They insisted that peace was in the planters' economic interests, not realizing that the planters preferred war to peace. Only through warfare could Carolinians obtain the slaves they desired to exchange for supplies to build their plantations. Peaceful coexistence with Indians might be fine for subsistence farmers or profit-making large plantations, but not for Carolinians hoping to amass capital quickly.

The proprietors instructed the Carolinians to make peace with the Westo on "equal terms."[56] The Westo must cease attacking the coastal Indians, but they should be supported to prevent other Indians from "daring to offend" the colony. Westo trade needs had to be met. The proprietors urged Councillor Andrew Percival to include in the "articles of peace" stipulations that the Westo would "be supplied by us with necessaries by way of Trade which will make us useful to them." And yet, the Westo must not have free access to the colony. Trade would be restricted to two plantations that were "strong in numbers and well fortified."[57] The Westo "must be plainly told that if they go to any other Plantations it shall be looked upon as a breach of the peace and they must take what follows." Colonists would have viewed these restrictions with skepticism. The two plantations where trade would be conducted belonged to the earl of Shaftesbury and Sir Peter Colleton—the earl a proprietor and Colleton the brother of one. Whatever humanitarian motives the proprietors had in calling for an end to the war, their obvious desire to protect their trade monopoly was not lost on the colonials.

The proprietors ordered Percival to keep all details of their proposals secret from everyone, including Woodward, illustrating their lack of trust in their own appointees. Maurice Mathews, who was to negotiate the peace, had to sign his instructions—agreeing to be bound by them. The proprietors urged Mathews to reestablish the beaver trade as quickly as possible with the Westo. If this was not possible, "with all your skill jointly endeavour to have the said Trade . . . restrained for as many years as you can obtain it to us" by "Act of the Parliament," meaning the Carolina legislature.[58] The proprietors worried over the legality of their monopoly, and they did not want the royal government interfering in their affairs. They hoped that the Carolinians would voluntarily preserve the proprietary monopoly over the Indian trade.

One of the more interesting recommendations conceived by the proprietors but not actually made to their officials was to have the peace treaty translated into the Westo language, with a written copy made in Westo that would be signed and given to them. Another copy would be kept in the colony to be read every time "they come amongst us." Someone must have informed the proprietors of the problems associated with transliterating such a document, but the sentiment illustrates their faith in treaties to settle differences—as long as the parties understood the terms.[59]

In his *History of South Carolina Under the Proprietary Government* (1897), Edward McCrady observed how unreasonable it was for the proprietors to restrict the Indian trade, "the principal source of gain to the industrious traders, among who were the chief men in the colony."[60] McCrady chided the proprietors for attempting to control Indian affairs from England. "It was scarcely to be expected that, situated as the colonists were, with their families exposed to the tomahawk and scalping-knife, they would leave the important matter of their relations with the savages to be governed by the diplomacy of any set of men on the other side of the Atlantic." McCrady then excused the colony's resident leaders' "disregard of instructions" as the acts of responsible men.[61] McCrady's point concerning the difficulties of conducting diplomacy from afar carries much water. And yet, this was always the excuse used by colonial officials and colonists in English, French, Spanish, Portuguese, and Dutch colonies when they disregarded their own imperial laws and enslaved Indians, stole their land, and abused them in any number of ways. Imperial officials beckoned their agents and their colonists to treat aboriginal peoples with justice, giving their people a moral and ethical framework for intercultural relations, not a detailed blueprint that would compromise the settlers' safety. These officials' motivations were not entirely moral, for they wished to avoid the costly expense of sending troops to extract colonists from local wars the purpose of which was not to aid the empire but to fulfill individuals' desire for gain at Amerindian and home government expense. In Carolina, as in other English colonies, rejection of proprietary rule (and then royal rule) was made in part to gain local control over Indian affairs, so that Amerindians could be exploited without outside interference, much as the southern states later rejected federal government authority so that exploitation of blacks could continue without outside meddling.

McCrady, in claiming the need for settler protection, also overlooked the fact that the Westo had become less of a threat to the colony than Carolina had become to them. McCrady's articulation of the standard shibboleths of his time depicting terrifying images of "savages" removing scalp-locks just does not apply to the Westo war. The Grand Council's records include alleged Indian abuses against colonists but do not cite the Westo as a source of settler complaints.[62] No doubt the proprietors were governed by self-interests, but at least their self-interested monopoly of trade was predicated on peace, in contrast to the colonists and local officials, whose self-interests led them to promote war. Irate over the renewed outbreak of war with the Westo, the proprietors demanded from the colony "Depositions to prove the matter of Fact upon which this war was grounded." They wanted to know whether the war was made for "preservation of the Colony, or to serve the ends of particular men by trade." They asked for depositions from the "Interpreters that they did truly interpret what was delivered by the Indians. Also a Copy of Dr. Woodward's Letter attested wherein he says if Trade were not permitted to the Westoes they would cut all your Throats. Also the Letter from the Spanish Governor of St Augustine's wherein he complains that the Doctor endeavoured to set the Chichimecas and other Indians to war upon the Spaniard."[63]

The proprietors defended their monopoly over the Indian trade as a source of peace with the Westo. They claimed to have monopolized the trade "not merely out of a design of gain: But with this further consideration, that by furnishing a bold and warlike people with Arms and Ammunition and other things useful to them, which they could not fetch from Virginia, New England, New Yorke, or Canider without great labour and hazard." By doing so, "We tied them to so strict a dependence upon us, that we thereby kept all the other Indians in awe: and by protecting our Neighbours from their Injuries would make them think our being seated near them a benefit to them; and that by them we should so terrify those Indians with whom the Spaniards have power." Unfortunately for the proprietors, this rationale would not convince the council to accept the monopoly over trade. The colonists were uninterested in making Indians dependent on trade to further the colony's political goals; they simply wanted to make money through the Indian slave trade. Still, the proprietors persisted. Learning that the Westo were "ruined," the proprietors considered whether another nation of Indians might be set up in their place—"one whose Government is less anarchical than theirs"— probably meaning one that could be more easily subjugated to English influence. The proprietors hoped that they "could furnish them with arms and ammunition but restrict them from selling to any other nation." In other words, the new ally would police other Indians, because they would have European arms, and be a defensive buffer to keep the "Northern and Spanish Indians from daring to infest you."[64]

The colony's leadership convinced the Savannah to move into the defeated Westo's vacated position along the Savannah River and become their chief partner in the enslaving of Amerindians. The proprietors were aghast that the colony had substituted the Savannah for the Westo; they feared this move would force other Indians to unite in resisting the Savannah and the colony. The proprietors rhetorically asked Governor Joseph Morton (September 1682–August 1684; October 1685–November 1686) why the colony had no wars with Indians when it was first founded and weak and then had warred with the Westo "whilst they were in treaty with that government and so under the public faith for their Safety and [then] put to death in Cold blood and the rest Driven from their Country"? The proprietors astutely recognized the Carolina elites' program: the "Savannahs not affording that profitable trade to the Indian Dealers that was Expected in beaver etc.," the Carolinians turned them to enslaving Indians. Reprehensibly, then, the colony began a war with the Waniah, a group of Indians who lived along the Winyaw River, "upon pretense they had cut off a boat of runaways."[65] The Savannah then captured Waniah and sold them to an Indian trader who shipped them to Antigua. The proprietors promised to collect depositions from both the Waniah and the trader. In the meantime, they learned that the Savannah were at first not going to sell the Waniah but had been intimidated by slave traders into doing so. The proprietors received testimony that a false alarm "was Contrived by the Dealers in Indians that they might have thereby an opportunity of Showing themselves at the sevanah Towne with forces and thereby frighten those people into a sole trade with themselves." The pretense of the alarm was that the Westo were going to attack the Savannah—but the proprietors wondered how that was possible. Not only were there no Westo near the town, but "the Indian Dealers have written us there are not 50 Westohs left alive and those Divided. Are the Savannahs so formidable a people as . . . you allege . . . that the whole English settlement must be alarmed and a great charge" incurred "to send out men to defend" the Savannah from fifty Westo?[66]

The proprietors also received word that the surviving Westo had wanted peace with Carolina and wished the Savannah to mediate, "but their messengers were taken and sent away to be sold." The same fate befell the messengers of the Waniah. Sarcastically, the proprietors rued "but if there be peace with the Westohs and Waniahs where shall the Sevanahs get Indians to sell the Dealers in Indians"? The proprietors were sure that the cause of both the Westo and Waniah wars, and the reason for their continuance, lay in the colonists' desire to sell Indians into slavery.[67] The governor and council responded to these accusations with a public letter, but the proprietors condemned their appointees' specious rationale that they had acted with great humanity by enslaving Indians, for otherwise, the Carolinians proclaimed, the Savannah would have put their captives to "Cruel deaths." Disingenuously, the enslavers pleaded that the Savannah had been too powerful to refuse: "having united all the tribes . . . it is dangerous to disoblige them."[68] First the leading men had raised an army to protect the "weak" Savannah from the Westo, but then they had had to buy their captives because the Savannah were too powerful to resist.[69]

The proprietors rejected all claims that the trade in Indian slaves was undertaken for the Indians' and the public good rather than for private gain. They received a letter from Colonel John Godfrey, one of the council, who along with former governor Joseph West apparently had refused to sign the public letter, disputing the governor's and council's interpretation of events.[70] Even some of the "Indian dealers" who signed the public letter wrote privately to the proprietors of the greed that had led to the enslavement of friendly Indians. The proprietors concluded from the evidence that the colony's leadership had induced the Savannah "through Covetousness of your guns, Powder and shot and other Europian Commodities to make war upon their neighbors, to ravish the wife from the Husband, kill the father to get the Child, and to burn and Destroy the habitations of these poor people into whose country we are cheerfully Received by them, Cherished and supplied when we were weak or at least never have Done us hurt." You have repaid their kindness by setting them "to do all these horrid wicked things, to get slaves to sell the dealers in Indians [and then] call it humanity to buy them and thereby keep them from being murdered." The proprietors questioned the morality of attacking all Waniah for the crimes of a few who had killed the runaways, so that "poor Innocent women and children [were] Barbarously murdered, taken and sent to be sold as slaves, who in all probability had been Innocent."[71] The Waniah should have been pressured to give up the guilty parties, for they had been too weak to resist.

The proprietors lectured the governor and council on the value of Indians to the colony. Without them, who would catch their runaway African slaves? Moreover, they should have more concern for God's approbation. They could not "Expect Gods blessing nor quiet in a Government so managed nor can we answer it to god, the King . . . Nor our own Consciences."[72] Remonstrations aside, the proprietors understood they could no longer rely on common sense, ethics, or their appointees' belief in the public good to stop them from waging war against innocents.

The proprietors tried a variety of tactics to reform the treatment of Indians. In 1680 they limited enslavement of Native Americans to those who lived more than two hundred miles from Carolina, though they left the door open to abuse by stipulating this applied only to Indians in league or friendly with the colony.[73] In their "Temporary Laws," given to the colony in 1682, articles 8, 9 and 10 specifically addressed colonial relations with Indians. Article 8 prohibited sending any Indian, "upon any pretense or Reason whatsoever . . . away from Carolina," while article 9 extended the area under which Indians were protected from within two hundred miles to within four hundred miles of Charles Town. No Indians in this area could be enslaved or injured by the inhabitants of Carolina. The proprietors hastened to add that colonists must obey these laws not as subjects of the proprietors but as subjects of the king.[74] Article 10 provided that the powers of the commission to hear Indian grievances were revoked.[75] The two-year experiment had failed,[76] since the powers of the commission were used "for the oppression [rather] than protection of the Indians." Once again they implored their officials to good treatment of Indians, reminding them of the Indians' value for catching runaway slaves, "and also for fishing, fowling and hunting." They warned the colonists against encroaching on Indian land, iterating the barring of settlement within "two miles of the same Side of the River of an Indian Settlement." They called on those settling near Indian towns to "help to fence in the Indians' Cornfield so that the Cattle and hogs of the English may not Destroy the Indians' Corn and thereby disable them to subsist amongst us." Adamantly, they insisted that Indians not be forced from the colony.[77]

Significantly, the proprietors chose to disband the commission rather than replace it with other men; neither did they punish those who had abused their power of office. The commission had included some of the most august men in the colony—West, Percival, Mathews, and Joseph Boone. The proprietors were not shy about replacing appointees; they just found that the replacements often were worse than those they had removed.

THE PROPRIETORS' FAILURE TO CONTROL INDIAN AFFAIRS AND PREVENT ILLEGAL ENSLAVEMENT OF INDIANS

The proprietors reproved their appointed officials for wrongheaded and immoral behavior, and they repeatedly juggled the pathways of power to prevent abuse of Indians. But they were never able or strong-willed enough to fire all disreputable appointees and replace them with honest men who shared their vision. The men who accepted appointments in Carolina had no reason to go there except to advance their estates. They were not career men serving the king out of loyalty or hope for a sinecure or a better appointment. Loyalty to one's king as might exist in a royal colony could not be equated with loyalty to a proprietor. Proprietary appointees had little or no hope of moving up the career ladder as was possible in the royal patronage system. The men who reached the pinnacle in a proprietary colony, the governor and members of the council, wanted only riches. If Carolina had been founded for religious or utopian reason, as had Pennsylvania, the proprietors might have found servants willing to work to fulfill a noble vision. But the offer of free land and religious toleration was noble only to the humble free colonists, not the "great" men or those who aspired to be great men, and who ruled in order to line their pockets, not serve the common good. Appointees by oath promised fealty to proprietary instructions and then disregarded directives to protect Indians, ensure justice, and preserve the proprietary monopoly over the Indian trade. For their part, the appointees and the colonists could not fathom why such profitable enterprises as the Indian trade should be restricted to men who lived three thousand miles away.

The proprietors lacked skill, funds, and will—the cornerstones of implementing a successful colonial policy. Skill was needed to rule over colonists, keep appointees on a leash, and treat with neighbors and foreign peoples incorporated into the new society. Funds were a prerequisite for defense, building an adequate economic infrastructure (a safe port to attract ships, for instance), purchasing trade goods for the conduct of peaceful relations, and giving or lending supplies to newly arrived settlers who were sick or needed help getting started. A strong will was necessary to see plans through to fruition, even in the face of strong opposition. Proprietary and royal officials lacked the firm resolve and resources to enforce compliance with the laws, though royal officials were more easily punished for their behavior.[78] Generally, the Crown and its officials in Europe turned their heads while their colonists and local officials engaged in illegal trade, enslavement of free peoples, and instigating and conducting unapproved wars. This was especially so in the English mainland colonies, where despite their self-perception as law-abiding people, colonists followed only those laws that suited them and held particular disregard for royal or proprietary directives regarding trade and relations with Indians. Laws were obeyed when convenient.

Royal rule did not guarantee better results than proprietary rule. The royal colonies, such as Virginia and New York, also had trouble controlling their officials and difficulty maintaining Indian relations beneficial to colony, empire, and Indians. But the Crown developed skills—a professional class of loyal bureaucrats and other imperial servants who believed in the empire. The Crown also had the funds to implement some of its policies. Ultimately, whether a colony was royal or proprietary probably mattered less than the expectations and goals of the colonists. Most sought ways to make money and improve their station. Some merely desired land to obtain independence, but others aggressively pursued wealth through any avenue available. America attracted the adventurous, the desperate, the impetuous, and the risk-taker. Even where only a small portion of the colonists disregarded colonial and imperial laws in the pursuit of wealth, that group had dramatic impact because neither fellow colonists nor government officials would or could stop them. Justices of the peace refused to arrest, juries declined to convict, and officials ignored malfeasance unless it affected their personal interests or they feared the wrath of the king and his ministers.

Carolina proprietors had the foresight to see that they needed to empower more colonists in order to reduce the abuse of Indians; not that one group of colonists would be more humane than another but that cells of power could counter the strength of governor and council. The proprietors looked to the elected assembly as a potential check on elites. In 1683, they instituted a licensing system to govern the exportation of Indians from the colony, commissioning the assembly to examine each group to be transported and obtain the names of every person and his or her nation. They would employ "sworn Interpreters" to verify "how and by whom" the enslaved were taken. Only Indians captured in a just and necessary war could be transported. The assembly would issue the license, but the governor, landgraves, and caciques all had to approve it—each providing a check on the other. If a law was broken, the proprietors promised to use all in their power to inflict the "utmost punishments the Law appoints to such offenders."[79]

Why the proprietors did not come up with another solution, such as banning the Indian slave trade, is worth asking. After all, the English colonies repatriated Spanish and French soldiers they captured in war. Granted, Waniah and Westo could not be repatriated if their villages no longer existed. South Carolina officials argued that Indians had to be sold into slavery to satisfy their Indian captors and to prevent them from being slaughtered. Carolina officials and proprietors were probably unaware that many Amerindian groups incorporated captives, particularly the women and children. In fact, saving captives from murder was a specious argument. Indians did kill and torture captives, particularly males, for a variety of cultural and ritualistic reasons, and purchasing women and children who otherwise would have been killed could be viewed as humanitarian, but by allowing "licensing," the proprietors opened the door for the same abuses that had existed before—Europeans setting Indians to capture other Indians for the purpose of obtaining captives to sell to the English.[80] Because the proprietors knew that most of those enslaved and transported were innocents, they should have closed the door right then. They could have instituted any number of alternative solutions, such as selling captives as indentured servants in other colonies or establishing new towns of Settlement Indians in distant areas where they could be of service to the colony, as was later done with the Apalachee in 1704 (resettled from Florida to the Savannah River) and the Tuscarora in 1712 and 1713 (resettled from North Carolina to South Carolina and New York).

All of this is not to say that English, or indeed European, enslavement of Indians was unusual at this time nor that we should condemn seventeenth-century slaveholders for keeping slaves. I am not trying to make a presentist argument against slavery. It is unfair to expect past peoples to consider an institution wrong that their generation viewed as legitimate and moral. But three factors must be emphasized in a discussion of European enslavement of Amerindians in the American South. First, the enslavement of Indians as practiced in Carolina was undertaken illegally by Carolina laws and moral standards. Enslavement of free people was a condition reserved for captives taken in a "just war" or prisoners who lost their freedom by conviction for a crime. The enslaved in Carolina were captured not in a "just war"[81] but in raids conducted for the sole purpose of turning free people into slaves. The enslavement of free people was considered morally reprehensible, so much so that no English colony or later state government of the United States permitted the enslavement of freeborn American people, including those of African descent. Slaves had to inherit their condition, arrive in America as slaves, or be war captives.

Second, nowhere in the English empire at this time was the enslavement of Indians undertaken on such a large scale as in Carolina. Puritan New England was just ending its period of large-scale enslavement of Indians, victims of the Pequot War (1636–1637) and King Philip's War (1675–1676). The Carolinians were neither less nor more moral in disregarding their own ethical values than English colonists living elsewhere. But they had the opportunity to enslave Indians on a scale not available elsewhere. New Englanders in the late seventeenth century had reduced much of the native population by enslavement and war and were blocked from expanding northward by the French and westward by the Iroquois. New York and Pennsylvania colonists were not in a position to enslave, except through purchase of other colony's slaves, particularly those of Carolina. New York made far too much from the profitable fur trade to alienate Indians through slaving, and Pennsylvania, when it did have the opportunity of purchasing slaves, outlawed slavery because of the neighboring Indians' objections.[82] Virginia participated in the Indian slave trade but by the time of Carolina's founding had developed a profitable plantation system and had to travel too far to organize a large-scale slave trade in the South. Yet even under difficult circumstances Virginia had established such a trade with the Westo, and the colony might have expanded it to the Mississippi were it not for Carolina's much more advantageous location. Nor can we ascribe religion as a differentiation in whether colonists would enslave, for High Anglicans as well as Puritans and other Dissenters equally participated in the Indian slave trade.[83]

Last, all the European powers enslaved Indians. Only the Spanish expressly outlawed enslavement, but as noted earlier, Spaniards found numerous ways to keep Indians in various conditions of unfree servitude to obtain their labor. The French enslaved Indians in Canada and Louisiana but did not practice slavery on the scale of the English because they were in a weak position to do so; their settlements lacked a strong population base to build a plantation society, leaving them utterly dependent on Native Americans for trade and military alliance.[84] Another difference between the English and the French and Spanish: the governments of the Spanish and French were both concerned with the ethical and religious ramifications of enslaving Amerindians. The Spanish outlawed it; the French even looked to incorporation of Indians in colonial society through intermarriage, as long as the Indians converted beforehand.[85] There was no broad-scale debate within the English imperial system or any of the churches or in the society at large on the expediency and morality of enslaving Native American peoples. The opposition raised by the Carolina proprietors to Indian slavery never extended to other English imperial or religious institutions or to other colonies because of the private nature of their ownership of Carolina. As in other proprietary colonies, the patentees hoped to attract as little attention as possible to their colony. They had constant fear of outside interference that might undermine their authority and right to rule. The Carolina proprietors intended to solve all their problems themselves.

The new licensing system in Carolina did nothing to alter the illegal enslavement of Indians. In November 1683, two of the proprietors' appointed officials, Maurice Mathews and James Moore, "most contemptuously disobeyed our orders about sending away of Indians and have contrived most unjust wars upon the Indians in order to the getting of Slaves and were Contriving new wars for that purpose." They were removed as deputies "by desire of the major part of the Lords Proprietors," and it was hoped that the two proprietors on their way to the colony, Seth Sothell and John Archdale, would not employ them.[86] But seven months later the proprietors complained that Mathews was still serving as surveyor general and in other civil and military capacities and was continuing to ignore their instructions. The proprietors again pleaded that only Indians taken "in a Just and necessary war" be transported from the colony, and only then as "Encouragement of the soldiers" who captured them. They had adjusted their restrictions so that even purchasing slaves from Indians to save them from death was no longer a legitimate justification: "we did not thereby mean that the parliament should license the transporting of Indians bought of other Indians by way of trade, nor are you to suffer it, for that would but occasion the dealers in Indians to contrive those poor people into wars upon one another that they might have slaves to buy."[87]

In 1685, the proprietors strictly warned the new governor, Joseph West, against allowing the enslavement of Indians except under the condition that they were captured in a war that Carolina itself was involved in, and only then as a reward for the soldiers. They reaffirmed the prohibition against transporting any Indian living within four hundred miles of Charles Town, hoping that this would prevent the colonists from fomenting wars with any Indians they could reach.[88] West was also ordered not to reappoint Mathews, Moore, and Arthur Middleton to the Grand Council because they had been removed from their positions for transporting Indians.[89] These three formed an antiproprietary party that the proprietors labled the "Indian Dealers."[90] By the 1680s Indian slavery had become the most important political issue in the colony and was representative of the division between the proprietors' and many of the colonists' vision of Carolina's purpose and future. The Indian Dealers were hell-bent on the exploitation of human resources—African and Amerindian—to make their wealth. Moore and Middleton became scions of two of the colony's most prominent families. Other families, too, would build their fortunes first on Indian slavery, then on African slavery. These men opposed the proprietors at every turn. When the proprietors tried to reapportion representation in the assembly, they met stern resistance from the "dealers in Indians [who] are the chief sticklers in it." The proprietors heard that these "dealers in Indians boast they can with a bowl of punch get who they would Chosen of the parliament and afterwards who they would chosen of the grand Councell." In control of Carolina's government, these men enacted laws that no one could "sell arms, etc., to the Indians upon forfeiture of all his estate and perpetual banishment . . . but brook it themselves for their private advantage and escaped the penalty." They also "made wars and peace with Indians as best suited their private advantage in trade," which cost the colony much money and resulted in the loss of lives. Who, the proprietors wondered, would want to live under a government led by such men? Who indeed but like-minded men.[91]

In spite of the proprietors' objections, Mathews and Moore were returned to the council. The proprietors demanded their indictment but got nowhere, probably owing to the instability that occurred during the governor's illness in the summer of 1685. Deputy Governor John Godfrey handled affairs for a short while until West resigned, and Robert Quarry took over for three months, appointed by the council. Joseph Morton then served his second term as governor. For a second time, the proprietors removed him from office. James Colleton (1686–1690), brother of one of the proprietors, was appointed. By his arrival in late 1686, piracy had temporarily replaced the trade in Indians as the proprietors' first order of business—the Crown was upset, understandably, that Carolina conducted a large trade with Caribbean pirates, some of whom operated out of the nearby Bahama Islands.[92] Colleton was given power to create deputies who would not only seize the illegal privateers and punish the guilty but also arrest those who sent "away the poor Indians."[93] Colleton tried to crush the pirates and the Indian dealers, who were about to invade Spanish Florida. Colleton prevented the invasion and arrested pirates but could not subdue the Indian dealers, who banished him.

The Carolinians and the Westo were two very different peoples. But as newcomers to the region they shared a method for carving out living space and improving their fortunes: the capture of humans for sale into an international market. Although the Westo held many advantages over the Carolinians, including greater military power and better skills for conducting slave raids, the Carolinians quickly prevailed over them. The Westo, by failing to ally themselves with any significant group of Indians, were unable to overcome the Carolinians' ability to unite Indian peoples against them. Whereas the Westo had alienated natives throughout the region by their slaving, the Carolinians enticed Indian groups to do their bidding. The Carolinians, for all their internal divisions, succeeded because they not only offered Indian peoples valuable trade goods but could also market Indians' commodities. The English did not have to become enslavers themselves, only middlemen between the raiders and the marketplace. To resist the Carolinians, the Westo would have had to compete against them: to form their own alliances and find someone else to supply their needs and purchase their commodities. But the Spanish were unwilling and unable, and Virginia was too distant to compete with Carolina on the Savannah River.

South Carolina's star was in ascension, and its influence quickly grew in the South. Yet in spite of the colony's favorable position for building a network of alliances that would secure and promote English interests in the region, internal divisions, ignorance, and greed kept South Carolina hovering near disaster. For the first fifty years of the colony, volatility characterized its Indian relations. The colony's leaders proved inept at maintaining stable alliances and preventing their people from exploiting allies. Native American peoples remained attracted to the Carolinians' trade goods, but to varying extents, they recognized the limitations of becoming partners with the English. New groups entered the South and went about establishing their own bases of power and networks of alliances, notably the French in Louisiana. Yamasee and Scots also played a significant role, emigrating to the Savannah River, where they established permanent settlements. Both followed the Westo and the English by becoming fully engaged in the Indian slave trade and the topsy-turvy politics that increasingly defined the region.

3

CROSSROAD OF CULTURES
SCOTS, YAMASEE,
AND THE CAROLINA COLONY, 1684–1701

The establishment of Carolina and the emigration of Westo, and then the Savannah, had made the South Atlantic Coastal and Savannah River subregions hives of activity. Through Charles Town entered European trade goods and more immigrants; leaving the South were animal pelts, livestock, wood products, and Indian slaves. Watching with great interest and trepidation were Spanish and Indians. English slaving threatened everyone, but English goods enticed interest from many. Much more than the Spanish, the English traded their wares with Indians. Metal tools, guns, alcohol, textiles, and fripperies led numerous Indians to seek out the English, just as the English sought out Indians for pelts and slaves. This trade activity played a part in luring more "newcomers" near the English. Large numbers of Yamasee and a much smaller number of Scots settled on the north side of the Savannah River, to the east of the Savannah Indians. Although both groups settled there for land, the opportunities for trade and alliance took precedence over agriculture. Other, smaller groups of Indians soon followed: Apalachicola, Chickasaw, and Yuchi all planted towns on the Savannah. The Carolina colonists welcomed the Indians as allies and trading partners, but they were none too happy about the Scots. In these last years of the seventeenth century, Carolina made its first attempts to regulate the Indian trade, to find other "uses" for both Settlement and neighboring Indians, and to assert its dominance over the Savannah River peoples. Although the colony largely failed in most of these endeavors, Carolinians established great influence in the area, which they quickly extended through the South.

THE EXPANSION OF CAROLINA

In July 1684 the 170-ton *Carolina Merchant,* carrying sixteen guns, departed western Scotland for South Carolina. As it set out for sea, a trumpeter aboard "sounded several times," which one observer thought "was truly pleasant." The Scots on board, many of whom were fleeing religious persecution, were convinced that God's providence guided them, and they anxiously awaited the revealing of God's design for them in the New World. As friends and relations watched from the shore, they reflected that they were witnessing a historic occasion, the beginning of what promised to be an important enterprise in Scottish overseas settlement. Both the passengers and those who wished them well dreamed of New World riches. Several on shore had invested in the enterprise by providing servants, goods, and money. For instance, John Erskine, brother of one of the expedition's leaders, Lord Henry Cardross, invested in one servant, £174 Scots currency, and about £4 sterling in goods.[1] Others invested much more, purchasing shares in Carolina plantations. Many were already making plans to follow their compatriots in the ensuing years. Like the Puritans who had settled Massachusetts Bay fifty years earlier, the Scots Presbyterians had long discussed planting a colony in the New World where they could control their destiny.

The Scots intended to settle apart from the English colony at Charles Town, on the Sea Islands to the north of the Savannah River. They believed the area to be virtually unpeopled, on the fringes of European settlement, with only a few Indians in the vicinity. In fact, large numbers of Indians were moving into the area at the same time. The Scots had no idea of the hornet's nest they would soon enter, as many people, Indians and Europeans, opposed their settlement.

The Spanish stood in the forefront of those who hoped to prevent any expansion of the Carolina colony. According to custom and international law, which provided first discovery as giving right to ownership, Carolina was clearly located on Spanish land.[2] The Spanish had extended their claims by settlements, many just abandoned after repeated attacks from pirates, English, and Westo, but they did not give up their rights to the territory. The English merely disregarded Spanish claims, as they later did in Georgia: England only accepted claims secured by force of arms.[3] The men of wealth and power in Carolina cared nothing for law because they had been nurtured by a society that bred disrespect for it. In seventeenth-century England force repeatedly prevailed over law. Kings ruled by divine right and proclaimed themselves above parliamentary law; Parliament went beyond its own laws to behead Charles I; and a nation engulfed in civil war learned that the greatest lesson of the century was that laws were malleable, issued by those in power of whatever stripe, to secure their rule and interests.

The English ached for stability with the Restoration of King Charles II, which coincided with the founding of Carolina, in what some would argue as the most corrupt period of English political history. Although the populace was unaware that its king treasonously sold English interests to the French for personal profit, the citizenry was aware of his sexual profligacy and numerous illegitimate children. Charles II's flaunting of conventional morality was easily matched by the political corruption of the period. The country's leaders abandoned political positions and ideas with incredible swiftness in search of place and profit. A "country" party emerged that denounced both individuals and the system, so that a reformist ideology of limiting government power and guarding to protect the people from perfidy grew in England and was carried to America.[4] It was not carried quickly enough. The men who served in Carolina's government, the merchant and planter elite, were unmoved by ideals of the virtuous public servant. They modeled themselves on what they saw at home in England. They held office not for any ideal of service to a monarch, a country, proprietors, or one's social inferiors but to attain and extend their wealth and power.

In 1688, England stood poised for the removal of yet another king, James II, a Catholic, and many in England wrote tracts to define the proper limits of authority, the importance of law, and the responsibilities of the governed and those who governed. The problems of the previous fifty years were laid at the feet of sovereigns who had disregarded the law—parliamentary and common—but save for the republicans, most English would not dispense with the monarchy. They simply wanted to rein in kingly power. The force of their argument was slow to take hold. Not until elites of all persuasions saw the need for regularity and the advantages of the law for upholding their authority and stabilizing the state did they actually begin to effect respect for the law through society. Even then, many questioned their motives, particularly as the rise of individualism led people to skirt the laws for self-fulfillment. Carolina's development was much along the same lines. The elite disregarded the laws until they got what they wanted. Once they had ensured their power in society over their inferiors and had rendered the proprietors' power null, they then portrayed themselves as upholders of fair and equitable laws that were good and just for the maintenance of all.[5]

THE SCOTS AND YAMASEE PREPARE
TO SETTLE ALONG THE SAVANNAH RIVER

In the 1680s the Savannah River's significance was just emerging. The most important river in the eastern half of the South, the Savannah connected Carolina to the western Indians. Much of the land that surrounded the river near its mouth was nearly impenetrable. Rivulets and swamps made for difficult terrain, forcing people to go nearly twenty miles inland to find a crossing place before proceeding north-south by land. Most, however, avoided the land route when going north-south, preferring the inland passage between the Sea Islands and the coast. The proprietors had initially intended to center the Carolina colony at Port Royal, just north of the Savannah, but the first fleet of colonists opted instead for the Ashley River. The Savannah River area retained its importance to the colony, however.

To protect Carolina from Indian attacks from the southwest and from the Spanish who could use the inland passage to invade, the colony encouraged Indians to inhabit the rich lands on the mainland along the north bank of the Savannah. Eventually, traders established Savannah Town at a spot formerly occupied by the Westo on the north bank of the river across from modern-day Augusta, Georgia. The trading post led hundreds of Indians to settle in the area. Many found employment in English enterprises as messengers, porters, scouts, trackers of runaways, enslavers, and carriers of goods for expeditions to the interior.

With the Westo and Waniah defeated and decimated, the Savannah were the first large Indian group to move to the Savannah River area in the 1680s. They shifted uneasily into a role as chief allies and slave catchers for the English as well as the colony's southwestern defensive buttress. Unexpectedly, the Yamasee vied for a similar position as ally while taking up land to the east of the Savannah. Just who the Yamasee were and when the group formed is a mystery to archaeologists and historians. They were probably a confederacy of diverse groups that formed in the protohistoric period, and the name Yamasee might have arisen from a town or group of towns within this new larger group. Many of these Indians had lived along the Savannah River until the Westo forced them to flee southward. Yamasee appear regularly in small pockets on the census returns of Spanish missions in central and northern Florida, and also in Guale and Mocama in Georgia. They usually did not convert to Christianity and were somewhat segregated from the Christian Indians in the same missions. The Yamasee were more adept than most of the region's people, except for the Savannah, at establishing contacts with other Indians along the southeastern Atlantic seaboard and the old southwest. In the early 1680s pirate attacks forced the Yamasee out of Guale and left the Spanish missions there untenable. Although some Yamasee moved to Florida, another migration from Florida and Guale went northward to reoccupy their former lands that became available with the defeat and reduction of the Westo. More than fifty years later, one Spaniard noted that a reason the Yamasee had left Florida lay in "a grudge against a certain governor of Florida on account of having ill treated their chief by words and deeds." The chief had fallen sick and failed to send "a certain number of men for the cultivation of lands as he was obliged to do."[6] Under the *repartimiento* (compulsory labor system), mission Indians were required to send laborers to Saint Augustine to work the fields and build and repair fortifications. The Yamasee might have become disenchanted, as other Indians did, with the arrangement, particularly when the Spanish failed to live up to their side of the bargain: to protect them from their enemies. The Spanish historian Andrés González de Barcía writing in 1723, blamed the English for luring the Yamasee away, though, he, too, noted the aforementioned chief's displeasure with the Spanish governor.[7] Most likely, the Yamasee, uninterested in Catholicism and mission life, simply took the opportunity of Westo defeat to regain their lands, though many (but not all) carried with them hostility to their former Spanish hosts. In 1683 or 1684 they informed the English of their intention to return to the Savannah, which the colonists welcomed as a buffer against the Spanish.[8]

The Yamasee quickly established relations with the Scottish settlers who migrated to Carolina in 1684, extending colonial settlement southward to Port Royal, where they built Stuart Town. The Yamasee numbered more than a thousand and lived on neighboring Sea Islands and on the mainland to the west. The two Scottish settler leaders, Lord Cardross and William Dunlop, described the Yamasee as the "most considerable" nation in the area. In a letter home they condescendingly noted how "we have consented to them that they remain here during their good behavior," but in fact the Scots had no say in the matter, realizing that "the truth is they are so considerable and warlike that we would not do otherwise" and "the whole nation is not yet come which we cannot well oppose." Fortunately, the Scots thought, the Yamasee were "Inveterate enemies" to the Spanish and their Indian allies, giving the Yamasee and the Carolina colonists a common interest.[9]

The Scots settlement at Stuart Town provides a case study, like the

Westo, of a new immigrant group's adaptation to the South. The settlement introduced an ethnic enclave of like-minded people who initially sought to carve out living space for themselves connected to, but separate from, their English neighbors. In the British Isles, the Scots were attached to the English through the person of the monarch, Charles II, a Scottish king who ruled both England and Scotland. His grandfather, James VI of Scotland, governed England as James I and dreamed of uniting his two kingdoms but failed. Scots and English were not predisposed to favor each other. The free movement of people between England and Scotland was obtained, but little else was accomplished. The governments remained separate; trade restrictions hindered economic integration; and except for Stuart kings bringing their favorites southward and generously bestowing gifts from English coffers upon them, about the only true integration achieved was in the shared carving up of parts of Ireland for Scots and English settlers. Prejudice in England against the Scots ran high, though by the time of Stuart Town's founding, it had waned considerably from earlier in the century.

In Scotland, the Presbyterians, like many of the Puritans in England, opposed bishopric control of the church and suffered for their beliefs. They opposed the hierarchical structure of both Catholic and Anglican churches, and thus the political power of the head of the established church, while vigorously favoring their own kirk. In the 1670s many west country Scots considered migration to Carolina, drawn by promises of religious toleration and free land, and also because one of the lords proprietors, the earl of Shaftsbury, publicly opposed their oppression in England's House of Lords.[10] Religious reasons were not the entire story. In the early 1680s growing political repression disenfranchised many leading Presbyterians: arbitrary government and political oppression pushed the Scots from their homeland.[11] To this must be added the economic malaise that resulted from poor soils. The Scots lived a much more primitive material existence than the English: their clothes were of rougher material, and their diet was more limited and contained less meat. Whereas the English were the center of a growing international trade economy, the Scots remained on the outside looking in, increasingly aware of the greater world and all it offered but practically barred from participating in England's profitable overseas colonies and trade. The search for better soils led to the movement of Scots to Ulster, one place they were allowed to colonize, but many sought other places to migrate, including England, where the English feared that Scots moving southward would cause economic problems. Yet England would not permit the Scots to have their own colonies or overseas trading companies.[12]

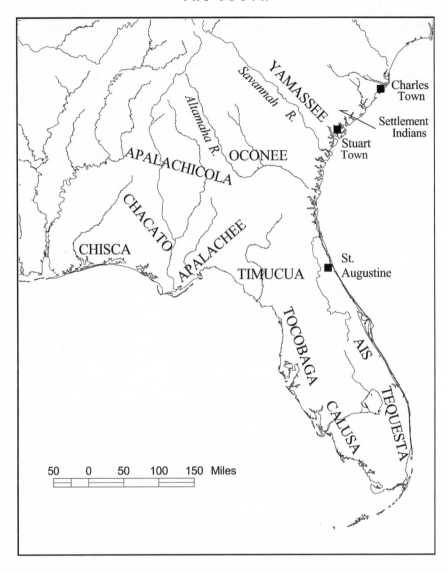

The South in 1684

Some west country Scots interested in the New World turned to the lords proprietors of Carolina, requesting a place to settle within their colony but apart from the English. In 1682, Sir John Cochrane and Sir George Campbell completed negotiations obtaining "two Counties in Carolina."[13] The proprietors agreed to purchase the land from Indian claimants, while the Scots would "take up" 36,000 acres each year for eight years[14] and would then be permitted more. The proprietors hoped to people their colony with

Scots because of their difficulty attracting English. Opposition to outmigration was on the rise in England, and there were more colonies for prospective colonists to choose from with the recent conquest of New Netherland (1664) and the founding of Pennsylvania (1682). Charles II permitted the Covenanters, as these Scots Presbyterians were called, to migrate "because they would carry with them disaffected people."[15]

The Scots and the lords proprietors expected thousands to flock to Carolina, but events conspired against them. Approximately 140 went on the first ship, the *Carolina Merchant*. The ship's owner, Walter Gibson, had to scramble for passengers, publishing broadsheets to advertise his terms. Relatively few paying passengers—who would receive fifty-acre headrights on reaching Carolina—were recruited. Gibson offered free passage to those willing to labor as indentured servants for three to five years.[16] Gibson's brother James, who captained the ship, purchased 35 prisoners to transport as laborers.[17] Only 35 free Covenanters were included among the passengers,[18] so that fully three-fourths of the passengers went as servants.[19]

The leaders, Cardross and Dunlop, both emigrated because of grave political problems that resulted from their religious activities; Cardross's brushes with the law were more serious than Dunlop's, but Dunlop found that his activities had made him unemployable. William Dunlop was a former tutor in Sir John Cochran's household and a recent university graduate. He was the Scottish colonists' religious leader (though he had yet to be ordained). Dunlop was very much a man of the world, and he provided the Scots with political and military leadership, economic vision, and entrepreneurial spirit.

One person died on the nine-and-a-half-week voyage because of a shortage of fresh water.[20] Worse was quick to come. The settlers arrived at Charles Town on October 26 in the midst of an unspecified epidemic that "quickly seized many of our number." Some of the "discouraged" survivors deserted their fellows as soon as they reached Port Royal and sold their servants. Cardross and Dunlop blamed some of Charles Town's "esteemed great men" for actively discouraging their settlement, though others treated them well.[21]

STUART TOWN

A recent Spanish attack on Providence in the Bahamas boded ill for Stuart Town, for the Spanish had grown more militant against English usurpation of Port Royal, which they still claimed.[22] The subsequent loss of a ship of Scots-Irish from Belfast on their way to settle with the Covenanters, and then the refusal of a second ship of emigrants to settle at Port Royal—they took one look at the place, changed their minds, and went elsewhere—left the colony's spirits and chances for survival even lower. In fewer than six months Stuart Town had only fifty-one people.

Cardross and Dunlop persevered, intent on living up to their obligations to the lords proprietors, their investors, and the colonists. They took great care laying out Stuart Town "in a very Convenient place." Each of the 220 lots had an adjacent garden and two acres of land. Forty-one town lots were taken up, and several English had "resolved to settle with us and are transporting their families hither." They also expected recruits from Antigua "and other plantations." A planter from Antigua who visited Port Royal pronounced the land good for indigo and sugar and promised to bring five or six families.[23]

To make the settlement more palatable to their desires and attractive to fellow Scots, Cardross and Dunlop asked the proprietors for substantial independence from Charles Town. The Scots believed that success depended on these concessions. They had yet to bring their wives and children, and they threatened "that nothing less than what we have demanded will confirm our stay here." They entreated the lords proprietors to "trust us," and they would make a "noble plantation" that would flourish more than Charles Town, or at least no worse. They promised to "be more for the lords' Proprietors' true Interest than any in Carolina."

Looking to the future well-being of the colony, Dunlop and Cardross expressed doubt about finding valuable ores—always the first item sought by colonists to procure wealth—and so they contemplated the rich mineral resources of New Mexico. They foresaw the opening of a "passage" from Port Royal to northern Mexico and of an alliance with the Indians there and along the way. They drew up a "method" for "laying down . . . correspondence" with those distant Indians, whom they heard had left the Spanish interest. Port Royal's location gave them much advantage over Charles Town, but they worried about their enemies provoking the neighboring Indians against them, which would hinder all commerce. The Scots generously offered the proprietors a share of the trade, apparently unaware of the proprietary monopoly over trade with distant Indians.[24] The Scots' ignorance or misunderstanding of restrictions on Indian trade also extended to their relationship to Charles Town and the Carolina government. Cardross and Dunlop were both intelligent men, so the blame for their confusion must be laid on the proprietors, who, although they expressed themselves clearly enough to Charles Town officials as to make no mistake about what could or could not be done in the colony, were surprisingly reticent with the Scots, whom they did not wish to alienate. The proprietors agreed to treat the Scots differently by giving them some control over their own affairs, but they never defined the extent of that independence. Perhaps they awaited the turnout of events at Stuart Town, for the Scots settlement had the potential to be a powerful counterpoise to Charles Town, one that might help the proprietors bring the Carolinians into line.

The vague independence of Stuart Town created great hostility between the Scots and the Charles Town government. Asserting their authority, the Scots arrested Henry Woodward and several others passing through Port Royal on their way to trade with Indians. The Scots and their local English allies claimed jurisdiction over the area's Indian trade, which angered those Carolinians chafing under proprietary restrictions and now challenged by upstart newcomers. Worse still, the newcomer Scots had apparently allied successfully with the Yamasee, who conducted a slaving raid into Florida and allegedly sold the captives to the Scots and not to Charles Town.

It had been only a matter of time before the Yamasee would strike against the Spanish and their Indian allies in Florida. Freed of the Westo threat, the Yamasee became a potent force on the Savannah River and a potentially valuable ally to Carolina. The Yamasee possessed enough military power to resist English intimidation and maintain for another twenty years a parity of sorts with Carolina. From the colony they obtained trade goods in exchange for deerskins, but their success as skilled raiders impressed the English and Scots even more. Yamasee knowledge of Florida, its people and topography, was a special threat to Florida and of great use to Carolina.

When the Yamasee invaded the Timucua in northern Florida in 1685, the English were not even sure who the Timucua were or where they lived.[25] The Yamasee "sacked the mission school of Santa Catalina, robbed the church and the convent of San Francisco of its precious ornaments, burned the village, inflicted pitiful deaths on many Indians, and carried away many others as prisoners to Santa Elena [Port Royal]."[26] Woodward, smarting from his arrest by the Scots, blamed Caleb Westbrook, an English trader who lived with the Scots, for having set the Yamasee "upon this Design." But it is likely that the Indians needed little push in this direction.[27] The plundering of church plate may have been as much an act of vengeance against the Spanish as an attempt to obtain valuable items for sale in Carolina.

The role of the Scots in the Florida raid remains unclear. Their enemies in Charles Town wasted no time blaming them for it. James Moore, one of the colony's premier dealers in Indian slaves, who led those who wished to overthrow the proprietary monopoly of the Indian trade, gathered evidence in depositions against the Scots, including from Woodward. With Woodward as interpreter, a Yamasee testified that Westbrook and Yamasee chief Araoma-hau had been the ones who encouraged the Yamasee to make war on the Ti-mucua, and that the Scots had given them twenty-three guns. He testified that the raiders burned several towns, killed fifty Timucuans, and took twenty-two prisoners, "which they delivered to the Scots as slaves."[28] One wonders where the Scots got the capital to purchase the Yamasee captives. Moreover, no mention is made of to whom the Scots sold the slaves, although the options were limited to Charles Town merchants or colonial officials—no ships went to Port Royal that could have purchased the captives for sale in other colonies, though it is possible that pirates bought the slaves. Whether the Scots sent the Indians on the raid, simply profited by it, or even were merely guilty of allowing slavers like Westbrook to join their community, Charles Town officials were intent on blaming the Scots. They knew that the proprietors would condemn any attack on the Spanish during peacetime and illegally enslaving Indians who lived closer than four hundred miles. The colony could not be expected to have stopped the Yamasee, if they had no hand in it, but they could not purchase their captives and booty except to return them to the Spanish.[29] Purchasing the slaves and not repatriating them made the colony complicit, or from Charles Town's point of view, it made the Scots complicit.

After blaming the Scots for the Yamasee raid, Charles Town continued its assault against Scottish pretensions by ordering the arrest of Cardross, West-brook, and another man in May 1685. They were not arrested for the Yamasee raid but for their interference with the claimed authority of the Carolina government. Cardross was too sick to travel and refused the warrant,[30] but the Scots conceded defeat and Dunlop patched things up by Scotch acceptance of Charles Town's jurisdiction. Still, much damage had been done, and the Scots could expect little help from the government in nurturing and securing their settlement.

For a year Stuart Town settled down and developed apace. Much of what is known about this period comes from Dunlop's letters to Sir James Montgomery, a major investor in the settlement, who had a debt of two hundred pounds to Dunlop, which Dunlop drew against to pay his bills. When Dunlop wrote Montgomery in May 1686, he was waiting impatiently for a 140-ton vessel that Montgomery and Lord Rosse, another investor, had bought specifically for Stuart Town traffic. Montgomery was going to accompany the ship to Port Royal and view his investment. Dunlop prepared for his arrival by cutting lumber for sale in Barbados or Jamaica, though he knew that this would hardly defray the ship's charges. More profit would be made from the goods brought from London, for prices were high in Carolina for many commodities. The chief purpose of purchasing the ship, however, was to bring more settlers and to carry away whatever the colonists had produced.

Dunlop sent instruction to Montgomery to bring free settlers and not white servants. For labor he instead recommended "negroes for they are the only servants for this country." These could be purchased in Barbados, so he suggested that they prepare a cargo for that island and when there to pick up rum, sugar, and melons before proceeding to Carolina; otherwise, if they sailed first for Carolina, whether from Scotland or England, they should bring "claret and other liquors," as well as clothing. Whichever course Montgomery chose, his chief care should be "to provide for negroes." Dunlop explained that of the twenty-two white servants he brought, only eight remained alive, and of seven others he had bought, all had died. In spite of this horrific death rate, Dunlop insisted that the country was healthy: domestic animals flourished, fruits were plenty—"this year the Indians brought us abundance of oranges from St. Katherines"—English grains grew well, also mulberries and olives. But, he warned Montgomery, do not let the emigrants think that settlement will be easy: they should "expect nothing but labor for the country is a wilderness." Montgomery should recruit freemen, preferably tradesmen, especially smiths, carpenters, tailors, ship chandlers, and shoemakers. Dunlop expressed his determination to maintain the colony as long as they had six men alive.

It might seem strange and callous that Dunlop could think so highly of the country and the enterprise in the midst of so much evidence to the contrary. He dismissed the deaths of the great majority who came as inexpedient and unrelated to settlement. The subsequent deaths of the passengers that came aboard an Irish ship he noted without comment. Smitten with Carolina, Dunlop never ceased talking of the colony's beauty and potential. He also was honored by the many offices that the new governor, Joseph Morton, bestowed on him. He proudly boasted how he was captain of the militia "answerable only to the governor," register of births and burials for the county, and one of the "Lords deputies," which involved him in important affairs of state. If the honors bestowed and the charm of the colony make him seem callous about the death that surrounded him, we should also remember that he believed that God was the author of all things and that the trials and tribulations that he himself, and the settlement generally, experienced had some greater purpose.

The success of Stuart Town depended on attracting settlers and obtaining capital to develop plantations through payment of surveying fees and the purchase of supplies, tools and labor. Dunlop, just short of exasperation, explained this to Montgomery when Montgomery's vessel failed to arrive as expected. He informed Montgomery that he would have to bear the blame for his investment suffering in Carolina. It had been up to him to bring the "recruits." Dunlop lectured him that "all new settlements are gone about with great charge at first and it takes time before profits come in." Montgomery risked losing his entire investment. In expectation of new settlers, Dunlop, on the investors' behalf, had run up surveyor fees of £120 for laying out twenty-four thousand acres. Dunlop vouched for half the sum and might have had to sell the investors' cattle to meet the debts but instead drew bills on Montgomery for money owed him. (In several letters, he prayed that Montgomery answer these bills so that his credit would not suffer, for if he did not, he would do the same to him.)

Dunlop put the best light possible on the colony: no one had died for six months and they had no fear of the Spanish. He and others intended a voyage south toward Saint Augustine to view the country, particularly Saint Catherine's Island, as a potential area of future settlement. His main concerns, however, were getting new settlers, without which the colony would wither and die; obtaining supplies from Montgomery; and third, persuading the king to alter the trade laws so that Scots could remove their goods, the very clothing they wore, to and from the English colonies without taxes placed on them. The Scots' enemies in Carolina ceaselessly reminded them that as foreigners they were subject to English navigation laws and taxes. Most everyone ignored the letter of the law, but the threat dangled over their head, and Dunlop was eventually confined aboard ship for breaking the law when he tried to return to Scotland.

When Montgomery failed to arrive Dunlop anxiously implored him to make haste without stopping anywhere, not even at Charles Town. He had prepared for him "a considerable parcel of cedar and will shortly provide squared pin and ship staves." Dunlop had spent much time and effort on the lumber and now expected some return. Alarmed at the ship's delay, he warned Montgomery that if it did not come "you shall pay for all for I might have employed my self much better."[31]

Dunlop had good reason for alarm: his suspicions were true and the ship never came. Disaster struck Stuart Town. On August 17, 1686, the Spanish attacked the settlement. Whether the attack was meant as an act of vengeance for the Yamasee raid of 1684 or simply as part of the overall strategy of the Spanish to check English expansion in the region, especially in areas still claimed by Spain, the Spanish showed that Spain would no longer remain on the defensive. Spain could not tolerate Carolina's expansion into Port Royal any more than it could the use of the Bahamas as a pirate base for attacks against Saint Augustine and the Spanish West Indies, and if the Spanish commonly thought of pirates and English as synonymous, they were somewhat correct. Carolina colonists were in league with the Bahamian-based pirates, buying their booty and selling them supplies.

In a revealing letter written two months later, Dunlop reserved mentioning to Montgomery the attack on Port Royal until he carefully recited his anguish in waiting for Montgomery's vessel to arrive. Dunlop had learned that the ship went to Antigua then returned to Scotland with its passengers—the colony's new recruits—because it "got a good freight" to take home. Dunlop declaimed how the ship had been engaged solely in a "trading Voyage to the West Indies." He did not know who had ordered it on this course, but Dunlop berated Montgomery that "you made me believe [it] was bought only for our service to advance the settlement at Port Royal." Distraught that it had not brought "that part of the cargo which belonged to me" and that no one had bothered to write him of its changed plans, he learned the truth only from someone who had been to Antigua. Then Dunlop lowered the boom, telling Montgomery of the Spanish attack and how if the ship had been there as promised the Spanish would never have succeeded. Dunlop relayed how in broad daylight they had to face "3 Spanish half galleys with 155 men." The Scots had fewer than 30, and half "were in the country and would not get to us." They did not have time to employ their three "great guns" and had to flee before the "multitude." The Scots ran for the woods, knowing the Spanish could not follow, but they turned the English guns on Lord Cardross, who had fled in a small boat, barely escaping. The Spanish stayed three nights at Stuart Town, leaving after they had "plundered all our houses," taking even their clothes. They burned the town to the ground, destroyed the fields and fences, killed hogs and cattle, and burned or threw into the water what they could not carry. The Spanish then went "toward the English settlement on the Edisto River" and plundered Paul Grimball's two plantations, carrying off "17 Ethiopians and white servants." They finally departed when a hurricane arrived.[32]

Dunlop lost several hundred pounds and two servants. Losses from Rosse's and Montgomery's investment exceeded five hundred pounds, but they still had fifty head of cattle, thirty hogs, and thirty acres of cleared, planted, and enclosed land. Dunlop had no intention of giving up, but he heaped blame on Montgomery for their predicament. The failure of the ship to arrive was threefold: it had not brought the recruits who would have paid the surveying fees; if the ship had been there the Spanish would not have dared to attack; and the Spanish had burned all the square cedar and other lumber that Dunlop had stored at the shore ready for export. Therefore Dunlop charged that Montgomery would have to bear the loss, because Dunlop had acted on Montgomery's "positive order" that the ship would come.

SCOTS AND YAMASEE:
UNEASY ALLIES AGAINST THE SPANISH

Committed as ever to building a settlement Dunlop negotiated with recently arrived French Huguenots to move to Port Royal.[33] But first the Spanish had to be taken care of, so the colony prepared an invasion force of four hundred to five hundred to go to Saint Augustine with Dunlop among the officers. Dunlop vowed "to take St. Augustine from the Spaniard in so just a quarrel."[34] In November 1686, just as the expedition was to set sail, new governor James Colleton arrived. He immediately canceled the invasion, threatening to hang anyone who dared to participate in it.[35] The proprietors applauded Colleton's actions and echoed his sentiment of hanging the belligerent, saying that former governor Morton and Colonel John Godfrey would probably have paid with their lives if an invasion had been sent.[36]

Most historians have assumed incorrectly that there was only one invasion of Stuart Town, but in fact a second occurred in December 1686, with the Spanish "utterly destroying what they left before at Port Royal."[37] Although the governor told the proprietors that he still refused to allow a counter invasion, in fact, four months later Dunlop led an armed party of thirty-five south of the Savannah River. It is unknown whether Colleton knew that Dunlop intended going all the way to Florida. The Scot was instructed to set up warning beacons on various Sea Islands to be manned by Yamasee—one fire for one Spanish galley, two for two, and three for more than two. Dunlop also was to "bribe" individual Indians to spy on the Spanish and to reconnoiter Spanish activities south of the Savannah River.[38] But how far south was he to proceed? Dunlop thought he had license "to go to the frontiers to see if the Spaniards were still lying within the province."[39]

On the way to Port Royal from Charles Town, Dunlop visited the Yamasee and "demanded" assistance in the form of forty warriors in six or seven canoes. The Yamasee agreed but refused to man the beacons. Nor could Dunlop induce anyone to deliver a letter for him to Saint Augustine. He tried to recruit the Ashepoo, a group of Settlement Indians, to join the expedition, but they refused. Dunlop was having his first but not his last lesson in Indian intransigence.

Dunlop would not need the Ashepoo because he saw his force swell to one hundred, including sixty-three Indians, almost all of whom were Yamasee under the leadership of Matamaha. Dunlop led the combined forces across the Savannah and found some of the Scots' cattle, which the Spanish had taken. The Yamasee saw evidence that other Indians had been there just a few days before. They identified these as the Huspaw, "their friends," who they believed had deserted to the Spanish. (The Huspaw were later known as one of the main groups of Yamasee, so it is possible that at this time they were an allied people and not part of the Yamasee proper, because Matamaha did not speak of them as Yamasee.) Almost as an aside, the Yamasee told Dunlop that on the Spaniards' last raid the Spanish had killed and taken away twenty-two Yamasee women. The divulgence of information about the Yamasee women and the Huspaw indicates that there had been little communication between the colony and the Yamasee, since four months after the invasion they were still learning essential details about what had happened.[40]

The invaders proceeded along the Sea Islands, stopping at Saint Catherine's Island and Sapelo Island, and continued toward Florida. Near Florida, they discussed "surprising" the Spanish lookouts on Amelia Island to gain intelligence, but Matamaha refused. He claimed that his Yamasee would not fight the Spanish, "for they had never killed any of his people." (Apparently, the twenty-two women killed and captured were from another Yamasee group. Matamaha's view adds credence to the view of the Yamasee as a loose confederacy of independent towns.) Some of the Yamasee berated Matamaha for his "unfaithfulness," but Dunlop decided to turn back. Earlier one of the canoes had disappeared, Matamaha explaining that it must have taken a wrong turn. Dunlop worried that Matamaha had sent the canoe ahead to warn the Spanish of their coming.[41] It will probably never be known what really went on among the Yamasee, but the episode illustrates how little these neighbors and allies understood each other. Dunlop certainly was ill prepared to contend with the vagaries of Indian diplomacy; his knowledge of his allies was too limited. The Yamasee all too well may have understood Dunlop's intentions and found a diplomatic way to avoid challenging the Spanish by feigning disagreement among themselves—in this way, they could reject Dunlop's desire to fight but still appear as if many supported the measure. The colony's weakness against the Spanish had probably made the Yamasee wary of raising the Spaniards' ire by yet another raid into Florida. But the Yamasee had also been misled about the purpose of the expedition. When Dunlop arrived at Matamaha's village, he told the Yamasee that he had been sent to defend them. In a later letter to Montgomery, Dunlop claimed that the expedition was initiated "when we heard they [the Spanish] designed a return Invasion." Dunlop let slip this same motive in his argument with Matamaha: "I told him we came to fight the Spaniard if we found them coming again."[42] In fact, they had not found any evidence of a third invasion. They had reconnoitered all the way to Florida, and Dunlop admitted that there was nothing to indicate that the Spanish had recently been in Georgia. It was clear to the Yamasee that the Carolinians did not care whether the Spanish were preparing to invade, they simply wanted to strike an act of vengeance to show Saint Augustine that Spanish raids would not go unanswered. Matamaha was unwilling to attack—the recent Spanish raids had made him think twice. And he might even have come not to trust Dunlop, who had misled him.

The Yamasee could not be easily manipulated. As colonists everywhere learned, Indian allies did not blindly follow Europeans. The Carolinians had to learn this lesson repeatedly, much to their dismay. Indians on European invasions insisted that their voice be heard, and they often dictated to Europeans the terms under which they would fight. In the South, the Europeans had little choice because Indian military power was stronger than their own; Indian tactics were better suited to local conditions, and Indians refused to fight when conditions did not suit them.

Fortunately for Carolina and for Dunlop, the invaders had not attacked the Spanish, for James II would brook no peacetime assaults against Spain. As a Catholic monarch who counted France's powerful Louis XIV as a first cousin, James drew England closer to Spain and sought a diplomatic solution to the Spanish attacks on Port Royal. Representations were made at the Spanish court, where the English learned that the king of Spain had not countenanced an invasion of Carolina and that the Carolinians "may have redress from their several Governors where they live"; Saint Augustine and Charles Town were left, somewhat, to work out their differences themselves.[43]

Governor Colleton chose Dunlop to represent the colony's case at Saint Augustine in June 1688. He instructed Dunlop to assure the Spanish governor that James II "hath vigorously resolved" to extirpate all pirates—of whatever nation—who harassed Spanish shipping in the West Indies and that Carolina's governor would effectively attack and punish any pirates who entered the province.[44] At that very moment Carolina had several in prison "who are speedily to be brought to their trials."[45] The king also sent a fleet to Carolina to root out "those ravenous Beasts (as his Royal Majesty is pleased to call these pirates)," but before doing so he must be assured that Florida had given satisfaction for the two invasions of Carolina. Dunlop threatened the

Spanish that if Carolina did not receive compensation, the fleet had instructions to assist the colony in "taking satisfaction."[46] Carolina demanded that the previous Spanish governor, Juan Marais de Cabrera, who had ordered the two invasions, be handed over, or they be assured that he would receive "some capital punishment" in Saint Augustine. They also required restoration of eleven slaves and the sum of fourteen thousand pieces of eight in Mexican or Spanish coin.[47] Dunlop was instructed to lie and claim that the eleven slaves were the property of the previous governor, Morton, to make it more likely that the Spanish would pay compensation.[48] It is also probable that Dunlop and the colony lied about the king's intention to use the fleet as leverage to gain compensation—James II was not looking for a war with Spain.

The Spanish refused to release the eleven slaves, whom they claimed were runaways, perhaps so they could not be accused of stealing them. They protected the slaves on the grounds that all had converted to Catholicism, and in return they offered to pay for them. One of the slaves, Mingo, was also accused of having murdered one of James II's subjects—if this were proven, then the Spanish governor agreed to inflict capital punishment on Mingo. After being warmly treated by the Spanish, Dunlop returned to Carolina believing that an honorable agreement had been made and that trade might soon begin with Florida. No money actually changed hands. The Spanish promised to send the compensation shortly, but they never did.

The deposing of James II in 1688 in England may have led both sides to reconsider patching up relations, for the ascension of the Protestant William and Mary boded ill for Anglo-Spanish relations. The colonists decided to try another course and asked Dunlop to go to England to represent their case for compensation, by which Dunlop could also restore his own sagging fortune.[49] Cardross preceded Dunlop home, and great pressure was brought to bear on the Presbyterian divine to abandon Carolina. In spite of his own constant entreaties, Dunlop's wife had never left Scotland to join him in America. Three of his friends begged him to return, telling him that it was the "opinion of all your other friends here." They reminded him that the investors had given up on Carolina, and no one else would invest. Their countrymen had a "great aversion" to build plantations "at that distance." Moreover, his account of the disasters "hath fully resolved all our people here to make no such adventure." They had persuaded his wife to stay in Scotland, but even if she went, "she would not get so much as one servant to come along with her." It seemed to them that the "unexpected ruin from the Spaniards" was "the clear voice of God not to press into it farther." They urged him not to oppose God's will and affirmed that no one would blame him for deserting the colony.[50]

Dunlop felt it necessary to justify his ostensible stubbornness. He had interpreted God's will differently. He could see no reason why God would "cast me here . . . under abundance of disappointments and difficulties" except for some greater design. Moreover, he had little chance for employment at home, but in Carolina he could "gather an estate of fortune for my family . . . if I designed worldly greatness I may have more of it here than ever I could expect elsewhere." But he accepted defeat and grudgingly gave up his dreams for a Scots settlement in Carolina. Dunlop returned to Scotland, where he uncovered and exposed a political conspiracy involving his two leading financial backers at Stuart Town, Lord Rosse and Sir James Montgomery; Montgomery, of course, Dunlop blamed for the Spanish success at Port Royal and had refused to answer bills Dunlop drew on him. In the so-called Montgomery plot, these disappointed office seekers had switched sides when William took the throne, plotting to restore James II as king. Rosse wound up in the Tower of London, and Montgomery had to flee the country.[51] King William rewarded Dunlop by making him principal of the University of Glasgow. But Dunlop never forgot his colonial adventures. He became a great promoter of Scottish overseas expansion into Africa and the Indies and one of the largest investors in the Scots' Darien colony on the coast of Panama. He even placed University of Glasgow funds into Darien, which proved an embarrassment when it failed, forcing Dunlop's sons to make up the university's losses out of their own pockets.[52]

At a glance, it would seem that the story of the Scots at Stuart Town is of minor significance. After all, as historians have noted, its destruction meant that it left no legacy; most of the settlers died, and its two most important leaders, Cardross and Dunlop, returned to Scotland.[53] But there is much to learn from the Scots' story. Stuart Town's failure illustrates the importance of new settlements' investors having deep pockets: new colonies required large amounts of capital and a steady influx of immigrants to replace those who died, as well as the need for quick economic success to attract more money and people. Once the Scots settlement earned a reputation for danger, it became too difficult to secure money and recruits. Stuart Town's brief history also shows the centrality of Indian-European relations to new European and Indian settlements—mutual interests against a common enemy did not guarantee success. The Spanish did not passively accept Carolina expansion and Yamasee attacks—the opening salvo in a long period of warfare between the belligerents. The Scots and the Yamasee failed to coordinate a policy of defense. Neither realized or knew how to bridge the cultural gaps between them for the good of both. Having chafed under treatment in the Spanish colonial system, the Yamasee were unwilling to give unilateral power to the Scots or to Carolina. And why should they have? They understood the region and had more knowledge of the Spanish mission system than the English and Scots. They thus refused to man the beacons to warn of impending Spanish invasions and rejected the offer to play second fiddle on Dunlop's foray into Florida. But if the English colonials were not ready to accept the Indians as equal partners, they had learned that the Yamasee were a force to be reckoned with: the Yamasee had become the most powerful group on the Savannah River.

There is more to consider in the Scots' settlement legacy. Most important is that the Scots did not completely disappear from the Port Royal area. Historians have always known that the Port Royal region attracted Dissenter emigrants, including Scots in the eighteenth century, but they have not realized the continuity in the Dissenter settlement. Stuart Town was no more, but some Scots never left Port Royal. Several played seminal roles in the future of South Carolina, and particularly in relations with the Yamasee, Creek, and Chickasaw. Two of Stuart Town's first colonists, George Smith and John Stewart, operating separately, opened Carolina's trade with the Lower Creek, the Upper Creek, and the Chickasaw. The son and grandson of Sir John Cochrane, who had negotiated the settlement of Port Royal with the proprietors, both filled important roles in the region as planters, Indian traders, and politicians.[54] Although it is unclear when fellow Scotsman Thomas Nairne arrived at Port Royal, he soon became the most important person to shape Carolina's Indian policies. The destruction of Stuart Town forced these men to come to terms with their predicament as isolated Europeans in an area dominated by Indians. All of them saw that their futures were indelibly linked to Indians. After establishing intimate relations with Native Americans, they came to appreciate them as trade partners and allies. Some began to better perceive both the Indians' and their own position in the geopolitics of the region—and they would articulate that vision for a large audience.[55]

In the aftermath of Stuart Town's destruction, many possibilities existed for the future of relations between Indians and Europeans along the Savannah. Both Scots and Yamasee were willing to experiment. In 1690, Scotsman John Stewart put forth a singular plan that had great potential for altering the nature of Yamasee relations with the colony. Stewart, the author of dozens of audacious projects,[56] approached Governor James Colleton with "a most enriching project": to contract Yamasee as agricultural laborers. He proposed "to enter in covenants with . . . 300 Indians yearly to work for me in silk and cotton." Stewart would "pay them [in trade goods] for every acre [of] cotton so managed as I should direct and inspect." The governor agreed "and offered

to be partner with me." But when Colleton negotiated with Altamaha, a Yamasee chief, he made "the bargain with himself."[57]

Stewart's plan to employ Yamasee labor was most unusual. Contemporaries and historians both note as a matter of course that Indians made poor
agricultural laborers, except when working their own subsistence plots. Indians, it was and is believed, at this time could not be disciplined to staple production, for their style of work was to use minimal labor in the fields. Weed-
ing was performed intermittently and haphazardly; fields were not planted in
a European monocultural manner; and men, in general, did not work fields,
except at sowing and harvesting, since many Amerindian peoples considered
fieldwork as women's and children's labor. Yet Altamaha had agreed to a
seven-year contract for three hundred Yamasee. Keeping in mind the Yamasee's difficult recent history, this arrangement might have been for them an
attractive way to earn European goods without having to enslave and to forge
a closer alliance with Carolina. Certainly, free Indian labor might have solved
some of the labor shortages faced by the colonists. Colleton's banishment in
1690 (described below) put an end to the project, however, and certainly
most landowners preferred slave and bonded white labor to Indian contract
labor. It was much easier to discipline slaves and servants who had difficulty
running away than free neighboring Indians who, for reasons of diplomacy,
could not be disciplined. Also, colonial leaders and other men of property
preferred to have Yamasee as armed allies to defend their borders, pursue runaways, enslave others, and bring in pelts and skins than as laborers on their
plantations. Nevertheless, there was nothing inherently impossible about
using free Indian labor. The difficulty lay not with the Indians, who were
very adaptable to European economic demands, but with the Europeans,
who wanted a labor force they could sharply discipline: free Indians would
have none of it, and enslaved Indians had means of escape unavailable to European and African laborers.

Although the plan failed, the fortunes of the Savannah River's Indian
and European population were irrevocably linked. Trade, not agriculture,
would be their bond. Living in and among one another for the next twenty-
five years, the Europeans who inhabited the Sea Islands on the southern
reaches of the colony came to understand the Yamasee in particular and Indian affairs in general better than any other Europeans in South Carolina.
They fought as allies, traded as partners, but ultimately ended as enemies. In
1690, however, no one could predict how their futures were linked. The Yamasee had more pressing concerns—fear of reprisals from Spanish Florida—

whereas the Scots had to pick up the pieces and build their settlements anew in a colony moving headlong toward anarchy.

CAROLINA'S SOLUTIONS TO ITS INDIAN PROBLEMS

As the last decade of the seventeenth century began, South Carolina was out of control. The Europeans colonists did as they pleased. They had little fear of punishment, even by the English royal government, as the persistence of piracy proved. Many of the colony's governors became involved in piracy, and the proprietors rued that juries could not be found to convict because so many colonists also engaged in illegal trade.[58] The proprietors begged the governor for the names of those who had neither countenanced piracy nor sent away Indians in order to call on these men to fill public offices.[59] They ceaselessly reminded appointees of the inhumanity of fomenting wars to obtain slaves, and they "resolved to break" this "pernicious Inhumane barbarous practice . . . though In order to [do] it We are forced to change all our officers there until we find men that will" stop it. They tried appealing to colonists' self-interests, reminding them of the need for free Indians to track down runaway black slaves.[60] Of course, these slaves would have had nowhere to run "Had the Spaniards been fairly dealt with in the business of the Timagoa [Timucua] Indians." The Spanish could not be blamed for their recalcitrance: the captured Timucua "ought to have been returned to them whosoever had bought them."[61]

Carolina's governor during the reign of James II (and shortly after his removal) was James Colleton. Colleton may have been the first governor who truly tried to make the local elite heel to proprietary wishes. Faced with opposition and fearful of invasion, he declared martial law. Colleton's suspension of normal government led the late nineteenth-century historian Edward McCrady to accuse him of being a poor governor.[62] Yet it is too easy, and incorrect, to associate Colleton with James II and arbitrary government. From Colleton's and the proprietors' perspective (there was no government operating according to law in Carolina), Colleton faced a corrupt council that blatantly disregarded Crown and proprietary laws, had to contend with officeholders who had been barred from office and were illegally appointed, and was charged with enforcing the laws of the Crown against piracy. Singlehandedly, he stood up against the elite by canceling the invasion of Spanish Florida and then arresting pirates. Granted, Colleton was no angel. He once murdered a man in Barbados, for which his brother had procured a royal pardon.[63] And he was as greedy as anyone else in the colony. Still, to have any chance of gaining control over Carolina, he had no choice but to declare martial law.

Colleton's enemies banished him in late 1690, but during his term the trade with distant Indians began. Carolina established trade with the Lower and Upper Creek, the Cherokee, and the Chickasaw.[64] Seth Sothell, who had recently purchased a share of the colony and become a proprietor, which gave him the right to the governorship on entering the colony, tried to bring the Indian trade under careful regulation. The proprietors had promised to open a trade that would "leave all men at liberty to have an equal share and advantage," but in such a way as to "secure the peace of the settlement."[65] Although the first Indian trading act passed in 1691 is not extant, a later act of that year to regulate the trade and tax skins and furs sheds light on government regulation. This act retained the restricted trading area desired by the proprietors. Carolinians were prohibited from trading south and west of Savannah Town (on the Savannah River), and they could not go north of the Winyaw River or west of the Congarees. In effect, colonists could trade with Settlement Indians, the Savannah, or the Yamasee or with Indians who brought their goods to Savannah Town. Yet even at Savannah Town trade was restricted. Smithing tools that could be used to repair Indians' guns were prohibited both there and among the Yamasee, probably to prevent Indians from learning how to repair their guns and to force them to keep buying new ones. In fact, no smithing tools were allowed outside of Colleton, Berkeley, and Craven Counties. The fine for illegal trading was fifty pounds—more than what most traders cleared in profits—and loss of goods at the time of the infraction. In addition, any person selling alcohol outside those same counties or who was found trading with the Creek or Cherokee was subject to twelve months' imprisonment. The illegal sale of alcohol also was punished by imprisonment without bail, while trading with the Creek netted the guilty an additional fifty-pound fine.

Whatever good intentions the government had in prohibiting alcohol, the bill was designed less to protect Indians and more to preserve the proprietary monopoly. Governor Sothell had purchased his share of the colony as a means to increase his riches. Unlike the other proprietors, he had been to America, having spent time in what is now North Carolina, and he hoped by becoming a proprietor and governor to monopolize as much of the Indian trade as he could for himself. Sothell was a man of immense greed, and his peculation and schemes were grandiose even by the standards of the day. Of the trade opened to the colonists, Sothell secured one third of all duties and one third of all fines.[66] His other schemes remain clouded by the length of accusations against him, some of which were self-interested. Sothell's fellow proprietors soon removed him from office, accusing him of holding an improper parliament, illegal imprisonment, and granting commissions to pirates.[67] He tried but failed to regain power and moved northward to either North Carolina or Virginia.[68]

New governor Philip Ludwell might have turned things around for the proprietors. He tried to enforce the ban on trading with distant Indians. Ludwell came up, however, against James Moore, the talented, forceful, and headstrong arch-foe to the proprietors who let no one stand between himself and profits from the Indian trade. During Colleton's administration, Moore had made two illegal trips to the Cherokee. Ludwell ordered him not to leave again,[69] but there was no stopping Moore, one of the "great heroes" of early Carolina for his Indian slaving, his later destruction of much of the Apalachee in 1704, and even for his failed assault against Saint Augustine in 1702.

Ludwell lasted little over a year, having alienated the proprietors by approving of laws they opposed, failing to prosecute pirates, and disregarding the proprietors' wishes in the granting of land.[70] He was followed by Thomas Smith, who served from mid-1693 until his death in November 1694. Smith was charged with promoting equality before the law for crimes committed by Indians and Englishmen. After Westbrook's murder by Indians, Smith was instructed to seek out the perpetrators by getting the Indians to turn in the guilty party. The proprietors urged Smith to take special care to find the correct group of perpetrators and to convince the Indians to mete out the punishment themselves, so that the guilty party's relatives would not try to avenge his death. The proprietors also lectured Smith that he must punish "such English as do violence" to the Indians or he could "not expect to have long peace" with them.[71] The proprietors had heard that some Indian traders had murdered Indians and been indicted by a grand jury but released for lack of evidence. Smith was told to punish the whites if he thought that they were guilty. This would "terrify others from committing the like Crimes for the future, by which the life of many an Englishman may be saved."[72]

At this time South Carolina's Commons House of Assembly stepped into Indian affairs. An assembly had existed as early as 1671, but its role was probably slight, and not until Smith's administration in 1692 did its potential power emerge.[73] In 1693 the assembly issued its first major report on the Indians, largely because of concern about Spanish interference with Indians friendly to Carolina. Spanish-allied Indians traded with the Yamasee, which the assembly forbade. The assembly also addressed problems concerning the migration of neighboring Indians out of the colony to the Creek in the southwest and considered the request by some of the surviving Westo to settle among Indians allied with the colony. The assembly opposed this settlement, for the members feared that "We may Expect [they] will take the first opportunity . . . to take Revenge" by uniting "our friendly Indians to war upon us." The Iroquois were another concern. They frequently traveled south, and the assembly believed that they were allied with the remaining Westo and that together they would attack the Savannah "to make way for a Trade with us and Consequently force us to Suffer for our friends to be Cut off or Engage us in a Certain war, which before all things ought to be Industriously avoided." Even more troublesome were the Savannah's attacks against the Cherokee, with the captives sold as slaves to Carolina traders. The colony hoped to establish closer relations with the Cherokee but did not know how to mediate between these "Long before enemies."[74]

Carolina also began to heed the proprietors' suggestions to employ Indians to capture runaway slaves. This had the dual purpose of protecting the slaveowners' investments and of preventing escaped Africans from establishing ties with Amerindians. Escaped slaves who lived outside government authority, known as maroons, had the potential to incite free Indians and enslaved Indians and Africans to destroy the colony. White Carolinians were already outnumbered by their Indian neighbors, and their slave population was steadily growing. In 1693, Governor Smith summoned the coastal Indians to discuss the return of runaways. The government envisioned the Indians' role as both police force and border patrol. Importantly, the government still considered local Indians as part of Carolina society, not external to it, for at the same meeting the governor proposed that Indians be taxed according to population—the natives would bring in "Wolves, tigers, or bear skins" as payment. The bill, as passed, condescendingly noted how "for several years Past" the colony had provided "the Indian Nations" who inhabited the province "with clothes and all sorts of tools necessary for making their provisions . . . [and had] protected and defended [them] from their enemies, at our trouble, expenses of time and charges by our forces." The Settlement Indians, according to this law, "have not hitherto been any ways useful or serviceable" except when individuals were rewarded. It was time for the Settlement Indians to pull their own weight. One wonders just exactly who the government thought it was protecting the Settlement Indians from? Indians from the north posed a threat, but the greater threat came from the Indian slave catchers in alliance with the colony. Did the colony feel that it alone protected Settlement Indians from enslavement? The government duly noted that the Settlement Indians had "voluntarily offered to be obliged to kill" the animals requested but declined to state why the assembly needed a coercive law. Forcing Indians to "volunteer" their labor seems reminiscent to the logic of enslaving only those Indians who had "freely" chosen bondage over death. Punishment for those who refused to labor voluntarily was a severe whipping on the bare back in front of the town's inhabitants; "nations" that refused compliance would be placed "out of the Protection of the Government," which invariably meant that they would be subject to enslavement.[75]

It is probably no coincidence that in a bill to tax Indians, and thus consider them as part of society, measures were taken to guarantee Settlement Indians equal treatment with Europeans. The act provided that the governor and any one member of the council would for the "time being" act as commissioners to "try and determine all differences and controversies" among Settlement Indians and between Settlement Indians and white men. The commissioners were charged to act "speedily" and "indifferently." They had the power to order Indians and whites "to make restitution in civil cases" and to commit them to jail, but whereas they had authority to punish Indians physically, "life and limb excepted," they had no right to order such punishments for white people.

The employment of the governor and a member of the council to act as a commission was a temporary measure. Still, twenty-five years after first English settlement, the governor was still being asked to settle personal disputes of colonists and Indians, illustrating not only the colony's failure to create a permanent mechanism to resolve differences but the face-to-face nature of a colony in which the governor arbitrated personal conflicts. The commission's charge to settle differences between Indians of the same group is also problematic. It is difficult to imagine Indians taking disputes to an outside commission, except as a means to challenge their own leaders. There is no evidence that Settlement Indians in the next generation, after a permanent commission was established to hear complaints, made use of it for either intratribal or intertribal disputes. It is indicative of the colony's claimed sovereignty over Settlement Indians that the colony would establish such a body and offer mediation to Indians, but is also indicative of Indians' independence and resistance to European cultural and legal traditions that they would not use the commission to settle purely Indian matters.

Although it is unclear just how much the commission did, if anything, it was the precursor of the commissions established early in the next century that did in fact mediate differences between Indians and Europeans, though the later commissions focused on differences among colonists and neighboring Amerindians, not Settlement Indians.

By the mid-1690s, guaranteeing Indians justice and allowing them to witness, if not to participate, in a "just" society that used law, the court system, and mediators to settle disputes had become a goal of many of the colony's leaders. Just a few years after the establishment of the commission, a case arose where three black slaves allegedly murdered "one of our Friendly and Neighbouring Indians." The victim was probably not a Settlement Indian because the government paid "Maintenance" for Indians attending the trial and the phrase "neighbouring" implies that the deceased hailed from the Yamasee or another group living near but not in the colony. The upper and lower houses of assembly agreed to have the trial take place immediately and to be governed by a new bill regulating slavery—one that had yet to be enacted into law, though it had passed its first two readings. The stated reasons for this extraordinary "Speedy Trial" were in part to save the expenses of putting up the Indians in town and in part to convict the slaves before they could escape jail, but the main purpose was "to give the friends of the Murdered Indjans as Speedy Satisfaction as Conveniently Can be."[76] Admittedly, the alleged perpetrators were black slaves, and this kind of "Speedy Trial" that disregarded colonial assembly law would never have been held if Europeans were the defendants; nevertheless, the colony had a chance to show Indians that justice could be attained, at least where the Europeans' slaves were concerned.

Government officials might have welcomed the murder of a few Indians by their African slaves, with the subsequent opportunity to punish the perpetrators, for another reason. The South Carolina government wished for Indians and Africans to develop a mutual hostility. The colony feared the possibility of Indians and Africans uniting against them and thus worked diligently to keep them apart. Punishing black slaves who attacked Indians was thus a way for the government to display to Indians that they were both on the same side against Africans. It is doubtful that Indians would have learned this lesson from one episode, but Europeans were quite persistent trying to instill in natives a racial ideology of African inferiority.[77]

South Carolina's elites had other reasons for setting Indians against Africans and for improving relations with Settlement Indians and the natives of the Savannah River Valley. The Savannah River peoples especially were crucial to the defense of the colony and for capturing slaves from distant tribes, particularly in Florida. The Spanish threat that had grown in the mid-1680s forced the colony to treat its neighbors better, particularly the Yamasee and Savannah. But threats from within Carolina also emerged. The colony's political leadership perceived Indians as having great value as a police force that could be used against slaves, indentured servants, and free whites. In March

1701 the assembly enacted one of its more unusual bills, "An Act for the Prevention of Runaways Deserting this Government." The bill referred specifically to those who left the colony overland to Virginia and elsewhere. Preventing free people from leaving a colony was a measure ordinarily taken only during wartime—for instance, South Carolina prohibited departures during the Yamasee War, and Georgia did the same during the Anglo-Spanish War of 1740–1744; during peacetime it was meant to prevent debtors from fleeing their creditors. The act of 1701 provided that anyone found without a pass north of the Santee River or south of the Savannah River was subject to seizure. To obtain a pass, individuals had to deposit a bond or give twenty-one days' warning so that creditors would have time to file a complaint. A hefty fifty-pound fine or six months' imprisonment awaited those who assisted runaways. Indians who apprehended runaways were entitled to the arms and ammunition in the runaway's immediate possession and a reward decided on by the governor; those assisting the captor could not receive more than twenty shillings. White captors could receive up to five pounds, but no limit was placed on what an Indian could receive.

Whites were also allowed to beat runaways, but Indians could beat them only if a white was present; neither would be held responsible for a runaway's death.[78] These provisions made it clear that Indians were not to be treated as the equal of whites, but in urging Indians to catch white runaways and allowing them to beat runaways to death (as long as a white person was present), the bill showed an elevated status for Indians over white runaways, who were either fleeing debtors or runaway indentured servants. This bill more than any other instituted Indians as a police force for South Carolina; the ruling elite had found a way to use coastal Indians to secure the internal order of the colony by allowing no one, African, Indian, or European, to leave without permission. Colonial and proprietary leaders envisioned Indians as the first line of defense against internal and external foes. Whether European Carolinians recognized it or not, they were growing increasingly dependent on Native Americans.

Spanish, English, and several Indian groups all sought to control the Savannah River subregion. South Carolina officials viewed the area as essential to the defense of their colony. They had allied temporarily with the Westo and then the Savannah to obtain dominance in the region, but when these allies proved dissatisfactory, the English forged an alliance with the Yamasee, who had established themselves as the most powerful group in the area. Many Carolinians had opposed the Scots colony at Port Royal as a threat to English

Carolina's interests in the Savannah River subregion. Charles Town officials rejected the Scots' claims to self-rule and opposed their competition in the Indian trade. Charles Town officials especially resented the Scots' perceived influence with the Yamasee and preferred to cultivate goodwill among the Indians than among the Scots.

The Spanish made little distinction between the Scots and the English, and they saw the new Port Royal settlement as a beachhead for an English push south of the Savannah River. But the Yamasee posed the more immediate threat because they had the will and the skills to conduct military operations against the Florida missions. The Spanish successfully reduced the Scots threat but could not uproot the Yamasee, who steadily increased their control of the area and, in league with their new English allies and with Indians from the west, threatened to topple not just the mission system but the entire Spanish presence in Florida. What weakened the Spanish even more—and at just the wrong time—was France's reentry into the South. The settlement of a French colony west of Florida forced the Spanish to devote money and men to build and defend Pensacola, diverting resources that they could have used to defend their northeast border.

PART TWO

ADJUSTMENTS, 1698–1708

Europeans and Indians had no choice but to interact in the American South. Although the Appalachian Mountains gave the Cherokee a modicum of isolation and the numerous bayous of the lower Mississippi Valley offered local peoples refuge from invasion, the region's extensive rivers and numerous trading paths facilitated mobility, trade, migration, and warfare. The establishment of Spanish, English and French colonies adversely enmeshed native peoples in European rivalries. Because the Europeans enjoyed limited military power away from their nascent colonies and their colonies were vulnerable to raids, they depended on indigenous peoples for both offensive and defensive operations. Conversely, the South's native peoples sought to enlist European aid in disputes with their own neighbors, and many Indians moved their towns to be near the Europeans for mutual protection and easier access to trade goods.

Over a vast cultural divide the peoples of the Old and New Worlds had to establish the means to communicate their ideas and desires. Each sought to convince the other to adopt their perspective on how, when, and under what conditions exchange and alliance should take place and what each should contribute to the relationship. Often they misunderstood the significance and meaning of ceremonies, motives, and behavior, but because so much was at stake, the parties persisted as best they could.

Each of three chapters in this part probes the adjustments made by Europeans and Indians in the South. In the first, through an examination of the initial French presence in the lower Mississippi Valley, we discover some of the ways Europeans and Indians learned to interact—the ground rules they laid for having positive relations and the difficulties they encountered in coming to terms with one another. The second chapter explores how the relationships forged between Europeans and Indians in the early eighteenth century led to military alliances that had devastating impact on the region, particularly in terms of the large-scale enslavement of native peoples. In this period, the English desire for slaves meshed with imperial designs for expansion against France and Spain, with the French and Spanish forced to counter by attempting to eradicate South Carolina. The connections among the subregions of the South became thoroughly intertwined as people went further than ever to conduct trade, alliance and warfare. And in chapter 6, we follow two Scots imperialists who, more than most, traveled through the South, recorded their observations, and theorized on the nature of both empire and relations between Europeans and Indians.

4

ARKANSAS, TUNICA, TAENSA, AND FRENCH MISSIONARIES

COMMUNICATION
ACROSS THE CULTURAL DIVIDE, 1698–1700

ll French activity centered on the Mississippi. Through the "father of waters," which connected Louisiana to Canada and Europe, the French explored and understood the region. Early French missionaries and soldiers did not stray far from the river. When they did edge away, it was always along confluent rivers. This meant that their initial contact with Indian peoples tended to be with the smaller groups who lived near the mouth of the Mississippi and the medium to larger groups, such as the Natchez to the Arkansas upriver, rather than the Choctaw, Chickasaw, and Creek, who lived inland. Although the Mississippi was unruly and unpredictable, it was an adequate means for transport, and if the French could have dealt only with the river, their chance for success would have been far greater. French devotion of effort and resources among just the Mississippi River and Gulf peoples would have allowed them to fulfill Amerindian desires for trade goods. Yet this was not to be. The inland peoples—Choctaw, Chickasaw, and Creek—were too powerful to be ignored, and the interconnectedness of the region forced the French to direct their attention, presents, and trade eastward and to plant their administrative and economic center at Mobile. Spread thin in the South, French political leadership focused on the inland peoples while the missionaries tended to the Mississippi groups.

THE MISSIONARIES:
INITIAL CONTACT WITH THE ARKANSAS

The Arkansas were among the first Indians the French encountered in the region. Father Jacques Marquette visited them when he descended the Mississippi in 1673, paving the way for the missionaries who followed almost a quarter-century later.[1] The Arkansas welcomed Marquette with the calumet ceremonies. The calumet was a pipe used by many Mississippi Valley Indians in the welcoming ceremonies that were essential in all intergroup relations. Marquette welcomed the Arkansas by speaking of his faith through an Illinois interpreter. The interpreter conveyed the priest's words in his own language to an Arkansas interpreter, who then translated the message into Siouan for his people. It would have been difficult for Marquette to make his theology understood to those uninitiated in French, let alone via translation through three languages, but the meeting illustrates the enormous linguistic and cultural gulf that gaped between the Indians and the French. Each could understand the other only in their own terms until they developed skills to communicate effectively across the barriers of language and culture.

When Marquette made his profession of faith, he sought to bridge the gap by stating what was most important to him: his faith in Christ. Catholic missionaries throughout the world made this same profession; lay Catholic explorers often did the same but added statements averring the temporal power of their living monarch. Dressed in his black robes, wielding the cross, and perhaps employing dramatic flourishes, the priest's performance would have been pleasing, and perhaps to some degree understandable, to the Arkansas. The Arkansas and the French each had prerequisites for establishing a positive relationship: the French demanded that their profession of faith be heard, the Arkansas demanded the ritual performance of the calumet ceremony. As long as each had their desire fulfilled, then good relations could be commenced and maintained.

The French learned the calumet ceremony from the Illinois, so that the French were prepared to share this particular cultural rite with the Arkansas to initiate friendship and exchange. Before we return to these ceremonies, we should see what Marquette learned from his encounter with the Arkansas, which abruptly ended his descent of the Mississippi.

Marquette discovered that he was ten days from the Gulf of Mexico, though it could be reached in five if he traveled quickly. He ascertained that the Arkansas had enemies to the south who prevented their access to the sea and to the Europeans who could be found there, undoubtedly referring to the Spanish presence on the Gulf. He found the Arkansas in possession of

European trading goods: hatchets, knives, and beads. These they obtained from an Illinois village four days' journey to the west (he may have misunderstood, since the Illinois lived to the north) and from natives to the east, who presumably obtained these goods directly or indirectly through the English in Carolina or Virginia. From this information, Marquette concluded that he had gone as far as he could and that more information would be needed about the Spanish and English presence in the South before the French could proceed further. Marquette recommended that when the French returned they should use the Arkansas as a base to explore the region. But the Arkansas warned Marquette that it was Indians, not Europeans, who prevented them from going southward. These Indians "had guns and were very warlike, we could not without manifest danger proceed down the river, which they constantly occupy." Mystery shrouded their identity. Marquette and his party had run into these Indians to the north, and he described them as wearing their hair long and tattooing "their bodies after the Iroquois fashion. The women wear head-dresses and garments like those of huron women."[2] This description led nineteenth-century historian John Gilmary Shea to identify the Indians as Tuscarora, but this seems highly unlikely.[3] It is not wholly improbable that the Tuscarora could be found so distant from their North Carolina home. Iroquois warriors from New York traveled even greater distances against their enemies, descending the Wabash and Ohio into the Illinois country, or south through the Piedmont and then west through the Cherokee country to attack the Chickasaw, but the Arkansas clearly stated that the Indians who prevented them from going south "constantly occupy" the land. This leaves the Chickasaw as the most likely candidates.[4]

The Chickasaw were the Indians of the Mississippi Valley with whom the English first established contact. Much has been made of Thomas Welch's visit to the Chickasaw from Carolina in 1698 as the first contact between them and the English, but this is clearly mistaken. Historians unfamiliar with the French records overlook the recorded presence of English traders among the area's Indians more than two decades before Welch. The French reported English traders in the 1670s on the Ohio and Wabash, particularly among the Savannah (Shawnee); these traders, almost certainly from Virginia, filtered west to the Illinois country and south to the Chickasaw. Scots traders operating out of Port Royal, who came from the south via trade with the Creek, followed them in the early 1690s.[5] Marquette referred to the Indians who blocked his way in the lower Mississippi Valley as having "guns, hatchets, hoes, knives, beads, and flasks of double glass, in which they put their powder. . . . they bought cloth and all other goods from the Europeans who lived to the east, that these Europeans had rosaries and pictures, that they played upon instruments; that some of them looked like me." The mention of rosaries and that they "looked like me" might lead to the assumption that these Indians had also traded with the Spanish, and met Spanish priests, but there is no evidence of the Chickasaw having gone to Florida. They could have acquired the rosary beads through exchange with Indians who traded with the Spanish in Florida or in New Spain.[6] There was already much contact through the Spanish operating out of New Mexico, the Missouri country, and Texas, by which Spanish goods could have entered the Mississippi Valley. The most likely source of goods, however, remains through the English traders who visited the Savannah and either encountered the Chickasaw there, or the traders moved on to the Chickasaw country.[7] Even though there was no permanent European settlement for hundreds of miles, European goods were in great supply among the Chickasaw.

Father Marquette provided the inspiration for the French missionaries who followed him twenty-five years later. They had read Marquette's account and intended to finish what he had begun by pushing south to the Gulf of Mexico. In 1698, a team of four French missionaries, with their French guide Tonti, who had been with the explorer René-Robert Cavelier, Sieur de La Salle, descended the Mississippi to embark on the establishment of missions among Indians along the Mississippi. Sent by the bishop of Quebec, they extended French Catholic influence south to the Tamaroas, an Illinois people, and then south again past the confluence of the Wabash and Ohio, down the Mississippi, perhaps all the way to the Gulf of Mexico. Leaving much of their gear at Chicago on Lake Michigan, they intended to review the country and peoples to determine where to build missions. Their expectations were shaped by their experiences in Canada among native peoples, as well as what they had read and heard about Marquette and of La Salle's trip to the mouth of the Mississippi, as well as his failed attempt to colonize just a few years earlier. They planned their string of missions separately from the near simultaneous establishment of a French colony by Pierre Le Moyne d'Iberville at the mouth of the Mississippi. In other words, Iberville and the priests knew of each other's intentions but operated independently and from opposite directions, one from the Gulf, the other from Canada. Iberville brought along his own missionary, the Jesuit Paul Du Ru.[8] Within a few years the Jesuits and the Canadian priests disputed jurisdiction in the Mississippi Valley, making their enterprise more difficult than necessary.[9] But as one group ascended the Mississippi and the other descended, neither could foresee their dismal prospects. The dreams of Iberville to build a great empire and of the priests to convert heathens would largely be exercises in futility, with the added short-comings of unknowingly spreading disease among the native peoples. None could know the misery they would bring; instead, it seemed the dawning of a divinely inspired enterprise for the glory of God and France.

Each of the missionaries recounted his journey in letters to superiors in Quebec, so we have a record of their thoughts and experiences.[10] Shared culture and mutual discussions contributed to a similarity in their perceptions about what they encountered. The French missionaries approached their journey with great excitement and expectation while understanding the importance of their task and its significance. They would extend God's glory by going beyond the explorers and traders who had preceded them, who sought only fulfillment of their own needs and those of the Crown. Their task was more ethereal, more important: they sought to bring God to the ignorant. They did not question the wisdom of God in denying these "savages," these wild people, the knowledge of Christ. Instead, they saw themselves as instruments of God's will, those who would complete the tasks of their mother church to bring Christ to all humankind. In their potential converts they saw an innate goodness that made them excellent proselytes. Conversion would encompass not so much a battle with the devil—the false Gods the Indians worshiped—but an unfolding of God's mysteries to people who simply needed the truths pointed out to them.

The missionaries were as well prepared for their task as could be expected. They understood the need for self-sacrifice and the difficulty of the work. Coming from Canada, they had experience with Native Americans, but their specific cultural knowledge of the groups they encountered was largely confined to what they learned from Marquette's memoirs. They generally recorded two types of information for their superiors. One was "factual" information regarding the peoples they met: location and distance of settlements and confluent rivers, demography, language families, availability of food, tribal health, and the presence of European goods. The other was their assessment of the Indians and their culture: dress, gender roles, religious practices, unusual customs, and degree of openness to the French.

THE CALUMET:
LINKING FRIENDS, STRANGERS, AND ENEMIES

From Chicago the missionaries made their way to the Illinois country and then south to the Kappa (Quapaw), one of four divisions of the Arkansas people. Indians carrying the calumet and provisions met the party. The French were shocked by many customs of the lower Mississippi Valley Indians, but they usually welcomed the calumet. Having encountered similar or identical ceremonies in the north, they had some familiarity with them. Yet they were much surprised by southern ceremonies, particularly by the importance attached to them, the vehemence with which the Indians insisted that they be conducted, and their sometimes far greater length. The calumet ceremony welcomed both friends and enemies while providing a truce from hostilities. It provided an opportunity to interact—to trade and negotiate—but it did not, in and of itself, comprise the making of an alliance between participants. Instead, it marked a moment pregnant with potential.

The ceremony began as the hosts met the visitors on their approach to a village. (Sometimes the visitors initiated the ceremony, but also before entering the village.) Songs were sung and visitors escorted to the village, sometimes carried on bearers' shoulders or in some other way physically helped along. Nearer the village emerged the calumet, held high. With a long stem up to four feet in length and a pipe bowl near its end, to which feathers were attached, the calumet contained tobacco by itself or mixed with other items. Guests then sat on mats or pelts and were feted, often with one of the pipes placed on "forked sticks."[11]

One of the earliest detailed descriptions of the ceremony comes from Father Marquette. Although his description refers to the ceremony among the Illinois, he specifically noted that it was the same among the Arkansas.[12] After all were seated, the chief who gave the dance placed on the mats his God, "which they call their Manitou. This is a serpent, a bird or other similar thing, of which they have dreamed while sleeping, and in which they place all their confidence for the success of their war, their fishing, and their hunting." Placed next to it was "the Calumet in honor of which the feast is given."[13] After weapons were placed around the calumet and the God, the dancers, men and women, emerged, and each "must salute the Manitou." This was done by "inhaling the smoke" from the pipe and blowing it "upon the Manitou, as if . . . offering it incense." Everyone handled "the Calumet in a respectful manner, and supporting it with both hands causes it to dance in cadence, keeping good time with the air of the songs. He [the chief] makes it execute many differing figures; sometimes he shows it to the whole assembly."[14] Then presents were exchanged and speeches given.

The French perceived the calumet as a mystical ceremony to the Indians, because the Indians beheld the calumet with awe and reverence *and* especially because they would not turn away enemies who carried the pipe. Archaeologist Ian W. Brown suggests, however, that the ceremony was somewhat foreign to the Southeast and may have been introduced by the French as a means of establishing friendly relations with the Indians.[15] Brown is clearly mistaken: the complexity of the calumet ceremonies and the depth with which they were practiced by indigenous peoples in the lower Mississippi Valley implies a long-term tradition, not a new introduction. Yet Brown's contention is persuasive that the ceremonies gained added importance in this period, as the topsy-turvy nature of life in the late seventeenth and early eighteenth centuries created great difficulties for the region's peoples. Warfare and sickness affected all, and with warfare arose situations where no one could be trusted. Villages dispersed and reformed, people turned on former cohorts, new alliances were made. The calumet ceremonies were much more than a way to meet strangers; they provided a temporary truce that allowed those who warred with one another to meet and trade, perhaps for food items and other goods that were desperately needed in weakened villages. Because southeastern enemies were often closely related by blood, they could and did maintain contact with one another even through time of war. In between the bloodshed, the Indians frequently socialized in one another's villages. (In much the same way, French and English in the Southeast exchanged goods during wartime, though this visiting between the two lacked the familial and social aspects that existed when Choctaw and Chickasaw parlayed.)

The calumet provided the means to postpone dangerous situations by making space for negotiation. For people of vastly different cultures and languages, like the French and the Indians, the calumet linked them across chasms of inscrutability, suspicion, and fear. It temporarily bound wounds by reminding people that differences could be overcome by the mutual sharing of ceremonies. An illustration of its mediating powers: after a three-day visit with the Ouma, Iberville left their village to check on his longboats about three leagues away. Anxious to get a good start in the morning, he sent his brother, Jean-Baptiste Le Moyne de Bienville, together with two Canadians back to the Ouma village to "fetch" his Bayogoula escort. Bienville found the Bayogoula "in a debauch with some women at the village." The Indians refused to come and told him they would be there the next day. Bienville left perturbed and returned to Iberville. About an hour later, "three Bayogoula and six Ouma came back bearing the calumet of peace to us all over again, believing us to be angry." Iberville beckoned them closer, food was shared, and the Indians explained that Bienville's "hasty departure from the village had thrown all the people into a turmoil . . . and that they had been sent to pacify us." Gifts were exchanged and all was forgiven.[16] In this way the Indians calmed what seemed to them to be a crisis. They had either misunderstood or simply disregarded the French while having a good time. Seeing Bienville react with anger for what must have seemed to them an irrational reason, they decided that for reasons unknown the French were mightily miffed. Note the wording that Iberville used when describing the Indians' approach to him: they came "*bearing the calumet of peace to us all over again.*" With the calumet literally held high to mark its entrance, the Indians created a setting in which differences could be discussed and amended.

Few French understood the "temporary" nature of the calumet ceremonies in establishing linkages between peoples. They thought that the ceremonies implied long-term alliances, whereas the ceremonies instead expressed the need for constant renewal between peoples. The French position of weakness, as outsiders who increasingly clashed economically and militarily with English competitors, led them to take the ceremonies seriously but sometimes as unwelcome. Frenchmen in a rush ascending or descending the Mississippi risked insulting their hosts if they refused to stop and celebrate. Every time a Frenchman in an official capacity passed a village, the Indians expected him to participate in the ceremonies. Father Du Ru was just one of many who found the ceremonies—the singing, gift giving, and eating—tiresome and overlong: "It is a slow process and makes us somewhat tired. . . . It was difficult to say farewell to each person. They had no idea that they were a nuisance to people who had to leave very early next morning. I had to hide in the brush to get rid of the man" who "during all the ceremonies always sat near me."[17] Father Jacques Gravier, who spoke glowingly of the calumet ceremony, also was bothered by having to stop for it when in haste. Ascending the Mississippi, Gravier stopped at the Kappa village to say hello and speak to an elderly chief who had met Father Marquette twenty-seven years earlier. Gravier told the chief that he had "come ashore merely to salute him in his cabin" and that he did not have time for the calumet ceremony. The chief insisted, offering to dance a special dance, "the chief's calumet with his young men." This was a special honor reserved for "persons of distinction." It irritated the French in Gravier's party that he would receive this honor. Gravier refused the request, but also in part because he believed the Indians' purpose was "to draw presents from me." To depart on good terms, Gravier had to convince the Indians that he was not worthy of a "Great Captain" ceremony.[18] He succeeded. The Arkansas had no need to perform the ceremonies once they learned that the French party had no important emissaries. As Father Marquette observed, "The Calumet dance, which is very famous among these peoples, is performed solely for important persons."[19] In other words, when individuals of different groups needed to interact, there was no need for the ceremony. Indians maintained relationships through many kinds of personal identities. Membership in a clan, such as Bear, Wolf, Fox, or Beaver, gave individuals identities of status when visiting from one group to another. A Choctaw bear would find hospitality among a Chickasaw bear, and a fox among the fox. The calumet operated on a different level, for it was a ceremony performed by one people for another. Honoring a "great captain" was an expression of honoring that person's people.

The French did not always understand the overlapping of identities or comprehend that the ceremony implied no permanent alliance and required renewal. This dismayed Iberville when he returned from France after a year's departure to find that the Bayogoula and Ouma had resumed their war. Iberville visited the Ouma to make a peace, telling them of "the distress I felt upon learning that they were at war with the Bayogoulas, after the alliance we had formed together last year."[20] Iberville did not understand that from the Indians' perspective no alliance had been formed. The calumet they had shared was temporary—an opening from which alliances might be forged. The Ouma were prepared to talk about ending hostilities, but the French again misunderstood the customs of the country. Iberville wanted to be the peacemaker, the mediator of their dispute. But the Ouma told him that "their custom was that the Bayogoulas, who had started the war, should come and sing the calumet of peace to them and give them presents to get back the prisoners" they had taken. Iberville insisted that he was conducting negotiations for the Bayogoula and that he would give the presents from them. In a twist on the Indian understanding of the calumet, Iberville promised that the Bayogoula would come to sing *after* the peace was made. Father Du Ru, who witnessed these proceedings, observed, "It has been extremely difficult to make the Oumas reasonable in the matter of prisoners." Of course, this was "reasonable" in French terms. Du Ru, too, noted that first the Ouma must agree to peace and then the calumet ceremonies could take place. The Ouma were in a difficult position. The French were angry with them for not accepting their mediation. Their own people were beset by disease that had killed half of them in the previous five months. Hearing of the Ouma's plight, forty "Little Taensa," Indian mercenaries described as "well-built men that live on the deer, the bear, and the game they hunt," traveled three days from their village to the west "to offer their services against the Bayogoula." Instead of employing the mercenaries, the Ouma accepted Iberville's terms and made peace with the Bayogoula.[21] But now Iberville did not trust them. When the peace was concluded, the French insisted on escorting the Bayogoula prisoners home. The offended Ouma "insisted that reliance should be placed upon their word." Iberville did not relent, but Du Ru was impressed by the Ouma avowal that their word was sacrosanct, for "it appears that the Savages are less savage than some nations of Europe."[22]

Relationships had to be continually renewed, with presents exchanged to secure renewal and as evocations of sincerity and goodwill. In this unstable world of ephemeral friendships and hostilities, where one's kin in another village could become an enemy overnight or where one's fellow villagers could turn on you, as when the Bayogoula attacked the Mougoulache, who had earlier invited them to join their village, or as when the Tunica attacked the Bayogoula, who had hosted them in their village,[23] nothing in this life could be seen as permanent. This explained the special fervor with which the lower Mississippi Valley Indians conducted the calumet ceremony.

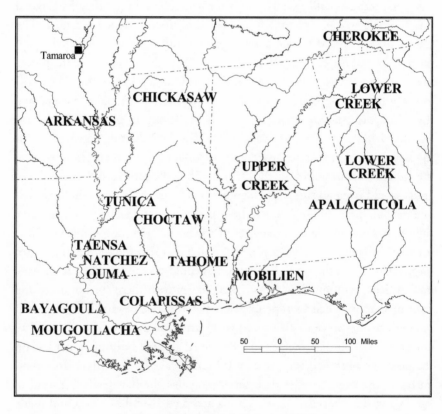

Indians of the lower Mississippi Valley

THE ARKANSAS AND THE FRENCH: A TENUOUS LINK

When the four missionaries from Canada went through the calumet ceremony at Kappa, the Indians rubbed their bodies, a rite practiced by other
peoples of the region, which they returned in kind. The Indians then carried
the priests on their shoulders into a cabin. After the visitors settled in, the
Kappa sang the calumet ceremony. The following evening, the calumet was
again brought out, but this time four chiefs each had a calumet. While the
missionaries and the chiefs sat, other Indians played drums, shook tambour-
ines, and danced. The sound was not "agreeable" to the French, but rather
more disconcerting was the Indian who stood behind them "bleating" through
the ceremony.[24] The French "suffered" this as long as they could before
"dropping off." The following day the French and Kappa exchanged presents,
the Kappa gave the French "a small slave and some hides," which the French
countered with "some knives and other things that they admired much." It
was an auspicious beginning. The French had allowed themselves to be honored, they had reciprocated with presents, and they had gotten to know each
other a little better. The Indians valued generosity, sharing, and patience, and
the French shined on all accounts.[25]

The French grew fond of the Arkansas. Father Jean François Buisson de
St. Cosme found the Kappa good-natured and extraordinarily loyal. The Indians transported all the French possessions, and the missionaries did not
worry about theft. When "one of our people having forgotten his knife in a
cabin, a savage came bringing it immediately."[26] Father François-Jolliet de
Montigny echoed St. Cosme: "these people, they are sweet, are largely receptive to the French and have a great esteem for them."[27] Whether culturally
disposed to provide warm hospitality or simply displaying proper etiquette to
guests, Kappa behavior can also be attributed to their desperate need for help
in the wake of unrelenting disease and repeated attacks from their enemies.
Among the Kappa, St. Cosme counted fewer than 100 men and noted that
they were ravaged by smallpox. Most of the Arkansas had died from disease,
and he sadly reported that "all the children were dead and a large part of the
women."[28] It is possible that the Kappa hid their women and children because Indians of the region did this as a matter of course when enemies
threatened, although none of the other Indians of the region, including the
other Arkansas villages, hid their women and children from the French.
Father La Source echoed St. Cosme's observation on the Kappa "dying in
very large numbers," but he observed two factors as the source of their ills:
"This beautiful nation of which much is spoken is nearly all destroyed by war

and by sickness." Montigny thought that ten years before the Arkansas had numbered twelve hundred warriors but were reduced "by war and sickness . . . to almost nothing." He estimated there were "scarcely 200 men and very few women and children."[29]

Population decline and external threats greatly affected the Arkansas identity, as they did other southeastern peoples. Today the Arkansas are known as the Quapaw. The Quapaw and modern scholars both believe that Arkansas was the Illinois name for the Quapaw, given to them by their Illinois interpreter. This is in all likelihood mistaken. The French in the Mississippi Valley were quite conscientious about calling Indians by the name they used for themselves. They might not have pronounced it correctly, but they did use the Indians' own name. When first meeting the Arkansas the French wrote and pronounced it as Acansas. Over time they learned to emphasize the "r" harder and adjusted the name to Arkansas. Quapaw actually derived from the Arkansas village Kappa. The Kappa inhabited one of four Arkansas towns, the others being Tourima, Tongigua, and Sitteoui. By 1700 many of the Tourima and Tongigua had settled with the Kappa.[30] Over time these people dropped the Arkansas cognomen for that of Kappa, which the French eventually learned to pronounce in its proper form as Quapaw. This distinction is easier to understand when Indian identity is better understood. To southeastern Indians, one's town (which could include several outlying villages) was usually a more important identity than the larger confederated identity to which people belonged. Many of the Indian "identities" of today began as towns that confederated with other towns, and for one reason or another the town identity became grafted on to the larger group, though the Indians themselves retained their town identity. The Quapaw may have dropped the Arkansas name because it no longer had any relevance once the Arkansas confederacy disintegrated and what remained was the town of Kappa.

Ethnicity meant different things to different people. "Arkansas" ethnicity was simply one identity held by an Indian among many identities, and its importance may have existed only in the context of these four towns' relationship to the outside world. Birth, clan, village, and town largely prescribed one's place in the social order and in the larger political order. The equation of ethnicity with nationhood is a modern construct used by people to lay claim to land. The deprivation of land by the later United States government forced Indians to give greater weight to a "tribal" identity than that identity otherwise deserved. Those who could not show specific identity in a tribal group were denied land and status as Indians. Eventually "tribe" and "nation" conflated. The United States has tried to alter normal historical processes by continuing to use tribal status as the sole determinant for recognition. Thus, when Indians of two groups merge into a new identity, they lose their tribal status, as if they had lost their Indian identity by intermarrying. If these ideas are applied to the English, under the U.S. government's understanding of ethnicity, the English must have lost their identity when the Romans or Saxons or Vikings or Normans invaded, conquered, and intermarried. This conception of inalterable ethnicity has now been adopted by many Indians, whose "ancient" claims to nationhood have little or no basis in historical reality. Forced to seek their political rights in a venue and with a language of the dominant American culture, these Indians have adapted to non-Indian concepts of ethnicity. Ethnicity has never been a monolithic, static source of identity grounded in biology and culture. It is a matter of political identity. The layered identities of Indians have parallels with the layered identities of Scotland, where clan and manor were akin to Indian clan and town. Scots knew they were Scottish only when faced with the English, who themselves were a conglomeration of Angles, Saxons, Normans, and others. The Quapaw, Tourima, Tongigua, and Sitteoui became Arkansas only when they faced outside enemies like the Osage and Chickasaw.

To the missionaries, the Indians' varied identities were of secondary importance: the only identity that mattered was whether they were Christian. The missionaries had their work cut out for them. To convert the Indians to Christianity, they had to learn the natives' languages and understand, to varying extents, their cultures. Those practices that they did not understand, or of which they disapproved, they could either ignore or try to alter. The cultural practices of the Arkansas did not scandalize the French missionaries as much as the practices of Indian peoples further south. Among the Arkansas they saw no human sacrifices, and St. Cosme, at least, was pleased to find polygamy rare. He was appalled, however, to learn of "unfortunates who dress in their youth as servant girls at [the] most shameful of all vices," which, however, was less common among the Arkansas than among the Illinois.[31] Reports of men dressing like women and performing feminine labor and having sexual relations with men have been found throughout the Southeast but diminish soon after initial contact. The Europeans reacted with disgust to the practice, and some scholars believe that this sent the custom underground and ended its commonness.[32]

One of the most promising aspects of missionizing among the Arkansas was the availability of game close to their towns. Missionaries ordinarily found it a hardship to travel with Indian peoples on their hunting expeditions, where it was difficult to turn the Indians' attention to religious instruction. La Source reported that from Chicago to Arkansas they came across great numbers of buffalo, bear, and deer; there were so many of the last that they even killed some with their sabers. Although game was abundant, sickness and fear of attack kept the Arkansas men close to home. The loss of 80 to 90 percent of their population—a devastation that certainly contributed to their warm welcome of the French, who might help them in any number of ways—had shattered their confidence and ability to hunt safely. They subsisted almost entirely on Indian corn.[33] Because provisions were scarce, the French did not accept any from the Arkansas for their journeys.

In spite of the sickness that plagued the Arkansas, Montigny thought he had not seen Indians so well made. La Source also waxed eloquently on Arkansas beauty: "These men are the best made, the most candid and of better nature than we have seen." The priests were somewhat taken aback by the Kappa's near nudity in their village, though when the Indians left their village the men wore buffalo hides and the women deerskins. Montigny attributed the Indians' nudity to the great heat, not to any moral shortcoming, though all the priests suspected a close relationship between the Indians' dress and their sexual behavior. Montigny thought their dress a problem of little matter, for the people were "sweet and have so much deference for what we tell them that I am persuaded that it cannot be difficult to reform them to the depths when I learn a little of the language."[34]

At the Kappa village the priests planted a cross to signify the union of their peoples, though one wonders if the Indians shared this symbolic meaning.[35] From there they proceeded to the next Arkansas village, Tongigua, nine leagues away (about twenty-two miles), where the calumet ceremonies began anew. The priests happily found more people in this village, including children, but thought it dangerous for the Arkansas to keep their villages apart. They should band together to better resist their enemies, recommended St. Cosme, and he felt strongly enough about it to tell the Arkansas, who were "impatient" to have a missionary, that they must first draw their villages together.[36] This may explain why the Tongigua and Tourima settled with the Kappa. The Arkansas agreed, offering to build a home for the missionary that the French promised to send the following spring.[37]

For the moment, the French decided to focus their missionary efforts to the south of the disappointed Arkansas, among the Tunica and Taensa. They bypassed the Arkansas, for whom they proclaimed much affection, because of their declining numbers and precarious military situation. The Indians to the south were more populous and less battered by attacks, but the French also hoped to move closer to the mouth of the Mississippi and eventually to spread out among all the Indian groups there.

TUNICA, TAENSA, NATCHEZ, AND FRENCH:
THE MEETING OF ANCIENT RELIGIONS

Sixty leagues (150 miles) south of the Tongigua, the French established a mission among the Tunica, whose villages lay four leagues (10 miles) from the Mississippi on the Yazoo River.[38] Montigny described this location as a beautiful place of "a few small villages of a few other nations who are with them, they are about 2000 souls."[39] They averaged six to eight per cabin, in "houses that are made of posts and earth and are very large."[40] The Tunica may have been recent migrants to the area. Archaeological evidence indicates that they inhabited eastern Arkansas in the prehistoric and protohistoric periods before migrating south to Louisiana and western Mississippi in the late seventeenth century. One scholar posits that they might have been forced south by the Arkansas, who themselves were recent migrants to Arkansas. According to Arkansas "tribal traditions," they had "moved from the north downstream into Arkansas, fighting and displacing Tunicans as they went."[41] La Source described the Tunica as "very peaceable people and of a very good disposition who much cherish the French."[42]

Father Antoine Davion was assigned to missionize the Tunica. "Davion is placed in a very beautiful place in the middle of all these small villages. This has caused quarreling . . . [among] the 4 different nations which speak different languages." Each apparently wanted close access to the missionary, who was placed in a difficult situation with three languages to learn, and he inept at learning any of them. The Tunica were the most numerous group there, having close to two hundred cabins and twelve hundred to fifteen hundred inhabitants, including women and children. Then there were the Yazoo and the Courouais,[43] who had only thirty-five cabins and "spoke the same language but different from that of the Tonicas," and the Couspe or Houspe, who had only fifteen cabins and spoke yet another language.[44] These last three peoples numbered fewer than three hundred. Montigny believed that there were other villages, "more remote," whose inhabitants also spoke like the Tunica, among which he included the Tioux, who lived on the Yazoo River, but Chickasaw attacks forced them south to the protection of the Natchez.[45] Many others, including the villages of the Koroa in the interior of Louisiana, Montigny thought, could be missionized, but he feared that these people spoke so many languages that it would require "a very large number of evangelizing workers."

Language difficulties precluded successful conversions, but the priests settled for baptizing dying children. A special plum was their being permitted to minister to a dying Tunica chief whom they deemed "very considerable." Through an especially skillful interpreter they "told him some of the principal mysteries of our religion." He seemed to understand, making a profession that "edified us much." The chief requested baptism, which they granted, renaming him Paul. "He died the next day and we hope that god will have the good wish to begin by him to open to this nation the door to heaven."[46]

Their enthusiasm restored, the French proceeded south to the Taensa, where they succumbed to an unidentified illness that gave them fevers and left them weak and without appetite. Montigny noted: "In descending the Mississippi one finds to the right a day's journey by path from the Tonicas, that is to say nearly 20 leagues from this village some Tahensa, which are one league from the shore of the Mississippi upon a small lake [Saint Joseph] which has scarcely only 6 or 7 acres of breadth."[47] About seven hundred Taensa lived in 120 cabins.[48] The cabins were close together, "not more than a quarter of a league apart." These "very large cabins of earth and mats made of cane" were thirty feet long and twenty feet high and were held up by poles. Like the Arkansas and Tunica, the Taensa did little hunting; instead, they "laboriously worked the earth sowing Indian corn."[49]

Later reports from the year 1703 indicate that the seven hundred Taensa comprised three hundred men and 150 families.[50] This indicates that there were relatively few women and children; fully half the adult men were single, many because there were too few women to become wives. Though disease could have caused some of the odd demographics among the Taensa and Arkansas, slaving probably produced much of the disparity. Slavers ordinarily focused on capturing women and children, believing men more capable than women and children of finding ways to rebel violently and escape.[51]

The French missionaries settled among the Taensa, Tunica, and Natchez, who presented a different challenge than other Indians in the South. These peoples had temples, priests, and idols—religious elements that the French both more easily identified with and felt threatened by in the competition over spiritual lives. The priests and temples, which the French had not seen among Amerindians in Canada, impressed the missionaries greatly. They thought these Indians superior, more civilized in certain respects. Perhaps, too, their task seemed clearer: they had to replace the temples with churches and the Indians' priests with themselves. These Indians already understood religious authority, service to a sanctuary, and veneration of holy people and places, whereas among other Indian groups, the French believed, they had to start from scratch to initiate religious life.[52]

Montigny admired the Taensa's beautiful temple of matted walls seven to eight feet high, which he thought more magnificent than the Tunica temple. The Taensa would do nothing of importance without carrying offerings to the temple, and "when they receive something they turn towards this temple with a special veneration." The Taensa restricted access to two people, the others believing that "they would die if they would enter." The French were barred but stole inside. Large wooden columns supported the temple, which had "wardrobes filled with figures of animals that no one sees." Wooden carvings of "gruesome things" were scattered about. There was a bed for the caretaker, who kept a fire burning inside, which Montigny thought might be ever burning. He was probably right, for the Natchez did not allow their fire to extinguish. The people offered "considerable presents" at the temple to their god, which Montigny believed was the sun, but he also saw many representations of snakes, which he thought could also be a deity. The priests regarded the Taensa and the Tunica as "very superstitious." They kept in their cabins "small manticores . . . figures of beasts to which they offer tobacco." The Taensa were deemed "more superstitious" than the Tunica because they had more of these figures.[53]

Although the Indians were attached to their gods and manticores, the French held high hopes for success. Montigny thought that "the savages of this country here are very sweet [and] are largely receptive and have great esteem for the French." La Source believed that they "could have much fruit at the missions among the Arkansas, Tunica and Taensa and several other nations who are near them," because the Indians found the French "good[,] saying that we have intelligence." From where they intended to missionize, "we can engage the principal things of this country. If we come among them, which doesn't seem very difficult . . . [it] will facilitate the means of sending missionaries in all these nations of savages." The French had to act quickly because English influence was already great. All the Indians of the region had English merchandise and the English traders had spread through the region, even to the Missouri River.

Like the Arkansas, the Taensa wore little, the men often going nude and girls as old as twelve also uncovered. Older females covered themselves with a skirt that covered the waist to the genitals, fringes hanging below. They sometimes wore dresses to their ankles, but these were very tight, so that when they sat the French priests thought their appearance immodest. Sometimes the women also wore a small cloak, though not when they were working.

The priests did not think much of the Taensa's military skills, an assessment they applied also to the Tunica and Arkansas. Montigny thought the Indians of the area "are not very brave nor great warriors, nevertheless they always war one against the other. They are content usually to take some prisoners, they nevertheless kill and even burn them, but not in a manner so cruel as the Iroquois." Montigny described the Taensa, like the other Indians of the region, as "Humane and Docile," probably because he perceived them as less aggressive than the Iroquois, whom the French viewed as a model of savagery. Montigny held this view despite the Taensa practice of human sacrifice, which horrified the French. When a Taensa chief died, many others were killed to accompany him to the afterlife as servants and companions. "Last year," Montigny reported, "the chief of the Taensa being dead there were 12 who were offered there and who had their head broken."[54] La Source said the Taensa told him that the people were "very content of dying" for their chief. The way the Taensa volunteered this information indicates that they were describing an event in which they took great pride. The region's Indians were ordinarily shy about disclosing religious beliefs to the French, but this action reflected on their good character—their inner strength and moral bravery in sacrificing themselves for their chief.

In January 1700, great sickness struck again at Montigny's Taensa mission, and the priest baptized many of the dying children.[55] He baptized adults only if they had some religious understanding, but now "improved in the language," he was able to baptize some of the adults he had instructed. As at the Tunica, he baptized one of the "great chiefs" and gave him the name Michel. He made the Taensa vow not to sacrifice Indians to accompany their chief when he died.[56] Two months later, while Montigny was away on an errand, the Taensa temple burned. An elderly man, according to Iberville a "chief priest," stood by the fire, shouting, "Women, bring your children and offer them to the Spirit as a sacrifice to appease him." Five infants were put into the flames. Three Frenchmen in the village stopped the Taensa from throwing in more. The French were shocked by Taensa behavior and the Indians' belief that their actions were "one of the noblest that could be performed."[57]

The Taensa priest blamed Montigny for the fire.[58] By preventing the ritual sacrifices when the chief died, the Taensa had offended the deceased, who then had the temple burned. It is easy to see that the Taensa priest would blame his competitor, a Catholic priest, for the burning of *his* temple.[59] Iberville thought that the priest was alone in his opposition to ending the sacrifice rituals—"everybody in the nation seemed highly pleased"—but Iberville could not conceive of the cultural value in human sacrifice, and like most Europeans, he viewed Amerindian people as superstitious simpletons who were gullibly fooled by the pseudo-magic and incantations of their priests to perform the most hideous practices and believe the most outrageous ideas. The Indians were awed by their priests, just as the French were awed by their clergy and the miracles they performed through the sacraments. Yet it is questionable whether the women so feared their priests that they felt compelled to sacrifice their children rather than believe that what they did was in fact a good and necessary deed. The Taensa women did not value their children any less by sacrificing them. Nor did the villagers, who honored the women. The sacrificing women were "caressed and highly praised by the old men; and each was clothed in a white robe made from mulberry bark, and a big white feather was put on the head of each." They sat in an honored place "at the door of the [new] chief's hut" and received presents from the villagers, who spent the day converting the hut into a temple.[60] The mothers had pleased the old men by continuing a cherished tradition, a necessary sacrifice that benefited all.

The French overlooked the Taensa belief that individual sacrifice benefited the community. These women loved their children, but they had a duty to offer them willingly—it is significant that the children were not turned over to the priest to sacrifice but tossed into the fire by the mothers themselves. Montigny reported that he learned when the priest made his call that "the mothers came with eagerness."[61] Christians certainly understood the concept of sacrifice for one's religion and one's God, and that rewards would be given in the next life. The Christian crusaders, for instance, were absolved of all sins and promised a place in heaven if they died in battle. Outside of the priests who suffered dearly in their quest to missionize, seventeenth-century French probably did not have the same spirit of enthusiasm of sacrifice for one's God and community that their ancestors a few centuries before had displayed. But the Taensa did. They were a closely knit community of believers for whom individuals bore responsibilities to kinfolk, clan members, town, ancestors, and gods.

The Taensa idea of an afterlife, probably identical to the beliefs held by their culturally similar neighbors, the Natchez, would have provided much comfort to them. As with Christians, the afterlife was much more important than this earthly life. They possessed, however, a stronger faith in the reality and bliss of an afterlife than most Christians. Cultures that sacrifice people of their own group must have an extremely strong faith. Europeans made the mistake of assuming that sacrifices occurred only because Indians could not resist the power of their chiefs and priests. The power of their leaders was great, but it worked on consensus—the chiefs and priests had no army or police to enforce compliance. In general, Indians accepted the sacrifice rituals because they believed that the sacrificed went to a better life, and they did so with honor. The Taensa understood that their time on earth was fleeting and that the pain to be endured would be by those left behind. Sure of themselves, sure in their beliefs, they welcomed rather than feared death. Only when their entire way of life began to crumble did Indians of the area begin to doubt their belief system. Even so, it is remarkable, in the face of repeated attacks by disease and enemies looking for captives to sell to the English, and the introduction of a market economy that rewarded individualism and loosened bonds of community, that decades of attempts by French missionaries yielded so few converts. Indians were unwilling to part with their spiritual beliefs even in the face of cataclysmic disasters and vast social change.

For American Indians in general, religious belief systems thoroughly integrated all areas of life. Hunting and warfare, good fortune and bad—all were connected with the past, present, and future. No human activity existed outside the scope of spirituality. Elements of Christianity could be incorporated within, grafted on to, their belief system. But the Catholic priests had great difficulties with Indians because they usually failed to understand the nature of Indian spirituality. They believed that Tunica, Taensa, and Natchez were religiously superior to other Indians because these people had recognizable religious forms that paralleled Roman Catholicism. Other Indians, the Christians thought, had either no religion or were devil worshipers. Those with temples seemed less primitive.

With a huge capacity for patience, the French priests set limited goals, to bring the Indians along step by step. They pressured the Indians to change only those practices that they found most reprehensible. When Montigny and Iberville traveled to visit the Natchez, Montigny found one of their great chiefs sick with the ague and expected to soon die. He was present when the chief died and convinced the people not to perform the usual sacrifice of companions and caretakers for the deceased.[62] Or at least he thought he did. As soon as Montigny left, the Natchez proceeded with their customary mourning rituals and sacrifices.[63]

Another burial practice that the French tried to alter in the South, as in Canada, concerned the interment of valuables with the deceased. The Jesuit missionary Paul Du Ru, who viewed many of the native customs with disgust, held special dismay for the Ouma's "evil" custom of burying "with the deceased all of his former possessions." Part of the missionary's anger arose from the Indians burying "a part of the presents which we gave to the tribe."[64] The French brought these presents a very long way and could not fathom why the Indians would part with such useful and valuable things. Montigny went so far as to obtain a promise from the Natchez, which they probably disregarded as easily as their promise not to sacrifice, to abstain from burying with the deceased "all that which was most precious, because not only did they bury the furnishings of the dead, but all the kin and friends were obliged" to do the same.[65]

Other rituals that surrounded death took the missionaries aback.[66] These rituals were easy for the missionaries to observe because virtually everywhere they went they witnessed death and dying. The period of mourning for the deceased lasted six days.[67] Bodies were left to dry for extended periods, until "the flesh drops from the bones." In periods of mourning, women left their hair unkempt and "bewail[ed] the dead day and night." The Indians, who ordinarily enjoyed gambling and athletic games, refrained "from all sorts of joy and diversions," including sex.[68]

Father Du Ru was particularly hostile to Indian mourning ceremonies. Du Ru found the Indians' dirge especially unappealing. The Indians knew of the missionaries' dislike of the dirge and used the "disagreeable" sounds as a ploy to remove Montigny from a Natchez village when they wished to resume mourning rituals that he detested.[69] Du Ru was disgusted that women in mourning drank as many as four pots of water to induce vomiting. When a torrential downpour temporarily abated outdoor mourning, it forced Du Ru to make a difficult choice "between being drowned outside or being smothered within the cabins which are like ovens." He went inside, pleased to find the women, some of whom were widows of the late Ouma chief, occupied with spinning bark and working looms. But soon they began to weep again. One woman exited to "boil a large pot of water with a handful of a certain herb in it which provokes vomiting." This was *Ilex vomitoria,* also known as black tea or black drink, a beverage drunk throughout the Southeast during many ceremonies. As the women sat and drank, Du Ru tried to convince them of the futility "of this ceremony and that the Great Spirit, to whom Heaven serves as a dwelling place, forbids it, that he does not wish the living to kill themselves for the sake of the dead," and that the deceased "is insensible to whatever they may do for him." The women vomited. Then they took away all of the pots of food and other items that they had left that day for the deceased. Thinking that they had finally changed their minds, Du Ru triumphantly noted in his journal, "It would not take much to abolish immediately these customs of drinking and offering gifts." Du Ru then began to preach to the women and show them "my images and to tell them about God." They gave him the impression that they were not so strongly tied to the notion of the sun as a spirit, and he concluded that in fact they had little theology or understanding of spirits: "As near as I can make out, their whole cult and religion is limited to the performance of their duties to their dead. This can easily be corrected by a little instruction."[70]

Beliefs in the Christian god, in the resurrection of Christ, and in redemption through faith, were central tenets of Du Ru's religion. The mourning ceremonies went right to the crux of "false religion" for Du Ru. An alternative heaven, whose boundaries were so amorphous that material could be transited from the earthly to the heavenly plane, where false Gods had to be appeased, where chiefs were deities who deserved to have living servants sacrificed to accompany them to the next world, where magical incantations were uttered and performed not out of any rationale belief but as a "cult" practice—to the French, these all indicated savagism and simplicity. Du Ru, having no inkling of the complex cosmology that lay behind these ceremonies, mistakenly assumed that the Catholic priests would have no trouble converting Indians to Christianity.

When the women took away their offerings and listened politely to Du Ru, he thought that he had won because their own beliefs were nothing more than superstitions that had fallen before the mantle of reason. He had no foresight that episodes like this would be repeated from one Indian group to the next, and from missionary to missionary, as Indians responded to the missionaries' nagging and berating by removing offensive icons, hiding religious practices, and nodding approval at missionary teaching. But Indians persisted in their religious practices. Few converted. Some incorporated aspects of Christianity into their religion, while others simply ignored it except to humor the priests.

FORGING ALLIANCES: THE LURE OF THE OTHER

Why, then, listen to the priests at all? Undoubtedly, the European strangeness piqued Indian curiosity. Much as the Indians fascinated the French, so the French fascinated the Indians. But interest went beyond fascination. The Indians in the area had had contact with the disastrous Soto expedition of the sixteenth century, when the Spanish spread a swathe of destruction through the valley. Alexandre de Batz claimed that the Indians maintained a long memory of hatred for the Spanish,[71] but their distrust probably extended to Europeans in general. La Salle had poisoned some Indians to the French by his barbarism, theft, and abduction of Indians.[72] The Mississippi River Indians also had contact with the English slave traders or their Indian agents, such as the Chickasaw who raided them. Because of the slave traders and their alliances, the Indians could not afford to ignore the French and had to welcome them as friends and allies. True, a few peoples kept their distance as best they could from all Europeans, but the French potentially had a lot to offer, though much about them remained a mystery.

The Indians must have viewed the French, at least initially, as very different from the English they had encountered. With the lines of trade crisscrossing the region, so that Spanish and English goods from the coast could be found along the Mississippi, Indians of the area likely had some knowledge of the mission system in Florida and of the English colonies in Carolina and Virginia. The actual Europeans encountered, however, would have been traders. It seems unlikely that the Taensa, Tunica, and other Indians of the area had traveled to the Atlantic coast—many had not even been to the Gulf of Mexico.[73] It was too dangerous to go from the Mississippi River to the Atlantic—one had either to pass through Chickasaw territory, to go north of the mountains through the Savannah Indians and the Cherokee to Virginia, or to head south through the Choctaw and the Creek. Fear of capture and enslavement would not have enticed many, if any, to make the trip. Thus contact was limited to the traders who hailed from Virginia and Carolina in search of Indian trading partners who dealt in pelts or humans.

The Frenchmen who followed La Salle and established a permanent presence brought a more vivid and varied picture of European life to the Mississippi River Indians. The missionaries, in their strange dress, with their religious icons, curiosity, celibacy, and devotion to particular—and perhaps to the Indians eccentric and mysterious—religious ideas and practices; the *voyageurs* and *coureurs de bois,* who must have seemed akin to the English traders in motives and character; the French soldiers and administrators, who the Indians would have understood in diplomatic terms: all these had something of value to offer the Indians, which enticed them into closer connections.

Acceptance of a missionary meant taking the friendship and trade possibilities of the calumet ceremonies one step forward, to where information and goods could more easily be exchanged. The French had knowledge of many things of which the Indians were curious and awed. In particular, the ships and cannons, which displayed power, knowledge, and perhaps magic, held special fascination. (The Indians of the area had not seen these items from their interaction with the English traders.) On hearing of the great ships of the French, several Natchez chiefs had Montigny take them to see the vessels and the French fort at Mobile. The French treated the guests graciously, knowing the powerful impression they could make. The Natchez were amazed at how heavy the cannon balls were. Iberville took the Indians with him on the *Renommée,* a fifty-gun frigate: "our savages could not but admire so great a canoe, and had been there surprised by our cannon." The noise was so loud that "a single one [is] capable of making flee all the natives of the Mississippi."[74] After Iberville departed, the man he left in charge, Sauvole, took "the chief of the Mobile to see the ships . . . . He was ecstatic to see such big contraptions, and he has been very satisfied with the reception that one has made him. He had with him two Chactas and the chief of the Pasco-boulas also." When they returned to the fort, they "told the others that they had been on the ships that went up to the clouds, that there were more than fifty villages on each one and crowds that one cannot pass through." They had gone down in the hold and were amazed that it had "a place where they did not see sun or moon; they have left to go to the Chactas to teach them these wonders. I hope they induce them to return."[75]

Sauvole obviously understood that French technology could lure the Indians into making contact with them and then into alliance. Like many Europeans, he overestimated the gun as a weapon for inspiring awe; although Indians coveted guns, they did not necessarily fear these weapons in light of their expertise with bows and arrows. Sauvole thus expressed surprise when he learned that years earlier, when the Quinipissa had attacked "La Salle for stealing his people, they ignored the effect of the firearms," though "when they noticed it, they retreated in disorder." Perhaps they had "retreated in disorder," but first they had attacked.[76]

Alliance with the French meant the possibility of obtaining their technology. Indians welcomed the new goods into their lives, though what they welcomed and in what quantity varied from group to group and among individuals. European trade goods were scarce and useful, so they were included in burials as among the deceased's and the mourners' most valued possessions. In the burial mounds of the precontact period, high-status burials are identified in part by the Indian produced goods that came from elsewhere. For instance, copper items produced in Missouri increased in value as they moved to the copper-short areas of the Atlantic seaboard.

From the Europeans, the Indians particularly valued knives, blankets, and guns. The last quickly became a much-desired status symbol and tool. The possession of all European goods, beyond their utility, symbolized the status of having access to the Europeans as well as the ability to earn the weapon. Thus, although the bow and arrow had many crucial advantages over the gun in the late seventeenth century, the owning of a gun symbolized an Indian's prowess as a hunter of deer, bear, and other animals or as a skilled warrior who could capture an enemy to sell to the Europeans as a slave. Not possessing a gun represented a lack of the much-valued martial and hunting skills. Yet the emphasis on European goods as symbols of power and accomplishment can be carried just so far—European trade goods had great utility. Although Indians sometimes ignored this utility and adopted items for other purposes, converting brass pots into jewelry and decorations, for instance, tools such as knives and hoes made labor easier, and scissors, thread, and iron pots soon entered Indian villages in great number, altering textile production and food preparation.

The trade goods and technology of the Europeans kindled Indian curiosity in the newcomers. Father Du Ru observed: "I am studying the character of these people, as much as I can, and I find that they are very much interested, that their whole desire is to get from everyone what they want, though without violence and without treachery."[77] The priests found the Indians attentive listeners, but their mistake was in assuming that the Indians' desire for European goods, technology, and ideas meant that they wanted to be like Europeans and would submit themselves to French authority. In fact, the Indians wanted simply to adopt and adapt what they found desirable and attractive from the Europeans. They had no intention of accepting the Europeans as a model for new behavior, or of exchanging their culture for a new one, or, not least, of accepting European dominance over them.

The Indians also actively sought out the French as military allies. The Tomé and the Mobile, for instance, sought protection from the Conchac, the Colapissa, "and other savages who have killed twelve of their men." Sauvole learned that he could provide Indians with military help in exchange for desperately needed provisions.[78] With the missionaries mediating between French officials and Indians, the two exchanged military assistance, trade, ideas, and technology. Both sought alliances to protect themselves from hostile forces and improve their regional position.

Many steps were required to cross the cultural divide. For French and Indians it involved the initial desire to make contact, mutual participation in each group's rituals of engagement, and the generosity of presents and hospitality. None of this could occur, nor would the relationship develop out of this stage, without each party striving to obtain something of significance from the other. In the case of the French, the priests wished to win the souls of heathen—but not any heathen, only those whose position would also promote France's position in the South. Louisiana's civil leadership needed Indian alliances to survive. It was impossible to build a colony in the Mississippi Valley without native assistance. Many Indians of the region welcomed the French because they needed assistance against slavers. They might not have been sure how the French could help them—whether through military assistance, trade, technological innovation, or other factors—but their enemies had forged connections to the English in Carolina or Virginia and that apparently had helped them. The unusual, useful, and awe-inspiring technology of the French illustrated their ingenuity and power. If these items inspired fear in indigenous people, it did not matter, given the grave circumstances they faced in the region from sickness and warfare. Isolation from or rejection of the French was not a choice.

At the dawn of the new century, the South's native peoples were probably unaware that the French, English, and Spanish envisioned a contest among themselves for control of the region—a contest to be settled primarily through alliances with Native Americans. The Spanish hoped to meet their goals by expanding the mission system. The English expected to accomplish their ends through trade. The French combined both methods, settling missionaries among some Indians and sending traders and agents to others. As the French increased their presence along the Gulf of Mexico and on the Mississippi River, the English considered ways to halt their progress and remove them. They contemplated a military assault to conquer Florida, which would give them a staging area for an assault on Louisiana. English aggression would help drive the French and Spanish together for their own attempted conquest of Carolina. Indians throughout the South enlisted in alliances with one European power or the other. Thousands were killed, enslaved, or displaced. From the Carolinas to the Florida Keys and west to the Mississippi Valley, the South was about to become engulfed in violence.

5

DIPLOMACY AND WAR, 1699–1706

The quest for Indian slaves shaped and distinguished the first decade of the eighteenth-century South. Slavers stepped up their attacks by organizing both large armies and small raiding parties that scoured the countryside in search of prey. Thomas Nairne, who participated in at least one of these raids, left a rare description of how such a raid was conducted in a legend for a map of Florida that he produced. The nineteen-part legend depicts the step-by-step process he and thirty-three Yamasee followed in Florida. Apparently, they took the inland passage from South Carolina to northern Florida, entering Saint Johns River, which they followed to a location six days from the river's mouth. They then headed south through "large inland lakes, some of them joined together." At "the furthermost place where the Indians have gone with canoes," they took a path "to go a Slave Catching." At Cacema town, south of modern-day Orlando, the raiders headed south, swimming "over a Deep River" to a place where they captured twenty-nine slaves. Continuing on, they captured six more slaves; at another spot they killed thirty-three men; and then they were attacked by "a very Numerous body of Indians," all painted, who were armed only with harpoons "made of Iron and Fish bones." They repulsed their attackers and headed home with their slaves. Nairne's account makes clear that the Yamasee knew exactly

where to go: their route "to go a Slave Catching" was well traveled. The inclusion of Nairne's map and its detailed legend in at least three widely published maps shows the British pride in these accomplishments—allying with
Indians who captured other Indians for sale to the British.[1]

The French and the Spanish spent much of the decade trying to stop the
British and allied Indian slave raids. Although not all of the Indians enslaved
were allied with either the French or the Spanish, their allies felt the brunt of
the attacks. For the Spanish, ending the slave raids was a matter of survival—
the raiders decimated their most powerful allies, leaving their colony almost
undefended. The French were not so greatly threatened, but ending the slave
raids was central to their diplomacy in the Mississippi Valley.

PIERRE LE MOYNE D'IBERVILLE
EXTENDS THE FRENCH EMPIRE

French imperial interests in the Southeast centered on controlling the mouth
of the Mississippi and securing alliances with the region's Indians against
both English traders and the Spanish in Florida. The Spanish did not welcome the French intrusion led by La Salle, who had discovered the Mississippi's mouth descending from Canada. Fearing that the French could drive a
wedge between Florida and New Mexico, isolating Florida to threaten New
Mexico, the Spanish failed to entrap La Salle, who was unable to relocate the
Mississippi and wound up in Texas.[2] The Spanish quickly established themselves at Pensacola to ward off further French incursions, but they were too
late. The French put their new colony into the hands of Pierre Le Moyne
d'Iberville, who had earned military fame in Canada by defeating the English
at Hudson's Bay.[3] Iberville arrived at the mouth of the Mississippi in 1699
and quickly established French power by turning back an English-sponsored
colony of French Huguenots at the aptly named "English Turn."[4] The
French were fortunate to have Iberville, rather than La Salle, to establish their
colony. The Canadian-born Iberville worked well not only with his own men
but with Amerindians. Iberville understood the value of the ritual exchange
of goods: the importance of following native ceremonies properly and of fulfilling aboriginal desires for European products. He also had an able assistant
in his younger brother, Jean-Baptiste Le Moyne de Bienville, a talented lin-
guist who smoothed communication with Amerindian groups and who also
appreciated the need to learn and follow native customs.

Commissioner Jean-Baptiste du Bois Duclos later described Bienville's
method of success for conducting relations with Indians: first, Bienville became "acquainted with the most powerful Indian nations and the ones that

could be most useful or do the greatest harm to the colony." Then he sent young men to live with these groups and learn their languages. The boys had the responsibility of spying on the Indians and keeping track of the English. When the English were about to offer the Indians gifts to lure them into warring with other Indians, Bienville quickly sent for the principal chiefs. Because the French were not in a position to counter English gifts with "similar ones, he would show them great friendship, regale them and very often succeeded by this means with the assistance of the Indian language which he speaks perfectly." The Indian chiefs were "delighted to see a French chief caress them and have them eat with him." They "would return home with a few little presents that M. De Bienville would give them and would assure their people that the French nation was the best nation in the world and that they must not quarrel with it or consequently destroy its allies." If this did not work, and the young men of a nation ignored their chiefs, then Bienville would stir another Indian nation against them. He would have them bring in many prisoners, whom he would then set free, and these would return to their nation to show their brethren "that the French nation was a friend of theirs and . . . that he hoped that henceforth their nations would pay more attention to the messages that he would send them." Bienville would then send for the "chiefs of both sides and make them make peace." Furthermore, "He also paid great attention to having the Frenchmen themselves punished who did them any wrong or defrauded them."[5]

Bienville gave France decades of service, and thus a modicum of stability in the sprawling colony they named Louisiana, which extended through the Gulf states west of Florida to east Texas, and north to the Missouri country. Assisting the brothers were Canadian voyaguers and coureurs de bois, woodsmen and traders experienced in frontier skills of trading, trapping, and warfare. What the French lacked in material resources they made up for with expertise and guile. Louisiana never attracted the anticipated large number of colonists, but the traders, missionaries, soldiers, and officials adjusted the best they could and secured France an important presence in North America from the Gulf of Mexico to Canada.[6]

The English threatened French interests more than the Spanish by sending traders into the Mississippi Valley as slave catchers who stirred up Indians to attack their neighbors. They armed the Chickasaw, whose towns became the central depot for slaving operations in the Mississippi Valley.[7] Together the English and Chickasaw engaged in expeditions to the south against the Choctaw and to the north against the Arkansas, and they terrorized Mississippi River peoples like the Tunica and Taensa. One French missionary among the Tunica reported that the Chickasaw acted not only against their enemies but also against their friends as they entered on a frenzy of slaving.[8] Iberville thought that he could simply apprehend the English traders and end the slaving.[9] But seizing another nation's traders was never an easy proposition—their Indian hosts would not tolerate it. Throughout the eighteenth century, the French, British, and Spanish had to compete with one another in Indian towns, because Amerindian peoples, particularly the larger groups, usually prevented any one group of Europeans from monopolizing trade. Those towns victimized by the slavers readily welcomed the French as a counter to the English, but they also were willing to negotiate with the English. The Arkansas, for instance, undertook slave raids for the English after having been subjected to slaving. For years, many Choctaw welcomed English traders even though they had lost thousands to slave raids; the Mississippi River peoples met the Welsh trader Price Hughes with much hurrah in 1714, even though they had been subjected to English-inspired slave raids for a generation.[10] Those peoples who welcomed the English to their towns probably had no choice. To oppose the English meant continued status as a potential victim of the slavers; to become a trading partner meant the possibility of survival.

The French had different ideas: their goal was to push the English out of the Mississippi Valley. As with the Spanish and English, the French at first believed only in exclusive alliances with the Indians. After establishing positive relations with many of the small Mississippi Valley groups near the Gulf, Iberville set his sights on the Chickasaw. As the chief slavers of the region they disrupted French hopes for peace and stability. The French hoped to unite the Indians in harmony, with themselves as mediators of differences among groups, to present a united front against the English. He tried to lure the Chickasaw from the English through presents and trade, for without allies like the Chickasaw, the English could have little influence in the trans-Mississippi. The English base in Charles Town was too distant to sustain their traders without Indian hosts. Iberville promised the Chickasaw merchandise at one fourth less than the English could provide and stated that the French would purchase not only deerskins but buffalo skins, which the English would not take. He warned the Chickasaw that the other Indians of the region were now friends of the French, and if the Chickasaw did not break off trade with the English, he would arm their enemies and "they would be unable to hold out against so many Indians equipped to fight them."[11]

The Chickasaw were understandably apprehensive about both the French entry into the South and the English desire for slaves. On one hand, their enemies to the north, the Illinois and the Arkansas, and those to the south, the Choctaw and the lower Mississippi peoples, would now have the backing of a European power—and one that was closer than the English, whose base at Charles Town was five hundred miles away. On the other hand, the Chickasaw also feared the English, who were expanding their presence by leaps and bounds. An English trader to the Chickasaw threatened to induce the Conchac (Abihka) and Alabama to attack them if they allied with the French.[12] Moreover, the English made inroads among the Choctaw in trying to lure them into becoming slavers. As early as 1699 the French received reports of English and Choctaw having "dealings together."[13] On the Chickasaw northwestern flank, the English armed the Arkansas to incite them to attack the Chakchiuma, a Yazoo River group who were Chickasaw but had separated from the main body in southwest Tennessee. Perhaps the Chickasaw had refused to attack their own people to procure slaves for the English; or maybe the Chickasaw asked the English to undertake this enterprise because they were unhappy with this band that had broken off—although if that were the case, they could have conducted the attack themselves. Whatever reason the English had for employing the Arkansas, the Chickasaw saw that the English could find other Indians to do their bidding and that Chickasaw could easily end up as slaves.[14]

Iberville used his knowledge of the Chickasaw situation to best advantage. In late March 1702, he convened the Chickasaw and Choctaw to make peace. The Choctaw had been urging the French to join them in a war against the Chickasaw, and the French seized the chance to tie both closer to them.[15] With Bienville as interpreter, Iberville, in a carefully prepared speech, implored the Chickasaw to realize their position of peril and accept the French and Choctaw hands of friendship. He told the Chickasaw that the English were using them for their own designs and had caused all their current problems. All the English cared about were "blood and slaves." Iberville assured the Chickasaw that when enemies captured them, the English bought and sold the Chickasaw captives in the West Indies, just as they did with the captives that the Chickasaw provided. Iberville recounted how for "the last eight to ten years . . . you have been at war with the Chaqueta [Choctaw] at the instigation of the English." During that time "you have taken more than 500 prisoners and killed more than 1,800 Chaqueta. Those prisoners were sold; but taking those prisoners cost you more than 800 men, slain on various war parties, who would be living at this moment if it had not been for the English." Where would it end? The answer was obvious: the "ultimate plan of the Englishman, after weakening you by means of wars, is to come and seize you in your villages and then send you to be sold somewhere else, in faraway countries from which you can never return, as the English have treated others, you know."[16]

If common sense could not convince the Chickasaw to embrace the French and their allies, then threats might work. Iberville warned the Chickasaw that he would arm all their enemies, as he had already begun arming the Natchez. He would incite their enemies to the north, the Illinois, to continue their war. The Chickasaw would not be able to hold out against so many. If they accepted the offer of peace, then the French would establish a trading post between them and the Choctaw. He reiterated the earlier offer of taking their buffalo, deer, and bear skins, adding: "those are the slaves I want. . . . To get them will not cost you your lives." After agreeing on prices, Iberville gave presents and promised that he would immediately send to the Illinois and have their Chickasaw prisoners released. The Chickasaw would have to induce the Alibamon and the Conchac to make peace with the Choctaw and other Amerindian allies of the French. This was Iberville's first step to unite all of the Mississippi Valley peoples, as well as those between Louisiana and South Carolina, into an alliance of peace.[17]

The Spanish grudgingly accepted French settlement and entered a period of mutual cooperation. Opposition to the English united the two powers, and the path of cooperation was smoothed when a French Bourbon took the Spanish throne. The French received food supplies from Spanish Vera Cruz and provided Pensacola with military stores. The Spanish improved their military presence in Apalachee by building a new fort and by sending three hundred men to do likewise at Pensacola. But conflicts with the Indians poisoned Spain's position in Apalachee, while desertion, death, debilitating disease, and frequent food shortages undermined their strength in Pensacola. Over the next decade the French tried to get the Spanish to cede Pensacola, and almost succeeded, but the Spanish would not part with this important base for protecting their New World possessions.[18]

THE ENGLISH RESPONSE

The English immediately recognized the repercussions of French settlement along the Mississippi. They chafed at the French enticing away their trading partners, complaining that the "Indians are in Love with their liberality." South Carolina's governor warned the General Assembly that even in peacetime the French posed the gravest danger; to look at New England's situation next to Canada "is to Say Enough on this Subject."[19] The French threat led Carolina officials to step up efforts to improve trade relations with Indians through reform of abuses, particularly in the area of spiraling Indian debts to the traders. Officials feared that if Indians were unable to pay their debts they would turn to other nations' traders. They toyed with forgiving old debts. Moreover, they took action to bar servants and slaves from participating in the Indian trade, so that if Indians did move from friend to enemy they would not find allies among Carolina's disgruntled population. The government also considered appointing an agent to monitor trader behavior and to remove those traders who abused Indians. Within a decade Carolina enacted all these measures into law, hoping to withstand growing French power and to calm the discontent expressed by their Indian allies.[20]

English fear of the French extended not just to their potential impact on Indians who lived in the Mississippi Valley but to the Creek and even to Carolina's closest allies, the Yamasee. The English knew that many Yamasee maintained relations with the Spanish and allied Indians in Florida and freely traveled there to visit friends and relations. The French were also presumed to be interested in luring Yamasee away and thus exposing the colony to attack. The English and French each held the belief that the other was capable of virtually any perfidy and would go to any length to undermine the other's position. The English suspected that French agents operated among the Yamasee, though no evidence exists. Carolina sent James Stanyarne to the Yamasee in August with presents and reassurances of the colony's friendship. Stanyarne was to take the unusual step of bringing the Yamasee to Charles Town, where they could be well entertained and where the governor could instruct them on what to do if the Spanish or French attacked.[21]

The Carolina government realized that intimacy and presents alone would not convince the Yamasee to become the colony's buffer and most important ally. The growing abuses of the Yamasee by the traders had to be addressed. That traders abused Indians was nothing new. The general complaints concerned running up Indian debts by getting the Yamasee drunk and then paying them a pittance for their skins, thereby alienating and impoverishing the hunters who sank ever deeper in debt. Earlier, in the 1680s and 1690s, the Yamasee and the traders had developed a good relationship. The traders depended on the Yamasee for skins and slaves, which minimized conflicts. But English traders soon expanded their operations westward and established strong linkages with the Creek Confederacy, with many Creek towns moving closer to the English and their trade goods. The traders' success among the Chickasaw in the Mississippi Valley gave them yet another source for human chattel and animal pelts. The Yamasee remained important to the traders, but they were no longer the sole or even primary source for slaves. Moreover, the number of deerskins they provided the traders declined as their hunting areas became depleted, and the Creek increasingly replaced the Yamasee as a source of skins. As had happened to the Westo and the Savannah, the Yamasee were becoming expendable to the traders, though not to the Carolina government, which recognized their importance as a first line of defense and appreciated their knowledge of Spanish Florida. The government feared that if trader abuses continued, the Yamasee would desert the Savannah River and move toward the French or Spanish.[22]

The Savannah also troubled the English. In spite of their declining importance along the Savannah River, the Savannah remained a significant force. They had connections and settlements throughout the East and a reputation as fierce fighters. Some Savannah had contacts with the French, and even if the English did not know the specifics of those contacts, they did know that their allegiance to the English was weak. Several Savannah traveled with Iberville and Bienville on their journeys through the Mississippi Valley, and we can assume that the English traders reported this to the Carolina government. By March 1702, when the English attempted to improve their relationship with the Savannah, the Savannah had convinced Iberville to counter the governor of Canada's directive to the Illinois to attack them. Iberville believed that the Savannah were "the single nation to fear, being spread out over Carolina and Virginia in the direction of the Mississippi." French goals in the interior could not be met without accommodating the influential Savannah. By ordering the Illinois to end their attacks Iberville hoped to attract the Savannah to settle on the Mississippi or at Mobile, where they would counter the English.[23]

The third key group for the English was the Creek, specifically the Alabama (about to become classified by the English as a Creek group but still acting somewhat independently), Cuseeta and Coweta subgroups, though the Creek included numerous other peoples. The Alabama, or Alibamon, lived at the confluence of the Alabama and Tallapoosa Rivers, much closer to the French than the Creek along the Ochese. Repeated attacks by the Choctaw and other Indians allied with the French threatened their subjection to Louisiana. As Carolina's governor noted, the Alabama must ally "themselves to the French or be Destroyed by them, nor can they be friends to them and us at the Same Time."[24] The governor overestimated French power and underestimated that of the Alabama, but the Alabama did indeed face a strong enemy to the west in the form of the Choctaw, with whom they often warred in the eighteenth century. Alabama conflicts with the Chickasaw, English trading partners, created the possibility of alienating the English while being unable to ally with the French. They also carried on warfare with the Tomé and the Mobilien, both of whom were becoming close allies with the French. In 1702 eight Alabama chiefs arrived in Mobile ostensibly to impress the French with the news that they had attacked the Chickasaw, only to learn that the Chickasaw were now considered French allies and to have Bienville urge them to make peace.[25] If the Alabama were confused about their difficult position regarding alliances, the English stepped in to clarify the situation. The Carolina government worked to end trader abuse among the Alabama, and the traders worked hard to convince the Alabama that their interests lay with them. In the next three years, the English successfully enlisted the Alabama to attack Florida Amerindians and to war with the French.

Opening a two-front war, both east (Spanish Florida and allied Indians) and west (French and allied Indians), was less hazardous than it might seem for the Alabama. The Spanish threat from Florida receded dramatically in the first decade of the eighteenth century as the English and their Indian allies, including the Alabama, repeatedly battered the Spanish and their allies. The English offensive drew the Alabama closer to the nascent Creek Confederacy, making both stronger.[26]

The English initiated attacks on Florida because of imperial, colonial, and economic concerns. The imminent outbreak of war in Europe between England on one side and France and Spain on the other was the worst-kept secret in America. Carolina had been waiting for more than a decade to pay Florida back for its two raids against Port Royal. The Bourbon accession now threatened Carolina directly, as it implied a united front of Florida and Louisiana against them. Opportunists in Carolina readily perceived that the Crown's and the colony's interests dovetailed nicely with their personal interests for retribution and to obtain Florida Indians for the slave trade.

Governor James Moore (September 1700–March 1703), one of the colony's largest slave traders, was not a man to let such opportunities slip away. He proposed to the assembly an invasion removing the Spanish from Florida.[27] The Carolina Commons House showed little interest in such an expensive campaign at first. Many distrusted Moore, whose desire for slaves was transparent. Before becoming governor, Moore had been barred from the Indian trade and had been the subject of numerous complaints by traders and colonial officials.[28] He became governor when Governor Joseph Blake (October 1696–September 1700) died and the council appointed him to the post until they could learn the proprietors' wishes. In spite of their objections to Moore, the proprietors allowed him to remain governor until they could decide on a successor, and he wasted no time making the best of his temporary power. Both houses of assembly assented to his plans to attack the Spanish.

They even ordered traders seized whom he suggested might defect to the Spanish, but as later events showed, these traders had simply opposed the governor.[29] Moore took command of the invasion forces. On this and future escapades into Spanish territory, plunder was the enticement to fill the ranks of soldiers.[30]

Perhaps as a result of the cancellation of the earlier expedition of 1685 as it was about to embark for Florida, this one took a remarkably short time to get under way. Only three months passed from the assembly's approval of the expedition to the troops' arrival in Florida in November 1702. As occurred in the later invasion of 1740, the English ransacked the environs of Saint Augustine and captured the town but were unable to subdue the Castillo de San Marcos, which gave refuge to soldiers and townspeople. Moore sent Colonel Robert Daniel to Jamaica to obtain additional artillery. Unfortunately for the English, Spanish reinforcements from Havana arrived first and "bottled up" eight of Moore's ships at Saint Augustine harbor. Calling an end to the two-month siege, Moore destroyed his ships and retreated overland forty miles, where relief ships carried home the disappointed invaders.[31] Moore was blamed for the disaster. His enemies questioned his competency, his cruelty to his officers (whom he accused of cowardice), and his greed.

Even more telling were the disputes that arose over the spoils. Moore and his allies tried to confiscate Yamasee loot, which included Apalachee Indians. That the tide of power had turned in the government was made evident in the choice of interpreters for the Yamasee: three of the four, Charles Morgan, Daniel Callahan, and Joseph Bryan, had been ordered apprehended before the invasion on the suspicion that they would warn the Spanish. Now that their friends had gained ascendancy in the assembly, they reemerged as respectable citizens. The contending parties worked out a compromise. The Yamasee apparently gave up some of their booty, which the governor exchanged for a barrel of powder and 250 weight of shot.[32] The Indians were unhappy, however, with restrictions that forced them to sell their captives to Moore's agents; the house amended the agreement so that the Indians could sell to whomever they pleased.[33]

Moore's enemies used the failed invasion to question the propriety of his governorship. They claimed that his selection had been fraudulent. Now they had sufficient ammunition for pressing their complaints to the proprietors over his venality and his agenda. The invasion itself they attributed to Moore's attempt to free himself of great personal debt. They alleged that he had controlled assembly elections to ensure a house favorable to his designs by allowing aliens, servants, and free blacks to vote—the Dissenters often accused the

Anglicans of obtaining elections through franchising the disenfranchised, including the colony's small Jewish population.

Only less scandalous than how Moore became governor and controlled elections was his ruining of the Indian trade. Some 150 irate Carolinians signed a petition claiming that the governor had been so obsessed with procuring slaves that the Indians gave up bringing in furs and skins. Although the critics' accusations must be taken with a grain of salt, Moore's quest for Indian slaves was undeniable before, during, and after the invasion. The remonstrators' other claim, that Moore granted commissions to whites to capture Indians for the slave trade, was also probably true. No one promoted and pursued the capture and sale of Indians more than Moore; in the aftermath of the failed invasion of Saint Augustine he embarked on a campaign to enslave thousands more.[34]

THE CREEK CONFEDERACY AND CAROLINA

Fully as important as Moore's swathe of destruction were the more immediate consequences of the invasion. Although the siege of Saint Augustine failed, many Indians did not consider it an English defeat. After all, the invaders had decimated the surrounding area and taken numerous captives, which many natives would have deemed a great success. The Indian allies of the English in 1702, and in later English invasions of Florida, opposed attacking the Castillo, a tactic they thought foolhardy. It was one thing to raid missions and Saint Augustine town to capture Indians and booty but quite another to extend great effort against a powerful fortress. Whereas the English sought total victory through removal of the Spanish presence, southern Amerindians saw nothing to gain from it. The English-allied Indians might have viewed the Spanish as a check to English power; but more important, there was no need to conquer the Spanish. The Spanish and their allies provided a convenient target for raids. If they were removed, the Indians would have to look elsewhere for plunder and captives.

The English display of power *did* convince the Alabama (whom the English and French still viewed as separate from the Creek) and the Creek to forge a closer connection with Carolina. In April 1703 the Alabama and numerous Creek groups asked the colony to send them drums and a stand of colors that they could display to proclaim themselves English allies. They also expressed their willingness to purchase ammunition for use against the French and Spanish.[35] Over the next three years the Carolina colony and the Creek Indians concluded an alliance that wreaked havoc on the Indians of Florida and threatened everyone else in the South. Menaced by the new

French colony at Mobile, which had armed the populous Choctaw and courted the Chickasaw, the Creek saw the English as a necessary counterweight to growing French power in the area. English success in Florida had proven their value as an ally. Many Creek towns moved their villages away from the French and closer to the English. In 1704 and 1705 they would join the English in the decimation of the Apalachee and Timucua. In between they signed an alliance with the English, which was given a title in England that misconstrued its contents when published as a broadside, *"The Humble Submission of the Kings, Princes, Generals, &c. to the Crown of England . . . ."*[36]

Broadsides were large sheets printed on one side for plastering on walls to publicize topics that ranged from public events to rewards for criminals. This broadside, printed in two parts, included a copy of the treaty with the Creek as attested to and signed by twelve Indian leaders, but it also described the treaty as a "Humble Submission" of the Indians. From a European perspective, of course, alliance with Indians could be on no terms other than as unequal partners with the English in the superior position. The English even interpreted the alliance to mean that the Indians had agreed to subjection, that is, to be subjects of England's monarch. Certainly the French and Spanish thought the same, for whenever Europeans made alliances with Indians, they then claimed sovereignty over those Indians' land—a fiction not to be admitted to the Indians, who had granted away neither sovereignty nor their land, but a claim appropriate to Europe's diplomatic tables when the ending of each war brought negotiations over colonial boundaries.[37]

The Indians issued no statement in the treaty implying that they accepted English sovereignty. Nowhere did they agree to submission or subjection; they did, however, promise fidelity to the Crown: "We do acknowledge our Protection depends upon the *English*." In return for that protection, the signers agreed to "behave" themselves toward the English, as they had in the past. They also declared that all friends and enemies of the English would be their friends and enemies, and in particular, that they would not allow the French or the Spanish to settle in their territory. It should be easy to see how the English would interpret this as a "submission" by Indians, from whom they rarely received such a bold statement of alliance. And yet, it is equally clear that the Indians never stated their submission, let alone accepted English sovereignty. Because the statement was unilateral—the English made no promises to accept the Indians' allies and enemies as their own—the document could be taken to infer submission. But no such statement had to be made. Given that these Indians were surrounded by Spanish, French, and hostile Indians, no clarification on the English part needed to be made: they already shared the same enemies. There was little chance that the English would become cozy with the French and Spanish, yet the Creek might settle matters with either of the European enemies of the English.

The document is revealing in another way. It never refers to the "Creek" Indians, though the signatures of leaders representing the chief towns that made up the confederacy are on the document. For each signer there is an English transliteration of their name, a symbol purportedly made or at least copied from the original by the printer, and an English title for the individual with the town they represented. Various "kings," "captains," and "head warriors" from both Lower and Upper Creek towns signed the document. The agreement was made at Coweta, and the "King of the Coweta" was the first signatory. Four other Lower Creek signatories represented Ockmulgee (a Hitchiti settlement), Cuseeta, Shufhatchee (a Chiaha settlement), and again Coweta, were joined by Upper Creek leaders of Tuchebatchee, Ockfuskie (a Coosa settlement), Poofchatche (probably referring to Okchai), and two from Alabama. The only major group unrepresented was Abihka. The absence of any reference to these Indians as Creek is significant, for the designation had virtually no meaning to the Indians involved. The signatories represented discrete groups, each with its own identity.[38]

The Creek, the name that described this confederacy to outsiders, were composed primarily of Muscogulge peoples. This meant that many of their languages were related though not mutually intelligible, much as are English and Italian. Coosa, Coweta, Cuseeta, and Abihka formed the core, but their language was not spoken by a majority of those in the confederacy. The Alabama were more closely related to the Choctaw in language, whereas Tuchebatchee and Hitchiti, two of the larger groups, also spoke two very different languages. Members of the confederacy spoke more than a dozen additional languages. The document clarifies the shared interests of these Indians; interests they would continue to have vis-à-vis outsiders: the English, French, and Spanish, not to mention the Choctaw, Cherokee, and Chickasaw. These Indian groups of varying linguistic and geographic backgrounds formed the Creek confederation as a response to the powerful outside forces that threatened them. They created a confederacy of convenience that gave strength against their enemies, while its diverse nature allowed each town to retain its independence. They could draw on their alliance with each other as needed or refuse calls as well. Sometimes the towns divided by their geographic division into Upper Creek and Lower Creek, which often operated as separate confederacies; sometimes each town formulated its own strategy and choices, opting to ally with others in a particular war or campaign, or to remain neutral. Some towns leaned to the Spanish,[39] some to the French, some to the English, and others to no European group. Thus, in a very real sense, the alliance was not between the "Creek" and the English but with many of the confederacy's key components.

At the bottom of the agreement an Englishman noted that the signatories had signed "In the Name of the rest." This was a wish and not a reality. Throughout the eighteenth century the English were frustrated at not being able to convince the Creek to act as a political unit. To them, the confederacy seemed like an anarchic collection of towns that united only when convenient. They were right—it was a confederacy of convenience that contained no mechanism to force all the towns to behave in any particular way to accept an alliance or agreement. This decentralized political structure was not confined to the Creek; the Cherokee, Choctaw, and others followed the same confederation system in which towns did as they pleased. The French and the English later tried to alter the system by creating medal chiefs, giving medals and presents to particular Indians who they hoped could build a following through disbursement of the presents. This scheme did not work. The medal chiefs were intimidated to turn over the presents by their opponents, and the Europeans made few inroads in placing their preferred men into leadership positions until well after the American Revolution. This document, then, was merely the first in a long series of agreements between the English and the peoples of the Creek Confederacy, but rarely did the English understand the nature of Creek polity or accept Creek refusal to make exclusive alliances.

POINT AND COUNTERPOINT:
THE VAGARIES OF DIPLOMACY

The French did not treat the Creek as a confederacy. Rather, they thought of them as groups of towns, then later treated the Upper Creek and Lower Creek separately. At the start of the eighteenth century, their most important relationship with a Creek group was with the Alabama, with whom they often warred but with whom they hoped to build a strong alliance. In 1702 the Alabama flirted with the French, having sung the calumet, but the French were mistaken to think the peace permanent, which the Alabama might have led them to believe. A party of Alabama visited Mobile and left with five Frenchmen who wished to trade for food at their villages. The combined group stopped at a Naniabas village outside Mobile and joined in a festival with Tomé, Mobilien, and their hosts. They left the village, and when they were about ten leagues from home, the Alabama murdered four of the five Frenchmen in their sleep. The fifth escaped and sounded the alarm to the French.[40]

The ruse was one of several to which the French fell victim that year. Forging alliances was painful and difficult, and Europeans were often overmatched by Indians who were practiced in the diplomatic arts and more familiar with both the terrain and the peoples. On learning what happened to his men, Bienville formed a force of seventy French and eighteen hundred Mobilien, Tomé, Naniabas, Choctaw, and others to pursue the Alabama. The army marched for two and a half weeks with Indians deserting every day—the French were unaware that their Mobilien guides were taking them in circles. When Bienville finally abandoned the quest, shorn of almost all his Indian support and unable to locate the enemy, the French returned to Mobile in just four days, having covered only "thirty leagues in eighteen days."[41]

The Mobilien might not have betrayed the Alabama to the French because of the fear of reprisals. They had much less to fear from the French than from the Alabama. An irate Bienville, bent on revenge against the Alabama and the need to show the Indians that the French were militarily competent and able to redress attacks, constructed ten boats and left secretly with fifty men—he did not want his allies to warn the Alabama. After several days he encountered his prey, a party of Alabama on a hunting expedition in fourteen boats. They escaped the French attack but had to leave their boats and goods behind.[42]

The war between the Alabama and the French lasted another decade. In the course of that war, the Alabama forged an alliance with the Mobilien and other Amerindian groups near Mobile. In this way the French learned the limitations of alliance. The Mobile-area Indians were good allies to the French, protecting their settlement and joining them on military expeditions that suited them. But they would not fight their friends, the Alabama. The French, however, gained experience in local politics and improved their relations with the Mobilien. After Pierre Dugué de Boisbriant led a raid taking six Alabama boats, killing several men, and capturing women and children for enslavement, the Mobilien begged Bienville to release the captives to them and he complied. André Pénicaut, a French carpenter and recorder of Indian life in early Louisiana, thought that this act of generosity led the Mobilien to a closer alliance with the French. Perhaps it did, but it also illustrates the power of *les petite nations,* the small Indian groups on whom the French depended.[43] The French had learned to adjust themselves and their expectations to their Indian neighbors.

War between the Alabama and the French also allowed the Choctaw to secure their position as the most important ally of the French. Their location and numbers assured them of that status. The Choctaw felt secure enough to conduct war on two fronts. Not only did they harass the Alabama, but they reopened hostilities with the Chickasaw, whom they had not forgiven for their slaving raids against them the previous decade.

Iberville's peace between the Choctaw and Chickasaw was chimerical. The Chickasaw were more intent on keeping the peace than the Choctaw, seeing the tide turn against them by the French ability to muster Mississippi Valley groups victimized by slaving. The Chickasaw tried to draw closer to the French, and on a trip to Mobile in 1702, they convinced the French to place a fourteen-year-old boy, St. Michel, among them to learn their language. In 1703, thirty-five Chickasaw returned to Mobile, though because of Choctaw hostilities, they had been forced to take the long way around to get there.[44] The Chickasaw asked the French to mediate again with the Choctaw, and Bienville instructed Boisbriant to take twenty-five Frenchmen to escort the Chickasaw to the Choctaw and negotiate a peace. When Boisbriant arrived, he was met by a chief, who asked him: "Where are you going with those Chicachas? Are you going to get yourself burned at their village the way a little French boy was burned whom M. de Bienville gave them last year to learn their language?"[45] Boisbriant doubted what the Choctaw said and informed them that he had come to mediate a peace. "I'll make peace with them," the chief promised, "if they will bring your little French boy back here." Two of the Chickasaw were given a month to retrieve the boy. While they were gone the Choctaw convinced Boisbriant to turn over the remaining Chickasaw if the boy did not come. Boisbriant, fifty leagues from Mobile, decided not to send to Mobile for advice. The time expired and the Choctaw pressed Boisbriant to turn over the Chickasaw. Boisbriant reflected on the weakness of the French, who "at that time were still no more than a handful of people in Louisiana," and with himself stuck "in the middle of a village of a populous savage nation of more than twelve thousand warriors—and also doubtful of being able to discover which side is the right." Boisbriant made his decision. He informed his men to prepare to leave, and realizing that he might have been hoodwinked by the Choctaw, he told them: "I leave them to you upon this condition—that your chiefs and all your nation shall always be friends of the French. Tomorrow I am going with my men back to Mobile." Boisbriant left. The Choctaw killed all the Chickasaw.[46]

Boisbriant realized, as his commander later did, that the Choctaw had manipulated the French into siding with them against the Chickasaw. Boisbriant, according to Pénicaut, felt "quite satisfied with having bound the most dreadful nation of all the savages to be friends of the French." Pénicaut considered that the policy of making a peace between the Chickasaw and the

Choctaw had been wrong all along, for then the two "most dreadful" nations "in all Louisiana," who between them had sixteen thousand warriors, "would have had the power to destroy our colony in its infancy." Allying with the Choctaw, the French rationalized, was better than allying with the Chickasaw because, as Pénicaut noted, the Choctaw were "the more powerful of the two nations and the one living closer to Mobile." It would have been nearly impossible for the French to ally with the Chickasaw against the Choctaw, precisely because of the Choctaw's location. As the French soon recognized, if they had not already, the success of their Louisiana enterprise depended entirely on Choctaw goodwill.[47]

As for the boy, St. Michel, he was alive and well. Ten Chickasaw brought him to Mobile and the Chickasaw were "placated as well as they could be with words" before being "sent back to their village."[48] The episode did not end Chickasaw hopes of remaining on good relations with the French. It is a common mistake of historians to assume that the Chickasaw were great allies of the English and enemies to the French. Certainly the French did not think so. Until the outbreak of the Natchez War in 1729, the French believed they were on an even footing with the English among the Chickasaw. In 1708, when the English thought they had great influence among the Chickasaw, Pierre d'Artaguiette reported that the "Chickasaws receive the French and English equally." The French realized that the Chickasaw played the English and French against one another, and simply accepted the situation.[49] The English perceived that employing the Chickasaw as slavers made the Chickasaw junior partners and the French just bit players without much of a hand to play. In reality, the Chickasaw continued to trade with the French, but they and the French realized that the French could not supply the Chickasaw with the goods they required.[50] The Chickasaw kept open the lines of communication and maintained friendship with the French because of their relationship with the English. The Chickasaw understood their geopolitical position and the threat posed by the English and their allies, as well as the Choctaw. In the fluid Southeast, friendships easily turned to dust, and diplomatic advantages could quickly disappear and realignments occur—especially when the English were involved. Bienville may have been bragging, but there was more than a little truth to his observation a few years later that "the English have spared nothing to attract the nation of the Chickasaws to themselves, but it is in vain. Although, to tell the truth, I do not give them any presents at all [and] they are more attached to us than to them."[51]

The hostilities between Chickasaw and Choctaw allowed the Creek to turn their attention elsewhere. Their enemy, the Cherokee, was being supplied by Virginia traders, and Carolina soon learned that these two allies of the English, Creek and Cherokee, were hostile toward one another. This created a situation that paralleled that of the French, Choctaw, and Chickasaw. When the Cherokee sold a captive Coosa (Creek) to Carolina, the government realized the potential peril and stepped up efforts to remove the Virginians from the Cherokee trade. If Carolina could control Cherokee access to English goods, they believed, the English would have the power to restrain the Cherokee.[52]

THE DECIMATION OF THE APALACHEE

The 1702 invasion of Florida had made Carolina more aware of both the imperial and strategic importance of the southern Indians and the need to direct Indian affairs in a rational fashion that would secure the colony and fulfill imperial goals while also lining people's pockets. The colonial government now found itself the center of attention as Indians both distant and near sought advice and approval of their actions, such as the relocation of their towns. In the aftermath of the invasion, there was some significant relocation of Indians. The Uhaw, about whom very little is known, requested land and permission to live among the Yamasee, which the colony granted.[53] As noted earlier, many Creek towns moved northward, in part because they may have feared Spanish retribution and French attacks and in part to draw closer to the sources of trade goods. Other Creek groups, including the Tallaboosa (the Alabama, or a town of the Alabama) and Coweta, were denied permission to move closer to the colony but were appeased by presents. The government urged them to "live where they now do," which "will as much Conduce to the Safety of this Colony as any thing [they] can do."[54]

To implement the colony's Indian policy, Governor Sir Nathaniel Johnson, a resident Carolinian, High Churchman, and good friend of former governor Moore, sent Moore to confirm the colony's "Friendly Indians to our interest, as well as Encouraging our friends, and destroying our enemies." Moore was instructed "to endeavor to gain by all peaceable means possible the apalaches to our interest," as they had learned that the Apalachee were so "inclinable."[55] Moore used this opening to enlist the colony's "friendly" Indians to accompany him on an officially sanctioned expedition into Florida. The government refused to provide funds for the campaign—plunder and slaves would recompense the adventurers. There was thus no way that a diplomatic solution could be achieved in Florida without the invaders' first fulfilling their desire for booty.[56] Moore had found a way to recoup his damaged reputation from the Saint Augustine expedition, obtain slaves, and earn kudos for fulfilling the Crown's and the colony's interests by raiding the Apalachee missions.

Moore's "diplomatic corps" of fifty whites and upward of a thousand Indians (some of whom sought revenge for devastating Apalachee attacks on them)[57] fell on the Apalachee in northwest Florida in January 1704. Accounts of the expedition vary—Moore himself wrote conflicting reports—but we can sketch in outline what happened.[58] Moore's attack initially focused on Ayubale, where about two dozen Apalachee were killed and two hundred were taken prisoner, with their Creek allies capturing another two hundred or so Apalachee in the surrounding countryside. What happened to the rest of Ayubale's people, who may have numbered more than five hundred, is unknown. Some of the Apalachee of Ivitachuco then agreed to go with Moore to South Carolina, while others apparently remained in Florida. Some Apalachee became rebels and attacked other Apalachee, and as many as four other towns agreed to relocate to South Carolina.

Moore could not have come at a better time. Many Apalachee were unhappy with the Spanish, for whom they labored but who were now failing to keep up their side of the bargain: they could not protect the Apalachee from their enemies. When the Spanish had first encountered the Apalachee in the sixteenth century, the aggressive Apalachee had handily defeated the early conquistadors. The Spanish muskets and lack of experience in the Florida terrain were no match for skilled Apalachee warriors. Their reputation was such that the Spanish named the Appalachian Mountains after them, though the Apalachee lived hundreds of miles to the south. After the Spanish established their permanent residence at Saint Augustine, the Apalachee, weakened by disease, moved into the mission system. In terms of converting to Christianity, they were a great success story for the mission fathers. No other Native American people east of the Mississippi acculturated as well to Christianity in the colonial period. This may have resulted from the unusually long time that the Apalachee spent on the missions and from the greater effort Catholic priests expended on them in contrast to other groups. When some of the Apalachee moved to Mobile after 1704, they told the French that they would not stay unless a priest was assigned to them. The Apalachee understood the usefulness of the clergy in their relationship with Europeans, but they were also very religious. They sang "the Psalms in Latin as is done in France" and were considered pious by the French.[59] The English noted this piety among Apalachee, whom they forced to resettle along the Savannah River. The ability and willingness of the Apalachee to acculturate can also be seen in the praise heaped on them by both the English and the French in nonreligious matters. Both found the Apalachee to be excellent scouts and warriors who completed tasks reliably. To Spanish, French, and English they displayed extraordinary fidelity, but only when they were treated well.

The English knew that many Apalachee were inclined to leave the Spanish in the early eighteenth century—their loyalty to the Spanish had its bounds and the Spanish had repeatedly crossed those bounds in the years preceding the English raid.[60] As early as 1699 the caciques of Ivitachuco and San Luis had written to the king of Spain for relief from abuses by soldiers and colonists. They had already "sought redress from various sources, [but] we have not had it, since they are so powerful, and we are without a person to protect and defend us." They complained that the Spaniards' cattle, swine, and horses roamed freely through their fields and that they labored for the Spanish without pay.[61] They had built a fort for the Spanish in Apalachee, but that attracted colonists, who confiscated their houses and placed labor demands on them, which forced them to flee to the woods or to Guale, "where many die without confession, because they do not understand the language of the missionaries of that province." Others had left to join the English.[62]

The caciques continued to write letters for relief, and the Spanish king responded with a *Royal Cédula* (a written order) in May 1700 demanding that the governor investigate.[63] The king informed the governor that he presumed the oppression of the Apalachee to be true and that when the governor had gathered the necessary evidence, he should make restitution and punish those at fault. Governor Zúñiga was also to provide a full account of all that happened and was reminded that "one of your principal duties is to exercise the greatest care so that the caciques and Indians of the said Province of Apalachee live without annoyance, . . . [that they] should be well treated, and that you help, protect, and defend them, as is your duty and as I have ordered in repeated cédulas to . . . your predecessors."[64]

The Apalachee were not the only ones asking for relief from forced labor. Timucua, Guale, Mocama, and Calusa also made these complaints. Apalachee had long been forced to work on the fortifications of Saint Augustine and they were willing to volunteer labor when necessary, but forced labor was an entirely different matter.[65]

Apalachee discontent helps explain the willingness of many to follow Moore to Carolina, but there is much confusion over the number enslaved and the number resettled. John H. Hann, the chief scholar of the Apalachee, shows that Moore's claim of four thousand enslaved is an exaggeration. And yet, Hann takes Moore at his word that he enslaved only the Indians of Ayubale, because that is what he admitted to the proprietors. But Moore, trying to show that he was doing the bidding of the empire by bringing the Apalachee to Carolina and that he had enslaved only the Ayubale, with whom they had fought—which convinced others to surrender—probably downplayed the number of Indians and the circumstances of their capture. First of all, as Hann has noted, we cannot be sure that Moore ever claimed to have enslaved four thousand—for we have only copies of what he had written, and in some of these documents he claimed to have taken far fewer than four thousand. His claim, "I did not make slave, or put to death one man, woman or child but were taken in the fight, or in the Fort I took by storm," remained constant. To the proprietors, it was not important how many slaves were taken but *how* they were taken. Only Indians captured in warfare could be enslaved. Indians who surrendered could not be considered slaves. The large numbers of Apalachee taken by Moore numbered well above the one thousand that Hann suggests; determining how much above is another matter. One difficulty with computing the number of enslaved is that a second raid conducted by the Creek occurred in July or August 1704. Between the two raids, Hann estimates that of a population of seven thousand Apalachee, hundreds were killed, "more than 2,000 were forced into exile in order to preserve their freedom or their lives," and an undetermined number were enslaved.[66] Spanish and French reports conflict as to the damage done, but we do know that about four hundred moved west to join the French, perhaps hundreds more remained in Florida and resettled in Apalachee or elsewhere on the peninsula, and others eventually made their way to Cuba and to Mexico.

Whereas the first attack on the Apalachee decimated five or six towns in the heart of the province, the second attack struck the more western towns and defeated the Spanish garrison of Pensacola. Lower Creek Indians killed twenty-eight Spanish soldiers in a launch and captured and sold many Apalachee into slavery.[67] The Frenchman Bénard de La Harpe reported that the attackers included three thousand Indians armed with guns who were led by five Englishmen and two Africans. The Apalachee, as on earlier occasions, asked the Spanish for guns but were refused. La Harpe noted that on this occasion the guns were withheld "for political reasons," but he did not elaborate.[68] Given Apalachee discontent and that some of the towns had "voluntarily" left with Moore on the first invasion, the Spanish might have feared that if they armed the Apalachee, the Apalachee could turn their guns on them.

A Spanish plea for French supplies came too late.[69] The mission system had been crushed, one Spanish report noting that twenty-nine missions were destroyed or forced to close.[70] La Harpe reported that "two thousand Apalachees surrendered to their enemies, who forced them to remove themselves to the coast of Carolina." From Mobile, Bienville reported the disaster of both raids as six thousand or seven thousand Apalachee killed or taken prisoner and six thousand head of cattle killed. Other French reports noted about two thousand Apalachee killed, thirty-two Spaniards captured, and seventeen Spaniards burned, including three Franciscans. Two hundred Chacato joined the four hundred Apalachee as refugees among the French. Bienville "asked them why they left the Spaniards. They told me that they did not give them any guns, but that the French gave them to all of their allies."[71]

How many Apalachee were enslaved? Hann and La Harpe both believed that about two thousand were forced into exile, but the census report of 1715 lists only 638 Apalachee in the Savannah River villages, and this was probably an increase over the number recorded in the census of 1708.[72] Although a few would have trickled back to Florida or to Louisiana and a few families joined the Creek, the vast majority remained on the Savannah River because they were, in effect, hostages. Thus, at least thirteen hundred to fourteen hundred Apalachee presumed to be refugees when they left Florida did not become refugees on the Savannah River. They were likely sold into slavery. Also overlooked is that on the second expedition, conducted by the Lower Creek, the Creek had no reason to turn over their captives as refugees, nor is there any record that the Carolina government compensated the Creek to release the Apalachee, which would have been a hefty sum and thus would have been recorded in the assembly's records. The Creek must have sold their captives to the slavers. All told, between two thousand and four thousand Apalachee were enslaved on both expeditions into Florida, with the high end the more likely number. The English and their allies captured and enslaved additional Apalachee and other Florida Indians in 1705 and 1706.[73]

The destruction of Apalachee province reduced the Spanish presence in northern Florida to Saint Augustine and Pensacola. In 1705 the Carolinians and their Amerindian allies destroyed the Timucuan missions of Florida. This attack is barely mentioned in the English records, and nothing is said about what happened to the captives, who were not settled into towns like many of the Apalachee but were apparently all killed or enslaved.[74] This assault opened the way for continued attacks by the English and their Indian allies, who attacked the Calusa on the Gulf Coast by Tampa Bay and then extended their slaving to the Florida Keys. All of Florida's Amerindians fell prey to the English desire for slaves.

As for the Apalachee, the Spanish tried to win back them and the Chacato who had settled near the French. They offered the Indians presents, but many stayed with the French, "who give more security to their allies."[75] The Apalachee provided the same immense value to the French that they had to the Spanish. They helped not only on military expeditions but in the construction of forts and the raising of supplies.[76] The Apalachee in Carolina negotiated with the French to move from the Savannah River to Mobile.[77] The French displayed their goodwill by returning to the Savannah River Apalachee those who had "been brought prisoners" to Louisiana. The Apalachee offered to pay for their kinfolk, but the French governor returned them without fee.[78]

Living with the French was preferable to semi-imprisonment on the Savannah River, but it was difficult and perilous to accomplish. If large numbers of Apalachee picked up and moved, the Creek or other Indians could easily have captured them and sold them as slaves. On the Savannah River they could at least live as a community and hope for the best. The Apalachee chance to escape the English came with the Yamasee War, when all the Indians between Mobile and Carolina fought with the English. Apalachee refugees then returned to Florida, moved to Louisiana, or assimilated into the Creek Confederacy.

AFTERSHOCKS

The Creek were the immediate beneficiaries of English success against the Spanish and the Apalachee. There is no telling how much they made from selling their captives, but their status as friends of the English secured their position in the South. English traders flooded into Creek towns to supply goods, and the French avidly courted them. The Chickasaw, who on occasion had brought Alabama scalps to the French to prove their fealty,[79] began to leave the Alabama and the Creek alone (they had the Choctaw to contend with); the Chickasaw might also have ceased attacks on the Creek when Carolina concluded their alliance with the Creek.

The French continued to make overtures to the Chickasaw, for Bienville recognized their importance. The Chickasaw could cut off communication between Canada and Louisiana. The French constantly had to weigh the relative value of having the Chickasaw at war with the Choctaw to keep the Choctaw dependent on them with the need to keep open the lines to Canada. In 1706, Bienville determined on improving relations with the Chickasaw because of the growing English presence among them and the threat that this posed to the colony. Bienville hoped to establish a French post among them. Bienville and the French learned that they could trade with both the Choctaw and Chickasaw and have the two remain at war, a concept of divide and conquer that the English and French had not previously considered. But the realization of that strategy lay in the future, and Bienville tried to patch things up between the Choctaw and Chickasaw, hoping then that the Choctaw would focus attention on the Alabama.[80]

The Chickasaw quest for slaves led them to continue attacks against the smaller Mississippi peoples who found refuge among the French downriver. In these endeavors, the Chickasaw often allied with the Natchez and the Yazoo, a combination that bode ill for the future of the French colony, for the Chickasaw would provide refuge to the Natchez in the Natchez War of 1729. The Taensa, Bayogoula, and Tunica were all forced to move southward by the attacks.[81] The constant movement of peoples and the realignment of alliances and enmities rarely moved smoothly for the French and their allies. The Taensa, for instance, after being pushed out of their villages by the Chickasaw, received refuge among the Bayogoula but then killed a great many of them. The attack on their hosts was allegedly undertaken as revenge for a "similar perfidy" by the Bayogoula against the Taensa's allies, the Mougoulacha. The Taensa feared reprisals from the small nations allied with the Bayogoula and returned to their village, but not before inviting "several families of the Chitimachas and the Yagenchitos . . . to come and eat with the Bayagoulas. By this ruse the Tensas had surprised and captured several of these Indians, carrying them off as slaves."[82]

The Tunica, to return to the good graces of the French—they had not protected a French priest, Nicolas Foucault, killed by the Koroa and the Yazoo—were told by the French that they had to avenge the priest's death and bring them the Englishmen who traded among these peoples. Bienville offered a detachment of French soldiers, weapons, and supplies to complete the task. It is unclear whether they were successful at this time, but in October 1706 they did capture "an Englishman engaged in the slave trade." Fearing retribution, the Tunica found refuge among the Ouma, but the Tunica turned on the Ouma and killed more than half of them.[83]

French inexperience in Louisiana gave them little chance of predicting Amerindian behavior. Each group had a history and culture of which the French had minimal knowledge. By contrast, the French understood the English only too well. While trying to mimic English colonization in the South by using trade to forge alliances and building plantations to create wealth, they also understood the inherent weaknesses of their numbers and their power. The English in the South had the advantage over the French in terms of numbers, experience in the region, and in trade goods. To shift the balance in their favor, the French realized that they must strike at the heart of English power in the region. The solution lay in an attack on Charles Town, with the ultimate goal the destruction of South Carolina.

FRENCH AND SPANISH DESIGNS AGAINST CAROLINA

The English attack on Saint Augustine in 1702 convinced the French government that it must conquer Carolina to protect not only Louisiana but also Cuba and Jamaica for the Spanish.[84] The English were bent on absolute domination of the West Indies and the American South, so the French believed that they must respond in kind. As early as 1703 a plan was hatched for the destruction of Carolina, and an itemized list was assembled of the vessels, cannon, and men needed for an invasion by sea and by land.[85] Iberville, who had returned to France, was chosen to lead the invasion. Through 1705 the French continued preparations. News of English success in Apalachee added urgency to the task,[86] for the French feared that Pensacola would soon fall and that Louisiana would follow.[87]

In Louisiana, the French stepped up efforts to secure their Amerindian neighbors through presents while also improving their fortifications at Mobile and sending more troops to the colony.[88] In Paris, Guillaume and Claude Delisle collected and collated information about Indians and geography to produce important maps of the South,[89] presenting their findings to the Royal Society and giving French imperialists a better idea of the situation in America.[90] Iberville envisioned a grand attack combining Spanish and French resources. A Spanish fleet at Vera Cruz would unite with one at Havana. Iberville planned to bring a fleet from France and enlist hundreds of filibusters from Martinique and Saint Domingue, as well as three hundred Spanish from Mexico, "of which 200 would be mulatto and free negroes." The French volunteered to cover most of the expenses and provide the supplies for the Spanish. To pay for the conquest of Carolina, Iberville intended to send the Spanish home after taking Charles Town, then proceed with his forces to Chesapeake Bay, capture three to four cities in Virginia and Maryland (and perhaps New York), and hold each for ransom, much as Drake had done to Spanish cities and colonial ports in the sixteenth century.[91] Lest we think that Iberville was imagining castles in the sky, it should be remembered that he was the Drake of his day, having defeated the enemy in the Atlantic, the Caribbean, the Gulf of Mexico, and at Hudson's Bay. The confident Iberville was willing to pay most of the expedition's expenses as well as organize and plan it. He needed the king's approval and the French government to negotiate with the Spanish, whom he would reward with a share of the booty. He also asked the king for some ships that were already stationed in America, promising to compensate the king with the great prizes he would take in English colonial waters.[92]

The invasion began on a high note. Iberville captured the small English islands of Nevis and Saint Christopher in the West Indies with ten vessels. He then went to Havana "to pick up a thousand Spaniards destined for Carolina." But Iberville and hundreds of men were struck down by disease, which La Harpe believed was the plague but was more likely yellow fever.[93] The invasion continued without him, yet shorn of his vision, skills, and strong hand, it became a sorry spectacle of Franco-Spanish military incompetence.

Five ships from Havana arrived in Saint Augustine, where they recruited a galliot (a small galley) that carried thirty local infantry and "fifty Christian Indians of the Timiquana, Apalachen and Tequassa [Tequesta] nations."[94] When they left Florida on August 31, 1706, they spotted an English sloop, which the flagship, *La Brilliante,* pursued. The flotilla proceeded without them, believing that *La Brilliante* would reach Charles Town first, but when they arrived on September 4, the flagship was not to be seen. The Franco-Spanish forces hesitated because *La Brilliante* "carried the best troops, the campaign guns, shovels, spades, shells, and the land commander," General Arbousset.[95] The waiting proved fatal.

The city had been warned by smoke signals sent by men stationed at nearby Sullivan's Island. Charles Town was in the midst of a yellow fever epidemic, but militia flocked in from the countryside. The invaders sat in their ships for four days awaiting the flagship, then demanded a ransom of fifty thousand pesos to not destroy the town. Governor Johnson was amused by the paltry demand and told the envoy that Charles Town was worth forty million pesos,[96] that they had been there thirty years, "and that it had cost much blood, so let them come."[97] Graciously, the governor treated the envoy to a night of drinking while his men prepared to resist the invaders.

Without Iberville at the helm, and missing their general, the invaders decided to seek plunder instead of conquest and divided into raiding parties to procure black slaves. On James Island, a combined force of militia and Indians turned back a Franco-Spanish raiding party, but another force of 160 Spanish destroyed two small boats and a small building on a spit of land between the Wando River and the Atlantic. The Spanish celebrated and rested overnight, expecting an easy victory the next day. However, the Carolina militia disrupted the celebration, surprised the invaders, and captured 60, with 12 others killed and a handful drowned. A few days later, the English sent seven small boats, including a fireship, against the French fleet, and the survivors retreated.

Soon after the fleet's departure, *La Brilliante* arrived with between 200 and 350 soldiers. The ship was late because it had missed Charles Town and had landed north of the city, when the crew thought that they were south, and now the men were eager for a fight. Embarrassed by his misjudgment,

Arbousset complied and landed his men east of Charles Town. Governor Johnson repulsed the attackers with militia, and another group captured their ship. The Franco-Spanish campaign thus ended with more than 320 of the invaders captured and approximately 30 killed. The French and Spanish prisoners were sent to Virginia for transportation to England, but the 90 to 100 Indians captured were kept as plunder and "Sold for Slaves."[98]

The grand designs of the French had come to naught. If Iberville had not died along with so many of his men in the Indies, and a major invasion rather than what amounted to a large sacking party had attacked Carolina, the French might indeed have conquered the colony, if not at least Charles Town. The colony's European population was vulnerable and could not count on its Indian allies, who might have deserted at any time. Whether the French could have held the colony is another matter, but it is not far-fetched to assume that the French could have followed up a quick victory with more Spanish help from Cuba and Saint Augustine and then focused resources designed for Louisiana on Carolina.

Still, the invasion had failed, and the French were on the defensive. In retrospect, they had lost their best chance to turn back English expansion in the South—a task that now lay almost entirely in Amerindian hands. But in 1706 southern Indians were concerned less with checking English expansion than with the slave trade—both the profits to be made and the danger to be faced as potential victims. The French understood that, barring the removal of the English from the South, they must continue to undermine the British traders to the Indians and reconcile (at propitious moments) the Chickasaw and Choctaw, a task that constantly hit snags.

In 1706 the Chickasaw attacked the Choctaw with great success and delivered three hundred captives to the English.[99] Thomas Welch, a Carolina trader among the Chickasaw, apparently provided the necessary powder and shot, for which the Carolina Commons House reimbursed him sixty-one pounds. The massive raid earned him a reputation as the colony's chief expert on the Mississippi River Indian peoples.[100]

Once he had the ear of the government, Welch proposed to wean the Choctaw and the Yazoo from the French by disbursing one hundred pounds' worth of presents.[101] He also wrangled a commission to lead an attack on the French at Mobile—this he declared was an urgent matter, for it must be done before a peace in Europe between the French and English would forbid an assault.[102] After conferring with Governor Johnson, the Carolina assembly agreed to raise eighty men, twenty of whom would be traders serving under Welch. Thomas Nairne would command the expedition. The soldiers would receive five pounds for enlisting and fifteen pounds after taking Mobile, and all would divide the plunder equally. (Officers would receive significantly higher pay.) The Commons House, however, directed that before Mobile was attacked, the troops should first try to bring the Choctaw and Yazoo into an alliance.[103] Although the expedition was not sent immediately,[104] the English had shifted their focus from Florida to the Mississippi; from the Spanish to the French; from the Apalachee to the Choctaw.

In the space of five years, 1702–1706, the South had changed forever. Disease and an alliance of English and Indians had decimated Florida's aboriginal population. The Apalachee mission system had collapsed. The Timucua had been driven from their homes, with many enslaved. The Alabama and the French engaged in raid and counterraid, which drew in the Choctaw and the Chickasaw. Forced from their homes, many of the small nations of the Mississippi Valley migrated toward the Gulf of Mexico and French settlements around Mobile. The English had confined the Spanish in northern Florida to the environs of Saint Augustine and Pensacola; they and their allies now raided for Indians to enslave to the tip of the Florida peninsula. The French and Spanish had countered with their own invasion of Carolina. In its aftermath, the English set their eyes on conquering Mobile. In the entire South, no one was immune nor could remain isolated from the European competition, and all Amerindians had to contend with the English quest for slaves.

Thousands of Florida Indians lost their liberty, were removed forcibly from their homes, and were shipped to ports throughout the Atlantic world to spend their lives in slavery. The English and their allies decimated the lives of thousands of others in the Mississippi Valley. The slave trade affected individuals, groups, and empires. The English empire provided the engine that set the wheels in motion. It enticed Indians to go slaving with valuable goods and offers of alliance. Yet some began to worry that slaving deterred the English from their imperial goals and that the manner by which Indian affairs were conducted threatened the empire. Concern among the English arose because of a growing plantation system they had to protect; Indian neighbors had to be appeased, French and Spanish power checked. Voices within the empire called for a rationalization of Indian affairs, and many still hoped that Indians could be incorporated within society. After 1706, reformers in Carolina called for new Indian policies, greater government control of trade, and a reconsideration of the meaning of empire. England and Scotland were about to unite as one nation, and perhaps it was no accident that two Scots, John Stewart and Thomas Nairne, had a different understanding of the future of the British empire, and of Indians' relationship to it, than many of their English peers.

6

BRITISH IMPERIALISM AND INDIAN
WARFARE IN THE SOUTH
JOHN STEWART
AND THOMAS NAIRNE

T wo Scots, John Stewart and Thomas Nairne, played seminal roles in
South Carolina's relationship with southern Indians. Nairne, the more
famous of the two, helped frame and implement the colony's policies
toward Native Americans—he fills a prominent place in the story that un-
folds in subsequent chapters. Stewart, by contrast, remains an obscure figure,
yet he initiated South Carolina's contact with many southern Indians and
paved the way for British expansion and influence in the region.

Stewart was older than Nairne. The prime years of his interaction with
southern Indians began in 1690, whereas Nairne became active about fifteen
years later. The two men were neighbors in Port Royal. It is easy to picture
Stewart regaling the younger Nairne with stories of the three most fascinating years of his life, his time with the Creek and Chickasaw, and of sharing
his vast experience with Nairne, who followed Stewart in trading with the
Chickasaw and then becoming the chief architect in South Carolina's reform
of the Indian trade.[1] As members of the small group of Scots at Port Royal
who lived in sustained and intimate contact with the area's Amerindian
peoples, particularly the Yamasee, Stewart and Nairne had much in common.
Both were imperialists who contemplated the relationship of Indians to the
British empire. Both analyzed Indians' culture and character and compared

them to Europeans. Yet they viewed Native Americans from different vantage points. Whereas Nairne articulated a vision of Indians that reflected a large segment of public opinion in America and Europe, Stewart transcended many of the stereotypes of his contemporaries and better understood native cultures on their own terms. Both men possessed penetrating minds, but whereas Nairne exhibited the intellectual discipline to connect his vision of Indian societies to his political ideology and the problems faced by his own society, Stewart systematized little of what he found. In part, perhaps, Stewart realized that Indian cultures were not easily reduced to terms Europeans would readily understand, but Stewart's thoughts also lacked rigor in their organization.

A comparison of Stewart and Nairne enlarges our understanding of the British imperial mind-set in turn-of-the-century South Carolina. Specifically, it demonstrates how imperial views of some of the powerful Indian peoples of the South (particularly the Creek and Chickasaw) evolved from the point of first contact with South Carolina in the 1690s to a time just fifteen years later when these Indians and Europeans fought together to decimate the natives of Florida and the lower Mississippi Valley. These ideas of empire—and of Indians' relationship to England's empire—create a framework for understanding the events that climaxed with the Yamasee War in 1715. Stewart and Nairne were among the first to recognize the centrality of Indian affairs not only to South Carolina but to British fortunes in America. Both men believed that Indians held the balance of power in the New World and that the competition among European nations would likely be won by the nation that held the most influence among key Indian peoples.

As imperial strategists, Stewart and Nairne assessed Indian culture largely in terms of martial prowess and skills. They analyzed military strategies and tactics, comparing one native group to another. Their observations permit an understanding of not only the Europeans but the nature of warfare for southern Indians, including raiding, defense against invasion, concepts of bravery, and the function of torture. Only by exploring the cultural values and meaning of native warfare can we understand the meaning and consequences of Indian engagement in slaving and in European-initiated wars.

JOHN STEWART: FROM SCOTLAND TO CAROLINA

Our understanding of the southern frontier in the late seventeenth and early eighteenth centuries is shaped largely by particular kinds of records. Most of what is known about Indians and Indian-European interaction comes from government documents: letters and reports produced by government appointees, soldiers, and missionaries and sent to the authorities in the mother country. Some are quite lengthy, but few are sustained analyses of Indian societies south of Virginia. In the early eighteenth century the French carpenter André Pénicaut's account of Indians in the lower Mississippi Valley and land surveyor John Lawson's book *A New Voyage to Carolina,* on the Indians in North Carolina and northern South Carolina, offer rare extended discussions of aboriginal life.[2] Lawson's study provides details on the environment while analyzing Indian politics, diplomacy, and economy. This contrasts with Pénicaut's penchant for recording cultural practices, particularly religious rituals, gender roles, and leisure activities. John Stewart's recollections of Creek and Choctaw life in the 1690s and early 1700s differ from both by providing extensive information unavailable in any other contemporary source. His experiences shed light on several important areas of Indian life, especially warfare, but they also show how one immigrant to Carolina, albeit a unique one, entered the Indian trade (after failing to make his fortune in other areas).

If Stewart had not been so unusual we would know little or nothing about him. He sought fame and fortune in his own time but is now only a footnote in history. Most historians have ignored his unpublished letters because of his nearly illegible handwriting, his archaic use of words, his extravagant claims, and his tendency to hyperbole. His stories often appear fantastic, and his bloated sense of self-importance, especially evident in letters he wrote before his involvement in the Indian trade, have steered scholars away from him. Historian Verner W. Crane briefly noted his existence as an imperialist, but it is not clear that Crane read much of what Stewart wrote. Peter H. Wood, who did read a selection of Stewart's letters published in the *South Carolina Historical Magazine,* described this "extraordinary" man in a footnote as "a Scottish frontiersman possessed of boundless energy, supreme vanity, and an outrageously florid prose style."[3] Indeed, this Scot's style, his whole manner of living, had a bit of the outrageous about it.

In scouring the French colonial records, I came across three additional letters written by Stewart in the eighteenth century, as well as one in the British Colonial Office Records (the letter that Crane had consulted). The three French letters were captured by France during Queen Anne's War and have been ignored by scholars. These epistles are lengthy—one is well over ten thousand words—and they form the basis for much of the second half of this chapter's discussion of Indians. First, however, let us turn to Stewart.

John Stewart's great-grandfather was James V of Scotland (1512–1542), and his father was nephew and heir to Patrick Stewart, earl of Orkney. During the English Civil War, Stewart's family fell on hard times. In his later years, he blamed the Presbyterian "party" for his family's misfortunes, averring in a letter to the earl of Dartmouth that they had been "ruined by the Scots Covenanters 70 years ago [1642],"[4] but Stewart himself may have been a member of the Presbyterian party in the 1680s. He emigrated to Carolina with the Covenanters in 1684 and was close friends with William Dunlop, with whom he kept a correspondence after Dunlop returned to Scotland. Stewart's refusal to take the Test Oath imposed on Scots in 1681 also signified his alliance, if not membership, with the Covenanters.[5] Only when asking for a pension from Queen Anne's government in 1711 did he suddenly proclaim himself anti-Presbyterian and High Church Anglican, a position designed to elicit sympathy from a Tory queen and her High Church government. Nor would it have been odd for Stewart to change sides in the dangerous game that infused Scottish and English politics. Political fortunes in Stuart England and Scotland were in large measure tied to religion, to one's family's position before and during the English Revolution as well as during and after the Restoration. With the accession of William and Mary to the throne in 1689, support or opposition to the Scots pretender James III affected family fortunes well into the next century. There was no such thing as neutrality for families of substance. Estates were won and lost based on religious and political allegiances, the very thing that had led the Scots to South Carolina in the first place and had then allowed them to return home with the enthronement of William and Mary.[6]

Unlike Dunlop and Cardross, Stewart did not return to Scotland after the Spanish attacks on Stuart Town. He remained resolute in his desire to build an estate in Carolina. He had suffered heavy losses from a shipwreck near England and initially hoped to accrue capital by managing Scottish investments at Port Royal.[7] When the Spanish attacks dried up Scottish capital, Stewart looked elsewhere for money. He did not have Dunlop's prospects in Scotland and was in no hurry to return to his wife and children, in spite of his expressions of concern for their welfare. Men often left their families behind when emigrating to America. All the Scots at Port Royal had done so. While they built shelters and established moneymaking enterprises, their families stayed in Europe supported by kin. Emigrants sent money home and expected their families to follow when success was clear. Stewart, in contrast, had no intention of bringing his family. He was forced to look after their interests to maintain his reputation in Scotland, but when he finally lined his pockets with money he begged Dunlop to keep his wife ignorant: "pray let not my wife know that I am worth a groat, for as she ruined me before by her folly to leave her all I had, and beggar and starve myself, I am resolved to do so no more."[8]

Stewart would have returned to Scotland temporarily if he could have found a "public office" where he could earn his keep and save three hundred to four hundred pounds Scots (twenty-five to thirty-five pounds British sterling) yearly, but he intended to return to Carolina to live permanently.[9] As it did Dunlop, the colony bedeviled Stewart as a place with an infinite number of economic opportunities. He fomented numerous moneymaking schemes to take advantage of the colony's environment.[10] Carolina had much to offer the industrious man who had a bit of capital. Even "the most clownish and poorest planter," he intoned, "may justly hope for an Earl's estate." And Carolina's beauty! Stewart waxed eloquently on whether "Windsor [Palace] or St. James Gardens shows so much variety, delight and native fertility, even when advanced by all that art and wealth can do, as rude nature spontaneously put forth with us?"[11]

Stewart's schemes covered a tremendous array of economic enterprise. He composed numerous papers and wrote books not only on the production of silk, cotton, and rice but also on the management of cattle, hogs, sheep, goats, rabbits, gardens, orchards, arable land and pastureland, vineyards, hops, and vinegar, as well as on the production of mead, bear ale, spruce beer, Madeira grapes, "swamp lands caviar," lime, four kinds of gum, turpentine, resin, treacle (both white and red), China turmeric, two kinds of snakeroot, five kinds of dye, hemp, "innumerable drugs," and a variety of fruits, grasses, and grains. He based his essays on experience and observation from his worldly travels, and many of his suggestions were tried to good effect in Carolina. Stewart's proposals for improvements in rice production arose from observations he made while in Russia; Governor Colleton earned great profits by following his instructions for the cultivation of rice and cotton.[12] Stewart also claimed to have introduced to Carolina peas, straw, rooks, and rabbits and he convinced others to use rice instead of Indian corn as a cheaper food source for slaves.[13]

Stewart's economic and intellectual interests extended beyond agriculture. In Carolina, he discovered mines and quarries for everything from isinglass (mirrors) to iron. He wrote prospective laws for England to promote colonial manufacturing and made so many legislative proposals that he expected it would take Britain a hundred years to get around to them all.[14] His knowledge was based on experience and reading, for his formal education had not advanced beyond grammar school. He read widely, particularly on government and law, and displayed enough learning and attention to detail that the proprietors chose him to conduct a comparison of the four constitutions they had produced for the colony, for which he received a reward of a thousand acres.[15]

Stewart's interests in politics went beyond the theoretical. He jumped into Carolina's political disputes with relish. From his pen we have personal portraits of many of the colony's leading men. He took pleasure in judging their talents and exposing their foibles. His description of elite posturing in Charles Town of the 1690s bears resemblance to the escapades Alexandre Dumas described in France in *The Three Musketeers*. Stewart prided himself on his wit and his skills with the cutlass. He cavalierly engaged his peers in verbal sparring, embarrassed those who lacked artifice, and took great pleasure in exposing hypocrisy. Those who took insult at his behavior he readily challenged or accepted a challenge to a duel. Scholars who look to the American Revolution for the origins of dueling and the code of honor in the South have not read Stewart's letters, which describe men calling each other out to redress real and perceived insults. In this way, the Charles Town of 1690 differed little from that of 1830.[16]

Stewart became enmeshed in the political machinations for control of the colony. His derring-do, experiences, political acumen, and general knowledge made him a valuable ally to the local elite, to which he had pretensions by birth and talent but not estate. Stewart's letters make clear that the lines between the colony's factions were not always strictly drawn: there were men whose support could be won or lost, negotiations to be made, alliances to be formed. New factors of politics, economy, and personality constantly entered the fray, personal enmities splintered factions, and the threat of violence was constant. Carolina politics was a high stakes game and the players were rather childish.[17] Yet Carolina did not differ so much from the other colonies, for factionalism and violence surfaced at this time in New York, Maryland, Massachusetts, and elsewhere.[18]

Stewart sided with Governor James Colleton, whose brother, Proprietor Peter Colleton, he held in high regard, but he chafed from the misuse he felt at the governor's hands. Stewart was miserable that his schemes for wealth made others, including Colleton, rich but not himself. Without capital he could do little to amend the situation. No capital meant no labor, and labor was the key to wealth. In 1690, Stewart hit upon the aforementioned scheme of contracting Yamasee laborers to work on the plantations, but Colleton, he wrote, "almost broke my heart" by stealing the idea for himself.[19] Stewart rued that Colleton's brother John was not governor, for then "I should quickly have a gallant estate. . . . could I ever [have] dreamed that he would snatch from me my darling projection and pregnant hope?" Colleton had the gumption to claim that "he thought on the project long before I discoursed it!" Stewart was not in a position to argue, and he retained hopes of obtaining a one-sixth interest in the agreement—perhaps the governor continued to lead him on, wary of losing Stewart's support.[20] In this instance, Stewart did well to hold his tongue, for he soon benefited from partnership with the governor.

Before Colleton was removed from office, his opponents, after rendering martial law "useless," approached the governor about opening a trade with the Cherokee. James Moore had gone to the Cherokee some time in 1689 or 1690. He realized little profit but wished to return with the governor's commission and fifty or sixty men.[21] Moore offered Colleton, who had legal control over the trade in the name of the proprietors, half of the profits, and said that the governor would not have to put "in any stock or deed of adventure." Stewart warned Colleton of "the people's inclinations" against the arrangement, but the compact was already "signed and sealed." According to Stewart, the common people resented Moore's "exemption from military obedience" and feared that his taking "60 white men" to trade for "private interests" would leave South Carolina nearly defenseless against the Spanish. (The colony was dangerously short of gunpowder, and the expedition was bound to remove a significant portion of what little remained.)[22] Colleton replied that his position was too weak to stop his enemies, but finally he acquiesced, telling Moore that he could not leave until the war ended. Moore ignored Colleton's order and left with fifty men.[23]

Disregarding the proprietors' monopoly and opening trade with distant Indians was like taking the finger out of the dike. It broadened Carolina's focus from a north-south axis, with Carolina north and Florida south, adding in southwest-northeast and west-east axes. The east-west axis connected the Cherokee to Carolina and developed slowly, for colonists judged Cherokee to be poor hunters, less interested in European goods than other Indians, and apparently less inclined to enslave their neighbors (though this later changed).[24] Moreover, the Carolinians faced competition with the Virginians for Cherokee trade, making this axis less important and less traveled than the one to the southwest that developed with the groups forming the Lower Creek. The line of trade was subsequently pushed west to the Upper Creek and then swept northwest to the Chickasaw. This axis of trade, more than any other, spread English influence through the South.

The expanding trade had already led the Lower Creek to begin moving some of their towns north to the Oconee River and other spots in northwest Georgia, where they would be nearer the English and their own supply of deer to hunt, process, and exchange. George Smith, a Carolina Scot who had arrived with the Covenanters as a prisoner-servant, began the process of closer alliance when he brought 2,800 dressed skins and "the Coweta and Cusheda

King" to Carolina, for which he received a reward of more than 400 dressed deerskins and thirty-six pounds.[25] The leaders of these two important Lower Creek towns were "loaded with presents" and agreed to desert "Spanish protection" and settle "10 days journey nearer us to enjoy the English freer protection."[26]

Impressed with Smith's trip and desiring skins for himself, Stewart vowed to return home if he could "master" eighty pounds' worth "of skins to carry with me."[27] Without capital, Stewart turned to the only man who had the authority and the capital to sponsor his proposed adventure to the Indians: Governor Colleton, the same man who had coopted his last moneymaking scheme.[28]

Colleton could not resist the chance for profits. Sometime during the summer of 1690, Stewart, "reduced to one single ryal," was employed to go "a Indian trading for Governor Colleton."[29] But before doing so, Colleton forced Stewart to go as supercargo on a vessel to Jamaica. The governor apparently liked to wring whatever advantage he could from whomever he could. On Stewart's return, Colleton charged him "to cross the mountains to go a trading to the Chickasaw." He would lead three caravans of goods, receiving a fifth of what he brought home after deduction of costs on one caravan and 2 percent of the other caravans, as well as the title of "Supervisor or Indian factor." Stewart thought the arrangement "a poor purchase for so hazardous, long, tedious and difficult a journey . . . but what shall I do without employment or stock?" He hoped, however, to learn the Indian trade, and the Indians' "Lingua," so that he could return on his own account. Moreover, there was the adventure. The "prompting motive," he declared, was "to discover where never Briton yet went." Ever the dreamer, Stewart also thought that the Jamaica and Chickasaw voyages would "put me in circumstances to go to Moldavia to procure goods that will make a rich staple here at the charge of grain."[30] Whatever his dreams, Stewart had before him the more mundane and difficult task of establishing a trade hundreds of miles away among unfamiliar peoples. Smith's visit to the Lower Creek apparently opened the door for Stewart, making the task a bit easier, but as he would find out, nothing could prepare him for what lay ahead. He would have to rely on his wits, his goods, and the hospitality of his Indian hosts.

For two years Stewart lived with the Cuseeta, a Lower Creek group "whose language I understand and can speak as well as that of the Yamasee and somewhat of the Savannah tongue." After these two years in service of the governor, "I traded another year for myself with the Talabusies, Canagies, Milawilaes and Chekesues, who are composed of 39 towns and kings and speak 3 several languages." Stewart claimed to be the first white man among them and that he had "opened a large trade thereby to Carolina." Of the above-mentioned groups, the Talabusies refers to the Alabama, later an Upper Creek people, the Conagies refers to Conaliga, which Woodward identified as an Upper Creek town,[31] the Milawilaes are harder to identify but were evidently another Upper Creek town, and Chekesues refers to the Chickasaw.

Stewart was very likely the first Carolinian to trade among the Chickasaw. Historians' claims that this trade was opened by Thomas Welch in 1698 is dubious, given the evidence found by the French in the 1670s of English traders in the area, who probably came from Virginia. There is no reason to doubt Stewart's claim of trading in the Chickasaw towns (six years before Welch), which he first mentioned in a letter of 1693 to Dunlop in Scotland (to whom he had no reason to lie about the matter). He computed the distance to the Chickasaw as 930 miles from Carolina, which is a good estimation given the roundabout route he had taken via the Lower and then Upper Creek settlements.[32] Certainly he understood their location, which he described "as far west of the Cherokee," who themselves lived "west of the Savannah."[33]

Stewart's three-year trading voyage enabled him to leave "Carolina without one farthing of debt" and in possession of two hundred pounds sterling in goods, as well as a stock he "left behind in partnership with Coll. Blake."[34] By his own account, he departed something of a hero. Three years among the Indians had allowed him to avoid the political turmoil of the colony, which then employed him to go to London to explain to the lords proprietors Carolina's problems with Governors Sothell and Ludwell. Ever scheming to enlarge his estate, Stewart wrote to Dunlop to find investors willing to venture five hundred or a thousand pounds sterling on goods for Indians and planters. He expected then to receive at least a 50 percent profit in skins and furs, but he effusively dangled the possibility of 100, "perhaps 200 per cent" profit. He assured Dunlop that even for investors of fifty or one hundred pounds he would "be as careful and faithful" as if the investment were one thousand pounds. Interestingly, Stewart had no intention of going to Scotland—he would stay five or six weeks in London, "and then return, God willing, for Carolina again."

Little is known of Stewart's affairs after 1693. He returned to Carolina, where he lived for at least another twenty years. According to his later letters, he went to Florida on one of the Carolina expeditions between 1702 and 1704. He also participated in an attack against the Choctaw in 1706. But he does not seem to have returned to the Indian trade, for his name does not appear as a trader in the colony's records. This is not hard to understand, for being a trader was only a means to an end. Stewart wanted to be a landowner, a gentleman with a landed estate; this was an esteemed position of honor in the British Isles and in the colonies. When he analyzed the various fundamental constitutions in expectation of receiving land, he volunteered "a plot of land rent free for ever is that which poor I gape for."[35] The Indian trade was a way to accumulate capital to purchase laborers and the goods needed to develop his land. It also brought a measure of status. When George Smith, who had arrived with the Covenanters as a transported prisoner, returned from trading with the Lower Creek, Stewart reported that even this humble man "dines when here with the Governor."[36]

THOMAS NAIRNE: A WHIG'S VIEW OF CAROLINA

Having achieved an estate and a higher status, Stewart settled down to the life of the country gentleman. In this way, Stewart's life contrasts with Thomas Nairne and other Indian traders of the Port Royal area. These men built estates through the Indian trade but actively continued as traders after becoming slave-owning planters. Indian affairs were an indelible part of their lives. Nairne, for instance, devoted his last decade to Indian relations in a variety of capacities. He helped write many of the laws that governed Carolina's Indian trade, served as the colony's agent governing the traders, formulated plans for and participated in military expeditions with and against southern Indians, researched and wrote about native peoples, and lobbied various groups in England to educate them on Indian affairs and gain support for his policies. In South Carolina, Nairne was held in high regard for his experiences on slaving raids and his understanding of Indians. After Moore's onslaught against the Apalachee in 1704, Nairne led a force of Indians into central Florida to capture more slaves.[37] Afterward Nairne bragged how "we the Indians and colonists have these past two years been entirely knifing all the Indian towns in Florida."[38] But profit was not his sole motive. Nairne was a warrior for the empire, and he saw slaving expeditions as a tool for imperial growth. He drew up plans and maps for imperial expansion through the South, advocated a militant offensive posture against the French, and sought to bring all of the region's Indians into the Carolina orbit. More than anyone else, he wished to improve relations with Carolina's Indian allies by reforming the Indian trade. While forging stronger bonds with native peoples in amity with the government, he also advocated harmonious relations among various groups within the colony. And although he was a strong supporter of the Anglican Church and worked to build churches in every parish, he opposed the bigotry of the Anglican party against Dissenters, from whom he derived political support.

Nairne expressed much of his philosophy about colonization and empire in a pamphlet he wrote in 1710 to attract Swiss settlers to Carolina. He (and others) considered Protestant Swiss soldiers to be the perfect colonists, and many emigrated to the Carolinas.[39] Famous for their martial skills, they were seen as especially suitable for settling on a dangerous frontier, where they would need to be soldier-farmers. South Carolina later adopted a policy of financing the emigration of soldier-farmers to settle frontier communities, and James Oglethorpe used the same strategy in establishing Scots Highlanders in southern Georgia.

Nairne's pamphlet, *A Letter from South Carolina . . . ,* reflected on his career as a soldier, though as a propagandist he claimed to be Swiss when he was actually Scots. The soldier, he asserted, had the noblest profession, as long as he followed it to protect free people, "destroy monsters, assist the Impotent, redress Injuries, oppose Tyranny, and root out Oppression from the face of the Earth." He chided those who followed war as a trade, the very group of Swiss mercenaries to whom he appealed, and derided those who would devote their children to the military life as soon as they were born, a practice common in Switzerland, the Germanys, and other parts of Europe. Nairne did not expect and perhaps did not want to attract the lifelong mercenary, but he wanted to encourage emigration of those who had tired of their profession and wished, as he had done, to take up planting. The colony needed settlers adept in the martial arts, given the military situation of Carolina and the experience of his fellow Scots at Port Royal. In a detailed discussion of the colony, in which he described how to manufacture tar and pitch, listed the expenses needed to settle both small and large plantations, and provided information on the climate, land, people, and medical condition of the colony, Nairne also assessed the colony's government and military situation. Expounding on government was not unusual in pamphlets of this sort, but Nairne put his own spin on Carolina. Discussion of the military situation was unusual: who wanted to frighten off prospective settlers? Yet Nairne's Swiss audience would of course want to know what they were getting into before arriving, and misleading mercenaries about their prospects could have grave consequences.[40]

Nairne evinced Whiggish views of government in his emphasis on the role of the Commons House in Carolina. The assembly, he assured his readers, not only imitated but "claim[ed] all the Powers, Privileges, and Immunities, which the House of Commons have in Great Britain." In particular, "'tis a received Opinion among them, that the Power of appointing, examining, censuring, and displacing those who have the Public Money in their Hands, is much better lodged in the House of Commons, who have so great an Interest in the Colony, than in the Hands of any Governour, for Reasons generally known in America." This Whiggish view could have been stated as easily in 1776 as in 1710. It clearly illustrates the Whig perception that colonial assemblies were the strongest safeguards of local interests and that appointed governors did not always have local interests at heart, nor might they be expected to because they represented outside interests, the Crown's or the proprietors'. Nairne was no revolutionary and gave the governor his due, noting the governor's supreme power over military affairs, his partnership in executive power with the council, and his veto over legislation. The Whigs in Britain and in America both wished a shared governance between the assemblies and the executive, whereas the Tories emphasized executive rule.

For Nairne, the success of South Carolina was dependent on its place within the empire, and his place was also dependent on the success of the empire. The Act of Union (1707) between England and Scotland promised that he, a Scot, would be treated equally with his English countrymen. This perception was crucial. In 1706 Governor Nathaniel Johnson had opposed Nairne's election to the assembly, alleging that "*Scots* had been declared Aliens, by an Act made a Year ago in *England*." A year later Johnson could no longer make that claim.[41] The Act of Union invested Scots like Nairne with a near holy respect for Great Britain. They felt a responsibility to nurture the empire to which they now possessed full access, which included the opportunity for advancement. Nairne understood the importance of good men stepping forward to make sure that Carolina forged ahead—that the greatest enemies to his imperial vision might not have been external, but internal. The Whiggish Nairne had no qualms about trying to crush obstructive leaders (like Governor Johnson) when the good of the colony and the empire was at stake.[42]

In his pamphlet for the Swiss, however, Nairne focused on South Carolina's external threats. He noted the ever-weakening position of the Spanish in Florida. As a result of "several foreign Expeditions; one against St. Augustine . . . and others against the Spaniards and Indians of Apalachia[,] . . . . our Forces entirely broke and ruined the Strength of the Spaniards in Florida, destroyed the whole Country, burnt the Towns, brought all the Indians, who were not killed or made Slaves, into our Territories, so that there remains not now, so much as one Village with ten Houses in it, in all Florida" that is not protected "by the Guns of their Castle of St. Augustine." Nairne exaggerated Carolina's success, but not by much. He assured the Swiss that Carolina's Indian allies continually pestered what remained of Spanish power, which was now rendered incapable of harming the colony. Moreover, the training of the colony's Indian allies "in the Use of Arms, and Knowledge of War" was a "great Service to us, in case of any Invasion from an Enemy: . . . by drawing to our Side, or destroying, all the [hostile] Indians, within 700 Miles of Charlestown." No European power could "settle on that coast, otherwise than as subjects to the Crown of Great Britain." Not that the colony had to rely completely on Indians for defense. All males from sixteen to sixty served in the militia, and no one thought himself "too good to be a soldier." All were "versed in Arms, from the Governour to the meanest soldier," since the people "think no body so fit to defend their Properties as themselves." As a "free People," they believed in trusting with arms "those who have the greatest Interest." Nevertheless, their militia enrolled "a considerable Number of active, able, Negro Slaves." In time of invasion, these slaves received freedom if they killed an enemy, the public compensating their owner for manumission. Thus, the colony's strong defense owed to the combination of "Indians with whom we are in Friendship," who answer every alarm under the leadership of colonial officers, "there being some thousands" of Indians "who are hardy, active, and good Marksmen, excellent at an Ambuscade, and who are brought together with little or no Charge," citizen-soldiers like himself, and slaves. The colony needed "no regular Troops . . . [and] desire none." The "Planter who keeps his Body fit for service, by Action, and a regular Life, is doubtless a better Soldier, upon Occasion, than a Company of raw Fellows raised in England."[43]

Nairne's vision of Carolina as an important and growing appendage of the British empire, peopled by citizen-soldiers, assisted by helpful Indians, open-armed to Protestant Europeans who could easily obtain naturalization by taking an oath of allegiance, depicted a place where Europeans could begin life anew with free land to cultivate and economic opportunity unavailable in the Old World; where all could enjoy the wise and generous governance of local laws and a beneficent monarchy; where hard work was rewarded by "no Taxes" and a fertile landscape. In Carolina, "the greatest Drudgeries" were reserved for the slaves, promising a prosperous future for all Europeans, even European servants, who upon the expiration of their term of servitude were "as much entitled to the Privileges of the Country, as any other Inhabitants whatsoever." The colony had everything going for it—good government, a rich environment, and a productive citizenry.[44] To Nairne, only the shortsighted men who abused the public trust and put their self-interest above the community threatened the idyll.

Nairne and Stewart shared a belief in a glorious imperial future for the British peoples. Nairne's vision was the more fully realized, ideological, and typical of other Euro-Carolinians. Stewart's vision was more global, diffuse and enmeshed in a wealth of detail that few could comprehend. Both articulated their views at the end of the first decade and the beginning of the second decade of the eighteenth century. By that time, Stewart was out of politics and largely expressed his views in long, rambling letters to the foremost personages of the British empire; but he probably had little influence there or in South Carolina. In contrast, Nairne was a leading man in the colony; he published some of his writings, and he would visit England, where his knowledge of colonial and Indian affairs made a favorable impression. Whereas Stewart's views would have appeared eclectic and eccentric to his contemporaries, Nairne, as a reformer, presented ideas of Indians and empire that reflected much of what many other Europeans already thought. His policies and views thus seemed reasonable and logical to his contemporaries.

THOMAS NAIRNE:
A WHIG'S VIEW OF SOUTHERN INDIANS

In the spring of 1708, Nairne visited the Choctaw and Chickasaw on an official visit for South Carolina. Nairne was charged with delivering presents to wean the Choctaw from their French alliance and to prevent the Chickasaw from moving closer to the French. He kept a journal of his trip, a valuable glimpse of Amerindian life in the region, but one that reveals even more about Nairne's views of Indians' value and their potential relationship to the British empire. His journal focuses on the Chickasaw, whom Nairne greatly admired—many Europeans, in fact, lauded them above other Indians. The Chickasaw, like most other southern Indians, lived in a matrilineal society in which clan identity descended through the mother. Marriages between two members of the same clan were considered incestuous, so one's father was always of another clan. As a result, the father played little role in the raising of the children, which was left to the mother and the mother's brothers. Succession was chiefly to one's nephew rather than one's son.[45] Nairne found that labor was sharply divided between men and women, as among the Savannah, but distinct from practices among many of the Creek, where men did some agricultural work. The Chickasaw women planted and hoed the fields, whereas the men hunted. Unlike the Ochese (the Lower Creek), according to Nairne, the men never assisted their wives in the fields nor helped them gather wood for the fire. Historians have noted that English colonists condemned Native Americans for their reversal of European gender roles—in which women rather than men worked the fields—but Nairne seems to have had more respect for the Chickasaw than the Creek because the Chickasaw maintained sharper divisions between male and female work roles. Nairne also noted without criticism that the Chickasaw men took ten or twelve women with them to war and that the women sang during engagements. When the men succeeded, these women "praise[d] them highly," but if they retreated, the women serenaded them with reproaches.[46] (The French also noted the presence of female singers during battle.)[47] The women had not fought—that was man's work—but they had spurred the men on and judged their performance.[48] It was one thing for women to assess bravery, however, and quite another for females to hold political power over men. Nairne thus expressed no disapproval of the Chickasaw convention that mothers-in-law should not converse with sons-in-law, and he duly noted that this situation compared favorably to the Talapoosa (the Upper Creek), among whom mothers-in-law "rule all the family." Nairne also saw fit to report that the Chickasaw made fun of this tradition among the Creek; they ridiculed Chickasaw men who married Creek women and adopted Creek gender roles and would tease these husbands: "have you been obedient to your wife and mother in Law this morning. Pray go carry home some wood [or] they'll be out of humor."[49]

The Chickasaw were superior in Nairne's eyes for other reasons, too. Nairne believed that the Chickasaw were the aristocrats of southern Indians. He respected the sexual practices of Chickasaw women because the women did not sleep with the traders.[50] Should an English trader "tempt the virtue of a young Chicasaw lady with a present, they usually reject it, with contempt, what (say they)[,] you think you're among the Ochesses now, how brutal a proposal you make."[51] In comparing them to the Tallapoosa, he declared Chickasaw to be "as men of Quality among us are to the peasants, [they] look much more brisk, airy and full of life and though in the same garb yet their mien is very distinguishing. Add to that both sexes of the Chickasaw are proper handsome people, exceeding the others," though not as "Civilized, quiet and good Natured." The Chickasaw were less polite and complacent than the Ochese but were more "morose and far less addicted to dancing[,] mirth and gallantry."[52] A prideful people, they refused to be burdeners for the Europeans—Thomas Welch had brought along on the trip twenty-five Apalachee burdeners, a people who seemed willing to fill this role, but the Apalachee had little choice, given their subservient relationship to South Carolina.[53]

The Chickasaw, according to Nairne, were of a "Whiggish opinion that the Duties of kings and people are reciprocal that, if [their chief] fails in his they've sufficient cause to neglect theirs."[54] The civil authority of the chiefs was limited to promoting "peace and quiet, and to be a Counterpoise to the fury of the Warriors." The chief made sure that the women planted enough corn for the nation and oversaw other domestic matters, but he had no military power. This power lay in the hands of the military chiefs, for whom the Chickasaw held great respect.[55] Other southern peoples also divided authority between civil and military leaders.[56]

Nairne displayed his greatest respect for the Chickasaw in the arts of war and hunting. As "excellent foresters, they never missed supplying the Camp with meat enough," and they shared with all. The Chickasaw were proud of their hunting skills. When they returned from the hunt, "they threw down" what they had killed for Nairne and his men.[57] Traveling with the Chickasaw was slow, for everywhere they went, they hunted. On the trip, "their whole discourse is, here's excellent ground for bears or Turkeys, in this canepiece we shall surely meet with Buffaloes, and it would in their opinion be perfect folly to pass by without hunting them."[58] Nairne accompanied the Chickasaw on a deer hunt and witnessed a manner of cornering deer that was common in forested areas of North America. The Indians would light a ring of fire four or five miles in circumference. Three or four hours later the hunters closed in on the deer, which were pushed to the middle, and usually captured seven to ten in the circle.[59]

As hunters and warriors, the Chickasaw excelled as slave catchers. Nairne recognized that the Chickasaw location led them to pursue slaving because "the difficulty of carriage makes their trade [in skins] of less Value." Human captives were easier to move and brought much more in the way of trade goods and with less labor than animal hides. Capturing slaves became a mark of prowess among them, while also bringing "them a whole Estate at once." In exchange for one slave, they received "a gun, ammunition, horse, hatchet, and a suit of Clothes."[60] Nairne exaggerated the compensation for captives because horses sometimes had higher value than slaves. Interestingly enough, Nairne derided the Chickasaw chief for participating in slave catching. As a civil authority, the chief, according to Nairne, should not join in the exploits of the warriors. Nairne believed that the chief lost his people's respect for slaving.[61] Here Nairne was projecting his own political beliefs on the Chickasaw. He had criticized Governor Johnson for profiting from the Indian trade, and he now criticized the Chickasaw civil leader for the same.[62]

INDIAN WARFARE: CULTURE,
GEOPOLITICS, AND EUROPEAN PERCEPTIONS

The Chickasaw deserved their reputation as excellent soldiers. We do not know the extent of that reputation and their skills before the European arrival, but members of Hernando de Soto's entrada in the 1540s experienced

Chickasaw military prowess firsthand, much to the Spaniards' dismay. The Chickasaw reputation grew as they began enslaving their neighbors for sale to the English in the last quarter of the seventeenth century. Slaving raids made them the scourge of the Mississippi, and their fame (or infamy) continued to grow in succeeding decades. Yet the Chickasaw were never as powerful as their admirers and victims portrayed. Europeans described them often as the most powerful nation in the region and sometimes as the most powerful on the continent. These observers never considered the limitations of Chickasaw power. The Chickasaw wreaked havoc on the small tribes of the lower Mississippi and terrorized the Choctaw, but their numbers ensured that they could never extend dominance over as large a region as the Iroquois had to the north or the Creek Confederacy would to the south. The Chickasaw did not have the people to conduct large-scale offensive operations without help from Europeans or more populous tribes, and their distance from the French and English, while allowing them some security from attack from these two, also left them vulnerable to supply shortages. They faced periodic raids from the Iroquois, which continued despite Nairne's claim that the English arming of the Chickasaw had ended these attacks. The Chickasaw also faced attacks from the northwest by the Illinois. Nairne criticized the Illinois as cowardly Indians who "dare not fight or attempt Towns as our allies do, but then are the slyest and most patient men stealers of the World, for they skulk close by the Towns until they have done some Murder, and fly off with all speed." It was peculiar for Nairne to criticize the Illinois in these terms, when this description also fits the Chickasaw. The Chickasaw were "men stealers" who used stealth to achieve their ends. They conducted lightening raids against small villages and attacked on the periphery of Choctaw power. They did not, and could not, conquer the Choctaw, but they kept the Choctaw on their heels by raiding for slaves. If the Chickasaw did have a military weakness compared to the Illinois and others, according to Nairne, it was that they were "no Water people," for they "know nothing what belongs to Canoes."[63] They compensated for this by a superb defense of their towns, which they situated in locales that were difficult to access in southwestern Tennessee and northern Mississippi. Sophisticated defensive works prevented enemies from penetrating to the core of Chickasaw power. The Chickasaw could not conquer the populous confederacies, but neither could the confederacies or the French conquer them, despite France's several attempts in ensuing decades.

The Choctaw were a greater threat to the Chickasaw than the Illinois and the Iroquois. They outnumbered the Chickasaw by four or perhaps five times. French alliance with the Choctaw turned the tide against the Chickasaw, who hoped for peace with the Choctaw. The Choctaw refused. They would not forgive the Chickasaw for the capture and enslavement of their people. Even when the slaving raids declined after the Yamasee War, the Choctaw-Chickasaw dispute continued, shaping the contours of life for both into the 1750s.

Kinship ties did not prevent wars between towns or confederacies, but they created a situation where positive relations could be maintained within the cycles of vengeance that kept peoples at war with one another. Warfare was an obligation; a necessity; a burning desire to acquit oneself honorably, revenge wrongs, and achieve glory. The Choctaw and the Chickasaw considered themselves originally to have been one people who had migrated from west of the Mississippi, with the Chickasaw moving north after crossing that river and the Choctaw migrating south.[64] We have no knowledge of why or when they began to war with each other, but despite the endemic warfare between them, they socialized with one another and had continuous contact, usually at certain villages where relations and friends could meet. Socializing between peoples at war was certainly not foreign in European history, nor was it in the American South, as French, Spanish, and English all maintained contacts, at least for trade both between and during conflicts. The contacts between Choctaw and Chickasaw, however, seem more personal and probably did not center on the exchange of goods. The ties of Choctaw and Chickasaw went beyond "ethnicity." Clan membership was more important, to many, at particular times than their town or confederacy identity. Towns and confederacies formed and re-formed, but clan membership devolved upon the individual at birth and never changed. Southern Indians belonged to such clans as bear, eagle, and turkey. When visiting other peoples, an Indian was welcomed by clan members as a "kinsman even though the 2 nations have wars together."[65]

From the time of first European contact with American Indians, Europeans had viewed Native Americans as peculiarly warlike people. Europeans were fascinated and terrorized by aspects of warfare they associated with Indians, including raids, scalping, torture, giving captives no quarter, and attacking in winter.[66] Europeans associated these forms of warfare with those of their ancestors, as characteristics of "primitive" peoples for whom warfare was sport or the product of feuds. The Europeans characterized their own warfare as noble and civilized; when fought between Christians it was viewed as a contest among gentlemen, albeit one fought by the lower classes. Their purpose in war was to serve monarch, lord, and country and attain honor (and plunder) for themselves. When Europeans fought with non-Christians, however, they deemed warfare a holy crusade. With the Reformation, Catholics and Protestants combined the idea of crusade for "true" Christianity with the concept of "noble" warfare. Non-Christians remained outside the "noble" ideal but could become allies against false Christians. Indians, in the European view, could have, at best, only a primitive nobility elevated by alliance with Europeans. Some Europeans recognized characteristics in Indian fighting that reflected their own martial values: they perceived both honor and courage in Indian warriors. The ends of Indian fighting, however, except when in defense of home and family, could never be seen by Europeans as noble, because Indians could fight only for false gods and had no "state" to serve; they had mere "tribal" animosities that made little sense to Europeans except as blood feuds perhaps akin to the famous family feuds of the Highland Scots.

Europeans were correct in their perception of cycles of vengeance between Indian groups that took on a life of their own in lasting for decades. Europeans also correctly perceived that not all Indians were alike in their martial qualities, though the qualities they applauded were the ones that seemed European, and they condemned those that appeared alien.

Too often people assess groups as "warlike" as if it were an ethnically genetic property. Military skills, however, are not biological and are only secondarily cultural. Groups develop martial skills to suit their geopolitical circumstances. Failure to adopt appropriate skills to defend one's group in a particular locale can lead to incorporation by more skilled groups and the end of a group's existence. Given a group's location and relations with neighbors, groups will develop offensive capabilities that allow them to extend their borders and conquer others. But the initial development must be defensive, to protect against outsiders. Just as societies define themselves as cultural units in relation to their neighbors, they also develop martial skills in the context of their neighbors' military capabilities.

Although warfare was important to southern native peoples, and played an important role in their intergroup relations, these were not military cultures. Warfare was but one factor in a cultural matrix, and the fact that most southern native peoples separated their civil leadership from their military leadership, granting military leaders power only in times of war, shows that the pursuit of war had not assumed control over their societies. Warfare was ritualized, with warriors seeking omens to guide when to fight and then following specific ceremonies to prepare for battle. Young men were trained to military tasks from an early age.[67] Making weapons, shooting, hiding, and tracking were finely honed skills.[68] In the period before contact with Europeans, the complex chiefdoms probably bore much similarity to the states that existed in many parts of the world, where military force played a significant role in external relations and in internal control over the populace. The dominant group in a chiefdom probably had better military organizational skills than the subservient groups, though political skills could have been just as important for maintaining a supreme chief's power. That is to say, a supreme chief's own group did not have to be the most militarily capable in the chiefdom, but he had to be able to unite enough groups to keep potential recalcitrants in line.

In the proto– and post–European contact periods, when the chiefdoms broke down, warfare appears to have become more limited. We might call this the tribal period, when group identities underwent great flux; the splintering of chiefdoms led to decentralization of authority and the collapse of political and administrative structures. The art of personal warrior skills persisted in the newly formed "tribes" for defense of home and town and as an extension of earlier cultural characteristics. But the fluidity of group identities, the lack of strong central leadership, and the impact of decimating diseases altered the nature of violent conflicts between peoples. From the Mississippi to the Atlantic, towns replaced chiefdoms as the most significant political unit, and these generally could not conquer neighbors until they formed or joined confederacies. As stability reemerged in group structures, preexisting cultural factors, location, population, and other geopolitical factors again combined to affect the military characteristics of each group. The Chickasaw, for instance, had developed excellent military skills by the protocontact period, which contributed to their strength in the postcontact period.

In the South, the formation of confederations of towns among such peoples as the Creek, Cherokee, Choctaw, Catawba, and others was a defensive strategy rather than an offensive one. Each confederacy had to contend with strong outside forces such as the Spanish, the Westo, the Chickasaw, and the English, and the only way to do so was through alliance. All of the southern Indian groups shared particular military characteristics that stemmed from their similar cultural history, but they varied one from the next in their military capabilities, tactics, strategies, and skills. To a large degree, the differences evident in the postcontact period resulted from geopolitical circumstances. The groups considered "warlike" by their neighbors, the Chickasaw, Westo, Yamasee, Creek and Savannah, all lived in peculiar situations that forced them to become militarily aggressive toward others. The Westo, as we have seen, had been forced from the North, then from Virginia, and were intent on settling along the Savannah. The Yamasee had tried to protect themselves from the Westo by entering the mission system, only to find no safety there. They became "warlike" when they reemerged on the Savannah River in an enlarged confederacy determined to protect itself against hostile outside forces and willing to take the offensive to accomplish their ends. The Creek, too, formed as a defensive response to the pressures placed on them by the Westo to the north, the Spanish and Apalachee to the southeast, and the Choctaw to the west.[69] The Chickasaw may have been in the most difficult position of all. Although their towns were secure from attack, they faced enemies in all directions whenever they emerged to hunt. The Illinois and the Arkansas from the north and northwest,[70] the Choctaw and Creek from the south and southeast, and, periodically, Iroquois from the northeast and other groups from the lower Mississippi Valley to the south surrounded the Chickasaw. The Savannah were more like the Westo than the Chickasaw, for they, too, were refugees who actively sought new lands and alliances and to do so became militarily aggressive toward others.

Being militarily aggressive toward one's neighbors should not necessarily be equated with military skill, an equation that both Europeans and Indians often made. The Choctaw and Cherokee, the two largest confederacies of Southern Indians, both of whom were considered militarily inferior to many of their neighbors, were as skillful as any other group in the South. Both the Cherokee and the Choctaw enjoyed geographical locations that were hard for their enemies to reach. They developed military strategies based on their location and had no need to conduct the kinds of offensive operations that the Chickasaw and Creek felt were necessary for security.[71] The Choctaw and Cherokee could overwhelm their enemies through their numbers, but their location encouraged them to turn inward rather than outward. To turn the general perception around, the Choctaw and Cherokee were probably the most powerful peoples in the South because of their invulnerability to conquest—Creek and Chickasaw raids against the Choctaw, and Creek raids against the Cherokee, were in large measure attempts to hold back the power of the Choctaw and Cherokee.

Europeans tended to view these tribal disputes only in relation to their own conflicts with other Europeans. They were aware of the "ancient" hostilities one Indian group had for another and often tried to play peacemaker in order to fulfill their diplomatic and military goals. Europeans attempted to forge exclusive alliances with Indians and to educate Indians or make them adopt their views, but they largely failed.

For an imperialist like Thomas Nairne, it was unacceptable that Indians did not form alliances with Europeans based on what he thought was right and just, a standard that Europeans certainly did not follow. Nairne criticized the French for their "endeavour to seduce our subjects [by whom he meant Indians] from their duty," but he blamed the Indians as well.[72] Referring to the Indians as "savages," a word he used when he felt that Indians were behaving in a particularly despicable manner, he complained that "especially those so remote have not a right notion of Allegiance and its being indefeasible. They're apt to believe themselves at Liberty, when they please to turn to those who sell them the best pennyworths." Although the "Traders take pains to instruct them, and by good arguments endeavour to draw them from that Erroneous doctrine, yet nothing but a much better trade and the reputation of far greater Courage than the French could have kept this Tribe [the Chickasaw] in any tolerable subjection." Nairne rued that self-interest was a "much more powerful" motive than "the Justice of our cause."[73]

Nairne and a host of frustrated European diplomats and officials could not accept that aborigines viewed themselves as independent peoples unbound to any nation. The Europeans expected Indians to be faithful allies (even vassals) out of friendship and loyalty, though they themselves did not act out of friendship and loyalty. They labeled Amerindians as inconstant, if not treacherous, for negotiating and trading with supposed enemies. They bewailed how Indians formed friendships with those who provided the best goods. Yet the Europeans behaved similarly, especially when trade was concerned. They, too, formed friendships and alliances with those who could provide the best military assistance and trade, and they easily exchanged one ally or partner for another. Europeans wanted Indians to consider themselves subject to their own monarch, and Nairne even referred to the Chickasaw as subjects, but *they* never made this concession. Yet Nairne might have realized his own inconsistency. On one hand, he condemned the French for trying to lure these "subjects" from the English, but on the other, he immediately followed this complaint by noting how the Chickasaw were "independents by trimming between the French and us." Perhaps this inconsistency was due in part to the common European perception that Indians in contact with Europeans became subject to them: if you traded with Indians you could claim them as an ally, which magically transformed them into subjects, whose land you could then claim sovereignty over at the diplomatic tables of Europe. Nairne's concept of Indian subjection anticipated an ideal future. At the time, he admitted that the Chickasaw were independent of "our power," for the English and the French "in these parts is something nigh a Balance." He expected this to end, however, and the Chickasaw would become "subjects of course, when we have put the French out of any capacity to raise an Indian army."[74]

JOHN STEWART:
SELF-PROCLAIMED EXPERT ON ALL THINGS

Stewart's views of southern Indians were never so cavalier as Nairne's. In spite of Stewart's constant promotion of British imperialism and his understanding of Indians as central to British designs, he had greater respect for Indians as independent peoples. Stewart's views may have contributed to his political isolation in the colony, for he seems to have had little to no political role in South Carolina after returning from London in the mid-1690s. Certainly many of his opinions and the topics he discussed put him out of step with his contemporaries. Yet this did not prevent him from putting forth his opinions, schemes, and recollections.

In his declining years Stewart had time to reflect on his many accomplishments—in fact, he spent much time writing to others recalling his contributions and offering recommendations and plans. We have already heard his claims to have almost single-handily proposed and designed nearly every agricultural experiment attempted in Carolina.[75] Yet these assertions barely compare to those he made later. Stewart wrote incessantly to the empire's leaders with all sorts of proposals, fourteen of which, he maintained, had been enacted into law by Parliament and others used as well. Given what we know of his earlier activities, it is not difficult to imagine that Stewart thought himself expert on any number of subjects and that as the great-grandson of a king he had every right and duty to make suggestions for the good of his country.

In 1712, Stewart claimed that for the previous twenty-one years he had sent four hundred sheets containing his proposals and ideas to various correspondents. (Each sheet held about three pages of text.) His recipients included Secretary of State Peter Trenchard, Admiral Peter Mitchell, William Legge, earl of Dartmouth, and none other than his cousin Queen Anne. Among those items he took credit for: the first draft of the Act of Union between England and Scotland; the sending of the Iroquois chiefs to London; a plan to send boys to sea and girls to woolen manufactories; a new system of postage and packet boats between America and Britain; a measure to protect seamen from impressment in America—a great bone of contention in the colonies; plans for the conquest of Canada and Louisiana; a plan to build a million tons of shipping at Port Royal, South Carolina; a plan for the investment of British funds in foreign nations; a program to have native artists produce "all sorts of toys, fripperies, and curious mechanicky" for sale abroad; a design for the employment of one million mechanics in Britain; and the preparation of "100,000 manifestos printed in the French tongue ready to be dispersed over France upon our descent or march into France when that happens." There were other schemes as well. It is questionable whether any of Stewart's proposals were actually discussed and acted on, and some, like the Act of Union, certainly proceeded independent of any input from Stewart.

Stewart made these claims when seeking financial help from the government: "I am very old and very poor and therefore in [need of] charity." His proof that he sent these proposals lay in "receipts" he had "for my packets." We can hardly doubt that he sent these packets because not only do we have a few of these letters, but Dartmouth, who received this request, could easily check in London with other recipients.[76] None of this proves, however, that Stewart was anything more than a crank who sent letters to leading figures of the realm, making recommendations on virtually anything under the sun. Fortunately for us, the French captured three of his letters, which they preserved among their official colonial documents because they included Stewart's recommendations for invading New France—yet they also contain a wealth of material about southern Indians.

Stewart's observations about Indians are extremely important, and to understand them we must analyze his purpose and methods in recording Indian life. Stewart left no systematic text to analyze, as did John Lawson. Nor did he have Pénicaut's gift for documenting social and religious activities. He also lacked the clarity and forethought of the French priests who dwelled among the lower Mississippi Valley peoples. His writing displays a distinct lack of discipline. He wanders from point to point, though he often carries an overarching theme or idea ad infinitum, and thus there is method to what often seems like madness. Stewart so valued himself and his thoughts that he felt no obligation to organize his ideas into a coherent whole. But Stewart's vivid memories persisted from three uninterrupted years among the Creek and Chickasaw. These memories possessed an immediacy and a lack of detachment not evident in Pénicaut, Lawson, Nairne, or most other observers of southern Indians. As in his letters of 1690 that recorded the minutiae of political affairs in Carolina, and rarely the larger picture, Stewart recalls fascinating tidbits of Indian life he witnessed firsthand. The effects are wondrous and baffling—wondrous because he provided extended discourses and speeches made by Indians that go on for so long that one can easily forget that he was reporting through another man's voice. Stewart consciously tried to be true to the Indians by letting them speak for themselves, by giving their thoughts weight above his own. Yet it takes patience to hear these voices, for Stewart allowed them free reign to move as he did, from point to point, often without clear markers when he changed subject matter.

Stewart recognized his propensity to babble, yet he explored issues with detailed examples not available elsewhere. In two lengthy epistles to Queen Anne, he painstakingly reported episodes of torture. Stewart thought it important not to hide the realities of Indian life from the queen; she must understand them as he did, for Britain's fortunes in America depended on the Indians who held the balance of power on the continent.[77] As the great-grandson of a king he thought himself entitled to speak his mind on all affairs of state, but his candor also arose from his sense of duty to inform the queen on Indian matters, because no one in her administration, he believed, could possibly know Indians as thoroughly as he.

JOHN STEWART: THE POWER OF THE CHOCTAW

Some of the letters Stewart wrote in 1711–1712, during Queen Anne's War between England and France, included proposals for conquering the French in America. He believed that the winner would be the one who had "the most warlike and numerous body" of Indians to command in North America. Because French influence among the Indians was strong, Quebec and Montreal had to be conquered to save the northern colonies (and Port Royal in Nova Scotia maintained), and Mobile had to be destroyed. Stewart was convinced that the powerful Choctaw, allies of the French, threatened to destroy the southern English colonies. He feared that although the southern Indians allied with Carolina were far more martial than the northern Indians were, the Choctaw could easily destroy them. Once this occurred, Carolina, Virginia, and Maryland would fall.[78]

Stewart's judgments regarding the Choctaw were unusual for a European. Britons had few contacts with the Choctaw and wrote little about them until the 1730s. The French, by contrast, were intimately concerned with the Choctaw, their most important ally in Louisiana, because they defended French settlements by occupying much of the land east of the Mississippi and northwest of Mobile. Yet the French had no intention of employing the Choctaw in an invasion of the English. They knew that the Choctaw could not conquer Carolina, which could be subdued only by sea, by a Creek-Yamasee invasion by land, or by a slave rebellion. Stewart based his opinion of Choctaw power in part on his experience living among the Creek and the Chickasaw, who must have expressed great fear of the Choctaw, with whom they frequently warred. Like Thomas Nairne, historians tend to view the Creek and Chickasaw as much more martial peoples than the Choctaw, largely because of the disparaging remarks made by later French and English alike. The Creek and Chickasaw displayed the kind of bravery and tactics that the Europeans respected, whereas they interpreted Choctaw military behavior as cowardly.[79] Stewart's in-depth discussion of Choctaw power thus provides a different and earlier view from contemporaries and historians.

Stewart first encountered the Choctaw while living among the Creek in 1692. He believed them the most militarily capable of *all* Indians the Europeans had yet to meet in North America. Comparing them to peoples he had seen in his far-flung travels across Europe, China, Turkey, Persia, and eight American colonies, "I do know that never was any Indian nation or race of mankind more savage, fierce, and brutal than the Choctaw." He considered them invincible. "They cannot be fatigued" or intimidated, for they would "run up to the very muzzle of their enemy's guns with unparalyzed and undaunted resolution." No army could withstand them. If they were in Europe, they would win there, too, as "nothing but fortified places can stand before them."[80]

Stewart assumed that the Cherokee and Chickasaw would join the Choctaw against the English. He might have thought that because the Creek were on the English side, the Cherokee would naturally gravitate to the Choctaw and French. Many historians would dismiss the possibility of a Chickasaw-Choctaw alliance in this period, but the French never gave up hope of reconciling the two, and as discussed earlier, the Chickasaw wanted the French to mediate a peace between them and the Choctaw. Stewart thus envisioned that a force of five thousand Choctaw, combined with four thousand Cherokee and one thousand Chickasaw, would bring the southern English colonies to their knees.[81] In this he overestimated the offensive capabilities of the Choctaw. He knew from the English-led invasions of Spanish Florida that large armies of Indians from different groups could be united in wars of conquest. He also correctly assumed that Indian armies could destroy the Carolinas, for the Tuscarora War and the Yamasee War later showed how vulnerable those colonies were to inland attacks. But he overestimated the ability of the Choctaw to vanquish the Creek and move a large army to the Carolinas. He realized that this would be possible only with the help of the Cherokee and the Chickasaw, and such a coalition must have been the greatest nightmare of the Creek. Their alliance would have formed a semicircle of power around the Creek. Yet the forming of the coalition was unlikely. The Cherokee had little interest in an offensive alliance with the Choctaw and Chickasaw, for they could meet their goals without involving themselves so heavily to the southwest. And a Chickasaw peace with the Choctaw did not assure an offensive alliance against the Creek, from which they could reap no benefit.

Still, given Stewart's experiences, it is easy to see why he would think that such an alliance was possible and boded ill for the British. Stewart thought the Choctaw the most "savage and barbarous" Indians he had met. These Indians, he wrote, "can endure more hunger, travel, toil and fatigue" and were the most "cunning [and] daring nation known."[82] In short, they were unconquerable, "never to be in reality beat or overcome by any aggressive whites or Indians." Because their towns were located along cane swamps, the Choctaw easily fled into an almost impenetrable environment where they could not be followed. It mattered not, Stewart thought, to defeat them in battle or to burn their fields and towns, for they simply disappeared without a trace. Also, the Choctaw placed their towns about ten to twelve miles apart, so it was easy for them to sound the alarm. Enemies soon learned that to retreat from the Choctaw was more dangerous than to attack, for the Choctaw pursued invaders more swiftly than the attackers could flee. Stewart mentioned Choctaw speed on several occasions—he was convinced not only that they were the fastest of all Indians but that they could outrun horses at "top gallop for many miles on end."

To illustrate Choctaw prowess and athletic ability, Stewart recounted an episode in which he saw a Choctaw outrun horsemen during an invasion of Choctaw territory in 1706. On the return, "12 of our nimblest Indians," armed with carbines, pistols, and cutlasses on horseback, "gave chase to a Choctaw Indian in a pine barren at top gallop for 4 miles." He outran them all "with meandering twists." Skirting from tree to tree, he would stop and shoot, killing or wounding every horse, wounding most of the riders, even "pinning one of the white men's thighs to his horse's side." His arrows spent, the Choctaw jumped into a river, swam to the other side, and then "in derision" berated his pursuers as "women, children, and chicken cowardly-hearted felons." This anecdote provides a cogent reminder of the advantage of the bow and arrow over the gun. Lightly armed, the Choctaw could wend his way through thick woods more easily than his heavily laden pursuers, and he could load and fire more quickly than they.

After this episode and others like it, Stewart lamented, "Our Indians are so discouraged that they will never more attack the Choctaw, they thinking them invincible." How do we reconcile Stewart's assessment of Choctaw prowess with the standard view of them as militarily incompetent victims of Chickasaw slaving? Stewart has an answer for this. The slavers' attacks on the Choctaw were not on their towns, for "they never attack them before but by stealth stragglers in the woods at great distances from home."[83] In other words, the Chickasaw had not been conducting raids against Choctaw towns in the way we might envision a slaving raid in Africa, or even in Florida, but were picking off individuals or small parties away from home, perhaps on hunting trips. Assaults on their towns were too difficult, given the defenders' ability to hide and then attack the invaders on their retreat.

The variance in views of Chickasaw and Choctaw can be seen in comparing Nairne and Stewart. Whereas Nairne reflected English and French opinion that praised the Chickasaw as masters of the craft of warfare, Stewart lauded the Choctaw. To illustrate Chickasaw prowess, Nairne related a story of Chickasaw disdain for their Choctaw enemies. He reported that when the Chickasaw traveled through enemy territory, instead of hiding their presence, at night they lit huge bonfires, beat loud drums, sang, and danced. Nairne thought that this was done "to show the Chactaws how little we valued them." Nairne celebrated Chickasaw courage as warriors who did not lurk in shadows but proudly announced their presence wherever they went. However, Nairne did not see that Chicaksaw strategy was to feign fearlessness. The Chickasaw were no fools. Although a war party with huge bonfires might *deter* an enemy, the Chickasaw kept their guns close by. If the encampment was attacked, the warriors would take their "Arms, [and] presently fly off from the fires and wait the Issue." Then, if the Choctaw entered their camp, the Chickasaw would turn around and use the "light of the fires" to have "a sure shot."[84]

This story of Chickasaw tactics in enemy country must be reconciled with a similar description by Stewart. Stewart also related that at night the Choctaw liked to surround the camps of enemies who had entered their territory. Yet Stewart asserted unequivocally, "Indians never stop without fires in the night." The Choctaw then let loose a hailstorm of arrows on the unsuspecting invaders—their victims not knowing from which direction the assault came. Stewart's rendition adds a crucial point missing from Nairne's account. This strategy worked only if one used arrows: "for if it were gunshot," then their enemies would know from which direction the attack came (because of the flash and resulting smoke).[85]

Nairne and Stewart wrote at approximately the same time, but Nairne was referring to events in 1708, whereas Stewart was recalling his experiences from fifteen years earlier—before the French arrived in Louisiana and had armed the Choctaw. The Choctaw attack thus would not have worked in 1708, because the tactic was predicated on bows and arrows. Yet Nairne did not state whether the Choctaw actually "fell" for the ruse—his emphasis was on Chickasaw bravery in making their fires and ridiculing their enemies by not employing stealth. Stewart, however, gainsaid Nairne's assessment: making fires was not bravery, it was merely typical of Indians. Having lived with Indians for three years and having joined several war parties, Stewart was probably correct on this point. Nairne's involvement with Indian raiders was much more limited, as in his raid into Florida at the head of thirty-three Yamasee—where he might have wielded enough influence to prevent night fires.

The time differential between Nairne and Stewart may also have contributed to their varying conceptions of military prowess. Stewart viewed Choctaw power from "inside" Indian culture, as a long-term resident in Indian towns that had great difficulty making headway against the Choctaw. His experiences occurred before the Chickasaw and Creek had been buttressed by English power, and before those peoples had improved strategy and tactics sharpened by the slaving expeditions and armed forays they participated in at the end of the 1690s and in the early eighteenth century. Nairne wrote in 1708, during sustained attacks on the Choctaw by the English, Creek, and Chickasaw. The Choctaw were on the defensive. In spite of the continued French-Choctaw threat, Nairne and others believed that they and their allies soon would prevail in the South, whereas Stewart maintained a healthy respect (and fear) of Choctaw power.

Stewart's purpose in recounting Choctaw prowess was to convince the royal government to invade Mobile and remove the French from the South. Because the Choctaw could not be defeated, the ties between the two had to be broken by some other means. Already the French had employed the Choctaw to "oblige" the Chickasaw "to keep no more correspondence with the English and to seize on an English trader that was there." It did not matter how many troops the French sent to Louisiana, for the secret of their power was Choctaw warriors, not French soldiers, as Stewart valued them of more use "than a million of Frenchmen would be if they were at Mobile." The other great French advantage over the English was their location. Easy water carriage from Mobile allowed them to undersell the Carolinians by 100 percent and more, through which advantage they made inroads luring the Abihka and Alabama from the English.

The main chance to win over the Choctaw had been missed years earlier when promises and one thousand pounds' worth of gifts could have enticed them to move northward, to "settle on the old Cusseda river between the

Tacobagy river and Flint river," in effect, to have occupied the location later taken up by Lower Creek who wished to live closer to Carolina. Choctaw chiefs should have been sent to London "to view our strength" and tie them closer to Britain.[86] But now, Stewart reflected, they disdain the English and had no need for their goods. Only the entire removal of the French could solve Britain's problem. Otherwise, Stewart predicted, the French soon would be masters of all the Indians, then the English colonies, and then Europe, with Britain reduced to enslavement by the papacy and the Bourbon monarchy. This domino effect was not entirely military, for Stewart did not postulate that the French conquest of English North America would lead to the conquest of Europe, though he did think that the Choctaw would do quite well fighting in Flanders. But French Louisiana, when developed, would give France a great advantage over Britain in the marketplaces of Europe. Louisiana's superior location to the southern English colonies would lead the French to produce the same commodities, but in a warmer climate and on better land. Stewart expected Louisiana to attract settlers from France and from Canada, for who would not want to emigrate to such a wonderful country?[87]

Stewart, the imperialist, also wrote to the heads of the Turkey and East India Companies with recommendations for countering the French elsewhere in the world. As was common with many Protestants, he feared the rise of French power because it meant the rise of Roman Catholic influence, and he held the common notion that Rome stood behind France in a great conspiracy to effect world domination. But Stewart's true interests lay in North America, and since he believed himself to be the foremost British expert on Indians, he had a duty to give those in power both information and recommendations. For this reason, he devoted one of his longest letters to Queen Anne to "some observations on American Indians."[88]

JOHN STEWART: INDIAN INVASIONS

In both letters to the queen, Stewart described how Indians conducted invasions. One of the important aspects he addressed was provisioning—which also affected Europeans. He had accompanied the Creek on an invasion of the Choctaw that took thirty days and was amazed to find that the Indians brought no provisions for an army of twelve hundred to thirteen hundred men. The entire time they had not one "grain of corn or pulse."[89] On the march, hunters scattered in a circle from two to twelve miles from the army, hunting deer and occasionally buffalo and bringing in their haul every night. (These same hunters may have formed a protective ring to warn the large body of warriors if the enemy was spotted.) Sometimes 100, but as many as 250, deer were brought in. On the retreat, however, no hunters could be sent out because they would have been killed. Instead, the Indians fasted on their ten-day retreat to Abihka. Going for days without food was not unusual for eastern woodlands Indians, whose stoicism during lean times is well known.[90] Many preferred to travel light. Carrying provisions such as corn would have slowed them down and reduced their mobility. In the southern heat raw meat would not have lasted long, hence the need for daily hunting. When an army of two thousand Carolinians and Indians, "the greatest force that ever Carolina brought into the field," invaded the Choctaw in 1706, they spent ten days burning Choctaw towns and provisions without ever seeing a Choctaw.[91] On their retreat to Abihka, the Carolinians refused to go without— they sent out hunting parties and the Choctaw killed or captured fifty. This taught the English that invading forces must travel lightly, as well as the need to rely heavily on Indians for distant invasions, because few Europeans were prepared for the hardships of retreat.

For these reasons Stewart recommended that the destruction of Mobile take place by sea rather than by land. Carts and wagons could not transport supplies to Mobile, for the difficult terrain meant slow going by both horse and man. Rain delays and the need to hunt while traveling led Stewart to estimate that it could take an army two hundred days going to and returning from Mobile. They could not count on purchasing supplies from the Indians along the way, for he had "been in Indian towns where a peck of corn has cost 2 buck skins dressed and when we travel we [must] trust only to our guns for deer and buffalo."[92]

On the return from an invasion, Stewart asserted, "every night 2 or 3 of their prisoners is put to death with great and lingering torments and burnt alive." Elderly women, infants, small children, the lame and wounded— those who could not march—were simply killed and scalped "in the twinkling of an eye." A knife "cuts round the skin of the head . . . [and] with one pull [the warrior] takes up all the skin and hair with it which he stuffs full of moss or dry grass and dries it at the fire then ties it to his girdle at his back and dances with it, with songs and beat of drum." The victim was not always dead when scalped, and sometimes the "poor creatures" have "hot fire ashes and ambers" put on their "naked scalp" and were sent home to show their people this "badge of his value." This humiliating and painful torment had another purpose: the afflicted was to tell his "countrymen" to be sure and come for a similar treatment. "I have seen," Stewart reported, "some well and alive that have been so served."[93]

Stewart also described his experience on the receiving end of an Indian invasion. In 1692 he resided with the Creek when a party of a thousand Apalachee attacked. Our historical memory of the Apalachee, based largely on the events of 1702–1706, when the Creek joined the English and Yamasee in devastating Florida, portrays the Apalachee as the victims of a sustained campaign of eradication and enslavement. Stewart's discussion enlarges the story and shows that the Creek were not merely hired mercenaries doing the bidding of Carolina to obtain trade goods by killing and capturing Florida Indians, but that the disputes between the Apalachee and the Creek went back decades. In the cycles of revenge the Creek had many long-term memories of themselves as victims of Apalachee aggression.[94]

During this invasion, the Apalachee burned two Creek towns, including one neighboring on Cuseeta, where Stewart lived. The Apalachee had killed "100 women, old men and children, scalping the slaves, ripping up the bellies, having out their hearts and guts and bowels." They strewed "these about trails" and threw "the carcasses in the high way to be devoured by our dogs, vultures and wolves. The hearts they either eat or dried and so carried with them as tokens of their victory."[95] We shall return to this invasion later, when Stewart details the Creek reaction to it, but first let us examine the characteristics of Indian invasions that Stewart recorded.

Stewart stressed that the size of an invasion force had little relationship to the probability of its success or failure. Having been wounded, he observed during the six months he spent recovering at Cuseeta, twenty-six separate parties that went against the Apalachee. War parties numbered as few as two men, and some of these returned more "loaded with spoils and scalps" than entire armies. These small parties of "2 or 3 men go out and stay three moons." They remained within "3 or 4 miles of their enemy's towns every day and night watching [for] an opportunity to catch slaves or kill and scalp." If the enemy detected them, they killed their captives and took the scalps. Before the English arrived, he added, they mainly kept as slaves the children they had captured. Once the children learned their captors' language "and grown up, they emancipated them to add numbers to their nation, or they adopt them for children or cousins to their particular families." Stewart related the story of an Iroquois who had been enslaved and then emancipated and adopted into a "King's family and growed to be King." Stewart knew the man personally, for "he was my landlord 2 years and I called his wife my mother for she fed and maintained me in the days of famine."[96] The famine was so bad that mothers killed their infants when they had no milk to offer. The famine had resulted from invasions by the "Spanish Indians," that is, the

Apalachee (and possibly Chacato and Timucua), who the season before had burned nineteen towns "with all the provisions."[97] Thus, large invasion forces were useful for burning towns and destroying crops but not necessarily for capturing slaves. Smaller groups, which could easily hide, were much more adept at picking off "stragglers." This reinforces Stewart's earlier explanation of how the Choctaw could lose people to enslavement but not be forced to succumb to large invading armies.

Another invasion Stewart participated in during his time with the Creek included an army of fifty Indian gunmen, fifty-one bowmen, and two whites besides himself, one being "an old Buccaneer of Sir Henry Morgan's." Before proceeding far they discovered an enemy force "1,000 strong," with Creek women, children, the elderly, and the lame fleeing before them. Recalling a story he had read in "Buchanan's Scots Chronicle," a sixteenth-century book that had been translated from Latin into English in 1690, Stewart and his party lit "quadruple fires to what we needed." They kept the fires blazing all night and covered six-foot logs with deer, bear, and buffalo hides to make their force appear much larger. Ordinarily, twenty-five fires signified one hundred men, four per fire, so by making one hundred fires they implied a force of four hundred men. The enemy fled by six different paths, perhaps because they feared not only the four hundred before them but that other Creek were on their way. Whatever the reason, "our Indians" followed them "10 days march to their own country and [in] country that I marched 10 years afterward."[98]

JOHN STEWART: THE CHARACTER OF THE INDIANS

Among other reasons, an invasion or raid sought captives on whom vengeance could be obtained in a highly ritualized fashion. Many Indians commonly practiced torture. Not all southern Amerindians or Indians in other regions of North America practiced torture, however. Victims were usually men but could include women and children. Captors expected their victims to sing their "mourning" song for as long as they could and to display both courage and disdain for their tormentors. Victims who did not display courage or who did not behave properly, they immediately killed as unworthy of torture. Victims believed that maintaining their courage and a show of disdain for their tormentors reflected on the character of their people; many thought that dying courageously under torture, like dying in battle, would gain them entry to an afterlife. The tormentors believed that they honored the victims by torturing them, though their hope was to break the victims' spirit so that their "performance" would redound poorly on their people.

Stewart's extensive accounts of torture, which include victims' speeches, provide one of the earliest written records of this practice in the South.[99] He reported hearing "excellent speeches" by tortured captives. In a composite or typical speech, he noted how the victim eyed his tormentors "with a scornful look and a disdainful air." Then he related a history of his exploits, telling of the women and children whom he had scalped and those whose brains he had "dashed out" because he could not take them home; of individual warriors or great captains that he had put to death by torture, how he had cut their body parts and eaten them before their eyes. If he lived, he promised to kill their entire nation and to "eat part of you all"; and if he did not live, his countrymen would do it for him. Then he informed his tormentors that they were "less than women and boys," for he had only fallen into their "snares by my wounds and your tricks, not by your courage and manhood." Stoically, he reasoned, "I know I was born to die. I was not born to live always." Referring to the next life, he discussed the rewards that awaited him "beyond the mountains, up where those stars are," where he would meet with his "fore-fathers and be full of all my Country's delights." Gratefully, he informed his captors, "had I not met with your cowardly womanly tribe perhaps I had died at home with colick stone or grip." Then his relations and "women friends" would have been "6 moons lamenting his absence." Instead, they should be ignorant of his destiny—"nor do I see any misfortune in this my fate." Like the eagle, "the badge of my family," he soared above them with "so high a pitch of thought that I govern you and all your nation." His tormentors had "neither heart nor contrivance or art to make me fall a victim of pity . . . do your worst. I am above you all."

To his correspondent, Stewart commended the tortured men who behaved with "Roman bravery" and sarcastically wondered at "the British interest to be masters of a million of [these] people." How could they conquer people so brave? It would be "just as profitable to the mechanics, merchants and mariners [and] to the crown" of Great Britain to have Indians as allies and trading partners rather than subjects. While urging the British government to make alliances with these most worthy people, he cautioned against fickle behavior on the part of the British. Indians made the most steadfast friends and "implacable" foes. Once Indians became enemies, he warned, it was almost impossible to end the hostility, though "fear or reward" sometimes, but "seldom," worked. To earn their friendship, "They love those that speak truth and deal justly in compacts," but they despise those who lie, whom they describe as "a man with two tongues." Their friends received the utmost hospitality, for they will share all they have and perform all sorts of service; they expected returns in kind, which if they did not receive, "they cool and by degrees neglect you."

If one's friends were always honored with loyalty, gifts, and help, one's enemies received no quarter. Stewart frequently returned to the theme of Indians' lacking pity for their enemies, though it was not something he criticized but merely noted and expounded. Indians expected no mercy and gave none. Enemies tried to destroy your town and crops and humiliate and humble your people by scalping and mutilating corpses, torturing prisoners, and enslaving women and children. (Stewart notes one important change in this regard "since the Britons" arrived—now they "sell all the young ones of both sexes" for profit.) The feelings of hatred and vengeance by one people for another were personalized, as if each member of the other group had killed one's own parent or sibling. From Stewart's descriptions we can better understand the cycles of vengeance that made it hard for Indian peoples to make lasting peace after long periods of enmity. These "ancient" enmities characterized the eighteenth-century relationships between Choctaw and Chickasaw, Creek and Choctaw, and Creek and Cherokee, for their long periods of war were interrupted only briefly by truces, much like the relationship between France and England from 1689 to 1815.

Stewart combined the themes of vengeance, raiding, torture, and bravery in a lengthy speech delivered by a Creek headman in 1692. The oration given by this warrior was not meant as a literal representation of what he said, though Stewart would have heard the anecdotes many times, for warriors often recounted their exploits. The event that led the warrior to make this speech was the Apalachee invasion of the Creek described above. Stewart had been in a neighboring town when the Apalachee struck in 1692. Expecting the invaders to arrive shortly at their town, the people were overcome with fear as the "war captain" tried to calm them and rally the men to take the offensive. The occasion was deeply etched in Stewart's memory.

The captain told the people what the Apalachee had done, destroying the neighboring town, brutalizing and mutilating the dead, and taking prisoners in tow to torture in their own town, where they would give "the same sauce" to them. The Apalachee would "make their mockeries with the prisoners and . . . dance and sing and beat their drums round the fires." They would "roast" them, their wives and children "abused before your eyes . . . them tormented with weeping eyes, sighing hearts, and inexpressible groans and screeches for anguish of pain." The speaker continued in this vein, describing how the men would have to watch helplessly as their families were brutalized—his description here went longer than most, reflecting the impact it had on him and the importance of the situation, where an impassioned speech was needed to rally the dispirited against a much larger force. The war captain implored the men to stay and fight, for he feared worse if they fled: a "sad spectacle that is more keen and cutting than ten thousand stakes in at the heart." He reasoned: "let all of us with heart and hands resolve to live and die together." If we die, he said, we neither hear or see all this, if we live, we will have fame all over the land, from the "great white sea" (the Atlantic Ocean) to the "great quiet waters where the sun sets called Mississippi, that great rich water over which our forefathers crossed when the Spaniards first came to the great lake, the Gulf of Mexico, where our great King had houses and palaces like the English King or Governor in Charles Town." Let us "behave like our forefathers . . . and hope of revenge." We must "march and find our enemies" and turn their "fury and conquests upon themselves." Then we will have victory, and "our wives and children shall dance, whoop and sing to see them dying and howling with the bitter points of knives, sharp flints and canes, fires [burning] slowly and leisurely till we are glutted and feasted with their miseries and destruction."

The war captain then recounted his exploits at length to instill confidence in those who would follow him as well as to remind his hearers of his right to lead. He prefaced his remarks, "You all know me and my forefathers, their blood runs in my veins." From boyhood he had been bred to "hunting and war" and had become the "cock of the town."[100] He had earned a "singular character of distinction" for children's games—athletic competitions such as wrestling, leaping, and playing chunky.[101] He always excelled at hunting and shooting matches: his arrows brought down flying birds and any variety of vegetables and fruits tossed in the air.

Now the "black cut King," their cousin, lay wounded in his house. He barely escaped the Apalachee—those who had not seen him "may go see his wounds." Forty of the enemy chased but failed to kill him. They would soon "see more tragedies when we come to the towns burned." Calling for courage in the face of adversity, he summoned the men to "let all our losses add to our fame of courage and revenge."

The war captain, chosen by the other Indians, hoped that he would live up to his past deeds. He recited a catalog of those he had killed, beginning with a "Chara" whom he had helped his father slay when he was a boy and for which he "got a piece of the scalp" that he proudly "wore . . . as a trophy." This heroic deed impressed his "mistress," who "would not look at me before." Suddenly popular, "all the girls in our town had their hopes set on me." He was then ready to pursue scalps on his own. "I began with the slaughter of women and children" and then moved on to men. In his life, he had killed a "Jimassees" (Yamasee), "a great many" Apalachee, "some Cherokee," a Chickasaw, Seneca, Illinois, Savannah, Timucua, and a Towasa, among others. He also claimed to have "killed two of the French Choctaw [who] ran swifter than rabbits or deer and [are] fiercer than bears when they are wounded with arrows in a cane swamp." He described killing an Indian from the Great Lakes region, a Tonuhi (whom I cannot identify), whose scalp he still had with its "curious head of hair"—which he displayed for all to see—and a "tobacco pouch I made of the skin of his thigh," on which he had a tiger (mountain lion?) painted. Of the fifteen scalps hanging on his girdle, he valued this one most.

Until then he had never killed in front of a white man. They now had the chance to show the English "what men we are," and if we do well they will trade with us and become friends. But let us revenge ourselves for "our little ones." Exhausted and hoarse, he excused himself and reeling like "a drunk, sunk down and fell as one dead upon the next cabin." Another captain took his place, foaming at the mouth "as he made his speech with rage, fury and vehemence like one mad and distracted." Stewart had never seen anyone fume like this, and it caused his listeners to cry out. The first speaker had appealed to the need to fight and for the warriors to place their trust in his military skills; the second now whipped the warriors into a frenzy, winning their commitment to the march. The next day, "the women and children retired into cane swamps" with canoes laden with their "goods and corn" as well as "raw skins." The men went off to war. (This was the episode earlier recounted, when their force of 104 made fires to appear like 400 and turned back the Apalachee force of 1,000.)

JOHN STEWART: THE IMPORTANCE OF TRADE

Later in this letter to the queen, Stewart returned to the theme of being the first white man among these Indians, providing the third, and longest, oration he gave by an Indian leader. This speech explained why it was so important to treat Stewart and future Englishmen well: to earn trade and alliance that would change their lives for the better. Stewart provided a few anachronisms in the speech, but through his lenses appears an Upper Creek perspective on the value of a permanent trade at the very point when it was initiated.

In this speech the chief used an orator, possibly a *heniha,* to relay his thoughts.[102] The speaker told the gathering that Stewart had come a long way, bringing axes, hoes, hatchets, and knives. These tools would make it much easier to clear land, cut timber, and build piraguas and canoes. With iron instead of stone hatchets they could construct a piragua[103] in half a moon instead of three. Knives would replace cane reeds and flint stones for the skinning of hides. Saws to "cut the grass and weeds" were superior to their former wooden saws and clubs. Guns that "roar . . . like claps of thunder frightening their enemies into flight" would allow them to "get more hides and furs in one moon" than the bow and arrow procured in twelve. Then they could trade for "matchcoats . . . soft and thick" for wearing and bedding. Their slaves, he announced, will be better dressed than the war captains are now. They will never have to worry about provisions, for in the very worst times the iron tools would help them dig roots, and they would have guns, powder, and shot to procure meat.

"Let us open a trade" with the English, the chief urged, exchanging "our skins and peltry" that have no value to us. These will procure "stone kettles." (Here Stewart inserted a parenthetical note that the Indians called all metals "stone," even silver coin, which they labeled "stone beads.") These kettles do not break like the ones we make, he continued. And, too, we should welcome the white man's red paint, vermilion, for our bodies and faces in time of war. "Let us entertain these strangers, this Englishman trader that has travelled so far." We will feed him "dainties," and regale him with dances, music, games, "and with our masquerade . . . of warring and with our war dances." We will show him how we "surprise camps and take towns and forts." We will make him comfortable with "buffalo and beaver skins to sit and lie on and feather matchcoats to sleep in." We will feed him all sorts of dishes in the "public great house and in private families." His tired feet will be washed every night. We will give him our parched corn, "sweetest bears oil," honey-preserved chestnuts and walnuts, and nectarines. "Be not covetous of your chickens, hens, and cocks, and if you have any dried turtle doves, and barbecued fish and barbecued deer and buffalo flesh, pray bring it to those white men with your finest lobl[oll]y of purest flour dumplings and cakes fried in bears oil." Unless he likes deer and buffalo fat better, then give him loblolly dishes of both. And let him sleep in the great house or wherever he pleases, for when he returns to the English he will tell them how he has been entertained. Then, continued the chief, we can expect others to visit yearly. You boys remember what you see now, for you see strange things brought by these men 2 or 3 moons across the great waters, things our forefather never saw. "Not one of them ever thought on us or our trade till this Captain Stewart having leisure and an itch of curiosity" traveled to see us.[104]

According to Stewart, the orator then spent a great deal of time outlining to his people the terms of English trade, especially proper treatment of the traders, the consequences of theft, and the reasons why the cost of European goods could rise. The traders' safety was of the utmost importance, and the Indians were warned that if they killed any trader then none would return. That raises the question: Why would Stewart have to warn the Indian chief, who in turn warned the others, not to kill traders? For one thing, to the Indians, the traders were "others," outsiders who could be stolen from or killed. In Native American terms there was nothing inherently immoral about stealing or killing someone with whom you were not friends or kin. Members of one's town, moiety, or "ethnic" identity were not to be robbed or harmed. "Others," however, could be treated in any number of ways, with indifference or charity, with hostility or friendship. The Mississippi River peoples conducted trade with "others," even with enemies, through the calumet ceremony, but the Creek did not use the ceremony, though they had other rituals that involved imbibing "black drink" and smoking tobacco, as means of facilitating interactions with outsiders.[105] The traders had to find ways to ensure their own safety and continuity in the trade relationship.

Repercussions for harming "others" were not personal, for the victims of "crimes" sought not to punish the individual perpetrator but rather to achieve vengeance against a member of his or her group. Thus, between groups of Indians, individuals did not commit crimes, groups did. To commit a crime within a group, however, was individual. Usually shame was used to punish the perpetrator, as in the case of theft, but serious crimes against a group's ethical standards could lead to banishment, in effect turning the member into an outsider, an "other."

The traders thus had to be perceived as insiders, and many were incorporated into kin and group networks through adoption and marriage. Yet Stewart made sure that the Upper Creek understood that the traders could not be considered as "others" before incorporation took place. Their people, the English, would not accept such treatment and would end the trade relationship if treated in this manner. Thus, the two cultures found a place to meet in the middle. English traders' lives would be sacrosanct before they established personal kinship relations with Indians; but the traders would do so as soon as possible, which meant achieving a clan identity that they could use in conducting trade with other Indian peoples.

This demand for the inviolate safety of the traders was necessary for conducting trade. Traversing the South with their slow-moving pack animals, the English made easy targets. Yet giving them status as untouchable was disastrous for the future of Indian relations with South Carolina. The traders were an arrogant lot, and many abused and exploited their Indian trading partners, knowing that the Indians would not risk attack. This refusal to attack was not because the Indians feared military reprisals from the Europeans but because they thought that the Europeans would never return—and the whole group was responsible for trader safety. Indians did not want to lose the trade that they valued dearly and, if withdrawn, would weaken them in relation to their neighbors.

To explain the importance of not stealing from the traders, Stewart informed his Indian friend, who then informed the others, of the English view of theft. He instructed them not to "lie or deceive them nor steal nothing." Do not become, he begged, like the Cherokee, Cheraw, Esaw, and Tuscarora, of whom the "white men living north," the Carolinians, and also those who live "where they make the Tobacco," the Virginians, do "so much complain that they all are thieves."[106] Except for the Cherokee, the other three lived near and among the English, where the situation for each had led to *not* establishing the kind of kinship relation that might have prevented theft. The Esaw and Cheraw did not have their own traders and purchased goods anywhere in Carolina, including from Charles Town merchants and shopkeepers. They would have adopted somewhat to English trade relations as practiced by the English in their own communities. The Tuscarora were in a similar position in North Carolina. As for the Cherokee, with whom close trade relations had yet to be established, they would have had no compunction in robbing traders.

As for the English side of the relationship, the orator promised that Stewart's prices "will always be the same, so long as he lives or the sun shines." But the Indians must understand that "when the white waters are angry" and bring storms to the sea, the large "house canoe (that is a ship) is lost and all the goods and people in it is drowned": that would raise the price of their goods. Or if "the French house canoes full of men . . . fall on our canoes and take the goods by fight or surprise then the goods are dear, otherways [otherwise] the old price will ever be the same." Thus the Indians learned, somewhat crudely, the vagaries of the world market. Yet no mention was made about the Indian supply rising or falling; perhaps Stewart assumed a constant supply or that the market for Indian goods in Europe would not expand or contract.

To test Stewart, the Indians would "send this and that man to pump him," with a variety of skins, in a variety of conditions, to see if he priced them consistently. Skins varied in color, size, weight, and whether taken in summer or winter. If Stewart disregarded whether the seller was young or old, wily or ignorant, friend or stranger, they would know that "he is good and has a good heart," making him a worthy trade partner.

Stewart then returned to the issues at hand: the need to use trade to gain influence with Indians, for the Indians' military power was too great to resist. He informed Queen Anne that Indians, if they chose, could drive "the Britons in the sea in one year." The English would have to build garrison forts every half-mile for twelve hundred miles to stop them, and even then they could "pass these in the night and fire the outhouses of plantations." The Europeans could never track down Indians, who were so skilled at hiding in cane swamps and the like that searching for them was like looking for a needle in a haystack. Horsemen were useless for pursuing Indians on their own terrain. But the greatest problem for the British was to protect persons and property. Indian raiders could easily kill cattle, hogs, and horses and capture and scalp people. Many Europeans would flee the colonies, and the rest would have to find refuge in forts. Pondering his twenty-six years in America, Stewart concluded that the Indians could as easily accomplish this destruction as "kiss my hand."

After yet another extended discussion for the queen concerning Indian bravery and skills in war, Stewart's concluding paragraph summarized and characterized Indians as "the most patient of mankind, the most contented, the most merry." They loved to game, were the "most hospitable, ingenious in every thing they delight in [and] of wonderful memory." They possessed exceptional eyesight, quickness, and physical endurance. They were "true to their friends [and] furious to their enemies." The best hunters, above all, they were particularly suited as trading partners, for their products complemented what the English could provide them. Their "friendship and alliance is the sure safety and enriching of the nations that have them"; their enmity was to be avoided. Stewart reminded the queen that none of her councillors could provide her "so particular, so true a narrative of Indians as this aforesaid, as lithe and babbling as it is."[107] It is fortunate that he took the time to do so.

In each his own way, Thomas Nairne and John Stewart tried to understand southern Native Americans. The two had wide-ranging and unusual experiences of Indian life: they joined native war parties, traveled hundreds of miles in Indian territory, received warm welcomes as cherished diplomats, had profitable adventures that brought them acclaim in the service of colony, monarch, and empire, provided important contributions to the Indian trade— Stewart as an initiator, Nairne as a reformer—and thus had the opportunity to leave a constructive mark on the course of intercultural relations in the South. Both men perceived Indian affairs as crucial to the good fortunes of South Carolina and the British empire, and they worked tirelessly to educate others and to shape and reform colonial and imperial policies. By the second decade of the eighteenth century, Stewart's influence in Carolina had waned, and so he extended his efforts to the leading personages of the British empire—on whom he had no impact. Stewart was unable to articulate a context by which others could understand his recommendations and observations. Neither Whigs nor Tories could have translated his obscurely rendered vision of Indians as independent peoples of practical knowledge and impressive power. His vivid recollections of Indian culture, if read at all, would have been interpreted, at best as exotic depictions of culturally unfathomable peoples, at worst as voyeuristic portraits of violent savages. Stewart had hoped to portray Indians realistically, without condemnation, so that others would understand them as he did. In this he failed.

Thomas Nairne, too, depicted Indians for a larger audience, but he was far more successful. In his hands, noble Indians appeared as natural adherents of Whig political philosophy, but as savages they could not resist acting treacherously in their own narrow self-interests. Britain would have to employ a firm hand and great forethought to force them away from French and Spanish influence and alliance and into alliance and dependence on Great Britain. Nairne's mixture of bravado and bluff, sympathy and arrogance, justice and power characterized South Carolina's Indian diplomacy from 1707 to 1715, when he played the leading role in shaping colonial Indian policies. Nairne based those policies on the continued gathering of knowledge of Indians, the institution of equity in relations, and the formation of a rational policy of trade. Had he and the other reformers not been so hypocritical and self-interested, they might have avoided the grave consequences that followed.

PART THREE

INTENTIONS, 1707–1711

The years 1707–1711 were a transitional period. After the swirl of invasions that began with the English failure to take Saint Augustine in 1702 and ended with the Franco-Spanish fiasco against Charles Town in 1706, the Europeans scurried to secure alliances with native peoples. Louisiana and Florida were in no position to undertake another invasion of South Carolina and had to shore up their defenses. South Carolina's phenomenal success in destroying Spanish missions raised English prestige and facilitated the recruitment of large Indian armies for campaigns against their enemies. The Carolinians had learned that they could make greater profits by attacking and enslaving a European foe's allies than by assaulting the Europeans directly. Moreover, invasions conducted by Indian armies with non-Europeans or a few Europeans were cost-effective. European invasions required the costly moving of heavy ordnance and months of supplies, whereas Indian armies could be provisioned with personal arms and "presents" of clothing, blankets, and trinkets: all of which could be carried by individuals.

The importance of Indian peoples to security and profits induced Carolinians to reassess the colony's relations with its native neighbors, for many recognized the fragile nature of alliances. The colony's political leaders still wanted to make profits through the Indian trade, but they had to consider the impact of the trade (and the traders) on military and imperial affairs. These were not viewed as mutually exclusive, for the invasion of Apalachee proved that imperial goals and private profits were compatible. Nevertheless, the pursuit of profits threatened imperial goals when it had first priority.

Part Three reveals the various methods South Carolina undertook to reconcile public and private interests in Indian affairs. Chapter 7 shows how South Carolinians set about enumerating and categorizing Indian peoples. Knowledge of their neighbors was an essential step in the process of gaining control over Indian relations—and there remained many challenges to that control. The South Carolina government sought to reduce not only the power of its French and Spanish enemies but that of its sister colony, Virginia, which had its own traders and interests. Yet the biggest challenge lay within the colony, where factions were at loggerheads over who should direct the Indian trade. Many in the assembly determined to wrest power from the governor. These Whig politicians had a different view of Indian relations than the Tory governor and his supporters. They hoped to "rationalize" the trade through regulation and oversight.

Chapter 8 then explores the Whig-Tory split over the meaning of empire and the proper way to conduct Indian affairs by focusing on the divisions that arose over the conversion of Native Americans to Christianity. Again, the root issue encompassed not just relations with Indians but the potential incorporation of Native Americans into society. With the growth of African slavery, the debate had evolved from its initiation by the proprietors: both clergy and laity wondered whether Indians or Africans would be easier to assimilate and Christianize.

Chapter 9 examines the colony's attempts to put words into action: reining in the traders through the combined powers of an Indian agent and a commission to oversee the trade and hear Indian grievances. The floodgates opened as Savannah River Indians flocked to Charles Town to register complaints. But the impetus and apparatus for reform were undermined by the colony's political divisions, which spilled into a severe factionalism that erupted among the traders and those who oversaw the trade, paralyzing South Carolina's quest to reform its Indian affairs.

7

INDIANS, TRADERS, AND
THE REFORM OF THE
INDIAN TRADE, 1707–1708

To reform Indian affairs, it was necessary to collect information about the South's native peoples. Thomas Nairne did his part by recording his observations and drawing maps of southern Indians; John Stewart contributed his expertise through letters to the queen and other leading personages of the empire; colony officials collected and collated census data—not just of Indians but of Europeans and Africans, too—through which they created a profile of the colony and the region's Indian population.

An examination of the demographic data South Carolina officials generated in 1708 and 1715 allows us to place in greater context the geopolitical relationships of that colony to its trading partners and to reconstruct how Carolina understood these peoples. Accompanying the colony's quest for knowledge was its first real attempt to reform Indian affairs, a contest that pitted the governor against the assembly and many of the traders against the government. With information at their disposal, new theories of empire to transform into programs, and a growing consensus to initiate real reforms, South Carolina's leaders undertook to assume a new and vital role in the British empire.

THE POPULATION OF CAROLINA'S
NATIVE NEIGHBORS IN 1708

In September 1708 the governor and council of Carolina sent to England descriptions of the colony and its neighboring Indians as well as a census.[1] The population of Carolina was set at 9,580; this figure included "whites" (in one of the first documents in the colony to use the term), "negroes," and enslaved Indians, but not the Settlement Indians. Although the Settlement Indians clearly lived within colony boundaries, the document reflects the officials' view that they were not part of the colony. Their exclusion also reflects how little colonial officials knew about Settlement Indians, people who fished and hunted on the Sea Islands and in and around the plantations, occasionally finding employment in service to the Europeans. At times ubiquitous in Charles Town, and at other times elusive, these Indians came and went as they pleased, and by 1708 the government either could not count them or did not care to try.

The report noted that the colony was evenly divided between whites and blacks, who each comprised 42.5 percent of the inhabitants, with enslaved Indians making up the other 15 percent. Children accounted for more than 41 percent of the white population, 29 percent of the black population, and just 21.4 percent of the Indian population. Black women outnumbered white women by 1,100 to 960, illustrating that the colony was better able to import black women than to attract white women immigrants.[2] Among white servants, male and female lived in equal though relatively small numbers. The census recorded only 120 white servants, 60 men and 60 women, most of whom would have been indentured.[3] Indian slave women outnumbered Indian slave men by six to five, a surprising number because so many contemporary observers noted Indian slavers' preference for capturing women and children and killing the men. The relatively large number of males might reflect the participation of Europeans in the raids against the Florida Indians and the Choctaw. The Europeans did not have the same tradition of murdering and ritually torturing the male prisoners and would have welcomed the higher prices brought by males they captured.[4] Also, the Europeans used iron implements to secure their slaves, whereas Indians did not, and thus had less fear of their male captives escaping or overpowering them.[5]

The report explained the growth of the colony's Indian slave population as a result of "our late Conquest over the French & Spaniards and the success of our Forces against the Appalaskye and other Indian Engagements." But it noted as a matter of course the colony's export of Indian slaves, as part of its ordinary trade: "We have also Commerce with Boston[,] Road Island, Pennsilvania[,] New York & Virginia to which places we export Indian slaves." The low number of Indian slave children in the report is hard to explain, because their numbers should approximate the numbers of women in the census, as in the numbers of African slaves. Perhaps many more Indian children succumbed to the diseases of the low country or of their villages before enslavement, but it is also possible that the colonists exported relatively more children than women to other colonies; evidence exists for the retention of Indian females in Carolina as domestic servants. Another reason for the low number of Indian slave children may have been the practice of birth control, particularly abortion, with which southern Indian women were very familiar. They had knowledge of which plants could expel the fetus and might not have wanted to bring children into a life of slavery.

In estimating the population of the colony's Indian neighbors, that is, those who were not Settlement Indians, the report did not include the numbers of women and children. Europeans typically calculated only the number of adult males in their estimates of aboriginal population, and usually only those who bore arms, since their purpose was to measure Indian military power. Nevertheless, the later census of 1715 included separate figures for women and children, though only of groups with which the colony was most familiar. Together, the two censuses allow us to reconstruct the demographics of some Indian peoples with fair accuracy.

In the 1708 census, the Yamasee, the colony's most important ally, were understandably the first Indian group mentioned. The Yamasee were reported as having but five hundred men, their recent decline in numbers owing in large measure to their military activities. The report merely stated, "They are become great Warriors & continually are annoying the Spaniards and the Indians their allies." South of the Yamasee were the Naleathuckles, who had eighty men "settled in [a] Town about Twenty miles up the Savannah River and are very serviceable in furnishing with provisions the Englishmen who go up that river." These were the Apalachicola, a Creek group who had migrated from the Apalachicola River just two years earlier. Further up the Savannah River, 150 miles from Charles Town, were three towns of the Savannah, which included 150 men. Just a few miles from them were located the Apalachee, who "deserted the Spaniards and came with our Forces." They had 250 men. The governor and council noted that the Apalachee "behave themselves very submissive to the Government" and "are seated very advantageous for Carrying our Trade" to the Indians that are "seated upwards of seven hundred miles off [and who] are supplied with Goods by our white men that Transport them from this River upon Indian's [sic] backs." The submissiveness of the Apalachee and their loyalty to the Europeans has already been noted; the report did not state that the Apalachee were there under duress and could not leave.

Next described were the eleven towns of Creek Indians living in northern Georgia on Ochese Creek, a former name of the upper Ocmulgee River.[6] The ethnic disparity of the settlements, and in general of the people who came to be known as Creek, was conceptually and probably linguistically too difficult for many English to contend with. So they either did not give them a name at all, as in this report, or lumped groups together as a single entity, such as Abihka, Coweta, or Cuseeta, or, as became more common in later years, simply labeled these Indians as Creek and designated differences by geographic settlement, such as Lower Creek and Upper Creek. The Ochese settlements actually included Cuseeta, Coweta, Oconee, and Hitchiti, among others. The report estimated six hundred men among the Ochese, which included several families of Apalachee, a group the officials could identify. Although they could not identify town or group distinctions among these Indians, the governor and his council recognized those characteristics most important to Carolina: these Indians, they noted, "are great Hunters & Warriors & Consume great quantity of English goods."

Another unlabeled Creek town was located 150 miles west of the Ocmulgee on the "Chochtakucky [Chattahoochee] River." A traditional area of Lower Creek settlements, most of the towns had moved to the Ocmulgee, but some would return during the Yamasee War. The report did not state how many Indians lived there, noting simply that there was a town "settled for Conveniency of Carrying on Trade who are very serviceable . . . these people are seated about midway between Ochasee River and the settlement of the Tallabousees and the Allabamees." The latter two peoples refer to the several groups who the Carolinians would soon lump together as the Upper Creek. The Upper Creek were located along the Coosa, Tallapoosa, and Alabama Rivers and comprised the Coosa, which included the Okfuski and the Tuchebatchee, the Abihka, who might also have been Coosa, or at least closely related, the Hilibi, the Holiwahali, the Eufaula, the Atasi, and many others.[7] In addition, the Alabama lived there, already recognized as one of the groups of the Upper Creek. The report counted thirteen hundred men among these Indians; like the Creek on the Ocmulgee, they "are Great Warriors & trade with this Government for a great quantity of goods."

West of the Upper Creek, about two hundred miles, were the Chickasaw, "who are [at] least in number six hundred Men." They were characterized as "stout and warlike." The report noted correctly, "They are divided part in the

English interest & part in the French." The French had the advantage of being nearer to Chickasaw than the English, and the great distance of the Chickasaw from Charles Town meant that "we have but few skins or furs from" them. Trade was maintained with the Chickasaw by purchasing their slaves, which they had "taken from several nations of Indians that live beyond them." In fact, many of the slaves they took lived between the Chickasaw and Carolina, but the proprietors had said that no slaves could be taken within five hundred miles of Charles Town, so it behooved the governor and council to say that they came from much further away.

The discussion of the Cherokee that followed was understandably vague. Although the Cherokee lived much closer than the Chickasaw—the report noted that they were just 250 miles away—the colony had little trade with them. The report did not even state the basic geographic divisions among the Cherokee. It estimated their population at five thousand men. Trade with the colony was "Inconsiderable," because, the report stated, the Cherokee were "but ordinary Hunters & less Warriors." This "Inconsiderable" trade, however, was because the Cherokee had not developed a taste for English goods to the same extent as the Creek and the Chickasaw. Moreover, Virginians dominated the European trade with the Cherokee, leaving less for Carolina, though in the next decade the Carolinians made great inroads and pushed out many of the Virginians.

The Cherokee, having few contacts with Carolina, were somewhat immune from the dangers affected by the European arrival until the end of the first decade of the eighteenth century, when they, too, began raiding for slaves and became enmeshed in the wars of the region. The location of their upper towns in the mountains allowed them respite from the damage inflicted by both raids and warfare, and the Cherokee towns of the Piedmont provided a further buffer. The Spanish were too far away, the English were too weak militarily, and the French had yet to expand their power bases from the south and north to threaten them directly. Their main threat of attack came from the Creek to the south and from Iroquois raiders to the north.

The 1708 census reported 5,000 Cherokee warriors, but this seems to be an overestimate—4,000 to 4,250 seems more likely. The more refined census made in 1715 by John Barnwell, which collated and corrected reports by Thomas Nairne, John Wright, and Price Hughes (Nairne and Wright were the colony's agents to the Indians and had access to more accurate information on the Cherokee than was available to Carolina in 1708), tallied 4,000 Cherokee men.[8] Barnwell also calculated 731 Ochese Creek, an increase over the 1708 report of 131 warriors that could have been due either to adoption or mobility among Creek groups. Barnwell's census also raises the number of Alabama and Upper Creek men slightly from 1,300 to 1,352.

The Chickasaw are much harder to estimate.[9] Iberville's calculation of 2,000 men seems rather high, given the numbers reported by the English in 1708 (600) and 1715 (700), but circumstantial evidence indicates that he may have been correct. It will be recalled that in a speech to the Chickasaw he attributed their precipitous decline to their slaving expeditions, and in his journal he did not say that the Chickasaw disagreed with this assessment.[10] There is no evidence that Chickasaw numbers declined at this time from disease, and given the Chickasaw hopes for peace with the Choctaw, who far outnumbered them, we may conclude that Iberville was correct: slaving had decimated them, as it had their victims.

THE DEMOGRAPHICS OF CAROLINA'S NATIVE NEIGHBORS

Barnwell's 1715 census presents more detailed data on the demographic composition of Indian groups than the 1708 census, and it also provides data on the northern or Piedmont Indians and some low country Indians, which the earlier report does not. In addition, Barnwell provided data on numbers of women and children, though for the Piedmont, low country, Yuchi, and Chickasaw, these numbers are combined into one category. For the other, more familiar groups—those on the Savannah River, the Creek, and the Cherokee—data on children is divided by gender.

The numbers provided in the report are much more precise for the Savannah River groups and the Creek than for other Indians. Numbers usually are rounded to the nearest hundred for Chickasaw and Cherokee. For the less numerous Piedmont peoples, the combined number of women and children in each group is rounded to the tens column, but the number of men is usually not rounded. The familiarity of the agents with the Savannah River groups and the Creek permitted greater demographic precision than for other Indian groups. The agents might never have visited the Cherokee, for instance, and thus had to rely on secondhand information from the traders (hence the rounding to the nearest hundred) for each Cherokee division and demographic category. As for the Piedmont peoples, Barnwell and other Carolinians fought alongside the men in the Tuscarora War, permitting them to figure their numbers more precisely than they could the women and children, whom they collapsed into one category.

The most trustworthy data from the 1715 census, that which exists for the Savannah River peoples (Yamasee, Apalachicola, Apalachee, and Savannah),[11] the Lower Creek (labeled Ochesee), and the Upper Creek (divided as

Abihka, Taliboosa, and Alabama), reveals a demographic profile of the Indian peoples in and west of the colony. In all of these groups, except the Savannah and Apalachee, adult males comprised 27 percent to 34 percent of the population. If we exclude the Yamasee, there is even greater consistency, as the adult males of these groups comprised from 27 percent to 30 percent. The Apalachee had a much larger percentage of adult males (43 percent) and the Savannah a smaller percentage (24 percent). The relatively few Savannah adult males might be explained by the migration of many Savannah to Pennsylvania, Maryland, and elsewhere, though warfare could also have had an impact. There are other incongruities in the Savannah numbers, which include an especially large number of adult females and very few children. Among the Savannah, the number of children (50) added to the number of adult males (67) almost equals the number of adult women (116). The absence of adult males probably explains the absence of children, but not why so many adult women chose to remain on the Savannah River and not migrate to other Savannah Indian towns. If they had recently been widowed, the disparity in the number of children should not have been evident yet. It is possible that an unusual number of Savannah women had established relationships with the traders, but if that had been the case, then the children would probably have been recorded in the census.

Among the Apalachee, the disproportionate number of adult males, in this case, a large number, is not countered by an unusual number of women— the proportion of women to men among the Apalachee is similar to the other Indian groups. What makes the Apalachee so unusual is the low number of children, which parallels that of the Savannah. The number of children ordinarily found in the Savannah River and Creek groups is from 36 percent to 52 percent of the population, but among the Apalachee they comprised only 17 percent. As a people held in a semihostage situation, the Apalachee likely practiced birth control, for in 1715 they had been along the Savannah River for more than a decade, so most of the children there probably were born after their move in 1704. Whereas the other Indian groups averaged from 1.0 to 1.4 children per adult female, the Apalachee women numbered slightly fewer than one child for every two women.

To summarize, in most of the Indian communities recorded by Barnwell, the number of men and women approximated each other, with women comprising 53 percent to 56 percent of the adult population, adult males comprising 27 percent to 30 percent of the total population, and women averaging more than one child each. Those communities that experienced traumatic upheavals varied from the norm. The Apalachee had been moved

TABLE 1. Census of Indians of South Carolina and nearby, 1715

Group	Villages	Men	Women	Boys	Girls
Yamasee	10	413	345	234	228
Apalachicola	2	64	71	42	37
Apalachee	4	275	248	65	55
Savano	3	67	116	20	30
Yuchi	2	130	{270 women and children}		
Ochesee or Creek	10	731	837	417	421
Abihka	15	502	578	366	327
Taliboosee	16	636	710	511	486
Alabama	4	214	276	161	119
Cherokee					
Upper	19	900	980	400	480
Middle	30	2,500	2,000	950	900
Lower	11	600	620	400	480
Chickasaw	6	700	{1,200 women and children}		
		Northern			
Catawba	7	570	[900 women and children]		
Saraw	1	140	[370 women and children]		
Waccamaw	4	210	[400 women and children]		
Cape Fear	5	76	[130 women and children]		
Santee	2	43	[60 women and children]		
Congaree	1	22			
Wereaw	1	36	[70 women and children]		
Sewee	1	[57 men, women, and children]			
		"Mixt with English Settlement"			
Itwan	1	80	[160 women and children]		
Corsaboy	5	95	[200 women and children]		

Source: SC Transcripts, 7:238–239, based on the journals of Nairne, Wright, Hughes, and Barnwell, who corrected them

to the Savannah River by force; many of the Savannah recently had fought against the colony, while others, more males than females, had migrated away. Of the other peoples, the Yamasee were the one group that appears to have strayed from the norm and thus could also have experienced recent difficulties. They fell outside the average statistics by having a 34 percent adult male population and more men than women (who comprised just 46 percent of the adult population). What happened to these women? If Yamasee numbers had been similar to those of most other groups, which typically had 53 percent women in the adult population (only the Alabama, which had 56 percent women, strayed from the norm) then the Yamasee would have numbered 447 women rather than 345. Since Yamasee women bore a normal number of children, 1.35 per woman, and the number of female children approximated male children, as in other groups, there must be another explanation for the low number of adult women. It is possible that Yamasee complaints about illegal enslavement (discussed in later chapters) had a more dramatic impact on this group than historians have estimated.

When we apply the demographic model of Creek and Savannah River Indians to other native peoples in the 1715 census, only two groups fit its characteristics. Generally, the percentage of males is much greater in the other Indian groups, which is probably, in large measure, owing to the census takers' more limited information on women and children among these Indians. The Lower Cherokee, by contrast, fit the model. Males comprised 28.5 percent of their population, whereas the estimates for males among the Upper and Middle Cherokee were respectively 33 and 39 percent. Carolina had far greater contact with the Lower Cherokee than the others who lived further away, and thus counted women and children more efficiently, which would explain the disparity in the statistics.

Among the Piedmont and low country Indians, as previously noted, the census takers combined the numbers of women and children, probably because they did not have accurate information and were merely guessing. Among the Catawba (39 percent), Waccamaw (34 percent), Cape Fear (37 percent), Santee and Congaree (52 percent), Wereaw (34 percent), Itawan (33 percent), and Corsaboy (32 percent), the male population is greater than the model. Although the figures could be accurate, they are probably not and instead indicate a different relationship between the colony and these Indians than with those along the Savannah River and the Creek. Whereas South Carolina conducted trade in the Indian communities of the Creek and the Savannah River peoples, Indians of the Piedmont towns often traveled to the traders on the Savannah River for their wares. Colony business with Piedmont Indians also was conducted on the Savannah River. The Piedmont and low country Indians had a distinct talent for "lying low" and avoided contact with Europeans except when it suited them.[12] Lying low was a strategy practiced by these Indians for the next 150 years, and it played a role in their survival in the South, in contrast to so many other Indians who were removed to the west. Europeans rarely knew where these Indians were and how many were in their group—often they appeared out of nowhere and then slipped away.

The other large southern Indian group, which the report does not mention but which was important to South Carolina, was the Choctaw, and they numbered anywhere from 3,500 to 5,000 warriors at this time. Iberville estimated between 3,800 and 4,000 Choctaw men. Drawing on French documents, Delisle thought that there were 6,000 men in 1703.[13]

Lacking extensive trade with the Choctaw, the Carolinians knew little about them. As far as the government was concerned, the Choctaw were either to be lured from the French or enslaved. Although it went unmentioned in the report, the government actively formulated plans to contend with the Choctaw and thus "solve" the French problem. To do so, they had to secure their Indian alliances, and this meant restructuring Indian affairs.

REFORM OF THE INDIAN TRADE

The government had attempted to control the Indian trade since the first English settlement in Carolina. These attempts arose from the proprietors' desire to monopolize profits from the trade as well as to protect the colony from warfare with neighboring Indians. The colony's history was one of abject failure where regulation was concerned. The proprietors' minimal influence over their governors prevented them from regulating the trade, and even if they had had the influence, they would probably not have spent the resources necessary to administer it effectively. By 1707 the proprietors had largely withdrawn from colonial affairs, particularly from Indian relations. Yet their power over the choice and tenure of governors remained. Governors continued to do as they pleased until their removal, and by then they had usually wrested the profits they desired out of the trade and the colony. To reform the Indian trade, the first step was to transfer the governor's power to the assembly. Many who supported this transfer were gentlemen traders. These men had used the trade to capitalize their plantations, but they remained committed to the trade, perhaps because of the continued high return on investments and because it brought them personal fulfillment. They served in the Carolina assembly and held other positions of prominence, including, in the case of James Moore, the governorship.

Another group heavily engaged in the trade consisted of Charles Town merchants who worked with the gentlemen traders or employed newer men who lacked capital. The merchants played an important role in the economy and in the assembly, where they assumed positions of power. Many merchants and gentlemen traders worried that continued abuse of Indians would ultimately harm the Indian trade, threaten the plantation system, and increase the power of France and Spain. Yet not all of the gentlemen traders wished to see greater government control. Some feared that government control would translate into favoritism; others saw no need for reform because they were already profiting from the system. But another strong force drew men toward regulation: imperialism. For many Britons, the empire meant the introduction of order in their lives and their society. Some, like the Whigs, saw order as a practical result of a more balanced sharing of power among Commons, Lords, and monarchy, while others, like the Tories, looked to kingship and the established church as the true sources of societal stability. Both thought more closely about the benefits of a well-regulated empire, though Whigs emphasized parliamentary regulation through the Navigation Acts and a strong army to complement the navy, whereas the Tories conceived of an empire led by the king and protected by the navy. Both groups believed that their interests and those of the colony were dependent on good relations with particular groups of Indians and on crushing the French and Spanish. James Moore, Thomas Welch, and Thomas Nairne all shared this imperial vision. They aggressively attacked their European enemies and pushed Britain to extend its colonial claims throughout the South. Welch and Nairne, in particular, dreamed of building colonies on the Mississippi and hatched plans in England to fulfill their vision. From Wales arrived Price Hughes with a scheme to settle his countrymen on the Mississippi; Englishman Daniel Coxe received a grant to colonize in French and Indian territory to the west of Carolina in his proposed colony of Carolana.[14] The Franco-Spanish invasion of 1706 confirmed what the Carolina gentlemen already suspected—that the struggle for control of the South would be a fight to the finish. They never once contemplated peaceful coexistence with France and Spain.

In Carolina, the imperialists were generally the strongest proponents of a controlled trade, partly because they perceived that imperial ends would benefit all and partly because they recognized that many of the traders had no concern for the empire or the colony and cared only about profits—a dangerous situation that could and would lead to disaster. Those of Whiggish inclinations supported regulation more than the Tories, but even many Tories believed in regulation. Common traders were irked by governmental regulations yet often complied. They chafed, however, under the hypocrisy of government men who talked about protecting Indians and then committed abuses. They also saw how the leading men themselves were divided, in part, from the religious factionalism that had weakened the colony for decades, and that their personal and petty disputes led to confusion, irrationality, and inconsistency in regulation and its enforcement.

Carolinians were united, however, against the Virginia traders, who not only directed profits away from the Carolinians but also interfered with Carolina's potential use of the trade for diplomatic purposes. When the Savannah Indians "Revolted" against Carolina by deserting the Savannah River in June 1707, the government alleged (probably mistakenly) that the Virginia traders were behind it.[15] The Commons House authorized James Moore to take twenty men and seize the traders' goods. Moore also was authorized to settle the Savannah "in any proper place for the present year," until the government had a chance to confer with their "Chief" and reach an agreement.[16]

It is not clear what led to Savannah discontent, but the relocation of the Apalachee only a few miles from the Savannah might have irritated them, and if nothing else, it made the colony less dependent on the Savannah and more inclined to abuse or neglect them.[17] Still, the colony did not want to lose the Savannah, and Thomas Nairne, the most vocal member of the assembly in favor of regulation, considered their defection grave enough that he asked the assembly to address the matter before all others. As noted above, the assembly responded by sending Moore to seize the Virginia traders' goods and to convince the Savannah to stay.[18] Many Savannah had already moved north to Maryland and Pennsylvania, where the governor of Pennsylvania encountered them. On a visit to a Savannah village on the Susquehanna River, Governor John Evans met with "several of the Savannah Indians from the southward [who] came to settle Here," because, as one told him, 450 Catawba had "besieged them." The Catawba was a name the English used to describe many of the Piedmont Indian groups of both South and North Carolina. A trader who acted as interpreter added that the Savannah had killed "several Christians," which led the Carolina government to set the Catawba upon them under the leadership of "some Christians."[19] Presumably, these were Moore and his men, for they were reimbursed 173 pounds from the assembly for their expedition against "the Deserted Savannas."[20] The Catawba, under Carolinian beckoning, official or otherwise, had preyed on the Savannah, as the colony had done to its erstwhile Westo ally. The Savannah, probably in revenge, then attacked some of the "Northward Indians," a designation the colony used to describe the Catawba and other Indians of the Piedmont, and they also "Carried Several of our Indian slaves away with them."[21]

The Savannah towns on the Savannah River were distant from white settlement, but because of the value of their location as a way station to the western tribes, some traders may have tried to establish themselves there. Circumstantial evidence further supports the contention that Savannah land was threatened, for in the lower house report made immediately after news of the Savannah attack on the "Northward Indians," a motion was put forth for a bill to protect Indian land because when "the Inhabitants run out land among Indians [it] will occasion the Indians to leave us."[22] The assembly requested that two traders, John Bull and Edward Wooky, appear before them with information about the Savannah, but the traders asked for protection from arrest in coming to and going from the house. Thomas Welch was also ordered to appear and granted immunity from arrest.[23] Granting traders protection from arrest going to and from the assembly was common, especially given traders' propensity to disobey the laws. Even so, the traders might not have done anything wrong yet still could fear arrest. With so many high government officials involved in the Indian trade and illegal activities, and with Carolina officials' history of arresting opponents under dubious, false, and sometimes illegal pretenses (which continued through the next decade), the two traders had every reason to demand protection. Bull appeared in October 1707 and reported that he had learned from the Shutteree, a Piedmont group, that 130 Indians "Calling themselves Savannah & Sen'atuees" (Santees?) fell on them, "Their Bows & Arrows on their backs pointed with brass & Iron." The force carried away forty-five women and children, but mostly children. A Cheraw Indian (from a group then in the Piedmont) informed Bull that the attackers traded with "white men at their own Homes & that they Live but 30 days Journey from us."[24] Apparently, if the report was correct, the Savannah were selling their captives in Virginia, Maryland, or Pennsylvania. If the "Northward Indians" of the Carolina Piedmont had had trouble getting weapons from the colony before, the attacks of the Savannah now changed officials' minds. They were sent fifty guns, a thousand flints, powder, and bullets to attack the Savannah. Whoever brought in a Savannah scalp would be allowed to keep his gun.[25] As for the Savannah, not all of them would leave the colony.[26] About a third of the population remained in their settlements along the Savannah River.[27] Those who left would continue their attacks on the Piedmont peoples.[28]

Carolina's problems with the mobile Savannah illustrated the necessity of controlling Indian affairs in as wide an arc as possible. Carolina redoubled its efforts to remove the Virginians from the Indian trade. Carolina law did not provide for seizure of the Virginians' goods, but the assembly thought that seizure might be legal by the laws of England. The colony passed a law in 1707 by which it hoped to control the Virginia traders by making them and others pay a duty on all deerskins exported from the colony. The Carolinians claimed that skins coming from the Cherokee and all the Indians south of the colony were subject to this tax. The Virginians, however, asserted that most southern Indians were not located in South Carolina, so that the colony had no power to lay a tax, which led to a dispute that lasted for years. Carolina seized traders' goods for nonpayment of the tax, which led Virginia to complain and instigated an inquiry by the Board of Trade, which administered England's colonies. To the Board of Trade, Carolina's proprietors claimed ignorance of the law their colony had passed! They placed all blame on the colonial assembly—but they promised to inform the Board of Trade of the reasons for the law as soon as possible. Three months later, in February 1709, the proprietors had still not put forth an explanation, even though Carolina had representatives in England who could have clarified the situation. The board threatened to take the matter to Queen Anne, but the proprietors seem to have been in no rush to investigate or explain and did not appear before the board for another six months. The proprietors explained that the duty on the Virginians was small and intended to support the clergy—always dear to Queen Anne's heart—and that some traders had been stopped by Carolina but they had paid the duty and had their goods released. The proprietors asserted that they "know of no Law that Prohibits any of the Queens Subjects Trading in Carolina but that all Her Majesty's Subjects have the Same Liberty and Freedom of Trading there as any of the Inhabitants of the Province of Carolina have and that it shall be our constant Care not to allow of any Law to the Contrary."[29] (In fact, the Carolinians had considered a law barring the Virginians from the trade, but it failed in 1701.)[30] This skirted the issue of jurisdiction, which the proprietors assumed they had over Indians west of the colony. In 1712, Virginia again made representation against South Carolina's prejudicial laws against Virginia traders, and the queen ordered the lords proprietors to instruct their governor neither to levy duties on the Virginia traders nor to permit any "hindrance or molestation whatsoever."[31] The Carolina government persisted, however, "discouraging" Virginia traders through regulations, seizure of goods, and taxes.[32]

ABUSIVE TRADERS

Placing a duty on skins was nothing new, and neither was the attempt to regulate the trade. Governor Seth Sothell had combined the two goals unsuccessfully in 1691, in a law he had the assembly pass, but he was removed from office a little over a month later, and the law apparently never went into effect.[33] In 1698, Governor Joseph Blake informed the proprietors that he would attempt to get the assembly to regulate the trade so that abuses would not lead to war, but he added, "we have no Reason to expect any Mischief from the Indian Trade, [for] the Small-Pox hath Killed so many of them, that we have little Reason to Believe they will be Capable of doing any Harm to us for several Years to Come." The "Distemper" had "Swept off great Numbers of them 4 or 500 Miles Inland as well [as] upon the Sea Coast as in our Neighbourhood, which must Needs lessen the trade very much."[34] Despite the ravages of disease, Indians still took the time to complain about the traders, which kept the issue before the assembly. In 1700 the traders and "Several of the Indian Kings" were ordered to appear before the assembly to discuss the traders' abuses and their "Lewdness and wickedness," which are "a Scandal to the Religion we Profess."[35] But the assembly's main concern was to convince Indians to capture runaway black slaves and to find ways to bar the Virginians from the trade.[36]

By 1701 the legislature still had not regulated the trade but was moving toward a licensing system, which would force traders to provide security for their good behavior.[37] The legislature also discussed limiting the debt load of Indians, for if the traders allowed Indians' debts to accrue or tricked them into large debts they could not pay, they would be forced into extreme measures that threatened the peace. The assembly also began considering establishing an agent to overlook the trade, that is, "a Judicious man be sent Among the Indjans [sic] to inspect into the Regularities of the Traders, with Power to Send them down, if he Think fit."[38]

By Nathaniel Johnson's administration (1703–1709), the government was ready to enact legislation, but the war with Spain and France forestalled action until after the failed invasion of Carolina in 1706. The great abuses of the traders were then brought before the assembly in the example of John Musgrove. Musgrove's prominence was growing—in 1705 he was one of two translators employed by Carolina to interpret for the Creek at the Coweta meeting where the alliance was consummated—but in December 1706 he was charged with a series of abuses against a variety of Indians. In the assembly, it was charged that Musgrove had taxed each Creek four deerskins, "under pretense of making a Present to the Govern[or], and that this had "hindered them from going to War" for the colony. This was precisely the kind of activity that Nairne and his fellow imperialists hoped to prevent— they wanted Indians to fight for the colony when called upon, and they did not want the governor, or people in the governor's name, to employ Indians for personal profit before imperial interests. Musgrove also was accused of enslaving sixteen free Apalachee and of having sold another six free Apalachee. Additional charges included enslaving a free woman of Coolene town, a free woman of Tomela (an Apalachee town), and eight Westo. He had also threatened the "Tuckesaw Indian King," demanding of him four slaves for his and William Steads's Indian wives. The Tuckesaw and Musgrove agreed to a compensation of three slaves to release the two wives, but trader John Pight rescued two of these slaves from Musgrove, which raised Musgrove's ire. In addition, Musgrove was charged with taking a number of slaves or free Indians from the Ilcombe (an Apalachee town) or Wacoa Indians because they presumably had killed some of his cattle. Moreover, even though the governor had given the Apalachee land on the Savannah River, Musgrove had "hindered and given the greatest discouragement" to their settlement, "which Abuse their Casseiques did Complain." The final charge against Musgrove was that he had used the governor's name to prevent the Indians from going to war. The assembly voted not to apprehend Musgrove on these charges but ordered him to remain in Charles Town.[39]

Charges in the assembly were then presented against traders Anthony Probat, James Lucas, and John Pight. They were arrested for purchasing ten free Indians from "Tomichee" (possibly the famed Tomochichi who befriended Oglethorpe twenty-five years later). An additional twenty free Indians, most of them Apalachee, were also enslaved by the three. The governor ordered the Indians released, which the traders had "Contemptuously and willfully disobeyed . . . to the great danger and Hazard of this Colony."[40] Apalachee on their way to Charles Town to testify against the traders were met by Probat and a party of Indians in his company, who threatened the Apalachee that if they did not go home they would kill them all when they got there. Probat, Pight, and Lucas were accused by the assembly of attempting to suborn witnesses. The assembly directed the attorney general to prosecute them, as well as Musgrove and James Child (a notorious trader discussed below). Probat and Lucas gave security, but Musgrove and Pight, as men of power, did not. Apparently, none of the men were prosecuted and all returned within six months to trading with the Indians—and again were accused of abuses.[41]

Why the traders were not adequately punished is not known. Perhaps the attorney general thought that the laws of the colony were inadequate for prosecution. Certainly many doubted, as did Governor Johnson, that crimes against Indians should be treated with the same severity as crimes against Europeans. Killing and enslaving an Indian was not considered on a par with killing and enslaving a European. Even the laws that were soon passed against enslaving Indians provided only fines as punishment. Nevertheless, assembly reformers, led by Thomas Nairne, used Musgrove's and the other traders' abuses as justification for introducing measures to regulate the trade.[42] They iterated their frustrated attempts to "Redress" problems, laying the blame upon the "Interest that the Upper House have had in the Indian Trade."[43]

THE COMMONS ASSERTS
CONTROL OVER THE INDIAN TRADE

When members of the Commons House blamed the upper house, they meant the governor, who controlled that house, which comprised his council. The key item of reform for Nairne and his followers concerned regulation, over which they clashed with the governor and upper house. Johnson complained about his proposed loss of power in Indian affairs, but the house countered that its bill would merely prevent abuses and regulate trade, not divest the governor of his power in Indian relations. The crux of the argument was money. The governor adamantly opposed the legislature's attempt to deny him the presents that Indians gave to the colony. Gift-giving was part and parcel of Indian relations, for presents bound people in amity and cooperation.[44] Carolina's Indian trading partners gave the colony, or the governor, gifts, and the colony returned gifts of equal value to the Indians. The Indians gave pelts and other commodities, and after the government calculated their value it exchanged clothing, guns, and other items in like proportion.[45] The assembly complained that it was inequitable for the Indians' gifts to the colony to go to the governor, because the return gifts were paid for out of tax revenue. Many believed that the presents belonged to the public. Moreover, traders had been extorting presents from Indians in the governor's name. The simple way to correct the abuse, according to the assembly, was to consider all Indian presents public property, and then it would be easy to identify those engaging in extortion. Governor Johnson refused, however, to give up what he felt was rightfully his and threatened to veto legislation that denied him the presents. The assembly threatened to take its case to the proprietors.[46]

The Commons's attempt at reform went so far as to propose complete government control of the trade; the government would prohibit all private traders and manage the trade by hiring traders to sell public goods. Governor Johnson believed that this "grand monopoly" was contrary to the colony's charter. The assembly countered that no less a personage than the "Late Governor Moore" had recommended this course in a public speech to the house, and he "certainly understood the Nature of That Trade as well as any man."[47] Without this bill, the house warned, the colony could expect "Our Utter Ruin and Destruction from a Continuance of the hurried Abuses and grievous mismanagement of the Trader Amongst the Indians." Unfazed, the governor and his council rejected the bill, claiming that they had already rejected another trading act earlier in the session and that a rejected bill could not be read again in the same session. Afraid that the assembly would appeal to the proprietors, who could remove the governor at their pleasure, Johnson tried to curry favor with the lords by demanding of the assembly a bill to settle the colony's debts.[48] The lower house responded that the new trade bill was so different from the last it had offered that there was "nothing Common to both" except the "Words (Indian) and (Trade) are used in Each." The lower house could be as difficult as the governor. As for priorities, the lower house scolded the governor that the Indian trade bill was more important than "Some Peoples being without the money due To Them." A brief stalemate occurred in which the governor and upper house refused to meet with the lower house. Resolutely, the lower house offered a bill declaring its rights, but gave in slightly by offering a bill to establish the colony's credit. All bills had to be voted on three times before they became law—so the house could vote once, even twice for a bill, but then oppose it on third reading to prevent its enactment into law. Thus the house offered the credit bill while waiting for the governor to act on the trading bill. The governor finally negotiated with the lower house. He demanded compensation of four hundred pounds per year for the lost Indian presents. They finally agreed on a one-time gift of four hundred pounds and annual compensation of two hundred pounds, with the public receiving all future Indian presents.[49] Somewhere in the negotiations the government monopoly over the trade was also dropped in favor of a plan of regulation and oversight.

The act of 1707 regulating the Indian trade was far-reaching. Its title stated its purpose: "An Act for Regulating the Indian Trade and Making it Safe to the Public." The bill's preamble took a high-minded and moral tone while stating the need for strong government overview of the trade and the traders: "WHEREAS the greater number of those persons that trade among the Indians in amity with this Government, do generally lead loose, vicious lives, to the scandal of the Christian religion, and do likewise oppress the people among whom they live, by their unjust and illegal actions, which if not prevented may in time tend to the destruction of this Province," the following measures would be enacted. All traders had to purchase a license, renewable each year, for eight pounds. They must also give a one-hundred-pound bond to ensure their good behavior while trading and their obeyance of the law. The penalty for trading without a license was a hundred pounds. The license did not concern trade with Settlement Indians, with whom anyone could trade. There were no restrictions on whom the traders could trade with, though ammunition could not be sold to enemy Indians, and liquor was barred.[50]

To oversee the traders and the trade, the act established a commission to hear Indian grievances. The commissioners would "frame general instructions to be given to all the traders who take out licenses." Those who did not obey the commission's orders and instructions were subject to forfeiture of their license. The commission was to meet in Charles Town twice a year, for three days per meeting, to "dispatch of the business of this Act." It could and did meet more often than that.[51]

The new trading law forbade traders and all other persons from selling free Indians as slaves. Extorting Indians to give skins, slaves, or other items as gifts to the governor was also expressly prohibited. The commission would hear complaints that Indians had to make in these matters, and they could refer cases to the courts. Unfortunately, the penalties were not severe. A trader found guilty of selling a free Indian was subject to a sixty-pound fine—thus selling a free Indian was not deemed as bad as trading without a license. If the culprit could not pay the fine he was subject to corporal punishment, though the act stated that this could not include the loss of life or limb. To oversee the daily operation of the traders, the act also provided for the selection of a resident Indian agent, and this was Thomas Nairne.

The Indian agent's job was full-time. The agent had to be at his post ten months of the year—more specifically, he was not allowed to "be in the English Settlement above two months in the whole year," and never this at one time. The agent would hear disputes between Indians and traders, which he could determine in any case not above ten pounds. He could also settle disputes between traders, though his findings were not binding. He was empowered to examine witnesses and to send to Charles Town those who refused to give testimony. Traders who did not execute the agent's warrants, orders, and decrees were subject to a £10 fine. The agent also had all the powers of a justice of the peace, and could collect sureties from those traders in debt to persons in the settlements. The agent had to provide a £200 bond for fulfilling the functions of his office, but he would receive a hefty salary of

£250 (equivalent to £166 sterling in 1708), one that compared favorably with other high government offices. On the other hand, the agent, under oath, had to swear not to engage in any trade with the Indians and thus could not have any income in the Indian country outside of his agency; Nairne supplemented his income through his slave-manned plantation. To prevent conflicts of interest, the commissioners, too, were barred from participating in the Indian trade and from receiving presents from the traders or anyone else associated with the trade.

Regulating the trade and the traders' behavior through the close oversight of an agent and commission was combined with another act to protect the land of the Yamasee, the colony's most important ally.[52] Carolinians valued Yamasee land highly because of its potential for rice production. The Europeans who lived in the southern portion of the colony were limited to the Sea Islands, whereas the Yamasee had the mainland to the southwest as far as the Savannah River, much of which was perfect for rice. Traders had been infringing on Indian land, and the assembly took steps to prevent encroachment. The title of the bill stated the problem succinctly: "An Act to Limit the Bounds of the Yamasee Settlement, to Prevent Persons From Disturbing Them With Their Stocks, and to Remove Such as are Settled Within the Limitation Hereafter Mentioned." Again the preamble averred how the bill was necessitated by the threats the colony faced: "WHEREAS nothing can conduce more under God to the repelling of an enemy which shall attempt to make an invasion in the south part of this Colony on the sea coast, by giving us timely notice thereof, than that nation of Indians called Yamasees, and all other Indians within the limitation, hereafter mentioned, be encouraged to abide in their present settlement; and that all reasons for their removal may be taken away." The Yamasee land was defined as all the mainland bound by the Combahee to the north, by the marshes and islands of the Coosa and Port Royal Rivers to the southeast, to the southwest by the Savannah River, and to the northwest by a line drawn from the head of the Combahee River to the head of the Savannah River, as well as an island inhabited by the Yamasee between their Pocosabo town and the Coosawhachee River. The act provided that no one could survey Yamasee land under penalty of a one-hundred-pound fine, except if the land was to be laid out for a church and a glebe for a minister to be used "to instruct the said Indians in the Christian religion." All persons who already had settled on Yamasee land or used it for their stocks or agriculture, even if they had titles to the land, had to vacate within one year of ratification or pay a fine of a hundred pounds. Those removed would be reimbursed their expenses for both removal and improvements.[53]

With the new Indian trade bill in place, Thomas Nairne, as the colony's Indian agent, was ready to push forward his plans to regulate the trade, rationalize relations with the Indians, and fulfill the designs of the Whig-imperialist faction in the colony.

WHO HAS THE POWER?
GOVERNOR JOHNSON VERSUS INDIAN AGENT NAIRNE

One of Nairne's first measures was to capture and make an example of James Child, of whom complaints had been made as early as 1706. On that occasion Child had taken captive some free Indians, who were released by the assembly, which also ordered him not to leave Charles Town. The house requested that the governor restrain Child from the Indian trade—a bill granting the governor the power to bar those who had committed any "misbehavior or abuse" against the Indians was enacted for this purpose.[54] A year and a half later, even before his appointment as agent, Nairne, as a justice of the peace had seized Child for "making war on his own Accord against the Indians, and for Several other enormous, and very notorious crimes." The crimes were so "horrid" that they went beyond "the power given to the Commons by our Indian Trading Act," and thus Child was "put in Irons" to be tried by the attorney general "according to law."[55] The assembly noted that Child's crimes included torture and murder of Indians,[56] but Nairne was more specific in a later petition he made to the proprietors. He noted that the traders had "contracted a habit . . . [of] inciting one Tribe of our friends to destroy others, merely to purchase the prisoners taken for slaves. Kidnapping and selling free people of such weak Towns as were unable to resent the Injury."[57] Nairne was in no ways opposed to the enslavement of Indians; as noted earlier, he had participated and led slaving raids.[58] He later told the earl of Sunderland: "It is our custom in this Province to make merchandise of such other savages as [our Indian allies] take in wars."[59] Nairne praised "our friend the Talapoosies and Chicasaws [who] Employ themselves in making Slaves of such Indians about the Lower parts of the Mississipi [sic] as are now Subject to the french." The English encouraged the Indians to go slaving with "good prices . . . and some men think that it both serves to Lessen their numbers before the french can arm them and it is a more Effectual way of Civilising and Instructing, Then all the Efforts used by the French Missionaries."[60] However, Nairne criticized "those English traders, who live among them," who had "a trick of setting them to surprise one another's towns, by that means to have the quicker sale of their goods for the prisoners taken." In other words, slaving should be done only against enemy, not allied, Indians.

Although illegal, these traders had learned "to procure a present to be made to the Governor of the booty so got." This, Nairne believed, was the case with Child, who, with the governor's support, had led a force of Cherokee against "two or three small towns of our friends . . . they destroyed the towns, took about 160 slaves," and killed others.[61]

The governor and council requested depositions concerning Child's malfeasance but questioned whether a person who killed Indians in friendship with the government "ought to be proceeded against: as a Murderer of any of the Queen's Liege Subjects."[62] Thus, the position raised by the proprietors thirty years before was still unsettled—were Indians and Europeans equal before the law? The lower house faced other problems in pushing their case against Child. The three Cherokee they questioned provided no helpful information as to Child's crimes. The lower house believed that these Cherokee had "had their Lesson aforesaid"—that is, they were told what to say by Child or his confederates. Two traders also were examined before the house, and "after Sometime" one "Acknowledged that Child has been Guilty of Sever[al] crimes, but the other tried to vindicate Child. The house dismissed the trader's story, believing him to be involved in Child's "Irregularities."[63] The Indians wrongly enslaved were freed.

Governor Johnson had had enough of Nairne. The agent had dragged the governor's name through the mud by constantly pointing out his approval of the illegal wars in exchange for "booty." The attack on Child, however, placed Johnson's involvement in a premeditated light as the mastermind behind these wars. For Child was employed by Thomas Broughton, son-in-law of Governor Johnson. Child would not have acted on his own in fomenting these wars, so it was easy to peg Broughton as having a guiding hand and to put the governor behind Broughton. Nairne located the governor squarely behind Broughton by accusing Broughton's traders of illegally obtaining presents for the governor. Nairne seized from Broughton "1,000 skins for the use of the Public which" the governor "pretended a right to," and "set free some Cherecies whom [Broughton's traders] kept slaves, though they have been our friends these Twenty years."[64] Nairne was now a marked man, and Johnson employed all his power to crush him. In June 1708, Nairne returned to Charles Town from his visit to the Chickasaw (discussed in Chapter 6). The governor immediately imprisoned him on charges of treason.[65] Two traders, John Dickson and Edward Griffin, provided depositions against the agent. They alleged that in November 1707, Nairne had said that Queen Anne had no right to the Crown, which properly belonged to the Prince of Wales.[66] As Nairne languished in jail for six months, he and his friends sought a variety of means of recourse. He offered to post a twenty-thousand-pound bond to go free until trial, but the governor refused. Nairne petitioned the lords proprietors, relating the irregularities of the proceedings against him: he protested that even if he was guilty of speaking against Queen Anne he could not be charged with treason, because he had committed no treasonous act, for it was merely alleged that he had spoken treasonous words (which he denied having said). Nairne asserted that his imprisonment occurred because the governor wished to prevent him from protecting Indians from illegal enslavement at the hands of people like the governor's son-in-law and that the governor sought revenge for Nairne's role in passing the legislation that stopped the governor and his men from extorting deerskins from the Indians as presents.[67] The men who testified against Nairne were Johnson's son-in-law Broughton's traders, "Two very infamous Wretches . . . one a perfect Lunatic and the other a mere villain whom I formerly put in prison for Buggery."[68] Nairne's claim that one of his accusers was a lunatic is questionable, for both remained traders for years. There can be no doubt, however, that Johnson was out to get him. Johnson prohibited his own council from examining the depositions against Nairne. Nor would he allow Nairne to come to trial.[69] Sixty-two inhabitants of Colleton County petitioned for Nairne's release and offered a bond of ten thousand pounds. The petition derided the character of the witnesses against Nairne, praised Nairne's integrity and bravery, affirmed that the charges against him were bailable, and warned of the "many bad consequences [that] may follow his being detained from that service wherein he had engaged himself for the safety of the country."[70]

Despite imprisonment, Nairne was elected to the Commons House. He was temporarily released from jail, and the Commons then debated whether he could sit in their body with the charges pending against him. Nairne testified in his defense. The house resisted deciding the matter in fear of the governor's wrath—after all, Johnson had successfully imprisoned Nairne, one of the colony's most powerful men. The governor's blatant disregard of the law in Nairne's case, his illegal enslaving of free Indians, and his continued obfuscation of the new trading laws made the Commons wary of challenging him. Johnson sought to stiffen the resolve of the assembly by informing it that he intended to prosecute Nairne as soon as he heard from the queen and the secretary of state, and he chided the house members for allowing Nairne to sit in their august body. Still, he said, it was their decision.

The Commons followed the governor's cue and expelled Nairne from the house. It also resolved that Nairne's defense and the dissent of his supporters could not be entered into the Commons House journal.[71] Nairne then petitioned for his salary as Indian agent. The Commons demanded that first he turn over the journal of his travels among the Indians and a map he had made. Nairne told the assembly that he could not comply for he had sent the map to the queen. After further argument and Nairne's refusal to appear again before the assembly, he was jailed for contempt and for not giving the house the map he had produced in its employ, and he was removed as Indian agent.[72] Nairne gave bond and fled to England to seek exoneration. Further reform would have to proceed without him.

In just two years, South Carolina had made huge strides in reforming its relations with Native Americans. The assembly had taken over regulation of the Indian trade, developed a body of rules to govern trader behavior, and created a commission and an agent to study Indian peoples and their problems, hear Indian complaints, and punish malfeasance. Nathaniel Johnson and his cronies, however, continued to block reform efforts, as the governor personally engaged in fomenting egregious wars that illegally enslaved Indians. Johnson successfully removed his nemesis Thomas Nairne by illegal imprisonment. In spite of the loss of the chief architect and voice for reform, the assembly, though cowed by the governor, continued to work for the regulation of the trade and the general improvement of Indian affairs through its appointed commission. The chief issue remained how to secure justice for Indians in their relations with Europeans. But the nature of that relationship had yet to be determined, for the hope of the proprietors to incorporate Indians within society had not been decided: it would be up to the clergy to take the first steps toward assimilation of Amerindians into South Carolina society.

8

DEFINING THE EMPIRE
CAROLINA AND
THE CONVERSION OF INDIANS

CHRISTIANITY AND
COMPETING VIEWS OF EMPIRE

The religious divisions that plagued Carolina in the late seventeenth century continued into the early eighteenth century. These divisions paralleled the Tory-Whig partisan politics of the mother country. In both the British Isles and Carolina, definitions of the nation, the political system, and the relationship between church and state were hotly contested. Although people hoped to avoid the violent political upheavals of the past, religious prejudices and civil disorders were rife. In England, individuals channeled their political energies into factions that evolved into parties, defining their positions through broadsides, pamphlets, books, and newspapers.

When historians examine the impact of these divisions in party and ideology on American society, they tend to emphasize the political philosophy that Americans inherited from England concerning the workings of the state and proper government, not the contemporary issues that lay foremost in people's minds. They also focus on the response of New Englanders to English politics, which provided a Puritan slant on issues of church and state, the monarchy, and the responsibilities of ruler and ruled.

Yet Carolina reflected the divisions within Britain more fully than New England. More ethnically and religiously diverse than the Puritan colonies or, for that matter, any colony save Pennsylvania and New York, Carolina experienced wrenching divisions almost as sharp as those of the middle colonies. Its political violence paled in comparison to the Leislerian tumults of New York, where the absence of a colonial assembly frustrated political factions and individual desires for power in ways that did not exist in Pennsylvania and Carolina. These two proprietary colonies shared a political culture of opposition to the proprietors. Ethnic divisions stratified their populace, but their class divisions differed immensely. The clearly marked social divisions of Philadelphia, between bourgeois merchants and free working people, found voice in local political organizations by the 1690s. In Charles Town, the interests of free working people found political expression only intermittently through their social betters, as in legislation to protect their economic interests vis-à-vis slave labor. Free workers were neither numerous enough nor powerful enough in Carolina to compel any political organization to focus on their interests.

In Carolina, the elite jockeyed for power and appealed to common folk only when necessary. The political factions, reflecting the basic lines of demarcation in the British Isles, had very different views of empire. The Tories represented large landed estates and supported a strong established church with favoritism toward Anglicans within government and society at large. Devoutly monarchical, suspicious of the movement for unification of Scotland and England, hierarchical in temperament, and exclusive by nature, the elite's vision of the future was countered by the "Whiggish" disposition that accepted more diversity by inclusion of many, but not all, Dissenters. The Whigs also had less fear of incorporating the Scots into a "Great Britain." The Tories, by contrast, tended to be less interested in the affairs of Europe than the commercially oriented Whigs, who promoted the expansion of imperial power, which meant engagement on the Continent as well as in America.[1]

The Tory-Whig divisions in Carolina resembled those in England in their contesting the modes and meanings of government and empire. In Carolina, these divisions reflected a dispute over the future of the colony's relations with Amerindians. More mundanely, however, they erupted in petty disputes between High Church Anglican Tories and Low Church Anglicans and Dissenting Whigs. The Tory-Anglicans sought to establish the Anglican Church as the state church and to counter the growing power and presence of Dissenters.[2] Anglicans numbered about 1,800 of the colony's 4,200 white inhabitants in 1708 and, curiously, found allies among the colony's 400 French Huguenots. The Huguenots' Calvinism should have placed them squarely in the cup of dissent, but by the end of the seventeenth century many refugee French Protestants in England and America found Anglicanism more appealing, perhaps as an extension of their quest for full acceptance in English society.[3] Carolinian Dissenters responded with discrimination against the Huguenots, because they feared that the Huguenots would increase the political power of the Tory-Anglicans. The Dissenters found allies among Low Church Anglicans, some of whom wanted to promote the church in the colony, but not by diminishing the rights of dissent.[4] Low and High Church Anglicans promoted the building of churches in each parish and the recruitment of ministers with the help of the Society for the Propagation of the Gospel in Foreign Parts (SPG). Low Church Anglicans believed that their goals could be met without state establishment of the church or, if the church was established, that it should not enjoy the favoritism that the Tories believed was necessary. Low and High churchmen appealed to the SPG (formed in 1701) for missionaries, which the society sent, but they had different ideas on how those missionaries should be employed. The intent of the organization and the Low Church people was that missionaries should convert Indians, but the High Church people wanted them to administer to the needs of whites.

Neither side had a monopoly on bigotry and underhanded politics. Many of the High Church Anglicans tried to disenfranchise the Dissenters, or at least keep them from holding political office, which was the same program they had in England. By contrast, the Dissenters, who had sought disenfranchisement of the Huguenots, complained that their opponents were trying to enfranchise non-Protestants in order to control elections. (Catholics and Jews probably found the High Church Anglicans more to their liking than the Dissenters, since it was the Dissenters who complained about the political participation of non-Protestants.)[5]

Although religious beliefs and prejudices undoubtedly played a role in the political factionalism, so, too, did geography. The Church party's center of power lay in the parishes surrounding Charles Town. Their faction is often referred to as the Goose Creek men, for much of their leadership lived along the Goose Creek branch of the Cooper River. The center of power for the Dissenters and their Anglican allies lay in Colleton County, on the southern frontier of the colony, where the Scots Presbyterians of Stuart Town united politically with newly arrived Dissenters and Low Church Anglicans. Their families intermarried, engaged in business with one another, traded with the Yamasee, and found mutual interest in promoting the defense of their exposed position on the southern frontier. They tended to support reform of the Indian trade and adopted a position of toleration in religious and political matters.

Governor Nathaniel Johnson, a stout Anglican, invigorated the bitter religious divisions in the colony in 1704, when he called an emergency meeting of the assembly. Before most of the Colleton County members could arrive, Johnson pushed through the Exclusion Act to effectively bar Dissenters from holding office in the assembly—all those elected were required to take an oath that they "took communion in the Church of England or that they conformed to Anglicanism and had not taken communion in any other church for a year."[6] This last stipulation was to prevent the common practice of Dissenters in England of receiving communion once a year in an Anglican church but attending their own chapels the remainder of the year. With the Dissenters disenfranchised, the Church party enacted the Church Act, which both established the Anglican Church and created a government body to oversee religious affairs, such as the building of churches, the paying of ministers' salaries, and prohibition of marriages performed in the colony by Dissenting clergy.[7] The Dissenters responded by sending Joseph Boone to London to seek support for overturning both the Exclusion Act and the Church Act.[8] The Dissenters also disrupted the colonial government. They and their allies were elected to the assembly and then either were barred from serving by the religious qualification or refused to be seated. In January 1706, the assembly session lasted but three days, as there were not enough persons qualified to make a quorum.[9] In England, the Whigs in the House of Lords refused to approve the colony's Church Act, which led the proprietors to reject the measure. In late 1706, the South Carolina assembly passed a new act of establishment less odious than the last, which calmed tempers somewhat.[10]

SAMUEL THOMAS: THE INCONVENIENCED MISSIONARY

In the context of these religious disputes, attempts were made to missionize Carolina Indians to Christianity. The attempt to convert was an important step in Euroamerican-Amerindian relations. If nothing else, it held the potential for creating a group of men, the missionaries, who would have intimate contacts with Indians and possibly serve as mediators between native and European peoples. French priests in Louisiana and Spanish priests in Florida filled similar roles, much to the advantage of their colonies. Although the Catholic clergy had limited success in converting Indians to Christianity, they provided indispensable service to the civil governments in intercultural relations. The priests became diplomats and cultural brokers. They explained the culture, needs, and desires of Indians to the colonial authorities and transmitted information about Europeans to the Indians. Language skills were necessary for success, but the priests' abstention from trade, Indian women, and military affairs also helped them.

Although they were in a position to mimic French and Spanish success by using missionaries to tie Amerindians closer to them, the English had a comparatively dismal record. The Protestant clergy shared the Catholic clergy's determination to convert foreign heathens. The Protestants, however, lacked such disciplined religious orders as the Jesuits, Franciscans, and Dominicans, who had much experience with Indian conversion elsewhere in the Americas. The Catholics also had a more universal perception of their religious goals, wishing to include all within their fold, whereas for Anglicans, religion could not be separated from the state and was thus exclusive rather than inclusive. The Catholic hierarchy sent individual clergy to learn the languages of small Indian groups, which seemed too much of a bother to most Protestant clergy. Yet the SPG brought much initial enthusiasm to the task in the first decade of the eighteenth century. Few could foresee the miserable outcome. SPG opponents predicted failure, but in retrospect those predictions seem based only in part on the belief that Indians could not be converted and much more on the fear that the missionaries might succeed—for if Indians became Christians, Euroamericans would have to consider treating them better.

Samuel Thomas arrived as the first SPG minister in Carolina in December 1702. Sent specifically to convert the Yamasee, he instead took up residence at Governor Johnson's house. Thomas justified his disinclination to go to the Yamasee by informing the SPG that as a result of the recent attack on Saint Augustine and the outbreak of Queen Anne's War, it was too dangerous to dwell with the Indians, for the colony expected a Spanish counterinvasion. This situation also precluded the Yamasee from having the time to attend to religious instruction. Governor Johnson promised Thomas that he would send for some Yamasee chiefs so that they could determine whether their instruction in Christianity was feasible,[11] by which Johnson planted the seed in Thomas's mind that missionizing might not be possible. No doubt the frontier situation of the Yamasee presented difficulties, but French priests, for instance, often joined their proselytes no matter what the danger. Of course, the priests were single men and Thomas had a family to consider. Still, the SPG expected Thomas to missionize, and he made no such attempt.

Reverend Thomas enjoyed his stay with the governor. He became Johnson's personal chaplain, reading prayers daily at his home. Thomas took pride in noting in his letters that they were written "From my study at Sr N. Johnson's in Carolina." He saw to the needs of the local Anglican community, to whom he preached on Sunday, and he found time to instruct twenty black slaves in reading. He even baptized one African. In explaining his failure to missionize Indians, Thomas withheld informing the SPG that the local parish already had a minister, Thomas Kendall, who had fallen out of favor with the congregation. The SPG learned the truth, and Thomas's critics called for him to proceed with his original assignment. Robert Stevens wrote from Carolina with disgust over Thomas's failure to go to the Yamasee and belittled the minister's claims to have converted African bondpeople: "I live at Goose Creek, but know no Negroes that [Thomas] converted or instructed any other way than by his now & then preaching to the Gentlemen of that Quarter in their church where there might be 5 or 6 Christian Negroes . . . they were Christians before he preached there, 3 or 4 of those Negroes may read[,] yet it is but sorrily." Stephens also criticized the suggestion that the SPG provide black slaves rather than Indians with the Bible and the Book of Common Prayer, for the slaves in need of the books belonged to former Governor Moore, who could buy them himself.[12] Thomas Nairne echoed Stevens's criticism, adding that if the Goose Creek men really desired the conversion of their slaves they would use the labor of one slave of each twelve "to raise a Sum for that purpose."[13] Instead, they employ "little Tricks and Sponging upon the Society whose Charity ought rather to be employed to help them who are not otherwise able to help themselves."[14]

When the SPG sent the Indians a gift of cloth for making match coats, Thomas found himself in the embarrassing position of not knowing any Indians to give the fabric to. The governor had the material appraised and sold, the proceeds to go wherever the SPG wished.[15] Displeased with Thomas's failure to fulfill his charge—or even attempt it—the society "Resolved that it be a standing order of this Society that if any Minister sent over to the Plantations with an allowance from this Society to any particular place shall fix himself in any other place by the direction of the respective Governor or otherwise this society will not continue the allowance of the said Minister until the said change shall be approved by the Society."[16]

Thomas returned to England, in part to fetch his family and in part to lobby the society to continue his salary. He arrived with testimonials from the four leading Anglicans in the colony, Governor Johnson, Johnson's son-in-law Thomas Broughton, Nicholas Trott, the chief justice and a leading bigot against Dissenters, and former governor James Moore—all men of questionable moral character but possessing great prestige.[17] Thomas recounted at length the state of religion in the colony, which, he believed, suffered from a growing proliferation of Dissenting clergy and a dearth of Anglican ministers. He argued that it was necessary for him to return to Carolina to tend to the needs of white people. Thomas proposed that his efforts to convert heathen be redirected from Indians to the African slaves on the plantations. The society excused Thomas from not going to the Yamasee, renewed his salary, and gave him its blessing to return to Carolina.

The episode was not over, however. Edward Marston, the Anglican minister of Charles Town, filed a complaint against Thomas. Marston had opposed the Church party and even delivered sermons against the assemblymen who supported the act that had disenfranchised Dissenters.[18] Marston labeled Thomas a sycophant who lacked the courage to reprove vice among his parishioners. He berated the minister for not settling among the Yamasee. Thomas's reply to the charge of failing to missionize illuminates his perceived difficulties in converting Indians. He told the society of the misinformation they had labored under in thinking that the Yamasee were "a sort of civilized Indians well disposed for the reception of Christianity." Although he did not know any Yamasee, he had learned from those who did that "they had neither leisure or dispositions to attend to Christian Instructions" and that it would be too dangerous to attempt it, for if he was to move to the frontier, he would hazard his life and face the possibility of being captured or "burnt alive" by the Yamasee's enemies. Even more problematic was the difficulty of language, for the Yamasee did not speak English, and their language was too "barbarous, savage and extreme difficult to attain." It would take him a year to obtain a "tolerable knowledge" of their tongue, which would be of little use to him because their language was "utterly void of such terms as we [have to] express the most necessary truths of Christian religion." For they "have no word for God or Heaven, or Kingdom for a Mediator or for his death and satisfaction." A trader had translated the Lord's Prayer into Yamasee, and the best he could make of it, according to Thomas: "'Our Father which art a top,' and instead of Thy Kingdom come, he translates 'thy great Town come.'"[19] These, Thomas argued, "are very improper expressions to convey to them the genuine sense of this most divine prayer." Converting the Yamasee, he believed, could hardly be worth the effort. Most of the Indian nations near the colony had fewer than fifty people, though he heard that the Yamasee numbered near two hundred—he underestimated their population by more than 600 percent![20] Thomas argued that if a missionary could learn and converse with one tribe of Indians, he could at best convert only that group, and if they refused to "hearken to Instruction (as we have just reason to fear) then all his labour in attaining their tongue is lost." So, why, he wondered, should he have "denied myself the comforts of my life as a Christian, the benefits I mean of God's ordinances publicly dispensed, and had hazarded my life and health by living among these poor Savages," when there are many others to whose needs he could minister, particularly the slaves.

Thomas affirmed that there were "great numbers of Heathens who stood in equal need of christian Instruction . . . the Negroe and Indian Slaves in our Parishes." Of the thousand slaves in Carolina—he again underestimated the population, for the number of slaves approached three thousand—at least eight hundred "can speak English tolerably well," and many wished to obtain Christian knowledge. In his parish alone, he thought there were more slaves than there were Yamasee in Carolina. But this was based on his faulty calculation of Yamasee numbers. Thus, he asserted that he had a larger field of heathen to convert in his parish and that these were better able and more willing to receive instruction. Lest the SPG forget, he reminded them that whites required spiritual nourishment, too. "I doubt not but you will grant that to prevent the growth of impiety and heathenism among Christians," he wrote, "is as highly honored as . . . propagating Christianity among heathens."

Thomas took the offensive by attacking two Anglicans who complained about his decision to convert blacks instead of Indians. One of these was Thomas Nairne. Nairne had provided much of the original impetus in recommending that the SPG send ministers to the Yamasee.[21] Nairne understood the value to the colony of ministers converting the Indians to Christianity. His trips through southern Indian towns had shown him the advantageous place occupied by the French and Spanish clergy in Indian communities. He held up "the Spanish Friars" of Florida for emulation. Referring to the devastation wreaked upon the Florida Indians, particularly the Apalachee, whose towns were razed and who were killed or carried into slavery, Nairne explained that these Indians "maintained their fidelity & friendship to the Spaniards to the very last"—despite the Spaniards' inability to protect them. "Nothing but downright force brought them over to our side." After recounting how "we have . . . been entirely knifing all the Indians Towns in Florida which were Subject to the Spaniards, . . . and by that means brought about 1600 souls to settle among our Indians and be Subject to our Government, besides the great numbers killed and sold for slaves, these people have had Christian Churches among them for an 100 years past." Nairne, who had participated in the Florida slaving expeditions, rhetorically questioned the "good fight . . . we [have] been fighting to bring so many people from something of Christianity to downright Barbarity & Heathenism." Conversion, Nairne averred, would not be so difficult, for "their Language is enriched with abundance of Spanish words p[ar]ticluarly those p[er]taining to Religion, the want of which often troubles Missionaries." Moreover, Nairne believed that a missionary, "disinterested from all the wrangles of trade . . . would be a Protector to represent their Grievances," while also giving the government "good Intelligence of what passed among the Indians."[22]

Nairne's imperial vision included reducing some Indians to slavery, while forcing others to abandon their Spanish and French allies and move to Carolina's frontier where they would defend the colony. The latter would become subjects of the Crown as part of English expansion and dominance over the entire South. As Indian agent, former trader, imperialist, and frontiersmen he perceived Indians not as external to European society but as potential and useful subjects who could provide military assistance and a trade partnership. Other Nairne supporters, among them John Barnwell, Thomas Welch, and Theophilus Hastings, shared this vision. Conversion was deemed a noble way to elevate heathens while preparing them for incorporation into the empire. Organizations like the SPG also considered Indians as subjects of the Crown to be included in society and whose assimilation would be hastened and effected by conversion to Christianity. Unhappily for them, the High Churchmen in Carolina had different ideas.

HIGH ANGLICANISM AND
THE EXCLUSION OF INDIANS FROM THE EMPIRE

Johnson, Moore, and other High Anglicans regarded Indians as incapable of incorporation into European society. Indians were to be used and exploited for both personal and imperial aims, and they could not be converted to either Christianity or European culture. The High Churchmen opposed the reformers as misguided, and many resented their attempt to expand government power into the Indian trade because it would lower private profits. They were imperialists of a different sort. They wore no paternalistic garb in their relations with Indians, for they did not see the Indians as needing or deserving of protection. Indians were "others" beyond the pale of civilization, and it was quixotic, if not foolhardy, to treat them otherwise.

The High Churchmen would not enlarge their conception of empire to include Indians. They focused instead on more fully incorporating Carolina into the empire by making the colony a bit more like England. The establishment of the Anglican Church was a first important step. They then hoped to attract ministers who could assist in the campaign to reform morality and to combat dissent. They held a traditional view of empire, a Tory view, where the church upheld the state and the state upheld the church. Together the two provided order and stability. In contrast, the Dissenters and the Low Churchmen of Whiggish disposition looked toward an England that was less exclusive, particularly toward Dissenters. The state-church tie was not as important, though not completely rent, because Whigs generally supported restrictions on Catholics. To the Whigs, the church should support the state, but not necessarily the other way around. For many Whigs, the state was becoming a religion in and of itself. The enemy was easy to identify: the Catholic French and Spanish stood in the way of national glory, which was no longer English glory but British glory. Whigs considered Indians as inferior peoples who were only enemies inasmuch as they misguidingly allied with the French or Spanish. As Nairne had earlier commented, if not for the French, the southern Indians would be able to see the rightness of the British cause. With guidance, they could be properly assimilated into the British state. By defeating the French and Spanish, the English could then subject all the South's Indians and then incorporate them into some as yet undefined way into the empire.

The High Church party of Carolina did not share this dream. Thomas criticized Nairne and his Anglican ally, Robert Stevens, for "pretend[ing] to a great zeal for propagating Christianity among the Yamonsea Indians, [but who] have not evinced the least Christian concern for their own ignorant slaves at home, of which they have many." The SPG, he asserted, had "little reason to credit their complaints," for they "are so backward in that . . . which they would have another attempt."[23] It made more sense to Thomas to proselytize among the whites and blacks who lived *within* their society than to convert neighboring Indian peoples who could never be included within, except as slaves.

Competing visions of the future clashed in Carolina. The conflict stemmed from the growth of two societies within a single colony whose ruling class lay divided. On one hand, the Whig imperialists possessed an expansive view of the colony. Their intimate contacts with Amerindians on the southern frontier, their fear of French and Spanish power, and their welcoming of the Act of Union with Scotland, pushed them to a more modern view of the state and to the rationalization of government policies, particularly in regard to Amerindians and trade. They upheld responsibility for promoting the welfare of the colony within an imperial context. They rejected the self-interests of governors and other appointees, who had in earlier days conspired with pirates, abused their positions for large financial gains, and employed underhanded measures to obtain their political ends. The administration of Nathaniel Johnson provided all the evidence they needed as to the kind of political leaders and government that could no longer be tolerated. Johnson's calling the assembly to meet and to pass laws establishing the Anglican Church and preventing Dissenters from serving in the assembly, all done before the Dissenters could reach Charles Town; his repeated foiling of assembly attempts to reform the Indian trade because of his personal interests; his arrest of the opposition leader Thomas Nairne on trumped-up charges of treason—all these rallied the Whigs to oppose the governor and to slowly and steadily assume the high ground of principle, which led to defections in the ranks of the Church party. Johnson's removal from office (1709) and his successor's death shortly after arriving in the colony led to a power struggle among the Church party to control the governorship. Robert Gibbes (1710–1712) temporarily won the position, but only through bribery. This so disgusted many in the Church party that they defected to the Whig vision of government, with its heavily tinged "Country party" philosophy that opposed political corruption.[24] The lords proprietors, although steadily fading into the background in colonial affairs, helped the assembly reformers by appointing as governor the capable and conscientious Charles Craven (1712–1716).

Carolina had yet to develop a united ruling class, but interest groups increasingly formed around large economic issues rather than the petty disputes of a few individuals who hoped to control the entire pie for themselves. The Goose Creek men no longer relied on the Indian trade or trade with pirates or the perquisites of office, for profits from African-cultivated rice plantations filled their coffers. The reformers also owned slaves and plantations (albeit smaller ones), but their more southerly location and business interests left them more squarely in two economies and two worlds. They were wealthy frontiersmen who held high political offices in Charles Town. They conducted trade with Indians and learned their languages. The Goose Creek men also remained engaged in the Indian trade, but increasingly through agents. They no longer traveled among the Indians themselves but hired others to do so. They devoted themselves to their plantations and to the cultural life of Charles Town. Some fretted about religion and morality among their neighbors and their slaves and sought to regularize society to secure their position at the top of the hierarchy. The frontier planters, however, were so busy with Indian affairs that they had no time to devote to Charles Town. They lambasted the High Churchmen for being so narrow-minded as to not realize the danger the colony faced from its external enemies and the need to keep good relations with their Indian friends.

The High Churchmen were not ignorant of external dangers and were ready to challenge France and Spain. After all, Moore had led the 1702 invasion of Saint Augustine and the 1704 attack on Apalachee, but his behavior was guided by personal interest rather than service to the colony and empire.

The reformers were not above combining personal and public interests, but they espoused excluding self-interests from public affairs. Thus, their reform of the Indian trade had barred commissioners, the governor, and the agent from participating in the trade. They began a process and adapted an ideology that guided the ruling class of South Carolina for the next 150 years: the colony's elite incorporated "republican" ideals of public service to the community, with suspicion of those who wielded political power. They predicated their ideas on the patriarchal belief that only wealthy men of affairs could understand the larger interests of society and thus that they possessed the right and obligation to rule. They dismissed shared governance with common people, for in their minds, as in the minds of the elite throughout the British empire, commoners' interests were too narrow, a product of the smallness of their estates. As men of wealth and vision, the elite believed that they should rule for the good of all, for they best understood duty to God, king, empire, and their social inferiors. The desire for stability and reform guided their political behavior. In Carolina, they wished to stabilize the Indian trade and secure the plantation economy. This meant reform born of public-spiritedness. They would reform government while also improving relations with Native Americans. They would tolerate in office only like-minded public-spirited men. They had yet to come to terms with how African slaves fit into their society, as more and more arrived in Carolina directly from Africa, speaking a variety of languages, and displaying alien customs and hostility to their condition. Increasingly confined to the rice plantations, the planters gave them little thought except to control their labor. Indians remained a greater concern to the reformers because they seemed to pose a greater threat. They had the power to bring down the colony by themselves or in league with the French or Spanish. Tying Indians closer to Carolina would secure the colony from external threats. In Francis Le Jau, they found a minister who might lead the way in converting Indians and opening the way for their ultimate incorporation.

FRANCIS LE JAU: THE INQUISITIVE MISSIONARY

When Samuel Thomas died in 1707, Le Jau took his place at Goose Creek parish. Unlike Thomas, Le Jau actually hoped to convert Indians. Like Thomas, he had, or at least thought he had, little opportunity to do so, but unlike his predecessor, Le Jau made an effort to learn from and about Indians. Where Thomas saw Indians as incapable of civilization, Le Jau thought their manner of life worthy of emulation. Le Jau believed that the Indians "do make us ashamed by their lives, conversation and Sense of Religion [though] quite different from ours; ours consists in words and appearance, theirs in reality. I hope they will soon worship Christ."[25] Whereas Thomas relied on a trader to paint a picture of Indians as incapable of conversion, Le Jau fell in with those who believed that the traders oppressed the Indians, "which makes them surly." Excited to learn that the Yamasee had sent for a clergyman to baptize their children, Le Jau rued that his physical weakness prevented him from going, and he resolved to do what he could by inviting "Servant Slaves and free Indians to come and be Catechized."[26]

Le Jau realized the difficulty of learning so many Indian languages, but throughout his decade of life in Carolina he frequently expressed hopes of finding a trade language, a lingua franca that would augment Indian conversion. For years he investigated the possibility that the language of the Savannah was "the transcendent Language of America, spoke everywhere through' the continent." Le Jau believed Savannah to be "understood as far as Canada," though he only had the traders' assurances for this. (He wanted it so much to be true that he mentioned it nine times in his letters to the SPG over a period of a little over four years.)[27] Of all Indian languages, Savannah was the most likely to be understood below the Great Lakes and east of the Mississippi because the Savannah had towns north and south and were one of the most peripatetic of peoples. When Tonti was among the Chickasaw in 1702, an English trader asked him to make his speeches in Savannah, presumably so that all could understand him.[28] Furthermore, Father Gravier reported in 1700 that a Taogaria [Yuchi] he encountered spoke Savannah fluently.[29] At a minimum, Savannah was used to facilitate trade and communication. Le Jau provided an important clue here. On February 10, 1710, he wrote that several traders had told him that Savannah "is understood in this Northern Continent, though not spoken by a great many Nations who have all of them different Dialects; but they affirm to me that if any person speaks the Saonah [Savannah] Language he may travel and be understood from hence to Canada inclusively."[30] This was important information to Le Jau, because mastery of Savannah would allow the missionary to overcome the problem of linguistic diversity, which Thomas had claimed deterred him from attempting to convert Indians. How universal the understanding of Savannah was in the east is difficult to say, but given the Savannah's propensity for travel, it is likely that many native people understood enough of their language to communicate on a basic level for conducting trade. Many of the traders achieved competency in Savannah, especially since the Savannah had been one of the colony's oldest and most important trading partners. It would have been difficult to use Savannah for the conversion of aboriginals, however, since non-Savannah people might not have been fluent in it nor wished to interact with a missionary in Savannah.

If Savannah did not work, then perhaps the language of the Creek would do, for Le Jau heard from a "rational and honest" Indian that "The Crick Indians Language, [that is, the] Nations that border near fflorida [sic] is also understood in the southern parts."[31] Le Jau preferred the Creek to the Savannah, because the Savannah were "dull and mean" in comparison to the Creek, who "are honest, polite and have Noble and Virtuous principles."[32] The Creek language was also understood by the Yamasee, according to Le Jau. Mastering both Creek and Savannah would allow communication with all because, according to Le Jau, they were "the two Languages of the North and South [and] are understood by the respective Inhabitants [for] the most part."[33] Little has been written on how the multilingual Creeks communicated with one another in the early eighteenth century. It is probable that one of the Muskeegee tongues served for communication purposes between Creek groups who spoke more than twelve languages.[34]

That the Indians wanted ministers, Le Jau had no doubt. The Apalachee, as their brethren had when migrating to join the French, entreated Carolina's governor to send them ministers. One chief, after visiting the governor with his request, visited Le Jau for the same reason. Le Jau heard frequently of the Apalachee and Yamasee desire for a clergyman.[35] They both had had Spanish priests in Florida and now requested baptism for their children. Beyond any religious desires they may have had, from their Spanish experience they understood the practical benefit of having European clergy represent their interests to the imperial and colonial governments, the military, traders, and others.

According to Le Jau, the traders opposed having missionaries among the Indians.[36] "It appears they do not care to have Clergymen so near them who doubtless would never approve those perpetual wars they promote amongst the Indians for the only reason of making slaves to pay for their trading goods."[37] Railing against the traders was a common theme in Le Jau's letters. He opposed "our manner of giving Liberty to some very idle Men to go and Trade in the Indian Settlements 600 or 800 Miles from us where they commit many Enormities & Injustices [which] is a great Obstruction to our best designs."[38] Only two miles from his home "one of those Traders caused a poor Indian Woman, a slave of his, to be Scalloped [scalped] . . . she lived 2 or 3 days in that miserable Condition and was found dead in the Woods."[39] The greatest crime, however, and one Le Jau often discussed in his letters, was that of the traders inspiring the Indians to go to war to obtain slaves: "how we shall behave ourselves that we answer not before God for the Wars promoted by some of our Traders to get Slaves for their profit"?[40]

Part of the problem, as Le Jau perceived it, was that the Europeans considered Indians and Africans as subhuman. He was astonished that whites did not differentiate "between slaves and free Indians, and beasts."[41] This "strange reasoning of my Neighbours" puzzled him. One woman, he remarked, "Considerable enough in any other respect but in that of sound knowledge," asked him, "Is it Possible that any of my slaves could go to Heaven, & must I see them there?"[42]

Unable to join the Indians as a missionary, Le Jau tried to convince "some free Indians to live with me." He offered to "Clothe them but they will not consent to it, nor part with their Children though they lead poor miserable lives."[43] He did not give up. Le Jau visited free Indian villages in the low country, observed their festivals, and chatted with them about their traditions and lives. Sometimes they visited him. Le Jau admired their sense of justice and their patience, rued their lack of ambition, and had difficulty comprehending "their sense of God." His lack of understanding he attributed to language differences, as he was sure "they agree with me about the duty of praying, and doing the good and eschewing the evil." Of their "perpetual murdering one another which some of them cannot to this day . . . conceive to be evil," this the Indians told him was due to the devil, a concept with which Le Jau could hardly disagree.[44]

Le Jau saw what he wanted to see. The cosmological differences between Europeans and Indians went beyond language difficulties, although language was indeed a great barrier. Le Jau seemed not to grasp that the absence of words also meant the absence of concepts. The abstractions of Christianity were unintelligible without long-term enmeshing in Western culture; similarly, Europeans could not even approach understanding Indian religiosity because of their inability to grasp aboriginal culture. Le Jau was an optimist: "Could we make them capable to understand what is meant by Words commonly used by us when we speak of Religion, we would find them other than We imagine; or could we understand their meaning." He had high expectations for the next generation of Indians, as "The Indian Children of our Neighbourhood speak English, there is hope that in Process of time they may be Instructed."[45]

In the meantime, Le Jau looked for religious parallels between Christians and Indians that would justify his optimism not only that Indians could be molded into vessels of Christian piety but that they already possessed some of the concepts and characteristics of Christianity and knew some of the most venerable Christian stories. At one Indian festival held near the glebe land, he rejoiced to learn that his Amerindian neighbors believed that man was created first and woman from his rib.[46] At an Etiwaw festival an Indian related a story similar to that of Noah and the ark.[47] Like James Adair, a Carolina trader of the next generation who wrote a book about the North American Indians that attempted to prove they were descended from the ten lost tribes of Israel, Le Jau affirmed the Indians' common humanity with Europeans by stressing a common heritage. Moreover, for Le Jau, the truth of the biblical stories seemed confirmed when recited by Indians—how else could Indians have learned the stories except from God, unless they were the descendants of the ten lost tribes?[48] Either way, their common humanity was confirmed.

Yet Le Jau's difficulty in attracting free Indians to religious instruction continued, which he initially blamed on their "perpetually changing places to get food, having no provisions laid up."[49] This led him to focus his missionary efforts increasingly on black slaves, as many came to him for baptism and religious instruction. Some masters also began bringing their slaves to Sunday services, after which Le Jau, with a few masters looking on, instructed them in "the Creed, the Lords Prayer, and the Commandments." Religious instruction had the added value of occupying the slaves' time on Sunday, which otherwise they spent "idly and criminally." Le Jau foresaw that Christian slaves would "do better for their Masters profit than formerly,"[50] but many owners opposed his teaching.[51] Slaves often approached Le Jau to baptize and marry them "according to the form of our holy church," but he "could not comply . . . without the Consent of their Masters," who would not permit them officially sanctioned marriages.[52]

Le Jau also faced opposition when he declared that people should keep the holy days through rest and worship, from which local slaves took their cue "and would not work, which made the Masters angry and none Came to Church." Le Jau's parishioners made sure he understood their anger by suspending "the building of Our Church and the finishing of my house." This left Le Jau "Spare hours" to devote to his memoirs, and particularly to "the Conversations I have had concerning the Indians."[53]

In spite of growing mistreatment, Le Jau did not give in, but he did warn the SPG that the society must properly prepare its missionaries for life in Carolina. The missionary must expect "to suffer great hardships and Crosses" and to receive little help from parishioners, "who have much ado to maintain themselves." His family ate meat but once a week and relied on Indian cornbread and water as their "Common food and drink," though his children also had milk sometimes. He had been forced to purchase three slaves on credit to keep his house in order, and he rued that they could only do the work of one English maid.[54] Although sympathetic to his parishioners' inability to support him better, he was unhappy with their behavior toward him. He resented the Carolinians' "ambition to rule and Command their Ministers; and for Peace sake I in my own District must bear pretty rough usage: I see that if I should be too earnest in shewing the Evil and opposing it, it would be worse." One of the evils he noted in this and other letters concerned the enslavement of peaceful Indians, which threatened the harmony of the province. One can almost hear him sigh with resignation when he recorded: "I hear that our Confederate Indians are now sent to War by our Traders to get Slaves."[55]

Although the colony's relations with Indians were worsening, the interest of African slaves in Christianity greatly encouraged Le Jau. He baptized many, though masters continued to bar church attendance and opposed baptism, for they feared that baptism "makes the Slaves proud and Undutiful."[56] Carolinians also feared bringing slaves together for worship because it allowed them the opportunity of "caballing." Yet if they were not in church while the whites worshiped, the slaves would have the opportunity of meeting and perhaps planning insurrection. The legislature considered a bill to prevent blacks from caballing *and* working on the Sabbath, but masters would not give up the power of having slaves work seven days a week.[57]

Even as blacks began attending church, Indians rarely were seen there, whether slave or free. And no wonder. They either were doing the government's bidding in fighting enemy Indians, the traders' bidding in capturing free Indians for enslavement, or being hunted themselves. When Le Jau rued the "Bloody Wars this last Year" promoted by the traders "to get slaves," he and other sympathetic souls wondered what was to be done with all the "unfortunate slaves" who were captured. Le Jau hoped his neighbors would use Christian charity to "render their Condition as tolerable as we can." In his letters, he immediately followed this reflection with one on the absence of Indians from his church. "I don't know where the fault lies," he puzzled, "but I see 30 Negroes at church for an Indian slave, as for our free Indians—they go their own way and bring their Children like themselves with little Conversation among us but when they want something from us."[58]

Le Jau's optimistic outlook for Indian-white relations quickly faded. The missionaries did not entirely give up the attempt to convert Indians—they tried a new method of sending a single Yamasee man to England for education who could then return and missionize his people[59]—but other, more basic problems had to be addressed first. Assimilation could not occur in an atmosphere of distrust, gross exploitation, and injustice. The government, not the clergy, had to improve relations between the European colonists and the indigenous peoples. Although Governor Johnson had undercut reform efforts by his prosecution of Nairne, the assembly was prepared to move forward. There was a commission to rectify injustices against Indians, a new agent to oversee trader behavior, and enough support to enact laws to govern the trade. On the surface, a new age in the history of Indian-European relations in South Carolina beckoned, but reform was not easily accomplished.

9

CAROLINA'S INDIAN TRADERS

The European powers depended on their Native American neighbors. Indian military power in the South was too strong for Europeans to resist without other Indian allies to protect their settlements. As the wealth of Carolina grew through the spread of plantation agriculture, defense of the sprawling colony became more and more difficult. The government sought ways to stabilize Indian affairs by diffusing the powder keg of native discontent. The sources of this discontent and Carolina's response to the problem are the subject of this chapter.[1]

The assembly did not doubt the importance of Indians to the colony. In 1709, after learning of an expected invasion by the French and Spanish, the assembly made plans to send for three hundred Indians—one hundred Creek, Esaw, and Cherokee, respectively—to be "Entertained at the Public charge." The governor would position the Indians in places designated to protect the southern and western flanks, while Indians from the northward would be moved to protect the northern flank.[1] As the threat of invasion grew, the assembly raised the number of Indian recruits to four hundred. The governor objected to the large public expenditure to support these troops, but the Commons House repeatedly voted to send for the Indians so that they would be within a twelve-hour march of the settlements. When the rumored invasion proved false, the house backed down, but not before ordering the construction of a refuge surrounded by a great swamp for women and children in case of attack. The refuge was to be designed so that only a few Indians would be needed to defend it. Neither slaves nor white laborers would construct the refuge or its buildings, but forty to fifty Indians were to be relieved by a like number when necessary. It was indicative of the colony's trust and dependence on Indians that they employed Indians not only to scout, warn, and defend the colony from invasions and erect a haven to defend their families, but also place their families in Indian hands during an attack.[2]

The assembly fully understood the colony's dependence. It relied on Indians to secure the colony from within and without. Indians prevented African slaves from escaping and, as discussed earlier, were given police powers to demand passes from Europeans found outside settler areas. In effect, they acted as a buffer, keeping hostile Indians and Europeans out of Carolina and hemming in individuals whom the government wished to contain. Yet "friendly" Native Americans came and went as they pleased in Charles Town and among the plantations, giving them ample knowledge and easy access, which presented a strategic nightmare to the colony. South Carolina had no choice but to trust its Indian allies. With the colony's existence at stake, profits could no longer be Carolinians' chief concern. Aware of the need for bringing harmony to Indian affairs, the assembly inserted itself over the governor in its legislative program to rein in abusive traders and bring justice to Indians. Assembly reform involved three areas: establishing laws and regulations to govern the trade and the traders; appointing an agent to oversee trader compliance with laws and regulations and to apprise the assembly and the commissioners of the Indian trade of problems and individuals who broke the law; and empowering the commissioners of the Indian trade to hear Indian complaints and arbitrate frontier disputes.

THE COMMISSIONERS OF THE INDIAN TRADE:
GIVING VOICE TO INDIAN COMPLAINTS

The commissioners of the Indian trade met first on September 20, 1710, in Charles Town. They swore in new commissioners and directed agent John Wright to bring in the next day Apalachee Indians who had arrived in town to express their grievances. The appearance of the Apalachee at the initial meeting of the commission evinces the importance of the board: the Indians had been promised justice and wasted no time demanding it.

The commission undertook a flurry of business, mostly hearing complaints against traders for illegal enslavement of free Indians. Thus, Ventusa and his wife were ordered "to continue as free People till Philip Gilliard," a trader, could prove otherwise "by a Hearing before the Board." Masoony, "another Indian of the Appalchias," also was ordered free until the infamous Captain John Musgrove could prove otherwise. The same judgment was passed in favor of Diego, Wansella, and "Coloose, a free Indian Woman given Mr. Pight by their own People," as the commission thought it "unreasonable for her to be a Slave." Illegal enslavement was not the only crime or complaint discussed before the commission. Apalachee headmen requested that the commission restrain Apalachee from leaving to live at Assapallago (Apalachicola?) town. They likewise complained against Captain John Musgrove for coming to their town last spring and demanding that the "Indians to go and hoe his Corn and if they did not answer his Demands he would beat them." Another trader, Jess Crosley, was accused of "being jealous of a Whore of his," and then "beat and abused an Apalachia Indian Man in a barbarous Manner." Crosley also beat their translator, John Cockett, "till he spit Blood, for only desiring him to forbear beating the Indian." The commissioners directed Agent Wright to seize Crosley and bring him before the commission. Finally, the trader Philip Gilliard, earlier accused of illegally enslaving two Indians, was then charged with taking a "young Indian against her Will for his Wife, and cruelly whipped her and her Brother for accepting a few Beads from her." Another man, Carpenter, testified that Gilliard had "made a Woman drunk with Rum and locked her up from her Mother," threatening to kill the mother "because she would not leave her Daughter behind her."[3]

The establishment of the commission opened a floodgate of grievances against the traders for crimes ranging from assault and battery to kidnaping, rape, and the enslavement of free people. By listening to Indian grievances and taking the advice of the agent and sympathetic traders, the commission and the South Carolina assembly worked together to bring justice to Indians and regulate trade. For instance, a few weeks after the commission's first meeting, a Captain Maggott appeared before the assembly to report abuses of the Yamasee. Maggott stated that "it was a General thing amongst the Traders" to meet Indians on their return from war, before they got to their towns, and to get them drunk from rum by which means they were able to get them drunk from rum by which means they were able to get their slaves and skins "for little or nothing, to the great dissatisfaction of the Indians when they are sober." This practice led the traders to run up great debts among the Indians, which "if not timely prevented will Occasion Murder to be committed amongst them."[4]

The commission's and the agent's assertion of power challenged the traders and brought many to heel. Two men received retainers to prosecute traders who had not taken out licenses or had done so but had disregarded trade laws and regulations.[5] When several traders refused to execute warrants given them by the agent, having "contemptuously tore" them, the commission ordered their prosecution.[6]

The successful wielding of power by the commission and the agent had to be combined with an ability to arbitrate fairly the disputes between Indians and traders, as well as between Indians and Indians and traders and traders. John Musgrove tested the power and impartiality of the commission when he asked them to force the Creek to pay for powder and bullets he had provided them and to reverse their decision setting free the Apalachee named Masoony. In the former case, the commission determined that Musgrove had forced the supplies on the Creek and that they already had compensated him sufficiently; as for Masoony, unless one of the three traders came forth who allegedly heard the Tomela king, an Apalachee, declare Masoony a slave, Masoony would remain free.[7] When Tobias Fitch reported that after the Apalachee stole one of his rams he confiscated two of their guns, the board ordered him to release the guns and they would compensate him for the ram.[8] In this last case, the property in dispute was of relatively little value, but it was brought before the board and the board gave justice to the white complainant. Perhaps this was a planted case. Tobias Fitch rarely appeared in the colonial records at this time—he was not a man whom Indians complained about, and in future decades he became an emissary to the Indians who was much trusted by the Carolina government. It was possible that the board used this case to show the traders that they also could receive justice for their complaints against Indians. Whatever the case, few complaints were lodged against Indians, save when they were partners with Europeans who were complained against; the overwhelming majority of cases heard by the commission were lodged by Indians against Europeans.

Some of the traders, as might be expected, resisted the commission's and agent's power. Musgrove entered complaints against Agent Wright directly to the assembly, to which Musgrove shortly thereafter received election, though he refused to serve because he would not take the necessary oaths that barred Dissenters.[9] A greater problem, which undermined the entire attempt at reform, concerned Captain Richard Peterson, who did take his seat in the legislature. Peterson, by order of the assembly, had brought to Charles Town eight traders to be prosecuted for trading without licenses.[10] The Commons House wished to reward Peterson fifty pounds "for his extraordinary care, trouble and personal attendance in bringing down the Southern Traders." His "extraordinary care" seemed a brave act that foreshadowed a new age in regulating the traders. The reformers' euphoria was fleeting, however, for it soon became clear that Peterson had used his governmental authority to his advantage when both the traders and Agent Wright accused him of malfeasance. Apparently, he only brought traders to Charles Town who had not bribed him while also unjustly sentencing one trader for an unspecified crime and himself committing abuses against the Yamasee.[11] The commission alluded to other complaints, as well, which they described as the "highest Crimes he could be guilty of."[12] The Commons asked the governor to have the attorney general prosecute Peterson for the "breach of his duty," and the governor agreed.[13] (That same day, the house removed Peterson from his seat in the assembly, claiming that he was not a resident of the county that elected him.) Punishment did not include a long imprisonment, for only nine months later, trader Thomas Simonds appeared before the commission accusing Peterson of extorting an Indian slave from him.[14] Reform proceeded in a checkered pattern, always subject to the political disputes that divided Carolinians and at odds with the traders' quest for profits, which lured them into behavior unacceptable within their society but which they had no qualms about committing when among Indians.

INDIAN AGENT JOHN WRIGHT

The government was by no means united in its view of the Indian trade. Many reformers, particularly the Colleton County men, refused to support John Wright, who had replaced Thomas Nairne as agent. Dissenters wanted Scotsman John Cochran to succeed Nairne, but Acting Governor Robert Gibbes refused to appoint him and forced fellow High Church Anglican Wright upon the house.[15] The Colleton County men thus waited for Wright to falter and took every opportunity to undermine him. Landgrave Thomas Smith, an enigmatic dissenter from New England who generally formed a party of one, despised Wright. Smith, on general principle, did not believe that the colony had the right to regulate trade with Indians who lived outside its boundaries.[16] Yet Smith claimed on at least one occasion that he thought the Indian trading act a good measure but would oppose it as long as Wright was agent.[17]

The choice of Wright was fraught with difficulties. Selecting a High Anglican and rejecting the assembly's choice shadowed his agency; Wright's self-interest and abrasive personality alienated many. Moreover, Wright was a moneylender who frequently sued debtors. His money-lending can be documented to some extent in the Court of Common Pleas, where he appeared in more than twenty-five cases. Several cases involved Wright as defendant or as plaintiff in his role as agent, but in most he appeared when suing those who defaulted on loans. Wright's activities as a borrower and lender allow us to explore the importance of credit in early Carolina and to look more closely at the man who played a preeminent role in the colony's Indian affairs.

Obtaining capital in a frontier society was difficult but necessary for rising above subsistence levels. Farmers used the promise of future crops to obtain credit; planters did the same but on a larger scale. They obtained credit or capital from the growing class of Charles Town merchants, who in turn obtained credit from British merchants. The Charles Town merchants provided the conduit for the export and import of goods for the Indian trade, the export of plantation commodities, and the import of goods from Great Britain and its colonies.

Obtaining credit was the most important factor in an individual's ability not only to expand but to maintain an estate. Drought, pestilence, and numerous other factors could mean a year of disaster in an agricultural society— credit kept planters and farmers afloat during lean times. If crops failed, the agriculturists could not pay their bills to the Charles Town shopkeepers, and then many of the merchants would default on loans.[18]

Indian traders also relied on credit. They received a year's supplies from the merchants and then traveled to Indian towns, returning months later to pay their bills and receive another cargo of goods.[19] Oversupply of deerskins might mean a precipitous drop in prices; warfare and bandits added peril; competition from inside and outside the colony also affected prices. Many accepted the risks because of the great chance of earning high profits. To hedge against disaster, Carolinians' invested in a variety of economic enterprises, all of them uncertain. Diversity did not make credit any less necessary, just more complicated. The wealthy were all lenders and borrowers, calculating the beginning and ending of overlapping projects so as not to spread themselves too thin and jeopardize their financial solvency. Yet these were long-term financial enterprises. It could take months to deliver European goods to Amerindian communities and months or years to be repaid for the goods; an expedition to capture slaves could likewise take months, with additional time to deliver the captives to market. Agricultural production ran on yearly cycles. Carolinians lived on credit; neighbors lent to neighbors.

The terms of credit were steep. Lending agreements bore similarity of conditions, as the court records show. Interest was ordinarily 10 percent per year. The length of a loan varied and was clearly specified. It could be a few days, a few months, a year, or longer. Failure to pay by the specified date *doubled* what was owed. The stiff penalty of debt doubling was to ensure prompt repayment, though it is clear that some lenders hoped for default as a way to earn profits.

Many Carolinians did not push the default clause when it occurred, for in addition to personal ties between lenders and borrowers that prevented lenders from taking advantage of every borrower misfortune, not pressing for repayment might mean future and more profitable transactions. It was not unusual for men to lend and borrow from each other in order to engage in a variety of joint investments in hiring or purchasing ships, providing goods for the Indian trade, or selling cargoes of African slaves. Nevertheless, not all lenders were inclined to extend time. Carolina's Court of Common Pleas was full of cases for nonpayment of debt. Debtors sometimes refused to pay, or a debtor might have died, leaving creditors to hound the estate's administrators for repayment, or a personal falling-out might lead to court action.

John Wright, variously agent, planter, Indian trader, and merchant, borrowed large amounts of money. He also lent small amounts to a great variety of people. Just when Wright began lending money is unknown, but his first three suits in the Court of Common Pleas occurred in 1704 and 1706. In one he sued a mariner for fifty pounds (judgment unknown), a second time he sued his overseer and lost, and a third time his partner, William Smith, sued him—Wright lost the case in arbitration. Wright did not appear again in this court until 1711, when he was agent, and then he appeared with regularity. From 1711 to 1715, Wright brought to court men (and sometimes their wives) from a variety of trades—butchers, yeomen, planters, Indian traders, tailors, and coopers—most of whom reneged on loans. It is doubtful that the sudden rise in cases during his tenure as agent was indicative of money troubles. At the time of these suits Wright successfully borrowed £2,000 SC from a London merchant through bonds to three Charles Town merchants on collateral of eleven slaves, five of whom were Indians, and he secured £2,200 SC without collateral from three other South Carolina merchants. Able to command large amounts of capital, Wright nevertheless hounded those who could not repay him piddling debts. His court appearances and his career as agent suggest that Wright was narrow-minded, ornery, and cantankerous, though perhaps made more vengeful by his experience as agent, when so many Carolinians created problems for him. When it suited him, Wright was a stickler for the letter of the law and agreements, and he never let the smallness of a perceived injustice against him stand in the way of his desire for exoneration and compensation.

In the Court of Common Pleas, Wright sought judgment against yeoman John Sebrell for a debt of £6 10s; Cooper David Galloway for £20 on a debt of £10; tailor William Weston for £22 16s 2p on a debt of £11 8s (plus £4 damages); and Samuel Rusco for £5 15s 6p—all these in South Carolina currency, at the time, two-thirds the value of British sterling.[20] Most men would have given lengthy extensions for repayment, but Wright did not have the personality or temperament. Interestingly, his wife, Eleana, appears to have been cut from the same cloth, at least in financial matters. Her court cases after Wright's death display the same kind of petty, litigious character. As administrator of her husband's estate she tried to hide his assets to avoid paying his debts, became involved in a complex series of suits and counter-suits that arose from an argument over skim milk from her cows, and then sued her business partner, with whom she had opened "a Shop of Goods of Ship Chandlery Ware."[21]

John Wright had the skills to convince the assembly to make him agent, albeit at the governor's beckoning—the same governor who had bribed his way into office—and to retain him in that position in the face of intense personal hostility from his opponents. One can imagine him as a humorless but efficient and stern servant of the colony. From the start, Wright tried the Commission of the Indian Trade's patience. He alienated even those commissioners who supported him. They grew exasperated when he refused to leave the settlement to undertake his agency. Many Indians who had visited the commission awaited Wright's departure, for he was to escort them to their respective towns (and probably was to inform guilty traders of the commission's determination of justice for wronged Indians). Wright claimed that he had not left because he was busy furnishing materials to the Goose Creek church for the completion of its construction and that he also had been pursuing blacks who had robbed him. The commission refused to accept his excuse, for the law required him to be out of the settlement ten months of the year, and his offer of being docked a month's salary failed to appease them. They thereby threatened to execute his bond, but no one could find it![22] Apparently, the man who had it had died and it was lost among his papers.[23] After much delay, Wright agreed to undertake his agency while the matter was being settled.

In the meantime, the assembly hoped to pass new bills to regulate the Indian trade. Many deficiencies existed in the 1707 act, and the assembly asked the commission to prepare a new bill while the assembly worked on a new act to regulate the Virginia traders. A new trade act passed two readings in 1711 but either failed to pass or was not brought up for a third reading.[24] This likely occurred because Wright pointed out deficiencies that still had not been addressed.[25] He recommended that better ways be found to "oblige the

Inhabitants to Take License to Trade" and to ensure that traders obeyed the laws. A new trading act had to provide stronger mechanisms for punishing the traders and those who illegally settled on Yamasee land. Wright also requested that a penalty be placed on traders who failed to execute the agent's warrants, and he asked that all traders be barred from trading at Dawfusky (a Yamasee town) and other towns, where their behavior could not be controlled.[26] Wright also suggested, on the recommendation of Indians and traders, that trade be restricted to within the towns and that some way be found to discharge "the Indians in our friendship" of their great debts to the traders, which he estimated at 100,000 deerskins, and calculated as 250 skins per man.[27] (Wright probably was referring only to Yamasee debts.) The agent was ordered by the assembly to attend the commission to discuss creating a new bill.[28]

The commission did not wait for the new trade bill to act. When Wright returned to the commission, as ordered, with bonds from twenty-one traders, he brought with him Yamasee chiefs to make their complaints. The chiefs wanted to know if they would be forgiven their debts for rum, which was illegal for the traders to sell, and the commission assured them that the assembly had approved this but "that it was impossible at this Distance wholly to restrain the Traders from carrying up Rum" and that they must prevent their people from purchasing it. The commission also promised to prosecute those who settled on their land.[29] The following day Wright and the Yamasee made complaints against individual traders, also naming those who had settled on their land. One of the men accused of selling a free Indian was Wright's competitor for the position of agent, John Cochran, whom Indians and traders would accuse of numerous misdealings in the coming years. William Bray, who served as one of two interpreters for the Yamasee, also was accused of having sold a free Indian woman and child into slavery. Bray was ordered to "send to New York" to bring them back.[30] Another Yamasee grievance: the Yamasee chief of Pocataligo asked the board if they were required to take white men with them when they went to war, to which the commission replied no, unless they had a specific order from the government.[31] The commission thus confirmed Yamasee independence, which the traders had been bent on preventing; besides, the commission probably suspected that if traders did interfere, it would be to encourage war parties to abandon goals good for the colony in order to go slaving.

A few days later, the commission instructed the traders that no slaves could be purchased from Indians who had not been in their towns for three days: this would allow Indians time to reflect on the traders' offers and to negotiate with different traders. It also allowed town elders to observe the trans-actions and report trader misbehavior to the agent or commission. Indians also would not be responsible for rum debts, nor could they be held account-able for relations' debts, unless the headmen of the town had given a guaran-tee for those debts; and traders were authorized to seize "Slaves or Goods of any Person trading without a License."[32] A week later the commission gave Wright detailed instructions. The agent had to leave within two weeks for the Yamasee towns, where he was to "hear and determine all such Wrongs and Injuries as are not yet determined" and to collect bonds from those traders who had yet to give them. Wright would publicly proclaim the forgiveness of the Yamasee from all rum debts, and those traders who had contracted such debts before the 1707 trading act, which had prohibited the sale of alcohol, could present their claims to the assembly. Wright would then proceed to the Apalachicola, hear their complaints, and send messages to the Waxhaw, Esaw, and Catawba to send their headmen to meet him at Savannah Town, where he would listen to their complaints and those of the Savannah.[33] Un-fortunately for all concerned, the commission had a difficult time assessing these grievances—for they became a venue by which Indians allied with one trader faction or another and leveled accusations against traders of the op-posing faction.

TRADER FACTIONALISM

Not all traders belonged to a faction. Doctor Edmund Ellis was one such man. Ellis lurks in historical shadows, though he appears in a variety of offi-cial records. He seems unconnected to allies and patrons. His circumstances were humble, and one might assume from the number of his appearances in the Court of Common Pleas as both plaintiff and defendant that he was a contentious man. In fact, he appears to be a schemer, a man on the make, looking for advantages that might come his way. In 1711–1712 he appeared in seven common pleas cases, where he was variously identified as a surgeon, Indian trader, and yeoman. The amounts disputed were generally small, even insignificant to the large traders. Planter John Alston sued Ellis over a debt of £12 SC, to which Ellis confessed £9 7s, but refused to pay more. Merchant John McPherson sued him for a debt of £25, to which Ellis confessed owing £13. On the other hand, Ellis sued a hatter, Adam Travers for a debt of £3. Some of the cases involved significant amounts of money, as in Ellis's claim that yeoman John Sebrell, owed him £100, for which he attached his prop-erty in the form of an Indian girl. He also was sued for £80 by Dove Williamson, Esq.[34] Ellis even sued the public receiver. In November 1712 he had hired several Indians to transport Edward Nichols by boat on colony business. The Commons House promptly paid him £3 for his labors. Ellis was dissatisfied, and two years later he brought suit for £8. The suit was continued three times until it was ended by the plaintiff's death in the Yamasee War.[35] Whatever Ellis's skills as a surgeon and trader, he was clearly something of a cantankerous individual. When the Tuscarora War broke out, Ellis petitioned to be made surgeon for South Carolina's relief expedition. The assembly politely referred the matter to John Barnwell, who headed the expedition to North Carolina.[36] Barnwell apparently declined Ellis's services, for he was still in Charles Town when the troops went to North Carolina.

Barnwell, in close contact with the Yamasee, knew of Ellis's activities as a trader. Ellis ran afoul of the laws governing the Indian trade on several occasions. The Yamasee identified him as a special source of complaint.[37] Additionally, the commission punished him for illegally selling rum to Indians and trading without a license. Ellis did not deny selling rum but used as his defense that the "Rest of the Traders" also did it; he gave the commission the names of several alleged offenders. Ellis accused traders from both major factions, which no doubt isolated him further and did not gain him any favor with the commission. Without patrons he had to post bond to appear at his later prosecution for rum dealing, and he was not allowed to "return among the Indians" to collect his debts. Usually traders unable to return to Indian country sold their debts to other traders or had associates collect them, but Ellis was apparently a man without friends. He took the unusual step of asking the commission to buy his debts.[38]

The commission's punishment of Ellis on this and a later occasion exemplify the problems of isolated traders. The commission made an example of Ellis. They followed up his punishment by sending Wright to collect bonds from nineteen traders to the Yamasee "disclaiming Rum & Relations Debts." Only Ellis, however, was prosecuted. Two years later they again punished him, this time for trading without a license, a crime of which many traders were guilty. Ellis, however, was confined to jail, probably because he could not post bond. He had to petition the assembly for release.[39]

An unsympathetic character of little influence and few friends, Ellis's experiences differed vastly from those of John Cochran. Cochran, even more than Ellis, ran afoul of the commission and the colony's agent to the Indians. But Cochran hailed from one of the leading families of Colleton County. His father, Sir John Cochran, had negotiated with the proprietors for the Scots who settled Stuart Town. John, himself was a captain in the militia and widely recognized as a man of substance—it will be recalled that he was the assembly's choice for agent over John Wright. The commission matched wits with Cochran on numerous occasions over the coming five years but rarely got the better of him.

John Cochran's ability to escape the law was evident as early as February 1703, when he was accused of plundering the Yamasee on their return from the failed siege of Saint Augustine.[40] It undoubtedly helped Cochran, who was found innocent of the charges, that one of the Yamasee's interpreters was his brother-in-law, a man earlier accused of having abused these same Indians.[41] Cochran apparently did not stand opposed to all reforms by the commission, as he took out licenses and joined with three other prominent traders, including John Barnwell, in petitioning the assembly to rectify abuses against the Yamasee.[42] Yet his career, as much as anyone's, illustrates the difficulty of elite reform when the elite desired reform of lesser men but not themselves. Cochran and Wright were two of a kind—in both men, self-interest and public duties clashed. The inability of these men and their factions to mend their differences undermined the government's ability to solve the problems of the Indian trade.

The arrest of Samuel Hilden brings to light not only the self-interests of these men but the hostile factionalism that divided traders and government. Seven traders, mostly from Cochran's faction, reported to the commission that Hilden had disregarded the directive that all trading had to be conducted within the Indian towns three days after the Indians had returned. Although this was a difficult rule to enforce, it was important for the commission to do so, for it represented an attempt to conduct the trade in an utterly fair manner—not just to protect Indians from being swindled but to allow traders equal opportunity to bid for the Indians' slaves and skins. Cochran, Bray, John Frazier, Cornelius Meckarty, and George Wright testified that not only had Hilden purchased slaves from the Indians out of their towns but he had done so even after the commission had ordered him to appear before them to answer the same charges.[43] Hilden professed ignorance of the commission's order to appear and of the restrictions against trading out of town—he claimed to have thought that the order only concerned trade with the Yamasee, whereas he had purchased the slaves from the Apalachicola. Two of the traders who signed the complaint against Hilden did not testify against him when the case came before the assembly. Cornelius Meckarty and George Wright both had a change of heart—probably because they learned what Cochran and his allies knew all along—Hilden was covertly financed by agent John Wright. By law the agent was barred from the trade; so he illicitly funded Hilden and John Cockett to the sum of £651.[44] Thus, Wright's own factor had disregarded the very law he had prompted the government to pass. The Cochran faction was up in arms against the self-righteous Wright and hounded him throughout his career.

The dispute over Hilden festered and exploded when the Cochran faction produced more evidence of Wright's peculations and maladministration. Accusations were rife that Wright had been buying up Indian debts from the traders to his advantage. The House of Assembly warned him to desist, and in the midst of their investigation, Wright resigned his agency. Perhaps the most damning charge concerned the Yamasee traders' agreeing to settle an annual salary on him. Wright disingenuously claimed that the salary was voluntary and that the traders were just trying to encourage him to settle with them.[45] That he could see no conflict of interest is hardly creditable.

Wright wasted no time in seeking vengeance against the Cochran faction. One of Wright's underlings, John Cockett, an interpreter for the Yamasee and Apalachee, who had just given bond to take out a license to trade (in Wright's service), charged Bray, Daniel Callahan, and Frazier with forcing Yamasee of Pocataligo town to sell their slaves the day they brought them to town. They had skirted the law by having "obliged them to keep the said Slaves till the three days were expired."[46] Cockett had other reasons to seek vengeance. John Charleton had seized Cockett's slaves and goods for trading without a license, for even though Cockett had given his bond, he had not yet received his license.[47] Cockett unsuccessfully sued Charleton, whom the commission praised for his actions: we "are glad," they wrote him, "to find a Man so active and hope you will not give reason to the Sufferer's Friends to say he is the only Person you put our Powers in force against." Charleton was ordered to return Cockett's goods to him, since he had taken out a license, but he was allowed to take something from them for his efforts.[48] Commissioner Benjamin Quelch, a supporter of Wright, refused to sign these orders, probably because he thought Cockett should lose nothing—Quelch soon lost his seat on the commission and in the assembly as a result of making disparaging remarks about assemblymen. (John Musgrove, a member of Cochran's faction and a man whose notorious treatment of Indians was discussed earlier, provided testimony against Quelch.) As for Wright, his motivations continued to come under scrutiny. Apparently, he had interfered with Charleton's attempt against Cockett by seizing Charleton's letter to the commission about the case, and he had forced another trader, Richard Slade, who owed him money, to deliver writs for him. More damaging, however, was the suspicion that Wright had been trading illegally with the Indians through Cockett.[49]

Wright took none of this lying down. He appeared before the commission with his own sundry complaints against his enemies. He accused Cochran (for a second time) of selling a free Indian into slavery. Wright asked the commission to call his witnesses, which included members of Cochran's faction. Wright's growing isolation became more evident as one witness, Thomas Simonds, retired from the Indian trade the same day Wright named him as a witness: Simonds would not testify against Cochran; Bray, his wife, and Frazier never testified against Cochran; this left Captain William Maggott, who was called as a witness against Cochran the year before.[50] Wright urged the commission to send for Maggott, "a material" witness then present in town. It does not appear, however, that he was called. Maggot's future behavior indicates that he would join, if he had not already, Cochran's faction.[51] Thus, none of Wright's witnesses against Cochran were willing to testify.

Wright's resignation as agent did not disrupt his faction, as they continued their offensive against Cochran and his allies. Wright appeared as a private citizen before the board against William Bray, accusing Bray of illegally sending a slave to war.[52] Bray countered that Wright had approved his action when he was agent: the slave had half his freedom, and by going to war he would earn the other half. Bray also accused Wright of having set a slave free whose master owed Bray two hundred skins.[53] Wright denied the charge. Wright then filed charges against John Frazier.[54] The most substantial attack, however, occurred when Cochran, Bray, and Frazier appeared before the assembly to testify against Hilden. As soon as they left, the three were arrested "to answer sundry offences committed by them." The assembly, however, requested that the governor order the Court of Sessions to release the men, for they "ought not to have been arrested or bound over at such a time when they were come to serve the Publick"[55]—no one could be arrested on their way to or from the assembly.

The Cochran faction did not prevail completely, for Wright again was appointed agent in June 1712, though with restricted powers. Whether Wright's reappointment resulted from support by the colony's new governor, Charles Craven, or from a resurgence of support in the assembly is unknown. It is clear, however, that Wright used his reappointment to harass his old nemesis John Cochran. The new trading act provided that traders must go to the agent when summoned, and when Cochran refused to do so, Wright took him to the Court of Common Pleas, seeking a twenty-pound fine that would go to the proprietors and twenty pounds to himself as informer.[56]

Wright also went after Cochran by having traders level charges against him. Trader Cornelius Meckarty appeared before the commission and accused John Cochran of demanding a slave from Nenehebau in exchange for the use of a canoe the year before. Meckarty claimed that Nenehebau had neither used the canoe nor promised to pay for those who had used it, but Cochran nevertheless threatened to knock him down and take his wife. Meckarty also claimed that Cochran had received rum debts from Nekebugga, contrary to the agent's instructions.[57] Stephen Beadon confirmed Meckarty's testimony, and added testimony against Frazier and Warner, accusing them of buying a slave from an Indian when they knew that the Indian was on his way to give the slave to George Wright in payment of a debt.[58] George Wright then appeared and accused Cochran of extorting Indians over another canoe. George Wright and Meckarty, perhaps to add legitimacy to their claims, also told the commission that the Yamasee were frightened of losing their land. It always helped, when accusing one's fellow traders of misdeeds against Indians, to express sympathy in more general terms for Indians. Yet if anything is true of both factions—all of their members were involved in abusing Indians. Cochran, Bray, Frazier, and Warner all had long histories of abusing Indians, as did their accusers, George Wright, Cornelius Meckarty, and Stephen Beadon. John Wright, too, was driven by greed to abuse Indians even while charged with their protection. Almost every man with power in the Indian trade took advantage of his situation. Duty to the Indians and the colony was compromised by self-interest and factionalism.

Two events at the end of 1711 complicated the factionalism among the government and the traders. First, in October, the colony learned of the outbreak of war between North Carolina and the Tuscarora. North Carolina desperately needed assistance and called on its sister proprietary colony to provide aid. The South Carolina governor immediately called the Commons House into emergency session. Five days later the second momentous event occurred—after a two-year absence, Thomas Nairne returned to the assembly. Exonerated in England, Nairne was rewarded with an appointment as vice admiralty judge and on his return to Carolina received election to the assembly, representing Colleton County. With great energy he reentered Indian affairs and led the Cochran faction against Wright while simultaneously directing the relief expedition for North Carolina and continuing to promote his imperial plans.[59]

The government thus had a brief respite from its Indian trade problems. It went about recruiting Indians who lived in and near the colony to send to North Carolina, an opportunity to forge stronger bonds between South Carolina and its indigenous neighbors. While on the expedition, ordinary trade could not take place, but Indians and Carolinians would learn more about one another, as they traveled distant miles from their homes to fight a common enemy. The results were not what either expected.

PART FOUR

REPERCUSSIONS, 1712–1717

The Indian slave trade placed South Carolina at the center of southern
Indian affairs. The colony's influence extended from one end of the
region to the other. Neither French nor Spanish could counter the
British position. The Tuscarora War gave South Carolina a venue to display
its power, as it rallied diverse groups of Indians to save North Carolina from
its enemies. Simultaneously, the colony undertook military operations against
the Choctaw, and to many, the English juggernaut might have appeared un-
stoppable.

Success led to growing arrogance. Traders believed themselves indispensable to the colony and to the Indians. They thumbed their noses at government directives and treated Indians as servile dependents. South Carolina's
political leaders viewed with trepidation their lack of control. But severe factionalism within government, especially among the "reformers," sabotaged
efforts to regularize trade and bring justice to the colony's Indian partners.

Those who fell victim to the slavers were usually shipped to distant
colonies to spend their days laboring for others with no hope of returning to
their families and homes. Not that they passively accepted their condition:
in several colonies the variously termed "Southern" or "Spanish" or "Caro-

lina" Indians earned a reputation as troublemakers and instigators, leading several provincial governments to bar their importation. Not that it mattered: in a few years South Carolina so alienated its allies that they banned together in a pan-Indian movement that ended the large-scale slaving of native peoples.

10

THE TUSCARORA WAR

SOUTH CAROLINA RESCUES NORTH CAROLINA

In at least one sense, the Tuscarora War was South Carolina's finest moment, for the colony overcame numerous obstacles to help its neighbor to the north. Although South Carolina was beset by harrowing epidemics that included smallpox, malaria, yellow fever, and various influenzas,[1] the colony did not blink from its duty to a sister colony. Virginia, in sharp contrast, waffled over providing aid, promised to send two hundred troops, and then argued with North Carolina over provisioning before withdrawing its offer. Virginia did play an active role in attempting to keep the Upper Tuscarora neutral, but the Old Dominion preferred not to spend money to help its neighbor. In February 1712, the Neuse River inhabitants of North Carolina begged Virginia for relief, fearing starvation and desperately needing "men, arms and Ammunition." Virginia governor Alexander Spotswood and his council assured the petitioners that they no longer needed relief, because a peace treaty that Virginia had promulgated was imminent, and the colony had nothing to spare "by reason of the low state of the public Revenue." They sent the treaty to the Neuse River inhabitants to show them the care Virginia had taken on their behalf and "to encourage the petitioners to defend themselves" until the peace was ratified. Virginia was willing, however, to send "one horse load of trading goods (arms and ammunition excepted) . . . to be applied towards the payment of any Charges they have been at in redeeming the English Captives or for discharging the Rewards promised" to Indian allies for bringing in the "heads of the Indian Enemy."[2]

Virginia government's revenue was low, but so was that of South Carolina, which found a way to raise money for its neighbor. The peace Virginia expected was not forthcoming. By the time the Old Dominion assented to sending one hundred Virginians and one hundred tributary Indians to help North Carolina, South Carolina forces already had forged a peace with the Tuscarora.[3] The North Carolina government thought that Virginia delayed assistance out of disgust with North Carolinians' "not seeing their own danger" in provoking the Tuscarora. They also blamed the internal divisions within the colony that resulted from the recent Cary Rebellion.[4] Moreover, the Virginia government was upset with the failure of North Carolina to work toward the settlement of their boundary dispute, an item of great importance to both colonies.[5] Governor Spotswood also complained about the North Carolina Quakers' refusal to fight. Spotswood believed that the Quakers were major fomenters of the Cary Rebellion—"they were the most active in taking arms to put down that Government"—and then refused to defend their colony against the Indians: "they now fly again to the pretense of Conscience to be excused from assisting against the Indians."[6] Whether North Carolina Quakers took up arms against their government is uncertain, but there is evidence that they maintained their pacifist principles during the Tuscarora War. The monthly meeting of the Society of Friends of Paquotank Precinct rebuked one member for reputedly "assisting the Soldiers to defend himself and others with carnal weapons contrary to our known principles."[7]

To assist North Carolina, South Carolina's acting governor Robert Gibbes bid the assembly to raise an army of "warlike Indians" to be led by the colony's officers.[8] How much aid Gibbes had in mind was unclear, and in fact, little was done until Thomas Nairne returned to the colony. The day after he took his seat in the assembly Nairne proposed a plan. The colony would raise four thousand pounds SC. Nairne headed a commission to instruct the traders on raising levies of Indian soldiers and to supervise the preparation of an expedition to relieve North Carolina.[9] South Carolina now had the opportunity to display its prominence in southern Indian affairs. The fiasco of 1702 against Saint Augustine had done nothing for the colony's reputation, and the decimation of the Florida Indians had been little more than slaving expeditions—at least on the surface—but now the colony could show its ability to raise and lead an Indian army to save a sister colony from disaster. Wealthy and powerful Virginia had shown itself too penurious to the task, and that colony could not call on as many Indians as South Carolina could. If South Carolina was successful against the Tuscarora it would demonstrate to the Crown that in Indian affairs the colony was on a par of importance with New York. From Albany, New York, the English conducted trade and diplomacy that affected the entire northern frontier, from the Atlantic through the Great Lakes, south to Virginia and beyond. The French in Canada were kept in check through the position of New York in Indian affairs. Now South Carolina, which already had to contend with French Louisiana and Spanish Florida, could prove that its influence was just as broad geographically, economically, and politically.

John Barnwell, an ally and neighbor of Nairne's in Colleton County, was selected by the assembly to lead the expedition. Barnwell shared with Nairne the desire to strengthen imperial power, end abuses in the Indian trade, and increase the standing of the Colleton County men in the government against the Goose Creek men. Barnwell emigrated to Carolina from a prestigious English family in Ireland in 1701. John Page, an alderman in Dublin who later became lord mayor, described him as an adventuresome sort, a man who had emigrated "out of a humor to go to travel, but for no other Reason." Like Nairne, he was both a member of the Church of England and a leader of the Dissenter party.[10] In opposition to the Church Establishment Act of 1707, he led a mob against Chief Justice Nicholas Trott, one of the colony's foremost High Church Anglicans.[11] The use of violence through crowd activity led by the elite was commonplace in South Carolina (as in many places in colonial America), so Barnwell fit right in with the patterns of the colony's political behavior. His peers recognized his talents, and he steadily climbed the political ladder. Barnwell's expertise in Indian affairs became apparent from his participation in raids against Florida. Later he produced several important maps of the South, with much valuable information about the migration of Indian towns;[12] he also collected the most detailed census of Indians east of the Choctaw.[13] Unlike many of his neighbors, however, he does not appear to have taken an active role in the Indian trade. Elected to the assembly from Colleton County, he became politically active, and in 1711 was appointed commissioner of the southern Indians, a supervisory position over those who traded with the Yamasee and other Indians along the Savannah River.[14] Perhaps in response to his rise in power, Barnwell wrote home for his coat of arms in 1709, which bore the motto *Malo moriquam foedari*— "I would rather die than be disgraced."[15] As leader of South Carolina's relief expedition, he received the chance to live up to his motto.

THE CAUSES OF THE TUSCARORA WAR

Colonists, like historians since then, were unsure as to what caused the war, in which the Tuscarora initiated hostilities. Land encroachment seems the most likely reason, because those Indians in the path of European expansion comprised the vast majority of those who attacked the colony, whereas those who lived far from European settlement remained neutral. In a letter written seven months before the war's outbreak, Governor Spotswood of Virginia warned Governor Edward Hyde of North Carolina about the potential threat of whites settling too close to Indians. Spotswood believed that the natives had just cause for complaint because of those "daily trespassing upon them," and he found perfectly "excusable" their retaliations, since "your people have been the first aggressors, by seating without Right on the Lands of which the Indians had first possession." Spotswood had "received private advertisement of some in Your government intending to fall upon the Indians, and to compel them by force to yield to their unreasonable pretensions." Spotswood predicted that a general Indian war would result "when they find the English have broke their faith with them, and that there's no Dependence on our Treaties, which would be a great reproach on us."[16]

Spotswood's prophetic words went unheeded. Part of North Carolina's problem lay in the recent migration of four hundred Swiss and German Palatines to the colony. Led by Baron Christoph von Graffenreid in September 1710, they settled on land along the Trent and Neuse Rivers sold to them by the colony's surveyor, John Lawson. A year later, in September 1711, these new settlers comprised about one half of the more than 130 victims killed by the Tuscarora and their allies. The war began when Lawson and Graffenreid explored the Neuse River and were captured by a party of Indians. Graffenreid, who later was released, blamed the war on the supporters of Thomas Cary, who violently opposed the government of Edward Hyde. These "*few rioters,*" he wrote, "kindled" the hostilities by telling the Indians that the Swiss and Palatines "had come to expel them from their land."[17] Governor Spotswood also believed that the Cary rebels instigated the Tuscarora against North Carolina—he made this charge a month and a half before hostilities began.[18] When war erupted, Spotswood placed the blame on "the invitation given those Savages some time ago by Colonel Cary and his party to cut off their fellow Subjects, [this] has [not] been the only occasion of this Tragedy, . . . Yet it appears very reasonable to believe that they have been greatly encouraged in this attempt by the unnatural Divisions and Animosities among the Inhabitants."[19] Graffenried's and Spotswood's blame of an antigovernment party must be viewed with skepticism, but the Indians' fear of settler encroachment on their land was real. Still, it was not the only source of dispute. As a Tuscarora prisoner, Graffenreid thought that he had succeeded in disabusing the Indians of the notion that his settlers had come to North Carolina to take their land, but he believed that the Indians remained upset with the North Carolinians for taking advantage of them in trade and not allowing "them to hunt near their plantations." Graffenreid also mentioned the killing of an Indian, as an act that had "most incensed them, and not unjustly."[20]

The war might have been averted, according to Graffenreid, if not for the behavior of surveyor John Lawson while the two men were prisoners. At Hancock's Town, a Tuscarora settlement, a lengthy assembly of Tuscarora deliberated on the fate of the prisoners and possible action to be taken to "avenge themselves for the rough dealings of a few wicked English Carolinians who lived near the Pamptego, News and Trent Rivers." The Tuscarora also had "to feel their way as to the help which they could expect from their Indian neighbors."[21] Indians from other towns arrived at Hancock's Town, and the two prisoners were questioned before an "Assembly of forty Elders."[22] Lawson and Graffenreid successfully explained that their trip up the Neuse was not undertaken to scout out new land for expanding European settlements. The Indians then focused their complaints on the abuse they received at the hands of "the inhabitants of the rivers Pamptego, News, and Trent . . . [which] could not be suffered any more." Thus warned, the Tuscarora voted to release the prisoners to relay the message to their people.[23]

The following day "two foreign Kings came" and again questioned Graffenreid and Lawson. One of the kings, of Coree, a group that played a large role in the ensuing hostilities, got into an argument with Lawson. Lawson recently had published *A New Voyage to Carolina,* a book that displayed impressive knowledge, sympathy, and respect for Carolina Amerindians. His familiarity with the Indians did him ill here, for he arrogantly ignored the danger of his situation and, according to Graffenreid, acted with great bluster. In spite of Graffenreid's pleadings, Lawson berated the headman, Core Tom, telling him, "we would avenge ourselves on the Indians."[24] This performance led the Indians to reverse their decision and sentence Lawson and Graffenreid to death. After much further discussion, the visiting Indians told Hancock, a Tuscarora chief, that they only desired the death of Lawson; Graffenreid received a respite from execution.[25]

After Lawson's execution, Graffenreid learned that the Indians had decided to attack the North Carolinians, though not the Swiss and Palatines of New Bern. The attacking force consisted only in part of Tuscarora, and even then, probably not even a majority. In spite of their earlier assurances, Indians attacked Swiss and Palatines, but Graffenreid believed that he could still save his settlers from further damage. He proposed a separate peace between the Swiss and Palatines and the Tuscarora and their allies. The Indians agreed to refer their complaints to magistrates, and Graffenreid assented to keep his settlers neutral by allowing neither English nor Indians to pass. Graffenreid also assured the Indians that they would "take no more lands from them without due warning to the King and his nation." They declared a fifteen-day truce so that "fit and able persons may be selected and appointed to propose good and reasonable terms of peace." Also, the Indians were permitted "to hunt wherever they please, unmolested, except that they shall not enter our plantations, for fear they should scare away the cattle, and on account of the danger of fire."[26] Finally, Graffenreid guaranteed that trade goods would be sold to the Indians "at a reasonable price." Afterward, the Indians added the further provision that they be provided various presents, which he called securities but which might simply have been the normal exchange of goods that accompanied agreements. Just how Graffenreid would get these presents to the Indians in the midst of war proved a problem, which held up his release, but fortunately for him a messenger arrived from the governor of Virginia demanding the baron's release. The threatening tone of the message upset the Indians, and Graffenreid was sent with an escort to another Indian village to meet with a Virginia trader—and for the Tuscarora and their allies to learn where Virginia and other Tuscarora stood concerning the dispute with the North Carolinians. The Indians from Hancock's Town decided not to free Graffenreid; he believed that they would not do so until his ransom— that is, the goods he had promised—was paid. Their refusal illustrates that they were unwilling to acquiesce easily to the demands of Virginia and perhaps, too, to the neutral Tuscarora.[27]

On his return to Hancock's Town, Graffenreid learned that the Indians had defeated a small force of Europeans who had reached within four miles of the town. Graffenreid convinced the Indians that the Swiss and Palatines were not among the attackers, though he knew otherwise.[28] Celebrating the triumph, the captors, in a good mood and desirous of the presents Graffenreid promised them, released him.

Encroachment on Tuscarora land and disputes over hunting comprise but two factors of many that led to the Tuscarora War. As in most wars initiated by Indians against Europeans, the sources of hostilities were long-standing, and their grievances fell into numerous categories. It is likely that any one set of grievances could have been overcome by negotiation, for Indians did not lightly undertake wars with Europeans. Rather, the wars occurred after long periods of insults, trade abuses, land encroachments, and, in the South, slaving.

John Barnwell claimed to have learned from some prisoners that the dispute began over a quarrel between an Indian man and a white man in which the Indian received punishment for something he had done to the other man's drink. Twelve Senecas who were visiting with the Tuscarora at the time (the Tuscarora were Iroquoian people related to the Seneca and afterward joined the Iroquois, becoming the sixth nation of the confederacy) ridiculed the Tuscarora "and told them that the Whites had imposed upon them . . . [and] that they were fools to slave and hunt to furnish themselves with the white people's food, it was but killing of them and possessed of their substance." The Seneca analysis, that the Tuscarora were losing "their substance" by eating the white men's food and doing their bidding, may have hit a raw nerve.[29]

The Iroquois connection with the Tuscarora should not be overlooked—certainly, colonial officials and other observers perceived its importance. The *Boston News-Letter* reported that the Tuscarora "were put upon that Bloody Action [their attack up North Carolina] by the Sinnecke Indians, one of our five Nations."[30] Pennsylvania and New York officials also recognized an Iroquois role in the conflict. One year before the outbreak of war, the Tuscarora sent eight wampum belts to a conference of Shawnee (Savannah) and Conestoga chiefs with Pennsylvania officials. Each of the eight belts signified a message from the Tuscarora to the other parties of preliminary steps to an agreement that would allow them to move to Pennsylvania. Through these belts the Tuscarora complained of their situation in North Carolina and their desire for a new home. They expressed the need for a place where their children could play and their young men could hunt without fear of attack *and* enslavement. Pennsylvania officials agreed to provide sanctuary for the Tuscarora "since they are of the same race and Language with our Seneques, who have always proved trusty," though they insisted that they bring a certificate from the North Carolina government confirming their "Good behaviour."[31] At the end of the conference the Conestoga sent the belts to the Five Nations in New York, which led the confederacy to assume a position of protection over their southern Iroquois brethren.

The connections among the Conestoga, Shawnee, the Five Nations of New York, and the Tuscarora were frequent and ancient. The Conestoga of Pennsylvania were a Seneca group who lived along the Chesapeake Bay when John Smith arrived in Virginia in 1607. In 1675 they moved north to the east bank of the Potomac in Maryland, and some of them later moved north again into Pennsylvania. Although Iroquoian, they had allied with Algonquins in Virginia and faced attacks from the Five Nations until submitting to their dominance in the late seventeenth century. As for the Tuscarora, it is not known how long they lived in North Carolina, but the New York Iroquois stated that they had lived with them before migrating southward. During the Tuscarora War, the Five Nations became advocates for their southern brethren and gave them sanctuary against the wishes of New York officials.[32] The Shawnee probably also played a role in convincing the Tuscarora of the expediency of moving north. Many of the Pennsylvania Shawnee had moved there only recently from South Carolina—they understood the precarious position of the Tuscarora in dealing with the Carolinians and the Carolinians' unquenchable thirst for Indian slaves. Pennsylvania officials sympathized with the Tuscarora plight. Pennsylvania had been the only English colony before the Tuscarora War to prohibit the importation of Indian slaves from other colonies. The preamble to this 1706 act noted that the importation of slaves from South Carolina and elsewhere offended the Indians of their province. During the Tuscarora War, Pennsylvania passed another act prohibiting Indian slave importation to shore up loopholes in the first law.[33]

Tuscarora discontent thus was deep-seated. As with many other Indian groups near Carolina whites, fear of enslavement was a major grievance. This fear, combined with the Tuscarora's fear of losing their land, created an explosive situation in North Carolina. The influence of the Five Nations strengthened the Tuscarora resolve to resist the many offenses offered by the North Carolinians. In the heated context of 1711, a dispute between two men over a drink may have been the catalyst for war.[34]

Graffenreid, after a vexatious journey home through difficult terrain, found his position at home as "dangerous" as it had been among the Indians. Determined to fulfill the terms of his agreement, including the giving of presents to the Indians, he was widely reviled by the Swiss and Palatine settlers. Some of his opponents desired "no less than to have me hung," for "I had strong reasons not to side with them and make war so inconsiderably against the Indians." The settlers urged him not to pay his ransom, but Graffenreid did not want to break his promise and the peace agreement he had made, and he hoped by his action to obtain the release of fifteen Palatine prisoners. The baron felt that he was not bound to keep his word to the Tuscarora, because he gave it at a time when "constrained and in danger of life." But he believed the agreement a good one for the colony, by which "many evils and murders could have been avoided."[35] Spotswood supported the baron, affirming that the Swiss and Palatines should keep the agreement because his people were in such a weak military position and "it would be madness to expose his handful of people to the fury of the Indians without some better assurance of help than the present Confusions in that Province gives him reason to hope for." Otherwise the Tuscarora would destroy their entire settlement or "starve them out of the place by killing their stocks and hindering them from planting Corn." Moreover, by their neutrality the Swiss and Palatines had "an opportunity of discovering . . . all the designs of the Indians." Their reasons were thus practical, not moral, for the baron assured Spotswood of "his readiness to enter into the war as soon as he should be assisted to prosecute it."[36]

All was not well for the baron, however, for he found himself brought in front of a tribunal that compared rather unfavorably with the one at Hancock's Town. In the Tuscarora town, "I had my accuser unmasked; every thing was done in good order, nothing in a clandestine way, nor turbulently or seditiously," but among his own people he found much artifice, "the very blackest perfidy" from one of the three members of the tribunal who wanted to avenge a punishment that Graffenreid had earlier inflicted on him.[37]

Graffenreid survived the attacks of his opponents, but they succeeded in breaking the peace with the Tuscarora that he had worked so hard to maintain. The arrival of Barnwell's army in North Carolina also guaranteed that hostilities would resume regardless of whether the Swiss and Palatines participated.

JOHN BARNWELL AND HIS INDIAN ARMY

Barnwell's forces, traveling by land, entered North Carolina in late January 1712. Starting with about 528 men, desertions reduced the number to a little over 400 by the time the troops reached Cape Fear River.[38] Almost the entire army was composed of Indians. As historian James Merrell observes, Barnwell's forces combined diverse Indians of the low country, Piedmont, and Savannah River, opening the way for their future military cooperation against South Carolina.[39] Divided into four companies, Captain (Robert?) Steel commanded one, a body of 30 white men.[40] The second, the "Yamasse Company," composed of 158 men, was apparently led directly by Barnwell or his second in command, Major Alexander Mackay. Although labeled Yamasee, only half the contingent was such; most of the rest were Apalachee, with the remaining 15 labeled by Barnwell as Hog Logees (a Yuchi band from along the Savannah River) and Corsaboy (also known as Cusabo, who lived on the island of Palawana, near Saint Helena Island in Granville County).[41] A third contingent bore the label "Essaw Captain Jack's Compa[ny]" and contained 155 men: Waterees, Sagarees, Catawbas, Suterees, Waxaws, Congarees, and Sattees (Santee?), all of whom lived in the Piedmont and were ordinarily referred to by the South Carolina assembly as the colony's "northern Indians."[42] The commander of this company, Captain Jack, was a Catawba whose military skills were much admired by his own people and the Europeans.[43] The Indians in the third company lived along the Santee and Wateree Rivers. Anthropologist John R. Swanton has correctly noted that Barnwell grouped neighboring and related Indians together.[44] The Esaw also lived along the Wateree River close to the Catawba, whose name was sometimes used by the Europeans to refer to the Esaw. The fourth company, where so many of the early desertions occurred, was led by Captain (Burnaby?) Bull. These Indians, also called "northern Indians" by the South Carolinians, lived in the Piedmont, but to the north or east of the Indians in the third company. Swanton does not identify all of them, but most can be found on early maps. They appear so infrequently in the colony's records that it can be assumed that these small bands had relatively little contact, at least beyond trade, with the colony. This group included Peedees, Weneaws, Cape Fear, Hoopengs, Wareperes, Saraws, Saxapahaws, and Waterees.[45] The Peedees lived on the Peedee River about eighty miles west of the coast. The Cape Fear Indians probably received that name from the colonists because of their location along the Cape Fear River. The colony's 1715 census placed them two hundred miles northeast of Charles Town in five towns of 206 inhabitants. The Hoopengs and Wareperes I cannot identify, while the Waterees, who also appeared in the third company, probably belonged to a band of that group that lived between or along the Cape Fear and Peedee Rivers. The Saraws and the Saxapahaws were listed by Barnwell as part of Bull's company, but separate from them. Although this could be owing to cultural differences between them and the others of the company, he might have listed them separately because when he made the company rosters the mass desertions from Bull's Company in the large group had already occurred, a fact that he hid from his army in order to avoid more desertions. (He simply told the army that these Indians had been sent by another route and that they would meet again later. They probably left because they were the groups, due to their towns' location and size, most likely to be attacked by the Tuscarora in vengeance for their support of the colonists.) The Saraws and Saxapahaws would also leave, but they had yet to do so. The Saraws lived about sixty miles upriver from the Peedees, while the Saxapahaws lived on the Saxapahaws River, a westward extension of the Cape Fear River.[46]

The colonists deemed Indians necessary for fighting not only because they cost less than European soldiers but because they were better than Europeans at battling other Indians. As Christopher Gale reminded Governor

Gibbes when making North Carolina's request for assistance: "I believe your honors will be of opinion, that it is altogether impracticable to attempt" to subdue the Tuscarora "without Indians who are acquainted with their manner of fighting. . . . I earnestly entreat your honors to permit and encourage so many of your tributary Indians as you think proper, to fall upon those Indian enemies." North Carolina could not rely on its own tributary Indians, as they had "joined with the enemy" or sympathized with them.[47]

Barnwell was unsure of the loyalty of many of the Indians who made up his army, but he had great confidence in the Yamasee. Whereas other Indians, he wrote, "are unwilling to proceed into unknown Country, where they may be hemmed in by a numerous Enemy and not know how to extricate themselves . . . my brave Yamassees told me they would go wherever I led them. They will live and die with me, Indeed I have that dependence on them that I would not refuse to give battle to the whole Nation of the Tuscaruros with them."[48] The Yamasee were willing to follow Barnwell, but they did not turn over all authority to him. As Barnwell himself noted of an attack on a Tuscarora fort, the Yamasee *told him* when to attack and would not follow his direction. Barnwell described their behavior as "mettlesome," but he acquiesced and ordered the attack as the Yamasee prescribed.[49]

Barnwell also learned to his dismay that when the English took a Tuscarora fort, his Indian allies gathered all the slaves and plunder they could while the whites put the enemy to the sword. The speed with which Indians gathered booty greatly disappointed the white soldiers, especially when the Indians succeeded in taking much of what the Tuscarora had stolen from the North Carolinians, but they rued even more the Indian captives who fell into their Indian allies' hands. Barnwell complained: "Our Indians [are] presently loading themselves with English plunder of which these Towns are full, and running away from me, nothing left for the white men but their horses tired and their wounds to comfort them."[50]

In spite of this initial victory and the haul of slaves and plunder, Barnwell recognized that they had a long way to go to end the war. The Tuscarora easily fled their pursuers and then quickly erected substantial forts.[51] At the beginning of their march through Tuscarora territory, the Carolinians discovered nine forts, each built a mile from the next. This made it difficult to surprise the enemy, for as soon as one fort was attacked, the alarm was sounded and passed along. At night the Tuscarora men slept in the forts while the women and children slept in the woods. Barnwell found "to our great surprise" when attacking one fort that no sooner had they breached the walls "within the Fort [than there] were two Houses stronger than the fort which did puzzle us and do [us] the most damage." Inside, "the enemy were so desperate, the very women shooting Arrows, yet they did not yield until most of them were put to the sword." The fighting of the women probably explains the high casualties among women, for Barnwell saw ten of them killed. It also accounted in part for his army's disappointment in not obtaining captives to sell as slaves, for traditionally the men were killed and the women sold into slavery.

From Torhunta, a Tuscarora town north of the Neuse River, Barnwell proceeded to the fort at the Tuscarora town of Narhontes. He lost seven killed and thirty-two wounded in taking the fort on January 30, 1712. The next day the Tuscarora town of Kenta attacked the invasion force, with little success, Barnwell's army taking nine scalps and two prisoners, whom Barnwell ordered "burned alive." His force suffered two wounded.[52] Barnwell continued on, harassed by the enemy and, lacking a pilot, finding the way difficult. He decided to head for the English settlements along the coast and to reduce or extirpate the enemy along the way. Hancock's Town lay ahead, and the English believed Hancock to have been chief instigator of the war—not all of the Tuscarora had been involved, and several bands under the leadership of Tom Blunt remained neutral in the conflict.[53]

Barnwell realized that his early attacks were not against the main body of Tuscarora responsible for hostilities. He knew that Hancock led the hostile Tuscarora, but he had yet to find Hancock's fort. His task became harder when the remainder of Captain Bull's company departed along with almost the entirety of Captain Jack's company, save for twenty-three men. In other words, virtually all of the "northern Indians" had left, and only those from the Yamasee Company and Steel's thirty white men remained. The Indians would not stay despite Barnwell's entreaties, but they promised to return with more men. They gathered up "their plunder which was very considerable and their slaves," and carried away ten bags of bullets, which left Barnwell short of ammunition. The Yamasee also wished to quit the expedition, but with so many wounded and distant from home they had to rely on Barnwell to lead them to the coast to reach the boats to transport them. Barnwell promised to undertake no more attacks and fight only in defense. Still, instead of leading his troops through the woods, he chose a route through Indian settlements to spread terror among the Tuscarora. Along the way he found abandoned towns and half-finished forts, his Indian allies dropping off their plunder in exchange for better. Tuscarora attacked the invaders along their way but on February 10, Barnwell and his army reached Bath on Pamlico Sound.[54]

Barnwell spent the next two weeks recruiting men and supplies to go again against Hancock. The elusive Tuscarora leader's town was but sixty miles away, and Barnwell could not return to South Carolina without meeting the main body of the enemy. To his force of two hundred he added sixty-seven North Carolinians but could only obtain enough shot for ten bullets per man. Barnwell clashed with the North Carolina authorities over their inability to provide him with provisions, and he became enmeshed in local politics. The civil disorders of the Cary Rebellion still divided elite factions, and Edward Mosley, one of the "rebels," befriended Barnwell, which reinforced Barnwell's hostility to the government. But Barnwell had every right to be hostile, for the government could not or would not give him the corn necessary to feed his men. For their part, many North Carolinians were dismayed to find much of their property in the hands of Barnwell's men, which they had taken from the Tuscarora. The North Carolinians were in little position to negotiate, because they were dependent on the South Carolinians for defense, but the corn was not forthcoming. Because the transports had not arrived to carry them to South Carolina, Barnwell headed for Hancock's Town on Contentnea Creek, though defeating the enemy was only half his motivation—he was forced to attack in order to capture Tuscarora provisions to feed his men. On March 1, 1712, he led his army of 94 whites and 148 Indians west along the Neuse River, and the following day they entered the deserted town of New Bern, where they found "plenty of corn," though they still lacked meat. Continuing west, they spent the next few days seeking a place to re-cross the Neuse River. His Indian allies refused to cross until, much to Barnwell's amazement, some of the enemy attacked and fled, which prompted the Yamasee to jump in the water and pursue them across the river. The North Carolinians balked at crossing but finally assented.

On March 5, Barnwell's forces marched through the woods and reached Hancock's Fort. This fort was even more impressive than the others. With "a large Earthen Trench thrown up against the puncheons," it featured two tiers "of port holes" for firing at attackers. If they succeeded on breaching the outer fort, the lower tier could be easily plugged to prevent them from firing in or from access to the inner portion. Yet Barnwell did not expect to get that close. An abatis of strewn limbs from large trees interspersed "with large reeds and canes to run into people's legs" blocked the approach. Only briefly did Barnwell consider burning, for "The Earthen work was so high that it signified nothing to burn the puncheons." Moreover, the enemy had four tall "round Bastions or Flankers" from which to fire at Barnwell's troops as they neared.[55]

Later, Barnwell learned that the fort had been designed by a South Carolina African slave, Harry, who had been sold to Virginia and had run away.[56] Native Americans built forts before the Europeans appeared in the New World, and the other forts that Barnwell had attacked apparently were of Tuscarora design. Harry in all likelihood had worked on one of the many fortifications in South Carolina built by colonists and thus had firsthand knowledge of European design. The fort at Hancock's Town combined both Native American and European styles. The fort itself and the abatis were of Native American design, while the high bastions were probably European. Combining both styles proved very effective, for Barnwell and his forces had little clue as to how to subdue the defenders.[57]

One method Barnwell attempted was to have German Palatines construct fashines, long wooden shields that lines of soldiers could march behind as they approached the fort.[58] (The French later used this tactic with the same lack of success against the Chickasaw.)[59] When they advanced to within thirty to forty feet of the fort the Tuscarora fired. The bullets failed to penetrate the shields but so frightened many of the North Carolinians that they dropped the fashines and their weapons and fled. The South Carolinians behind the fashines held their ground, along with twenty-three North Carolinians as Barnwell tried to rally the "runaways." He failed. Mauling several with his cutlass, they refused to return to battle. Barnwell ordered retreat and the men removed to their lines under the fashines.

Barnwell then tried various feints against the different sides of the fort and ordered a night attack, but only sixteen men agreed to participate. As a result, Barnwell sought terms with the Tuscarora. He gave many reasons for this decision: his men were short of ammunition; he heard rumors that the Seneca would soon arrive to assist the enemy;[60] their wooden tools were insufficient for digging their way closer to the fort; he had but thirty men he "could entirely depend upon, which if some of them were killed or wounded the rest of them would leave me in the lurch." Still, Barnwell might have laid siege to the fort but for one overwhelming factor: the captives inside. Barnwell feared that the Tuscarora would kill them if he breached the fort. Inside the fort the Tuscarora were nearly as terrified as their prisoners. Many Tuscarora considered slipping away, but Barnwell had surrounded them. This forced the Tuscarora to send a captive to fetch water, from whom Barnwell learned that an eight-year-old girl was being tortured and put to death. The Tuscarora then allowed other captives to talk with Barnwell, who "came crying and begging of me to have compassion of the innocents." The Tuscarora demanded that he raise the siege or they would kill all and fight to the last man.[61] Barnwell made a truce, exchanged captives, and agreed to hold peace talks in twelve days. Barnwell's men "spoke kindly" to the Tuscarora "and told them they hoped before long to be good friends."[62]

A CHIMERICAL TRUCE

Barnwell and his men returned to the coast. The North Carolina government still failed to provide the South Carolinians with food, and Barnwell and many of his men fell ill. Barnwell asked a gentlemen visiting from the Swiss canton of Bern, Francis Michel, to represent him at the peace talks with the Tuscarora, which was unnecessary because they failed to show. By March 25, Barnwell had recuperated enough to lead a party of fifteen Europeans and thirty Indians back to Hancock's Fort, outside of which they captured some corn. The Tuscarora diligently had built a new fort that extended from the old one to where Barnwell had conducted his previous attack. Barnwell retreated southeast seven miles to near where Contentnea Creek meets the Neuse River, "a place so naturally fortified that with a little Labour 50 men could keep off 5000." He sent to New Bern for tools and the rest of the men, and they proceeded to build Fort Barnwell. Over the next week Barnwell received supplies and additional men, and on April 7, the troops returned to Hancock's Fort, which they besieged for ten days. According to Barnwell, "This siege for variety of action, sallies, attempts to be relieved from without, can't I believe be paralleled against Indians." At one point, after several failed attempts, Barnwell's forces at last made it to the entrenchment outside the fort, only to find that the "enemy had a hollow way under their palisades," through which they crept and stole the fashines! Both sides, exhausted, were ready for peace. Running short of food and having learned from North Carolina's governor that the Tuscarora had received ammunition from Virginia and were thus not likely to run out anytime soon, Barnwell offered the Tuscarora terms, though it "leaves above 100 murderers unpunished."[63]

By the terms of the treaty, the Tuscarora had to deliver all of the plunder, captives, and black slaves in the fort, and the remainder within ten days. The Tuscarora immediately turned over to Barnwell twenty-four captive children and two blacks, one of whom he deemed a "notorious Rogue" and had "cut to pieces." There were few spoils in the fort, for most of it had been sold to Virginia traders. The little corn that was left he gave to forty of his Catawba and Apalachee soldiers for their return home—to his dismay, one of his slaves escaped with the Indians. The Coree and Tuscarora argued over treaty provisions by which they had lost hunting territory and been confined in their planting—the Coree opposed these terms. Barnwell rued that if he had more provisions available he could have "oblige[d] the Tuscaroras to have de-livered all the Coves [Coree] for slaves." As for the fort, after entering it with colors flying, Barnwell was even more impressed than before, as he "never saw such subtle contrivance for Defence," though he then realized that fire would have wreaked more damage than he earlier had thought. Barnwell did not allow the North Carolinians to accompany his army on its triumphant entry march—relations between him and their government had so disintegrated that they had barely any contact. Inside the fort "Some base people" urged Barnwell to kill all the Tuscarora. Barnwell said he would "sooner die," but he considered it. Fearing the loss of his own men and that if he broke his word "our Indians [would find] that there could be no dependence in our prom-ises," and also knowing that those outside the fort would then renew the war, he decided not to "take this opportunity."

The war with the Tuscarora was not over. The peace was soon broken. Just who was to blame is a matter of some controversy. Governor Hyde of North Carolina and Governor Spotswood of Virginia blamed Barnwell. Ac-cording to them, the South Carolinians did not want to go home empty-handed—as Barnwell himself noted, his Indian allies got all the booty, in-cluding the slaves—and so, according to Spotswood, they attacked "some towns and carried off a great many captives," which led to the renewal of hostilities.[64] Governor Hyde claimed that Barnwell had broken the peace by "taking several of the Indians . . . who being along with the Tusqueroras in Hancock's fort were equally concerned in peace with them."[65] Graffenreid, too, noted that the Indians attacked and seized by Barnwell's men were not Tuscarora but their Coree allies, as well as other allied Indians.[66] Given Barn-well's admitted temptation to enslave the Coree with Tuscarora help, it ap-pears at first glance that he had followed through on his earlier plan.[67] There is no denying that Barnwell and his men were disappointed in not obtaining plunder—and *everyone* knew how much they coveted Indian slaves. When Governor Hyde sent James Foster to South Carolina to obtain more help, the governor told his agent that to convince the colony to send a second expedi-tion, he should use as bait "the great advantage [that] may be made of slaves there," as there were "hundreds of women and children," perhaps "3 or 4 thousand," that the South Carolinians could enslave.[68]

There is much evidence, however, to doubt that Barnwell attacked the Coree. There is no hint in the South Carolina records that he caused all the trouble. Barnwell wrote an ingratiating letter to North Carolina's governor asking for compensation for his services, and he would not have done so if he thought he might be blamed for enveloping North Carolina into another war. There is also a danger in accepting at face value the criticisms of Virginia's Governor Spotswood and North Carolina's successive governors Hyde and Pollock. All three adamantly opposed the supporters of Thomas Cary and associated Barnwell with Cary through his friendship with Edward Mosley.[69] As William L. Saunders noted more than a century ago, the surviving records of North Carolina from this period almost all come from the pens of Cary's opponents and must be assessed accordingly.[70] Hyde's request that South Carolina should not send Barnwell to lead the second relief expedition because of his unpopularity in North Carolina was contradicted by an address composed by the North Carolina assembly. This address to the proprietors, drawn up around February 1713, well *after* Barnwell had left North Carolina and hostilities with the Indians had resumed, requested the appointment of Barnwell as governor! According to the new acting governor, Thomas Pollock, Barnwell had support from the pacifist Quakers. The Quakers opposed the Hyde and Pollock governments, but we might also presume that they approved of Barnwell's behavior while in the colony. Finally, it must be noted that Barnwell became embroiled in a nasty dispute with South Carolina's new governor, Charles Craven, over the expedition to relieve North Carolina, but Craven never suggested in his criticism of Barnwell that his behavior might bear responsibility for the resumption of the war.

There is no doubt that the Coree had been attacked. Hugh T. Lefler and William S. Powell are probably right that North Carolinians were responsible.[71] Did the Tuscarora resume the war out of faith to their Coree allies? In other words, did Barnwell overestimate the rift between the Tuscarora and the Coree? This certainly seems possible. The influence of the Coree among the Tuscarora might have led the Tuscarora back into war, just as they had convinced the Tuscarora to fight in the first place.[72] We might also wonder whether there was a second attack, however, this one against the Tuscarora and unreported in the extant evidence. North Carolinians, no doubt, thirsted for revenge against the Tuscarora. After all, the Tuscarora and their allies had attacked and killed more than 130 Euro-North Carolinians. The colonists may have thought that they had not been adequately avenged. The North Carolina government is on record as having *opposed* Barnwell's peaceful settlement, because it desired the extirpation of the Tuscarora, at least those "towns actually joining with Hancock in the massacre." The governor and the council did not have far to look for a model for this kind of settlement, as they noted in their journal that the extirpation of Indian enemies was the "laudable custom of South Carolina."[73]

The first phase of the Tuscarora War was over. South Carolina had shown itself generous in helping its neighbor. South Carolinians had also learned again some of the drawbacks of employing Indian armies. As in the invasion of Florida in 1704, Indians were as interested as Europeans in plunder and they were unwilling to follow a European's command blindly, often insisting on the conditions under which they would fight. The Europeans also showed that they were far from unified. Virginia scarcely helped North Carolina, and the North Carolinians were divided among themselves. Yet the Indians, too, were divided. Tuscarora did not all unite against North Carolina, and in retrospect, the war probably should not be labeled the Tuscarora War, because a majority of Tuscarora might not have fought and of the Indians who did fight, a majority might not have been Tuscarora. The confusion over the renewal of hostilities and the role of John Barnwell, ever afterward known as "Tuscarora Jack," reflects the difficulty of contemporaries and historians in discerning what actually happened. The attack on the Coree was confused with an attack on the Tuscarora; the North Carolina government had little interest in distinguishing one Indian from another, and even less for distinguishing one Tuscarora from another. The North Carolinians were simply bent on revenge, having lost so many of their people and so much of their property, and they might not have cared where or on whom they vented their rage. To complicate matters, domestic turmoil from the Cary Rebellion and the arrival of the Swiss and Palatine settlers, who had no natural affection for English North Carolinians nor any understanding of Indian affairs, prevented clarity and unity of action and thought. The desire for vengeance and the hope of obtaining Indian deaths, property, and land united the Euro-North Carolinians.

What lessons did the participants learn? The North Carolinians learned from the South Carolinians that plunder and extirpation were the proper ends of warfare with Indians. Their Indian enemies learned that they had to fight to protect their interests; that a peace made by Europeans could not be trusted; and that although Europeans were militarily weak and their settlements were easy to attack, their ability to draw on outside resources, such as distant Indian peoples, made them formidable foes. The South Carolinians might not have learned much of anything from their foray into North Carolina, except of the threat posed by abusing Indians, which they already knew to some extent, and of the weaknesses of their sister colony. South Carolina's Indian allies might have learned the most important lesson of all. The invasion gave them new intimacy and knowledge of the British colonies (and other Indians). They saw North Carolina up close and better understood how that colony treated its Indian neighbors. South Carolina Indians had fought alongside the English on many expeditions into Florida and to the Mississippi, but that was against the Spanish and French and their Indian allies. This was different. Now they were fighting in an English colony against Indians they had long lived with as neighbors. It reinforced what most of South Carolina's allies already thought or suspected: the English were untrustworthy allies and dangerous neighbors. They had the peculiar habits of treating all Indians as inferior and alike, of infringing on their land, and, all too often, of enslaving their friends.

THE RESUMPTION OF WAR IN NORTH CAROLINA

In August 1712, word arrived in South Carolina that war had again erupted in North Carolina between that colony and the Tuscarora and their allies. In spite of all the problems Barnwell's army had in receiving cooperation and supplies from North Carolina, Governor Craven urged the assembly to "act upon nobler principles than to involve the innocent with the Guilty" and to come to their sister colony's aid. South Carolina had not spent all of the four thousand pounds allotted for the first campaign, and Craven believed that enough money remained to mount another. As a condition for providing relief, the Commons House demanded to see Governor Edward Hyde's instructions to his messenger Foster, to which Foster agreed. These instructed Foster to counter any "misrepresentations and false aspersions [that] may have been cast upon the governor and Government (if any such be) by Colonel Barnwell or any other" and to request that Carolina appoint someone other than Barnwell to lead the expedition. The colonel, he said, was "much disliked" in North Carolina, though the North Carolina assembly's request to appoint Barnwell governor, previously noted, gainsaid Hyde's assertion. Hyde ascribed the colony's failure to supply Barnwell's army with provisions on drought and on the political disturbances caused by the Cary Rebellion and, in part, to the feeble excuse that they did not know when Barnwell would arrive. By that time, the governor explained, the people had sent their corn out of the country, but the government had done all it could under the circumstances.[74]

In spite of the conflicts among the Carolinians, the recent Tuscarora massacre of people on the Neuse River "and the shooting of some Negroes at Movettice" demanded a response.[75] The governor of New York, Robert Hunter, offered to send Iroquois to North Carolina, but Hyde feared that as conquerors, they would claim the land and "become bad neighbors to their Indians, either to destroy or join with them against the Government." Hyde asked the South Carolinians why the Iroquois should "have all the advantage of" making the Tuscarora slaves. Surely the Carolinians would want this opportunity for themselves.[76] The North Carolina governor saw no hope that peace could be made with the Tuscarora, so whoever came to the colony's rescue first would have "3 or 4 thousand" slaves.[77] Such a potential windfall made Hyde less reticent about his warning that they could offer no subsistence to the relief force. Instead he told South Carolina that the relief expedition could have the corn planted by the Tuscarora.

A Commons House committee met with Barnwell to hear his recommendations. Barnwell could not lead the expedition because he had been shot in the leg, apparently by one of his men, shortly before boarding the sloop that returned him and the army to South Carolina.[78] Barnwell heartily supported a relief expedition and suggested that they immediately send its commander to North Carolina to prepare the way for the arrival of recruited Indians. He supported Hyde's suggestion that a thousand Indians be enlisted and that they "be encouraged by giving them ammunition and paying them as before for every scalp, otherwise they will not kill many of their enemy." The Indians must have white men lead them, he advised, otherwise they "will never of themselves attempt the taking of any fort," a recommendation contradicted by the action of the Yamasee on the first expedition but conveniently forgotten. Barnwell opposed Hyde's suggestion as "morally impossible" of "totally destroy[ing] the enemy" and thought that a "lasting peace" could be made with the Indians. Barnwell made a huge mistake, however, when he suggested "that the Traders having liberty to trade with our Indians," this should "be a sufficient encouragement" to enlist their help in recruiting and serving on the expedition, and that they deserved no "further gratification from the Public."[79] Many of the traders were so irritated at the lack of reward for themselves that they actively discouraged Indians from enlisting.

Finding a commander was another matter. The first choice, Colonel Robert Daniel, made the terms of his monetary compensation so extravagant that the upper house rejected him.[80] The lower house then nominated Robert Lorey, but the governor and council rejected him as "[un]acquainted with the way and manner of Indian war." They suggested instead either Colonel John Fenwick or James Moore, the former governor's son. The lower house agreed to Moore's nomination.[81]

In November 1712, Governor Craven traveled to the Congarees to see the South Carolina army before its departure for North Carolina and "to encourage our men and likewise to see that neither provisions[,] arms or ammunition were wanting." There he learned that the recruitment of Indian allies fell far short of expectations and that "The failure in our number of forces is wholly owing to some of our Traders," who discouraged the Indians from going. Contrary to his orders, they had "prevailed on several to stay at home, and . . . to go to war where they thought fit." This, he told the assembly, was "the highest contempt that can be shown to the Government, and what is more a growing Evil & of so pernicious a consequence, that if not timely prevented will endanger the safety of this province." He described these traders as "profligate wretches" who "for sordid gain would betray their country," and he demanded "punishment due to their crimes."[82] Nairne and Barnwell formed a committee to prepare a response to the governor. They thanked Craven for his care in preparing the expedition and condemned those who would not assist North Carolina, amazed "that any who have British blood in their veins should regard the destruction of their neighbours as a tragedy in a Theatre." The house asked the governor to provide the names of the traders who deserved punishment, which the governor promised to give them the next day.[83]

TRADER FACTIONALISM AND INTRANSIGENCE

The same day that the governor requested that the traders be punished, Cochran, Frazier, and Bray appeared before the house to present grievances against John Wright, who had seized their bonds for trading with elapsed licenses. The house supported the traders against the agent. It declared that the Yamasee and Apalachicola traders had a three-month grace period to pay their fees, and all other traders (because they operated at towns more distant) had six months to renew; on payment of their license fees, the traders could have their bonds returned.[84] It was obvious to the assembly that Wright's seizure of the bonds arose from his hostility to these men, and the Cochran-Nairne faction immediately took the offensive against the agent. Barnwell demanded to know from the commissioners of the Indian trade whether Wright had instructions for visiting the Yamasee, which he did. The assembly then voted that Wright had no power to act as agent to the Yamasee and Apalachicola, which they followed with another vote removing Wright as agent.[85] The next day Wright submitted depositions, copies of warrants, and letters against Thomas Nairne, but the house voted that Wright's letters and supporting papers "were false and scandalous."[86]

Again, Wright did not accept defeat without a response. He returned to the Yamasee towns and seized the goods and slaves of three of his opponents, Maggott, Bray, and Frazier, "under pretense of their disobedience in not attending the said Jno [John] Wright as agent or upon any other account whatsoever." The three traders petitioned the house to stop Wright, who "had put

9 [of their] slaves in Irons, one of which was an Indian woman newly brought to bed." He had since been trying "to sell them at Vendue." The House ordered the slaves released,[87] and if Wright failed to comply, then his old nemesis, John Cochran, had the power to free the slaves.

A few days later the house selected Nairne as agent and reconfirmed him as commissioner of the Yamasee and Apalachicola Indians.[88] Nairne's victory seemed complete. When the Cusabo Indians asked the governor to affirm their title to one of the Sea Islands along the southern coast, Nairne immediately supported Craven by bringing in such a bill—one that also compensated the claimed owner, John Cochran, an ally of Nairne's.[89] Both Nairne and Craven undoubtedly agreed on the next measure of the house, the punishment of the traders who had prevented the Indians from going to North Carolina. All of the eleven so accused traded with the Creek or Cherokee. The assembly asked Nairne to bring in one group of these traders and presumably someone else to bring in the other. The attorney general received instructions to prosecute.[90]

None of the traders who stopped the Indians from enlisting appear to have been members of either the Wright or the Cochran-Nairne factions. These Creek and Cherokee traders could be described as unaligned. The factionalism, for the most part, involved the traders who operated among the Yamasee, Apalachee, Apalachicola, and other groups that lived near the colony. Of nearly one hundred traders who can be identified in the colony's records, almost 40 percent traded with the Yamasee, while another 20 percent traded each with the Creek and the Cherokee. Some of the 20 percent who traded with the Cherokee were Virginia traders who took out South Carolina licenses, and there would have been a number of additional Virginia traders among the Cherokee who lacked licenses. The Creek and the Chickasaw also received unlicensed French traders. Some English traders operated among more than one group of Indians.[91] The number of traders exceeded one hundred, but by how much is uncertain.[92]

Traders of the Creek and Cherokee towns, farther from the colony and the view of the agent, came under less scrutiny than the Yamasee traders. Some traders appear to have kept an unofficial eye on their fellows and their activities, for the government called on them periodically for information. Benjamin Clea and Robert Card apparently fulfilled this function among the Cherokee. Yet their powers were limited. Occasionally they seized the goods of Virginians trading illegally or provided information in cases against traders. As is evident by the concerted effort of the eleven Cherokee and Creek traders who used their influence to stop the Indians from enlisting in the second expedition, the government exercised little real power over the distant traders. The traders willingly opposed government directives of important consequence. For instance, when Captain Theophilus Hastings went to the Creek and demanded that trader John Dickson (or Dixon) help him recruit warriors to go against the Choctaw, Dickson tore up and burned the governor's order. (He later claimed that he did not realize that Hastings's commission came from the governor.) Dickson was one of the two traders who had testified several years earlier to Thomas Nairne's treason, yet Nairne did not associate him with the Wright faction when he called on him to deliver a warrant to Thomas Welch to set free three Indians that Welch had enslaved. Dickson delivered the warrant but turned around and accused Nairne of illegally interfering with the traders by seizing their skins and forcing them to "pay double Pay to the Indians for the Carriage of Skins."[93] Dickson was brought before the commission at least twice for trading without a license, and he operated his business with little fear of the commission and its agents. The punishment provided by the commission for tearing the governor's order comprised his acknowledging to the governor his offense and then making a public acknowledgment to the Creek—the board did not specify what form this acknowledgment would take but spent some time discussing it. He probably had to publicly affirm to the Indians the preeminence of the government's power over him. Whatever the punishment, Dickson's activities among the Creek could be observed only intermittently, and he probably did as he pleased.

The government needed the Creek and Chickasaw traders to keep the Indians supplied and to prevent the French from strengthening their influence. John Dickson's behavior may have been reprehensible to the governor, but this was the same John Dickson whom the government had just called on to deliver trade goods to Thomas Welch in the government's quest to lure Choctaw from the French.[94] Welch himself, the key British figure among the Chickasaw, had been accused of irregularities involving the enslavement of free Indians.

The factionalism only grew worse. Before Nairne could leave on his agency in the winter of 1712–1713 (he apparently did not wish to leave until the legislative session ended), Wright submitted yet another memorial, which the house rejected.[95] A week later, George Logan and Benjamin Godin, two members of the house, entered their objections in strong language to Nairne serving as both Indian agent and commissioner to the Yamasee and Apalachicola, an objection Nairne and his faction had previously made of Wright. They found it "repugnant & contradictory . . . to the Said Act a Commissioner amongst those Indians, inconsistent in itself, impractical in the execution & directly opposite to the design, true intent and meaning of this House." The governor and council agreed and suggested that the house repeal the relevant clauses of the Indian trading act if they wanted him to serve in both functions.[96] Nairne could not have been happy at this turn of events, and as usual, one political measure enmeshed with another. The same day that Logan and Godin entered their objections to Nairne, Governor Craven publicly humiliated John Barnwell; the Nairne faction was now on the defensive.[97]

On August 9, 1712, the house had asked Craven to write to North Carolina about compensation owing to Barnwell. Many of the men on the first expedition had been rewarded by South Carolina for their services. The assembly forestalled rewarding Barnwell until they found out how North Carolina would compensate him. According to Barnwell, North Carolina had agreed to reward him when he returned to the colony and an act had been passed there in his favor. It provided that he should receive twenty shillings per day "during the time he continued in that Govern[men]t." He also sought compensation for several horses lost in the colony's service. As a result of his wound, he could not return to North Carolina and thus asked the South Carolina assembly to represent his interests, and the assembly then turned to Craven.[98]

Craven probably refused to write, for nine days later Barnwell himself petitioned North Carolina.[99] Barnwell told Governor Hyde that South Carolina's sending of a second expedition was entirely his own doing. Governor Craven, he informed Hyde, supported sending a relief force, but the assembly would have refused if not for him. Barnwell also promised to be North Carolina's and Hyde's friend if he received the rewards due him. Barnwell planned a trip to Great Britain and offered to speak in Hyde's behalf with the proprietors, suggesting that Hyde would be rewarded with the governorship of South Carolina. Barnwell then asked that North Carolina reimburse him £84 for the loss of five horses, £50 for money disbursed "at several public works, of which he has a voucher for £39"; £16 for "rum & other necessaries" for the wounded; and 20s per day, as the North Carolina assembly provided, for the entire time he was in North Carolina—approximately one hundred days—thus £100. These reimbursements and rewards were quite reasonable. Some of Barnwell's officers had received rewards of £50 from South Carolina, and the South Carolina assembly had voted him a £60 reward in early December.

Barnwell's claim to control the House—that sending the second relief force was utterly owing to him—galled the governor and probably many

Carolinians.[100] The assembly resolved that Barnwell's letter was false and scandalous, derogatory to the assembly and the governor. They also suspended the reward they had voted Barnwell just one week before.[101] The arrogance of Barnwell's letter is certainly understandable—for without his support the assembly might well have refused to send the second expedition. Craven was a new appointee and as such may not have been viewed by Barnwell as either powerful or influential. Governors came and went, but local members of the elite like Barnwell remained. The letter illustrates poor judgment on Barnwell's part and a bloated sense of self-importance, but having ignored his affairs while in North Carolina, Barnwell might have needed money desperately. The injury he suffered might also have affected his judgment—as he noted of his injuries, "I suffer inexpressible torments." Yet for the moment, the assembly was displeased, and he was not reelected in 1713—though given the circumstances he might not have sought election. The setback was temporary. The assembly soon urged the governor to approve compensation for him, and Barnwell reemerged as one of the most important men in the colony with the outbreak of the Yamasee War, when the colony again called on his leadership.

THE END OF THE TUSCARORA WAR

The second expedition performed ably in North Carolina. Arriving in the autumn of 1712, the troops faced the same problems as Barnwell's army, lacking provisions to conduct an effective campaign. North Carolina had hopes of ending the war in November when it negotiated a preliminary peace with the Tuscarora by which the Tuscarora agreed to bring in Coree and Coteching Indians "and all others that had any hand in the massacre of the English" by January 1, 1713.[102] The Tuscarora did not comply, but a heavy winter snow kept Moore's men idle until March, when they attacked Hancock's fort.

More than seven hundred Indians and slightly fewer than a hundred Europeans comprised Moore's army. The Catawba and the Yamasee again made up much of the ranks, but this time hundreds of Cherokee joined in. The attackers used artillery to bring the Tuscarora to submission, and in the fight that ensued two hundred of the enemy were burned to death inside their fort, with another nine hundred to a thousand killed or captured.[103]

In spite of Moore's victory, the war did not end immediately. Many of the previously "neutral" Tuscarora—Spotswood estimated the number at two hundred—joined Hancock's forces. Iroquois from New York also entered the dispute, attacking Virginia traders on their way to that colony's "Western Indians" and capturing more than a thousand pounds' worth of merchandise.[104] Spotswood feared that even if peace were soon concluded with the Tuscarora, the Five Nations would continue their attacks.

Tuscarora refugees were left in a difficult situation. Many sought refuge in New York with the Iroquois,[105] while upward of fifteen hundred headed west. Spotswood sent fifty of Virginia's tributary Indians to sound out the refugees as to the prospects of their making peace. They found the Tuscarora "dispersed in small parties upon the head of [the] Roanoke [River], and about the Mountains in very miserable condition, without any habitation or provision of Corn for their Subsistence." The Tuscarora despaired over whether "to return to their old Settlements in No. Carolina and run the risk of being knocked in the head by the English and So. Carolina Indians or to submit themselves to the Senecas." The Iroquois reputedly agreed to assist them in revenge against the English, "upon condition of incorporating with them."[106]

In New York the Five Nations firmly rejected that colony's insistence that they not provide refuge for the Tuscarora.[107] Decanisora, a Seneca spokesman of great influence throughout the Five Nations, urged the English to make peace with the Tuscarora. At a conference held among the Onondaga he implored the English to "have compassion on them." The Tuscarora, he said, are "dispersed . . . and have abandoned their Castles and are scattered hither and thither; let that suffice." Decanisora recommended that New York mediate a peace between the Indians and North Carolina, so that the Indians "may no longer be hunted down." He promised the government that if they made peace, the Five Nations "will oblige them not to do the English any more harm; for they are no longer a Nation with a name, being once dispersed."[108]

North Carolina grew desperate for peace with the Tuscarora. Only a few weeks after Moore's victory, the Mattamuskeet captured and killed twenty Europeans on Roanoke Island, and two Tuscarora killed a European on the mainland. North Carolina feared that the war would continue indefinitely, for the Indians could hide in the swamps and the forest.[109] Neutral Tuscarora leader Tom Blunt made a show of good faith to the colony by turning over the two Tuscarora murderers, and Virginia recommended to North Carolina that they conclude a peace with the Tuscarora through Blunt, whereby he would be declared king over all the Tuscarora and would thus be responsible for their behavior.[110] Governor Spotswood also recommended that Blunt not be pressed too hard on terms because the Tuscarora would not keep the peace if it proved dissatisfactory. The Tuscarora, he reminded the North Carolina government, had already suffered greatly—North Carolina should demand punishment for only two or three of the ringleaders.[111]

Moore's victory had thus proved inconclusive. Most of Moore's Indian forces had taken slave captives and gone home.[112] Moore remained in North Carolina with approximately 180 Indians, enough to protect North Carolina if the colony faced no major attack. The departure of the bulk of the forces was welcomed by North Carolinians because the troops devoured so much that many colonists were unsure where the greatest threat lay: the Tuscarora or the hunger of Moore's troops.[113] Provisions were so low that when South Carolina sent additional troops to the colony at the end of the summer, North Carolina sent them home immediately because they could not feed them.[114] North Carolina was forced to come to terms with Blunt, who agreed to defend the colony against hostile Tuscarora. Blunt, Moore, and a force of twenty Yamasee under a Colonel Mackey then had the responsibility of hunting down the Coree, Mattamuskeet, and all other Indians who remained at war with the colony.[115]

The agreement with Blunt, however, did not cover all the Tuscarora— only those who accepted his leadership. Spotswood tried to lure the others to settle permanently in Virginia. Irate with North Carolina for not including Virginia in the agreement with Blunt, Spotswood hoped that those Tuscarora who did not accept Blunt's leadership would become a buffer for Virginia against hostile Indians, which presumably included the New York Iroquois.[116] Most Tuscarora, however, chose either to return to North Carolina, where a peace was made in February 1715 that included the Coree and other North Carolina Indians,[117] or to go to New York, where they later became the sixth nation of Iroquois.[118] Another group of Tuscarora, carried away by the South Carolinians, were settled in that colony, where they later had opportunity to seek vengeance against the Yamasee and other Indians who had played a part in their subjugation.[119] Others were sold into slavery.[120]

In New York, the Five Nations told Governor Robert Hunter the facts of the Tuscarora adoption, leaving that government with no choice in the matter except to risk Iroquois hostility:

We acquaint you that the Tuscarore Indians are come to shelter themselves among the five nations. They were of us and went from us long ago and are now returned and promise to live peaceably among us and since there is now peace among us and since there is peace now everywhere we have received them, do give a Belt of Wampum, we desire you to look upon the Tuscarores that are come to live among us as our Children who shall obey our commands & live peaceably and orderly.[121]

In the coming years, the Iroquois continued as an important party in the southern colonies' affairs, as their influence and their war parties extended not only south through the Piedmont but west to the Mississippi. Native American peoples, in particular the Iroquois, helped bind the entire region east of the Mississippi through their familial connections, trade networks, and ancient enmities. Throughout the Tuscarora War and the ensuing Yamasee War, English officials recognized the continental threats they faced from Native Americans who could combine against them. The Tuscarora War had threatened to engulf the Atlantic coast by Five Nations participation. The Iroquois had to be constantly consulted about events in the South and were a key factor not only in that conflict but also in the Yamasee War, in the later Chickasaw Wars with the French, and in relations between the Catawba and the English colonies. The Iroquois traveled freely, and their communication network ordinarily operated more efficiently than that of the English. During the Tuscarora War, they knew before the New York government did of the state of relations between North Carolina and its Indian neighbors.[122] During the Yamasee War they easily countered the New York government's false claims concerning Catawba reasons for fighting South Carolina—although the Iroquois were enemies with the Catawba, their informants provided different reasons and the New York government looked silly trying to convince the Iroquois otherwise.[123]

The South's affairs were increasingly imperial in nature. The Tuscarora War had brought together the three southernmost English colonies to deal with the Tuscarora and allied Indian threat, though with limited success. The war tied New York and the Iroquois into southern Indian-European relations. It brought distant Cherokee, Yamasee, and Piedmont Indians together as a fighting force and, in particular, paved the way for a closer relationship between the Cherokee and Carolina. South Carolina gained confidence from its importance and role in southern Indian-British imperial relations and from its ability to mobilize Indian forces. Yet British policy-makers were deluded if they thought that their Indian allies cared about their empire. On both invasion forces into North Carolina the vast majority of their Indian recruits fought to obtain the spoils of war. Contrary to Nairne's and the other reformers' hopes, Indians continued to serve their own interests, as the Europeans served theirs. The only way for South Carolina to have had a chance of convincing their Indian allies that the empire worked for their benefit, beyond their uneasy trade relationship and the military alliance to gain slaves and weaken enemies, was to forge a more equal partnership based on justice. But the traders and the government's poor administration of the trade stood in the way. When John Barnwell, in preparing for the second expedition against the Tuscarora, recommended that the traders not be compensated for their help against the Indians, as the "liberty" provided them to trade was compensation enough, the colony opposed men who had great skills and little respect for a government both ineffectual and corrupt in Indian affairs. Apart from the military expeditions, which were mostly slaving enterprises led by greedy men who hoped to fill their own pockets while also forwarding the interests of empire, the government had accomplished little to its credit in Indian relations. Its feeble reform efforts repeatedly smacked of hypocrisy, for the factions that administered Indian relations seemed equally corrupt. Carolina's inability to control its traders and bring justice to Indian relations led to the near destruction of the colony in a few short years.

11

CONTOURS OF THE INDIAN
SLAVE TRADE

Whatever pretensions the South Carolinians had for reforming relations with their Indian allies, they had few qualms about destroying and enslaving those whom they classified as enemies: natives aligned with the French. Although these natives posed little or no direct threat to the colony, South Carolina's government, factions, and Indian allies all agreed on the expediency and profitability of attacking and capturing French-allied Indians. The slave trade thus continued to play a preeminent role in shaping South Carolina diplomacy: it linked the colony and its allies while distracting both from the problems between them.

CAROLINA AND ITS ALLIES GO SLAVING
AGAINST THE CHOCTAW

During the Tuscarora War, South Carolina had resumed its "laudable custom" of Indian extirpation by sending an army against the Choctaw.[1] The Carolina government, fearing the French, sought to reduce French power by subduing the Choctaw, much as they had devastated the Apalachee to strike at the Spanish. In both cases, the imperial goal of colonial defense through invasion was compromised by the quest for slaves and profits. But in the case of Florida, destruction of the missions effectively constricted the Spanish, while defeating the Choctaw was unnecessary for reducing the French. To defeat the French, the English had only to attack them and their allies (Mobilien and Tomé) at Mobile on the Gulf Coast. Dependent on the Gulf for receiving supplies from Europe, the French had no other post on the Gulf of significance outside Mobile.

To remove the French, South Carolina had two choices. The first was an overland invasion against Mobile. Fort Louis, which guarded Mobile, was hardly a defensive bulwark. Poorly maintained and undermanned, it could not withstand a concerted attack. The English were fully aware of its weakness. In 1709 an English-led Indian army of five to six hundred attacked the Tomé and Mobilien within five leagues (12.5 miles) of the fort, capturing twenty-six to twenty-eight women and children and losing but fourteen.[2] The Indians gave chase to regain their families, leading the attackers to kill all their captives "in order to be more free to protect themselves."[3] The foray, if not sidetracked by slaving, might have done more damage, but it showed the English, and the French, that an even larger army could conquer the entire area.[4] As an alternative, the English could attack by sea. French vulnerability to such an attack had been made apparent by an English privateer from Jamaica, which in September 1710 wreaked havoc at Dauphin Island in Mobile Bay. It destroyed more than fifty thousand livres (more than £3,500 sterling) worth of property, suggesting that a seaborne invasion would have great chance for success in capturing Mobile.[5] A naval attack, however, would yield few slaves, and coordinating a naval and overland invasion was nearly impossible, given the difficulty and unpredictability of travel conditions.

If the English had wished to defeat the French they had the means. The French colony hung by threads, its manpower scattered through the South, its military posts almost always short of supplies, particularly clothing and rations, the men forced periodically to live with the Indians to prevent starvation.[6] Supply shortages meant that the French could not wean the Chickasaw from the English interest (although a pro-French faction remained among the Chickasaw). In February 1711, Jean-Baptiste Martin d'Artaguiette Diron, a commissioner in charge of supplies, reported to Louis Phélypaux Pontchartrain that "the savages decrease every day in the esteem that they have for us. Our neighbors are all firm in our party, those who are more remote are faltering." The English informed the Indians that the French had no supplies, trade goods, or presents because they had lost all their ships to the English and been defeated in Queen Anne's War. D'Artaguiette rued, "They back these talks with good presents which can only in the long run have the result that [the Indians] resolve . . . against us and we are closed out of the Mississippi."[7] Eight months later Bienville gloomily echoed the bad news, complaining of the French inability to furnish "our allies" with "any assistance that can protect them against the raids that the allies of the English make upon them." Even the "Chickasaws with whom I have always maintained a perfect understanding have let themselves be won over to . . . the English and have excused themselves to me for it on the ground that not being able to obtain from us their needs which have become indispensable to them they find themselves obliged to take from the English." The inability to supply the Chickasaw meant that their other Indian allies would fall prey, for "the Chickasaws have no commerce except that in slaves which they carry on with the English."[8]

The English made inroads among the Choctaw at several of their villages closest to the Chickasaw. There, the English could be found "daily . . . to get slaves" but also to close off the Choctaw as a refuge for runaway African slaves. At these villages the English exchanged captured Choctaw for their African slaves who had absconded.[9] Keeping the lines of communication and trade open mutually benefited the Choctaw and English, especially the English. It suited their interests to lure some Choctaw, but not all. This tactic created confusion and division among the Choctaw, weakened the French, provided a window for gathering intelligence, and kept open possibilities for future rapprochement.[10]

The English might have used presents to wean other Choctaw towns from the French if they were serious about peace, but they offered only smatterings to accomplish more limited ends. The desire for Choctaw slaves was too strong to sway the Carolinians from their preference for Choctaw as enemies rather than allies. The Carolina government might have rationalized that slaving weakened their enemies and paid for itself, but the Carolinians' actions speak for themselves: instead of attacking Mobile to root out French power, the government raised an expedition to march against the more distant Choctaw. Francis Le Jau, writing in his journal as the expedition prepared to leave, never mentioned the French threat as a reason for its undertaking. In July 1711 he succinctly recorded: "This Province is at present quiet enough. I hear that our Confederate Indians are now sent to War by our Traders to get Slaves."[11] He should have added that the traders organized these forces under government auspices.

The South Carolina assembly did not record in its journals that the quest for slaves instigated the invasion. Instead they discussed a letter from John Wright that informed them of a Choctaw-Chickasaw rapprochement that might be directed against the colony.[12] The source of Wright's fear was apparently a letter from Thomas Welch, the foremost slave trader among the Chickasaw, who had the most to gain from an invasion of the Choctaw.[13] The South Carolina assembly formed a committee to examine the Choctaw threat and rapidly prepared an expedition to be led by Theophilus Hastings. The house intended to raise a force of two thousand Indians, fifteen hundred of whom would be armed with guns.[14] The preparations were well under way, if not completed, by the time word reached the colony four months later of the Tuscarora War.

The traders loved these expeditions. In addition to the slaves they hoped to procure, they supplied the army with powder, bullets, flints, paint, presents, and anything else the assembly deemed necessary.[15] In many ways the assembly was at the mercy of the traders, for they had the responsibility of raising the Indian forces; if the assembly tried to rein in the traders and restrict their profit making, then the traders persuaded the Indians not to fight for the colony. Everything went well with the Choctaw invasion because traders and Indians happily cooperated in the expectation of profits.

The invasion began in the winter of 1711. The force was divided into two parts. Thomas Welch led a force of two hundred men, mostly Chickasaw. Reports of damage to Choctaw towns or how many they killed do not exist in the English records. Rather, the "important" information reported to Charles Town was that they had carried off about two hundred Choctaw into slavery.[16] Theophilus Hastings led the much larger force of thirteen hundred, more than a thousand bearing guns, while the rest used bow and arrow. His army was composed mostly of Creek, but it may have included Yamasee as well. According to his report, "he marched into the Chuctau nation where he ravaged the whole country by burning their Houses . . . killing about 80 men and taking about 130 prisoners most of which were old men and young children."[17] The Creek apparently were happy with their pay, the stores provided by the colony; in fact, they were so pleased with what they received "that in Gratitude the Emperor Brims," a Cuseeta and the most important Creek leader, sent his men on the hunt to bring in a present of skins.[18] Thus, the Carolinians conducted a war against the Choctaw while fighting another against the Tuscarora because the Choctaw campaign cost them so little. The white men received plunder as their reward, while the Creek were paid in trade goods; the Creek willingly worked "cheap" because it suited their interests to wage war on the Choctaw with Carolina's help. They might also have been skittish about the English courting of the Choctaw, so that the colony's engagement in war against them would be a strengthening of ties, a reassurance that they shared the same enemy.

Though successful in terms of spoils, the invasion of the Choctaw tightened the connections between the Choctaw and the French instead of driving them apart. Presents and trade goods would have worked to separate the two, but the Creek would not have tolerated an Anglo-Choctaw rapprochement and the Carolinians could not afford to alienate the Creek. There had been no need for the expedition except to obtain slaves. The enemies of the English were the French, not the Choctaw.

AGENT WRIGHT, COMMISSIONER NAIRNE, AND SOUTH CAROLINA'S INABILITY TO CONTROL ITS TRADERS

The relief expeditions to North Carolina and the invasion of the Choctaw increased the importance of the traders, who were responsible for enlisting, organizing, and directing the Indian recruits, particularly those natives who lived far from the colony. The traders' ability in raising an Indian army and satisfying the recruits with trade goods and military success bloated their sense of self-importance. Traders offered their services for personal benefit, not from patriotism or a sense of duty to the government. The government's dependence on and trust of these men was compromised by the traders' greed, again forcing South Carolina to seek solutions to what must have seemed a never-ending problem: control of the traders' behavior. Thus, while fighting both the Choctaw and the Tuscarora, the Carolina government attempted to reform the Indian trade and improve relations with their allies.

A new trading act was prepared in the spring of 1712 and ratified in June. Although the Indian Trading Act of 1712 is not extant, its problems were immediately apparent.[19] Soon after passage the governor called for yet another bill to rectify the act's shortcomings. Though the assembly spent much time discussing a new bill, none was passed until 1716. The dispute between Wright and Nairne resurfaced more bitter than ever, reinforced by their respective interpretations of the 1712 trading act.

Wright had been accused of maladministration of the agency in November 1711—apparently he bought Indian debts from the traders and then used his authority to secure payment. Nairne was one of three members of an assembly committee appointed to investigate.[20] Wright also came under suspicion of trading, from which he was barred by virtue of his position as agent.[21] One of the commissioners, Richard Berresford, leveled other unspecified charges against Wright—on the very eve of the new trading act's ratification—probably a last-ditch effort to prevent Wright's reappointment as agent.[22] The attempt failed, but under the new trading act his powers were restricted by virtue of Nairne's appointment as commissioner to the Yamasee and Apalachicola Indians.[23]

The commissioners of the Indian trade decided that since Nairne was designated "commissioner" to the Yamasee and Apalachicola, then Wright was not agent for those Indians. Wright objected to this limitation on his powers, and the commission asked Chief Justice Nicholas Trott to interpret the new trading law. An archenemy of Nairne, Trott supported Wright. Where the new governor, Charles Craven, stood on the matter is unclear, but in June, Craven assumed a more active role in Indian affairs by taking a seat on the board of commissioners, which then elected him president. Craven likely preferred Nairne to Wright, for Nairne promoted a legislative program favored by the governor. Nairne had introduced a bill to build a statehouse for the colony, and the governor must have appreciated Nairne's knowledge of Indian affairs, particularly as complaints continued to flood in during the Tuscarora War. Also, the two saw eye to eye on the question of religious dissent. In the governor's message to the Commons House of April 1712, he had urged tolerance of Dissenters and allowance of their liberties.[24] Nairne might have been under suspicion for his role in promulgating the factionalism that existed in Indian affairs, but the two agreed that Indian affairs were the highest priority for the colony, because the "friendship" of the neighboring Indians "is so necessary to the well being of this Province."[25] Craven's attendance at commission meetings was short-lived, however, as they became a venue for members of the Wright and Cochran factions to accuse each other of all kinds of malfeasance. Craven, either out of disgust or in an attempt to remain above the factionalism, refused to return to the meetings despite an assembly request.[26]

Wright and Nairne served side by side as agent and commissioner to the Yamasee and Apalachicola Indians. The commissioners of the Indian trade gave the two men nearly identical instructions.[27] They had to travel together (how they were to resist slitting each other's throats was unstated) to both the upper and lower Yamasee towns, where Wright would "confirm them in their Rights to their Lands" and gather the names of whites illegally settled there. At each place Wright was to tarry no longer than three days, for Nairne would remain there to regulate relations. Wright was to continue on to the Alabama to hear their grievances and "do them immediate and impartial Justice on all Traders that have abused them." The French had mended relations with the Alabama,[28] and Wright had to "do whatsoever in you lies to hinder their Desertion." If "persuasive Arguments" did not work, Wright should "excite all our friendly Indians to your Assistance to hinder their Departure from this Government, sending some of the chief men as Hostages into the Settlement." Fortunately for all, this tactic was not attempted.[29]

Wright never went on his agency, but his instructions shed light on the South Carolina government's intentions of having both an agent and a resident commissioner, as well as on how unrealistic the commission on the Indian trade remained in regard to Indian-white relations. Wright, after visiting the Alabama, was supposed to continue to the Creek, Cherokee, and the Chickasaw, if possible, and solve all their grievances. The sheer length of the trip was not the only problem he faced. Somehow, Wright and Nairne were supposed to learn the customs of each group; give the headmen advice on "managing their People the better to keep them in Subjection" (using the South Carolina government as a proper example); help the headmen maintain their authority; lecture to and regulate all traders; gather information on the French and Spanish; secure unlicensed traders and other whites who had no business among the Indians; and complete numerous other tasks.[30] One agent and one resident commissioner could hardly do it all. The colony needed to have a commissioner each among the Upper Creek, the Lower Creek, the Cherokee, the "Northern Indians," and the Chickasaw. Instead, they expected miracles. Lecturing the traders on behaving like good Christians would have had little effect. And providing unenforceable restrictions undermined the government's creditability. The traders, for instance, were prohibited from receiving presents from the Indians under any pretense. The extortion of presents was an age-old abuse, but the commission ignored the cultural and business functions of gift-giving. The traders had to take up residence in Indian villages and establish personal relations with Indians on the Indians' terms, which included the exchange of gifts, but the Carolina government expected Indians to conduct trade in a European manner, as an impersonal transaction. The traders, for all their faults, understood much better than the government the cultural aspects of the trade, though their greed led them to exploit this knowledge for personal ends rather than to benefit the colony.

CALCULATING THE NUMBERS

The trade in Indian slaves formed a part of a larger movement of peoples from one locale to another, and from one continent to another, to fulfill the desire for labor by those who commanded capital to develop the resources of European colonies. The largest exportation comprised the millions of Africans wrested from their homes and enslaved throughout the Americas. Tens of thousands of European laborers were also pulled into the trans-Atlantic passage as indentured servants and convict laborers. Less known is the enslavement and transportation of American Indians.

The use of Indians as laborers in the colonial empires was quite common, particularly in Mexico and South America. North of Mexico, however, Indian labor was harnessed infrequently for use in the mines or on plantations. Instead, Europeans ordinarily made use of Indian labor in terms of clientage—as soldiers, slave-raiders, and police forces—and as hunters and processors of pelts, but thousands were also sold as slaves. The Carolinians' use of Indians as slaves was not unprecedented, only unusual in the scale of the colony's commitment to pursue and enslave Amerindians. Though some of the enslaved were employed on the plantations, most were shipped elsewhere. As with the trade in African slaves and European bonded servants, the dealers in unfree Indian labor were engaged actively in an intercolonial trade network, in which they possessed a commodity desirable at any colonial port.

The surviving documentation on this trade is scanty. British imperial and colonial officials had few reasons to record the intercolonial exchange of Indian labor. Yet enough survives to provide glimpses too valuable to be ignored. First, let us summarize the data on who was transported and in what numbers.

The first place to examine is Florida. As discussed in Chapter 5, perhaps as many as 4,000 Florida Indians were captured and enslaved in the period 1704–1706. Many more were enslaved *after* this period. In 1708, Governor Francisco de Córcoles y Martinez estimated that the Indians the slavers had taken "must number more than ten or twelve thousand persons."[31] Father Joseph Bullones, a witness to James Moore's second invasion, reported that four-fifths of the Christian Indians who remained in Florida after 1704 were "annihilated" in subsequent attacks, by which he meant killed and enslaved.[32] Historian Amy Turner Bushnell adds that the Spanish authorities could only document the decline in the Christian Indian population and "had no accurate way of knowing how many Florida Indians were being consigned to slavery." Thus, Córcoles's estimates might only include Christian Indians—how many non-Christian Indians were taken? Once the Apalachee and Timucua were defeated, the slavers went all the way to the Florida Keys. In Calusa, on Florida's southwest coast, thousands of Indians sought transport to Cuba to escape the raiders. One ship captain who carried 270 Florida Indian refugees to Cuba noted in 1711 that he could have brought 2,000 more Christian Indians from the Keys and that 6,000 more sought baptism (and probably protection). The bishop of Cuba, Gerónimo Valdés, learned from the refugees "that the Yamasees have killed some of the aforementioned

Keys Indians; have made others flee; and that they have captured the greater part of the latter, whom, it is said, they carry off and sell, placing them into slavery at the port of St. George [Charles Town]."[33] When we add in the hundreds of Spanish-allied Indians in Georgia who were forced into slavery in the 1670s and 1680s, and the hundreds more from Florida who were taken in the seventeenth century, it is easy to conclude that Córcoles was well within reason in suggesting that 10,000 to 12,000 were the minimum number enslaved by 1708. If we extend the time-frame to 1715, when so many of the Indians below Timucua and Apalachee were enslaved, then 15,000 to 20,000 is the probable low range for the number of enslaved from the Florida peninsula. There is no estimating the impact of slaving, warfare, and disease on Florida, which was nearly depopulated of Indians in the early eighteenth century.[34]

In the Lower Mississippi Valley it is even harder to estimate the number of enslaved. We know that the Chickasaw preyed on Indians all the way to the Gulf of Mexico and across the Mississippi into Arkansas. Many raids probably yielded small numbers of slaves, anywhere from one to a few dozen, and small parties or individuals conducted others.[35] The aggregate result, however, was the enslavement of many Indians. Some losses occurred before the French settled permanently in the Mississippi Valley. The French missionaries learned when arriving among the Arkansas that their population had declined 80 to 90 percent in a decade and that disease did not account for all the losses. The Arkansas probably lost hundreds to the raiders. The Tunica and Taensa were similarly victimized and may have lost as many.[36] Given what is known about the Arkansas, Tunica, and Taensa, these people alone lost at least a thousand souls before 1715.[37]

Information about the enslavement of the peoples near the mouth of the Mississippi and along the Gulf Coast is largely anecdotal, but it is worth describing a few episodes because they illustrate the slavers' vast impact on the region. For instance, the Colapissa, who numbered around five hundred in 1700, lost eighty that year in a Chickasaw-English slaving raid.[38] The petite nations were easy targets for the raiders. André Pénicaut related how the English "had incited the nations to war among themselves so that by this means they might find a good number of slaves to buy and take back to Carolina."[39] He recalled an episode in 1713 in which a "strong party" of Chickasaw, Yazoo, and Natchez combined to raid the Chaoüachas, who lived south of New Orleans. The slavers killed their grand chief and carried off his wife and ten others. The Yazoo, who had themselves been victimized by the slavers, were now slavers. But it is the scheme by which the slavers had captured their enemies that illustrates most pointedly how the English desire for slaves had so dramatically affected the culture of the region. The slavers had entered the Chaoüachas's village "under the pretext of singing the calumet of peace."[40] The Chaoüachas, a small group, had probably been quite excited by the opportunity of entertaining a mixed delegation of Indians from upriver. Why should they suspect malfeasance when the calumet was being sung? Ever so quickly the ceremony had lost its sanctity and much of its meaning as the Chaoüachas were attacked and enslaved. To protect themselves, the petite nations moved closer together and nearer the French. This resulted in ghastly massacres among those forced by circumstances to share towns, as when the Bayogoula turned on their Mougoulache hosts, the Taensa turned on their Bayogoula hosts, and the Tunica turned on their Ouma hosts.[41]

Petite nations losses could easily have been over a thousand. When added together with the Arkansas, Tunica, and Taensa, the number of enslaved in the Lower Mississippi Valley falls between two and three thousand.

A few more clues exist concerning numbers when discussing the Choctaw. Iberville stated in 1702 that the Choctaw had lost five hundred to Chickasaw enslavers, with another eighteen hundred killed.[42] The Choctaw gave these numbers to Iberville, who mentioned them in a speech to the Chickasaw, and Iberville made no statement in his journal that the Chickasaw denied these numbers. Patricia K. Galloway, in her study of the formation of the Choctaw people at the end of the seventeenth century, provides no numbers for how many Choctaw were enslaved before 1700, but she does say that the slavers' attacks were the catalyst for bringing together the several peoples who converged to make up the Choctaw.[43] Keeping in mind the Westo assaults on the peoples who combined into the Creek Confederacy, the attacks of slavers were key in forming the two largest ethnicities in the Lower South as well as in destroying several ethnicities in Florida.

After 1702 large armies made three major attacks on the Choctaw—in 1706, 1708, and 1711—to obtain slaves. Bénard de La Harpe reported that the Chickasaw and English carried off 300 Choctaw women and children in the 1706 raid.[44] The details of the raid in 1708 are murkier. The major English excursion that had been planned for that year was scratched, substituted by two invasions of Indians with minor English participation. One of these armies went against the Indians who lived in the environs of Mobile.[45] The other force was led by Thomas Welch, and thus probably comprised Chickasaw but might also have included Creek. How many Choctaw they captured is unknown, but Welch complained in December 1708 that Governor Johnson had confiscated 15 Choctaw slaves that he and others had taken.[46] The invasion of 1711, discussed at the beginning of this chapter, yielded 330 slaves. If we add Iberville's numbers of Choctaw taken before 1702 to the numbers carried off in 1706 and 1711, Choctaw totals reach 1,130. When the unknown number carried off in 1708 and the large number carried off in raids between 1702 and 1715 are also added, it is reasonable to conclude that between 1,500 and 2,000 Choctaw were enslaved.

Many Tuscarora and their allies in North Carolina were also sold into slavery. Enslavement had been one of the causes of the outbreak of war, but there is no way of knowing exactly how many were enslaved. John Barnwell admitted to having taken 36 captives on his expedition, but this does not include those taken by his Indian allies. Governor Pollock thought that Barnwell and his forces took 200 women and children.[47] On the second expedition into North Carolina, James Moore was very specific about Indian casualties. He reported having taken 392 prisoners and 192 scalps. He thought that at least another 200 were killed and burned inside their fort, and 166 others killed and taken who had fled the fort.[48] Other sources report 800 casualties inflicted by Moore but do not break down the numbers.[49] Governor Hyde of North Carolina bragged in a letter of May 1712 that he had "cut off and took prisoners betwixt 3 or 400 Indian Enemies."[50] Some of these would have been those seized by the North Carolinians as soon as the war broke out.[51] The seizing of Tuscarora and their allies continued long after Moore's Nohoroco campaign. Pollock made arrangements for shipping the prisoners to the West Indies, some of whom were brought in by neutral Tuscarora.[52] There is no way of knowing how many in total were taken, for we do not know how many Indians were carried off for sale in Charles Town or Virginia. Nor do we know how many were sent off at the end of the war. At least 1,000 to 1,200 Tuscarora and their allies were enslaved as a result of the war, though it is quite possible that the figure could be as high as 1,800 to 2,000.

There is no telling how many Piedmont and low country Indians as well as Creek, Westo, Savannah, Chickasaw, and Cherokee were enslaved. Hundreds of Westo were taken, and there is evidence that members of all these groups were enslaved, but there are no numbers. Almost no records of the late seventeenth-century raiding exist outside the Spanish sphere. The lords proprietors frequently complained of illegal enslavement. All of the evidence points to wide-scale enslavement from the 1670s through 1700, so much, in fact, that the numbers taken in this period could have outnumbered the later years of enslavement. It seems clear that, excluding the Creek, Savannah, Cherokee, Chickasaw, and Piedmont Indians, approximately 25,000 to 40,000 southern

TABLE 2. Southern Native Americans
sold in the British slave trade, c. 1670–1715

Place/Peoples	Low range	High range
Florida	15,000–20,000	30,000
Arkansas, Taensa, and Tunica	1,000	2,000
Petite Nations		
(lower Mississippi Valley)	1,000	2–3,000
Choctaw	1,500–2,000	2,500
Tuscarora and allies	1,000–1,200	1,800–2,000
Westo	500	1,500
Subtotal	20,000–28,200	41,000
Piedmont, Creek, Savannah,		
Chickasaw, Cherokee,		
Mocama, Guale, and others	4,000	10,000
Total	24,000–32,200	51,000

Amerindians were enslaved; if we include the excluded peoples, plus the Mocama and Guale in Georgia, we can add in several thousand more. All told, 30,000 to 50,000 is the likely range of Amerindians captured directly by the British, or by Native Americans for sale to the British, and enslaved before 1715.

THE EXPORTATION OF INDIAN SLAVES

What is surprising about these figures is that Carolina exported more slaves than it imported before 1715. There may not have been a single year in the colony before 1715, except for 1714, when the number of slaves imported exceeded the number of Indians exported.[53] Charles Town, as Peter H. Wood incisively shows, was an Ellis Island for Africans arriving in the New World; but it also marked the point of deportation for thousands of Native Americans.

Scholars have underestimated the size of the Indian slave trade for two reasons: there is little record of where large numbers of Indians were shipped, and the sole extant "official" Carolina document recording exports for the period (which covers the year June 1712–June 1713) lists only seventy-five slaves exported.[54] Moreover, most contemporaries listed the West Indies as the destination of Carolina's Indian slaves, but there are few records of Native Americans arriving in these islands. There are shipping returns from some islands, but not enough to support a systematic analysis. For instance, Barbados was the most likely destination for Indian slaves because South Carolina conducted an extensive trade there in its first five decades. But many surviving Barbadian shipping returns list only outbound goods before 1718. (For example, there are no inward returns from 1704 to 1709.) Those years that do have inward returns usually list only items liable to pay a duty, and there is often no column on the ledgers to record commodities not on the dutied list. There was thus no reason and often no space to record Indian slaves. Yet a few scattered relevant references are found in the records. For example, the *St. Christopher,* an eighty-ton ship owned in London, carried from South Carolina to Barbados in September 1682 a cargo of cedar, three hundred bushels of corn, thirty barrels of tar, ten barrels of pork, and thirteen Indians.[55]

Jamaica is the next likely port to consider, but there are shortcomings in that island's records for most relevant years. There are fairly complete records, however, of Jamaican exports and imports from 1709 to 1711. For this almost two-year period from mid-1709 to spring 1711, South Carolina sent or received numerous cargoes from that island. From Jamaica sixteen ships brought African slaves to Carolina totaling 297 individuals. Carolina shipped in return garlic, staves, candles, butter, peas, pork, tar, and rice. No Indians appear in the records, though the Mosquetos, on the coast of South America, sent a shipment of thirty in 1709.

A few records exist for Nevis, particularly for 1685–1686 and 1704, but often these do not identify the cargo. Other islands, such as Antigua, Bermuda, and Saint Christopher, are equally unhelpful. The records either do not exist or, where they do, imperial officials seem to have been peculiarly uninterested in recording South Carolina Indians.[56] This does not mean that Indians were not shipped to these islands. In 1698, the Board of Trade in London got wind of the large number of Indians being shipped to Bermuda. In the board's journal, under the heading *American Indian Slaves,* it was recorded that "upon observation made that it is commonly said there are many Americans at Bermuda kept as slaves; ordered that the governor be required to give an account, what number there are of them, from whence they are bought and by whom imported." According to historian Almon Wheeler Lauber, Bermuda's governor merely replied with information on slaves "without any special reference to Indian slaves." The board did not follow up with another request.[57]

When we place the Indian slave trade into the context of the African slave trade, the lack of records in the West Indies and the frenzy with which Carolinians pursued Indian slaves begins to make sense. West Indian planters had no reason to draw attention to the supply of Indian slaves from Carolina—why should they publicize an important commodity that was regulated and taxed by the mother country when obtained from Africa? The sugar-producing islands of the West Indies were dependent on the Royal African Company, which had a monopoly over the shipment of Africans to the islands before 1698. The company was rarely able to supply the huge labor needs of the planters, who would take labor from wherever it came. In response to planter political pressure, in 1698 Parliament passed an act that lasted until 1712 that opened the African trade from Cape Mount to the Cape of Good Hope. Noncompany traders had to pay a 10 percent duty on all that they imported into Africa, as well as a 15 percent duty on exported goods and 15s per African. These taxes were to pay for the forts that the Royal African Company maintained in Africa. Opening the trade actually raised rather than lowered the price of Africans, K. G. Davies argues, because competition among traders raised the price they had to pay in Africa for slaves. Also contributing to the rise in prices was war with France. Davies calculated that in 1688 a slaver paid only £3 for an African and £5 to transport him or her to Barbados. During Queen Anne's War, from 1702 to 1712, "the purchase-price trebled or quadrupled, and the transport-cost doubled." Thus it cost the traders £19 to £22 per slave, which they sold for about £25.[58] Importing slaves from Carolina thus had great advantages over Africa. Transport costs were probably half or less, and there were no imperial taxes to pay, although South Carolina placed its own 20s tax (13s sterling) in 1703.[59] Also, Indians could be purchased for half the cost or less from North American suppliers. With periods of drop-offs in the supply of Africans, as in 1706–1708, prices would have risen for what purchasers would pay for Indian slaves. Carolinians found it profitable to ship not only their Indians but occasionally their Africans as well.[60]

The rise in prices for African slaves affected the northern mainland colonies even more than it did the West Indies. The northern colonies were farther from Africa and could not pay what the islanders could afford. Into the breach stepped the Carolinians. The South Carolina governor's and council's 1708 report on the colony specifically referred to the northern mainland colonies as a destination for their Indians: "We have also Commerce with Boston[,] Road Island, Pennsilvania[,] New York & Virginia to which places we export Indian slaves."[61] The author of *A Description of South Carolina* . . . (1710) echoed the earlier report. He observed, "The Commodities sent from South Carolina to other Northern Colonies, are tanned hides, small Deer Skins, Gloves, Rice, Slaves taken by the Indians in War, some Tar and Pitch."[62] It is impossible to determine how many Indians were shipped northward. New York's and Pennsylvania's extant shipping returns do not begin until 1713, and Maryland's do not include imports. We also run into the same problem of customs agents not reporting or reporting accurately the import of Indian slaves. For instance, in 1715, the *Royall Anne* arrived in New York with a shipment of Indian and black slaves. The number of blacks was recorded but not the number of Indians.[63] Royal officials were very interested in numbers of Africans brought into each colony but not Indians.

Many northern colonies determined the importation of South Carolina's Indian slaves to be a growing threat after the Tuscarora War. Massachusetts (1712) and New Hampshire (1714) followed Pennsylvania's earlier barring of the importation of Indian slaves. Any master who brought an Indian slave to Massachusetts or New Hampshire, whether by land or sea, had to post a fifty-pound bond for the Indian's good behavior and remove the Indian from the colony within one month.[64] Although these laws stopped the importation of all Indians, they were specifically drawn up to prevent importation from Carolina, from where the vast majority of Indian slaves came. The preamble of the Massachusetts law specifically described the southern Indians brought to their colony as "malicious, surly, and revengeful."[65] In 1715, Connecticut and Rhode Island passed laws against the importation of Indians as a result of the Yamasee War. The Connecticut governor and council passed the prohibition as an emergency measure until the assembly could next meet and affirm a more permanent law—which it did. The emergency situation arose when "a considerable number of Carolina Indians, as they are commonly called, that is to say, Indians of those nations in and about South Carolina, which are in open hostility against his Majesty's subjects there," and who had "committed many cruel and bloody outrages upon them," were captured and sold in Connecticut. The governor and council feared that "our Indians may be tempted to draw off to those enemies, and many other great Mischiefs may ensue thereon, to the great hurt both of this and other [of] his Majesties Colonies upon this Continent." The Rhode Island law described in more detail the "great Mischiefs" referred to by Connecticut: "conspiracies, insurrections, rapes, thefts, and other execrable crimes."[66]

Indian slaves exported from Carolina to New England often retained their identity in their new homes. This is evident from advertisements for runaways and sales of Carolina Indians printed in the *Boston News-Letter*. Carolina Indian runaways were identified as such—presumably they had features distinctive from New England Amerindians. Southern Indians had hairstyles, tattooing, and head shapes that differentiated them one from the other. For instance, the Catawba bound a board to infant heads to extend and flatten the forehead and were often called "flatheads."[67] Traders, too, noted differences in stature and facial features from one group to the next,[68] though it is questionable whether New Englanders would find features of stature distinct enough to differentiate New England from southern Amerindians. Still, hairstyles and such cultural mannerisms as gait, facial features, and expressions might have been more significant in distinguishing southern from northern Indians. When the authorities took up an Indian woman in December 1711 and an advertisement placed in the *Boston News-Letter* announced her seizure, the announcement made it clear that this woman who spoke "very little English" was readily identifiable as "A Carolina Indian Woman."[69] She must therefore have possessed some physical feature(s) that marked her. Clothing is unlikely to have been used for identification, because almost all the ads for Carolina Indians noted their English clothing.

The maintenance of cultural identity among New England's Carolina Indian slaves is evinced in many ways in newspaper advertisements. One ad offering a Carolina Indian for sale noted that he had been "Nine Years in the Country and hardened to our Climate and Diet."[70] This Indian could speak and read English and was nineteen or twenty years of age, which meant that he had been captured when ten or eleven years old around 1708. The regional identity of the slave may have been important to a prospective buyer because a Carolina Indian slave was less likely to run away than a New England Amerindian. Still the retention of features from childhood distinct enough to indicate this Indian's origins nine years after arrival in the region, if not arising solely from physical features, suggests the survival of cultural identity in other ways.[71] Another advertisement making a similar point was placed for Moll, aged twenty, who had run away from her master (and "has carried away considerable Money"). This "Carolina Indian Maid-Servant, . . . Speaks good English." The vast majority of slaves exported from South Carolina would not have spoken English. Moll's English skills are evidence that she had been away from her home of origin for quite some time, probably since adolescence. Her employment as a maid is further circumstantial evidence that she had been purchased as an adolescent and trained for domestic duties. Finally, her theft of a substantial amount of money and a hefty wardrobe of clothes indicates that she must have planned escape with forethought and been quite familiar with her environment. Only a lengthy life in Boston would have created this situation. In spite of her likely arrival in adolescence, her "good English," and her skills as a maid—which would make her similar to any number of New England young women, or at least New England Indian women—the description of Moll included the adjective "Carolina," thus showing that her cultural identity was retained in either physical or cultural features.[72]

Even stronger proof of the maintenance of cultural identity came from two ads for runaways placed in the *News-Letter* of September 1711 and September 1716. The former notice announced that five Indians of five different masters had run away together. Three of the runaways were described as Carolina Indians, the other two as Spanish Indians. We may assume that the Spanish Indians had been exported from Carolina, because it is unlikely, though not impossible, that they came from elsewhere. The Spanish Indians likely hailed from Florida and would have had much in common both culturally and from life experiences with the Carolina runaways. The ages of the Spanish Indians, Boston, aged eighteen, and Manway, aged nineteen, make it likely that they were taken as children during the raids into Florida of 1702–1705. The Carolina Indians, Toby, aged twenty, Jenny, aged forty, and Phillis (age illegible), may also have been enslaved around the same time. The anglicized names of four of the five suggest that they had been in New England for some time. Just when they arrived in Boston, however, is less important than the establishment of ties among them after arrival. Obviously, they had been drawn to one another through their cultural ties and shared experiences both before and during enslavement. It is noteworthy that they did not run away with either black slaves or New England Indian slaves.[73]

The second runaway announcement also referred to three Carolina Indians who escaped together. Again, each of the runaways had a different master. In 1716, the three were "about 30 Years of Age or above" and spoke "but broken English." The limited English skills imply a fairly late arrival in the colony. Massachusetts outlawed the importation of slaves in 1712. The slaves' broken English could have been the result of about five years of residence in the colony, which would have meant that they were exported as a result of the Tuscarora War or one of the attacks on the Choctaw. Two were "menServants," James and Robin, and the other, Amareta, was simply identified as a "Woman Servant . . . pretty Lusty." Again, that they absconded together and did not run away with other servants denotes the strong retention of cultural ties several years after arrival in the colony.

Craftsmen owned all three runaways in this case; either their owners' work or propinquity had brought them into contact with one another. Their masters were, respectively malter, ship carpenter, and cordwainer.[74] The masters of the five runaways in the ad of September 1711 were minister, ship's captain, tailor, leather dresser, and someone of unidentified occupation. Moll's master was a mariner. Most of these masters were of middling means. They likely purchased these servants to assist in their trades or to work as house servants. Although Indian slaves were probably more expensive than indentured servants, they provided better value. Female children could be trained to domestic work without the worry that they would soon have their freedom; Indian slave apprentices would not leave their masters' employ except at sale for great profit. Finally, the ownership of slaves would have given status to those seeking to move upward in the local social hierarchy.

Some of the Indian slaves of Carolina also wound up in Virginia. The scarcity of evidence makes it hard to document numbers. In spite of its proximity, or partly as a result of it, Virginia was not an important market for Carolina traders in Indian slaves—southern Indians could run away from Virginia, at least from the frontier areas, more easily than they could from more distant colonies. Presumably, the Tuscarora and their allies in North Carolina were not sold in Virginia, for it would have been relatively easy for them to escape and it would have invited retribution from neutral Tuscarora and Five Nations peoples. The North Carolinians preferred to sell their Indian captives to the West Indies, so that they would not face meeting them again.[75]

Virginia did, however, import some Carolina slaves, and documentary evidence exists from which analysis of a portion of this trade can be made. Import records were kept for the period of December 10, 1710, to December 10, 1718, for each of the major Virginia rivers. The starting date of 1710 excludes what could have been two periods of heavy exportation from South Carolina to Virginia—the late seventeenth century and the period 1702–1706, but it does cover the years of the Tuscarora and Yamasee Wars. During these eight years, 4,415 black slaves entered Virginia. In this time only 72 Indian slaves (.016 percent of slaves) were brought into the colony, all but 1 from Carolina.

Of the 72 Indian slaves Virginia imported, 66 went to just one of the five Virginia points of importation. They were sold at neither the closest nor the farthest river from Carolina, but at a location that did not import large numbers of Africans. Whereas 2,657 Africans arrived at the York River, 675 at the Rappahannock, and 743 at the James, only 166 arrived at the "Upper

District of York" and 174 at the Potomac River. The Carolina traders who sold their merchandise in Virginia usually chose to do business at the Upper District of York. (In choosing between the Potomac and the Upper York, the traders probably chose the Upper York because it was much closer.) The Upper York district attracted just under 6 percent of the slaves brought into the York. The planters there thus turned to Indian labor, which accounted for 28 percent of their slave imports.

Whereas the Africans were imported in large ships, the Carolina Indians arrived in small coastal vessels. (Entry records include the name of the ship's captain, the owner of the cargo, and often the name of the ship—but none of the names of the Carolina vessels are included, most likely because of their small size.) Indians exported from Carolina by the large merchants to the northern colonies or to the West Indies generally would have gone on larger trading vessels; those carried into Virginia went in small lots by individual owners, though some companies exported medium-sized lots. Of the 66 Indians imported into the Upper District of York, all but 1 came from South Carolina and were transported in twelve vessels. The largest single cargo of Carolina slaves was the 12 exported by the firm of Jones and Clay, then 11 by Coleman and Thweet, and 10 by Robert Hix. Seven of the twelve vessels brought in fewer than 5 slaves. Thirty-nine of the 66 slaves entered in 1711, before the Tuscarora War. What does all this tell us? For one, Virginia was not a destination for the large exporters who used seagoing vessels. It was, however, a destination for individual entrepreneurs and firms dealing in small parcels who used the smaller vessels that plied the coastal trade. To sell their slaves elsewhere than in Virginia or the Carolinas, individuals and small firms would have had to consign or sell their parcels of slaves to the larger merchants, who then would have shipped them to the West Indies or the more northerly colonies. By taking their parcels to nearby Virginia, however, they could cut out the merchant middleman and sell their cargoes themselves. Those who took their Indian slave cargoes to Virginia probably knew of the market at the Upper District of the York River or learned of the market as they headed northward to conduct their sales after stopping at one of the closer Virginia ports. Even at the Upper District of York, the market for selling Indian slaves might not have been considered that advantageous because none of the owners returned to make a second sale there—perhaps the owners of these small parcels rarely handled the sale of Indian slaves, or they might have learned from their experience in Virginia that it was more profitable to sell or consign their merchandise in Carolina to the large merchants, who obtained higher prices in more distant colonies.[76]

There also existed an overland trade between Virginia and the South. Both Virginia and Indian traders traveling on the corridor east of the Appalachians carried slaves northward. No reliable data indicates how many Indians were transported in this manner, but one important document has survived relating the sad story of a single Indian captured in the vicinity of Mobile near the Gulf of Mexico and conveyed overland to Virginia. Lamhatty was a Towasa Indian, aged twenty-six, seized by a party of Tuscarora and transported northwest through Creek territory in 1706. Put to work in agricultural fields for three to four months at Talapoosa, an Upper Creek town, he was then taken by the Tuscarora on a six-week journey east to Oconee, a Lower Creek town. They then spent a month heading north through the southern Appalachians, where Lamhatty was sold to the Savannah, who took him further north into Virginia. At the foot of the Blue Ridge Mountains, on a branch of the Rappahannock River, Lamhatty escaped eastward, crossing branches of the Rappahannock three times, until he reached the Mattapony River, which he also crossed three times. Exhausted, he "surrendered himself" at Andrew Clark's house, where he was "violently" seized and restrained although he offered no resistance. After shedding tears and displaying "how his hands were galled and swelled by being tied before," he received gentler treatment. Not knowing what to do with him, his captors, who had never encountered a Towasa Indian and could not communicate in his language, brought him before a Lieutenant Colonel Walker of King and Queen County, where he remained "at liberty & stays very contentedly."

Lamhatty's account was recorded by Virginia's first historian, Robert Beverley, who had just published a book, *The History and Present State of Virginia* (1705), that included valuable ethnographic information on the local native population. Beverley interviewed Lamhatty, and one or both of them drew a map of Lamhatty's trip. Beverley does not say how he communicated with Lamhatty, but either Lamhatty had learned enough English to relate his story, or Beverley, who had many contacts with Virginia's native peoples, was adept at bridging linguistic gaps.

Lamhatty's story reveals a bit about the Virginians' views of native peoples. Their initial reaction was one of fear and hostility, followed by sympathy for Lamhatty's condition. Yet they would not determine Lamhatty's fate, and took him before a local elite, Walker, who was probably a magistrate. Viewed as a unique individual, Lamhatty was permitted his freedom. But the story does not end there. Beverley provided a "Postscript" to his unpublished record of Lamhatty. The Virginians learned that "some of his Country folks," other Towasa, were or had been kept as "servants"—that is, slaves. Lamhatty was no longer considered unique, but a member of a group that other Europeans deemed worthy of enslavement. His treatment changed, and he was "ill used by Walker." Lamhatty "Became very melancholy after fasting and crying several days together, sometimes using [a] little Conjuration & when warm weather came he went away & was never more heard of."[77]

FRENCH ENSLAVEMENT OF INDIANS

The English were not the only Europeans to enslave Indians in the South. The French enslaved Native Americans in Louisiana as a matter of course. They were familiar with enslaving Indians from their settlement in Canada.[78] They also kept in chains large numbers of Africans on their plantations in the West Indies. Carolina, however, gave the French their model for Louisiana's economic development, particularly where slavery was concerned. The French did not expect Louisiana to provide furs like Canada (nor did they want or need it to), nor did they model their economic plan after the sugar islands of Martinique and Saint Domingue. Initially, they hoped that Louisiana would bear the mineral wealth that the Spanish had reaped in the Southwest. But as the discovery and exploitation of mines did not bring immediate returns—the French had trouble locating mines and extracting their wealth—many eyed the Carolina plantation system as a more viable model.[79] The climate and latitude were similar, and the French thought that valuable commodities like silk and tobacco, experimented with on Carolina plantations, would be produced more easily in Louisiana. A plantation system required slaves, but with limited capital, the French eyed Carolina's method of obtaining labor—capture Indians to sell in the West Indies. It was as if one could create capital out of thin air; the only effort lay in capturing the prey and transporting it to market.

The French faced the same problems as the English in regard to enslaving Indians: enslaving was not an activity that lent itself to easy state control and orderly procurement. With potential profits so enormous, and so many people available to enslave, a *frenzy* of enslaving threatened to destroy the colony. French officials could not control their frontierspeople, particularly, the coureurs de bois, from inciting Indians to war against one another to make slaves. These French woodsmen had been enticed from Canada with the prospect of work but failed to find the high-wage income they expected. A census of 1708 stated that sixty lived in Indian villages along the Mississippi.[80] The actual number was probably much higher, because it does not include those who lived along the Red River, among the Choctaw and Chickasaw, or those who simply were too transient to be counted. Commissary Nicolas de La Salle complained that they had become "very harmful in Louisiana. They only excite the Indian nations to make war in order to buy the slaves . . . [which] stirs up wars among all the nations who [then] oppose the passage of the French." La Salle blamed the murder of the missionary St. Cosme upon these wars. Forced to employ coureurs de bois and sixty Towasa to hunt down the murderers, the French not only had to compensate the coureurs de bois for their work but felt it necessary to pay 220 livres each for the twelve children prisoners they now claimed as slaves.[81] The coureurs de bois had created their own employment opportunities.

La Salle had other reasons to oppose Indian slavery. He thought Indian slaves the cause of "much of the disorder" in the colony. Louisiana received "very little service" from them, Indians "not being at all appropriate to hard work like the negroes." La Salle proposed that the directors of the assiento at Havana "send Negroes of both sexes . . . and allow ourselves to pass on Indian slaves" in exchange.[82]

To transform Louisiana into a plantation colony laborers were needed. Looking around him at the sorry state of the colony in 1708, d'Artaguiette observed that the colony's free residents could be counted in handfuls; the others were "pledged to the king" as soldiers and other public servants. D'Artaguiette echoed the recommendation to exchange Indian slaves for black slaves, "such as is practiced by the English." The French colonies of Saint Domingue and Martinique, he stated, should exchange two Negroes for three Indians: "if this exchange takes place it is one of several means to establish this colony." The West Indies planters would gladly make the trade for "it is certain that in the islands an Indian is worth a Negro, it is not likewise here." D'Artaguiette noted that Indians could escape enslavement in Louisiana more easily than Africans, thus diminishing their value in the colony. The Africans had nowhere to escape and "will be here without retreat from the scorn that the Indians make of them."[83]

Pontchartrain took d'Artaguiette's suggestions to Michel Bégon, the intendant at La Rochelle, asking his advice on "the proposition that allows the inhabitants of Louisiana to exchange savages of North America taken in war, for some blacks." He wondered how it would be executed, its practicality, and its potential benefit to both Louisiana and the West Indies.[84] Without waiting to hear from the home government, Bienville opened a slave trade with the West Indies. He informed Pontchartrain: "A small French boat from Santo Domingo has arrived at this port to attempt to open a traffic in Indian slaves with the colonists of this place." Bienville promised to buy fifteen in his cargo and that if he brought more he would exchange Indians two for one, to which the captain agreed.[85] Bienville had promoted the exchange with the

West Indies as early as 1706. The Louisiana colonists, he reported, were willing to pay cash for Negro slaves. The Indians, he affirmed, were "very good for cultivating the earth but the facility they have for deserting prevents the colonists from taking charge of them." Thus, it was "quite necessary" to follow the English practice of trading Indians for blacks with the West Indies.[86]

Not all French in Louisiana were thrilled by the prospect of slave exchange. A colonist named Robert lobbied Pontchartrain to bar the trade because he feared that the islanders would send only the most vicious slaves. He argued that the English got their slaves from "the coast of Guinea" in exchange for cargoes of flour, salt, and meat. The Indian slaves, he affirmed, were exchanged in the islands for cash, not Negroes.[87] Thus, Robert did not oppose selling captured Indians, only exchanging them for island slaves— better to use the proceeds to buy new slaves from Africa. Pontchartrain, for the moment, sided with Robert and told Bienville that the Louisianans must buy Africans and that when peace was made ending Queen Anne's War with England, French vessels would be sent with cargoes.[88]

The French enslavement of Indians in Louisiana proceeded apace. Although the French were not in a position to enslave indiscriminately on the scale of the English, they did purchase slaves from their Indian allies. The French gave a gun for each scalp or slave, but they could only give fifteen or twenty guns per year, which limited how many Indians they could purchase. According to d'Artaguiette, Bienville "demonstrated" to the Indians "that nothing is owed them when they avenge their particular quarrels, they appreciate this reason and are contented."[89] But even if the French market for slaves was limited, English traders were always willing to buy Indian slaves, particularly from the coureurs de bois. Even so, Louisiana had a significant Indian slave population, for these slaves provided a big chunk of the colony's labor. In August 1708, Nicolas de La Salle's census of Louisiana counted 279 persons, not including the 60 Canadians residing in Indian villages along the Mississippi. Eighty of the 279, or 28.7 percent, were Indian slaves, a much larger percentage than in Carolina that same year.[90] These slaves were probably not widely distributed. There were few free people to own these slaves in Louisiana. Most probably lived near Mobile. D'Artaguiette himself owned more than ten. Other officers may have owned more than a majority of the slaves, with a few individual soldiers and coureurs de bois possessing one or two.[91] The high number of Indian slaves did not mean that the French could build their colony on Indian bondage. Most of those enslaved would have been brought by the coureurs de bois and voyageurs from distant nations. The enslaved had difficulty escaping because of their lack of familiarity with the terrain and their physical appearance. The various peoples' distinctive hair styles, tattooing, head shape, and other physical markings demarcated "Strange" Indians from allies of the French, and escapees would most likely have been returned by allied Indians for rewards, at least in the colony's early years.[92] Yet Indian slaves were also considered troublesome property, thus the desire of the French to get permission to export them. In 1709, Nicolas de La Salle reported the case of "a woman of the nation Yamagoyochée [?]"[93] who murdered a Canadian and his two slaves—she killed them en route to Mobile, where he was intending to sell her. She was captured by a Frenchmen, brought to Fort Louis at Mobile, and executed. La Salle cited this as a specific example of why black slaves were preferable to Indians.[94]

The exchange of slaves took place despite Pontchartrain's reservations. In early 1711 a ship from Cap Français, Saint Domingue, arrived for this express purpose. D'Artaguiette suddenly realized the necessity of a certificate system to prevent the "terrible abuse" that could occur if friendly Indians were shipped instead of enemies.[95] *Whose* enemies remained the question. The French believed that if they were to compete with, if not replace, the English as trading partners with many southern Indians, then they would have to be willing to buy their Indian allies' captives, whether or not the French were at war with the victims. To bring the Indians to the east of the colony into alliance, one memorialist noted, the French must make "a few presents," offer protection, and "trade with them for the slaves that they make from the nations which inhabit the cape of Florida with which they are already at war." These should be shipped to the islands because they come from "hot countries" and would presumably be acclimated to the environment.[96]

ENGLISH AND FRENCH VALUATION OF INDIAN SLAVES

The purchase price of slaves from Indian sellers varied widely from the French to English. D'Artaguiette thought that the English paid fifteen or sixteen trade muskets per slave in 1708, which would equal about £10 or £11 sterling. This was a little high, but even if they offered £5 in trade goods they could turn a handsome profit and still pay more than the French, who could offer but one gun for a slave or scalp.[97] Still, Bienville had compensated the coureurs de bois 220 livres for the Indian children they captured, which was more than the English paid, though this occurred under special circumstances—the coureurs de bois could have sold their captives to the English traders, always a fear of the French.[98] In 1714, however, new governor Antoine LaMothe de Cadillac claimed that the French could pay only between 100 and 150 livres, or £6 and £10 sterling, which was comparable to what the English paid in Africa that year plus the cost of transportation. Cadillac claimed that the English paid up to 50 pistoles for an Indian slave, which in 1722 equaled about £37 sterling. This is much exaggerated. Nevertheless, the Carolinians could pay more than the Louisianans: their economy was so much stronger—their profitable plantations could employ unfree laborers in a variety of moneymaking operations; they could more easily ship Indian slaves to the West Indies or the northern mainland colonies—they were closer to the islands than the French and had many ships plying trade from there and also from Massachusetts southward; and they were stronger at sea—particularly during wartime, the British enjoyed more security in shipping than the French, which lowered costs and risks. Whether the cost of slaves was £5 or £10 or even more, both English and French could turn a hefty profit through sale to other colonies.

We must be careful of accepting at face value Bienville's offer of two Indians for one African, for this could have been two women or children for one adult male African. If Bienville meant two Indians of similar age and gender to the Africans, then he contradicts d'Artaguiette's observation that Indians would be worth the equal of Africans in the West Indies. We must thus address comparable value of African and Indian slaves.

The cost of Indian slaves to purchasers is difficult to determine. Historians have stated and contemporaries believed that African slaves were much more highly valued than Amerindians because they were better field-workers, they were less likely to die in captivity from diseases, and on the mainland they were less able to run away. But circumstances varied from place to place, and we must examine who was for sale, when they were sold, and where.

Most Indian slaves were women and children, whereas the majority of African slaves were adult males. In the West Indies and the southern mainland plantation colonies, the men were far more valued than women and children for their ability to perform heavy physical plantation labor. William Robert Snell has separated men from women in valuating Africans and Indians in colonial South Carolina and found Africans to rate 25 percent higher than Indians when gender is removed as a consideration. Snell's figures, however, are based on the period after the Yamasee War, when changing factors might have influenced alterations in prices, one way or another, from before the war.[99] Also, using Carolina as a measuring stick for valuation of Indian slaves is problematic—they would have cost less at their source of supply in Carolina than elsewhere, whereas Africans in the colony would have cost more than in the West Indies, from where they were transshipped.

Almon Wheeler Lauber has examined inventories for several northern colonies to assess valuation placed on Indian slaves, many of who had Carolina and Spanish origins. Although Lauber made no attempt to systematize the evidence, he concludes that black servants were of higher costs than Indian servants. Yet from his scattered evidence a different conclusion could be drawn. To illustrate low value placed on Indian slaves, for instance, Lauber points to an estate in New Jersey where an Indian man was valued at eleven pounds, five shillings, in 1714. Yet among his list he included an Indian woman and her two children valued at one hundred pounds in 1711.[100] Lauber should have pointed out that this woman must have had some skill that brought her relatively high valuation, whereas the man referred to might have been elderly or otherwise physically incapable of doing skilled or heavy physical work. Skills, age, gender, and physical fitness must all be taken into consideration when assessing the value of slave laborers.[101]

Indian slaves probably were less valued in Carolina than African slaves because they could escape more easily. It is not clear, however, that Indians were valued much less than Africans when shipped to other colonies. In the West Indies, the value of Indian slaves depended on a variety of factors— availability and cost of other forms of labor and the physical abilities of each slave. Men were valued more than women and children. The Carolina slave traders could afford to undersell the African slave traders because of their lower transportation costs. Much would also depend on how much they paid for each slave from their supplier. Additionally, because the Indians were exported in smaller vessels than those that plied the African trade and were often shipped alongside other commodities in relatively small parcels, the shippers of Indians were more flexible in seeking markets. They could afford to ply their trade among the smaller islands where the African slavers rarely went and where they could receive higher prices than the African slavers received in Barbados and Jamaica. The African slave traders required a reliable market where they could expect high but not necessarily the highest prices; such a market had to have an almost limitless demand for labor to guarantee a sure and quick sale before too many of the victims died from the horrible travel conditions.[102]

The Carolinians thus took their slaves to the northern mainland colonies, where African slavers rarely ventured. There, Indian women and children probably brought higher prices than they fetched in the Caribbean. Northerners were less interested in field hands for whom Caribbean planters paid top dollar and more interested in purchasing domestic servants and trade apprentices. As noted earlier, middle-class households were typical purchasers in the cities, as tradesmen sought assistants and families sought household help. Africans could have filled these positions as easily as Indians, for they also worked as tradesmen and domestics in other colonies, but slave traders were less likely to bring Africans to these ports.

Buyer preference also played a role in slave sales. In Carolina, planters had preferences for Africans of particular ethnicities, especially for those familiar with rice production in Africa.[103] Whether an African was newly arrived, seasoned, or second generation also affected prices. Purchasers often paid more for slaves familiar with plantation agriculture in the West Indies than for those arriving from Africa.[104] Prejudice against the productive capability of Indian slaves in plantation agriculture was probably not as strong before 1715 as it grew later, when many Europeans thought that Africans were the best suited of all peoples to the difficult labor of staple production. This bias against Indian laborers might not have existed in the West Indies and would have been largely irrelevant in New England, where Europeans usually did not seek plantation slaves. In short, except in locales where it was perceived that Indians could escape among familiar peoples and terrain, whether a slave was Native American or African probably had little impact on his or her valuation by Europeans in the seventeenth and early eighteenth centuries. More significant would have been matching the age, gender, and skills of individuals to the labor needs of purchasers.

After King Philip's War ended in 1676, which was the peak of New England's export of Indian slaves, Charles Town became the main port of departure for Indians on the North American mainland. The broad array of destinations probably resulted in a great range of prices realized for Indian cargo. In this regard, the Indian slave trade was akin more to the resale of Africans from the West Indies than to the African slave trade. Slaves sold from the West Indies to the mainland and small islands tended to be in much smaller parcels than those from Africa. They also went to a wider variety of ports. West Indian slave parcels also included "troublemakers," slaves the planters wished to get rid of because of their behavior, which bore similarity to those Indians complained about by the New Englanders shipped as a result of the Tuscarora War.

Statistics can never do justice to recapturing the horrors of the slave trade. It is nevertheless important to discuss numbers as a way to begin to reconstruct this important trade in human cargo that had such a deleterious impact on so many and played such an influential role in the South's and the Atlantic world's development. The end result for Africans and Indians was the same: removal from their homes, denial of their rights and basic humanity, subjection to lifelong servitude, and the passage of slave status from mother to child.

12

THE YAMASEE WAR

INDIAN COMPLAINTS, TRADER FACTIONALISM, AND THE FAILURE OF REGULATION

While the second expedition was on its way to North Carolina, the factionalism at home continued unabated. Indians, too, took sides in the factionalism. Thomas Nairne represented the interests of King Lewis of the Yamasee town of Pocataligo at a commission meeting in March 1713, asking the board whether the Chehaw, "who were formerly belonging to the Yamassees and now settled" with the "Creek, might return."[1] That same day King Lewis and other Pocataligo Yamasee made a variety of complaints against members of the John Wright faction. They complained about Wright intimidating them to build him a house and sell him an island. After failing to pressure the Yamasee into giving him a house already built for one of their chiefs, Wright demanded timber for a house he would build by their "Great House," but they told him "he must not expect any Help from them or from their people." The Indians understood that Wright did not pretend to have a government order for him to settle there, but they feared the repercussions of refusing his request. The commission assured the Yamasee that they would not have to suffer anyone settling on their land or to build a house or provide timber for any person.[2] Other complaints registered that day included two against Wright's associate John Cockett: that he sold a slave he received from the Yamasee without paying for the slave and that he had gotten a slave from King Lewis for which "he had only an old Coat, and that Mr. Wright knew of the Debt."[3] White men lodged two other complaints against Wright concerning his having freed enslaved Indians. The commission upheld Wright in one of the complaints; the result of the other is unknown.

The following day the Wright faction took the offensive, making accusations against members of the Nairne (formerly designated Cochran)[4] faction. An Indian named Owitka accused William Bray (who had filed a complaint against Wright the day before) of seizing a free Indian woman, and Ianoia accused Bray of taking his slave as payment for hire of a canoe "which went to war, though he did not go in her."[5] In another case, ultimately brought to the assembly, Cornelius Meckarty accused Nairne of taking one of his slaves, whom Nairne gave to John Cochran and John Frazier, contrary to Wright's earlier orders.[6] The dispute took over a year and a half to settle, when the assembly finally decided that Nairne had been impartial in giving the slave to "Captain Cochran's family."[7]

The Nairne faction struck hard at former agent Wright, apparently trying to frame him, though the truth of the matter might never be known. Nairne issued a warrant to John Cochran to seize Wright's trading goods (valued at two hundred pounds SC currency) at Dawfusky, a town that Wright, as agent, had convinced the commission to declare off-limits to trading. Wright claimed in defense that he had sent the goods to Daniel Callahan— an ally of Nairne—for delivery to Joseph Wright (no relation to the agent). Joseph Wright had instructions to take the goods to the Alabama but instead took them to Dawfusky. The commission debated the matter and told Wright that the goods were forfeit according to law but that the commissioners would not use "the utmost Rigor [of the law] against him" if he paid the charges, which were insubstantial. Wright refused "and said if he had done any Thing against the [Trading] Act, he must abide by it." The commission affirmed that Nairne had done his duty in seizing the goods and that it would decide how to dispose of Wright's property at the next meeting,[8] at which the commissioners told Wright he could have his goods returned if he paid Cochran six pounds for his troubles in seizing the goods and up to six pounds more later when the commission determined the final amount owing. Wright also had to promise not to trouble Cochran or anyone else about the matter. Wright refused to pay because he believed that it would be an admission of guilt.

Meanwhile, the board made several attempts to have Joseph Wright present his side of the story, and he finally appeared before it in May 1713.

Wright admitted that the former agent had not given him orders to take the goods to Dawfusky. The board proposed that Joseph Wright pay Cochran's expenses and that John Wright could have the goods returned if he promised not to molest Cochran over the affair.[9] Wright refused. He went to his ally, Chief Justice Nicholas Trott, a man as punctilious, arrogant, narrow-minded, and self-centered as Wright, and received from him a writ of delivery issued to Cochran to deliver the seized goods to Wright. Cochran refused the writ because it did not state on what grounds he should return the goods or to what particular goods the writ referred. In the Court of Common Pleas, Trott ruled in Wright's favor, but the chief justice and the former agent could not obtain release of the goods. (Trott's authority in the colony was undoubtedly undermined by the near universal hatred of him.) Refusing to budge on point of principle, Wright would not comply with the commission's recommendation to pay six pounds to retrieve his goods or have Joseph Wright pay the fee; nor would he promise not to molest Cochran, which he had now done with his court case. More than a year later the commission ordered the goods condemned by the attorney general.[10] As for the dispute between Cochran and Wright, Cochran obtained several continuances (probably granted by judges other than Trott) until the matter finally was settled by the deaths of both plaintiff and defendant in the Yamasee War.[11]

John Wright had a modicum of revenge against the Nairne faction when he successfully prosecuted William Bray for "selling two free Indians." As both "Informer and Prosecutor" he received a reward of sixty pounds.[12] Yet the accusations against Wright continued. Colonel Alexander Parris claimed that Wright told the traders not to pay their arrears to the government,[13] and John Musgrove complained of Wright selling Ahele, a Creek Indian woman whom he had previously declared free.[14] Other accusations concerned Wright canceling traders' bonds and his purchase of slaves (when he was agent) the previous year, which had alienated the Alabama to strike an alliance with the French.[15]

By the summer of 1713 the entire attempt to regulate the trade was falling apart. The constant bickering and accusations of the two factions, in which charge and countercharge exposed the perfidy and self-interest of both, undermined any attempt to bring or keep the traders under control. Moreover, the legality of the licensing system, which stood as the cornerstone of regulation, lay threatened by England. The commission warned Nairne to "be very cautious how you deal with the Indian Traders about paying their Arrears of License Money." He could threaten them with warrants, "but upon Considering the Act of Parliament we do not think we have a sufficient

Power to prosecute the same." The board feared that it might even have to refund the traders' license money. They instructed Nairne to do all that was in his power to "oblige" the traders to purchase licenses and to "suffer not the Traders to cheat and use" the Indians "with Insolence inconsistent with the Amity we profess." As Nairne already well knew but the board felt necessary to iterate: the Indians "are the Bulwark of this Settlement."[16]

As the commission's power weakened, rum flowed illegally into the Indian towns and the traders stepped up their abuses.[17] Even Thomas Welch, the government's trusted trader among the Chickasaw, came under suspicion of illegally enslaving "two free Indian women and their brother."[18] The commission issued a warrant for his arrest, which Price Hughes, an imperial adventurer and friend of Welch, tried to stop. Hughes wanted the trader to accompany him on "his designed journey among the Indians" to establish a colony of Welsh along the Mississippi, but the board adamantly opposed releasing Welch.[19] Meanwhile, King Lewis and other Pocataligo Yamasee returned to the commission with complaints against members of the Wright faction, some of whom might have taken revenge on the Yamasee for their earlier testimony against them. King Lewis claimed that Cornelius Meckarty and Samuel Hilden had stripped and beat Indians "at one of their Plays," also taking their cloth;[20] Meckarty produced affidavits from two of his trader allies that he had not beaten or misused the Indians.[21] The matter was referred to the next meeting, but the outcome was not stated in the commission records.

Exasperated with the conduct of the Indian trade, in November 1713, the governor called for yet another act of regulation, one that would amend the "many absurdities and contradictions incautiously inserted" in the 1712 act. A new act was necessary to "restrain the exorbitant practices of the Traders, and confine them (if possible) within the bounds of reason and justice." He also wished for a revision of the "Negro Act," which "next to keeping up a good understanding and friendship with the Indians in amity with this Government," is of the "greatest consequence." The black slaves, he wrote in an address to the assembly, "must be reduced to order and subjection . . . by the strict severities of the Law."[22] In spite of the governor's directions, the assembly passed neither a new bill to regulate the trade nor a new slave code. Part of the reason for the slowness of the assembly arose from the difficulty of framing a bill that would eliminate loopholes and solve deficiencies. With no clear idea of the government's authority over the Indian trade, this was difficult to accomplish. The house put the matter to the Indian commissioners and came up with a bill in May 1714.[23] After passing a first reading, however, John Wright and Price Hughes made recommendations and the entire matter was put off to the next session, when it again was discussed and postponed.[24] Many in the house also may have obstructed the bill because of their displeasure with the governor's behavior toward John Barnwell: the governor had countermanded the assembly's order to the public receiver to pay Barnwell for his service in the Tuscarora War.[25]

The assembly's main preoccupation through 1714 remained the Indian trade—both the abuses of the traders and the political divisions between the Wright and Nairne factions. The Indian commission proved increasingly impotent to solve the abuses and to regulate the trade, which led the various factions to take their cases to the assembly. These distractions deflected the government from acting swiftly to prevent serious problems from exploding.

THE CHEROKEE DESTRUCTION OF CHESTOWEE YUCHI

In May 1714, as the petty squabbling continued, two traders fomented the destruction of the Indian town Chestowee Yuchi to obtain slaves. Yet the circumstances differed somewhat from the slaving that had taken place in the previous two decades. This time a free town in amity with the government was victimized. The Carolinians had gone against free towns in friendly commerce with the colony in the seventeenth century, and they had victimized individual Indians in amity with the government on numerous occasions since then. The wholesale attack on a free town in alliance to the colony was an entirely different matter in 1714—one that greatly threatened the existence of all free Indians in and near South Carolina.

The origins of the Yuchi (spelled in contemporary South Carolina documents as Euchee) are a subject of much debate, though anthropologist John Swanton claims that they migrated from the southern Appalachian Mountains to the south and east. (They are referred to as the Chisca by the Spanish and some of the early English explorers.) Some Yuchi temporarily settled in Virginia in the 1650s, while others had migrated west toward the Mississippi in the 1680s, but their permanent settlements in the early eighteenth century lay in three distinct areas. A small band had resided since at least the last quarter of the seventeenth century in Florida, west of the Choctawhatchee River. A much larger number resided on the Savannah River. After the Westo War with the colony, other Yuchi moved to the Savannah, the location of two of their towns in the second decade of the eighteenth century. After the Yamasee War, these towns moved to the Chattahoochee and lived with the Lower Creek, while the Florida Yuchi may have settled with the Upper Creek. The third group of Yuchi lived on the Upper Tennessee, just west of the Middle Cherokee, in a town called Chestowee. It is to their fate that we now turn.[26]

In 1711 or 1712, the trader Alexander Long had a dispute with some of the inhabitants of Chestowee over debts he thought they owed him. The Chestowee refused to pay, and in an ensuing scuffle Long was either humiliated or hurt when his hair was pulled severely. Long swore revenge against the town.[27]

Trader James Douglas later testified that in 1712 he had heard "grumbling against the Euchees" by the Middle Cherokee "but Nothing about War." Two years later, the Cherokee, under the urging of Long, decimated Chestowee.

Numerous witnesses, both Cherokee and Carolina traders, testified to the plot among the Cherokee, Long, and Long's partner, Eleazer Wiggan. Long provided the powder and ammunition. He also promised the Cherokee a huge supply of trade goods, valued between £300 and £320. In return, the Cherokee would attack Chestowee, pay the Chestowee's debts owed Long (which he calculated as amounting to the value of one woman and five children), and turn over the captives to be sold as slaves in exchange for a "Cargo" of goods.

The planned attack was hardly a secret. Long bragged about it to one and all. Robert Card testified that Long said he "would have some of the Euchees' Heads on a Pole," and others testified that Long boasted he would cut off the town "before Green Corn time." Word of the impending attack reached South Carolina, and the governor sent an express message to the Cherokee not to attack Chestowee. Somewhere along the lines of transmission the governor's message was detained by one of the conspirators until after the attack. Price Hughes, who learned of the plot on his way westward, received promises from some Cherokee chiefs that they would not "molest the Euchees till the Agent came." Hughes returned east, probably to report the grave situation. On his way, he came across the governor's orders to the Cherokee to not attack the Yuchi and returned to Euphase, the Cherokee town Long had enlisted in his plot. Hughes was too late. The attack already had occurred, though Hughes arrived in time to convince the Cherokee not to extend their war against the Savannah River Yuchi.

According to witnesses, Long had pestered the Cherokee for some time to attack the Yuchi. Long and Wiggan promised the Cherokee that "there would be a brave Parcel of Slaves if Chestowee were cut off." Long pretended to have an order from the governor to "cut off" Chestowee, but one of the defendants, Wiggan, claimed that the Cherokee headmen, Flint and Caesar, aimed at attacking Chestowee whether the governor approved of it or not. Both of these Cherokee were particular favorites of the government. In 1713 Caesar had been a slave of John Stephens, from whom he had run away.

When Flint and Caesar delivered letters to the colony regarding French traders among the Cherokee and Yuchi (whom the Yuchi had captured), the Board of Commissioners of the Indian Trade urged that Caesar's freedom be purchased from Stephens, as Caesar "may prove serviceable on Occasion," and in fact, Caesar had a long and profitable association with the colony, particularly as a supplier of Indian slaves and captor of runaways.[28]

Wiggan blamed the Cherokee for the attack by claiming that they "were dissatisfied for the Loss of some of their People and for that Reason cut off Chestowe." The commission was unconvinced. Several traders testified that the Cherokee "would not have cut off the Euchees if they had been expressly ordered to the Contrary" by the governor.[29] Partridge, a Cherokee chief who refused to go against the Yuchi, testified that none of the white men had "used any Endeavour to prevent" the attack. Partridge did not put all the blame on the traders, though he singled out Long as the instigator. He reported Long's sadistic murder of a Yuchi who had come to him to purchase powder just before the attack—Long put the powder behind the Yuchi "and set fire to it and blew him up." Partridge also blamed Flint and Caesar, who had kept the impending attack secret from the Lower Cherokee towns because they did not want to share the spoils.

During the attack, the Yuchi "killed their own People in the War House to prevent their falling into the Hands of the Cherikees." Nonetheless, many were taken captive and others escaped. (The survivors later joined the Creek.) Long tried to convince the Cherokee to attack the Yuchi at Savannah Town "or else there would be no Traveling" in that area, but the Euphase Cherokee thought better of it.[30] All but a few abandoned their town, perhaps fearing retribution from the Yuchi or from South Carolina. One trader testified that Long had convinced them to leave, but Partridge claimed that Long had berated the Cherokee as "old Warriors" and threatened to get an order from the governor to "have them cut off as the Euchees had been."[31]

The commission ordered the confiscation of Long's and Wiggan's licenses and the prosecution of their bond. They also asked the governor to prosecute the two traders. The commission then ordered six Cherokee traders and any other white men who held Yuchi captives to turn them over to the government "with all convenient Speed." Long fled the colony and found refuge among the Cherokee, with whom he remained for several decades. Wiggan, whatever prosecution he faced in 1714, remained active in the trade for years afterward.

The South Carolina government could no longer deny the importance of the Cherokee to the South's geopolitical future. Until the second decade of the eighteenth century, this populous group played little role in colonial affairs, and only a secondary role in relations among southern Amerindian peoples. Their trade with South Carolina in Indian slaves and deerskins was insignificant in comparison to the more southerly Indians. Virginians controlled much of the Cherokee trade, though the French had a portion as well. As the Cherokee desire for European goods increased they more actively hunted deerskins and established stronger ties with the Carolinians. Their participation in the invasion against the Tuscarora led by James Moore brought them into closer contact with English colonial society. The growing military power of the Cherokee and their geopolitical importance to the French and English ensured that they would play a key role in the South in the coming years.

As Cherokee power emerged as a force in the region, the Creek, Yamasee, and other allies of the English grew more wary of their neighbors—both the Cherokee and the English. South Carolina's attempts to ameliorate the unhealthy relationship between the traders and the Indians, and to reassure the "friendly Indians" that the English believed in justice and considered their trading partners as friends, were gravely shaken. The Indians in amity with South Carolina knew exactly where to place the blame for the horrendous attack on the Yuchi: the traders and the Cherokee, with the Carolina government once again impotent or negligent in controlling its people. In the coming year, Indian relations continued on their course; the commission and the government remained unable to discipline the traders or to diminish the factionalism that threatened to paralyze the government.

SOUTH CAROLINA'S INABILITY
TO CONTROL THE INDIAN TRADE

Although Indians continued to complain to the commission, it was clear by mid-1714 that the commission had become little more than an arbitrator between the factions that sought to dominate the Indian trade. The commission was unable to settle the traders' differences, which usually involved the illegal sale of Indians or overlapping claims to particular slaves. The more powerful traders turned to the assembly for justice, and both the commission and the agent had to defend themselves and their decisions. This kept them from handling growing Indian discontent, tying their hands and slowing their response to the traders who took advantage of their impotency.

Landgrave Thomas Smith and John Pight, two powerful traders who walked an independent line, challenged the commission on points of law. Smith sent traders to the northwest without licenses and argued that because

"he traded without the Limits of the Government," no licenses were required.[32] The outcome of his challenge is unknown, but certainly the traders
followed Smith's case closely, for it questioned the legality of whether Carolina could regulate the trade outside its boundaries. The assembly charged
the commission to produce a draft for a new law to govern trade, but Smith's
argument went beyond the manner of regulation to a question of jurisdiction: how far did the colony's jurisdiction extend? The colony's right to regulate the trade had already been challenged in Britain, and Governor
Spotswood of Virginia had long fought Carolina's claim of jurisdiction over
the Indians outside the colony.[33] If Spotswood and Smith were right, then
the only trade that could be regulated lay in the bounds of the colony, cover-
ing the Settlement Indians, the Savannah River tribes, and some of the Cherokee, but excluding the Creek, the Chickasaw, most Cherokee, and many
other Indians south and west of the colony.

Pight's complaints against the board revolved around a dispute he had
with John Musgrove, a former trader and current member of the Commons
House and the commission, contesting the ownership of an Indian boy.
Pight argued that the commission had gone beyond its jurisdiction in granting the boy to William Steed, who sold the boy to Musgrove. The commission countered that it had never made this decision; rather, it had gone to
court, where two arbitrators (one of whom happened to be a commission
member) had decided against Pight. Pight complained to the governor in
June 1714 that the commissioners of the Indian trade were unjust to him.
The commission then vowed to prosecute Pight "for his scandalous Reflec-
tions on them."[34] The matter was referred to the assembly, which scolded the
commission for responding to Pight's charges by a letter delivered to the assembly by messenger: they were ordered to bring in their letter themselves.[35]

After denying Pight's charges, the commission asked the assembly for justice against him, "as may incourage us to stand by the Indian Trading Act purchased and procured with so much Difficulty by your Predecessors and so apparently advantageous for the Good and Safety of Carolina." Clearly, the
commission believed that Pight threatened its power over the Indian trade,
and the commissioners looked to the assembly to stand behind them. The Indian Trading Act, they told the assembly, "is now vilified and ridiculed by the
said Pight," who traded without a license and committed "other Things
against the said Law for which this Board has ordered him to be prosecuted."[36]

Both sides brought to the assembly legal counsel to argue points of law,
but the outcome of the dispute was not reported in the journals of the assembly or the commission—perhaps they reached some settlement out-of-

doors.[37] But Smith's and Pight's opposition to the trade laws led many if not most traders to disregard the licensing system. In the summer of 1714, almost all of the traders, according to the commission, operated without licenses, which led the board and the agent to redouble their efforts.[38] In November, Nairne successfully brought in bonds for licenses from twenty-three traders, and in a show of power, the commission prosecuted one of these men, Roger Hoskins, for "great indecencies" against Nairne, demanding of him to beg pardon and promise future good behavior and threatening to revoke his license if he repeated the offense.[39] Meanwhile, the assembly stepped up efforts to improve relations with the colony's Indian allies by rewarding Indians who had performed well during the Tuscarora War. Four Indians who had "signalized themselves in the late expedition" received cash payments, five Yamasee headmen received coats valued at seventeen pounds, ten shillings, and others who were injured also received compensation.[40] When a party of Chickasaw arrived in town to ratify a peace with the colony, the assembly might have thought that the future boded well for Indian relations.[41] They were wrong.

The dispute between the Nairne and Wright factions flared anew. William Bray, Nairne's ally, again was accused of selling free Indians. His case came before the assembly, where John Cochran, another staunch Nairne ally and a member of the assembly committee examining the matter, provided evidence for Bray.[42] Meanwhile, Wright accused another of Nairne's allies, John Frazier, of having obstructed the Yamasee from going to North Carolina the year before.[43] The governor supported Wright and employed another Wright ally, Cornelius Meckarty, to bring in Frazier. Meckarty received a hefty reward of twenty pounds for completing his task.[44]

In the summer and autumn of 1714, Nairne and Wright squared off against each other with charge and countercharge, their dispute in the assembly interrupted only occasionally by complaints (such as Pight's) against the commission's power and intermittent discussion of reforming the trade laws. Wright began the onslaught in May when he accused John Jones of disobeying the laws stipulating a three-day wait before purchasing slaves from Indians who had just returned home.[45] Most of Wright's attack, however, was reserved for Thomas Nairne, whom he accused of incompetence and negligence as agent. Nairne had allegedly allowed traders without licenses to collect their debts from Indians and tolerated the operation of a "Punch Hous[e] for the Indians" run by John Jordine on Captain John Cochran's land.[46] (Cochran's land lay very close to the Yamasee.) Nairne countered by accusing Wright of carrying rum to the Indians, and the commission ordered

Wright's prosecution by the attorney general. The commissioners also used the occasion to sell Wright's long-disputed goods at Dawfuskey, which the former agent had never reclaimed. As for the confiscated rum that Nairne had stored at the "Pocatalligo King's Hous[e]," a Portuguese and a Spaniard who both worked for Wright broke in and stole the alcohol. The two were indicted, but Nairne was rebuked for having not "staved the Rum," instead placing it in a way that gave "them the Opportunity to have got it away."[47]

Having lost all creditability with the commission, Wright took his case to the assembly. The very day Wright was ordered prosecuted for carrying rum, he appeared before the Commons House to recommend changes in the administration of the Indian trade. He also attacked Nairne's conduct as agent.[48] Because the session was soon to end and the interested parties needed time to call their witnesses, the dispute was put off until the following session, which met in November 1714. When the assembly reconvened, the governor again called for a new "Negro Act" and a new Indian trading bill, but instead the assembly took up Wright's remonstrance against Nairne.[49] The Commons House met as a grand committee to examine at least nine articles Wright had presented concerning the agent's behavior. After nearly a month investigating the charges, the house sided with Wright against Nairne on the first article, the substance of which is unknown, and on part of the second article, whereby Wright "effectively proved" that Nairne had issued illegal warrants to seize traders' goods. (Nairne later called more witnesses to prove the warrants were not illegal, but the outcome of the matter is unknown.) The house found in favor of Nairne on all other charges it acted on. The nature of these charges was unspecified in the assembly journals, except for one in which Nairne was found innocent of showing partiality in declaring an Indian slave the property of John Cochran and not Cornelius Meckarty.[50] Wright was not finished. He had more grievances against Nairne and petitioned the governor for redress. The governor and assembly, however, put aside all consideration of the remaining charges as the parties again gathered witnesses. In the meantime, the government had more pressing matters to consider: a new trading act had to be passed.

The problems of the old Indian trade act apparently had to do with enforcement. In December 1714 a new act was introduced similar to the act of 1711, but with much of the wording changed apparently for clarity and to remove loopholes. Both factions agreed on the need for a new bill: one that would help end the bitter factionalism. The complaints of the Wright faction against Nairne, and much of the long-running dispute in general, had to do with unequal enforcement of the regulations and favoritism, complaints similar to those lodged against Wright when he was agent. The traders looked for ways to circumvent the regulations, and if the agent was their friend, they did so. Both Nairne and Wright prosecuted regulations to the letter of the law when it suited them. Also, in the many disputes that arose between traders, the agents invariably decided in favor of the trader of their faction. These disputes were often over ownership of Indian slaves, so the monetary stakes were high. And both factions used Indians to register complaints against members of the opposing faction. This last act was the most dangerous because it showed Indians the politicized nature of the grievance process for achieving justice.

Once again, the colony tried to amend relations with Indians through words—producing another document to define trader activities. The first two weeks of December 1714 were taken up with consideration of a new trading act, which made it through two readings. By the third reading a bizarre event led to the bill's postponement until the next session. The house desired to compare the wording of the new bill to that of the old only to find that someone had borrowed or stolen the current trade act. Then, as mysteriously as it had disappeared from the secretary's office, it reappeared. Each member of the house was required to take an oath that he had not removed the act, knew nothing of how it disappeared or when, nor who had it and how it came to be returned. It was insinuated that Chief Justice Nicholas Trott was responsible. Trott, whose family had recently become shareholders in the colony, had procured for himself the remunerative perquisite of making copies of all the colony's laws, for which he charged the assembly the exorbitant sum of £350.[51] With the current act safely returned, the assembly postponed the new act's passage to give the commissioners of the Indian trade time to make sure that the new bill was drawn to meet their specifications.[52] The time wasted searching for the 1711 act and then trying to find the culprit proved fatal to the colony: the assembly would not have the opportunity to pass a new trading act for a year and a half.

When the assembly again met in February 1715, it had no chance to consider the new bill because the proprietors, in a fit of anger over the colony's enactment of a bank act, gave the despised Nicholas Trott veto power over all laws passed by the colony. Governor Craven defended the bank law as one almost universally approved of in the colony and bragged about the "addition of slaves [that] has been acquired by it." Craven believed, and the assembly seconded his notion, that giving Trott the veto allowed one man "a power unknown" and "unheard of in other Plantations abroad." It helped matters little that the proprietors had chosen to elevate Trott, "a person acceptable to very few in Carolina."[53] The assembly thought Trott's unusual power as "ruining our Constitutions" and "unheard of in any of the British Dominions, or for ought we know in the whole world."[54]

With the chief justice now installed above the governor, Craven wished to resign, but the assembly begged him to stay until they had remonstrated in England.[55] The house sent two agents to the proprietors; they then passed a bill prohibiting the chief justice "from giving advice in matters of Law." On February 25, 1715, Trott vetoed the legislation.[56] The house then prepared detailed instructions for their agents in Great Britain, including the charge that if the proprietors did not redress their grievances, then the agents should appeal to "a superior power" namely, the king. The last act of the assembly, passed that very day, was an address of congratulations by them and signed by the governor, on the accession of King George I to the throne of England. The assembly was prorogued until June 14, but it would be called back into session before then.[57]

THE EARLY STAGES OF THE YAMASEE WAR

The commissioners of the Indian trade also convened sooner than expected. They received a report from Samuel Warner that he had learned from the Apalachicola that the Creek "were dissatisfied with the Traders that were among them, particularly John Jones." The Creek "had made several Complaints without Redress and . . . upon the first Affront from any of the Traders," they would "down with them"—presumably, kill them. William Bray then told a similar story. Bray was on his way "towards St. Augustine" to pursue "some of his slaves" who had run away, when "a Yamassee Indian came to his Wife and told her . . . that the Creek Indians had a Design to cut off the Traders first and then to fall on the Settlement, and that it was very near." This Yamasee told Bray's wife of the impending attack because "he had a great Love for her and her two Sisters and when it was very near he would come again and . . . [then] they must go immediately to their Town."[58]

Alexander Hewitt, writing in the late 1770s, related another warning given before the attack. This came from Sanute, a Yamasee who reputedly had visited Saint Augustine, where he and other Yamasee received guns, ammunition, and additional supplies for attacking South Carolina. Hewitt relates that Sanute told Frasier (probably John Frazier) that the Yamasee had agreed to accept the Spanish king's sovereignty. The Spanish would support a Yamasee attack by bottling up Carolina's harbors. Sanute told Frasier's wife that the English "were all heretics, and would go to hell, and that the Yamassee would also follow them, if they suffered them to live in their country." The Creek,

Cherokee, "and many other nations" had joined with the Yamasee, and soon they would destroy "all the English inhabitants of the province." Sanute informed them of the plot only out of friendship and begged Frasier to take his family to Charles Town. If they refused, he promised to kill his family when the attack came so that they would not be tortured.[59]

The governor took the warnings seriously enough to meet immediately with the Indians. Bray and Warner returned to the Yamasee, where Nairne, former agent Wright, and John Cochran met them. The governor expressed his concern by sending the leaders of both factions to negotiate and appease the Indians, so that no faction of Indians among the Yamasee would be omitted. Carolina's negotiators promised redress of all grievances and that the governor would soon arrive to meet with them in person. The Indians "appeared satisfied." All shook hands, drank, and retired for the night.

The next morning, Good Friday, April 15, the Indians attacked the traders and representatives of Carolina. That the Yamasee painted their bodies in the middle of the night while the white men slept indicates that the attack was premeditated. Almost all the resident traders were killed. A Captain Burage escaped: he was shot twice, one bullet piercing his neck and exiting his mouth, yet he swam to John Barnwell's home on Port Royal Island and sounded the alarm. Fortunately for the island's inhabitants, a ship that had been seized for illegal shipment of goods provided refuge for the four hundred people who escaped the Indian army that soon arrived.[60]

A trader who escaped the initial attack by hiding in the marsh witnessed the fate met by many of the Europeans. The captives were apparently tortured. The irony that Wright and Nairne, bitter enemies but also the foremost spokesmen for reform, would share the same gruesome death was probably not lost on the Indians. According to George Rodd, who wrote the fullest account of the initial attack, death was slow and painful for the agent: "the criminals loaded Mr. Nairne with a great number of pieces of wood, to which they set fire, and burnt him in this manner so that he suffered horrible torture, during several days, before he was allowed to die." John Cochran and his wife were kept prisoners but slain a few days later.[61]

The governor counterattacked, and Carolina forces captured the Yamasee town of Pocataligo. The Indians went into hiding, giving Carolina a brief respite, but then the colonists learned that the Creek, Cherokee, and many Piedmont and low country Indians had joined against them. Resident traders were killed, plantations burned, and civilians killed or taken to Saint Augustine. The southern parishes were abandoned, and people throughout the colony sought refuge in Charles Town. A Captain Barker led a company of one hundred horsemen to the Congarees and was ambushed by the "northern" (Piedmont) Indians, with thirty dying, including Barker. The leader of these Indians was a "war captain" who previously fought alongside Craven against the Yamasee but had now changed sides.[62] Shortly thereafter, the Indians subdued a garrison of seventy whites and forty blacks.[63] Indian raiding continued through the year, but Carolina effectively organized its defenses. The colony raised an army of about six hundred whites, four hundred black slaves, and one hundred free Indians, and this force was later joined by three hundred whites sent by Virginia and North Carolina and seventy Tuscarora.[64] The colony was constricted to Charles Town and its environs, but the Indians did not attempt to eradicate the colony.[65] Hundreds of colonists had died and South Carolina was thoroughly demoralized.

No one was in for a greater shock, however, than the "Yamasee Prince," a young man sent to England for schooling and religious instruction in 1713. The Society for the Propagation of the Gospel had hoped that Prince George, as he was called in England, would become the means by which other Yamasee would be converted and Anglicized. By January 1715, he had learned to read and write, been baptized by the bishop of London, and met King George. The prince returned to South Carolina during the war to find that his family had fled south. Later his family was captured and sold as slaves. The fate of the prince, left "Extremely Sunk and dejected," is unknown.[66]

CAUSES OF WAR

The ministers, recognizing their own failures in converting Yamasee, did some soul-searching to find the causes of the colony's misfortune. But generally, they blamed the traders. Francis Le Jau thought that the traders' oppression of the Indians and their running up huge debts that the Indians could not repay had left the Indians no choice.[67] Gideon Johnston also blamed "the barbarous usage these poor Savages met with from our villainous traders."[68] Another SPG minister, William Treadwell Bull, provided a more detailed assessment. As with Le Jau and Johnston, Bull believed that the attack was a judgment from God against the colony for its voluminous sins. Bull, however, added that though the sins were general, one in "particular" was worth noting: the "gross Neglect of the poor slaves amongst us," in not teaching them the "Faith and Principles" of Christianity.[69] Through the next generation, Carolina ministers would uphold the denial of Christianity to slaves as the root cause of God's having inflicted drought, disease, pestilence, military defeat, and other punishments on the colony.[70]

Bull also pointed the finger at the "profligate & debauched" traders, but he thought that their behavior was no different than in years past, so he questioned their abuses as a cause of war. Instead, he noted the Indians' growing poverty, which had arisen alongside the rising wealth of the English. In "late years" the colonists had "prodigiously increased their estates" and established a "genteel way of Living" made evident "both by Gayety of Dress and handsome furniture of Houses, whilst the Indians," through either "Natural Laziness, or more properly I think the extortion and Knavery of the Traders can hardly procure ordinary Clothing to cover their Nakedness." The envious Indians grew resentful and burdened by debts they could not repay for years. But, at long last, as a response to British perfidy, the Indians had learned to live in peace with each other and thought that they were "a Sufficient Match for us."[71]

Historian Richard Haan echoes Bull's rejection of the idea that trader abuses led to war. Haan emphasizes that the Yamasee had run out of victims to enslave and that with a declining deer population they could not hunt to pay off their debts, which amounted in 1711 to a hundred thousand deerskins.[72] Haan overlooks the profits the Yamasee made by slaving and plundering during the Tuscarora War, particularly on the second expedition led by James Moore, but he points out the long-term problems the Yamasee faced in residing in an overhunted area.[73] Haan believes that a census of Indians taken by the colony in 1715 frightened the Yamasee into thinking that the English were preparing to enslave them as a means to recoup the exorbitant debts they owed the traders.[74] Given the colony's history of turning on its neighbors, this was certainly a possibility.

Trade abuses, envy, mounting debts that could not be repaid, and fear of enslavement are but part of the story behind the Yamasee decision to strike.[75] Putting the blame on a census taker implies that the Yamasee were impulsive and that they chose to attack the colony without forethought. Yet there is much to suggest that Yamasee plans were premeditated and long planned. Was there a "conspiracy" among the southern Indians, and if so, was it in league with the French or Spanish? To answer this question we must look further at the Yamasee's role in the conflict.

The factor most overlooked in considering Yamasee motivation was the threat of the colonists to their land. The traders and others had long eyed the valuable mainland occupied by the Yamasee. In response, in 1707, the colony had prohibited Europeans from settling between the Combahee, Port Royal, and Savannah Rivers. The colonists near Port Royal were confined to the Sea Islands. Two factors led to continued encroachment on Yamasee territory— the growing importance of rice in the colony and the declining importance of the Yamasee trade in slaves and animal pelts. The Sea Islands were not conducive to rice production, but the Yamasee land was perfect. With many freshwater rivers and creeks, the mainland could be diked to flood fields with freshwater.

The Carolina government understood that the Yamasee were their most important ally and that they must be protected from the traders' perfidy and the settlers' encroachment on their land. The traders, in contrast, had little use for the Yamasee. Once the trade declined they wanted nothing better than to provoke a war between the colony and the Yamasee, to force the Yamasee from their lands.[76] The Yamasee had no choice but to fight, and the question was not whether they should attack but when. If they were going to retain their lands they would have to forge new relations with the region's Indians and organize an alliance against Carolina. In 1715, no war against the colony could have taken place without their involvement.

The smaller Indian groups of the South Carolina coastal plain were too small and weak to attack their Carolina neighbors without the assistance of the Savannah River peoples—the Yamasee, Apalachicola, and Apalachee. The last two and the northern Piedmont peoples would also not have attacked South Carolina without Yamasee assistance. These Piedmont Indians had just witnessed the power of the colony with its Yamasee allies against the Tuscarora and were certainly also aware of the power of Virginia. Many of these groups were coalescing with the Catawba, and in any war with the colony they also had to fear that the Europeans would call on the Catawbas' ancient enemy, the Iroquois, and that they could also face attacks from the Cherokee. South Carolina coastal and Piedmont Indians could not attempt a war with the English without wider support, particularly from the Yamasee and possibly from the Cherokee.

What motivations would the Piedmont Indians have for joining the Yamasee? David Crawley, a Virginia trader among the "northern Indians" and the Cherokee, addressed this question in an analysis he prepared for William Byrd to deliver to the Board of Trade and Plantations in London, before which they both appeared to discuss the war. Although Crawley naturally bore resentment against the Carolinians for trying to exclude Virginians from the Indian trade, his detailed observations have the air of truth about them. Crawley claimed that the Carolina traders did what they pleased among the Indians, arrogantly lording over them by taking their animals and corn and physically abusing them. Traders forced the Indians to work as carriers and messengers, humiliated them with senseless tasks, and barely compensated them for their labor. Crawley named former agent Wright as a particular source of grievance, who "would when out amongst the Indians have a great number only to wait on [him] and Carry his Luggage and packs of skins from one town to another purely out of ostentation." Crawley heard Wright say that he "would make them Honour him as their Governour and would be often threatening them on purpose to make them present him with skins." The traders aped Wright's behavior and played silly games with one another at the Indians' expense. Crawley claimed that traders would "send some of their Indians 2 or 300 miles with a Letter to Each other that hath had Little in it only to Call one another names and full of Debauchery." Crawley did not think that this behavior was the entire cause of the war, merely a "part . . . of their present Sufferings."[77] His observations illustrate the power of the traders, and partially explain in part the burning resentment of Carolina's Indian trading partners. Under the weight of the traders' oppression, many of the Piedmont peoples joined the Yamasee against South Carolina.

Another perspective on the war came from New York, where the government grew fearful that Indian hostilities would spread northward and that the French would join the belligerents.[78] Rumors had spread that the reasons for the Indian attacks lay in South Carolina's having taken Indian lands and also that Indian children given to the Christians for education had actually been sold into slavery.[79] To assist Carolina, New York governor Robert Hunter tried to recruit the Iroquois to go against the "flatheads," meaning the Catawba and other Piedmont Indians.[80] Hunter told the Iroquois that the Flatheads attacked Carolina because the colony refused to assist them in an attack on the Iroquois.[81] Two days later the Iroquois replied to Hunter that he was wrong about the Carolina Indians' reason for fighting: "we are informed quite otherwise," they replied. The Flatheads had assisted the colony in the Tuscarora War under promise of a reduction in the price of trade goods. They "received no satisfaction, but found the goods as dear as formerly." All they received for a beaver skin was "a handful of powder . . . and other goods proportional."[82] Nevertheless, the Iroquois agreed to go against these Indians, their "ancient enemies," whom they had made peace with earlier only at English bidding.[83]

The Creek, Chickasaw, and Cherokee were in a very different position than the Indians in and near Carolina. They had little or no reason to fear enslavement and were unconcerned about losing their land to the English. Many may have lost patience with the traders' behavior, but their resentments probably also grew as the inequality of the trade became more apparent. Creek, Chickasaw, and Cherokee recently had visited the colony and seen it as never before. The Chickasaw had just ratified a peace in Charles

Town, while Cherokee served with Moore on the second expedition to North Carolina. Creek visited Carolina with increasing frequency. All would have taken note of the colony's wealth. The clothing and buildings of wealthy colonists indeed, as Bull suggested, inspired enmity in the Indians. None of these Indians considered themselves inferior to the Europeans, so the disparity in the trade relationship would have been entirely irksome. In the early days of trade the disparity would not have been apparent. The traders, even the gentlemen traders, were a ragtag bunch, the colony's wealth was limited, the primitive buildings aptly reflected Carolina's condition, and the Indians were satisfied with the European goods they received. On the eve of the Yamasee War it had become obvious that the colonists were no longer poor. The free Indians recognized that some of this wealth was produced by slave labor on plantations, but they also realized their role in creating these riches.

Yet they did all the work. Their effort and skills brought in the animals; their wives' hard labor turned the skins into valuable pelts. They risked their lives hunting enemies; they received little in return compared to the Europeans. Should they not, too, be rich? As one headmen recalled to John Stewart: in former days "our great King had houses and palaces like the English King or Governor in Charles Town."[84] Southern Indians remembered their past. The great chiefdoms of a century before lived in their memory. They also were aware of their present: these were not beaten peoples cowed by enemies and neighbors. They had pride in themselves as accomplished in the arts of war, hunting, and diplomacy. Their cultures were rich and vibrant. Their enemies feared them. The Europeans posed new challenges. But European technological supremacy did not lead the Indians to assume an inferior position. The Europeans borrowed some of their technology, such as the piraguas that traversed southern waterways. And no one could gainsay the English desire for Indian-produced goods, particularly pelts. The Europeans also expressed the desire to learn from Indians the secrets of their medicines and the many uses of native plants. The Indian forts, too, showed the Europeans their construction and design skills, as did the housing that they could erect, dismantle, and transport at a moment's notice.

The Creek, Cherokee, and Chickasaw did not fear the English as much as they feared one another. No English army could come against them. To attack them, the English had to employ an Indian army. Fear did not lead the powerful Indian peoples to attack the traders. Pride and resentment did. But many questions remain. What did the Indians hope to accomplish by attacking the traders, and were their plans coordinated ahead of time? Were the Spanish and French involved?

The Spanish had much to gain by an Indian war with Carolina and would gladly have nourished Yamasee and Creek discontent. Yamasee frequently visited their relations in Florida, and it would not have been unusual to find Yamasee in Saint Augustine. When the war broke out, Yamasee found immediate refuge in Spanish Florida, which welcomed them as added defense for their settlements. Perhaps the Yamasee had received promises of help, supplies or otherwise; the Spanish had nothing to lose by making promises to the Indians—especially if they entangled the Indians in a war with the English.

According to eighteenth-century historian Alexander Hewitt, the Yamasee's decision to strike Carolina had been made long before the actual attack. Hewitt reports that Sanute told Frasier that more than a year before the war the Yamasee had approached the Creek "with a Spanish talk for destroying all the English inhabitants."[85] We also know that Creek discontent was long-standing because of Samuel Warner's warning to the colony of their dissatisfaction with the traders. When the Yamasee attacked, the Creek immediately murdered their Carolina traders, though it is not known whether they did this on a prearranged day or after hearing of the Yamasee attack on the English. It seems reasonable to assume that the Creek forestalled acting until the Yamasee committed themselves, though the Yamasee probably would not have attacked without some assurance from the Creek that they would not actively support the English.[86]

By attacking the traders, the Creek risked losing their English trading partners. They would not have done so without securing other avenues of trade. The Spanish and the French were both potential partners. There is no evidence that the French inspired the Creek to attack the traders—in fact, the French seemed surprised at war's outbreak—but there is plenty of evidence that the French hoped to improve relations with both Upper and Lower Creek and that as early as 1713 they had fomented plans for building a fort among the Alabama.[87] The Creek knew they could turn to the French for trade goods.

The Chickasaw, too, hoped for better relations with the French and joined in against the English. The Chickasaw attacked a cabin in one of their villages filled with fifteen Englishmen.[88] George Chicken also reported the death of English traders to the Chickasaw, though he asserted that the Creek had killed them in Chickasaw villages without the Chickasaw's cognizance. But the Creek never would have assaulted the traders without Chickasaw acquiescence, and the Chickasaw used this flimsy excuse only when attempting a rapprochement with Carolina.[89]

Creek and Chickasaw attacks on the English traders did not mean that these Indians expected warfare to erupt. They had little to fear in the form of military reprisals; loss of trade was their main concern. Only the Choctaw and Cherokee posed a danger to each, and there was little possibility that the Choctaw would ally with the English, while many Cherokee apparently also supported war against Carolina. Even when the Yamasee assaulted Carolina, Creek, Chickasaw, and Cherokee warriors did not attack the colony—they only attacked the traders. In killing the traders they had taken extreme measures to get their point across, but these were men whose behavior was condemned by their own government. These attacks were not desperate actions but a statement of power that the Creek were not to be trifled with. English promises for reform were no longer acceptable. Alliance was no longer appropriate or possible. The Creek and the Chickasaw had asserted themselves, announcing to the English the need to negotiate a new relationship.

THE CREEK, THE CHEROKEE, AND THE FAILURE OF CAROLINA DIPLOMACY

The Creek were prepared either to settle their differences with the English or to escalate the assault on the traders into war. They approached the Cherokee to find where they stood. The Cherokee stood divided. A desperate South Carolina focused its diplomatic efforts upon them. The colony sent emissaries to enlist Cherokee support or to at least obtain neutrality.[90] In December 1715, George Chicken arrived among the Cherokee to learn their decision. The Conjurer told him that the Cherokee and English were as one but that they would not fight the Yamasee or the Creek. The Creek had accepted the "flag of truce that was sent to them and had promised to come down when we came up." In other words, the Creek were willing to negotiate with the English, with Cherokee mediation. Perhaps they could yet prevent the expansion of hostilities.

The Conjurer also told Chicken that the Cherokee refused to fight both the northern Indians, who had been misled into fighting by the Waterees, and the Catawba, who he believed had done no wrong.[91] They were willing to fight only the Savannah, Apalachee, and Yuchi—the three Savannah River groups who had joined with the Yamasee against the colony.

On New Year's Eve, the Conjurer "sent a message to the Head men of the Crick to come to Speak with us [the Cherokee and the English] concerning peace." They should bring their white prisoners and meet in fourteen days. While they waited, the Cherokee told Chicken that some of the whites killed among the Cherokee were actually killed by the Creek—as with the Chickasaw, the Cherokee found it convenient to blame the Creek for attacks on English traders in their own villages.[92] Another Cherokee explained that the reason for "several of the wars first breaking out," by which he probably meant separate attacks by the Cherokee on the English, was that Alexander Long, the trader responsible for the assault on the Yuchi, who had since fled Carolina for refuge among the Cherokee, "came up here and told these people that the Einglish was going to make wars with them and that they did design to kill all their head warriors which was the reason he ran away and loved them and could not Indure to see it."[93]

The longer Chicken waited for the Creek to arrive, the more optimistic he became that a general war could be averted. He sent a message to the Chickasaw absolving them for what had happened to the whites among them and accepted their excuse that they had had no hand in the traders' murder and would have prevented it if they could. Chicken also believed that he had made a peace with the Cherokee and he expected soon to bring the Creek headmen to Charles Town, "to make Peace So that in all Probability we shall have a Peace with all our Indians again in a little time and our Trade with them may flourish again as it has done in time Past."[94] (Chicken's assertion that peace with the Creek could be made even after they had killed many traders provides further evidence that these assaults did not preordain a general war.)

When the fourteen days had elapsed, Chicken grew nervous and sent men to see if the Creek were coming. Meanwhile, Chicken went to one of the westernmost Overhill Cherokee towns to speak with the headmen, particularly Caesar, who wanted to discuss "where to go to war."[95] On January 23, inside the "war house," Chicken asked Caesar and the other "head men of those parts what their Business was in sending for us there." They replied that they had been to Carolina and been "very well pleased" at being told that the colony wished them "to go to war against any nation of Indians that were our Enemies." They were ready to attack the Creek, whom they claimed were "the first that began the war against the English."[96]

Chicken tried to persuade them not to go, for he intended to make peace with the Creek. He told them that Creek women, children, and property were well hidden, so "they could not at present make any advantage of taking slaves or any plunder." The Cherokee curtly responded that it was not plunder they were after, "but to go to war with them and cut them off." The Cherokee complained that it was only "but as yesterday that they were at war" with the Creek, and they had made peace only because of English "persuasion." After the Creek did "damage" to the English, the government reversed itself and asked the Cherokee to prepare for war against them. But once again, the English changed their mind, as Chicken forestalled them, entreating the Cherokee to wait fourteen days for the Creek to arrive so that peace could be made. But the Creek had not come, so the Cherokee sent the red stick through the nation to prepare for war.

The Cherokee, not the English, desired war with the Creek. Chicken told the Cherokee that if they attacked the Creek without his approval, then they were going against the peace the Cherokee had just made with the colony. Caesar replied that it was too late. The Cherokee were so "resolved" on war that they would fight with their "Short knives" if the English did not supply them with the necessary accoutrements.[97] The Cherokee considered going to Savannah Town to procure ammunition from the traders, but Chicken begged them not to go. He reiterated that he had not given up on making peace with the Creek. The Cherokee told Chicken that they could not have peace with the "Southward Indians," the Creek, because "they should have no way in getting of Slaves to buy ammunition and Clothing and that they were resolved to get ready for war." After lengthy discussion, the Cherokee claimed to have changed their minds and said they would not attack the Creek.

Chicken and his party traveled to Chote, a major Overhill town at the Fork of the Little Tennessee and Tellico Rivers. There he learned that the Cherokee had just killed 11 to 13 Creek at Toogaloo.[98] These were leaders of a party of 280 to 300 who had come to meet Chicken. The Cherokee also captured 2 Creek scouts and killed them both. The Cherokee killed the headmen and the scouts so that the Creek would not have the opportunity to make peace with Carolina. The Cherokee rationalized to the Carolinians that the Creek had come to kill Chicken and his men. Of course, if that had been true, the Cherokee could have taken the Creek hostage. Chicken learned from an "Indian King" captured the next day that the Creek were totally befuddled by the murder of their chiefs, when they had been invited there to make peace.[99]

Disgusted with the Cherokee, Chicken decided to leave only fifty men with them, upsetting Caesar with the paucity of English support for the war against the Creek. At the Conjurer's request, Chicken agreed to supplement these with a company of thirty blacks under a white leader. They would be used for "Running after the Enemy."[100]

The Cherokee had hoodwinked the Carolinians into war with the Creek, and Chicken was forced to pacify them now that the deed was done. Chicken's activities in pursuing peace with the Creek show that their killing of the traders had not created an irredeemable situation of hostility between them and Carolina. Negotiations could have prevented the escalation of hostilities.

The Creek situation differed from that of the Yamasee and the "Northern" Indians because the northern Indians and Yamasee had attacked settlers and plantations whereas the Creek had only assaulted traders. The Creek had come to the Cherokee towns expecting to resolve their differences with South Carolina—why else send their headmen unprotected to meet Chicken?

The Cherokee had succeeded in using the English to murder the Creek and to reopen the war against them, but in the long run, this course had more deleterious effects on them than on the English, who began the peace process with the Creek despite the Cherokee's ploy to wedge them apart. For the better part of the century, the Creek and Cherokee remained at war; the Creek would not forgive the Cherokee for what they had done at Toogaloo. Forty years later, in 1755, Edmond Atkin, who later became Britain's agent to the southern Indians, would recall: "The Creeks have an old Grudge against the Cherokees, for joining the Carolina Army in the Indian War in 1715, and falling on them unexpectedly."[101]

REPERCUSSIONS OF WAR

The Yamasee War gradually ended as Carolina made peace with most of the Indian groups by 1717, though the Yamasee and some of the Piedmont peoples refused. Many Indians who had lived near Carolina moved away, leaving the colony practically bereft of Indian allies and neighbors. With its borders largely undefended, and the colony incapable of prosecuting a war against Indians more than one hundred miles west of the colony, Carolina was forced into new relationships with the South's Native American peoples. The Yamasee War was thus an end and a beginning. It reconstructed the South in a way that few events have—only the end of the Civil War compares—for this war marked the birth of the Old South, just as Appomattox later marked its death.

The chain of events that the Yamasee initiated by attacking the English affected the entire South. The trade in Indian slaves went into quick decline, after the English shipped off as many prisoners as they could. The trade did not cease entirely, but the wars to obtain Indian slaves ended abruptly.[102] No longer could South Carolina enlist Indian peoples to conduct slave raids. Indians were too discontented with the English to do their bidding and only slowly, and at arm's length, reconstituted trade relations; a generation of traders had been wiped out, leaving the colony shorn of men skilled at inducing groups to "go a-slaving."

The government took firm control over the Indian trade by initially prohibiting private traders. The trade soon regained its economic importance to both Indians and colonists, but it revolved around the exchange of animal skins and foodstuffs for manufactured goods. Though governance underwent numerous alterations in the colonial period, the Indian trade became an extension of colonial and imperial diplomacy rather than simply a way for entrepreneurs to make money. The Indians' losses in no longer providing slaves for sale to colonists were compensated by annual presents given by colonial governments to Indian peoples. This distribution of presents gave English, French, and Spanish an opportunity to establish patronage networks in Indian communities by which they hoped to direct Indian politics and diplomacy. The Europeans' success was limited because Indian political and military power grew in the aftermath of the Yamasee conflict, and the more powerful groups adopted political strategies that kept the Europeans at bay while maintaining the flow of goods into their communities.

The Indians became stronger, in part, because the Spanish and French were stronger. Queen Anne's War ended in Europe, so the English could not attack the Spanish in Saint Augustine or the French in Louisiana except through Indian clients, and the Indians were uninterested in clientage to the English. The French and Spanish warred in 1719–1721, with the French capturing Pensacola, only to lose it again to the Spanish.[103] It is indicative of the declining English position that Britain could not take advantage of the Spanish-French split.

The Spanish in Saint Augustine did not rebuild their mission system, but they had valuable new allies in both the Yamasee and the African slaves who had either run away or been liberated by the Yamasee. Spain granted freedom to these Africans and formed some into a free black militia to help defend Saint Augustine.[104] Saint Augustine became a thorn in Carolina's underbelly as a haven for runaways and as a base from which Indian–free black raids were conducted. This led Carolina to attack Saint Augustine in 1728 and again in 1740, but the Spanish withstood the onslaught and even counterattacked in 1742.[105]

The French benefited even more by the Yamasee War because it reduced pressure on Louisiana. Creek and Chickasaw both improved relations and trade with France, and the Creek invited the French to build a fort among them as a counter to English influence.[106] Yet in spite of an influx of settlers, the establishment of New Orleans, and the beginning of a plantation economy, the French were unable to maximize their good fortune. War with the Natchez in 1716 and an inability to maintain the flow of trade goods from Europe limited French expansion. The colony was too sprawling for the paucity of resources allotted by the home government. Another devastating war with the Natchez in 1729 and then a series of wars with the Chickasaw further retarded Louisiana's development.

The Chickasaw emerged more powerful after the war because their slaving ended. With their numbers severely reduced, they focused on hunting, increasing trade with the French, and patching things up with the English. The Chickasaw became less harassed on almost all fronts. Creek-Cherokee preoccupation with each other allowed the Chickasaw to focus on the Choctaw, with whom they warred periodically. The Illinois threat was reduced from the north but occasionally arose. The Chickasaw also received attacks from the Iroquois, though these were infrequent. They secured their towns with impenetrable forts and enjoyed relative security, turning back repeated French invasions after their falling out during the Natchez War of 1729.

After the Yamasee War, the Chickasaw, Cherokee, and Creek all followed the same basic diplomacy in relation to the Europeans: entangling alliances with none. For the next half-century, the Creek and the Cherokee, and often the Chickasaw, balanced the competing European powers against one another. They traded and accepted presents from all while refusing to create exclusive alliances.[107] Their military power allowed them to retain independence, and as long as they could obtain European commodities from more than one source, they could withstand any European attempt to impose influence by withholding trade goods. The Europeans chafed under the system yet had no choice but to accept it.

The Choctaw, however, failed to master this system of diplomacy. Their location next to the French precluded the independence other Indian peoples enjoyed. To the Choctaw's advantage, the French were dependent on them, but Choctaw needed the French to help them withstand the Creek and Chickasaw. The Choctaw tried to play the French against the English, but ultimately a brutal civil war weakened them greatly.[108]

The Yamasee War had devastated South Carolina. The colony not only had to rebuild but found its frontiers defenseless. The Creek abandoned northern Georgia and returned to their settlements on the lower Chattahoochee and Flint Rivers, to put some distance between themselves and the English. The Savannah River buffer of Yamasee, Apalachicola, Apalachee, Yuchi, and Savannah was gone: many of the survivors moved to Florida or joined the Creek Confederacy. The Piedmont peoples made peace with the colony, but many of the coastal Indians left and joined the Creek and Catawba. The infrastructure of the colony remained strong because the colonists still had most of their slaves, and they were supported by the English imperial system, which allowed them continued protection and access to capital, trade goods, and markets. The proprietors were put on the defensive, however, as forces in England and South Carolina both worked to transform Carolina into a royal colony. The proprietors acquiesced (somewhat unwillingly) by relinquishing the colony to the Crown in 1729, giving Carolina even greater access to the imperial system. It took years for South Carolina to rebuild after the Yamasee War, but by 1730 it had emerged in a dramatically new form. It then had a plantation-based economy that revolved around rice while continuing to produce cattle, food, and wood products for West Indian markets. Changes in the Navigation Laws in 1731 allowed for further economic expansion by permitting the Carolinians to ship rice directly to some ports outside the empire. Its economy was more diverse and healthy than Virginia's,[109] but both colonies were utterly dependent on slave labor.

JOHN BARNWELL'S HOPE FOR PEACE WITH THE YAMASEE

The frontier remained of paramount importance to the safety and economic development of Carolina. In the aftermath of the Yamasee War, the colony had to find new ways to protect its borders that lay open to raiders. Indians could strike the plantations at will and slaves could run away.

No one had more concern for the safety of the colony than John Barnwell, who worked tirelessly to solve South Carolina's defensive problems. Barnwell lost ten slaves to Saint Augustine during the war and understood the threat posed by a Spanish-Yamasee alliance. He hoped to mend relations with the Yamasee and as late as 1719 still tried to affect a peace with them. Learning through three Creek Indians who were relations to the Huspaw king that the king wished to return to Carolina, Barnwell and a small party went to the Saint Mary's River in Florida to parlay at a spot designated by the Yamasee. The three Creek went into Saint Augustine to get the Huspaw king, but they "found him in such a temper, that they durst not deliver their Errand; The Spaniards having made him Chief Generall of 500 and odd Indians to come immediately against us." What had gone wrong? Had the Huspaw king decided to stay with the Spanish, perhaps as a result of his being given command over the local Indians? And why had Barnwell traveled to the environs of Saint Augustine in the first place? He trusted the Huspaw King enough that he had risked his life to negotiate under circumstances where he could easily have been captured or killed. They could have chosen a more neutral place to meet, but Barnwell accepted the invitation to go to the Huspaw king—a man who it was then believed had actually initiated the war.[110] Was Barnwell feeling guilty over what had happened between Carolina and the Yamasee? More than likely, the two, who had lived near each other, had been good friends: they at least knew and respected each other enough that the Huspaw king expected Barnwell to come if he beckoned.

In 1721, Barnwell's map of "The Northern B[ra]nch of Altama River . . . ," which depicts an area in southern Georgia, made reference, perhaps wistfully, to the Huspaw town during the Yamasee War. On the map, Barnwell included information on how the Huspaw had relocated temporarily during the war to the site he then depicted, "An old Indian Town containing about 10 Acres of Land." It was "At this Place" that the "huspaw People (belonging to the Yamafees) lived all the summer of the Year 1715." They "deserted the Same upon advice of the English coming to attack them in November 1715."[111] It was not unusual for Barnwell (and others) to include information about Indians on the maps they produced, but it is interesting that he chose to include these particular tidbits—details about a people whose lives had been so intertwined with his own. This was the same John Barnwell who had praised the constancy of his Yamasee soldiers during the Tuscarora War, the only Indians who persisted through the entire campaign and who he believed would follow him anywhere.

In reconstructing the past, we sometimes forget, beyond the carnage that is documentable by the physical damage wrought, that personal relationships, too, were destroyed in the violent disputes between peoples. If we knew more of these gray areas, the history would emerge with richer textures. We are apt to think that when Indians and Europeans fought they became inveterate enemies and that neither could forgive or forget. Yet here was Barnwell, representing South Carolina, on an important mission of peace to the Yamasee. The colony was willing to forgive and forget, to accept its responsibility in bringing on the war, because it had assessed that it was better to have the Yamasee as allies on the Savannah River than as enemies in Florida. The colony was not in a position to hold a grudge.

The peace attempt having failed, Barnwell traveled to London to represent the colony's interests. While there, he lent support to Sir Robert Montgomery's scheme to establish a new colony below the Savannah River.[112] Ironically, Montgomery was the son of Sir James Montgomery, who had invested in the Stuart Town community and then fled from Scotland for treason against King William. Barnwell also promoted a township system to protect the colony's southern and western frontier.[113] Under this plan, impoverished Protestants from Europe would be settled in fortified communities. In both instances, Barnwell was trying to solve Carolina's problem of not having Indians available or willing to protect its borders. Because Indians could not be found, the Carolinians turned to poor Europeans. In 1721, Barnwell pushed Carolina's frontier southward by building a fort for Carolina practically in the Spanish backyard on the Altamaha River. Fort King George was too distant from Carolina to be properly maintained and was abandoned in 1727, but Barnwell's plans to push against the Spanish, settle the land below the Savannah River, and bring poor Protestants to populate frontier outposts were all adopted by the English a few years later in their plans to settle the new colony of Georgia.[114]

Lest anyone think that all Carolinians had turned conscientious and diligent in working to protect the colony from outsiders, one need only consult an unusual law that the Carolina government passed in December 1717.[115] This statute was enacted to prevent colonists from trading "with our Indian Enemies living in and about Saint Augustine, Pansacola, Mobile or the River Mississipi, and for laying a Duty on all Indian Corn and Pease exported from this Province." Apparently, Carolinians were exporting food in the midst of wartime shortages because they expected greater profits elsewhere. But most of the bill concerned the "great Quantities of Goods" being traded with Carolina's Indian enemies, "whereby they have been enabled to continue their hostilities against us." It was not the poor or the Indian traders who were betraying the colony but some rich merchants and politicians who served in the government—those people wealthy enough to own ships to carry goods to Saint Augustine or the Gulf of Mexico. Part of the penalty for conviction was that the person would be "rendered incapable of exercising any Place of Trust in this Province forever" and, if already in government, would be expelled. The commissioners of the Indian trade were charged with examining mariners and captains to investigate what had been traded at the ports they had visited. Trading at Mobile, Pensacola, and Saint Augustine was not illegal, but trading Indian goods was. Owners of vessels found to be illegally trading would be fined two thousand pounds each. The statute provided a lengthy list of prohibited goods, illustrating how different the Indian trade was from that conducted with Europeans. More than thirty items were barred, for they were exclusive, or characteristic of, goods bought by Indians. These included hawk's bells and horse bells that Indians used in dancing, brass wire and beads, vermilion, red lead, tinseled or copper-laced hats, tinseled lace, tin or lacquered buttons, Jew's harps, leather girdles (plain or gilt), and coarse neckcloths. Because Indians preferred red and blue cloth over all other colors, red and blue cottons, kerseys, half-thicks (a coarse cloth), and duffels striped red or blue were also barred—presumably, these items in colors other than blue or red were not prohibited. All kinds of weapons and their accoutrements were also barred from the trade—whatever their color. Ships arriving from these ports could not bring with them animal skins or pelts, for that would indicate Indian trading. The statute was to remain in force for only six months. Perhaps that is as long as the Carolina government felt that it could go in preventing their people from trading with the enemy.

AFTERWORD

INDIANS AND AFRICANS

The threat Native Americans posed to the burgeoning plantation system did not disappear after the Yamasee War. The specter of Native Americans uniting with African Americans against Europeans haunted South Carolina and Louisiana colonials. The elite of both colonies worked strenuously to keep Indians and Africans apart and mutually hostile, and to do so, they sought to impose their racial ideology on them. In particular, the colonists wanted Indians to adjudge African slaves as inherently belonging to an inferior and debased caste, while they taught Africans that Indians were savages who would scalp, torture, and cannibalize them. In spite of these and other actions taken by British and French leaders to prevent positive interactions among Indians and Africans, the blacks had numerous occasions to forge relationships outside of those proscribed by the Europeans.

Africans and Native Americans had interacted since the arrival of the first Spanish conquistadors in the sixteenth century. Records exist of several instances in which blacks joined southern Indian nations. One African, Johan Biscayan, was left behind by the Soto expedition and lived with the Coosa for eleven to twelve years. Two African slaves escaped the Spanish and married into the Ais in Florida. Another allegedly married a Yuchi "queen."[1] Africans also accompanied the first English colonists to Carolina and played a varied

345

and significant role in the colony's development. These African pioneers filled virtually every economic need of the colony, working as lumberjacks, carpenters, fishermen, soldiers, traders, farmers, sailors, pilots, and so on. African expertise and labor helped transform Carolina from a frontier to a plantation economy based on rice production.[2] Even before the Yamasee War gave economic precedence to the plantation over the Indian trade, colonists understood that the colony's future lay in agriculture. The Indian slave trade was destined to decline because the pool of potential victims was diminishing. The deerskin trade remained significant, but most free Carolinians preferred to invest in African slaves and quality land. Even if the Indian slave trade had continued to flourish, Carolinians would have continued to export most captives and invested the profits in African labor. In spite of the vagaries of plantation agriculture, where drought or pestilence could destroy a year's crop, staple production yielded excellent returns, and many Europeans hoped to become gentlemen planters through the possession of landed estates and the ownership of large coteries of unfree laborers.

The black population of Carolina numbered just over 4,000 in 1708, roughly equivalent to the white population, and larger than the number of Indian slaves, estimated at 1,400. The largest population group, however, consisted of the free Indians who lived in and near the colony. More than 6,300 free Indians lived within 200 miles of Charles Town, along the Savannah River, in the low country, and Piedmont. If we extend the area westward and include the Lower Creek (250 miles) and Lower Cherokee towns (320 miles), then the number of free Indians reaches 10,875.[3] As a result of the Yamasee War, many of these free Indians moved away, died, or had been enslaved and sold elsewhere. Through importation the number of Africans then grew by leaps and bounds to form the largest sector of the colony's population.

Importation figures also illustrate the changing character of Carolina's economy just before and after the Yamasee War. On the eve of war few blacks were imported (most had been slaves in the West Indies). In 1706, just 24 blacks entered Carolina; ten years later, in 1716, only 67 entered; in between those two years the yearly number of imports exceeded 170 only once, in 1714. In 1717, however, the number jumped to 573. Ten years later, yearly imports exceeded 1,700, and by the 1730s, more than 2,400 arrived in four separate years, and the number fell below 1,500 only twice.[4] The Yamasee War marks a watershed: from then until the Civil War, South Carolina's wealth lay in its ownership of black slave labor. Slaves were the most substantial form of capital and the means for increasing capital through their sale and labor. In the colonial period, securing that labor—keeping slaves from running away and revolting—was essential to the well-being of the slave-owning class.

In the aftermath of the Yamasee War, slaveholding Carolinians yearned to stabilize their political system by removal of the lords proprietors in exchange for royal colony status. From the colonists' perspective, the proprietors added nothing to the colony except interference with profit-making and the local legislative process. Royal government, it was thought, could provide no worse, and at least it had the wherewithal to defend the colony. Colonial interest groups also preferred to lobby Crown and Parliament for local needs than an increasingly insouciant proprietorship. With the government taking over the Indian trade, colonial elites no longer competed for frontier profits, and they found a unity of interests building a planter society.[5] The elite formed a police system to keep their slaves at bay. Their political system kept nonslaveholding whites powerless, for ownership of slaves was a prerequisite for holding office in the assembly and most free adult males could not meet the property-holding requirements for voting. The elite created slave codes to regulate and control blacks' behavior and to force all whites to participate in upholding the institution of slavery. As they attempted to secure their safety and wealth by exerting control over all sectors of the population, the elite recognized the necessity of enlisting free neighboring and distant Indians to maintain the system. The neighboring Indians would track down runaways and inhibit African slaves from escaping; distant Indians, it was hoped, would deny runaways sanctuary and turn them over to Carolina authorities.

At the end of the seventeenth century European officials had contemplated instituting policies to prevent contacts between Native Americans and African Americans.[6] Laws were passed barring Indians from entering the plantation areas and restricting the employment of blacks in the Indian trade.[7] Nonetheless, the Europeans failed to keep escaped African slaves from entering Indian villages. During the Tuscarora War, John Barnwell insisted that the Tuscarora hand over twenty-five runaways under their protection. After the war many Tuscarora who remained in the Carolinas continued to harbor runaways. More than twenty years after the war, South Carolina officials contemplated solving the problem of Tuscarora liberating slaves from their plantations by a program of extirpation of these Indians.[8]

Even greater cooperation between Indians and Africans occurred in the Yamasee War.[9] Caught in a desperate situation as a result of the war, South Carolina armed African slaves to fight against Indians, but the Yamasee countered by liberating many Carolina slaves who accompanied them to Florida.

The freed blacks and Yamasee conducted raids against the plantations in the coming decades.[10] Black slaves also worked with other Indian peoples against South Carolina. During the early stages of the Yamasee War, the governor of South Carolina expected the Cherokee to join them against the Creek, but he learned to his dismay that "2 Rogues of Negroes run away from the English and came and told them [the Cherokee] a parcel of lies which hindered their coming."[11] Another people who joined South Carolina's enemies in the war were the Waccamaw, of the South Carolina Piedmont, a people who numbered fewer than one hundred men in 1720. The single source recording the origin of the Waccamaw conflict with the colony noted that blacks had instigated the Indians against the colonists.[12]

Military alliance was but one of many ways in which African-Indian cooperation threatened European interests. Blacks were privy to a great deal of information valuable to Indians. They could give Indians knowledge of European military forces and forts, a colony's politics, diplomacy, current events, gossip, and even information concerning crimes.[13]

To prevent this sharing of information, South Carolina officials enacted laws barring African-Americans from employment in the Indian trade, where they could learn Indian languages and gain familiarity with Indians. Nevertheless, traders often employed blacks in the Indian trade despite the stiff penalties. Colonel George Chicken was one of many British officials to note the hazards of the employment of blacks in the Indian trade and their accrual of knowledge of native languages and culture. As Chicken wrote to Arthur Middleton, chairman of the South Carolina Council in 1725, "I must take Notice to your Honour that [traders] Sharp and Hutton have brought up [to the Indian villages] their Slaves although by law they are to forfeit one hundred pounds for so doing." It is "my Opinion that the Law ought to be punctually Complied with . . . because the Slaves that are now come up talk good english as well as Cherokee Language and I am Afraid too often tell falsities to the Indians which they are very apt to believe, they [the blacks] being so much among the English."[14] Europeans feared that if blacks talked to Indians, the two would recognize their mutual interests against Europeans. In July 1751, Indian trader Richard Smith observed the potential for cooperation among blacks and Indians. After learning that three runaway blacks had told the Keowee "that the white People was coming up to destroy them all, and that they had got some Creek Indians to assist them," Smith asserted that the Indians believed that the runaways spoke the truth, "and the more [so] for that the old Warrior of Keowee said some Negroes had applied to him, and told him that there was in all Plantations many Negroes more than white People, and that for the Sake of Liberty they would join them."[15]

South Carolina's attempts to keep blacks out of the Indian country met with both success and failure. Government officials disregarded their own policies and employed African-American interpreters to the Indians and traders persisted employing blacks despite the fines.[16] The government had much success in obtaining the return of runaways. Many Settlement Indians found employment capturing runaways. Bartholemew Gaillard informed the commissioners of the Indian trade in 1716 "that some of the Wineau Indians were seated at Santee, and have been found beneficial to that part of this Province, for their Safety, by keeping the Negroes there in Awe." In exchange for this service, the Indians requested the colony place a trading post there.[17] More than forty years later Edmond Atkin could report that that there were almost four hundred "Ancient Natives . . . still living in our Settlements among the plantations." Their "chief Service" to the colony lay "in hunting Game, destroying Vermin, and Beasts of Prey, and in catching Runaway Slaves."[18]

The treaties and the handsome rewards Europeans offered did not ensure that Indians would return runaways. For much of the colonial period Indians could and did resist pressure to turn over slaves who sought sanctuary. For instance, when relations deteriorated between the Creek and South Carolina in the mid-1750s, agent Daniel Pepper found to his dismay that the Upper Creek virtually ignored his pleas to return runaways. He reported to the governor of South Carolina, "I made a Demand of all Negroes and Horses belonging to white People in their Possession, which they agreed to deliver up to me, but after sending for them several Times they made sham Excuses and I could not get them at any Rate to fulfill their Promises. I have left orders with the Traders to get them, but I am apt to believe they will have no success."[19] The ability to resist pressure to return escaped slaves depended on a variety of factors, not the least of which was the Indians' ability to play the European powers against one another in order to keep open multiple lines of trade.

The end of the Indian slave trade largely freed Native Americans from their own enslavement, but it increasingly involved many in the enslavement of African-Americans. The growth and prosperity of the plantation system and the military power of Native American peoples led the British and French to focus their "Indian affairs" on preserving their African slave economy. The South's Native Americans could not escape the international market forces that pervaded the South and influenced their lives, but they held a position in which, to a large degree, their autonomy was little threatened. Native Americans adapted European trade goods and technology and reached diplomatic "understandings" with European colonies; they experimented with new ideas and forms of social and political organization; they continued to evolve as they always had—with one foot in the past and another in the present.

ENGLISH AND INDIANS: RELATIONS AFTER THE YAMASEE WAR

South Carolina's survival depended on its relations with the South's native peoples. Europeans lacked the military capability to conquer the large inland groups who outnumbered them; they could not move artillery over difficult terrain, nor could they travel as quickly and with as much stealth as the indigenous peoples. Typically, the English employed natives to do battle for them, but no powerful native group was willing to forge alliance with Carolina, though occasionally warriors could be recruited for attacks on Spanish Florida.

To convince Indians of their greatness, the English (and French) periodically took Indians to Europe, for it was hard for Indians to believe that Europeans were as special as they asserted themselves to be.[20] On one of these excursions, James Oglethorpe, in 1734, escorted Tomochichi, leader of the Yamacraw, who lived near modern-day Savannah, and a small party of his people to the British royal court.[21] Uncowed by British splendor, the Indians exasperated the British by refusing to sign any cessions of land. To please Oglethorpe, Tomochichi and his party agreed to dress in European garb, as their native dress was deemed inappropriate for the court.[22] But the Yamacraw refused to dispense with face paint. At court, the British aristocracy treated the Indians with condescension, as a spectacle to be enjoyed for their viewing pleasure. When one Indian was asked to select the most attractive lady at court, he politely declined, informing his hosts that "all white people were so much alike to him, that he could not easily distinguish one from another." Turning to the large-headed Oglethorpe, a most distinctive-looking individual, who had placed them in this uncomfortable situation, the Indian added "that it was some time before he could distinguish their friend Mr. Oglethorpe from the rest."[23]

Oglethorpe is usually viewed by historians as a master of Indians whose skillful diplomacy saved Georgia and paved the way for improved relations between the Creek and the British, as he manipulated hostile "savages" into making peace and then lured them into assisting him against the Spanish. In fact, Oglethorpe's success resulted from the education Indians gave him on the terms of diplomacy. Georgia's existence was impossible without Indian, particularly Creek, acquiescence. The Creek wanted British trade goods to keep French and Spanish pretensions in check; Oglethorpe wanted Georgia to survive. The Creek held the better hand, and Oglethorpe understood this. A telling episode in 1743 illustrates not only the give and take in Creek-Georgia relations but the inability of most Europeans to see and understand the nature of those relations. In March 1743, Oglethorpe led a combined Indian-European force on a raid against Spanish Florida. Edward Kimber, recently arrived in America, joined the expedition, on which he later reported for *Gentlemen's Magazine* and in a pamphlet. Kimber repeated the shibboleths of the time concerning Oglethorpe having "tamed" these examples of "ancient roughness and simplicity." He thought the Indians considered the general their father, and he marveled at Oglethorpe's ability to convince forty-six of them to join him aboard ship for the invasion—Indians usually refused to travel on these vessels. In spite of Kimber's acclaim for Oglethorpe, his account reveals that relations between the general and the Indians were far different than what he described. For the Indians agreed to join Oglethorpe's forces only after negotiating the terms: he had to agree to their plan of action. Then, when all boarded the ship, Kimber expressed astonishment and dismay at "the rude manners of the Indians on board, who without ceremony took up the cabin and all the conveniences for lodging, and their arms and lumber were somewhat irksome, especially considering their nastiness." While the Indians enjoyed the cabin, all the Europeans had to remain outside exposed to the elements. Oglethorpe put as good a face as he could on the matter, Kimber observing: "as his Excellency himself was pleased with lying roughly on the deck, all the voyage, nobody else had the least reason to complain."[24]

Oglethorpe understood, as did most post–Yamasee War British colonial leaders, that diplomacy rather than force was the key to relations with southern Amerindians and that arrogance and haughtiness succeeded as tools of diplomacy only when employed properly and at the right moment. Virtually everyone engaged in Indian affairs knew that Indians could not be easily hoodwinked. Trader James Adair observed: "They are very deliberate in their councils, and never give an immediate answer to any message sent by strangers, but suffer some nights first to elapse." Issues were widely discussed among leaders and the people at large, especially because the confederacies had no mechanism to force recalcitrant Indians to obey agreements. Of southern Indian diplomacy and the decision-making process, Adair wrote, "When any national affair is in debate, you may hear every father of a family speaking in his house on the subject, with rapid, bold language, and the utmost freedom that a people can use. Their voices, to a man, have due weight in every public affair, as it concerns their welfare alike." In these decentralized confederacies, "Every town is independent of another. Their own friendly compact continues the union. *Any obstinate war leader will sometimes commit acts of hostility, or make peace for his own town, contrary to the good liking of the rest of the nation."*[25]

Europeans had to be ever watchful and deliberate in their diplomacy with Indians. The Europeans' limited military power and the vulnerability of their settlements to raids forced them to adjust to Indian demands as much as, if not more than, Indians adjusted to them to obtain trade goods. After the Yamasee War the British resorted to military solutions only when diplomacy failed or poor civil leadership drew them into conflict, as occurred when the incompetent William Henry Lyttleton (1757–1760) was appointed governor of South Carolina and immediately enmeshed the colony in a war with the Cherokee from 1759 to 1761.[26] The southern British colonies' biggest fear remained the Creek, who possessed the greatest offensive capabilities in the region. The Creek and British rarely fought after the Yamasee War, the two finding ways to accommodate to each other's interests.[27] Intermittently they squabbled, and the Creek learned that raids against frontier communities effectively brought the British to the negotiating table, for there was little way to prevent the Creek from destroying farms and plantations except through diplomatic means: trade and presents. The British grudgingly accepted Creek neutrality between them and the French, as the Indians welcomed French traders into their towns and the building of Fort Toulouse among them.[28] The Creek and the British neither liked nor trusted one another, but they learned to live with each other and prevented their disagreements from evolving into destructive wars.[29]

GEOPOLITICS

The geopolitical contours of the South began to change in the early nineteenth century, perhaps even earlier. The creation of the United States brought together people from the mainland plantation societies who shared similar economic and political interests. From the Constitutional Convention through nullification and secession, South Carolinians, in particular, sought to draw Virginians (and through Virginians, other people from what became known as the "border South" or "upper South") to their vision of the South as a geopolitical entity that must pursue its interests against an increasingly hostile outside world. Of course, areas of Virginia had much in common with the South, and many, though not all, Americans already considered Virginia as part of the South. But the Old Dominion was pulled in other directions as well. Some Virginians perceived that the state's future lay with an industrializing north, whereas those in the western areas, especially in the section that later formed West Virginia, had little in common with the area east of the Blue Ridge.[30] In 1860, Southern fire-eaters had to convince Virginians not just to stand with them against a powerful and "foreign" hostile government in Washington, D.C., but to join them in what they thought, all along, had been a separate country: the South. For generations, scholars have seriously questioned the Southern nationalists' claims to being a separate nation based on culture, geography, and history, and that Northerners and Southerners had too much in common to be two separate peoples: they shared the same form of government, history, and culture. Without venturing into the depths of this argument, however, it can at least be said that the South *did* have a largely separate history from neighboring regions for the thousand years that preceded the attack on Fort Sumter—in terms of cultural development, social organization, economy, and politics. The political uniting of this region with the North was a relatively recent and unprecedented event. And yet, creating one nation out of the South—the Confederacy—was also unprecedented. There is great irony in the Southern states confederating to survive against hostile threats, much as Indian peoples had done in the previous century. The Confederate nation lived only briefly, but the region remained, inescapably bound by history and continually shaped by its environment and its people.

South Carolina survived the Yamasee War and grew strong in its aftermath, though it took about twenty years to recover. The French and Spanish never again seriously challenged the British for supremacy in the region, though the British made little headway against their European rivals before the Seven Years' War (1756–1763). The Indians gained the greatest advantage from the Yamasee War. Warfare between Indians reverted to its more traditional forms, as violent conflicts resulting from any number of group enmities but in which generally the parties knew each other. Raids of distant Indians, sometimes led by English or French, whose purpose was to obtain captives for an international trade in humans rarely occurred in the South again. Wars between traditional enemies also altered in character. Creek and Choctaw, Choctaw and Chickasaw, and Creek and Cherokee continued their endemic warfare, but they tended to use limited raiding by small parties whose purpose was vengeance, not to obtain slaves to sell. If the Yamasee War had not left the English so isolated in the South, the slaving would probably have continued, but the raiders would have had to travel further to procure victims, most likely into Texas. Instead, the southern Indians remained focused on the region and their homes. The reduced nature of warfare allowed the confederacies to grow. Smaller groups continued to incorporate into larger ones, but the basic political structures of the confederacies barely changed: they remained decentralized. Towns thus possessed almost the same independence that they would have had unconfederated, but the confederacy meant security against outsiders.

The events surrounding the Yamasee War had prepared the way for southern Indians to survive the slaving, which enveloped hunter and hunted into a no-win situation. Most Indians learned to keep the Europeans at arm's length. In the end, demographics, geography, military power, and diplomatic skills allowed the southern Native American confederacies to survive, if not to flourish, in the midst of European imperial expansion.

ENGLISH IMPERIALISM AND THE INDIAN SLAVE TRADE

In this book, I have made no comprehensive treatment of the forces of imperialism and colonialism that brought the Europeans to the New World, a book in itself, or of the international market economy that introduced world trade to the South, but I have tried to suggest some of the forces that led many of the region's native inhabitants to capture and sell other native peoples to fill the labor needs of colonial societies. I also posited that raiding and capturing enemies was not new to Amerindian peoples but that the scale was enlarged by European labor demands and by Amerindians' willingness to meet those demands. This willingness did not grow out of dependency on trade goods but rather a desire for trade goods and closer relations with Europeans and as a means to inflict a devastating defeat on their enemies. Many Indians, moreover, probably feared that refusal to become slave raiders would have led Europeans to categorize them as potential victims, with their enemies then filling the role of slavers.

Southern Native American societies were already expansionistic before European arrival. The chiefdoms sought to expand at their neighbors' expense, and incorporated peoples assumed tributary status. Yet Native American expansion differed in significant ways from European imperialism. The sheer size of European empires gave their expansion a scope and nature unknown in the American South. The Choctaw would never have been enslaved in such large numbers, nor would they have landed in Massachusetts and Barbados, if European colonists had not instigated the Chickasaw to capture Choctaw and provided ships to carry Choctaw to distant colonies. European imperialism was characterized by the maturation of its international system of far-flung colonies, economically integrated and skillfully administered in terms of organizing labor and extracting resources. Few native societies possessed the skills to exploit distant peoples on such a grand scale, though certainly the Aztecs in Mexico had a similar understanding of government bureaucracy, organization, and exploitation.

European imperialism was also predicated more consciously on ethnocentrism than the expansion of Indian chiefdoms, and this difference gave European imperialism as much of its peculiar character in the South as any other attribute. Ethnocentrism provided European imperialists their rationale for moving to other people's territory and appropriating both their land and their bodies. Indians, too, possessed an ethnocentrism toward outsiders, and in the chiefdoms the elite sought to control and transform the ideology of their minions, but there was nothing deemed inherently evil or inferior about outsiders or nonbelievers to prevent incorporation and the granting of equal status within the class system. The Spanish and French toyed with this notion when bestowing upon converted Indians special privileges and status comparable to that enjoyed by Europeans in their society. Similar to the chiefdoms, the Europeans' hierarchical caste system placed every human into a category defined by birth. The imperialism of the Europeans, however, expanded categories so that the colonial nobility was deemed inferior to the nobility of the mother country, as if being born in or traveling to the New World somehow rendered humans inferior to those born and residing in the mother country. The Spanish and French also added gradations of skin color and mixed parentage to categorize peoples.[31] The only way for Spanish and French incorporation to have worked more equitably, that is, to not treat Native Americans and Africans as inherently inferior to Europeans, would have been to imitate contemporaneous native societies that placed adopted individuals into specific identities within the hierarchical structure. In many Indian societies, adoptees replaced deceased persons, but if not, they still were given clan and social identities, whereas Europeans *expanded* their caste system to create new, lower-status categories for non-Europeans and children of mixed marriages.[32]

The British, in much less sophisticated fashion, eschewed the categories of skin-color gradation, except in the crudest sense (black, white, red, mulatto, and mustee), but shared with other Europeans a belief in the inferiority of the colonial to the European-born. Also, the British never considered incorporation of native peoples with any of the seriousness of the Spanish and French, who investigated the issue in political, philosophical, and religious terms.

The English readily incorporated non-English Europeans into their society but had the greatest difficulty contending with Africans and Native Americans. As we have seen, some in England considered incorporation a desirable goal, but the colonists generally did not. Their cultural insecurity played some role here. Spaniards and French were relatively comfortable with their ethnicity, whereas the English were not. The British had feelings of cultural inferiority in relation to France and other continental nations, which in part resulted from the smallness and backwardness of the British Isles in the late Middle Ages and Renaissance. On their island, the English and Scots turned in on themselves, even as they reached out to the world, unlike the Dutch, who in similar circumstances as an outnumbered and surrounded people in Europe retained their cosmopolitanism, their cultural security, and their ease with the outside world.[33]

In spite of differences among Europeans in their willingness and ability to incorporate non-Europeans as equal, near-equal, or proto-equal citizens of their colonial societies, compared to Native Americans, European incorporation was an abject failure. Native Americans readily treated adoptees with full equality. This was most startlingly apparent after the American Revolution, when many African-American ex-slaves joined the Seminoles, some obtaining chiefly status, as did some of the "half-breeds," the children of Euramerican trader fathers and Indian mothers, among several southern Indian groups, particularly the Creek and Cherokee. In contrast, European ethnocentrism was peculiarly virulent. The exclusiveness of seventeenth-century Protestantism may explain why the English were less able than the Spanish and French to consider incorporation of all humans into their societies, for Catholicism asserted that everyone—slaves included—could and should be included in God's church, whereas Anglicans and Puritans thought the mass of humanity destined for hell.

For the English and other Europeans to incorporate non-Europeans into their society, they would have had to reorient their basic thinking and value system. When Catholics considered conversion of native peoples as important duty, they placed religious priorities first—that they did not succeed was largely a result of competing interests and values in their society, which wished to keep the newcomers in an inferior and subservient status. The Carolinians barely approached incorporation of Indians, though the proprietors had hoped for such, because greed was too strong among the colonists and local officials who understood personal fulfillment in terms of exploiting human beings for materialistic ends. The slave trade had been practiced by Europeans since Columbus's arrival in America, though the Carolinians had to look no further for an example than the Virginia traders who purchased captives from the Westo. Moreover, the colony's first settlers brought slaves with them from the West Indies, where they were familiar with the slave trade.

Understanding the international market for human cargo, all they needed was to find people with the skills to capture Indians.

The introduction of the slave trade convinced some Native Americans likewise to seek material gain by exploiting neighbors and strangers, but they had no organized slave trade until the Europeans came. The Carolinians, in comparison to Indians, were obsessed with the desire to own human labor. Wealth in England was based on ownership of land; but in Carolina land existed aplenty, and it was labor that free people ached to possess. Labor meant that vast tracts of land could be transformed into staple-producing plantations that would bring their owners wealth and status. Capital-hungry colonists, with no access to labor or mineral wealth as existed in other colonies, stole human beings to fulfill their self-gratification. That they succeeded resulted from the empire that nourished their nascent community, their single-minded ruthlessness to obtain their ends, their willingness to exploit humans in any number of ways, their ability to find Indians to do their bidding, and the inability of those who opposed them in their own society to enforce laws and restrict behavior that they saw as detrimental and unethical.

If the Carolinians were a God-fearing people, it was an exclusive God that permitted them to smite not just their enemies but people they had never met. If they were a law-abiding people, they obeyed only those laws that suited them and then used the law to secure their place in power and the subjection of their social inferiors. If they were a civil people, it was a civility of convenience.

NOTES

ABBREVIATIONS

AC	Archives des Colonies, Archives Nationales, Paris
AE	Archives du Ministère Etrangères, Archives Nationales, Paris
AM	Archives de la Marine, Archives Nationales, Paris
AN	Archives Nationales, Paris
ASH	Archives Service Hydrographique, Archives Nationales, Paris
CO	Colonial Office, Public Record Office, Kew, United Kingdom
Commissioners	*Journals of the Commissioners of the Indian Trade, September 20, 1710–August 29, 1718,* ed. William L. McDowell, Jr. (Columbia: South Carolina Department of Archives and History, 1955)
CRNC	*The Colonial Records of North Carolina,* 10 vols. (Raleigh: P. M. Hale, 1886–1890)
BL	Manuscript Room, British Library, London
HL	Henry E. Huntington Library, San Marino, Calif.
House Journals	South Carolina Commons House Journals, microfilm of original transcripts in South Carolina Department of Archives and History, Columbia
LC	Library of Congress, Washington, D.C.
Le Jau	*The Carolina Chronicle of Dr. Francis Le Jau, 1706–1717,* ed. Frank J. Klingberg (Berkeley: University of California Press, 1956)

MPA *Mississippi Provincial Archives: French Dominion,* vols. 1–3, ed. Dunbar Rowland and A. G. Sanders (Jackson: Press of the Mississippi Department of Archives and History, 1927–1932), vols. 4, 5, ed. Patricia Galloway (Baton Rouge: Louisiana State University Press, 1984)

Official Letters *The Official Letters of Alexander Spotswood, Lieutenant-Governor of the Colony of Virginia, 1710–1722,* 2 vols. (Richmond: Virginia Historical Society, 1882; reprint, New York: AMS, 1973)

Records *Records in the British Public Record Office Relating to South Carolina, 1663–1717,* 5 vols. ([Various publishers], 1928–1947)

SCCHJ *Journal of the Commons House of Assembly,* 21 vols., ed. Alexander S. Salley, Jr. (Columbia: Historical Commission of South Carolina, 1907–1946), and *The Colonial Records of South Carolina: The Journal of the Commons House of Assembly,* 14 vols., ed. J. H. Easterby et al. (Columbia: Historical Commission of South Carolina, 1951–)

SCHM *South Carolina Historical Magazine*

SCDAH South Carolina Department of Archives and History, Columbia

SC Transcripts "Records in the Public Record Office Relating to South Carolina, 1663–1782," 7 vols., Microcopy Number 1 (Columbia: South Carolina Department of Archives and History, 1971)

Sketch William James Rivers, *A Sketch of the History of South Carolina to the Close of the Proprietary Government by the Revolution of 1719; With an Appendix Containing Many Valuable Records Hitherto Unpublished* (Charleston, S.C.: McCarter, 1856)

SPG Society for the Propagation of the Gospel in Foreign Parts, Papers, Manuscript Division, Library of Congress, Washington, D.C.

SRO Scottish Record Office, Edinburgh

Statutes *The Statutes at Large of South Carolina,* 10 vols., ed. Thomas Cooper (Columbia: A. S. Johnston, 1836–1841)

PREFACE

1. On the importance of the Delisle maps, see William P. Cumming, *The Southeast in Early Maps* (Princeton, N.J.: Princeton University Press, 1958), 39–40, pls. 43, 47; and Marcel Giraud, *A History of French Louisiana,* vol. 1: *The Reign of Louis XIV, 1698–1715,* trans. Joseph C. Lambert (Baton Rouge: Louisiana University Press, 1974; originally published in France, 1953), 16. Of the 1703 map, *Carte du Mexique et de la Floride des Terre Angloises et des Isles Antilles du Cours et des Environs de la Riviere de Mississippi,* Cumming wrote: "In spite of the large area shown, the map has much detail and influenced subsequent continental mapmakers profoundly in their delineation of the Mississippi Valley and, to a lesser extent, of the southeastern region" (172). Delisle's 1718 map, "Carte de la Louisiane et du Cours du Missippi . . . ," is even more historically important as the basis for numerous other maps of the Mississippi Valley produced in the eighteenth century (186–187). Without the Delisles' copying of documents, we would not have many important documents of the period, including some important letters by Henri de

Tonti. See Patricia Galloway, "Henri de Tonti du village des Chacta, 1702: The Beginning of the French Alliance," in Patricia K. Galloway, ed., *La Salle and His Legacy: Frenchmen and Indians in the Lower Mississippi Valley* (Jackson: University Press of Mississippi, 1982). The Delisle documents are mostly bundled in ASH, 115–9, 115–10, and 115–11. I use several of these documents here. There is some controversy about the Delisle map—Jean Delanglez claims that Guillaume's father, Claude, was the actual author of the map. See Delanglez, "The Sources of the Delisle Map of America, 1703," *Mid-America* 25 (1943), 275–298.

INTRODUCTION

1. Peter H. Wood, *Black Majority: Negroes in Colonial South Carolina from 1670 Through the Stono Rebellion* (New York: Norton, 1974).

2. See James Merrell, *The Indians' New World: Catawbas and Their Neighbors from European Contact Through the Era of Removal* (Chapel Hill: University of North Carolina Press, 1989); John H. Hann, *Apalachee: The Land Between the Rivers* (Gainesville: University Presses of Florida, 1988), and *A History of the Timucua Indians and Missions* (Gainesville: University Press of Florida, 1996); and Patricia K. Galloway, *Choctaw Genesis, 1500–1700* (Lincoln: University of Nebraska Press, 1996).

3. Many of these works are discussed in Chapter 1.

4. Verner W. Crane, *The Southern Frontier, 1670–1731* (1929; reprint, New York: Norton, 1981), did unite the histories of the three European powers in the region and included much about native peoples. Crane's study remains highly useful but is limited, given all that we have learned in recent years. Gary B. Nash, *Red, White and Black: The Peoples of Early North America* (Englewood Cliffs, N.J.: Prentice Hall, 1972, with later editions in 1982 and 1994), is an important geopolitical survey of the American colonies that casts its net wide and in many ways has inspired this book. An ecological analysis of the South's Atlantic colonies in this period can be found in Timothy Silver, *A New Face on the Countryside: Indians, Colonists, and Slaves in South Atlantic Forests, 1500–1800* (New York: Cambridge University Press, 1990).

5. An important work on cultural exchange between native and European peoples is James Axtell, *The European and the Indian: Essays in the Ethnohistory of Colonial North America* (New York: Oxford University Press, 1981). On the exchange of goods and services in French Louisiana, see Daniel H. Usner, Jr., *Indians, Settlers, and Slaves in a Frontier Exchange Economy: The Lower Mississippi Valley Before 1783* (Chapel Hill: University of North Carolina Press, 1992).

6. An exceptional recent account that takes into consideration the geopolitical forces facing both Amerindians and Europeans in a specific geographic region is Richard White, *The Middle Ground: Indians, Empires, and Republics in the Great Lakes Region, 1650–1815* (Cambridge: Cambridge University Press, 1991). My account of the South differs from White's exploration of the Great Lakes region in several significant ways. Although an analogous situation existed in the South where refugee populations of Amerindians came together in new and various ways after contact with Europeans, the Indians themselves were culturally different, inhabited a distinctly different environment, and enjoyed geopolitical advantages in their relations to Europeans that Amerindians to the north did not possess. Many southern native peoples wielded far more military power than northern Algonquins, both defensively and offensively. The South was far less subject to excur-

sions from Indians external to the region than were Great Lakes region peoples, who, in particular, had to contend with a constant Iroquois threat. Moreover, the nature of interactions and exchange among Indians and Europeans took a far different character in the South as a result of the Indian slave trade connecting the region in more intricate and complex ways than in the area north of the Ohio River.

White's approach to the Great Lakes region differs substantially from my approach to the South. Although we are both interested in long-term developments in our respective regions, White paints broader strokes in examining evolutionary change from one period to the next, following a topical framework, while my analysis focuses more narrowly on a fifty-year period with special attention on year-to-year developments at key junctures.

7. Rachel Klein shows that these people entered the market economy as soon as they had the opportunity. See Klein, *Unification of a Slave State: The Rise of the Planter Class in the South Carolina Backcountry, 1760–1808* (Chapel Hill: University of North Carolina Press, 1990).

8. One of the few surveys of American colonial history to give a prominent place to the Indian slave trade is Nash, *Red, White and Black*. J. Leitch Wright, *The Only Land They Knew: The Tragic Story of the American Indian in the Old South* (New York: Free Press, 1981), recognized the centrality of the trade to the South's development. (In particular, see the chapter "Brands and Slave Cords"). The seminal study of Indian slavery in early America is Almon Wheeler Lauber, *Indian Slavery in Colonial Times Within the Present Limits of the United States* (1913; reprint, Williamstown, Mass.: Corner House, 1979).

9. On the South's Indian trade, see Kathryn E. Holland Braund, *Deerskins and Duffels: Creek Indian Trade with Anglo-America, 1685–1815* (Lincoln: University of Nebraska Press, 1993).

10. I have not provided an in-depth treatment of Native American alcohol consumption in this book. Alcohol was undoubtedly a problem in many southern Indian communities, particularly those close to the sources of supply in Carolina. As a response to the pleas of Indian leaders, the South Carolina government repeatedly banned alcohol from the Indian trade, though officials could not prevent its sale. Most complaints arose from groups along the Savannah River, and it remains unclear how much alcohol was carried further westward. The alcohol trade among the Creek, Choctaw, and Chickasaw is much better documented after 1730, which is beyond my scope. The best introduction to alcohol use among Native Americans in the eighteenth century is Peter Mancall, *Deadly Medicine: Alcohol in Early America* (Ithaca, N.Y.: Cornell University Press, 1995).

11. The rise of the modern state placed new "national" identities into conflict with local and regional ones; the Reformation added a religious identity that often competed with the claims of the state and monarch, as well as opposition to other religious identities; the rise of an international market economy created new class identities within European societies, as it also introduced to Europeans a vast array of non-European, non-Christian peoples, from whom they felt compelled to identify themselves as different.

12. My geographic division of the South generally follows that provided by Peter H. Wood, in "The Changing Population of the Colonial South: An Overview by Race and Region, 1685–1790," in Peter H. Wood, Gregory A. Waselkov, and M. Thomas Hatley, eds., *Powhatan's Mantle: Indians in the Colonial Southeast* (Lincoln: University of Ne-

braska Press, 1989). Wood defines ten geographic areas. I have excluded two of these, Virginia and Shawnee, as outside the region. I also have followed the suggestion in his essay that it might be useful to divide the Choctaw-Chickasaw subregion in two. Further, Wood avers that North and South Carolina (east of the Appalachians) might be combined into one. I have combined the two into one, but then redivided them by separation of the Piedmont from the Atlantic Coastal area. Another distinction I have made from Wood's divisions is removing the Savannah River watershed from the Creek-Georgia-Alabama subregion. Given the nature of relations between Georgia and the Creek after the colony's establishment in 1733, it certainly makes sense to follow Wood and put both in the same subregion. But from the era of pre-European contact to the 1730s, it seems to me that these were two different subregions. In fact, the meshing of these two areas largely results from the events portrayed in this work. Last, I have made one other adjustment from Wood's model, dividing his Natchez-Louisiana subregion in two. This division, too, would not be made if this book focused on the period after 1729 (when the Natchez War effectively brought this subregion into closer contact with the Gulf Coast). Culturally, the Indians of both subregions shared much in common, but before 1730, those of the Natchez area remained much more enmeshed in the religious, political, and social life of the "Mississippian" era than did the groups further south.

To clarify my alterations from Wood's divisions I provide the following chart:

Wood	*Gallay*
Virginia	Excluded
North Carolina (east of the mountains)	Piedmont
South Carolina (east of the mountains)	South Atlantic Coastal
Florida	Florida
Creeks–Georgia–Alabama	Creek
	Savannah River
Cherokees	Cherokee
Choctaws–Chickasaws	Choctaw
	Chickasaw
Natchez–Louisiana	Natchez
	Gulf Coast
East Texas	East Texas
Shawnee	Excluded

13. See the excellent study of the Catawba by James Merrell, *The Indians' New World*.

14. Control of the Mississippi River was critical to the new United States Independence. But even then, the river was not crucial to the South, for it was needed primarily as an avenue for farmers of the Ohio River and Tennessee River Valleys for shipping their goods to New Orleans. At that time, the Creek and Choctaw still retained control of most of the central South. Only with Indian removal and the invention of the steamboat did the Mississippi take on its great importance to the South.

CHAPTER 1: THE MISSISSIPPIAN ERA

1. Through stable carbon isotope analysis, scientists are able to document the "relative dietary contribution of maize" in measurements of human bone collagen. Combin-

ing this information with measurements made by the accelerator mass spectrometer, and analysis of "fine-grain archaeobotanical sequences," Bruce Smith concludes, "Maize was initially introduced into eastern North America by A.D. 200–300, but was not present in some areas for another 400 to 600 years, and does not appear to have been anything more than a minor crop before A.D. 900–1000." Bruce D. Smith, with C. Wesley Cowan and Michael P. Hoffman, *Rivers of Change: Essays on Early Agriculture in Eastern North America* (Washington, D.C.: Smithsonian Institution Press, 1992), 201–203. After 1100, maize became the region's predominant crop (294).

2. Smith, *Rivers of Change*, 294. For the cooking of corn, see Charles Hudson, *The Southeastern Indians* (Knoxville: University of Tennessee Press, 1976), 302–307.

3. Ordinarily, 1600 is used as the approximate marking for the end of the Mississippian period, but I have extended the date to 1730, when the Natchez lost their homeland and no longer lived as a chiefdom.

4. A good place to start for an introduction to Mississippian cultures is with three collections of essays: David Hurst Thomas, ed., *Columbian Consequences*, vol. 2: *Archaeological and Historical Perspectives on the Spanish Borderlands East* (Washington, D.C.: Smithsonian Institution Press, 1989); Bruce D. Smith, ed., *The Mississippian Emergence* (Washington, D.C.: Smithsonian Institution Press, 1990); and Patricia K. Galloway, ed., *The Southeastern Ceremonial Complex: Artifacts and Analysis* (Lincoln: University of Nebraska Press, 1989).

5. Hudson, *Southeastern Indians*, 365–375; Smith, *Rivers of Change*, 294. Although maize was important to Native Americans in other regions, it could not be relied on for subsistence. Richard White discusses the need for Great Lakes region Indians to turn to fishing rather than corn for survival in *The Middle Ground: Indians, Empires, and Republics in the Great Lakes Region, 1650–1815* (Cambridge: Cambridge University Press, 1991).

6. Lewis Cecil Gray, *History of Agriculture in the Southern United States to 1860*, 2 vols. (Washington, D.C.: Carnegie Institute of Washington, 1932), 1:171. Gray also noted that corn production remained central to the region in 1860, when per capita production was 35.63 bushels, whereas wheat was only 4.57 bushels. The South was by far the premier corn-producing region. In 1839, it produced more than half of the nation's crop, but it exported very little, preferring to reserve corn for humans and livestock (2:811–812). One reason for corn's continued prominence as a food crop might have been slaves' preference for corn over wheat (1:66–71, 171). Many southern farmers also believed that their land was unsuitable for wheat production (2:816–817).

7. An essay collection on southern Native Americans during the period of Spanish exploration and early colonization is Charles Hudson and Carmen Tesser, eds., *The Forgotten Centuries: Indians and Europeans in the South, 1521–1707* (Athens: University of Georgia Press, 1994). For a discussion of ritual sacrifice in the historic period in the lower Mississippi Valley, see Chapter 4, below.

8. Charles De Pratter, *Late Prehistoric and Early Historic Chiefdoms in the Southeastern United States* (New York: Garland, 1991), 39–56.

9. James A. Brown, Richard A. Kerber, and Howard D. Winters, "Trade and the Evolution of Exchange Relations at the Beginning of the Mississippian Period," in Smith, *Mississippian Emergence*, 264.

10. John H. Blitz, *Ancient Chiefdoms of the Tombigbee* (Tuscaloosa: University of Alabama Press, 1993), 178.

11. De Pratter, *Late Prehistoric and Early Historic Chiefdoms,* 41.

12. Blitz, *Ancient Chiefdoms,* 123.

13. Timothy R. Pauketat, *The Ascent of Chiefs: Cahokia and Mississippian Politics in Native North America* (Tuscaloosa: University of Alabama Press, 1994), 91.

14. Blitz, *Ancient Chiefdoms,* 121–122.

15. David H. Dye, "Warfare in the Sixteenth-Century Southeast: The de Soto Expedition in the Interior," in Thomas, *Columbian Consequences,* 211–222, provides an introductory overview. See also Lewis H. Larson, Jr., "Functional Considerations of Warfare in the Southeast During the Mississippi Period," *American Antiquity* 37 (1972), 383–392, and a response by Jon L. Gibson, "Aboriginal Warfare in the Protohistoric Southeast: An Alternative Perspective," *American Antiquity* 39 (1974), 130–133.

16. David G. Anderson, *The Savannah River Chiefdoms: Political Change in the Late Prehistoric Southeast* (Tuscaloosa: University of Alabama Press, 1994).

17. Anderson, *Savannah River Chiefdoms,* 81.

18. John A. Strong, "The Mississippian Bird-Man Theme in Cross-Cultural Perspective," in Galloway, *Southeastern Ceremonial Complex,* 211–238.

19. Jon Mueller questions whether similarities in symbols necessarily imply similarities in beliefs. "The Southern Cult," in Galloway, *Southeastern Ceremonial Complex,* 11–26. Two other essays in this volume that interpret Mississippian symbols are "Vernon James Knight, Jr., "Some Speculations on Mississippian Monsters," 205–210, and Robert L. Hall, "The Cultural Background of Mississippian Symbolism," 239–278.

20. A review of the comparisons made by scholars averring that cultural similarities "are due to parallel and convergent evolution" is found in Malcolm C. Webb, "Functional and Historical Parallelisms Between Mesoamerican and Mississippian Cultures," in Galloway, *Southeastern Ceremonial Complex,* 279–293, quotation on 281. It used to be assumed that maize and squash both moved from Mesoamerica to the South, thus providing a model of movement for culture as well. But archaeological studies have since shown that varieties of maize and squash developed independently in the southeastern United States. See the extensive discussion of this issue in Smith, *Rivers of Change,* especially chapters 4 and 11.

21. Anderson, *Savannah River Chiefdoms,* 9–10.

22. Anderson, *Savannah River Chiefdoms,* 21, 25–34.

23. Anderson, *Savannah River Chiefdoms,* 330–331.

24. Marvin T. Smith, *Archaeology of Aboriginal Culture Change in the Interior Southeast: Depopulation During the Early Historic Period* (Gainesville: University Press of Florida, 1987), 84. See also Smith, "Aboriginal Depopulation in the Postcontact Southeast," in Hudson and Smith, *Forgotten Centuries,* 257–275, which summarizes archaeological work on epidemics in the sixteenth- and seventeenth-century South.

25. Henry F. Dobyns, *Their Number Become Thinned: Native American Population Dynamics in Eastern North America* (Knoxville: University of Tennessee Press, 1983), is the best place to begin for discussion of disease and demography in Florida. Smith, *Archaeology of Aboriginal Culture Change,* 5, points out some of the problems with Dobyns's analysis, but Smith's study is also highly speculative. Jerald T. Milanich reviews much of

the work done on disease in sixteenth-century Florida in *Florida Indians and the Invasion from Europe* (Gainesville: University Press of Florida, 1995), 212–222.

26. A good introduction to the historical discussion of the relationship between pre- and postcontact peoples is Ann F. Ramenofsky, "Loss of Innocence: Explanations of Differential Persistence in the Sixteenth-Century Southeast," in Thomas, *Columbian Consequences,* 31–48.

27. Anderson, *Savannah River Chiefdoms,* 158.

28. Pauketat, *Ascent of Chiefs,* 186–187.

29. Anderson, *Savannah River Chiefdoms,* 101, cites an example witnessed by the Soto entrada where male captives were hamstrung to keep them working in the fields.

30. De Pratter, *Late Prehistoric and Early Historic Chiefdoms,* 52.

31. Theda Perdue, *Slavery and the Evolution of Cherokee Society, 1540–1866* (Knoxville: University of Tennessee Press, 1979), 11–18. The slaves of the Cherokee, *atsi nahsa'it,* a term applied not only to bondpeople "but to any animate thing which was owned by a person," Perdue writes, "were anomalies because they had the physical appearance of human beings but could not live as such because they lacked membership in a clan." She continues, "By maintaining *atsi nahasa'it* the Cherokees gave cognizance to these anomalies and also demonstrated daily through the operation of their kinship system why such individuals could not be considered complete human beings" (16–17).

32. A useful survey of the rise of the Spanish mission system in Florida is Milanich, *Florida Indians and the Invasion from Europe,* particularly chapters 3, 4, 9, and 10.

33. Bruce D. Smith discusses the problems faced by archaeologists and anthropologists in defining the South as a region in the precontact period in "The Archaeology of the Southeastern United States: From Dalton to de Soto, 10,500–500 B.P.," in Fred Wendorf and Angela E. Close, eds., *Advances in World Archaeology,* vol. 5: *1986* (Orlando, Fla.: Academic, 1986), 1–18. In charting seven interpretations of the South's geographic extent, three of the scholars Smith examines excluded Virginia from the region (see Smith's fig. 1.1). One reason for the disparity of opinion is the periodization in which the South is being analyzed, which elicits the geographic elasticity of the region.

34. Helen C. Rountree, *The Powhatan Indians of Virginia: Their Traditional Culture* (Norman: University of Oklahoma Press, 1989).

35. Even as late as the constitutional convention, James Madison could state: "Of the affairs of Georgia I know as little as those of Kamshatska." James Madison to Thomas Jefferson, Aug. 12, 1786, in Robert A. Rutland et al., eds., *The Papers of James Madison,* vol. 9: *9 April 1786–24 May 1787* (Chicago: University of Chicago Press, 1975), 95.

36. The traditional discussion of Virginia's impact, or lack thereof, on the South is in W. J. Cash, *The Mind of the South* (New York: Knopf, 1941), 8–14, and elsewhere. Cash argues that in the migration of Virginians to the cotton South in the nineteenth century, they were largely out of place and found it difficult to adjust and compete in the "tooth-and-claw struggle" that characterized the South (12). Throughout, Cash separates Virginia from the rest of the South as a place apart, of a different temperament and development. This, of course, is nothing new, as Cash himself noted that antebellum observers from Frederick Olmsted to Daniel Hundley made the same distinction between Virginia (or an upper South) and a lower South. In the last four decades of the antebellum period, political affairs drew the slaveholding areas of Virginia and Kentucky closer to the South, but before then they stood outside the region.

37. Peter H. Wood, *Black Majority: Negroes in Colonial South Carolina from 1670 Through the Stono Rebellion* (New York: Norton, 1974), chapter 1.

38. This is not to say that these Native American peoples were not adversely affected by European diseases that resulted in large numbers of deaths—only that the impact was not destructive enough to eliminate or significantly reduce the power of many groups, many of whom found new strength in forming confederacies. For a discussion of the impact of Old World diseases on the American South, see Russell Thornton, Jonathan Warren, and Tim Miller, "Depopulation in the Southeast After 1492," in John W. Verano and Douglas H. Ubelaker, eds., *Disease and Demography in the Americas* (Washington, D.C.: Smithsonian Institution Press, 1992), 187–195 (especially conclusions on 193).

39. See Chapters 2 and 5 for further discussion of the evolution of the Creek Confederacy.

40. Paul E. Hoffman, *A New Andalucia and a Way to the Orient: The American Southeast During the Sixteenth Century* (Baton Rouge: Louisiana State University Press, 1990).

41. Alan Gallay, ed., *Voices of the Old South: Eyewitness Accounts, 1528–1861* (Athens: University of Georgia Press, 1994), 6–7. The entire account is printed in Álvar Núñez Cabeza de Vaca, *The Narrative of Álvar Núñez Cabeza de Vaca*, in Frederick W. Hodge, ed., *Spanish Explorers in the Southern United States, 1528–1543*, trans. Buckingham Smith (New York: Charles Scribner's Sons, 1907).

42. Gallay, *Voices*, 11.

43. For a review of the literature on Soto, see David Sloan, "The Expedition of Hernando de Soto: A Post-Mortem Report," in Jeannie Whayne, comp., *Cultural Encounters in the Early South: Indians and Europeans in Arkansas* (Fayetteville: University of Arkansas Press, 1995), 3–37. For the Soto *entrada*, see Lawrence A. Clayton, Vernon James Knight, Jr., and Edward C. Moore, eds., *The De Soto Chronicles: the Expedition of Hernando de Soto to North America in 1539–1543* (Tuscaloosa: University of Alabama Press, 1993); Charles M. Hudson, *Knights of Spain, Warriors of the Sun: Hernando de Soto and the South's Ancient Chiefdoms* (Athens: University of Georgia Press, 1997); and Jerald T. Milanich and Charles M. Hudson, *Hernando de Soto and the Indians of Florida* (Gainesville: University Press of Florida, 1993).

44. Gallay, *Voices*, 12. Ranjel's narrative is published in its entirety in Edward G. Bourne, trans. and ed., *Narratives of the Career of Hernando de Soto*, 4 vols. (New York: AMS, 1904).

45. Gallay, *Voices*, 13.

46. Gallay, *Voices*, 14.

47. Juan Friede and Benjamin Keen, eds., *Bartolmé de las Casas in History: Toward an Understanding of the Man and His Work* (Dekalb: Northern Illinois University Press, 1971).

48. Charles M. Hudson, *The Juan Pardo Expeditions: Exploration of the Carolinas and Tennessee, 1566–68* (Washington, D.C.: Smithsonian Institution Press, 1990). For the Luna expedition, see Hoffman, *New Andalucia*, chapter 7.

49. Paul E. Hoffman, *The Spanish Crown and the Defense of the Caribbean, 1535–1585: Precedent, Patrimonialism, and Royal Parsimony* (Baton Rouge: Louisiana State University Press, 1980).

50. For the Spanish reoccupation of Florida, see Eugene Lyon, *The Enterprise of Florida: Pedro Menéndez de Avilés and the Spanish Conquest of 1565–1568* (Gainesville: University Press of Florida, 1976).

51. Gallay, *Voices,* 16, from Nicolas Le Challeux, *A True and Perfect Description, of the Last Voyage or Navigation, Attempted by Capitaine John Rybaut . . .* (London, 1566).

52. See Hoffman, *New Andalucia,* chapter 9, for the French settlement.

53. Hoffman believes that Ribaut went to England voluntarily. In either case, he was imprisoned there and also spread news of French exploits in Florida. *New Andalucia,* 212; Lyon, *Enterprise of Florida,* 33.

54. Gallay, *Voices,* 18.

55. Estimates on how many were put to death vary from 200 at the low end to 350 and more. See Lyon, *Enterprise of Florida,* 126n45, 127n47.

56. Gallay, *Voices,* 20.

57. For Roanoke, see David Beers Quinn, *Set Fair for Roanoke: Voyages and Colonies, 1584–1606* (Chapel Hill: University of North Carolina Press, 1985). For the relationship between English overseas expansion and privateering, see George Bruner Parks, *Richard Hakluyt and the English Voyages* (New York: American Geographical Society, 1928); and Kenneth R. Andrews, *Trade, Plunder and Settlement: Maritime Enterprise and the Genesis of the British Empire, 1480–1630* (Cambridge: Cambridge University Press, 1984), and *Elizabethan Privateering During the Spanish War, 1585–1603* (Cambridge: Cambridge University Press, 1964).

58. For the Spanish in Florida, see John H. Hann, *A History of the Timucua Indians and Missions* (Gainesville: University Press of Florida, 1996), Hann, trans. and ed., *Missions to the Calusa* (Gainesville: University Press of Florida, 1991), and Hann, *Apalachee: The Land Between the Rivers* (Gainesville: University Presses of Florida, 1988); Amy Bushnell, *The King's Coffer: Proprietors of the Spanish Florida Treasury, 1565–1702* (Gainesville: University Presses of Florida, 1981); and John Jay TePaske, *The Governorship of Spanish Florida, 1700–1763* (Durham, N.C.: Duke University Press, 1964). For the relationship of France and Spain on the Gulf Coast, see Henry Folmer, *Franco-Spanish Rivalry in North America, 1524–1763* (Glendale, Calif.: A. H. Clark, 1953); and Kimberly S. Hangar, "France-Spain Relations," in Alan Gallay, ed., *The Colonial Wars of North America, 1512–1763: An Encyclopedia* (New York: Garland, 1996), 232–234.

CHAPTER 2: CAROLINA, THE WESTO, AND THE TRADE IN INDIAN SLAVES, 1670–1685

1. A good overview of English colonization on mainland North America, particularly from the mother country's perspective, is Wesley Frank Craven, *The Colonies in Transition, 1660–1713* (New York: Harper and Row, 1968). This should be compared with Stephen Saunders Webb's view that the Crown sought to exert control over its colonies through establishment of garrison government in America. See Webb, *1676: The End of American Independence* (New York: Knopf, 1984). The best study of South Carolina politics in this period is M. Eugene Sirmans, *Colonial South Carolina: A Political History, 1663–1763* (Chapel Hill: University of North Carolina Press, 1966).

2. Marvin T. Smith, *Archaeology of Aboriginal Cultural Change in the Interior Southeast: Depopulation During the Early Historic Period* (Gainesville: University Press of Florida, 1987), 131–132.

3. For a discussion of Indian adaptation of seventeenth-century guns in New England, see Patrick M. Malone, *The Skulking Way of War: Technology and Tactics Among the*

New England Indians (Lanham, Md.: Madison Books, 1991). Unfortunately, Malone does not adequately address the question of the bow and arrow versus the gun.

4. John E. Worth, *The Struggle for the Georgia Coast: An Eighteenth-Century Retrospective on Guale and Mocama,* Anthropological Papers of the American Museum of Natural History, 75 (Athens: University of Georgia Press, 1995), 17.

5. Peter H. Wood, *Black Majority: Negroes in Colonial South Carolina from 1670 Through the Stono Rebellion* (New York: Norton, 1974), chapter 1, "The Colony of a Colony."

6. I have pluralized "constitution" because the proprietors employed several drafts, which created confusion for the colonists and themselves. Sirmans, *Colonial South Carolina,* 7–16, 37–38, 67.

7. *Records,* 1:204. The proprietors ignored this restriction on occasion. For instance, in 1686 they approved a thousand-acre grant to Maurice Mathews, a notorious abuser of Indians who had managed to obtain bills of sale to a tract of land from several Indian groups: the Stono, Ashepoo, Saint Helena, Cussah, Wichaugh, and Wimbee. See A. S. Salley, ed., *Commissions and Instructions from the Lords Proprietors of Carolina to Public Officials of South Carolina, 1685–1715* (Columbia: Historical Commission of South Carolina, 1916), 72–73.

8. For the proprietors' loss of their patent, see Sirmans, *Colonial South Carolina,* 127–129.

9. "Coppy of Instruccons annexed to ye Comission for ye Governr Councell," July 27, 1669, in *Sketch,* 348.

10. *Records,* 1:217.

11. For an excellent discussion of English concepts of Indian land rights, see William Cronon, *Changes in the Land: Indians, Colonists, and the Ecology of Colonial New England* (New York: Hill and Wang, 1983), 64–81.

12. Cronon, *Changes in the Land,* 52–53; James Axtell, "The Invasion Within: The Contest of Cultures in Colonial North America," in Axtell, *The European and the Indian: Essays in the Ethnohistory of Colonial North America* (New York: Oxford University Press, 1981), 52–53.

13. "Coppy of Instruccons," 348. Unlike the proprietors, Charles II did not intend Carolina to incorporate Native Americans. See Anthony Pagden, *Lords of All the World: Ideologies of Empire in Spain, Britain and France, c. 1500–c. 1800* (New Haven and London: Yale University Press, 1995), 37.

14. *Records,* 1:201. They allowed any seven persons to "constitute a Church or profession to which they shall give some name to distinguish it from others," extending this right to Jews, heathens, "and other deserters" from Christianity.

15. For instance, the 1682 version of the constitution stated in article 109, "Every Freeman of Carolina shall have absolute power and authority over Negro slaves of what opinion or Religion soever." *Records,* 1:204.

16. Kenneth R. Andrews, *Trade, Plunder and Settlement: Maritime Enterprise and the Genesis of the British Empire, 1480–1630* (Cambridge: Cambridge University Press, 1984), 116–128.

17. Nicholas P. Canny, "The Ideology of English Colonization: From Ireland to America," *William and Mary Quarterly,* 3d Ser., 30 (1973), 575–598. See also the anthology by K. R. Andrews, N. P. Canny, and P. E. H. Hair, eds., *The Westward Enterprise: English Activ-*

ities in Ireland, the Atlantic, and America, 1480–1650 (Detroit, Mich.: Wayne State University Press, 1979); and Angus Calder, *Revolutionary Empire: The Rise of the English-Speaking Empires from the Fifteenth Century to the 1780s* (1981; reprint, London: Pimlico, 1998).

18. According to Dauril Aulden, the first Portuguese law to deal with Indian affairs, enacted in 1570 in Brazil, "prohibited the enslavement of the natives of Brazil except for those taken in a just war." See "Black Robes Versus White Settlers: The Struggle for 'Freedom of the Indians' in Colonial Brazil," in Howard Peckham and Charles Gibson, eds., *Attitudes of Colonial Powers Toward the American Indian* (Salt Lake City: University of Utah Press, 1969), 25.

19. Prisoners were viewed as having lost their freedom by their voluntary commitment of a crime. On the rationales employed by Europeans for justifying enslavement, see David Brion Davis, *The Problem of Slavery in Western Culture* (Ithaca, N.Y.: Cornell University Press, 1966); and Winthrop D. Jordan, *White Over Black: American Attitudes Toward the Negro, 1550–1812* (Chapel Hill: University of North Carolina Press, 1968).

20. Jordan, *White Over Black*, 167–178; Thomas D. Morris, *Southern Slavery and the Law, 1619–1860* (Chapel Hill: University of North Carolina Press, 1996), 22–23.

21. Edmund S. Morgan, *American Slavery, American Freedom: The Ordeal of Colonial Virginia* (New York: Norton, 1975); Jordan, *White Over Black*, chapter 2.

22. Lewis Hanke, *The Spanish Struggle for Justice in the Conquest of America* (Philadelphia: University of Pennsylvania Press, 1949); Edward H. Spicer, *Cycles of Conquest: The Impact of Spain, Mexico, and the United States on the Indians of the Southwest, 1533–1960* (Tucson: University of Arizona Press, 1962); Amy Bushnell, *The King's Coffer: Proprietors of the Spanish Florida Treasury, 1565–1702* (Gainesville: University Presses of Florida, 1981); Kathleen A. Deagan, "Spanish-Indian Interaction in Sixteenth-Century Florida and Hispaniola," in William W. Fitzhugh, ed., *Cultures in Contact: The European Impact on Native Cultural Institutions in Eastern North America, A.D. 1000–1800* (Washington, D.C.: Smithsonian Institution Press, 1985), 281–318; Lolita Gutiérrez Brockington, *The Leverage of Labor: Managing the Cortés Haciendas in Tehunantepec* (Durham, N.C.: Duke University Press, 1989). On the Portuguese experience in Brazil, see Aulden, "Black Robes," 19–46.

23. An excellent discussion of the development of Spain's imperial policies is Geoffrey Parker, *The Grand Strategy of Philip II* (New Haven and London: Yale University Press, 1998).

24. Betty Wood, *Slavery in Colonial Georgia, 1730–1775* (Athens: University of Georgia Press, 1984).

25. *Records*, 1:55, 97–102. The commission could neither interfere with alliances or public treaties nor establish policy—it could only rectify injustice. The Grand Council, composed of the colony's governor and council, continued to administer proprietary rules. The council ascertained all complaints to be heard by the commission. The governor could play a large role in this system for he alone comprised the commission if the other commissioners were unavailable. To ensure compliance with proprietary rules, the proprietors sent the commission a book to enter Indian grievances and petitions as well as other relevant information about Indian affairs. The governor and council had to sign each entry, after which the book was to be forwarded to the proprietors yearly or earlier if circumstances warranted.

26. Quotation from "Coppy of Instruccons," 350; but also see "Instructions to Joseph West," 350–351; and "Instructions to the Governor and Council of Ashley River," May 1, 1671, in *Sketch,* 366–369.

27. Robert K. Ackerman, *South Carolina Land Policies* (Columbia: University of South Carolina Press, 1977); Sirmans, *Colonial South Carolina,* 12, 38–39, 54, 120, 123; David Duncan Wallace, *South Carolina: A Short History, 1520–1948* (Columbia: University of South Carolina Press, 1969), 25, 47, 53.

28. For the early economic development of South Carolina, see Converse D. Clowse, *Economic Beginnings in Colonial South Carolina, 1670–1730* (Columbia: University of South Carolina Press, 1971).

29. Council meeting, Dec. 10, 1675, in A. S. Salley, ed., *Journal of the Grand Council of South Carolina, August 25, 1671–June 24, 1680* (Columbia: Historical Commission of South Carolina, 1907), 80.

30. These instructions were given in 1671 and 1672. See "Temporary Laws," in *Sketch,* 353; and "Agrarian Laws or Instructions from the Lords Proprietors to the Governor and Council of Carolina," June 21, 1672, in *Sketch,* 358.

31. For examples of the intermixing of violence and politics among the elite, see "Barnwell of South Carolina," *SCHM* 2 (January 1901), 47–50, which notes John Barnwell's use of a mob against the colony's chief justice; "Letters from John Stewart to William Dunlop," Apr. 27, 1690, *SCHM* 32 (January 1931), 26–27, and June 23, 1690, *SCHM* 32 (April 1931), 105, which describes dueling and other violence among elites; and "Deposition of Samuel Everleigh . . . ," Oct. 8, 1706, Additional Manuscripts, 61647, folio 112, BL, in which Everleigh claims that Colonel William Rhett threatened to cut off the ears of political opponent Joseph Boone (when he returned from England, where he had taken Dissenter complaints against High Anglicans) and that Rhett had caned James Burt and John Toomer.

32. Shirley C. Hughson, *The Carolina Pirates and Colonial Commerce, 1670–1740* (Baltimore: Johns Hopkins University Press, 1894).

33. Two places to begin for study of Carolina's Settlement Indians are Gene Waddell, *Indians in the South Carolina Lowcountry, 1562–1751* (Spartanburg, S.C.: Reprint Company, 1980); and J. Norman Heard, *Handbook of the American Frontier: Four Centuries of Indian-White Relationships,* vol. 1: *The Southeastern Woodlands* (Metuchen, N.J.: Scarecrow, 1987).

34. "The Articles and Agreemt. of ye Lds. Proprietrs. of Carolina, Betweene themselves, concerninge the trade there," in *Sketch,* 390.

35. "Order concerning the Trade with the Westoes and Cussatoes Indians," in *Sketch,* 388–389; *Records,* 1:60–61.

36. "Articles and Agreemt. of ye Lds. Proprietrs. of Carolina."

37. Council meeting, Sept. 27, Oct. 4, 1671, *Journal of the Grand Council,* 8–9.

38. John R. Swanton, *Early History of the Creek Indians and Their Neighbors,* Smithsonian Institution Bureau of American Ethnology, Bulletin 73 (Washington, D.C.: Government Printing Office, 1922), 67–68.

39. Council meeting, Sept. 27, Oct. 2, 1671, *Journal of the Grand Council,* 8–9.

40. Council meeting, Aug. 3, 1674, *Journal of the Grand Council,* 71–72.

41. Council meeting, July 25, 1674, *Journal of the Grand Council,* 71. The colony

could not always identify enemy Indians—or those guilty of crimes. See, e.g., Feb. 23, 1673, 54.

42. Quoted in Swanton, *Early History,* 69.

43. Swanton, *Early History,* 69–70.

44. Carolina's efforts to remove the Virginia traders are discussed in Chapter 7.

45. Marcel Mauss, *The Gift: The Form and Reason for Exchange in Archaic Societies,* trans. W. D. Halls (1950; reprint, New York: Norton, 1990).

46. Council meeting, Oct. 7, 1673, *Journal of the Grand Council,* 64, emphasis added. According to James Merrell, Esaw was a term employed by the Carolinians to refer to a variety of Piedmont peoples in the Wateree-Catawba valley. See *The Indians' New World: Catawbas and Their Neighbors from European Contact Through the Era of Removal* (Chapel Hill: University of North Carolina Press, 1989), 47.

47. *Journal of the Grand Council,* Feb. 2, 1673, 66–67.

48. *Journal of the Grand Council,* Mar. 7, 1673, 67.

49. Henry Woodward, "A Faithfull Relation of My Westoe Voyage," Dec. 31, 1674, in Alexander S. Salley, Jr., *Narratives of Early Carolina, 1650–1708* (New York: Charles Scribner's Sons, 1911), 130–134.

50. For the opening of Virginia trade with the Cherokee, see Alan Vance Briceland, *Westward from Virginia: The Exploration of the Virginia-Carolina Frontier, 1670–1710* (Charlottesville: University of Virginia Press, 1987).

51. For the Iroquois Wars, see Daniel K. Richter, *The Ordeal of the Longhouse: The Peoples of the Iroquois League in the Era of European Colonization* (Chapel Hill: University of North Carolina Press, 1992); and Richter, "Iroquois Wars," in Alan Gallay, ed., *Colonial Wars of North America, 1512–1763: An Encyclopedia* (New York: Garland, 1996), 317–319.

52. For discussion of Savannah as a lingua franca, see Chapter 8. For the pan-Indian movement, see Gregory Evans Dowd, *A Spirited Resistance: The North American Indian Struggle for Unity, 1745–1815* (Baltimore: Johns Hopkins University Press, 1992).

53. Worth, *Struggle for the Georgia Coast,* 35.

54. Worth, *Struggle for the Georgia Coast,* 26–27; "Testimony of David Turner," Oct. 25, 1680, in "The Spaniards and the English Settlement in Charles Town," trans. José Miguel Gallardo, *SCHM* 37 (October 1936), 137–138.

55. Francis Le Jau would write of the Savannah in 1708: they "settled near this province Even before the Nation of the Westos were destroyed and to this day they keep about the places where the Westos lived, but perhaps are not so numerous" (*Le Jau,* 68).

56. *Records,* 1:106.

57. *Records,* 1:107.

58. *Records,* 1:112.

59. *Records,* 1:107.

60. Edward McCrady, *The History of South Carolina Under the Proprietary Government, 1670–1719* (1897; New York: Russell and Russell, 1969), 178.

61. McCrady, *History of South Carolina,* 178.

62. McCrady's nonsense also extended to his view of Indian land rights. A lawyer, McCrady came up with the interesting legal notion that since Indians did not understand land tenures they had "no rights" to the land. *History of South Carolina,* 179.

63. *Records,* 1:115–116.

64. *Records*, 1:116–117.

65. *Records*, 1:256. According to James Merrell, the Waniah (or Winyaw) later moved closer to the English colonists by settling on the Santee River. In 1716, during the Yamasee War, they returned to the Winyaw River. *Indians' New World*, 100.

66. *Records*, 1:257.

67. *Records*, 1:257–258.

68. *Records*, 1:255.

69. *Records*, 1:255.

70. *Records*, 1:255.

71. *Records*, 1:259.

72. *Records*, 1:260.

73. *Records*, 1:99.

74. *Records*, 1:142.

75. *Records*, 1:142.

76. *Records*, 1:98–99.

77. *Records*, 1:174.

78. The Board of Trade and Plantations made constant complaint against proprietary governments, hoping to transform all colonies to royal rule. The board accused them of countenancing illegal trade and "other Irregular Practices, to the great prejudice of her Majesties Revenue of fair traders, and otherwise." Although these criticisms were self-interested—the board hoped to expand its power through eliminating colonial proprietorships—in the case of Carolina, the charges were true. Quotation from "Report from the Commissioners of Trade and Plantations, of the 16th of December 1703," Manuscript Collection, University of London, Manuscript 78.

79. *Records*, 1:254, 261.

80. Both torture and incorporation of captives are discussed in Chapter 6.

81. For discussion of the concept of "just war," see John Morgan Dederer, *War in America to 1775: Before Yankee Doodle* (New York: New York University Press, 1990), 162–164, 167–169, 262*n*78.

82. See Chapter 10.

83. David Hackett Fischer makes the sophistical argument that slavery "was fundamentally hostile to the Puritan ethos of New England." This view is clearly contradicted by Puritans actively engaging in slaveholding wherever slavery flourished in the Atlantic world. *Albion's Seed: Four British Folkways in America* (New York: Oxford University Press, 1989), 53. See also Joanne Pope Melish, *Disowning Slavery: Gradual Emancipation and "Race" in New England, 1780–1860* (Ithaca, N.Y.: Cornell University Press, 1998), 11–49; Michael Zuckerman, "Identity in British America: Unease in Eden," in Nicholas Canny and Anthony Pagden, eds., *Colonial Identity in the Atlantic World* (Princeton, N.J.: Princeton University Press, 1987), 144–145, 148–149.

84. On Indian slavery in Canada, see Marcel Trudel, *L'esclavage au Canada français: Histoire et conditions de l'esclavage* (Quebec: Presses Universitaires Laval, 1960). See Chapter 11 for discussion of Indian slavery in Louisiana.

85. [Jean-Baptiste Le Moyne] de Bienville au Comte de Pontchartrain, Oct. 10, 1706, AC, microfilm copies, Manuscript Reading Room, LC, C13, B:1; [Nicolas] de la Salle au Comte de Pontchartrain, June 20, 1710, AC, microfilm copies, Manuscript Reading Room, LC, C13A, 2:519; le Cte de Pontchartrain à [Antoine Alexandre] de Re-

monville, Sept. 14, 1710, AC, microfilm copies, Manuscript Reading Room, LC, C13, B32:207; Jean Delanglez, S.J., *The French Jesuits in Lower Louisiana (1700–1763)* (Washington, D.C.: Catholic University of America, 1935), 394; Richard White, *The Middle Ground: Indians, Empires, and Republics in the Great Lakes Region, 1650–1815* (Cambridge: Cambridge University Press, 1991), 69–70; Pagden, *Lords of All the World,* 149.

86. *Records,* 1:266–267.

87. *Records,* 1:290.

88. *Records,* 2:20–21, 59–60.

89. *Records,* 2:28.

90. *Records,* 2:33.

91. *Records,* 2:34.

92. For the crackdown on piracy, see Robert C. Ritchie, *Captain Kidd and the War Against the Pirates* (Cambridge, Mass.: Harvard University Press, 1986); and Marcus Rediker, *Between the Devil and the Deep Blue Sea: Merchant Seamen, Pirates and the Anglo-American Maritime World, 1700–1750* (Cambridge: Cambridge University Press, 1987), 281–285.

93. *Records,* 2:181.

CHAPTER 3: CROSSROAD OF CULTURES

1. John Erskine, *Journal of the Hon. John Erskine of Carnock, 1683–1687,* ed. Walter Macleod (Edinburgh: Scottish History Society, 1893), 69, 72.

2. In 1493, Pope Alexander VI gave to Spain all the Americas, except Brazil, and the boundaries were refined the following year in the Treaty of Tordesillas. Henry VIII's break with the Catholic Church made the papal bull a moot point in England, which also did not accept Spain's and Portugal's bilateral agreement. On the evolution of European claims for sovereignty, including Spanish and English disagreement over what constituted rights of possession, see Anthony Pagden, *Lords of All the World: Ideologies of Empire in Spain, Britain and France, c. 1500–c.1800* (New Haven and London: Yale University Press, 1995), 89–94.

3. The English also disregarded French claims in Louisiana by their attempt to plant the colony of Carolana along the Mississippi. See Daniel Coxe, *A Description of the English Province of Carolana . . .* [1722], ed. William S. Coker (Gainesville: University of Florida Press, 1976).

4. On the political corruption of England under Charles II, see John A. R. Marriott, *The Crisis of English Liberty: A History of the Stuart Monarchy and the Puritan Revolution* (1930; reprint, Westport, Conn.: Greenwood, 1970), 365–366; Clayton Roberts, *The Growth of Responsible Government in Stuart England* (Cambridge: Cambridge University Press, 1966). George Macauley Trevelyan discusses the contours of corruption in seventeenth-century England, in *England Under the Stuarts* (London: Methuen, 1904), 125–126. For political corruption under James I and Charles I, see Linda Levy Peck, *Court Patronage and Corruption in Early Stuart England* (Boston: Unwin Hyman, 1990). Fear of political corruption contributed to the rise of an anti–standing army ideology in England and North America. See Lois G. Schwoerer, *"No Standing Armies!": The Antiarmy Ideology in Seventeenth-Century England* (Baltimore: Johns Hopkins University Press, 1974). For the response of the English to political corruption, see J. G. A. Pocock, *The Machia-*

vellian Moment: Florentine Political Thought and the Atlantic Republican Tradition (Princeton, N.J.: Princeton University Press, 1975).

5. Robert Olwell, *Masters, Slaves, and Subjects: The Culture of Power in the South Carolina Low Country, 1740–1790* (Ithaca, N.Y.: Cornell University Press, 1998), 57–101, esp. 99–100.

6. Fray Joseph Ramos Escudero, in a letter of Oct. 20, 1734, quoted in John R. Swanton, *Early History of the Creek Indians and Their Neighbors,* Smithsonian Institution Bureau of American Ethnology, Bulletin 73 (Washington, D.C.: Government Printing Office, 1922), 96.

7. Andrés González de Barcia Carballido y Zúñiga, *Barcia's Chronological History of the Continent of Florida* [1723], trans. and ed. Anthony Kerrigan (Gainesville: University of Florida Press, 1951), 312.

8. Lord Cardross and William Dunlop to Sir Peter Colleton, Mar. 27, 1685, in "Arrival of the Cardross Settlers," *SCHM* 30 (April 1929), 76.

9. Cardross and Dunlop to Colleton, Mar. 27, 1685.

10. George Pratt Insh, *Scottish Colonial Schemes, 1620–1686* (Glasgow: Maclehose, Jackson, 1922), 188–189.

11. Insh, *Scottish Colonial Schemes,* 190–191.

12. Originally, the Scots had hoped to have their own colony on "Cape Florida," notwithstanding that the Spanish were already settled there; or they would prefer one of the Bahamian Islands; or elsewhere in the West Indies. Denied this, they settled for land in Carolina. "Memorial concerning the Scottish plantation to be erected in some place of America," Feb. 28, 1681, in *Register of the Privy Council of Scotland,* 3d Ser., vol. 7: *1681–1682* (Edinburgh: Morrison and Gibb, 1915), 664–665.

13. Sir John Cochran, quoted in Insh, *Scottish Colonial Schemes,* 191. Members of the Privy Council in England believed that the Scots' negotiations in London for Carolina were a mere pretext for plotting treason against the state. *Register of the Privy Council of Scotland,* 3d Ser., vol. 8: *1683–1684* (Glasgow: James Heddlewich and Sons, 1915), 213–214; *Register of the Privy Council of Scotland,* 3d Ser., vol. 11: *1684* (Edinburgh: H. M. General Register, 1924), 256.

14. Insh, *Scottish Colonial Schemes,* 195.

15. Duke of York, quoted in Insh, *Scottish Colonial Schemes,* 197. Charles II to the Privy Council, Aug. 15, 1682, *Register of the Privy Council of Scotland,* vol. 7, 599–600.

16. Lawrence Sanders Rowland, Alexander Moore, and George Rogers, Jr., *The History of Beaufort County, South Carolina,* vol. 1: *1514–1861* (Columbia: University of South Carolina Press, 1996), 70.

17. Rowland et al., *History of Beaufort County,* 70; Insh, *Scottish Colonial Schemes,* 202–203.

18. "Arrival of the Cardross Settlers," 70.

19. Twenty-two of the servants belonged to Dunlop and his backers. William Dunlop to Sir James Montgomery, May 1686, Dunlop Papers, SRO, Scotland, GD 3/5/772.

20. Robert Wodrow, *History of the Sufferings of the Church of Scotland from the Restoration to the Revolution,* 4 vols. (1721–1722; reprint, Glasgow: Blackie, 1836), 4:10b.

21. "Arrival of the Cardross Settlers," 72–73.

22. The Spanish had abandoned Port Royal in the 1580s but had not given up their

claim to the area. For archaeological analysis of the Spanish settlements at Santa Elena on nearby Parris Island, see Stanley A. South and William B. Hunt, *Discovering Santa Elena West of Fort San Felipe*. Research Manuscript Series 200 (Columbia: University of South Carolina, Institute of Archaeology and Anthropology, 1986).

23. "Arrival of the Cardross Settlers," 73.

24. "Arrival of the Cardross Settlers," 75.

25. March 21, 1685, *Records*, 2:49.

26. Barcia, *Barcia's Chronological History*, 312.

27. March 21, 1685, *Records*, 2:49.

28. November 29, 1693, *Records*, 3:109. Westbrook was later killed by the Savannah, perhaps because of his promotion of the Yamasee into their position as Carolina's chief ally.

29. "Lords Proprietors to Governor Jas. Colleton," Dec. 2, 1689, in *Sketch*, 410.

30. [June?] 1685, *Records*, 2:75.

31. William Dunlop to Sir James Montgomery, May 1686, Dunlop Papers, SRO, GD 3/5/773.

32. Dunlop to Montgomery, Oct. 21, 1686, Dunlop Papers, GD 3/5/775.

33. Dunlop to Montgomery, Nov. 21, 1686, Dunlop Papers, GD 3/5/776.

34. Dunlop to Montgomery, Oct. 21, 1686, GD 3/5/775.

35. "Memorial of the Hostilities committed in the Province of Carolina by the Spaniards Represented by Major William Dunlop who is Commissioned to that effect," Leven and Melvile Muniments (GD 26), 26/7/277, SRO; "Early History of South Carolina," in *Sketch*, 144–145.

36. October 10, 1687, *Records*, 2:221.

37. An exception is Charles H. Lesser, *South Carolina Begins: The Records of a Proprietary Colony, 1663–1721* (Columbia: SCDAH, 1995), 143, which notes that there were two attacks. Quotation from "Memorial of the Hostilities."

38. "Instructions for Major William Dunlop from Landgrave James Colleton, June 15, 1688, on his mission to the Governor of Florida at St. Augustine," Dunlop Papers, CH 8456, National Library of Scotland, Edinburgh. A copy of this can be found in Dunlop Papers, MS 9255, National Library of Scotland, p. 42.

39. William Dunlop, "Journall. Capt. Dunlop's Voyage to the Southward. 1687," *SCHM* 30 (July 1929), 129.

40. Dunlop, "Journall," 129.

41. Dunlop, "Journall," 127–133; also see Dunlop to Montgomery, July 13, 1687, Dunlop Papers, SRO, GD 3/5/777, where he states they traveled 300 miles on this invasion.

42. Dunlop, "Journall," 129.

43. "William Dunlop's Mission to St. Augustine in 1688," *SCHM* 34 (January 1933), 21.

44. "Dunlop's Mission," 20.

45. "Dunlop's Mission," 2.

46. "Dunlop's Mission," 22.

47. Spanish pieces of eight were the most common form of coinage in the British colonies and may have accounted for approximately half of all coins. It eventually evolved

into the dollar and became the "basic unit of the monetary system of the United States." John J. McCusker, *Money and Exchange in Europe and America, 1600–1775* (Chapel Hill: University of North Carolina Press, 1978), 7. There were about four pieces of eight to the pound sterling, so Carolina was asking, in addition to the slaves, for a compensation of approximately 350 pounds sterling.

48. "Dunlop's Mission," 2, 23.

49. "Memorial of the Hostilities."

50. W[illiam] Mure, J[ohn] Hamilton and Ja[mes] Stewart to William Dunlop, [n.d., received May 1687], in J. G. Dunlop, *The Dunlop Papers*, vol. 2: *The Dunlops of Dunlop: and of Auchenskaith, Keppoch, and Gairbraid* (Frome: Butler and Tanner, 1939), 131–132.

51. Dunlop, *Dunlop Papers*, 2:136.

52. Dunlop, *Dunlop Papers*, 2:140. The story of the Darien colony is ably told in John Prebble, *The Darien Disaster* (London: Secker and Warburg, 1968).

53. For Cardross, see Rowland et al., *History of Beaufort County*, 74, and Erskine, *Journal*.

54. Descendants in Carolina often dropped the final "e" in Cochrane.

55. See Chapter 6.

56. See Chapter 6.

57. John Stewart to William Dunlop, June 23, 1690, "Letters from John Stewart to William Dunlop," *SCHM* 32 (April 1931), 83–84.

58. "The Lords Proprietors to the Governor and Deputies," Apr. 10, 1693, in *Sketch*, 436.

59. October 18, 1690, *Records*, 2:294.

60. October 18, 1690, *Records*, 2:294.

61. Quotation from "Lords Proprietors to Governor Jas. Colleton," Dec. 2, 1689, in *Sketch*, 410; see also M. Eugene Sirmans, *Colonial South Carolina: A Political History, 1663–1763* (Chapel Hill: University of North Carolina Press, 1966).

62. Edward McCrady, *The History of South Carolina Under the Proprietary Government, 1670–1719* (1897; reprint, New York: Russell and Russell, 1969), 227–228.

63. Lesser, *South Carolina Begins*, 106n127.

64. See the discussion in Chapter 6.

65. "Lords Proprietors of Carolina to the Grand Council of South Carolina," May 13, 1691, in *Sketch*, 416.

66. "An Act for Laying a Tax or Duty on Skins or Furrs, For the Publick Use of This Province, and Regulating the Indian Trade," Sept. 26, 1691, in *Statutes*, 2:64–68.

67. A. S. Salley, Jr., ed., *Commissions and Instructions from the Lords Proprietors of Carolina to Public Officials of South Carolina, 1685–1715* (Columbia: Historical Commission of South Carolina, 1916), 24–28; Council meeting, June 15, 1692, in A. S. Salley, ed., *Journal of the Grand Council of South Carolina, April 11, 1692–September 26, 1692* (Columbia: Historical Commission of South Carolina, 1907), 39.

68. Lesser, *South Carolina Begins*, 141.

69. Council meeting, Apr. 14, 1692, *Journal of the Grand Council*, 6–7.

70. *Commissions and Instructions*, 74; McCrady, *History of South Carolina*, 266.

71. November 29, 1693, *Records*, 3:109–110.

72. November 29, 1693, *Records*, 3:111–112.

73. Lesser, *South Carolina Begins*, 182–183.

74. *SCCHJ, 1693*, 11–13 (quotation on 13).

75. "An Act for Destroying Beasts of Prey, and for Appoynting Magistrates for the Heareing and Determineing of all Causes and Controversies Between White Man and Indian, and Indian and Indian," Mar. 16, 1696, in *Statutes*, 2:108–111. The bill provides a roster of Settlement Indians at the time of enactment in 1696, and given its nature, it may be the most reliable list extant. The act applied to "the nations of Sante Helena, Causa, Wimbehe, Combehe, Edistoe, Stonoe, Kiaway, Itwan, Sewee, Santee and Cussoes."

76. November 12, 1693, *SCCHJ, 1693*, 21.

77. See "afterword" for further discussion of relations between Indians and Africans.

78. "An Act for Laying an Imposition upon Skinns and Furrs, For the Defence and Publick use of this Country," Mar. 16, 1696, in *Statutes*, 2:110–112.

CHAPTER 4: ARKANSAS, TUNICA, TAENSA, AND FRENCH MISSIONARIES

1. "Voyage of P. Jacques Marquette [Toward New Mexico]," in Reuben Gold Thwaites, ed., *The Jesuit Relations and Allied Documents*, 73 vols. (Cleveland: Burrows Brothers, 1896–1901, hereafter cited as *Jesuit Relations*), 59:134–159.

2. *Jesuit Relations*, 59:149–153.

3. John Gilmary Shea, *Discovery and Exploration of the Mississippi Valley with the Original Narratives of Marquette, Allouez, Membré, Hennepin, and Anastase Douay* (Redfield, N.Y.: Clinton Hall, 1852), 44n.

4. B. F. French also thought that they were Chickasaw. See his edition of Shea's *Discovery and Exploration*, published as vol. 4 of *Historical Collections of Louisiana, Embracing Translations of Many Rare and Valuable Documents . . .*, 5 vols. (New York: Wiley and Putnam, 1846–1853), 43n.

5. See the discussion in Chapter 6.

6. The Chickasaw, of course, met the Spanish when Soto's entrada came through, but unless there were strong language difficulties, which is possible, than Marquette is referring to these Indians having met Spanish black robes in the immediate past.

7. Verner W. Crane disagrees. See "The Tennessee River as the Road to Carolina: The Beginnings of Exploration and Trade," *Mississippi Valley Historical Review* 3 (1916), 3–18, and *The Southern Frontier, 1670–1732* (1929; reprint, New York: Norton, 1981), 39–40, 45–46.

8. Richebourg Gaillard McWilliams, trans. and ed., *Iberville's Gulf Journals* (University: University of Alabama Press, 1981), 198; Ruth Lapham Butler, trans., *Journal of Paul Du Ru: Missionary Priest to Louisiana* (Chicago: Caxton Club, 1934).

9. For the Jesuits, see Jean Delanglez, S.J., *The French Jesuits in Lower Louisiana (1700–1763)* (Washington, D.C.: Catholic University of America, 1935). A good summary of the dispute is in Marcel Giraud, *A History of French Louisiana*, vol. 1: *The Reign of Louis XIV, 1698–1715*, trans. Joseph C. Lambert (Baton Rouge: Louisiana University Press, 1974; originally published in France, 1953), 26–30.

10. These letters are contained in "Copie d'un lettre a Mr. de l'Evêde Quebec, Par Claude Del'Isle le 2 Jan 1699. par J. F. Buisson de St. Cosme missionaire [Jan. 2,] 1699," in ASH, 115–10: no. 13. Also included here are three additional letters: M. de Montigny

to Mother Superior, Jan. 2, 1699, and to [Bishop of Quebec?], May 6, 1699, and from M. de la Source [to Mother Superior], Aug. 12, 1699.

11. *Iberville's Gulf Journals,* 61.

12. *Jesuit Relations,* 59:159.

13. There was more than one calumet. Many observers note that there was one for peace and one for war.

14. *Jesuit Relations,* 59:133, 135.

15. Ian W. Brown, "The Calumet Ceremony in the Southeast and Its Archaeological Manifestations," *American Antiquity* 54 (1989), 311–331. For calumet usage in the Great Lakes region, see Richard White, *The Middle Ground: Indians, Empires, and Republics in the Great Lakes Region, 1650–1815* (Cambridge: Cambridge University Press, 1991), 21–22. The purpose of the ceremonies, as depicted in White's discussion, varied considerably from those described here. White observes that in the Great Lakes region, the ceremony "formed a part of a conscious framework for peace, alliance, exchange, and free movement among peoples." If "negotiations were successful," then a "full calument ceremony ratified the peace and created a fictive kinship relation between the person offering the pipe and the person specifically honored by the calumet." By contrast, in the South, I observe that the calumet could lead to better relations, perhaps even an alliance, between peoples but that often it was meant merely as a respite from hostilities.

16. *Iberville's Gulf Journals,* 77–78.

17. *Journal of Paul Du Ru,* 32.

18. Father James Gravier, "Journal of the Voyage of Father Gravier," in John Gilmary Shea, trans. and ed., *Early Voyages Up and Down the Mississippi, By Cavelier, St. Cosme, Le Sueur, Gravier and Guignas* (Albany, N.Y.: Joel Munsell, 1861), 125–129.

19. *Jesuit Relations,* 59:131.

20. *Iberville's Gulf Journals,* 122.

21. *Iberville's Gulf Journals,* 114, 122.

22. *Journal of Paul Du Ru,* 31.

23. These attacks are discussed in the next chapter.

24. Shea, *Early Voyages,* 43–86, translated that St. Cosme wrote: "while an Indian who was behind rocked us." This translation loses the sense of the document—Shea's translations tend to remove the intent of St. Cosme by making the language more palatable for Victorian sensibilities. I translated *bêlot* as bleating, based on its use in the early seventeenth century, according to William S. Woods, comp., *A Dictionarie of the French and English Tongues* [1611] (Columbia: University of South Carolina Press, 1950). This dictionary is quite useful for translating French of the period, though it is of limited value for terms related to Native Americans, many of which entered French after the dictionary was published.

25. St. Cosme, in "Copie d'un lettre."

26. St. Cosme, in "Copie d'un lettre."

27. Montigny [to Bishop of Quebec], May 6, 1699, included in "Copie d'un lettre."

28. St. Cosme, in "Copie d'un lettre."

29. See letters included in "Copie d'un lettre."

30. W. David Baird, *The Quapaw Indians: A History of the Downstream People* (Norman: University of Oklahoma Press, 1980), 27.

31. St. Cosme, in "Copie d'un lettre."

32. Charles Hudson, *The Southeastern Indians* (Knoxville: University of Tennessee Press, 1976), 269.

33. La Source also contended that the Taensa's only subsistence was maize and that they did not hunt like other "savages."

34. Montigny, May 6, 1699, and La Source, Aug. 18, 1699, in "Copie d'un lettre."

35. Tonti, the woodsmen who had guided them there, left to return to the Illinois in 1699. The priests sang Tonti's praises—he was the most experienced French frontiersmen along the Mississippi, and they must have looked with trepidation at continuing without him, though they also welcomed the opportunity to be forced to rely more on themselves.

36. La Source, Aug. 18, 1699, in "Copie d'un lettre."

37. Montigny, May 6, 1699, in "Copie d'un lettre."

38. La Source, Aug. 18, 1699, in "Copie d'un lettre." Montigny thought the villages five or six leagues from the Mississippi (May 6, 1699, in "Copie d'un lettre").

39. Montigny, May 6, 1699, in "Copie d'un lettre."

40. La Source, Aug. 8, 1699, in "Copie d'un lettre."

41. Michael P. Hoffman, "Protohistoric Tunican Indians in Arkansas," in Jeannie Whayne, comp., *Cultural Encounters in the Early South: Indians and Europeans in Arkansas* (Fayettevelle: University of Arkansas Press, 1995), 73.

42. The best introduction to the Tunica is Jeffrey P. Brain, *Tunica Archaeology*, Papers of the Peabody Museum of Archaeology and Ethnology, 78 (Cambridge, Mass.: Harvard University Press, 1988).

43. The Courouais probably refers to the Koroa, who sometimes lived with the Yazoo; see *Iberville's Gulf Journals*, 70n104.

44. Montigny, May 6, 1699. The Yazoo are believed to be culturally and linguistically in the Tunican family, but the proof is fleeting. Montigny noted that their language differed from the Tunica. See John R. Swanton, *Indian Tribes of the Lower Mississippi Valley and Adjacent Coast of the Gulf of Mexico*, Smithsonian Institution Bureau of American Ethnology, Bulletin 43 (Washington, D.C.: Government Printing Office, 1911), 9, 307, 309. Gravier, "Journal," 132–136, also said that Tunica and Yazoo were two separate languages.

45. *Iberville's Gulf Journals*, 143–144nn.

46. Montigny, May 6, 1699, in "Copie d'un lettre."

47. Montigny, May 6, 1699, in "Copie d'un lettre."

48. *Journal of Paul Du Ru*, 42, estimated one hundred cabins. Iberville recorded 150 families. This and other estimates of Iberville can be found in "Memoir of Iberville on the country of Mississippi, Mobile . . ." [June 30, 1703], in Pierre Margry, ed., *Découvertes et établissements des français dans l'ouest et dans le sud de l'Amerique Septentrionale (1614–1754)*, 6 vols. (Paris: Jouaust, 1876–1886), 4:602.

49. Montigny, May 6, 1699, in "Copie d'un lettre."

50. These figures are taken from Guillaume Delisle's notes on the Indian tribes who lived along the Mississippi, which he garnered from Iberville and other visitors to Louisiana. See ASH, 115–10: no. 17.

51. European contemporaries frequently observed that Indian women and children were more apt to be enslaved than men. This is discussed at greater length in later chapters.

52. Richard White notes that the French preferred to deal with the hierarchically organized lower Mississippi River peoples rather than the more northerly Algonquins. The Algonquins lacked "class divisions and state and religious institutions," which the French

interpreted as signifying "an absence of social order." The French "clearly regarded authority as being at the heart of not only society but humanity." In comparing "Canada Indians" to the Mississippians, White cites one Frenchman as favorably describing the Mississippians as "men." *Middle Ground,* 57.

53. Montigny, May 6, 1699, in "Copie d'un lettre."

54. La Source thought that there were thirteen.

55. Although Montigny spoke highly of the Taensa, he was apparently dissatisfied with the assignment. Father La Source, who liked Montigny and described how he was loved wherever he went, thought that the priest envied his own assignment with St. Cosme at the Tamaroas. Even before he settled at the Taensa, Montigny began planning a mission among the Natchez, who spoke the same language as the Taensa. Montigny had not yet met the Natchez, but he knew they had many more people than the Taensa, perhaps as many as two thousand—a larger group to cultivate than any they had encountered in the area. The restless Montigny, however, stayed nowhere very long, and after a short mission among the Indians, he left to travel through the colonies, even some of the English ones, returned to France, then went to China, and eventually became head of the foreign mission office in Paris. See *Journal of Paul Du Ru,* 31*n37.*

56. "Lettre d'un Missionnaire [François-Jolliet de Montigny] aux Taensas au Comte de Pontchartrain, ministre de la Marine," July 17, 1700, Bibliothèque Nationale, Paris, Manuscripts 7485:127, from photostats in the Manuscript Reading Room, LC.

57. *Iberville's Gulf Journals,* 129. *Journal of Paul Du Ru,* 41, reports that four or five were killed; Montigny, Jan. 2, 1699, in "Copie d'un lettre," says four; Gravier, "Journal," 137, says five. Montigny also asserted that they happily sacrificed their children.

58. *Iberville's Gulf Journals,* 129.

59. "Lettre d'un Missionnaire."

60. *Iberville's Gulf Journals,* 129–130.

61. "Lettre d'un Missionnaire."

62. *Iberville's Gulf Journals,* 129–130.

63. Gravier, "Journal," 140–141.

64. *Journal of Paul Du Ru,* 27.

65. "Lettre d'un Missionnaire." On the French priests' reaction to Indian mourning rituals, see James T. Axtell, "Last Rights: The Acculturation of Native Funerals in Colonial North America," in *The European and the Indian: Essays in the Ethnohistory of Colonial North American* (New York: Oxford University Press, 1981), 101–130.

66. The missionaries were very curious about the medicines Indians used to heal people, but they scorned the incantations and ceremonies that accompanied these cures.

67. "Lettre d'un Missionnaire."

68. *Journal of Paul Du Ru,* 26; "Lettre d'un Missionnaire."

69. Gravier, "Journal," 140–141.

70. *Journal of Paul Du Ru,* 29.

71. "Addition au premier memoire du Sieur Le Bartz [sic]," AE, Mémoires et Documents, Amérique, 1:156, microfilm, Manuscript Reading Room, LC.

72. *The Journal of Sauvole: Historical Journal of the Establishment of the French in Louisiana,* trans. and ed. Jay Higginbotham (Mobile, Ala.: Colonial Books, 1967), 37; Patricia K. Galloway, ed., *La Salle and His Legacy: Frenchmen and Indians in the Lower Mississippi Valley* (Jackson: University Press of Mississippi, 1982).

73. The Arkansas had told Marquette that they had not been to the Gulf of Mexico. *Jesuit Relations,* 59:153.

74. "Lettre d'un Missionnaire."

75. *Journal of Sauvole,* 40–41.

76. *Journal of Sauvole,* 37.

77. *Journal of Paul Du Ru,* 52.

78. *Journal of Sauvole,* 45.

CHAPTER 5: DIPLOMACY AND WAR, 1699–1706

1. The legend in its entirety was included in Herman Moll's *New Map of the North Parts of America,* which was published in his *World Described,* in both the 1720 and 1736 editions (London: n.p.). Portions also appear in his *Map of North and South Carolina and Florida* [1715], Map Room, Crown Collection, Ser. 3, LC. Nairne's *Map of South Carolina Shewing the Settlements of the English, French, and Indian Nations from Charles Town to the River Missisipi,* shows only a general area where "the Carolina Indians leave ther [sic] Canoes when they goe to War against ye Florideans." The map is an inset published as part of Edward Crisp's *Compleat Description of the Province of Carolina* [1711], and reproduced in William P. Cumming, *The Southeast in Early Maps* (Princeton, N.J.: Princeton University Press, 1958), pl. 45.

2. The "enormous geographical dilemma" La Salle faced in finding the Mississippi's mouth by sea is expertly told in Peter H. Wood, "La Salle: Discovery of a Lost Explorer," *American Historical Review* 89 (1984), 294–323. Contemporaries and later historians have maligned La Salle's character because he failed to re-find the Mississippi (and because he was murdered by some of his men). Wood suggests that the depiction of La Salle as incompetent is patently unfair, for the tools at his disposal, particularly those of cartography, were limited. He shows that La Salle and his men dealt rationally and diligently with the obstacles they encountered. Wood implies that La Salle's murder by a dissident party was not necessarily the product of his misconduct or mistreatment, nor just punishment of a deceitful character, but rather a bitter end to an expedition lost, discouraged, and isolated.

3. Iberville's life is recounted in Nellis Crouse, *Lemoyne d'Iberville: Soldier of New France* (Ithaca, N.Y.: Cornell University Press, 1954).

4. These colonists eventually were settled in Virginia. See Indenture of Daniel Coxe, Rawlinson Papers, A 271, folio 26, Manuscript Reading Room, LC, copies from Bodeleian Library, Oxford University; Daniel Coxe, *A Description of the English Province of Carolana . . .* [1722], ed. William S. Coker (Gainesville: University of Florida Press, 1976), xxxii–xxxvii.

5. [Jean-Baptiste du Bois] Duclos to [Comte de] Pontchartrain, "Memoir," Oct. 25, 1713, *MPA,* 2:125–127.

6. The place to begin for early Louisiana is Marcel Giraud, *A History of French Louisiana,* vol. 1: *The Reign of Louis XIV, 1698–1715,* trans. Joseph C. Lambert (Baton Rouge: Louisiana University Press, 1974; originally published in France, 1953); and Daniel H. Usner, Jr., *Indians, Settlers, and Slaves in a Frontier Exchange Economy: The Lower Mississippi Valley Before 1783* (Chapel Hill: University of North Carolina Press, 1992).

7. "Extrait d'une au lettre du meme [Henri de Tonti] au meme [Pierre LeMoyne d' Iberville] Des Chacta," Mar. 14, 1702, ASH, 115–10: no. 20.

8. Pierre LeMoyne d'Iberville, *Iberville's Gulf Journals,* trans. and ed. Richebourg Gaillard McWilliams (University: University of Alabama Press, 1981), 110 (hereafter cited as *Iberville's Gulf Journals*). The missionary was Albert Davion.

9. *Iberville's Gulf Journals,* 119; Paul Du Ru, *Journal of Paul Du Ru: Missionary Priest to Louisiana,* trans. Ruth Lapham Butler (Chicago: Caxton Club, 1934), 43.

10. For Hughes, see Eirlys M. Barker, "Pryce Hughes, Colony Planner, of Charles Town and Wales," *SCHM* 95 (October 1994), 302–313; Giraud, *History of French Louisiana,* 324–329; Verner Crane, *The Southern Frontier, 1670–1732* (1929; reprint, New York: Norton, 1981), 100–107.

11. *Iberville's Gulf Journals,* 133.

12. "Extrait d'une au lettre," May 14, 1702.

13. *The Journal of Sauvole: Historical Journal of the Establishment of the French in Louisiana,* trans. and ed. Jay Higginbotham (Mobile, Ala.: Colonial Books, 1967), 35.

14. *Iberville's Gulf Journals,* 144.

15. Jean-Baptiste Bénard de La Harpe, *The Historical Journal of the Establishment of the French in Louisiana,* trans. Virginia Koenig and Joan Cain, ed. Glenn R. Conrad (Lafayette: University of Southwestern Louisiana Press, 1971), 59.

16. *Iberville's Gulf Journals,* 172.

17. *Iberville's Gulf Journals,* 172-173. He also had to work for peace between the Choctaw and the French allied tribes (*Journal of Paul du Ru,* 54).

18. There was much discussion of Spain ceding Pensacola in 1705. See [Pontchartrain au] Daubenton, Apr. 8, 1705, AM, B2, 181:157; [Pontchartrain au] Amelot, July 22, 29, Sept. 2, 1705, AE, Espagne, 153:58, 97, 226; AM, B2, 182:245, 465; Oct. 7, 1705, 183:47; Nov. 4, 1705, AE, Espagne, 154:96, in which cession was abandoned.

19. *SCCHJ, August 13, 1701–August 28, 1701,* 4.

20. *SCCHJ, August 13, 1701–August 28, 1701,* 5, 7, 20.

21. *SCCHJ, August 13, 1701–August 28, 1701,* 15, 24, 32.

22. *SCCHJ, 1702,* 6

23. *Iberville's Gulf Journals,* 132, 175.

24. *SCCHJ, 1702,* 47–48.

25. La Harpe, *Historical Journal,* 59.

26. The joining of the Alabama with the Creek, and the relationship of the Alabama with the French in Mobile, can be ascertained, somewhat, in the migration stories recorded by Louis Le Clerc Milfort, who visited the Creek in 1780. *Memoirs, or a Quick Glance at My Various Travels and My Sojourn in the Creek Nation,* ed. and trans. Ben C. McCary (1802; reprint, Kennesaw: Continental Book, 1959). See also Albert S. Gatschet, *A Migration Legend of the Creek Indians, with a Linguistic, Historic and Ethnographic Introduction,* 2 vols. (1884; reprint, New York: AMS, 1969), 1:227–228.

27. For the invasion of Florida, see Charles W. Arnade, *The Siege of St. Augustine in 1702* (Gainesville: University of Florida Press, 1959).

28. A. S. Salley, Jr., ed., *Journal of the Grand Council of South Carolina, April 11, 1692–September 26, 1692* (Columbia: Historical Commission of South Carolina, 1907), 6, 45. Also see the discussion of Moore in Chapter 6.

29. *SCCHJ, 1702,* 80, 82, 83.

30. *SCCHJ, 1702,* 84, 85, 87, 89. On the use of plunder as a method of recruitment for the 1740 invasion of Florida, see Alan Gallay, *The Formation of a Planter Elite: Jona-*

than Bryan and the Southern Colonial Frontier (Athens: University of Georgia Press, 1989), 24–27.

31. Arnade, *Siege of St. Augustine,* 5–7.

32. He later gave them an extra half-barrel. *SCCHJ, 1703,* 36, 38, 47, 51.

33. *SCCHJ, 1703, 75.*

34. "The Representation and Address of several of the Members of this present Assembly return'd for Colleton County, and other Inhabitants of this Province, whose names are hereunto subscribed," in *Sketch,* 453–460.

35. *SCCHJ, 1703,* 61.

36. *The Humble Submission of the Kings, Princes, General, &c. to the Crown of England,* Aug. 15, 1705, Broadsides, Great Britain, photostatic copy in Rare Book Room, LC, portfolio 267, no. 7d.

37. Dorothy V. Jones, *License for Empire: Colonialism by Treaty in Early America* (Chicago: University of Chicago Press, 1982).

38. For Creek ethnography see J. Leitch Wright, Jr., *Creeks and Seminoles: The Destruction and Regeneration of the Muscogulge People* (Lincoln: University of Nebraska Press, 1986); and John R. Swanton, *Early History of the Creek Indians and Their Neighbors,* Smithsonian Institution Bureau of American Ethnology, Bulletin 73 (Washington, D.C.: Government Printing Office, 1922).

39. See, e.g., "Letter from the lieutenant of Apalachee, Antonio Matheos, to the Seffer Governor and Captain-General of Florida, regarding the English having returned to the province of Apalachicola," May 19, 1606 [1696], in Manuel Serrano y Sanz, ed., *Historical Documents of Florida and Louisiana: 16th to 18th Centuries* (Madrid: General Library of Victoriano Suárez, 1913), 218, where the towns of Colome (Kolomi) and Tasquiqui (Tuskegee) express friendship for the Spanish, who have been warring with nearby Cuseeta and Coweta.

40. André Pénicaut, *Fleur de Lys and Calumet: Being the Pénicaut Narrative of French Adventure in Louisiana,* trans. and ed. Richebourg Gaillard McWilliams (Tuscaloosa: University of Alabama Press, 1953, 1981), 63–65; La Harpe, *Historical Journal,* 64.

41. Pénicaut, *Fleur de Lys,* 66.

42. Pénicaut, *Fleur de Lys,* 66–67.

43. Pénicaut, *Fleur de Lys,* 68–69.

44. Instead of traveling southeast through the river system, the conflict forced them to use the Mississippi and approach Mobile from the west.

45. Pénicaut, *Fleur de Lys,* 73.

46. Pénicaut, as in much of his account, misdates events. This episode he placed in 1703. La Harpe, *Historical Journal,* 136, correctly noted that it was 1705.

47. Pénicaut, *Fleur de Lys,* 74–78.

48. Pénicaut, *Fleur de Lys,* 79.

49. D'Artaguiette au ministre [Pontchartrain], "Memoir on instructions given the late De Muy," Feb. 25, 1708, AC, C13, 2:313. There is a memoir of the same date by d'Artaguiette reprinted in *MPA,* vol. 3, but that is a different document.

50. Nicolas de La Salle to [Comte de] Pontchartrain, May 20, 1703, AC, C13, 1:387.

51. [Jean-Baptiste Le Moyne de] Bienville to [Comte de] Pontchartrain, Feb. 25, 1708, *MPA,* 3:113.

52. *SCCHJ, 1703*, 75–76.

53. *SCCHJ, 1703*, 48.

54. *SCCHJ, 1703*, 105.

55. *SCCHJ, 1703*, 121.

56. Crane believed that the assembly's instructions that Moore should seek a diplomatic solution "laid a serious restriction upon a campaign which must pay its way out of slaves and plunder." But the fact that the assembly provided no pay shows that it fully expected the invasion force to obtain slaves and plunder. In the event, this is exactly what happened: first the invaders took slaves, then they discussed peace. Crane, *Southern Frontier*, 78–79.

57. See Chapter 6 for Apalachee attacks on the Creek in the late seventeenth century.

58. John H. Hann, *Apalachee: The Land Between the Rivers* (Gainesville: University Presses of Florida, 1988), provides the most detailed comparison of Moore's and Spanish accounts of the invasion.

59. Pénicaut, *Fleur de Lys*, 102–103, 133–135. As late as 1721 the Apalachee threatened to return to the Spanish if they were not provided with a priest. See "Minutes of the Council of Commerce of Louisiana," Feb. 8, 1721, *MPA*, 3:303.

60. A major revolt against the Spanish occurred in 1647, about which little is known of the causes. See John H. Hann, "Apalachee Revolt," in Alan Gallay, *Colonial Wars of North America, 1512–1763: An Encyclopedia* (New York: Garland, 1996), 37–38.

61. Don Patricio, Cacique of Ivitachuco, and Don Andrés, Cacique of San Luis, to the King, Feb. 12, 1699, in Mark F. Boyd, Hale G. Smith, and John W. Griffin, trans. and eds., *Here They Once Stood: The Tragic End of the Apalachee Missions* (Gainesville: University of Florida Press, 1951), 24–26.

62. Don Patricio and Don Andrés to the King, Feb. 12, 1699.

63. Don Patricio Hinachuba to Don Antonio Ponce de León, Apr. 10, 1699, Don Antonio Ponce de León to the King on behalf of Don Patricio Hinachuba, Jan. 29, 1702, and Royal Cédula, May 7, 1700, all in *Here They Once Stood*, 26–27, 27–29, 29–30.

64. Royal Cédula, May 7, 1700.

65. Andrés González de Barcia Carballido y Zúñiga, *Barcia's Chronological History of the Continent of Florida* [1723], trans. and ed. Anthony Kerrigan (Gainesville: University of Florida Press, 1951), 351.

66. Hann, *Apalachee*, 279. Hann discounts the exportation of large numbers of slaves, writing, "It seems that if they were as massive as would be required to meet the numbers claimed by Moore, they would have elicited some comment." I disagree with Hann here and discuss the exportation of Indians from the region further in Chapter 11.

67. La Harpe, *Historical Journal*, 66

68. La Harpe noted that only two Apalachee villages remained loyal to the Spanish, "the majority of whose inhabitants were Catholic." *Historical Journal*, 63.

69. La Harpe, *Historical Journal*, 66.

70. John H. Hann, *A History of the Timucua Indians and Missions* (Gainesville: University Press of Florida, 1996), 302.

71. Swanton, *Early History*, 123.

72. See Chapter 7 for a discussion of Apalachee demographics on the Savannah River. The 1708 census counts only males, of which 250 were recorded. That number increased to 275 seven years later. SC Transcripts, 7:238.

73. I discuss the overall impact of slaving on the Florida Indians in Chapter 11.

74. Several maps record the attacks on Timucua. Many of these follow John Barnwell's 1722 untitled map of the American South. Barnwell, who is discussed at length in later chapters, was among the most knowledgeable of men in the South on Indian affairs. In the aforementioned map he included the following notation in the center of Florida: "Province of the Timmoquas Wholy Laid waste being distroyed by ye Carolinians 1706." Photocopy, Map Room, LC, from original in Public Record Office, United Kingdom. Of the Gulf Coast raids he noted: "Tocobogga Indians Destroyed 1709." William Bull's untitled map of the American South includes the notation: "Province of the Timoquas destroy'd by the Carolinians in 1706." Photocopy, Map Room, LC, from original in Public Record Office. R. W. Seale's map *South Carolina and Georgia, and Parts adjacent; from the latest Improvements,* published in *A New and Complete History of the British Empire in America,* vol. 3 (London: n.p., 1756), 265, also notes: "Timooquas destroy'd by the Carolinians 1706."

75. "Proposition d'une entreprise sur la Caroline pour en chasser les Anglois," 1705, AM, B4, 29:213.

76. D'Artaguiette au Comte de Pontchartrain, ministre de la Marine, Feb. 20, 1711, AC, C13A, 2:641; de Bienville au Comte de Pontchartrain, ministre de la Marine, June 20, 1711, AC, C13B, 1:n.p.

77. [Unknown author], "Etat des sauvages qui habitent depuis les Alibamons, jusqu'à la Caroline," [1713?], AC, C13C, 1:358.

78. M. de Lamothe à M. le Gouverneur de la Caroline, June 3, 1714, AC, C13, 3:489.

79. La Harpe, *Historical Journal,* 66.

80. "Abstract of Letters from Bienville to Pontchartrain," July 28, 1706, *MPA,* 2:25; de Bienville au Comte de Pontchartrain, ministre de la Marine, Oct. 10, 1706, AC, C13B, 1:n.p.

81. La Harpe, *Historical Journal,* 75.

82. La Harpe, *Historical Journal,* 75.

83. La Harpe, *Historical Journal,* 68–69, 76.

84. "Proposition d'une entreprise sur la Caroline"; [Pontchartrain au] M. Amelot, July 29, 1705, AM, B2, 182:212.

85. [Unknown author], "Memoire grande d'Entreprises de Gaine Projet pour se rendre Maitre et Detruire la ville de Charleston [sic]" [1703?], AC, C13A, 1:445; [Iberville au Pontchartrain], June 26, 1704, AM, B4, 26:481.

86. "Proposition d'une entreprise sur la Caroline,"; [Pontchartrain au] Mon Coudray, Apr. 1, 1705, AM, B2, 181:10; [Pontchartrain au] M Le duc & Gramont, Apr. 8, 1705, AM, B2, 181:156; [Pontchartrain au] M. Amelot, July 29, 1705, AM, B2, 182:212.

87. [Pontchartrain] à M. Amelot, Oct. 7, 1705, AM B2, 183:47; [Pontchartrain] à M. Amelot, Oct. 7, 1705, AE, Espagne, 153:365; [Memoire], Nov. 3, 1705, AM, B4, 29:219; [Pontchartrain au] M. Amelot, Feb. 24, 1706, AE, Espagne, 163:129; [Pontchartrain au] M. Amelot, AM, B2, 187:518.

88. [Pontchartrain au Chateauguay], Mar. 8, 1703, AM, B2, 167:697; [Pontchartrain au] Mgo le Card[inal] d'Estrées, Mar. 21, 1703, AM, B2, 167:674.

89. [Notes by Guillaume Delisle on Indians near the banks of the Mississippi], [1703?], ASH, 115–10: no. 17. Other Delisle extractions are in the same source and in ASH, 115–10: no. 20, and 115–11: no. 12.

90. Giraud, *History of French Louisiana,* 16; Jean Delanglez, "The Sources of the Delisle Map of America, 1703," *Mid-America* 25 (1943), 275–298.

91. An excellent account of Drake's methods and the subsequent views of them can be found in John Cummins, *Francis Drake: Life of a Hero* (New York: St. Martin's, 1997).

92. "Proposition d'une entreprise sur la Caroline" provides one of the fullest accounts of French plans.

93. La Harpe, *Historical Journal,* 75–76; *Iberville's Gulf Journals,* 12. Nellis Crouse's biography *Lemoyne d'Iberville* provides background on the Canadian's imperial vision and details of the assault against Nevis and Saint Christopher.

94. "Affidavit and testimonio by the notary Juan Solana relative to the English of Carolina," Oct. 26, 1706, from Archivo General de Indies, Seville, Spain, AI 58–2–3, 32, trans. Edith Luther, Stetson Collection, P. K. Yonge Library, University of Florida, Gainesville (hereafter cited as Stetson Collection).

95. "Affadavit and testimonio by the notary Juan Solana."

96. Extract of "Autos de una carta del gobernador de la Florida del 28 de Febrero relative to the English and the natives," Stetson Collection, A1 58–2–33, Mar. 7, 1707.

97. "Affidavit and testimonio by the notary Juan Solana."

98. *Boston News-Letter,* Oct. 21–28, 1706. About twenty of the prisoners drowned. Shackled in pairs, they were transported in piraguas that capsized in the Atlantic.

99. La Harpe, *Historical Journal,* 73.

100. *SCCHJ, October 1707–February 1708,* Oct. 28, 1707, 27, 28.

101. House Journals, Book October [23]–November [11], 1707, Oct. 28, 1707, 116.

102. House Journals, Book October [23]–November [11], 1707, Nov. 11, 1707, 87–88.

103. *SCCHJ, October 1707–February 1708,* 13, 27, 28, 33, 36, 46, 48–50; House Journals, Book October [23]–November [11], 1707, Nov. 8, 12, 1707, 90–93, 98.

104. House Journals, Book October [23]–November [11], 1707, Oct. 12, 28, 31, Nov. 1, 3, 6, 1707, 111–112, 116, 134–135, 137, 139, 142; Book November 24, 1708–December 18, 1708, Dec. 9, 20, 1708, 105; Book February 1, 1709–February 19, 1709, Feb. 7, 19, 1709, 126, 137. According to John Stewart, when the expedition was sent it yielded nothing; see Chapter 6. This may be why the assembly did not discuss it in its records.

CHAPTER 6: BRITISH IMPERIALISM
AND INDIAN WARFARE IN THE SOUTH

1. Fellow Scots trader George Smith, who had inspired Stewart to undertake the trade, also befriended Nairne. Smith provided testimony for Nairne when he was arrested for treason. See Chapter 7. "Certificate . . . [regarding Captain Thomas Nairne] From George Smith," 9/22/08, Maggs 498, HM 1387, HL.

2. John Lawson, *A New Voyage to Carolina* [London, 1709], ed. Hugh T. Lefler (Chapel Hill: University of North Carolina Press, 1967); André Pénicaut, *Fleur de Lys and Calumet: Being the Pénicaut Narrative of French Adventure in Louisiana,* trans. and ed. Richebourg Gaillard McWilliams (Tuscaloosa: University of Alabama Press, 1953, 1981). Other lengthy accounts, such as the journals of Bénard de La Harpe and Pierre Le Moyne d'Iberville, have much valuable information but do not focus on Indian life and culture.

3. Peter H. Wood, *Black Majority: Negroes in Colonial South Carolina from 1670*

Through the Stono Rebellion (New York: Norton, 1974), 57*n83;* Verner W. Crane, *The Southern Frontier, 1670–1732* (1929; reprint, New York: Norton, 1981), 103.

4. Stewart to [William, Lord Dartmouth], June 18, 1712, CO, copies, Manuscript Reading Room, LC, Ser. 5, 9:53. Stewart's father's first cousin, Marie Stewart, daughter of the earl of Orkney, was reduced to poverty by 1616, so it seems that the family's misfortunes preceded the Civil War. See "Petition from Marie Stewart natural daughter of the deceased Patrick, Earl of Orkney, who was in a state of destitution," in *Register of the Privy Council of Scotland* (hereafter cited as *Register*), 2d Ser., vol. 8: *1544–1660* (Edinburgh: H. M. General Register House, 1808), 344–345.

5. Refusal to take the oath could result in imprisonment, banishment to the colonies, torture, or death. Many of the Scots prisoners banished to Carolina had refused to take the oath or were found attending illegal conventicles. A John Stewart was arrested for the latter in 1675, though there is no way of telling if it is the same one. See *Register*, 3d Ser., vol. 4: *1673–1676* (1911), 664. For the banishment of prisoners, most of who were religious dissidents refusing to take the oath, see *Register*, vol. 11: *1684* (1924), 16, 28, 70, 95, 102, 111, 130, 131, 319. One prisoner, Alexander Stewart (relationship to John Stewart unknown), refused to go to Carolina. He was executed a month later in March 1684. *Register*, vol. 8: *1683–1684* (Glasgow: James Hedderwick and Sons, 1915), 671–672. A boy of eighteen who had refused the oath petitioned the Privy Council to protect him from torture because he was so young. The council assented. *Register*, vol. 11: *1684*, 69.

6. See the discussion of Scots emigration in Chapter 3.

7. June 23, 1690, "Letters from John Stewart to William Dunlop," *SCHM* 32 (April 1931), 83–84 (hereafter cited as "Stewart to Dunlop").

8. October 20, 1693, "Stewart to Dunlop" (July 1931), 174. Earlier Stewart had asked Dunlop to deter his wife from following him to Carolina, for "she has no stock to bring with her," and her prospects for charity were much greater in Scotland, where this daughter of a bishop might obtain through Lord Cardross a "salary out of the Royal Treasury." June 23, 1690, "Stewart to Dunlop" (April 1931), 111–112.

9. "Stewart to Dunlop" (April 1931), 111–112.

10. Like the proprietors, Stewart expected silk to become the colony's main product, predicting that in a few years' time (he was writing in 1690) that a million trees would be planted for that purpose.

11. April 27, 1690, "Stewart to Dunlop" (January 1931), 6.

12. "Stewart to Dunlop" (January 1931), 15–17.

13. "Stewart to Dunlop" (January 1931), 17.

14. Some of the laws he recommended for Carolina covered post offices, juries, the destruction of wolves, Indians killing hogs, runaway slaves, perjury, and the stealing of cedar and fruit trees. "Stewart to Dunlop" (January 1931), 18.

15. June 23, 1690, "Stewart to Dunlop" (April 1931), 89.

16. After a duel with Robert Stevens, in which Stewart thought he was the victor, an ally of James Moore, Maurice Mathews, whom the Scotsman despised above all others, spread stories that disparaged Stewart's performance in the scuffle. Stewart informed Mathews by letter that Stevens was a lying rogue in nature and "dwarfy" like a "musketo" and that Stewart's sword "quickly shall justify my courage and his baseness." To Stevens he wrote a "stinging" note, "calling him puny hero and a villainous calumniator," re-

minding him that it was he who had disarmed Stevens. Stewart demanded that Stevens admit as much in a letter or the "2 pricks he gave me I would now repay with interest." If Stevens did not send a true account "of our duel I would post him in Charlestown and everywhere."

Stevens and Stewart made up their differences and became friends, but Stewart was soon challenged by Job How, their quarrel arising from a speech How had made in the assembly. They stood for six minutes "sword to sword" within two feet of each other before the duel was halted by the governor's order. In an ensuing melee, How fled. Stewart proudly proclaimed himself victor and called How the "mockery of the town." Stewart believed that all his enemies were now "unwilling to meddle at sharpers with me," but he remained on the alert, for "I shall far sooner sacrifice a life subject to so many misfortunes rather than enjoy life with dishonor, especially when it reflects on my country," Scotland. And so, "for a month on end," he lay at night "in bed with naked sword before me and charged gun."

Though he did not write of other duels, Stewart noted his continued need for a sword to defend himself from enemies, many of whom he accumulated in politics. Death threats against Stewart were common: "My vulgar friends gives me warning that some would kill me." But he would not back down: "I tells them to tell again I hated a coward, that a just cause or honor led the way and therefore I would be the more forward, bold and confident, and it added much to my mettle." When one man threatened him in a tavern, Stewart "turned him our of doors and jocked his senses to folly." When another attacked him "with blows," he threw him down and straddled him for a quarter hour, forcing him to "beg my pardon that night and next morning," and making him spend money on "the company." "Stewart to Dunlop" (April 1931), 105, 108–109, and Apr. 27, 1690 (January 1931), 26–27.

17. At one point, Stewart related how he once spent twenty-one hours in a room with his archenemy Maurice Mathews, neither man saying a word! "Stewart to Dunlop" (April 1931), 109.

18. Many colonists used the occasion of the overthrow of James II in 1689 to take over local government in the name of William III, but local and not imperial issues guided their actions. Jacob Leisler in New York was hanged for his usurpation of the government, his reprieve arriving too late from King William to save his neck. For Leisler's Rebellion in New York, see David William Voorhees, "Leisler's Rebellion," in Alan Gallay, ed., *Colonial Wars of North America, 1512–1763: An Encyclopedia* (New York: Garland, 1996), 370–372; for Massachusetts, see Viola Florence Barnes, *The Dominion of New England: A Study in British Colonial Policy* (New Haven: Yale University Press, 1923); for Maryland, see David S. Lovejoy, *The Glorious Revolution in America* (New York: Harper and Row, 1959).

19. See Chapter 3.

20. June 23, 1690, "Stewart to Dunlop" (April 1931), 94.

21. April 27, 1690, "Stewart to Dunlop" (January 1931), 29–30.

22. June 23, 1690, "Stewart to Dunlop" (April 1931), 105. Edward McCrady, *The History of South Carolina Under the Proprietary Government, 1670–1719* (1897; New York: Russell and Russell, 1969), 228, claims that Colleton had declared martial law "under pretence that some danger threatened the country" but actually to assert control over his opponents in the government. Later, McCrady adds, Colleton thought the

colony threatened by Spanish invasion. And yet, Stewart specifically states that the colony was at war, but he does not identify who with—though he probably meant the Spanish, with whom there was not an official war but who had invaded twice in the last decade and might be considering another strike. Stewart had no reason to state in his letter that there was a war when none existed, and McCrady's claims that Colleton had invented the danger should be discounted.

23. June 23, 1690, "Stewart to Dunlop" (April 1931), 107–108.

24. On Cherokee slaveholding, see Theda Perdue, *Slavery and the Evolution of Cherokee Society* (Knoxville: University of Tennessee Press, 1979), and *Cherokee Women: Gender and Culture Change, 1700–1835* (Lincoln: University of Nebraska Press, 1998).

25. June 23, 1690, "Stewart to Dunlop" (April 1931), 109; Apr. 27, 1690, "Stewart to Dunlop" (January 1931), 30.

26. Apr. 27, 1690, "Stewart to Dunlop" (January 1931), 30.

27. June 23, 1690, "Stewart to Dunlop" (April 1931), 112.

28. Colleton initially rejected the plan. Stewart had proposed venturing all the way to the Illinois country, where he would attack the French and seize their skins. Colleton feared that this would show the French the route to Carolina. "Stewart to Dunlop" (April 1931), 113.

29. October 20, 1693, "Stewart to Dunlop" (July 1931), 172. Ryal refers to a Spanish coin common in the English colonies.

30. June 23, 1690, "Stewart to Dunlop" (April 1931), 92.

31. John R. Swanton, *Early History of the Creek Indians and Their Neighbors,* Smithsonian Institution Bureau of American Ethnology, Bulletin 73 (Washington, D.C.: Government Printing Office, 1922), 284.

32. October 20, 1693, "Stewart to Dunlop" (July 1931), 171–172.

33. June 23, 1690, "Stewart to Dunlop" (April 1931), 92.

34. October 20, 1693, "Stewart to Dunlop" (July 1931), 171–172.

35. June 23, 1690, "Stewart to Dunlop" (April 1931), 89.

36. Lawrence Sanders Rowland, Alexander Moore, and George Rogers, Jr., *The History of Beaufort County, South Carolina,* vol. 1: *1514–1861* (Columbia: University of South Carolina Press, 1996), 70; quotation from June 23, 1690, "Stewart to Dunlop" (April 1931), 110.

37. See the discussion in Chapter 4.

38. Thomas Nairne to Doctor Marston, Aug. 20, 1705, enclosed with Robert Stevens to the Society [SPG], November 1705, in SPG, Ser. A, vol. 2, no. 156:347–357.

39. On the Swiss settlement at Purrysburg, see Arlin Charles Migliazzo, "Ethnic Diversity on the Southern Frontier: A Social History of Purrysburg, South Carolina, 1732–1792" (Ph.D. diss., Washington State University, 1982).

40. [Thomas Nairne], *A Letter from South Carolina* . . . [London, 1710], reprinted in Jack P. Greene, ed. and intro., *Selling a New World: Two Colonial South Carolina Promotional Pamphlets* (Columbia: University of South Carolina Press, 1989).

41. "'A Narrative . . . Of An Assembly . . . January The 2d, 1705/6': New Light on Early South Carolina Politics," *SCHM* 85 (July 1984), 184.

42. The dispute between Johnson and Nairne is discussed further in Chapter 7.

43. All quotations in the preceding, current, and following paragraphs are from Thomas Nairne, *Letter from South Carolina.*

44. Thomas Nairne, *Nairne's Muskhogean Journals: The 1708 Expedition to the Mississippi River*, ed. Alexander Moore (Jackson: University Press of Mississippi, 1988).

45. Nairne, *Nairne's Muskhogean Journals*, 39.

46. Nairne, *Nairne's Muskhogean Journals*, 43.

47. Nairne, *Nairne's Muskhogean Journals*, 69–70n26.

48. There are obvious parallels here with European bearing of arms in the Middle Ages, especially as professed in the Arthurian romances, where men performed at tournaments and in battle to serve individual women—poor performance could mean the loss of a lady's love.

49. Nairne, *Nairne's Muskhogean Journals*, 46, 48.

50. Nairne, *Nairne's Muskhogean Journals*, 44–45.

51. Nairne, *Nairne's Muskhogean Journals*, 45.

52. Nairne, *Nairne's Muskhogean Journals*, 38.

53. Nairne, *Nairne's Muskhogean Journals*, 51–52. Nairne also failed to mention that a town of Chickasaw had migrated close to the colony on the Savannah River, where they found employment working for Carolinians in the Indian trade as burdeners. The Chickasaw he visited looked down on these Savannah River Chickasaw.

54. Nairne, *Nairne's Muskhogean Journals*, 39.

55. Nairne, *Nairne's Muskhogean Journals*, 38–41.

56. See Charles M. Hudson, *The Southeastern Indians* (Knoxville: University of Tennessee Press, 1976), for an overview of southern Indians.

57. Nairne, *Nairne's Muskhogean Journals*, 51.

58. Nairne, *Nairne's Muskhogean Journals*, 53.

59. Nairne, *Nairne's Muskhogean Journals*, 52.

60. Nairne, *Nairne's Muskhogean Journals*, 47.

61. Nairne, *Nairne's Muskhogean Journals*, 38–39. On the use of horses by traders, see M. Thomas Hatley, *The Dividing Path: Cherokee and South Carolinians Through the Era of the American Revolution* (New York: Oxford University Press, 1993), 38–39. The cost of Indian slaves is discussed in Chapter 11.

62. See the discussion in Chapter 7.

63. Nairne, *Nairne's Muskhogean Journals*, 37.

64. There is no adequate history of the Chickasaw in the colonial period. For the Choctaw before 1700, see Patricia K. Galloway, *Choctaw Genesis, 1500–1700* (Lincoln: University of Nebraska Press, 1996).

65. Nairne, *Nairne's Muskhogean Journals*, 60.

66. For an introduction to European conceptions of Indian warfare, see the excellent essays in James Axtell, *The European and the Indian: Essays in the Ethnohistory of Colonial North America* (New York: Oxford University Press, 1981); and Francis Jennings, *The Invasion of America: Indians, Colonialism, and the Cant of Conquest* (Chapel Hill: University of North Carolina Press, 1974). On the culture of warfare among southern Indians, see James H. Merrell, *The Indians' New World: Catawbas and Their Neighbors from European Contact Through the Era of Removal* (Chapel Hill: University of North Carolina Press, 1989), 119–122.

67. For the creation of warriors among the Chickasaw, see Nairne, *Nairne's Muskhogean Journals*, 43–44.

68. Helen Rountree provides an extensive discussion of the training of adolescent

Powhatan males to military tasks. See Rountree, *The Powhatan Indians of Virginia: Their Traditional Culture* (Norman: University of Oklahoma Press, 1989), 79–87.

69. See below for discussion of Apalachee and Choctaw pressure on the Creek.

70. Three accounts of the La Salle expedition report the war between the Arkansas and Chickasaw. See John D. Stubbs, Jr., "The Chickasaw Contact with the La Salle Expedition in 1682," in Patricia K. Galloway, ed., *La Salle and His Legacy: Frenchmen and Indians in the Lower Mississippi Valley* (Jackson: University Press of Mississippi, 1982).

71. James H. Merrell makes a similar point about the Cherokee in comparison to the Catawba: the latter had a reputation as "fierce" warriors, while the former were "scorned." Merrell notes that whereas the Cherokee "could rely on their mountainous terrain for protection," the "Ancestors of the Catawbas lacked such natural defenses and may have compensated by developing superior martial skills." See *Indians' New World*, 119–122 (quotations on 119).

72. Nairne, *Nairne's Muskhogean Journals*, 50.

73. Nairne, *Nairne's Muskhogean Journals*, 56.

74. Nairne, *Nairne's Muskhogean Journals*, 50.

75. It is reasonable to believe that in his first six years in the colony (1684–1690) he conducted many, if not all, of the experiments he claimed to have conducted. Dunlop, his correspondent, would have known if Stewart was lying because he had been with him in the colony.

76. Stewart to [Dartmouth], June 18, 1712.

77. Decades later the Europeans remained dependent on Indians in the New World. The anonymous author of *State of the British and French Colonies in North America . . .* (London: A Millar, 1755), 70, would write: "Therefore, in case of any war, either with *Indians* alone, or where they are auxiliaries, we must have *Indians* oppose *Indians*. They must be fought with their own way. Regular forces being wholly unacquainted with their way of making war can be of no service against them: they are only of use to defend a fort, or to support *Indian* forces against regular troops. . . . The *French* of *Canada* know the importance of *Indians* on this account, and therefore never undertake any expedition without them."

78. Stewart to [Dartmouth], June 18, 1712.

79. Though writing later in the century, Edmond Atkin expressed a typical European view of Choctaw character in a lengthy report he drew up for the British government: "Of all the Indians the Choctaws bear the worst character. They are subtle, deceitful, insolent, lucrative, beggarly, vicious, and indolent to such a degree, that for want of planting corn sufficient, living for the most part miserably, they eat creatures and things untasted by other Indians. And withal they are less Warlike than those before described; insomuch that Govr. Vaudreüil, in a Letter to the French Secretary of State, said 'That he believed the Chicasaws, if they had to do with them only (tho' near 10 times their Number) would in the end Destroy them.'" Wilbur R. Jacobs, ed., *The Appalachian Indian Frontier: The Edmond Atkin Report and Plan of 1755* (Lincoln: University of Nebraska Press, 1967), 71.

80. Stewart to [Dartmouth], June 18, 1712.

81. John Stewart to Queen Anne, Mar. 10, 1711, AC, microfilm copies, Manuscript Reading Room, LC, C13C, 2:80.

82. Stewart to Queen Anne, Mar. 10, 1711.

83. Stewart to Queen Anne, Mar. 10, 1711.

84. Nairne to Robert Fenwick, Apr. 13, 1708, in *Nairne's Muskhogean Journals,* 53. Additional discussion of Chickasaw military culture by Nairne is in Thomas Nairne to Landgrave Thomas Smith, Jan. 20, 1708, in *Nairne's Muskhogean Journals,* 41–44.

85. Stewart to Queen Anne, Mar. 10, 1711.

86. Taking Indian leaders to England to impress them with British power was done with much fanfare during Queen Anne's reign. See Richmond P. Bond, *Queen Anne's American Kings* (Oxford: Clarendon, 1952).

87. The discussion above is based on Stewart to Queen Anne, Mar. 10, 1711.

88. He provided no introduction to these remarks other than addressing himself to the queen and identifying himself as "John Stewart of Carolina Gentleman, An European and American traveller." He expected the queen simply to pick up where he had left off in his previous epistle to her and never considered that she might not have read that or any other of his correspondence. He also was unaware that the French had captured his last letter to the queen, and he probably had not sent more than one copy because the letter was so long. But even if she had received correspondence from him, would she have read it? Stewart's lack of literary skills, poor handwriting, prolixity, and the subject matter—Indians described in gritty detail—would have deterred the queen. Yet King James V's great-grandson fully expected the queen to read his letters. They were a way for him to validate his worth. Who else but he could provide such important knowledge and such gruesome details as he had witnessed?

89. John Stewart to Queen Anne, October 1711, AC, microfilm copies, Manuscript Reading Room, LC, C13C, 2:72; pulse refers to the seeds of leguminous plants. Other European observers noted that Indian armies marched slowly so that they could stop and hunt—Nairne thought that it was because they loved the sport of hunting, but Stewart points out the necessity of the hunt. Nairne, *Nairne's Muskhogean Journals,* 53.

90. See, e.g., William Cronon, *Changes in the Land: Indians, Colonists, and the Ecology of New England* (New York: Hill and Wang, 1983).

91. La Harpe reported that the Chickasaw carried three hundred Choctaw into slavery in 1706. This might have been a different invasion. Jean-Baptiste Bénard de La Harpe, *The Historical Journal of the Establishment of the French in Louisiana,* trans. Virginia Koenig and Joan Cain, ed. Glenn R. Conrad (Lafayette: University of Southwestern Louisiana Press, 1971), 73.

92. Stewart to Queen Anne, Mar. 10, 1711.

93. Stewart to Queen Anne, October 1711.

94. See, e.g., the discussion of Apalachee attacks on the Coweta and other Creek groups in "Letter from the lieutenant of Apalachee, Antonio Matheos, to the Seffer Governor and Captain-General of Florida, regarding the English having returned to the province of Apalachicola," May 19, 1606 [1686], in *Historical Documents of Florida and Louisiana, 16th to 18th Centuries,* trans. Manuel Serrano y Sanz (Madrid: General Library of Victoriano Suárez, 1912), 217–222.

95. Stewart to Queen Anne, October 1711.

96. Stewart to Queen Anne, October 1711.

97. Stewart mentioned that the famine compelled Creek to go three hundred miles in search of corn. (He had to remain behind because of his injuries.) When Stewart returned to the Creek in 1706, he again had the misfortune of arriving during "calamitous

times." He joined them on an invasion, from which they returned home bringing a "rag-ing pestilence . . . from their enemy's country in their army." The Creek had killed three hundred men but refused to bury the dead despite Stewart's pleadings. They had stayed for six days among the unburied corpses, from which Stewart implies they ate, for "both Illinois and Iroquois have told me that the foot and cheek of a man was delicious food and the sweetest in the world," even better than "bear's paw," which he knew from expe-rience was the tastiest part of the bear.

98. Stewart to Queen Anne, October 1711. This leads me to believe that he is talk-ing about the Apalachee and that he participated in one of the invasion forces to Florida from 1702 to 1704, most likely the one conducted by the Creek against the western Apalachee and Chacato in the summer of 1704. He also mentions that when they got to the enemy towns they found crucifixes, which indicated that these were Spanish-allied Indians. Stewart may have participated in the later invasion not only for profit and be-cause he was on intimate terms with the Creek allies of the English but also because he had knowledge of the Apalachee country and its Indians from this earlier invasion.

99. We have several accounts by Frenchmen of torture in the Mississippi Valley, but these are from later decades. The French recognized that they would be viewed as cowards if they did not adapt to the Indians' conception of bravery under torture. Thus, in 1736, when seventeen Frenchmen, including a priest, were burned alive by the Chickasaw, the victims sang, "since it is the custom of the Indians, who only judge the bravery of a war-rior by the stronger or weaker sounds of his voice at the moment that they kill him." See Sieur de Crémont to Jérome Phélypeaux Maurepas, Feb. 21, 1737, and D'Artaguiette to Maurepas, Oct. 24, 1737, *MPA*, 4:141, 149.

100. The metaphor was probably Stewart's, though there were chickens among the Ouma and although Stewart asserted that the Creek had them, too; as with much of this speech, however, it is not a literal rendering but one that tries to recapture the gist of what was said.

101. Chunky was a popular game among southern Indians, sometimes pitting towns against one another. See James Adair, *History of the American Indians* [1775], ed. Samuel Cole Williams (New York: Promontory, 1930), 431; Hudson, *Southeastern Indians,* 221–222, 421–425; and Lewis H. Larson, Jr., "Historic Guale Indians of the Georgia Coast and the Impact of the Spanish Mission Effort," in Jerald T. Milanich and Samuel Proctor, eds., *Tacachale: Essays on the Indians of Florida and Southeastern Georgia During the His-toric Period* (Gainesville: University Press of Florida, 1978), 128–130.

102. Stewart does not identify the speaker as a *heniha.* I have drawn from the term used later in the century to describe the person who served as a chief's official orator. For the use of these speakers, see Alan Gallay, *The Formation of a Planter Elite: Jonathan Bryan and the Southern Colonial Frontier* (Athens: University of Georgia Press, 1989), 142.

103. Carved or hollowed by burning cedar or cypress trees, piraguas were the basic form of water-based transportation in the South. They could be quite large and manned by upward of thirty-five paddlers.

104. In much of this speech and others, the Indian orators spoke in the plural when referring to the white men then among them. I believe that Stewart must have brought one or two helpers or servants. Stewart would not have mentioned them by name unless they were involved in some event that made it necessary to identify them. As the man in charge, he assumed the role as the sole discoverer of the trade and as the first white man

among these Indians—in keeping with the spirit of the times—his dependents were deemed unworthy of credit or even an identity separate from his own.

105. On the use of black drink, see the collection of essays in Charles M. Hudson, ed., *Black Drink: A Native American Tea* (Athens: University of Georgia Press, 1979). I do not discuss black drink at length because virtually all of the primary sources on its use in the colonial period come from the second half of the eighteenth century. Charles H. Fairbanks, "The Function of Black Drink Among the Creeks," in the Hudson collection, is the best place to begin study of its ceremonial use. An excellent source that illustrates its ubiquitousness in Creek daily life and interactions with outsiders is "David Taitt's Journal of a Journey Through the Creek Country, 1772," in Newton D. Mereness, ed., *Travels in the American Colonies* (New York: Macmillan, 1916), 493–565.

106. Stewart to Queen Anne, October 1711.

107. Stewart to Queen Anne, October 1711.

CHAPTER 7: INDIANS, TRADERS, AND THE REFORM OF THE INDIAN TRADE, 1707–1708

1. The report is dated Sept. 17, 1708. *Records,* 2:203–209. The report was probably a response to the British ministry's request to the proprietors. See Apr. 17, 1708, and May 7, 1707, in A. S. Salley, Jr., ed., *Commissions and Instructions from the Lords Proprietors of Carolina to Public Officials of South Carolina, 1685–1715* (Columbia: Historical Commission of South Carolina, 1916), 203–204, 208–210. Peter H. Wood, in "The Changing Population of the Colonial South: An Overview by Race and Region, 1685–1790," in Peter H. Wood, Gregory A. Waselkov, and M. Thomas Hatley, eds., *Powhatan's Mantle: Indians in the Colonial Southeast* (Lincoln: University of Nebraska Press, 1989).

2. Males outnumbered females by approximately the same percentage among both adult whites (60–40 percent) and adult blacks (62–38 percent).

3. Warren B. Smith, *White Servitude in Colonial South Carolina* (Columbia: University of South Carolina Press, 1961); David Galenson, *White Servitude in Colonial America: An Economic Analysis* (Cambridge: Cambridge University Press, 1981).

4. Europeans practiced all sorts of torture on political and criminal prisoners but did not ordinarily torture their war prisoners except as a form of punishment for perceived wrongs.

5. Cherokee headman Ketagustah will tell South Carolina's governor in 1730: "Here stands the Governor of Carolina, whom we know; this small Rope which we show you, is all we have to bind our slaves with, and may be broken, but you have Iron chains for yours; however, if we catch your Slaves, we shall bind them as well as we can, and deliver them to our Friends again, and have no pay for it." Quoted in Verner W. Crane, *The Southern Frontier, 1670–1732* (1929; reprint, New York: Norton, 1981), 300.

6. John R. Swanton, *Early History of the Creek Indians and Their Neighbors,* Smithsonian Institution Bureau of American Ethnology, Bulletin 73 (Washington, D.C.: Government Printing Office, 1922), 220, believes that the Indians had inhabited the area since the early 1680s, but it seems that Creek migration increased after the English attack on Saint Augustine in 1702. Crane believes that the term *Creek* was given to these Indians and others associated with them as they gathered into a confederacy, because of their habitation on Ochese Creek, which was later shortened to Creek Indians. Verner W. Crane, "The Origin of the Name of the Creek Indians," *Mississippi Valley Historical Re-*

view 5 (December 1918), 339–342. What lends credence to Crane's surmise is that the 1708 report provides no name for these Indians.

7. Swanton, *Early History,* has the most extensive discussion of the peoples who made up the Creek Confederacy, but also see J. Leitch Wright, Jr., *Creeks and Seminoles: The Destruction and Regeneration of the Muscogulge People* (Lincoln: University of Nebraska Press, 1986).

8. For the 1715 census, see SC Transcripts, 7:238–239. Wood supports Barnwell's estimate of the overall population of the Cherokee as slightly more than eleven thousand in 1715. Wood, "Changing Population," 38.

9. For analysis of Chickasaw population, see Wood, "Changing Population," 66–69.

10. See Chapter 5.

11. I have excluded the Savannah River Yuchi from these calculations because the data appears rounded for the men, and the number of women and children have been combined together, suggesting guesswork.

12. On the Catawba, see James H. Merrell, *The Indians' New World: Catawbas and Their Neighbors from European Contact Through the Era of Removal* (Chapel Hill: University of North Carolina Press, 1989). The Western Abenaki employed a similar strategy. See Colin G. Calloway, *The Western Abenaki of Vermont: War, Migration, and the Survival of an Indian People* (Norman: University of Oklahoma, 1990).

13. [Notes by Guillaume Delisle on Indian tribes near the banks of the Mississippi], [1703?], in ASH, 115–10: no. 17.

14. On Hughes, see Marcel Giraud, *A History of French Louisiana,* vol. 1: *The Reign of Louis XIV, 1698–1715,* trans. Joseph C. Lambert (Baton Rouge: Louisiana University Press, 1974; originally published in France, 1953), 324–329. For Coxe, see Daniel Coxe, *A Description of the English Province of Carolana . . .* [1722], ed. and intro. William S. Coker (Gainesville: University Presses of Florida, 1976).

15. For Savannah relations with South Carolina, see Merrell, *Indians' New World,* 56–57.

16. *SCCHJ, June 5, 1707–July 19, 1707,* 26–29.

17. For the location of Apalachee and Savannah on the Savannah River, see Herman Moll, *Map of North and South Carolina and Florida* [1715], Map Room, Crown Collection, Ser. 3, LC.

18. *SCCHJ, June 5, 1707–July 19, 1707,* 26–27.

19. Quoted in Swanton, *Early History,* 317–318. Also see *SCCHJ, October 22, 1707–February 12, 1707/08,* 45.

20. November 6, 1707, *SCCHJ, October 22, 1707–February 12, 1707/08,* 28. The House Journals make an oblique reference to another reason for Savannah discontent. Richard Berresford, former surveyor general and register of the province, had done something "official" against the Savannah, which the governor and council complained was undertaken "without our Consent and Approbation." They agreed as to the necessity of the action and thus sent him a commission, but what the commission was for they do not say. *SCCHJ, June 5, 1707–July 19, 1707,* 50.

21. *SCCHJ, June 5, 1707–July 19, 1707,* 23, 38.

22. *SCCHJ, June 5, 1707–July 19, 1707,* 39.

23. *SCCHJ, October 22, 1707–February 12, 1707/08,* 99.

24. *SCCHJ, October 22, 1707–February 12, 1707/08,* 99.

25. *SCCHJ, October 22, 1707–February 12, 1707/08*, 68.

26. *Le Jau*, 35.

27. House Journals, Book April 20, 1709–May 6, 1709, Apr. 21; Moll, *Map of North and South Carolina and Florida* [1715], shows Indian settlement along the Savannah River; Swanton reproduces this map but makes many changes, not all for the better. Swanton, *Early History*, map 3.

28. Frank J. Klingberg, ed., *Carolina Chronicle: The Papers of Commissary Gideon Johnston, 1707–1716* (Berkeley: University of California Press, 1946), 35; House Journals, Book October 22, 1707–February 12, 1708/09, Oct. 31, Nov. 3, 12; Book June 12, 1711–June 22, 1711, June 14.

29. *Records*, 5:211–212, 236, quotation on 290.

30. *SCCHJ, August 13, 1701–March 1, 1701*, 16.

31. W. L. Grant and James Munro, eds., *Acts of the Privy Council of England*, Col. Ser., vol. 2: *A.D. 1680–1720* (London: Lords Commissioners of His Majesty's Treasury, 1910), 613.

32. For the desire to discourage, see *SCCHJ, August 13, 1701–March 1, 1701*, 8. For further discussion of the competition between Virginia and South Carolina to control the Indian trade, see Merrell, *Indians' New World*, 52–56.

33. "An Act for Laying a Tax or Duty on Skins or Furrs, For the Publick Use of This Province, and Regulating the Indian Trade," Sept. 26, 1691, in *Statutes*, 2:64–68. For Sothell's removal, see June 15, 1692, in A. S. Salley, Jr., *Journal of the Grand Council of South Carolina, April 11, 1692–September 26, 1692* (Columbia: Historical Commission of South Carolina, 1907), 39.

34. April 23, 1698, *Commissions and Instructions*, 105.

35. *SCCHJ, October 30, 1700–November 16, 1700*, 17–18.

36. *SCCHJ, February 4, 1701–March 2, 1701*, 3, 4, 5, 8, 14, 16.

37. *SCCHJ, February 4, 1701–March 2, 1701*, 3.

38. *SCCHJ, August 13, 1701–August 28, 1701*, 7.

39. *SCCHJ, November 20, 1706–February 8, 1706/7*, 21–23.

40. *SCCHJ, November 20, 1706–February 8, 1706/7*, 24–25, quotation on 28.

41. *SCCHJ, November 20, 1706–February 8, 1706/7*, 33–35, 43; *June 5, 1707–July 19, 1707*, 71.

42. *SCCHJ, November 20, 1706–February 8, 1706/7*, 29.

43. *SCCHJ, November 20, 1706–February 8, 1706/7*, 35–37, quotation on 35.

44. Marcel Mauss, *The Gift: The Form and Reason for Exchange in Archaic Societies*, trans. W. D. Halls (1950; New York: reprint, Norton, 1990).

45. House Journals, Book October 9, 1710–December 5, 1710, Oct. 18, 19.

46. *SCCHJ, November 20, 1706–February 8, 1706/7*, 37, 41.

47. *SCCHJ, June 5, 1707–July 19, 1707*, 77–78.

48. *SCCHJ, June 5, 1707–July 19, 1707*, 79.

49. *SCCHJ, June 5, 1707–July 19, 1707*, 79–83, 85, 97–98, 100–101. Crane, *Southern Frontier*, 149.

50. "An Act for Regulating the Indian Trade and Making it Safe to the Publick," July 19, 1707, Act 269, in *Statutes*, 2:309–316.

51. "Act for Regulating the Indian Trade."

52. *SCCHJ, October 22, 1707–February 12, 1707/08*, 39, 46.

53. "An Act to Limit the Bounds of the Yamasee Settlement . . . ," Nov. 28, 1707, Act 271, in *Statutes,* 2:317–319.

54. The actual act, offered by the lords proprietors to the assembly, was to be in effect for only six months. The short limit may have been because they expected to have a new trading act in place that would cover punishment of misbehaving traders. "An Act to Impower the Right Honourable the Governour to Restrain Persons Offending from Goeing Amongst the Indians," Apr. 9, 1706, Act 251, in *Statutes,* 2:274; *SCCHJ, March 6, 1705/06–April 9, 1706,* 47, 51, 56.

55. *SCCHJ, October 22, 1707–February 12, 1707/08,* 12–13, 16, 18, 29, 50, quotation from 13.

56. House Journals, Book October 22, 1707–February 12, 1708/09, Oct. 28.

57. Thomas Nairne, "Petition to William, Lord Craven, Palatine, and the . . . Lords Proprietors of Carolina," Oct. 16, 1708, HM 1385, Maggs 498, HL.

58. See the discussion in Chapter 5.

59. Thomas Nairne to Earl of Sunderland, July 28, [1708], in *Calendar of State Papers, Colonial Series, American and West Indies,* 45 vols. (London: Longman and others, 1860–), 24:662.

60. Thomas Nairne to Earl of Sunderland, July 10, 1708, in Thomas Nairne, *Nairne's Muskhogean Journals: The 1708 Expedition to the Mississippi River,* ed. Alexander Moore (Jackson: University Press of Mississippi, 1988), 75.

61. Nairne to Sunderland, July 28, [1708]; James Child's troubles with the law began in England, before his emigration to Carolina. See Henry A. M. Smith, "Childsbury," *SCHM* 15 (1914), 110–111.

62. *SCCHJ, October 22, 1707–February 12, 1707/08,* 29.

63. *SCCHJ, October 22, 1707–February 12, 1707/08,* 50.

64. Nairne, "Petition to William, Lord Craven."

65. Thomas Nairne, "Petition to Queen Anne," 1708, HM 1384, Maggs 498, HL. Secondary sources discussing the treason case include Crane, *Southern Frontier,* 92–93, and "Introduction," in *Nairne's Muskhogean Journals,* 16.

66. House Journals, Book November 24, 1708–December 18, 1708, Dec. 1. He also was alleged to have repeated the claim while in prison. See George Smith, "Certificate . . .[regarding Capt. Thomas Nairne]," HM 1387, Maggs 498, HL; see also Nairne to Sunderland, July 28, [1708]. J. D. Alsop accuses Thomas Nairne of fabricating an alibi in the treason episode. See "Thomas Nairne and the 'Boston *Gazette* No. 216' of 1707," *Southern Studies: An Interdisciplinary Journal of the South* 22 (Summer 1983), 209–211.

67. Nairne, "Petition to William, Lord Craven."

68. Thomas Nairne to Earl of Sunderland, Oct. 16, 1708, HM 22268, Maggs 498, HL. See also Nairne to Sunderland, July 28, [1708].

69. Nairne, "Petition to Queen Anne," and "Petition to William, Lord Craven"; Nairne to Sunderland, Oct. 16, 1708.

70. "The Petition of the Subscribers in the Name of themselves and the generality of the Inhabitants of Colleton County," Sept. 17, 1708, HM 1389, Maggs 498, enclosed in Nairne to Sunderland, Oct. 16, 1708.

71. House Journals, Book November 24, 1708–December 18, 1708, Nov. 25, 30, Dec. 1, 3.

72. House Journals, Book November 24, 1708–December 18, 1708, Dec. 3, 9, 10.

CHAPTER 8: DEFINING THE EMPIRE

1. One reason that Tories opposed a militaristic policy overseas was their belief that war taxes fell more heavily on them than on the Whigs. W. A. Speck, *The Birth of Britain: A New Nation, 1700–1715* (Oxford: Blackwell, 1994), 8. For Tory support of the monarch, see Christopher Hill, *The Century of Revolution, 1603–1714* (New York: Norton, 1961), 282. Hill also notes that there arose in England a popular Toryism that opposed the Whigs because the Whigs were "associated with the City and an aristocratic oligarchy" (301).

2. The best introduction to the Church of England in South Carolina is S. Charles Bolton, *Southern Anglicanism: The Church of England in Colonial South Carolina* (Westport, Conn.: Greenwood, 1982).

3. On the French Huguenots, see Jon P. Butler, *The Huguenots in America: A Refugee People in New World Society* (Cambridge, Mass.: Harvard University Press, 1983); and Arthur Henry Hirsch, *The Huguenots of South Carolina* (Durham, N.C.: Duke University Press, 1928).

4. Much of the discussion of the colony's religious disputes is based on M. Eugene Sirmans, *Colonial South Carolina: A Political History, 1663–1763* (Chapel Hill: University of North Carolina Press, 1934), 76 ff.

5. In England, too, Whigs were more actively anti-Catholic than Tories. The Whigs suspected the Tories of crypto-Catholicism and of plotting to put the Stuart Pretender on the throne. Speck, *Birth of Britain*, 5. Samuel Everleigh, of the Dissenter party, deposed against the Anglicans conducting illegal elections. He testified to being "present at the Election of assembly men in Charleston in Jan[uary]y Past and that he saw Sailors, Strangers, Negroes and Jews give in their Votes promiscuously with other freeman without exception by the Sherif." "Deposition of Samuel Everleigh . . . ," Oct. 8, 1706, Additional Manuscripts 61647, folio 112, BL.

6. Sirmans, *Colonial South Carolina*, 87. See also Speck, *Birth of Britain*, 4.

7. Sirmans, *Colonial South Carolina*, 88.

8. The opposition published the act with a statement of their reasons for opposing it. See Additional Manuscripts 61647, folio 89–92b, BL.

9. "'A Narrative . . . Of An Assembly . . . January The 2d, 1705/6': New Light on Early South Carolina Politics," *SCHM* 85 (July 1984), 181–186.

10. Sirmans, *Colonial South Carolina*, 89.

11. Samuel Thomas Smith to Rev. Dr. Bray, Jan. 20, 1702, "Letters of Rev. Samuel Thomas Smith, 1702–1706," *SCHM* 4 (October 1903), 227–228.

12. Robert Stevens to the Society [SPG], November 1705, in SPG, Ser. A, vol. 2, no. 156:347–350.

13. Thomas Nairne to Doctor Marston, Aug. 20, 1705, enclosed in SPG, Ser. A, vol. 2, no. 156:347–357.

14. Stevens iterates his claims about Thomas in Robert Stevens to SPG, Feb. 21, 1705/06, SPG, Ser. A, vol. 2, no. 158:359–363.

15. Samuel Thomas to SPG, Mar. 10, 1704, in "Letters of Rev. Samuel Thomas, 1702–1707," 278–280; "Documents Concerning Rev. Samuel Thomas, 1702–1707," *SCHM* 5 (January 1904), 21–22. Match coats were Indian coats, or mantles, originally of furs sewn together but then manufactured by Europeans of coarse woolen cloth and sold to Indians.

16. Quotation from "Documents Concerning Rev. Samuel Thomas," 24; Samuel Thomas to Mr. Hodges, May 3, 1704, in "Letters of Rev. Samuel Thomas, 1702–1707," 282. The SPG thought ministers not going on their assignment to the Indians a dangerous precedent. Eleven years later, Thomas's failure to go to the Yamasee was still a topic for discussion! Gideon Johnston, during the Yamasee War, reflected on his and the society's accomplishments—and lack thereof—in converting Yamasee. Johnston himself made little effort to convert the Yamasee beyond sponsoring the conversion and education in England of the "Yamasee Prince." Johnston reminded the SPG that this effort was far more than anyone else had attempted: "But however things have fallen out contrary to my Expectation, yet my Design was good, Since I attempted nothing, as to the Yammouseas conversion, but what I had ground for, from what the most Illustrious Society did before; when they Sent Mr. Thomas hither, for that very purpose, though after his arrival he was prevailed upon to turn himself an other way." Gideon Johnston to SPG, Dec. 19, 1715, SPG, B4, Pt. 1, 102–108.

17. "Documents Concerning Rev. Samuel Thomas, 1702–1707," 30–31.

18. Edward McCrady, *The History of South Carolina Under the Proprietary Government, 1670–1719* (1897; reprint, New York: Russell and Russell, 1969), 409–418.

19. The reference to a town as the largest political unit supports my contention that the confederacy was simply an alliance of towns and that it still had little meaning beyond towns coming together as occasion warranted for defensive purposes.

20. The earlier discussed census of 1708 counted 500 men, which translated to more than 1,500 individuals. Reverend Le Jau estimated 400 men five years after the 1708 census, in 1713, when warfare had reduced their numbers. John Barnwell's collated census data of Indians in South Carolina in 1715 and found 413 men of a total Yamasee population of 1,215. Because Barnwell was on intimate terms with the Yamasee and lived near them, his numbers are probably the most accurate. Thomas's estimates were well before the 1708 census, when Yamasee men probably numbered more than 500. For Barnwell, see SC Transcripts, 7:238–239. For Le Jau, see *Le Jau*, 134.

21. See Robert Stevens to the Society [SPG], November 1705, where he notes that he originally had recommended converting the Yamasee upon Nairne's request.

22. Thomas Nairne to Doctor Marston, Aug. 20, 1705, enclosed with Stevens to the Society [SPG], November 1705.

23. "Mr. Samuel Thomas's Remonstrance in Justification of Himself," in "Documents Concerning Rev. Samuel Thomas," 39–54, quotations on 47.

24. In England, a combination of opposition Whigs and Tories often espoused the Country party philosophy of reform. It represented the anticity and anticommercial element in both parties. The Country party philosophy was popular throughout the American colonies, particularly in the plantation areas where rural life was celebrated, the corruptions of the city were (sometimes) denounced, and men emphasized the importance of personal relationships in business over the impersonal nature of the marketplace.

25. Le Jau to SPG, Apr. 15, 1707, in *Le Jau*, 24.

26. Le Jau to SPG, Mar. 13, 1708, in *Le Jau*, 37.

27. Le Jau to SPG, Dec. 2, 1706, Mar. 13, Sept. 15, 1708, Feb. 18, Aug. 5, 1709, Feb. 1, 19, June 13, 1710, Feb. 9, 1711, in *Le Jau*, 19, 35, 41, 49, 57, 68, 73, 79, 87.

28. "Extrait d'une au lettre du meme [Henri de Tonti] au meme [Pierre Le Moyne d' Iberville] Des Chacta," Mar. 14, 1702, ASH, 115–10: no. 20.

29. Father James Gravier, "Journal of the Voyage of Father Gravier," in *Early Voyages Up and Down the Mississippi, By Cavelier, St. Cosme, Le Sueur, Gravier and Guignas,* trans., and ed. John Gilmary Shea (Albany, N.Y.: Joel Munsell, 1861), 124–125.

30. Le Jau to SPG, Feb. 1, 1710, in *Le Jau,* 68.

31. Le Jau to SPG, Feb. 1, 1710, in *Le Jau,* 68.

32. Le Jau to SPG, Feb. 9, 1711, in *Le Jau,* 87. Le Jau's bias against the Savannah was probably due, at least in part, to the fact that he obtained his information from traders and local Indians and that the colony recently had been warring with the Savannah.

33. Le Jau to SPG, Feb. 9, 1711, in *Le Jau,* 87.

34. On the development and use of Mobilian as a trade language in Louisiana, see James M. Crawford, *The Mobilian Trade Language* (Knoxville: University of Tennessee Press, 1978).

35. Le Jau to SPG, Apr. 22, 1708, Feb. 18, 1709, Aug. 3, 1712, in *Le Jau,* 39, 49–50, 121. Minister Gideon Johnston also reported that the Yamasee desired conversion to Christianity. Gideon Johnston to SPG, Jan. 27, 1711, in Frank J. Klingberg, ed., *Carolina Chronicle: The Papers of Commissary Gideon Johnston, 1707–1716* (Berkeley: University of California Press, 1946), 82.

36. Le Jau to SPG, Aug. 5, 1709, in *Le Jau,* 58.

37. Le Jau to SPG, May 27, 1712, in *Le Jau,* 116.

38. Le Jau to SPG, Sept. 15, 1708, in *Le Jau,* 41.

39. Le Jau to SPG, June 3, 1710, in *Le Jau,* 78.

40. Le Jau to SPG, Nov. 15, 1708, in *Le Jau,* 48. See also July 10, 1711, Feb. 20, May 27, 1712, Aug. 10, 1713, in *Le Jau,* 94, 109, 116, 134.

41. Le Jau to SPG, Feb. 18, 1709, in *Le Jau,* 52.

42. Le Jau to SPG, Sept. 18, 1711, in *Le Jau,* 102. Le Jau seems to have forgotten his own prejudices against blacks, for earlier he had stated that they "are generally very bad men, chiefly those that are Scholars" (Apr. 15, 1707, 24).

43. Le Jau to SPG, Sept. 15, 1708, in *Le Jau,* 41.

44. Le Jau to SPG, Oct. 20, 1709, in *Le Jau,* 61. See also Feb. 1, 1710, 67.

45. Le Jau to SPG, Oct. 20, 1709, in *Le Jau,* 61.

46. Le Jau to SPG, Feb. 1, 1710, in *Le Jau,* 68.

47. In 1712, a Chowan Indian in North Carolina related a story similar to Noah and the flood to a SPG missionary in North Carolina. G. Rainsford to John Chamberlaine, July 25, 1712, in *CRNC,* 1:859.

48. Le Jau to SPG, Jan. 4, 1712, in *Le Jau,* 105.

49. Le Jau to SPG, Feb. 1, 1710, in *Le Jau,* 67.

50. Le Jau to SPG, June 13, 1710, in *Le Jau,* 76.

51. For the introduction and opposition of Christianity to slaves, see Alan Gallay, "The Origins of Slaveholders' Paternalism: George Whitefield, the Bryan Family, and the Great Awakening in the South," *Journal of Southern History* 53 (August 1987), 369–394.

52. Le Jau to SPG, Mar. 22, 1709, in *Le Jau,* 55.

53. Le Jau to SPG, Feb. 9, 1711, in *Le Jau,* 86–87.

54. Le Jau to SPG, Apr. 12, 1711, in *Le Jau,* 89.

55. Le Jau to SPG, July 10, 1711, in *Le Jau,* 93–94.

56. Le Jau to SPG, Aug. 30, Dec. 11, 1712, in *Le Jau,* 121, 124–125 (quotation on 125).

57. There is irony in the legislature describing slave behavior as caballing. Cabal had just entered the English language in the 1660s from an acronym representing the initial letter of the names of five men who formed a secret group in support of King Charles II. The first "a" referred to Lord Ashley, Anthony Ashley Cooper, later the earl of Shaftsbury, one of Carolina's original proprietors (and a man who frequently changed sides in English politics). House Journals, Book October 22, 1707–February 12, 1708/09, Nov. 1. One solution to the problem was to have some whites stay at home to keep an eye on the slaves. But who wanted to spend their Sundays as policemen? Le Jau to SPG, June 13, 1710, in *Le Jau*, 78.

58. Le Jau to SPG, Feb. 20, 1712, in *Le Jau*, 109.

59. See the discussion of the Yamasee prince in Chapter 12.

CHAPTER 9: CAROLINA'S INDIAN TRADERS

1. House Journals, Book April 20, 1709–May 6, 1709, Apr. 21.

2. House Journals, Book April 20, 1709–May 6, 1709, Apr. 28.

3. *Commissioners*, 3–4.

4. House Journals, Book October 10, 1710–December 5, 1710, Oct. 12.

5. *Commissioners*, 4–5.

6. *Commissioners*, 6.

7. *Commissioners*, 5–6. James Lucas accused Musgrove of detaining two of his slaves—the case was postponed until Lucas could appear personally to give evidence.

8. *Commissioners*, 6.

9. House Journals, Book January 10, 1711–February 24, 1711, Jan. 11, Feb. 17. Musgrove would later become a reformer.

10. *Commissioners*, 5–6; House Journals, Book January 10, 1711–February 24, 1711, Mar. 1 (note: the March 1 entry was included in spite of the February 24 end date.)

11. House Journals, Book June 12, 1711–June 22, 1711, June 14.

12. *Commissioners*, 8–9.

13. House Journals, Book June 12, 1711–June 22, 1711, June 21.

14. *Commissioners*, 20.

15. House Journals, Book October 9, 1710–December 5, 1710, Oct. 12.

16. *Commissioners*, 56.

17. From Smith's behavior it was apparent that he opposed any attempt to regulate his trading activities. Smith, for instance, was sued for trading without a license three months before Wright became agent. House Journals, Book January 10, 1711–February 24, 1711, Jan. 31; Book February 1, 1709–February 19, 1709, Feb. 19.

18. For the procurement of capital in Carolina, see Russell R. Menard, "Financing the Lowcountry Export Boom: Capital and Growth in Early South Carolina," *William and Mary Quarterly*, 3d Ser., 51 (1994), 659–676.

19. Although it focuses on trade in the last half of the eighteenth century, a good place to start for examining the Indian traders and the trade in the South is Kathryn E. Holland Braund, *Deerskin and Duffels: Creek Indian Trade with Anglo-America, 1685–1815* (Lincoln: University of Nebraska Press, 1993).

20. Judgment Rolls, 1703–1790, Court of Common Pleas, SCDAH, 3A:226, 4B:250, 5A:275, 5B:385.

21. Anne King Gregorie, ed., *Records of the Court of Chancery of South Carolina, 1671–1779* (Washington, D.C.: American Historical Association, 1950), 208.

22. House Journals, Book June 12, 1711–June 22, 1711, June 14, 19; *Commissioners,* 7, 12. Wright sued Alexander Parris, the public receiver, over the bond Jan. 30, 1713, Judgment Rolls, 4A:8.

23. *Commissioners,* 18.

24. House Journals, Book January 10, 1711–February 24, 1711, Jan. 17, Feb. 1, 10, 14.

25. Wright's letters regarding the problems of the trade arrived while the assembly was considering the new bill.

26. Why Dawfusky was singled out is not explained. Dawfusky Island is a Sea Island just north of the Savannah River and distant from Yamasee towns on the mainland. Perhaps it was too far for Wright to keep an eye on trade there.

27. House Journals, Book June 12, 1711–June 22, 1711, June 14.

28. House Journals, Book June 12, 1711–June 22, 1711, June 21.

29. *Commissioners,* 10–11.

30. Bray asked for the return of his bond, which was refused as the Yamasee had "several other Complaints against him."

31. *Commissioners,* 11–12.

32. *Commissioners,* 12.

33. *Commissioners,* 14.

34. Judgment Rolls, 3A:231, 280, 3B:4A, 26A, 3A:228.

35. Judgment Rolls, 6A:498.

36. House Journals, Book October 9, 1711–November 10, 1711, Oct. 9.

37. *Commissioners,* 51.

38. *Commissioners,* 18.

39. *Commissioners,* 51.

40. *SCCHJ, 1703,* 36, 38.

41. *SCCHJ, 1703,* 47.

42. *Commissioners,* 10, 19; House Journals, Book January 10, 1711–February 24, 1711, Jan. 19.

43. *Commissioners,* 22–23.

44. Judgment Rolls, 2D:81A.

45. House Journals, Book October 9, 1711–November 10, 1711, Nov. 7.

46. *Commissioners,* 24.

47. *Commissioners,* 21.

48. *Commissioners,* 22.

49. *Commissioners,* 21.

50. *Commissioners,* 11.

51. *Commissioners,* 43; House Journals, Book Session Beginning November 18, 1712, Nov. 25, 1712.

52. *Commissioners,* 23.

53. *Commissioners,* 23.

54. *Commissioners,* 24.

55. House Journals, Book May 13, 1712–June 6, 1712, May 13. For cases initiated by Wright and the Public Receiver against Cochran, Frazier, and Bray, see also Judgment Rolls, 2D:3A, 5A, 29A, 30A, 5A:268, 6A:490.

56. Judgment Rolls, 5A:268.

57. *Commissioners,* 27.

58. *Commissioners,* 27–28.

59. Nairne also used his newfound power for augmenting attacks on Agent Wright, who in the midst of war preparations was brought up on charges of maladministration of the Indian trade. House Journals, Book October 9, 1711–November 10, 1711, Oct. 9. As soon as the relief expedition left for North Carolina, Nairne headed a committee that investigated Wright's activities.

CHAPTER 10: THE TUSCARORA WAR

1. Gideon Johnston reported in November 1711 that Charles Town was in the third month of an epidemic. He thought it "a kind of Judgment upon the Place (for they are a sinful People)." At the new year, he recorded that the streets were still deserted and that the only public business attended to was the Tuscarora War. The money raised for the Barnwell expedition "will be no small hindrance to me in obtaining relief for my present Necessities." Frank J. Klingberg, ed., *Carolina Chronicle: The Papers of Commissary Gideon Johnston, 1707–1716* (Berkeley: University of California, 1946), 98–99, 100–103. Francis Le Jau wrote of the epidemic, Jan. 4, 1712: "we have lost a great Number of White people and 3 or 400 Slaves in this Province within 4 months. The Town is almost desert, the Mortality Continues still, All our families in the Country have been Visited. Several of my People have been sick, I thank God none died in my house. . . . The distemper seizes suddenly, it is like a Pleurisy. I have used large doses of snake root Infused for us all (under God) with good Success." *Le Jau,* 104.

2. "Journal of the Virginia Council," Feb. 20, 1711/12, *CRNC,* 1:836–837.

3. Coll: [Alexander] Spotswood to the Lords of Trade, May 8, 1712, *CRNC,* 1: 839–841.

4. President and Council, the Speaker and Members of the House of Burgesses of the Government of North Carolina to Alexander Spotswood, undated, *CRNC,* 1: 837–838.

5. Alexander Spotswood to Council of Trade, May 8, 15, 1712, *Official Letters,* 1: 149, 160–161.

6. Colonel Spotswood to the Board of Trade, July 25, Oct. 15, 1711, *CRNC,* 1: 779–783, 812.

7. "Friends Monthly Meeting in Pasquotank Precinct," Sept. 16, 1711, *CRNC,* 1: 813.

8. House Journals, Book October 9, 1711–November 10, 1711, Oct. 27.

9. House Journals, Book October 9, 1711–November 10, 1711, Nov. 2. Part of the colony's preparation for the expedition included petitioning the proprietors to use their efforts to convince the Crown to allow Carolina to control the Virginia traders, for they claimed that enemy Indians would receive armaments and other supplies from Virginia (Nov. 3).

10. Barnwell is buried at St. Helena's Episcopal Church in Beaufort, South Carolina.

11. "Barnwell of South Carolina," *SCHM* 2 (January 1901), 47–50.

12. For discussion of examples of Barnwell's maps, see William P. Cumming, *The Southeast in Early Maps* (Princeton, N.J.: Princeton University Press, 1958).

13. See the discussion in Chapter 7.

14. House Journals, Book January 10, 1710/11–February 24, 1710/11, Feb. 21.

15. "Barnwell of South Carolina," 46.

16. Alexander Spotswood to Collo. Hyde, [February 1710/11], *Official Letters*, 47–48.

17. "De Graffenried's Manuscript," *CRNC*, 1:921.

18. See "A Proclamation for seizing and apprehending Colo Thos Cary and other Seditious and Fractious persons that have made their escape from North Carolina into this Colony," July 24, 1711, *CRNC*, 1:776–777; Alexander Spotswood to Lord Dartmouth, July 28, 1711, *Official Letters*, 105–106; Spotswood to Earl of Rochester, July 30, 1711, *Official Letters*, 107–108.

19. Alexander Spotswood to the Council of Trade, Oct. 15, 1711, *Official Letters*, 116–117; also see Spotswood to Lord Dartmouth, Oct. 15, 1711, *Official Letters*, 118–119.

20. "De Graffenried's Manuscript," 922.

21. "De Graffenried's Manuscript," 927.

22. "De Graffenried's Manuscript," 928, italics removed.

23. "De Graffenried's Manuscript" 928.

24. "De Graffenried's Manuscript," 929.

25. "De Graffenried's Manuscript," 932.

26. This refers to the method of hunting deer, mentioned earlier, by which a ring of fire channeled the prey to one spot, where they could be taken easily.

27. "De Graffenried's Manuscript," 936–938. For the Virginia government's demands for Graffenreid's release, see "Journal of Virginia Council," *CRNC*, 1:808–809.

28. "De Graffenried's Manuscript," 938–939.

29. Sometimes Europeans referred to all Iroquois as Seneca, so it is possible that the Europeans were using the term in this manner at this time.

30. *Boston News-Letter*, Mar. 24–31, 1712.

31. J. N. B. Hewitt discussed these belts in an essay on the Tuscarora, in Frederick Webb Hodge, ed., *Handbook of American Indians North of Mexico*, 2 vols., Smithsonian Institution Bureau of American Ethnology, Bulletin 30 (Washington, D.C.: Government Printing Office, 1910), 2:843–844; the source for his discussion is June 16, 1710, *Minutes of the Provincial Council of Pennsylvania . . .*, vol. 3 (Philadelphia: Joseph Severns, 1852), 511–512.

32. Governor Robert Hunter to Secretary Popple, Sept. 10, 1713, *Documents Relative to the Colonial History of the State of New York*, vol. 5, ed. E. B. O'Callaghan (Albany, N.Y.: Weed, Parsons, 1854), 371.

33. Almon Wheeler Lauber, *Indian Slavery in Colonial Times Within the Present Limits of the United States* (1913; reprint, Williamstown, Mass.: Corner House, 1979), 193–195.

34. Barnwell's report of Tuscarora discontent rings true in his cross-examination of prisoners taken on the expedition to North Carolina. Barnwell asked the captives whether any white men, particularly Virginia traders, might have "incited them," to which the Tuscarora "unanimously answered no." Barnwell would not have hesitated to blame the Virginians, but he could not find "upon the strictest enquiry that any Virginia Traders has been here with ammunition or goods since the Massacre." John Barnwell to [Governor Craven?], Feb. 4, 1711/1712, "The Tuscarora Expedition: Letters of Colonel John Barnwell," *SCHM* 9 (January 1908), 35.

For Le Jau's perspective on the causes of the war, see Le Jau to SPG, Jan. 4, 1712, in *Le Jau,* 103–104.

35. "De Graffenried's Manuscript," 945.

36. Colonel Spotswood to the Board of Trade, Feb. 8, 1711/12, *CRNC,* 1:834.

37. "De Graffenried's Manuscript," 941.

38. Barnwell to [Governor Craven?], Feb. 4, 1711/12, 30.

39. James Merrell, *The Indians' New World: Catawbas and Their Neighbors from European Contact Through the Era of Removal* (Chapel Hill: University of North Carolina Press, 1989), 69–72.

40. Barnwell to [Governor Craven?], Feb. 4, 1711/12, 30.

41. The Corsaboy, according to Barnwell's 1715 census, comprised 295 people in five villages. SC Transcripts, 7:238–239.

42. Barnwell also combined the Congarees and Santees in his 1715 census of the Indians. At that time there were 43 Santee men and 22 Congaree men, along with a combined 60 women and children. They had three towns, two Santee and one Congaree. After the Yamasee War, colonists often referred to many of the Piedmont Indians as Catawba. The 1715 census recorded 1,470 Catawba in seven towns two hundred miles northwest of Charles Town. This probably included some of the Indians listed in Esaw Jack's company, but not the Santee and Congaree who were listed separate and as living much closer to Charles Town. SC Transcripts, 7:238–239.

43. Chapman J. Milling, *Red Carolinians* (Chapel Hill: University of North Carolina Press, 1940), 118.

44. John R. Swanton, *Early History of the Creek Indians and Their Neighbors,* Smithsonian Institution Bureau of American Ethnology, Bulletin 73 (Washington, D.C.: Government Printing Office, 1922), 18.

45. Barnwell to [Governor Craven?], Feb. 4, 1711/12, 30–31.

46. Barnwell's 1715 census lists one Saraw town of 510 people, 170 miles north of Charles Town. SC Transcripts, 7:238–239.

47. "The Memorial of Christopher Gale from the government of North Carolina, to the Honorable Robert Gibbs, Governor and Commander-in-chief, and to the Honorable Council and general Assembly," undated, *CRNC,* 1:828–829.

48. Barnwell to [Governor Craven?], Feb. 4, 1711/12, 34.

49. Barnwell to [Governor Craven?], Feb. 4, 1711/12, 32.

50. Barnwell to [Governor Craven?], Feb. 4, 1711/12, 33.

51. The quickness with which the Tuscarora built forts, abandoned them, and built new ones is akin to the strategy of many Maori in nineteenth-century New Zealand. See James Belich, *The New Zealand Wars and the Victorian Interpretation of Racial Conflict* (New York: Oxford University Press, 1986).

52. Barnwell [Governor Craven?], Feb. 4, 1711/12, "Tuscarora Expedition," 33–34.

53. Historian Thomas Parramore suggests that Barnwell attacked neutral Tuscarora at Torhunta who "were not at all clear as to what the Tuscarora War was about or, indeed, precisely whom it was being waged against." But Graffenried made no mention in his journal that Barnwell might have attacked neutral towns, and given that he had been prisoner for an extended time among the Tuscarora, he would probably have noticed the alleged neutrality. The upper towns of the Tuscarora, far from Hancock's village, were neutral, but not the towns to the south. It is hard to believe that months after the outbreak of

the war all the Tuscarora, neutral or not, would not have known what the war was about. Parramore attributes the "white scalps and stolen articles" found in the allegedly neutral towns "to the fact that such items entered quickly into the Indian trade once they came into Tuscarora hands." If this was indeed the case, it adds weight to the premise that the Tuscarora would absolutely have known why the war had taken place—can one imagine Tuscarora trading with one another but not discussing such a momentous event as the war with North Carolina? Moreover, it is difficult to imagine the Tuscarora trading scalps with one another when such behavior seems unprecedented in Native American history. Indians sold scalps to the colonial governments for hefty bounties, but not to each other as commodities. They displayed scalps as trophies—but only those they had taken themselves. Scalps could also be given as compensation to families who had lost members to the group that was scalped, but if this were the case with Torhunta, then it implicates that town into having participated in the hostilities.

Moreover, Parramore argues that Barnwell, by attacking neutral towns, had "transformed a conflict of intermittent skirmishes and peace initiatives into a desperate war of survival," yet one can hardly argue that either side would interpret the killing of more than a hundred Europeans by the Tuscarora and their allies as any sort of "skirmish." Furthermore, the "peace initiatives" that Parramore refers to involved the Upper Tuscarora led by Tom Blunt, not those led by Hancock. These peace initiatives were designed to keep the war from escalating to the upper towns, not to make a peace with Hancock and the towns that supported him. As is discussed below, the North Carolina government had no intention of making any sort of peace with the "hostile" Indians and desired nothing less than their utter extirpation. Parramore, "With Tuscarora Jack," 122, 125, 128. Also see Parramore's essay, "The Tuscarora Ascendancy," *North Carolina Historical Review* 59 (October 1982), 307–326. For an excellent discussion of scalping, see James Axtell, "Scalping: The Ethnohistory of a Moral Question," in James Axtell, *The European and the Indian: Essays in the Ethnohistory of Colonial North America* (New York: Oxford University Press, 1981), 207–241.

54. Barnwell to [Governor Craven?], Feb. 12, 1711/12, 36–41.

55. Barnwell to [Governor Craven?], Mar. 12, 1711/12, 43–44.

56. Barnwell to [Governor Craven?], Mar. 12, 1711/12, 43.

57. It is also quite possible that Harry brought valuable military skills with him from Africa. John K. Thornton has shown that the Kongo provided South Carolina with many slaves and that many Kongolese "had training with modern weapons." Guns were common in Kongo by the 1660s, and by the 1680s, Kongolese already had switched from matchlocks to flintlocks. When a Capuchin visited Kongo in 1694, he was greeted by thousands of musket-equipped soldiers. The Kongolese would thus have been familiar with the weaponry used by the Europeans in the American colonies and perhaps how to respond tactically to these weapons. "African Dimensions of the Stono Rebellion," *American Historical Review* 96 (October 1991), 1101–1113 (quotation from 1109). Another essay that illuminates the transformation of knowledge from Africans to the Carolinas is Peter H. Wood, "'It Was a Negro Taught Them': A New Look at African Labor in Early South Carolina," *Journal of Asian and African Studies* 9 (July–October 1975), 160–179.

58. Barnwell to [Governor Craven?], Mar. 12, 1711/12.

59. [Jean-Baptiste Le Moyne de] Bienville to [Jean-Frédéric de] Maurepas, June 28, 1736, *MPA,* 1:305.

60. He probably carried this information from South Carolina, since Gale had reported this in his request for aid for North Carolina. "Memorial of Christopher Gale," 828–829.

61. Barnwell to [Governor Craven?], Mar. 12, 1711/12, "Tuscarora Expedition," 45–46.

62. Barnwell to [Governor Craven?], Mar. 12, 1711/12, 46.

63. Barnwell to [Governor Craven?], Mar. 12, 1711/12, 46–47.

64. Colonel Spotswood to the Board of Trade, July 26, 1712, *CRNC,* 1:862. Thomas Pollock's letter to the proprietors adds confusion to the matter. Pollock blames Barnwell for making a treaty that he *and* the Tuscarora immediately broke, but he seems to be referring to the first agreement between Barnwell and the Tuscarora, not the second. The breaking of the treaty, according to Pollock, took place only a few days after it was made, which if he was referring to the first or second attempt still makes no reference to the alleged later attack. Thomas Pollock to the Lords Proprietors, Sept. 20, 1712, *CRNC,* 1:875.

65. House Journals, Book August 5, 1712–August 8, 1712, Aug. 5.

66. Milling also notes the Coree identity of those attacked. *Red Carolinians,* 128.

67. Also see Graffenreid's account in "De Graffenried's Manuscript," 956.

68. House Journals, Book August 5, 1712–August 8, 1712, Aug. 5.

69. Mosley, it should be added, represented North Carolina with John Lawson in negotiations with Virginia over their boundary dispute and did not earn much favor with Spotswood.

70. *CRNC,* 1:xxxi.

71. Hugh T. Lefler and William S. Powell, in their *Colonial North Carolina: A History* (New York: Charles Scribner's Sons, 1973), categorically refute the charges against Barnwell as false and suggest that North Carolinians must have orchestrated the attack. They assert that the Indians could not have been taken by Barnwell because he "had boarded the sloop" that returned him to South Carolina before the incident occurred. They attribute the false charges to Barnwell's many enemies in North Carolina who were jealous of his success and had battled with him incessantly over provisions for his troops, manpower, and supplies. Thomas Parramore disputed these authors' assertion but misread the evidence. He claimed that Barnwell's attack and the counterattacks by the Tuscarora all occurred in June. On June 2, the North Carolina council had decided to send Foster to South Carolina to ask for further assistance against the Indians. Pollock also stated that the agent was sent to South Carolina in June. Foster, however, did not appear before the South Carolina assembly with North Carolina's plea for help until August 5. If he was traveling by canoe with hired paddlers, it could not have taken him two months to reach South Carolina. In fact, it would have been odd for him not to have taken passage with Barnwell on South Carolina's sloop which left July 5 and reached Charles Town three days later. The decision to send for help in early June had occurred not because war had broken out again but simply because North Carolina would be defenseless as soon as Barnwell departed. When Barnwell did return home on July 8, it would have been odd for him (or anyone else in the sloop) not to tell the colony that war had broken out anew. This would have been a mighty secret to keep, and no one in South Carolina ever accused him of such. How do we explain Foster's arrival a month later with news of the renewal of war? Either this was a return trip by Foster or he had just received a message from a

courier that hostilities had erupted. Also, it is doubtful that North Carolina would have waited so long—to August 5—to ask for help unless war had just broken out. Spotswood first mentions the alleged attacks by Barnwell on July 26, three weeks after Barnwell had left North Carolina. Graffenreid, whom Parramore relies on, was not in the vicinity of the attack and would have had to rely on rumors. Parramore, "With Tuscarora Jack," 134–135; Thomas Pollock to the Governor of Virginia, Oct. 5, 1712, *CRNC,* 1:880; South Carolina Commons House Journals, microfilm, Book August 5, 1712–August 8, 1712, Aug. 5; House Journals, Book August 5, 1712–August 9, 1712, Aug. 5, 1712; "Col. Barnwell's Letter to Governor Hyde," Aug. 18, 1712, *CRNC,* 1:904.

72. Graffenreid believed that Barnwell's "breach of [the] truce . . . did not fail to greatly incense the other Tuscaruros and Carolinian Indians, . . . [who] accordingly fortified themselves still better, and made terrible raids" against us. "De Graffenried's Manuscript," 956.

73. Minutes, February 1711/12, *Records of the Executive Council, 1664–1734. The Colonial Records of North Carolina* [2d Ser.], vol. 7, ed. Robert J. Cain (Raleigh: North Carolina State Division of Archives and History, 1984), 9.

74. House Journals, Book August 5, 1712–August 9, 1712, Aug. 5. Governor Hyde blamed Barnwell for the renewal of the war, claiming that he should have taken Hancock's fort and that the Carolinians had enough provisions to do so. He described Barnwell's treaty with the Tuscarora as a "sham." Hyde asserted that Barnwell had stated that he made the treaty only as a temporary measure to buy time until they could return better prepared to subdue the enemy. If it had been a sincere peace, the governor wondered, then why had Barnwell "broken it" by attacking the Tuscarora's allies? Hyde's successor, Thomas Pollock, also believed that Barnwell's peace with the Tuscarora had been a "sham." Pollock hoped to prove that Barnwell and Mosley had contrived together to make a peace with the Tuscarora that would "blacken Governor Hyde's administration, thereby to endeavor a change of Government"—with Barnwell as governor. He could never prove the charge. Thomas Pollock to the Lords Proprietors, Sept. 20, 1712, *CRNC,* 1:875; Pollock to Governor Craven, Feb. 20, 1712/13, May 25, 1713, *CRNC,* 2:20, 46.

75. House Journals, Book August 5, 1712–August 9, 1712, Aug. 5.

76. North Carolina again rejected Iroquois mediation in 1713, but this time out of poverty—the colony could not afford the presents and expenses needed to supply the Iroquois for such an undertaking. Thomas Pollock to [Governor Robert Hunter], Mar. 6, 1712/13, *CRNC,* 2:23.

77. House Journals, Book August 5, 1712–August 9, 1712, Aug. 5.

78. House Journals, Book August 5, 1712–August 9, 1712, Aug. 9. The house asserted that it believed that the shooting was not an accident and that it wished the perpetrator to be brought to justice.

79. House Journals, Book August 5, 1712–August 9, 1712, Aug. 7.

80. Daniel, it should be noted was nearing seventy at the time, but he could still lead military forces. During the Yamasee War, three years later, he led a force against the Yamasee. See Milling, *Red Carolinians,* 129; Edgar Legaré Pennington, "The South Carolina Indian War of 1715, as Seen by the Clergymen," *SCHM* 32 (October 1931), 260.

81. House Journals, Book August 5, 1712–August 9, 1712, Aug. 8.

82. House Journals, Book November 11, 1712–December 12, 1712, Nov. 20.

83. House Journals, Book November 11, 1712–December 12, 1712, Nov. 21.

84. House Journals, Book November 11, 1712–December 12, 1712, Nov. 21.

85. *Commissioners,* 30–34.

86. House Journals, Book November 11, 1712–December 12, 1712, Nov. 22.

87. House Journals, Book November 11, 1712–December 12, 1712, Nov. 25.

88. House Journals, Book November 11, 1712–December 12, 1712, Nov. 27.

89. House Journals, Book November 11, 1712–December 12, 1712, Nov. 28, Dec. 2, 3, 5, 6.

90. House Journals, Book November 11, 1712–December 12, 1712, Dec. 2, 3.

91. I have not been able to identify which group or groups had fifteen of the traders.

92. Some traders never appear in the commission's records for having taken out a license but do appear in other official records. On a few occasions the house punished men identified as Indian traders for remarks made about the assembly, but these men do not appear in the commission's records. The house made no note of these men having traded without a license, and it can be assumed from the haphazard nature by which licenses were reported in the commission journals that the men had licenses that were not recorded in the journals but were probably noted in the records kept by the public receiver. Therefore, there could have been other traders who do not appear in the commission's records for having taken out a license and who had not been accused of abusing Indians.

93. House Journals, Book November 24, 1708–December 18, 1708, Dec. 1; *Commissioners,* 50, 51. The demand of double pay for Indians illustrates Nairne's view of his role as commissioner and agent. He was willing to regulate trader activities even when there was no specific law governing particular aspects, such as wages paid to Indians.

94. House Journals, Book February 1, 1708/09–February 19, 1708/09, Feb. 7, 19. See the discussion of this episode in Chapter 11.

95. House Journals, Book November 11, 1712–December 12, 1712, Dec. 10.

96. House Journals, Book November 11, 1712–December 12, 1712, Dec. 11, 12.

97. House Journals, Book November 11, 1712–December 12, 1712, Dec. 11.

98. House Journals, Book August 5, 1712–August 9, 1712, Aug 8, 9.

99. The letter is dated Aug. 18, 1712. See House Journals, Book November 11, 1712–December 12, 1712, Dec. 11.

100. House Journals, Book November 11, 1712–December 12, 1712, Dec. 11.

101. House Journals, Book November 11, 1712–December 12, 1712, Dec. 12.

102. Thomas Pollock to [Governor Robert Hunter], Mar. 6, 1712/13, *CRNC,* 2:24.

103. For the second expedition, see Joseph W. Barnwell, "The Second Tuscarora Expedition," *SCHM* 10 (January 1909), 33–48; Milling, *Red Carolinians,* 113–134; Alexander Spotswood to the Earl of Dartmouth, May 15, 1713, *Official Letters,* 2:18–19; Spotswood to Lords Commissioners of Trade, June 2, 1713, *Official Letters,* 2:24–25; *Boston News-Letter,* May 11–18, 1713; Thomas Pollock to [Governor Charles Craven?], Apr. 2, 1713, *CRNC,* 2:229–230; James Moore to ?, Mar. 27, 1713, *CRNC,* 2:27; "Journal of Virginia Council," Apr. 16, 1713, *CRNC,* 2:36.

104. Alexander Spotswood to the Earl of Dartmouth, May 15, 1712, June 2, 1713, *Official Letters,* 18–19, 24–25.

105. Governor Hunter to Secretary Popple, Sept. 10, 1713, "Conference with Five Nations at Onondaga," and "Conference Between Governor Hunter and the Five Nations," Sept. 20, 23, 1714, all in *Colonial History of New York,* 5:371, 375–376, 382–383, 386–387.

106. Alexander Spotswood to Lords Commissioners of Trade, Nov. 16, 1713, *Official Letters,* 42.

107. Governor Hunter to Secretary Popple, Sept. 10, 1713, 371.

108. "Conference with Five Nations at Onondaga," 376.

109. Thomas Pollock to [Governor Alexander Spotswood], Apr. 2, 1713, *CRNC,* 2:30–31; Le Jau to SPG, Apr. 20, 1714, in *Le Jau,* 141.

110. [Governor Alexander Spotswood] to Colonel Thomas Pollock, [April] 1713, *CRNC,* 2:32–33.

111. Thomas Pollock to [Governor Alexander Spotswood], Apr. 25, 1713, *CRNC,* 2:37–39; [Governor Alexander Spotswood] to Thomas Pollock, May 1713, *CRNC,* 2:47–48.

112. Pollock to [Spotswood], Apr. 2, 1713.

113. Pollock to [Spotswood], Apr. 25, 1713.

114. Thomas Pollock to [Governor Alexander Spotswood?], Sept. 1, 1713, *CRNC,* 2:61.

115. Thomas Pollock to [Governor Alexander Spotswood], Apr. 30, 1713, *CRNC,* 2:39–40.

116. "Journal of Virginia Council," Aug. 12, 1713, *CRNC,* 2:57; Thomas Pollock to [Governor Alexander Spotswood], Nov. 16, 1713, *CRNC,* 2:73–75; Alexander Spotswood to Earle [sic] of Dartmouth, Mar. 9, 1714, *Official Letters,* 2:53; Alexander Spotswood to the Lords Commissioners of Trade, Mar. 9, 1713/14, *Official Letters,* 2:57–58.

117. "North Carolina Council," Feb. 11, 1714/15, 1675, *CRNC,* 2:168; "Minutes," in Robert J. Cain, ed., *Records of the Executive Council, 1664–1734: The Colonial Records of North Carolina* [2d Ser.], vol. 7 (Raleigh: North Carolina State Division of Archives and History, 1984), 51–52. The Coree would resume fighting with North Carolina during the Yamasee War. *Records of the Executive Council,* Sept. 13, 1715, 57.

118. In the ensuing century, the North Carolina Tuscarora would continue their migration to New York.

119. Pennington, "South Carolina Indian War of 1715," 255.

120. The sale of Tuscarora into slavery is discussed in Chapter 11.

121. "Conference Between Governor Hunter and the Five Nations," 387.

122. "Conference Between Governor Hunter and the Five Nations," 386.

123. "Reply of Five Nations to Governor Hunter," Aug. 31, 1717, *Colonial History of New York,* 5:443–446.

CHAPTER 11: CONTOURS OF THE INDIAN SLAVE TRADE

1. French intelligence knew of the impending invasion almost as soon as it was formulated, but the many cancellations relaxed their guard for when the attack finally came. D'Artaguiette au Comte de Pontchartrain, May 11, Aug. 26, 1709, AC, C13A, 2:427; de Bienville au Comte de Pontchartrain, 1709, AC, C13A, 2:457; d'Artaguiette au Comte de Pontchartrain, [1709], AC, C13A, 2:458.

2. D'Artaguiette au Comte de Pontchartrain, May 11, 1709, AC, C13A, 2:427; Dartaguiette [au Ministre de la Marine], May 11, 1709, AC, C13A, 2:461; Nicolas de La Salle [au Ministre de la Marine], May 12, 1709, AC, C13A, 2:395.

3. Nicolas de La Salle [au Ministre de la Marine], May 12, 1709.

4. The French estimated and believed that the English would come with an army of 1,500 to 2,500 men and that there would be little they could do to stop them. D'Artaguiette au Pontchartrain, May 11, 1709; Bienville au Pontchartrain, 1709.

5. Jean-Baptiste Bénard de La Harpe, *The Historical Journal of the Establishment of the French in Louisiana*, trans. Virginia Koenig and Joan Cain, ed. Glenn R. Conrad (Lafayette: University of Southwestern Louisiana Press, 1971), 82.

6. André Pénicaut, *Fleur de Lys and Calumet: Being the Pénicaut Narrative of French Adventure in Louisiana*, trans. and ed. Richebourg Gaillard McWilliams (Tuscaloosa: University of Alabama Press, 1953, 1981), 133; de la Salle au Comte de Pontchartrain, June 20, 1710, AC, C13A, 2:519; d'Artaguiette au Comte de Pontchartrain, Feb. 23, 1711, AC, C13A, 2:635. They were especially short of shirts and stockings.

7. D'Artaguiette au Pontchartrain, Feb. 23, 1711.

8. Bienville to Pontchartrain, Oct. 27, 1711, *MPA*, 3:159. Also see d'Artaguiette au Pontchartrain, Feb. 23, 1711, for other discussion of need for presents for the Indians.

9. D'Artaguiette, "Memoire de ce que J'ai pû apendre Concernant les Instructions de feu M. Demuy Gouverneur du forts de la Louisiane," Feb. 25, 1708, AC, C13A, 2:313. (Note: this memoir is different from the one of the same date by d'Artaguiette that is reprinted in *MPA*, 3.)

10. D'Artaguiette specifically mentions intelligence gathering as the reason the English gave presents to Mississippi River tribes allied with the French. Nicolas de la Salle au Pontchartrain, Sept. 12, 1708, AC, C13A, 2:193.

11. Francis Le Jau, July 10, 1711, in *Le Jau*, 94.

12. House Journals, Book June 12, 1711–June 22, 1711, June 20, 21, 22. The *Boston News-Letter* report on the invasion, Mar. 24–31, 1712, also notes that Carolina's fear that the French would "draw the Chickasaw Indians unto them" provided a major reason for the invasion.

13. Welch had previously headed up an unofficial slaving expedition against the Choctaw in 1708.

14. House Journals, Book June 12, 1711–June 22, 1711, June 21.

15. House Journals, Book June 12, 1711–June 22, 1711, June 21; Book May 13, 1712–June 7, 1712, May 24. See also Book November 11, 1712–December 11, 1712, Nov. 20; Book February 1, 1708/09–February 19, 1708/09, Feb. 7, 19; Book October 19, 1709–November 5, 1709, Nov. 4, 5.

16. House Journals, Book May 13, 1712–June 7, 1712, May 24.

17. According to a letter of Dec. 19, 1711, from Hastings to Governor Robert Gibbs, cited in the *Boston News-Letter*, Mar. 24–31, 1712, Hastings estimated to have "burnt near 400 Houses and Plantations."

18. House Journals, Book May 13, 1712–June 7, 1712, May 24.

19. A small portion of the act has survived in the South Carolina Judgment Rolls. When agent John Wright sued traders for noncompliance with the trading act, the relevant portions of the act were included in the court papers. Thus, Wright sued merchant John Beauchamp for one hundred pounds SC for trading with Indians "beyond Port Royal or the Yamasee settlement," outside of an Indian town or settlement, and before the Indians had been in town for three days. Judgment Rolls, 1703–1790, Court of Common Pleas, SCDAH, 5A:310. Wright also sued John Cochran under the 1712 act for failing to attend the agent when summoned. Judgment Rolls, 5A:268.

20. House Journals, Book October 9, 1711–November 10, 1711, Nov. 7, 9; Book April 2, 1712–April 8, 1712, Apr. 4.

21. *Commissioners,* 21.

22. House Journals, Book May 13, 1712–June 7, 1712, June 6.

23. Barnwell, who previously had been appointed as commissioner to the Southern Indians, probably could not serve because of his injury in North Carolina.

24. House Journals, Book April 2, 1712–April 9, 1712, Apr. 2.

25. House Journals, Book April 2, 1712–April 9, 1712, Apr. 2.

26. House Journals, Book November 11, 1712–December 12, 1712, Dec. 12; *Commissioners,* 38.

27. *Commissioners,* 30–37.

28. La Harpe, *Historical Journal,* 73, 84.

29. *Commissioners,* 31–32.

30. *Commissioners,* 30–34.

31. Governor Francisco Córcoles y Martinez to the King, Jan. 14, 1708, in Mark F. Boyd, Hale G. Smith, and John W. Griffin, trans. and eds., *Here They Once Stood: The Tragic End of the Apalachee Missions* (Gainesville: University of Florida Press, 1951), 90. See also Robert Allen Matter, *Pre-Seminole Florida: Spanish Soldiers, Friars, and Indian Missions, 1513–1763* (New York: Garland, 1990).

32. Bullones quoted in Amy Turner Bushnell, *Situado and Sabana: Spain's Support System for the Presidio and Mission Provinces of Florida* (Athens: University of Georgia Press, 1994), 194.

33. Bishop Gerónimo Valdés to the King, Dec. 9, 1711, in John H. Hann, trans. and ed., *Missions to the Calusa* (Gainesville: University of Florida Press, 1991), 336.

34. Peter H. Wood estimates the population decline of Florida Indians more conservatively, at 12,300 from 1685 to 1715. This figure includes those who succumbed to disease, warfare, and other afflictions. See "The Changing Population of the Colonial South: An Overview by Race and Region, 1685–1790," in Peter H. Wood, Gregory A. Waselkov, and M. Thomas Hatley, eds., *Powhatan's Mantle: Indians in the Colonial Southeast* (Lincoln: University of Nebraska Press, 1989), 38, 51–56.

35. See Chapter 6 for a discussion by John Stewart of why the raiders tended to work in small groups.

36. See the discussion in Chapter 4.

37. See Wood, "Changing Population," 75–77, for discussion of population decline in this area.

38. Paul Du Ru, *Journal of Paul Du Ru: Missionary Priest to Louisiana,* trans. Ruth Lapham Butler (Chicago: Caxton Club, 1934), 66.

39. Pénicaut, *Fleur de Lys,* 159.

40. Pénicaut, *Fleur de Lys,* 159.

41. La Harpe, *Historical Journal,* 68–69, 75–76.

42. See Chapter 5 for discussion.

43. Patricia K. Galloway, *Choctaw Genesis, 1500–1700* (Lincoln: University of Nebraska Press, 1995), 356.

44. La Harpe, *Historical Journal,* 73.

45. D'Artaguiette au Comte de Pontchartrain, May 11, Aug. 26, 1709, AC, C13A, 2:427, 461.

413

46. Thomas Welch to Earl of Craven, Dec. 4, 1708, HM 1257, Maggs 498, HL.

47. Thomas C. Parramore, "With Tuscarora Jack on the Back Path to Bath," *North Carolina Historical Review* 64 (April 1987), 135, thought that Pollock was referring to how many Barnwell captured just before he left North Carolina, but I believe that he is referring to the entire time that Barnwell's forces were in the colony.

48. James Moore to ?, Mar. 27, 1713, *CRNC,* 2:27.

49. Le Jau to SPG, Apr. 11, 1713, in *Le Jau,* 131–132; *Boston News-Letter,* May 11–18, 1713. A contemporary map of the campaign also notes that Indian losses were at least eight hundred. See Joseph W. Barnwell, "The Second Tuscarora Expedition," *SCHM* 10 (January 1909), 33–48; Graffenreid thought there were two hundred burned of nine hundred killed and does not note the number of prisoners. "De Graffenried's Manuscript," *CRNC,* 1:956–957.

50. Edward Hyde to Mr. Rainsford, May 30, 1712, *CRNC,* 1:850.

51. Christopher Gale to [his sister], Nov. 2, 1711, Additional Manuscripts 32496, folio 44b, BL, for instance, noted that twenty-nine women and children had been taken in October 1711.

52. Council meeting, June 25, 1713, *CRNC,* 2:52.

53. For African import figures from 1706 forward, see Peter H. Wood, *Black Majority: Negroes in Colonial South Carolina from 1670 Through the Stono Rebellion* (New York: Norton, 1974), 151. In 1714 there were 419 Africans imported, but from 1706 to 1713 no year had more than 170, and four of the years had fewer than 76.

54. CO 5, 1265:29; SC Transcripts 6:173–174.

55. CO 33, 14:14, 23.

56. These records are housed at the Public Record Office, Kew, United Kingdom. I consulted all of the other English islands in the West Indies but found almost no records available until the 1720s or later.

57. *Journal of the English Board of Trade,* 11:174, Aug. 19, 1698, cited in Almon Wheeler Lauber, *Indian Slavery in Colonial Times Within the Present Limits of the United States* (1913; reprint, Williamstown, Mass.: Corner House, 1979), 178–179*n*2. J. Leitch Wright provides a general overview of the factors that led both Spanish and French to export American Indians to the West Indies in *The Only Land They Knew: The Tragic Story of the American Indian in the Old South* (New York: Free Press, 1981), 129–133.

58. K. G. Davies, *The Royal African Company* (London: Longman, 1957), 132–133, 139, 144, 313–314, 364 (quotation on 314).

59. Act no. 204, "An Act for the Laying an Imposition . . . ," *Statutes,* 2:200–206. The tax was to help defray the cost of the expedition against Saint Augustine. It was renewed to defray the cost of the Yamasee War. See Act no. 359, "An Act for Laying an Imposition on Liquors, Goods and Merchandizes . . . ," *Statutes,* 2:649–661.

60. CO 33, 14:45, records four Negroes imported from Carolina to Barbados. In 1720, New York records a shipment of six Negroes and another of five slaves to Barbados, illustrating that market conditions could draw African slaves from the mainland to the islands. CO 5, 1222:224, 226.

61. *Records,* 5:205.

62. Printed in B. R. Carroll, *Historical Collections . . . ,* 2 vols. (New York: Harper and Brothers, 1836), 2:255.

63. CO 5, 1222:37.

64. *The Public Records of the Colony of Connecticut . . .* , 15 vols. ([various publishers], 1850–1890), 5:534–535; Lauber, *Indian Slavery,* 189. The Indian could be confined during the entire month.

65. Cited in Lauber, *Indian Slavery,* 188.

66. Governor and Council, July 8, October 1715, *Public Records of the Colony of Connecticut,* 5:516, 534–535; "An Act prohibiting the importation, or bringing into this colony any Indian servants or slaves," July 5, 1715, in John Russell Bartlett, ed., *Records of the Colony of Rhode Island and Providence Plantations in New England,* 10 vols. (Providence, R.I.: A. C. Greene and Brother, 1856–1865), 4:193–194. Most Indian slaves in Connecticut likely were imported from Carolina. A 1711 law regarding freed slaves refers to slaves as comprising "negro, mulatto, or Spanish Indians." See "An act relating to Slaves, and such in Particular as shall happen to become servants for Time," May 1711, in *Public Records of the Colony of Connecticut,* 5:233.

67. Choctaw also flattened their heads; see James Adair, *History of the American Indians* (1775), ed. Samuel Cole Williams (New York: Promontory, 1930), 305.

68. Extensive discussion of features by eighteenth-century observers can be found in Adair, *History of American Indians;* and William Bartram, *Travels* [1772], ed. Francis Harper (New Haven: Yale University Press, 1958).

69. *Boston News-Letter,* Dec. 10–17, 1711.

70. *Boston News-Letter,* Mar. 11–18, 1717.

71. Other advertisements identifying Indians as from Carolina can be found in *Boston News-Letter,* Nov. 15–22, 1708, Aug. 13–20, Dec. 10–17, 1711.

72. *Boston News-Letter,* Aug. 13–20, 1711.

73. *Boston News-Letter,* Sept. 10–17, 1711.

74. *Boston News-Letter,* Sept. 17–24, 1716.

75. Thomas Pollock to [Governor Charles Craven], May 25, 1713, *CRNC,* 2:44–45; Council meeting, June 25, 1713, *CRNC,* 2:52.

76. Elizabeth Donnan, ed., *Documents Illustrative of the History of the Slave Trade to America,* 4 vols. (Washington, D.C.: Carnegie Institute, 1930–1935), 4:175–180. In 1711 Virginia placed a twenty-shilling tax on slaves imported by land and a five-pound tax on those imported by sea (4:93).

77. Lamhatty's story, recorded by Robert Beverley, is reprinted in David I. Bushnell, Jr., "The Account of Lamhatty," *American Anthropologist* 2 (October–December 1908), 568–574. It is worth noting that Lamhatty told Beverley that he was the last of the Towasa people, though in fact they continued to exist. As noted below, the Towasa were allies of the French, so it is possible that Lamhatty was astute enough to hide from the English not only this fact but the existence of his people to deter the slavers from seeking them out.

78. Marcel Trudel, *L'esclavage au Canada français: Histoire et conditions de l'esclavage* (Quebec: Presses Universitaires Laval, 1960).

79. "Memoire du s. Dartaguette . . . ," Feb. 26, 1708, AC, C13A, 2:57; "Memoire," 1714, AC, C13A, 3:655; Duclos au Comte de Pontchartrain, Apr. 17, 1714, AC, C13A, 3:623; Le Bartz, "Mémoire . . . ," [1716–1717], AE, Mémoires et Documents, Amérique, 1:156; "Memoire e Crozat sur l'état de la Louisiane et ses projets," Feb. 11, 1716, AC, C13A, 4:907.

80. "Census of Louisiana by De La Salle," Aug. 12, 1708, *MPA,* 2:32.

81. De la Salle au Comte de Pontchartrain, July 25, 1707, AC, C13, B:4. The sum of 220 livres equaled about £14 sterling.

82. Nicolas de la Salle to [Pontchartrain], May 12, 1709, AC, C13A, 2:395. The assiento refers to a contract between the king of Spain and other countries for the sale of African slaves in the Americas.

83. "Memoire du s. Dartaguette . . . ," Feb. 26, 1708.

84. Pontchartrain à Bégon, Nov. 30, 1708, AC, C13A, C13B, 30:77.

85. Bienville to Pontchartrain, Oct. 12, 1708, MPA, 2:37.

86. "Abstract of Letters from Bienville to Pontchartrain," July 28, 1706, MPA, 2: 23, 28.

87. Robert to Pontchartrain, Nov. 26, 1708, MPA, 2:45–46.

88. Pontchartrain to Bienville, May 10, 1710, MPA, 3:141. Robert's assessment helps clarify a point made by his contemporaries. Although Bienville and other French and English officials discussed exchanging Indians for Africans, in fact, this rarely occurred. Instead, Indians were sold to one buyer, and the cash could then be used to purchase Africans from another slaver. See discussion below for valuation placed on Indian slaves.

89. D'Artaguiette, "Memoire de ce que J'ai pû apendre . . ." Feb. 25, 1708.

90. "Census of Louisiana by De La Salle."

91. For d'Artaguiette, see d'Artaguiette au Comte de Pontchartrain, Jan. 10, 1711, AC, C13A, 2:633.

92. In 1726 the attorney general of Louisiana, referring to the need to capture runaway Indian slaves, recommended that "neighborhood Indians watch out for such runaways and arrest them." He made this call after three runaways had murdered Louis Congo, an African employed as an executioner. The attorney general feared that "prompt and sweeping action against runaways" must be taken "lest soon the community be raided by whole gangs." "Records of the Superior Court of Louisiana," Aug. 17, 1726, in Louisiana Historical Quarterly 3 (1920), 414.

93. This might be the group that La Harpe describes as the Yaguénéchiton, who lived with the Chitimacha in 1706. See John R. Swanton, Indian Tribes of the Lower Mississippi Valley and Adjacent Coast of the Gulf of Mexico, Smithsonian Institution Bureau of American Ethnology, Bulletin 43 (Washington, D.C.: Government Printing Office, 1911), 270, 337.

94. Nicolas de La Salle to [Pontchartrain], May 12, 1709, AC, C13A, 2:395. In 1728, Commandante Périer added another objection to Indian enslavement. He feared "that these Indian slaves being mixed with our negroes may induce them to desert with them, as has already happened, as they may maintain relations with them which might be disastrous to the colony when there are more blacks." Périer to [Abbé Raguet], May 12, 1728, MPA, 2:573.

95. D'Artaguiette au Comte de Pontchartrain, Jan. 10, 1711, AC, C13A, 2:633.

96. [Unknown author], "Etat des sauvages qui habitent depuis les Alibamons, jusqu'à la Caroline" [1713?], AC, C13C, 1:358.

97. D'Artaguiette, "Memoire de ce que J'ai pû apendre . . . ," Feb. 25, 1708; d'Artaguiette, "Memoire . . . ," Feb. 26, 1708, AC, F3, 24:53; Cadillac au Comte de Pontchartrain, [July or Sept.] 18, 1714, AC, C13A, 3:511.

98. [Minutes of Council], Mar. 28, 1716, AM, B1, 8:255. See also the career of Jean

Couture, recounted in Verner W. Crane, *The Southern Frontier, 1670–1732* (1929; reprint, New York: Norton, 1981), 42–44.

99. William Robert Snell, "Indian Slavery in Colonial South Carolina, 1671–1795" (Ph.D. diss., University of Alabama, 1972), table 5, 144.

100. Lauber, *Indian Slavery,* 300.

101. Verner W. Crane thought that planters preferred African workers to Indian workers because Indians "were at best poor workers in the fields." But the evidence Crane cites to show that Africans were considered more valuable than Indians was a comparison of African males to Indian females. *Southern Frontier,* 113 and *n20.*

102. Davies, *Royal African Company,* 313–315, discusses the rising costs of the trade to the slavers, which was not accompanied by a similar rise in the sale price of Africans in the period 1702–1712.

103. Wood, *Black Majority;* Daniel C. Littlefield, *Rice and Slaves: Ethnicity and the Slave Trade in Colonial South Carolina* (Baton Rouge: Louisiana University Press, 1981).

104. Health would have been another issue.

CHAPTER 12: THE YAMASEE WAR

1. *Commissioners,* 42.

2. *Commissioners,* 41–42.

3. *Commissioners,* 42.

4. I have changed the designation of the Cochran faction to the Nairne faction because of the latter's emergence as their leader.

5. *Commissioners,* 43. He had "only sent home a Slave" in it.

6. *Commissioners,* 42–43.

7. House Journals, Book November 9, 1714–December 18, 1714, Nov. 18.

8. *Commissioners,* 43.

9. *Commissioners,* 43, 44, 46.

10. *Commissioners,* 59. Wright's refusal to reclaim his goods by paying what amounted to 3 percent of their value, and a possible 3 percent later, remains puzzling, as was his refusal to allow Joseph Wright to pay the fine. Wright's actions are consistent, however, with his behavior and personality; he had a predilection for hounding his enemies, even when it hurt his interests. Likewise, his expressions of moral outrage must have offended the many who took umbrage at his self-righteous hypocrisy. Yet I wonder if Wright's willingness to risk losing his goods to government appropriation might be, in part, because they belonged to a silent partner whom Wright wished to punish.

11. Judgment Rolls, 1703–1790, Court of Common Pleas, SCDAH, 5A:268. There were four continuances in the course of the trial.

12. *Commissioners,* 44, 47.

13. *Commissioners,* 44. Previously, Wright had either sued or arrested Parris. The assembly paid a lawyer, John Robinson, to defend Parris. House Journals, Book November 17, 1713–December 18, 1713, Dec. 18.

14. *Commissioners,* 47–48.

15. *Commissioners,* 48–49.

16. *Commissioners,* 47.

17. *Commissioners,* 49–50.

18. *Commissioners,* 50.

19. *Commissioners,* 51–52.

20. *Commissioners,* 50–51.

21. *Commissioners,* 52.

22. House Journals, Book November 17, 1713–December 18, 1713, Nov. 19.

23. House Journals, Book November 17, 1713–December 18, 1713, Nov. 13; Book May 4, 1714–May 13, 1714, May 6, 12; Book June 1, 1714–June 12, 1714, June 8, 9.

24. House Journals, Book November 17, 1713–December 18, 1713, Nov. 19.

25. House Journals, Book November 17, 1713–December 18, 1713, Nov. 27.

26. For the early history of the Yuchi, see John R. Swanton, *Early History of the Creek Indians and Their Neighbors,* Smithsonian Institution Bureau of American Ethnology, Bulletin 73 (Washington, D.C.: Government Printing Office, 1922), 286–312.

27. All of the information concerning the attack on the Yuchi comes from *Commissioners,* 52–57.

28. *Commissioners,* 45, 186, 232, and throughout the journal.

29. *Commissioners,* 52–54.

30. *Commissioners,* 52–54.

31. Another trader claimed that Long had threatened the Cherokee when they refused him meat and oil, but this could only be emblematic of the dispute between them. *Commissioners,* 57.

32. *Commissioners,* 56.

33. Board of Trade to Alexander Spotswood, 1711, *Calendar of State Papers,* Col. Ser., America and West Indies, 45 vols. (London: Longman and others, 1860–), 25:364; Alexander Spotswood to the Council of Trade, Sept. 5, 1711, *Official Letters,* 1:110–112. He sums up his arguments in Alexander Spotswood to Mr. Popple, Apr. 16, 1717, *Official Letters,* 2:230–236.

34. *Commissioners,* 58.

35. *Commissioners,* 61–62.

36. *Commissioners,* 62.

37. House Journals, Book November 9, 1714–December 18, 1714, Nov. 18, 19, 23, Dec. 1, 3, 4, 7, 10.

38. *Commissioners,* 61.

39. *Commissioners,* 63.

40. House Journals, Book May 4, 1714–May 13, 1714, May 13; Book June 1, 1714–June 12, 1714, June 12. The colony also provided provisions for Indians on their return from North Carolina: Book April 2, 1712–April 9, 1712, Apr. 9, 10 [sic]; Book November 11, 1712–December 11, 1712, Nov. 20; Book November 17, 1713–December 18, 1713, Dec. 17.

41. House Journals, Book June 1, 1714–June 12, 1714, June 4, 8.

42. House Journals, Book May 4, 1714–May 13, 1714, May 12; Book June 1, 1714–June 12, 1714, June 9, 10.

43. House Journals, Book June 1, 1714–June 12, June 12.

44. House Journals, Book June 1, 1714–June 12, June 12.

45. *Commissioners,* 57.

46. *Commissioners,* 58.

47. *Commissioners,* 59.

48. *Commissioners,* 59; House Journals, Book June 1, 1714–June 12, 1714, June 8, 9, 12.

49. House Journals, Book November 9, 1714–December 18, 1714, Nov. 10.

50. House Journals, Book November 9, 1714–December 18, 1714, Nov. 10, 12, 16, 17, 18, 19, 23, Dec. 1.

51. House Journals, Book November 9, 1714–December 18, 1714, Dec. 17. They also complained about how long it took him to make the copies. House Journals, Book February 8, 1714/15–February 25, 1714/15, Feb. 11. He eventually published the colony's laws in 1736. Nicholas Trott, *The Laws of the Province of South Carolina . . . ,* 2 vols. (Charles Town: Lewis Timothy, 1736).

52. House Journals, Book November 9, 1714–December 18, 1714, Dec. 18. The house also wanted to reconsider whether Nairne should be both agent and commissioner of the Yamasee and Apalachicola.

53. House Journals, Book February 8, 1714/15–February 25, 1714/15, Feb. 9. Trott, through his wife, Ann Amy Trott, had a proprietary share in the colony. William S. Powell, *The Proprietors of Carolina* (Raleigh, N.C.: Carolina Charter Tercentenary Commission, 1963), 68–69.

54. House Journals, Book February 8, 1714/15–February 25, 1714/15, Feb. 11.

55. House Journals, Book February 8, 1714/15–February 25, 1714/15, Feb. 11, 22.

56. House Journals, Book February 8, 1714/15–February 25, 1714/15, Feb. 19, 23, 24, 25.

57. House Journals, Book February 8, 1714/15–February 25, 1714/15, Feb. 19, 23, 24, 25.

58. *Commissioners,* 65. We may assume that Bray's wife was Yamasee; the Yamasee would not tell her to go "to their Town" when the attack came if it referred to Charles Town, because the attack would also have been against there.

59. Alexander Hewitt, *An Historical Account of the Rise and Progress of the Colonies of South Carolina and Georgia,* 2 vols. in 1 (London: Alexander Donaldson, 1779), reprinted in B. R. Carroll, *Historical Collections . . . ,* 2 vols. (New York: Harper and Brothers, 1836), 1:192–194. Sanute's warning of the Frasiers formed the basis for an important part of the plot in William Gilmore Simms's novel *The Yemassee: A Romance of Carolina* (New York: Harper and Brothers, 1835).

60. Le Jau says that two hundred escaped. Le Jau to SPG, May 10, 1715, in *Le Jau,* 155.

61. For the initial attack, see Charles Rodd to his employer in London (forwarded by him to the king), in *Calendar,* 28:166–169, but compare with the original in French, SC Transcripts, 6:74–85; *Boston News-Letter,* June 6–13, 1715; Governor Craven to Lord Townshend, May 23, 1715, in *Calendar,* 28:227–229; William Treadwell Bull to SPG, Aug. 10, 1715, in SPG, B4, Pt. 1, 49–57.

62. Bull to SPG, Aug. 10, 1715, in SPG, B4, Pt. 1, 49–57.

63. For an overview of the military events, see Chapman J. Milling, *Red Carolinians* (Chapel Hill: University of North Carolina Press, 1940), 141–152.

64. Thomas Hasell to SPG, Dec. 1, 1715, SPG, B4, Pt. 1, 93–96.

65. Hasell said the Indians got within twenty miles of Charles Town. Hasell to SPG, Dec. 1, 1715.

66. For a summary of the Yamasee prince's life, see Frank J. Klingberg, "The Mystery of the Lost Yamasee Prince," *SCHM* 63 (January 1962), 18–32; Gideon Johnston to SPG, Dec. 19, 1715, Apr. 4, 1716, SPG, B4, Pt. 1, 102–108, 226–230; Prince George to SPG, Dec. 8, 1715, SPG, B4, Pt. 1, 97.

67. Le Jau naturally interpreted the war as God's judgment against the colony. Le Jau to SPG, May 10, 1715, in *Le Jau*, 153.

68. Gideon Johnston to SPG, Dec. 9, 1715, SPG, B4, Pt. 1, 98–99.

69. Bull to SPG, Aug. 10, 1715.

70. Alan Gallay, "The Great Sellout: George Whitefield on Slavery," in Joseph F. Tripp and Winfred B. Moore, eds., *Looking South: Chapters in the Story of an American Region* (Westport, Conn.: Greenwood, 1990), and *The Formation of a Planter Elite: Jonathan Bryan and the Southern Colonial Frontier* (Athens: University of Georgia Press, 1989), 38; and Harvey H. Jackson, "Hugh Bryan and the Evangelical Movement in Colonial South Carolina," *William and Mary Quarterly*, 3d Ser., 43 (October 1986), 594–614.

71. Bull to SPG, Aug. 10, 1715.

72. Richard L. Haan, "The 'Trade Do's Not Flourish as Formerly': The Ecological Origins of the Yamassee War of 1715," *Ethnohistory* 28 (Fall 1982), 341–358.

73. Donald A. Grinde and Bruce E. Johansen challenge Haan's assumption that the Yamasee faced an "ecological collapse accompanied by declining deer populations." They argue instead that Yamasee were not eating deer. Grinde and Johansen overlook the need of the Yamasee to pay off their debts with either captured slaves or deerskins, so that even if they did not rely on the deer as a food source, they still had to find some way to pay debts and earn credits for trade goods.

Grinde and Johansen offer many fascinating tidbits on the Yamasee that are not available elsewhere, but their ahistorical slant mars their work. For instance, one would never know from reading their work that the Yamasee were heavily involved as enslavers of other Indians: they conveniently avoid discussion of anything that would add gray areas to their portrait of the Yamasee. Moreover, there are peculiar mistakes of fact. For instance, they criticize John R. Swanton for omitting reference to the Yamasee in his *Early History*, but Swanton devotes a chapter to the Yamasee. They mistakenly identify the Yamasee neighbors, the Palachicola, as the Apalachee, instead of the Apalachicola, and they make many dubious and unsubstantiated claims about Yamasee settlement in Georgia and South Carolina. Unfortunately, their goal is not to seek the history of the Yamasee but to create an artificial history to suit their personal political vision that casts Europeans as evildoers and Native Americans as peace-loving ecologists. "Pre- and Post-Columbian Native Ecology: The Yamasees," in Grinde and Johansen, *Ecocide of Native America: Environmental Destruction of Indian Lands and Peoples* (Santa Fe: Clear Light, 1995), 79–103.

74. Haan, "'Trade Do's Not Flourish as Formerly,'" 343.

75. See the discussion of problems of Yamasee demographics in Chapter 7.

76. See Gallay, *Formation of a Planter Elite*, 12–15. La Harpe thought that the Carolina Indian attack on the English was done in imitation of the Choctaw, who had recently pillaged and sent running the English traders among them. La Harpe is undoubtedly mistaken in thinking the Yamasee were simply taking their cues from Choctaw bravery in standing up to the English. Jean-Baptiste Bénard de La Harpe, *The Historical*

Journal of the Establishment of the French in Louisiana, trans. Virginia Koenig and Joan Cain, ed. Glenn R. Conrad (Lafayette: University of Southwestern Louisiana Press, 1971), 91–92.

77. David Crawley to William Byrd, July 30, 1715, SC Transcripts, 6:110–111. Also printed in *Calendar,* 28:247–248. Thirty years later Edmond Atkin alluded to the abuses of an agent against the Yamasee as a cause of the war, in which he probably was referring to former agent Wright. See Wilbur R. Jacobs, ed., *The Appalachian Indian Frontier: The Edmond Atkin Report and Plan of 1755* (Lincoln: University of Nebraska Press, 1967), 18.

78. Colonel Heathcote to Lord Townshend, July 16, 1715, in E. B. O'Callaghan, ed., *Documents Relative to the Colonial History of the State of New York,* vol. 5 (Albany, N.Y.: Weed, Parsons, 1854), 432–434.

79. Heathcote to Townshend, July 16, 1715, 433.

80. Governor Robert Hunter to Secretary William Popple, July 2, 1715, and "Conference of Governor Hunter with the Indians," Aug. 27, 1715, *Colonial History of New York,* 415, 437–438.

81. Hunter to Popple, July 2, 1715, and "Conference of Governor Hunter with the Indians," Aug. 27, 1715.

82. "Reply of Five Nations to Governor Hunter," Aug. 31, 1715, *Colonial History of New York,* 443–444.

83. "Reply of Five Nations to Governor Hunter," Aug. 31, 1715, "Message of Five Nations to Commissioners of Indian Affairs, Oct. 3, 1715, Cors Urom to Governor Hunter, Oct. 17, 1715, Governor Hunter to Lords of Trade, Apr. 30, 1716, July 1717, and Governor Hunter to the Five Nations, June 13, 16, 1717, all in *Colonial History of New York,* 444–446, 463–464, 464, 475–476, 483–484, 485–487, 485–491.

84. John Stewart to Queen Anne, October 1711, AC, C13C, 2:72.

85. Hewitt, *Historical Account,* 193–194.

86. Some Creek did turn against the Yamasee several years later. After South Carolina and the Creek made peace in 1717, some Creek towns agreed to attack the Yamasee. Milling, *Red Carolinians,* 156–158.

87. [Unknown author], "Etat des sauvages qui habitent depuis les Alibamons, jusqu'à la Caroline" [1713?], AC, C13C, 1:358.

88. La Harpe, *Historical Journal,* 91–92. Verner W. Crane and Chapman Milling believe that the Chickasaw did remain loyal to the English. See Crane, *The Southern Frontier, 1670–1732* (1929; reprint, New York: Norton, 1981), 169–170; and Milling, *Red Carolinians,* 142.

89. George Chicken, "A Letter from Carolina in 1715, and Journal of the March of the Carolinians into the Cherokee Mountains in the Yemassee Indian War, 1715–1716," in Langdon Cheves, ed., *Year Book of the City of Charleston, 1894* (Charleston, S.C.: n.p., 1895), 333.

90. House Journals, Book May 6, 1715–May 13, 1715, May 9; Book August 2, 1715–August 27, 1715, Aug. 6, 8.

91. I have not been able to identify the Warwees.

92. Chicken, "Letter from Carolina," 334.

93. Chicken, "Letter from Carolina," 334–335.

94. Chicken, "Letter from Carolina," 337.

95. Chicken, "Letter from Carolina," 341.

96. Chicken, "Letter from Carolina," 342.

97. Chicken, "Letter from Carolina," 343. A recent history of the Cherokee in this era, by M. Thomas Hatley, provides a different interpretation of Cherokee behavior and the passage in Chicken's journal that records these affairs. Hatley argues that the Cherokee were frustrated with the English for expecting them to fight the Creek alone. He believes that Caesar, head of the anti-Creek faction, "sensing the hesitation of the colonial force, refused to take up the invitation of the English to fight unilaterally against their neighbors." My reading of Chicken's journal leads me to believe that Chicken wished the Cherokee to *not* fight the Creek and that he wanted to *prevent* the resumption of warfare between the two. M. Thomas Hatley, *The Dividing Path: Cherokee and South Carolinians Through the Era of the American Revolution* (New York: Oxford University Press, 1993), 25–26.

98. Chicken, "Letter from Carolina," 345.

99. Chicken, "Letter from Carolina," 346. Historians have mistakenly thought that the Creek headmen visited the Cherokee in order to enlist them against the colony. But they overlook the fact that the Creek were coming to meet Chicken. The colony chose to accept the Cherokee interpretation that the Creek were trying to enlist them against the English, because the murder of the Creek headmen had created a *fait accompli,* with the Cherokee as their ally and the Creek as their enemy. But the behavior of the Cherokee headmen in fomenting a war is obvious in Chicken's journal, and their murder of the Creek headmen a clumsy but effective ploy in making sure that peace was not made. For the colony's interpretation, see SC Transcripts, 6:157–159.

100. Chicken, "Letter from Carolina," 348–349.

101. Jacobs, *Appalachian Indian Frontier,* 62.

102. English and French still shipped Indians out of the region, as when the French enslaved Natchez during the Natchez War, but the wars themselves were not conducted to obtain slaves, and the trade no longer had economic importance.

103. Henry Folmer, *Franco-Spanish Rivalry in North America, 1524–1763* (Glendale, Calif.: A. H. Clark, 1953). Jeanne T. Heidler, "Pensacola and the War of the Quadruple Alliance (1718–1722)," in Alan Gallay, ed., *The Colonial Wars of North America, 1512–1763: An Encyclopedia* (New York: Garland, 1996), 554–556.

104. Jane Landers, "Gracia Real de Santa Teresa de Mose: A Free Black Town in Spanish Colonial Florida," *American Historical Review* 95 (February 1990), 9–30. Also see her book *Black Society in Spanish Florida,* foreword by Peter H. Wood (Urbana: University of Illinois Press, 1999).

105. Verne E. Chatelaine, *The Defenses of Spanish Florida, 1565–1763* (Washington, D.C.: Carnegie Institute, 1941); Larry E. Ivers, *British Drums on the Southern Frontier: The Military Colonization of Georgia, 1733–1749* (Chapel Hill: University of North Carolina Press, 1974); Gallay, *Formation of a Planter Elite,* 23–29; Jane Landers, "Battle of St. Augustine (1728)," in *Colonial Wars of North America,* 648–649; Doris B. Fisher, "Battle of Bloody Marsh," in *Colonial Wars of North America,* 68.

106. For the history of this fort, see Daniel H. Thomas, *Fort Toulouse: The French Outpost at the Alabamas on the Coosa,* intro. Gregory A. Waselkov (Tuscaloosa: University of Alabama Press, 1989).

107. The Chickasaw and Cherokee had little interaction with the Spanish, but

played the French and English against one another. The Creek, however, were able to negotiate with all three.

108. Patricia K. Galloway, "Choctaw Factionalism and Civil War, 1746–1750," in Carolyn Keller Reeves, ed., *The Choctaw Before Removal* (Jackson: University Press of Mississippi, 1985), 120–156; Michael James Foret, "Choctaw Civil War (1746–1750)," in *Colonial Wars of North America*, 135–136.

109. For the comparison of Virginia's and South Carolina's economies, see John J. McCusker and Russell Menard, *The Economy of British America, 1607–1789* (Chapel Hill: University of North Carolina Press, 1985).

110. SC Transcripts, 7:186–188.

111. John Barnwell, *The Northern B[ra]nch of Alatama River which joyns ye main River 3 miles higher up . . . ,* 1721, Map Room, LC, photocopy of original in Public Record Office, Kew, United Kingdom. The naturalist William Bartram recorded a fantastic story he heard from the Creek before the American Revolution about the Yamasee in the Okefenokee Swamp. The Creek told him that there was in the swamp "a most blissful spot of the earth . . . inhabited by a peculiar race of Indians, whose women are incomparably beautiful." Some of the Creek hunters, when lost in the swamp and "perishing, were unexpectedly relieved" by these women, whom they call daughters of the sun. . . . their husbands were fierce men, and cruel to strangers." From "the elevated banks of an island" the Creek could see these Indians' settlements, but "like enchanted land . . . it seemed to fly before them, alternately appearing and disappearing." One time, the "young warriors were inflamed with an irresistible desire to invade, and make a conquest of so charming a country; but all their attempts have hitherto proved abortive, never having been able again to find that enchanting spot, nor even any road or pathway to it; yet they say that they frequently meet with certain signs of its being inhabited, as the building of canoes, footsteps of men, etc. They tell another story concerning the inhabitants of this sequestered country, which seems probable enough, which is, that they are the posterity of a fugitive remnant of the ancient Yamases, who escaped massacre after a bloody and decisive conflict between them and the Creek nation (who, it is certain, conquered, and nearly exterminated, that once powerful people) and here found an asylum remote and secure from the fury of their proud conquerors."

The Creek did indeed fight the Yamasee, but many, as we have seen, moved to Florida, others joined the Creek Confederacy, and another group returned to the vicinity of the Savannah River. It is certainly possible that Yamasee lived in the Okefenokee as well. William Bartram, *Travels Through North and South Carolina, Georgia, East and West Florida* (London: n.p., 1792), 24–25.

112. Sir Robert Montgomery and Colonel John Barnwell, *The Most Delightful Golden Isles: Being a Proposal for the Establishment of a Colony in the Country to the South of Carolina* [1717] (Atlanta: Cherokee, 1966).

113. Robert L. Meriwether, *The Expansion of South Carolina, 1729–1765* (Kingsport, Tenn.: Southern, 1940).

114. Gallay, *Formation of a Planter Elite*, 18–23.

115. This is Temporary Acts #21 in Trott, New Collections, SCDAH. The original copy of the act was long thought to be lost and thus was not printed in either Trott, *Laws of the Province of South Carolina,* or *Statutes. Statutes,* 3:44, Bill #392, notes it as having been lost. In recent years the bill was discovered in the archives.

AFTERWORD

1. John R. Swanton, *Indians of the Southeastern United States*, Bureau of American Ethnology, Bulletin 137 (Washington, D.C.: Government Printing Office, 1946), 60, 84; Daniel F. Littlefield, *Africans and Creeks: From the Colonial Period to the Civil War* (Westport, Conn.: Greenwood, 1979), 8; Theda Perdue, *Slavery and the Evolution of Cherokee Society* (Knoxville: University of Tennessee Press, 1979), 36.

2. For the role of Africans in building the colony, see Peter H. Wood, *Black Majority: Negroes in Colonial South Carolina from 1670 Through the Stono Rebellion* (New York: Norton, 1974).

3. Figures drawn from Barnwell in SC Transcripts, 7:238–239.

4. These statistics are drawn from Wood, *Black Majority,* 151.

5. I do not mean to imply here that the elite did not jockey for power, only that they united in terms of securing the slave system to their benefit and that they united when they needed to keep slaves and free whites in line. I have argued elsewhere that the slave-holding elite of the northern parishes were at odds with the elite of the southern parishes as late as the 1740s. Alan Gallay, *The Formation of a Planter Elite: Jonathan Bryan and the Southern Colonial Frontier* (Athens: University of Georgia Press, 1989), 55–59.

6. A good place to begin for examining Indian-African interactions is Daniel H. Usner, Jr., *Indians, Settlers, and Slaves in a Frontier Exchange Economy: The Lower Mississippi Valley Before 1783* (Chapel Hill: University of North Carolina Press, 1992), 58–59, 72–75, 86–87. A more general study of these interactions throughout North America can be found in Jack D. Forbes, *Black Africans and Native Americans: Color, Race, and Caste in the Evolution of Red-Black Peoples* (New York: Blackwell, 1988).

7. For the barring of Indians from the plantation areas, see David H. Corkran, *The Creek Frontier, 1540–1783* (Norman: University of Oklahoma Press, 1967), 68, and Wood, *Black Majority,* 116; SCCHJ, *May 18, 1741–July 10, 1742,* 420–421. For restrictions on the employment of blacks in the Indian trade, see *Statutes,* 3:145, 332; W. L. McDowell, Jr., ed., *Documents Relating to Indian Affairs, May 21, 1750–August 7, 1754,* Colonial Records of South Carolina Series 2 (Columbia, S.C.: SCDAH, 1958), 86–89, 136, 199; and Verner W. Crane, *The Southern Frontier, 1670–1732* (1929; reprint, New York: Norton, 1981), 203.

8. Chapman J. Milling, *Red Carolinians* (Chapel Hill: University of North Carolina Press, 1940), 121, 123, 126, 127; SCCHJ, *November 8, 1734–June 7, 1735,* 235. To promote enmity between slaves and Tuscarora, slaves were offered a reward of fifty pounds if they killed a Tuscarora and sixty pounds "per Head for every Tuskerora Indian that shall be taken alive" (233).

9. Africans and Indians could unite with each other, not because they had any special cultural affinity, but out of mutual interests. Neither had a racial consciousness similar to that developing among Europeans. Indians understood people in a variety of ways and in a variety of conditions that involved kinship, alliance, and culture. They judged people not by how they looked but by the connections or lack of connections that existed between them. They were fully aware of the European obsession with skin color and of the Europeans' attempt to press their racial ideology on them—at least in terms of seeing Africans as worthy only of enslavement. A meeting between an Indian and an escaped African was thus filled with innumerable possibilities, some of which depended on the con-

ditions under which they met. A runaway who "discovered" a party of Indians was more likely to be treated as a free agent than a runaway discovered by Indians, who then might be returned for the reward. Other circumstances and the runaway's skills and personality also affected the outcome.

10. SC Transcripts, 13:64–65.

11. George Chicken, "A Letter from Carolina in 1715, and Journal of the March of the Carolinians into the Cherokee Mountains in the Yemassee Indian War, 1715–1716," in *Year Book of the City of Charleston, 1894*, 344.

12. Cited in Milling, *Red Carolinians*, 226. The 100 men in 1720 was a large decline from the 210 reported in Barnwell's census of 1715. According to one source, by late 1716 some Waccamaw had made peace with the colony, but those who did not fled to the Saraw. SC Transcripts, 6:241, 7:239.

13. When in 1758 four Cherokee were killed while visiting among South Carolina whites, the Cherokee asked the Chickasaw if they knew anything of the matter. A Chickasaw meco told the Cherokee that he was "very sorry to hear that [y]our people have been killed." He "apprehended a Negro Fellow" to question him about the murders. This man related that he was at Fort Augusta, where a white had received a letter reporting how the killings occurred near his house. Moreover, the black "told the Chickasaw," it "was the opinion of the White People" that "the Cherokees were fools and that it [the murderers] would never be found out." W. L. McDowell, ed., *Documents Relating to Indian Affairs, 1754–1765* (Columbia, S.C.: SCDAH, 1970), 444.

14. "Journal of Colonel George Chicken's Mission from Charleston, S.C., to the Cherokees, 1726," in Newton D. Mereness, ed., *Travels in the American Colonies* (New York: Macmillan, 1916), 116. Captain Daniel Pepper echoed Chicken's sentiments. The agent to the Creek Indians wrote Governor William Henry Lyttleton, Mar. 30, 1757, complaining that seven traders had brought eight slaves with them. He concluded, "The carrying of Negroes among the Indians has all along been thought detrimental, as an Intimacy between them ought to be avoided." See McDowell, ed., *Documents Relating to Indian Affairs, 1754–1765*, 357. Similarly, when "one of the Cherokee Chiefs" arrived in South Carolina in the 1740s accompanied by two blacks, the Commons house begged Lieutenant Governor William Bull to purchase and transport them "from thence to the West Indies or Northern Colonies to prevent any Detriment that they might do this Province by getting acquainted with the Cherokees." Apparently, Bull was unable to make the purchase, for there is no record in the assembly journals of money set aside for this purpose. *SCCHJ, May 18, 1741–July 10, 1742*, 45. Also see Daniel Pepper to William Henry Lyttelton, "Some Remarks on the Creek Nation" [1756], Lyttelton Papers, William L. Clements Library, University of Michigan, Ann Arbor.

15. "Deposition of Richard Smith," July 12, 1751, in McDowell, ed., *Documents Relating to Indian Affairs, May 2, 1750–August 7, 1754*, 103.

16. See, e.g., McDowell, ed., *Documents Relating to Indian Affairs, 1754–1765*, 190.

17. *Commissioners*, 80. For French use of Indians to return runaway Africans, see *MPA*, 2:563.

18. Wilbur R. Jacobs, ed., *The Appalachian Indian Frontier: The Edmond Atkin Report and Plan of 1755* (Lincoln: University of Nebraska Press, 1967), 44–45.

19. Daniel Pepper to Governor Lyttelton, June 28, 1757, in McDowell, ed., *Documents Relating to Indian Affairs, 1754–1765*, 387–388.

20. In 1725, Indians from the Missouri country were sent to Paris. The French had also intended to send Choctaw and Alabama, but the great expense forced the authorities to cancel their debarkation. Those who went to Paris were duly impressed, but on their return other Indians could not believe their stories of French grandeur because of the abject condition of the French they knew in America. "Minutes of the Council," Jan. 10, 1725, *MPA*, 3:476–477; Frank Norall, *Bourgmont: Explorer of the Missouri, 1698–1725* (Lincoln: University of Nebraska Press, 1988), 81–88; Eric Hinderaker, *Elusive Empires: Constructing Colonialism in the Ohio Valley, 1673–1800* (Cambridge: Cambridge University Press, 1997), 38.

21. The Yamacraw lived in the vicinity of modern-day Savannah, Georgia. Their origins are obscure, but it is generally believed that they had been part of one of the many Creek peoples and then either banished or removed voluntarily for reasons unknown.

22. Louis XV of France likewise denied the French queen the opportunity to see the visiting party of Indians in 1725 because of their "savage and too bizarre attire." Quoted in Norall, *Bourgmont,* 86.

23. John T. Juricek, ed., *Early American Indian Documents: Treaties and Laws, 1607–1789,* vol. 11: *Georgia Treaties, 1733–1763* (Frederick, Md.: University Publications of America, 1989), 23.

24. Edward Kimber, *A Relation or Journal of a Late Expedition to the Gates of St. Augustine, in Florida . . .* (London: T. Astley, 1744), 18, 29, 31. Also printed in Alan Gallay, ed., *Voices of the Old South: Eyewitness Accounts, 1528–1861* (Athens: University of Georgia Press, 1994), 53–54.

25. James Adair, *History of the American Indians* [1775], ed. Samuel Cole Williams (New York: Promontory, 1930), 461, emphasis added.

26. William L. Anderson, "William Henry Lyttleton (1724–1808)" and "Cherokee War," in Alan Gallay, ed., *The Colonial Wars of North America, 1512–1763: An Encyclopedia* (New York: Garland, 1996), 406–407, 121–123.

27. Corkran, *Creek Frontier;* Alan Gallay, "The Search for an Alternate Source of Trade: The Creek Indians and Jonathan Bryan," *Georgia Historical Quarterly* 75 (Summer 1989), 209–230.

28. Gregory A. Waselkov, "Fort Toulouse," in *Colonial Wars,* 745–746; Daniel H. Thomas, *Fort Toulouse: The French Outpost at the Alabama on the Coosa,* intro. Gregory A. Waselkov (Tuscaloosa: University of Alabama Press, 1989).

29. The South Carolinians also used the establishment of Georgia to defend their colony from external enemies, particularly the Spanish. With the English push into Georgia in the 1730s, the Spanish, almost powerless to stop the expansion, stepped up cold-war tactics, publicizing their offer of freedom to slaves who escaped the British plantation system. Carolina sent a representative to ask the Spanish to desist: to convince them that racial solidarity against African slaves should take precedence over any dispute between Europeans. The Spanish refused. When Carolina Angolan slaves shortly thereafter rebelled in September 1739, the British blamed Saint Augustine for inspiring the slaves to violence in the hope of freedom. The English once again tried to eliminate Spanish Florida, but a combined land and sea invasion against Saint Augustine failed in 1740, and though the Spanish half-heartedly counterattacked a few years later, stalemate ensued between the two until the Spanish ceded East Florida to Great Britain in 1763. Larry E. Ivers, *British Drums on the Southern Frontier: The Military Colonization of Georgia, 1733–*

1749 (Chapel Hill: University of North Carolina Press, 1974); Wood, *Black Majority,* 308–323; Gallay, *Formation of a Planter Elite,* 23–29.

30. William G. Shade, *Democratizing the Old Dominion: Virginia and the Second Party System, 1824–1861* (Charlottesville: University of Virginia Press, 1996).

31. For discussion of the expansion of categories of people in New Spain, see Anthony Pagden, "Identity Formation in Spanish America," in Nicholas Canny and Anthony Pagden, eds., *Colonial Identity in the Atlantic World, 1500–1800* (Princeton, N.J.: Princeton University Press, 1987), 51–93, esp. 69–70. On French incorporation of Native Americans, see Anthony Pagden, *Lords of All the World: Ideologies of Empire in Spain, Britain and France, c. 1500–c. 1800* (New Haven and London: Yale University Press, 1995), 149–151.

32. James Axtell, "The White Indians of Colonial America," in *The European and the Indian: Essays in the Ethnohistory of Colonial North America* (New York: Oxford University Press, 1981).

33. English in the sixteenth through mid-eighteenth centuries were very conscious of their cultural backwardness in terms of art, music, fashion, and other cultural forms. The general acceptance in Europe of the superiority of French language and culture, particularly in comparison to English, especially rankled. For Dutch relations with Indians, see Allen W. Trelease, "Dutch Treatment of the American Indian, with Particular Reference to New Netherland," in Howard Peckham and Charles Gibson, eds., *Attitudes of Colonial Powers Toward the American Indian* (Salt Lake City: University of Utah Press, 1969); Donna Merwick, *Possessing Albany, 1630–1710: The Dutch and English Experiences* (Cambridge: Cambridge University Press, 1990). On Dutch culture in the period, see Simon Schama, *The Embarrassment of Riches: An Interpretation of Dutch Culture in the Golden Age* (New York: Knopf, 1987).

INDEX

Abhika, 125, 131, 139, 183, 185, 202; demography of, 205–206

Act of Union (*1707*), 166, 177, 232

Adair, James, 238, 351–352

African slaves: and Cherokee, 348; arrival in South, 345–346; carried from Carolina to Florida in *1686*, 83; conversion to Christianity, 45, 228, 230, 238–239; cost of, 301; demography of in South Carolina, 200–201, 346–347; in early South Carolina, 43; employed in Indian trade, 348–349; English fear alliance with Indians, 94; exchanged for captured Choctaw, 290; lords proprietors' views of, 45–47; and Native Americans, 94, 345–350, 416*n*94, 424–425*n*9, 425*n*17; and refuge in Florida, 339; and refuge with Tuscarora, 272, 347; Scots' desire for in Carolina, 81; Settlement Indians capture, 62, 91, 94–95, 347–349; as soldiers, 167, 407*n*57; and Tuscarora, 272, 424*n*8; Yamasee liberate, 347–348; in Yamasee War, 329, 347–348

African slave trade, 46; in context of Indian slave trade, 294–295, 299, 300–302, 305–306, 312–314; cost of slaves, 301; duties on, 301

Agriculture, 23–24, 48, 89

Ahele, 317

Alabama, 14, 33, 131, 139, 140, 144, 149, 154, 163, 183, 202, 294, 316, 317, 334; and Choctaw, 141–142; demography of, 205, 206; and English, 137–138; and French, 134–135, 137–138, 293

Alabama River, 17, 134, 202

Albany, 261

Algonquins, 30–31, 265–266, 380–381*n*52

Alston, John, 250

Altamaha, 90

Altamaha River, 342, 343

Amareta, 304

Amelia Island, 85

Anderson, David G., 28

Anglicans, 66, 158; Church establishment in Carolina, 226; and missionizing Indians,

429

Anglicans (continued)
228–231; politics of, 224–226, 232–233;
views of empire, 231–234. *See also* Le Jau,
Francis; Thomas, Samuel
Anglo-Spanish War (*1740–1744*), 97
Anne, Queen, 177, 195, 212, 220–221
Antigua, 78, 83, 300
Apalachee, 16, 29, 65, 132, 138, 152, 175,
191, 200, 202, 233, 273, 288, 293, 331,
335, 340, 394*n*98; and Christianity,
145–146, 236; attack Creek, 186–187;
complaints against traders, 214, 242–244;
demography of, 201, 204–206; employed in
Indian trade, 169; enslavement of, 146–149,
295–296; and French, 148–149; illegal
enslavement of, 214; invaded by English and
allied Indians, 144–149; move to Savannah
River, 149; and Spanish, 33–34, 145–146;
and Tuscarora War, 267. *See also* Commissioners of the Indian trade; Indian traders
Apalachicola, 16, 70, 250, 279, 331, 340;
demography of, 201, 204, 206
Apalachicola River, 55, 201
Appalachian Mountains, 31, 32, 99, 145, 307,
319
Araomahau, Chief, 80
Arbousset, General, 152
Archdale, John, 67
Arkansas, 129, 175; and calumet ceremony,
102–103, 108–109, 111; characterized
by French missionaries, 111–112, 114;
enslavement of, 296–297, 299; ethnicity of,
112–113; Marquette visits, 102–104; mis-
sionaries among, 106, 108–109; as slavers,
130; town divisions, 112
Arkansas River, 101
Artaguette Diron, Jean-Baptiste Martin D',
289, 309–310, 312
Ashepoo, 84–85
Ashley River, 51, 52, 73
Assapallago, 243
Atasi, 202
Atkin, Edmond, 338, 349, 392*n*79, 421*n*77
Augusta, 73
Augusta, Fort, 425*n*13

Ayubale, 145
Aztecs, 27

Bahama Islands, 68; Spanish attack on, 77
Barbados, 31, 80, 91, 300, 301, 313
Barcía, Andrés Gonzalez de, 74
Barker, Captain, 328–329
Barnwell, Fort, 273
Barnwell, John, 231, 251, 252, 287, 328,
347, 400*n*20; blamed for resumption of
Tuscarora War, 274–276, 408*n*71, 409*n*74;
leads Euro-Indian army in Tuscarora
War, 267–276; political career, 261,
371*n*31; produces census of Indians,
203–204; promotes defense of South
Carolina, 342–343; pursues peace with
Yamasee, 341–342; reputation suffers, 282
Bartram, William, 423*n*111
Bath, 270
Batz, Alexander de, 122
Bayagoula, 297; attacked by slavers, 150; attack
Mougoulacha, 150; conflict with Ouma,
107–110
Beadon, Stephen, 255
Beauchamp, John, 412*n*19
Bégon, Michel, 309
Belfast, 77
Bermuda, 300
Bern, 273
Berresford, Richard, 292
Beverley, Robert, 307–308
Bienville. *See* Le Moyne de Bienville,
Jean-Baptiste
Biscayan, Johan, 345
Black Cut King, 190
Black Drink (*Ilex vomitoria*), 121–122,
395*n*105
Blake, Joseph, 135, 163, 213
Blitz, John H., 25
Blue Ridge Mountains, 307, 353
Board of Trade and Plantations, 212
Boisbriant, Pierre Dugué de, 141–143
Boone, Joseph, 62, 226, 371*n*31
Boston, 200
Boston (Indian), 304